MILLER'S
COLLECTORS CARS
PRICE GUIDE

1991-1992
(Volume I)

Compiled and Edited by

Judith and Martin Miller

General Editor: Robert Murfin

MILLERS PUBLICATIONS

MILLER'S COLLECTORS CARS PRICE GUIDE 1991-1992

Created and designed by
Millers Publications Limited
The Mitchell Beazley Group
Sissinghurst Court, Sissinghurst
Cranbrook, Kent TN17 2JA
Telephone: (0580) 713890

Compiled and edited by
Judith and Martin Miller

General Editor: Robert Murfin
Production Team: Sue Boyd
Marion Rickman, Sue Woodhouse, Chris Huggett
Jody Taylor, Jacqui Small
Advertising Executive: Elizabeth Smith
Display Advertisements: Trudi Hinkley
Index compiled by: DD Editorial Services, Beccles

Copyright © 1991 Millers Publications Ltd

A CIP catalogue record for this book is
available from the British Library

ISBN 0-905879-69-4

Typeset by Ardek Photosetters, St. Leonards-on-Sea
Illustrations by G.H. Graphics, St. Leonards-on-Sea
Colour origination by Scantrans, Singapore.
Printed and bound in England by William Clowes Ltd.,
Beccles and London

Introduction

As the antiques market has developed and changed over the past 10-20 years, 20th century furniture and ceramics and all sorts of nostalgia and memorabilia from this period have become very collectable; it is not surprising, therefore, that automobiles and anything connected with automobiles are now very sought after as well. There has always been a good trade in 'Classic' cars but the market only consisted of real enthusiasts up until a couple of years ago when speculators realised what terrific value old vehicles represented and the mad free-for-all started. The market crashed to earth last year but now appears to have settled down at a more sensible level. We felt that this was a good time to tackle the classic car market with a Miller's Price Guide.

Miller's Price Guides are exactly that, they are not definitive price lists. We have, in conjunction with Peter Card and Malcolm Welford of ADT Auctions, produced a listing of all the major pre- and post-war motor cars considered collectable. We have given a price banding dependent on condition and have illustrated that price list, where possible, with relevant examples that have been sold, or have been offered for sale, during the past year. Do not forget the many factors that can influence the price of motor vehicles; originality, right or left hand drive, restoration, provenance, racing or competition history and so on. Equally important to the price band is the source of information — this is indicated at the end of the caption and can be cross referenced to the list at the front of the book. We have also included many other features which we feel will be extremely useful and interesting, for example, car clubs and a directory of specialists as well as conversion tables and a comprehensive glossary of terms. If you feel we have missed anything please let us know — as with all our price guides we do look forward to feed-back from our readers. Our aim, as always, is to make our books as 'user friendly' as possible.

A word of warning, although fake cars exist they are usually well documented and your friendly dealer, auctioneer or car club will point you in the right direction. However, automobilia, car mascots in particular, is a very different case. There has developed a thriving industry in reproduction car mascots, which is quite acceptable as long as they are not passed off as the real thing. It is imperative that you buy from reputable dealers and auctioneers, and always seek their opinions before buying. As we say in our antiques and collectables books, if in doubt, walk away.

As I said, this is a price guide not a price list; we have endeavoured to cover as much as we can and we sincerely hope this book will be, as our antiques books have become, not only of great interest and full of readily digestible information, but also of great use to both amateur and professional.

Judith H. Miller

5

Acknowledgements

The publishers would like to acknowledge the great assistance given by our consultants.

Peter Card
Malcolm Welford

ADT Auctions Ltd, *Prospect House, The Broadway, Farnham Common, Slough*

David Baldock

Chequers Garage, *North Road, Goudhurst, Kent*

Robert Brooks

Brooks, *81 Westside, London SW4*

Adrian Hamilton

Duncan Hamilton & Co Ltd, *The Square, Bagshot, Surrey*

Malcolm Barber

Sotheby's, *34-35 New Bond Street, London W1*

1956 Daimler Conquest DJ 250/1 Four Door Saloon, 6 cylinder in line, water-cooled monobloc engine, 3in bore x 3½in stroke, 2433cc, overhead valves, preselector 4 speed gearbox plus reverse, fluid flywheel clutch, laminated torsion bar front suspension, semi-elliptic rear, wheelbase 104in. Est. **£3,800-4,800** *S(A)*

1923/1924 Gardner Radio Special Tourer, Lycoming 4 cylinder in line, water-cooled monobloc engine, side valves, 3¹¹⁄₁₆in bore x 5in stroke, 3400cc, 3 speed gearbox, dry plate Borg and Beck clutch, semi-elliptic spring suspension, wheelbase 112in, tyres 33in x 4.5, right-hand drive. Est. **£16,000-20,000** *S(A)*

7

Key to Illustrations

Each illustration and descriptive caption is accompanied by a letter-code. By reference to the following list of Auctioneers (denoted by *) and Dealers (●), the source of any item may be immediately determined. In no way does this constitute or imply a contract or binding offer on the part of any of our contributors to supply or sell the goods illustrated, or similar articles, at the prices stated. Advertisers in this year's directory are denoted by †.

ACO †● Anthony Coyne, 161-165 Churchill Parade, Birchfield Road, Perry Bar, Birmingham. Tel: 021-523 6363.

ADT †* ADT Auctions Ltd, Prospect House, The Broadway, Farnham Common, Slough. Tel: (0753) 645622.

AMR ● A.M. Restoration Service, 1 Firswood Road, Lathom, Skelmersdale. Tel: (0695) 21849.

APP ● Richard Appleyard, Sunderland House, Sunderland Street, Tickhill, Doncaster, S. Yorks. Tel: (0302) 743782.

AUT †● Autodrome, Omega Palace, Caledonian Road, London N1. Tel: 071-833 2076.

B * Brooks, 81 Westside, London SW4. Tel: 071-228 8000.

BC ● Beaulieu Cars Ltd, Beaulieu, Hants. Tel: (0590) 612444.

BEE ● Bruce Beer, Bruce Beer Classics, 51 Colchester Road, Weeley, Essex. Tel: (0255) 831122.

BLE ● Ivor Bleaney, Lords Oak, Landford, Salisbury, Wilts. Tel: (0794) 390895.

C * Christie's, 8 King Street, St James's, London SW1. Tel: 071-839 9060.

C(A) * Christie's Australia Pty Ltd, 1 Darling Street, South Yarra, Melbourne, Victoria 3141. Tel: (03) 820 4311.

CARH ● C.A.R. Howard, 14/16 Queens Gate Place Mews, London SW7. Tel: 071-584 4701.

CC ● Collectors Cars (Mr D. Connell), Drakeshill, Birmingham Road, Kenilworth, Warks. Tel: (0926) 57705.

CD ● Chris Drake Collectors Cars Ltd, 21 Brook Mews North, London W2. Tel: 071-723 1881.

Cen * Central Motor Auctions, Barfield House, Britannia Road, Morley, Leeds. Tel: (0532) 527722.

CFC ● Classic Fun Cars (Peter Laine-Toner), 3a Warwick Road, Beaconsfield, Bucks. Tel: (0494) 670154.

CGO ● The Capital and General Omnibus Co Ltd, Gawsworth Hall, Gawsworth, Macclesfield, Cheshire. Tel: (0260) 223456.

CLC ● Country Lane Classics, The Barn, Macclesfield, Cheshire. Tel: (0625) 860149.

CLG ● Clarke Gammon, 45 High Street, Guildford, Surrey. Tel: (0483) 572266.

C(M) * Christie's (Monaco), S.A.M., Park Palace, 98000 Monte Carlo. Tel: 010 339 325 1933.

CMA * Classic Motor Auctions Ltd, P.O. Box 20, Fishponds, Bristol. Tel: (0272) 710370.

CMa ● Classic Match (Mr A. D. McWilliam), High Green, Mark Way, Godalming, Surrey. Tel: (0483) 415928 or (0322) 864576.

CNY * Christie, Manson and Woods International Inc, 502 Park Avenue, New York, NY 10022. Tel: (212) 546 1000.

CTC †● Classic Transport Co, Brewood Road, Coven. Wolverhampton. Tel: (0902) 790666.

CW ● The Chelsea Workshop, Nell Gwynn House, Draycott Avenue, Chelsea, London SW3. Tel: 071-584 8363.

CZ † The Classic Z Register, Mrs L. Godber (Chairman), Thistledown, Old Stockbridge Road, Kentsboro, Wallop, Stockbridge, Han Tel: (0264) 781979.

DB †● David Baldock, North Road, Goudhurst, Ke Tel: (0580) 211326.

DDM ● Dickinson, Davy and Markham, Wrawby Street, Brigg, S. Humberside. Tel: (0652) 53666.

DF ● David Foster, 87 Foxley Lane, Purley, Surre Tel: 081-668 1246.

DHA ● Duncan Hamilton & Co, (Byfleet) Ltd, The Square, Bagshot, Surrey. Tel: (0276) 71010.

DJ †● Derek James, Oakwood House, Charles Hill Elstead, Surrey. Tel: (0252) 702909.

ELD ● Malcolm C. Elder, Unit 5, Enstone Airfield, Enstone, Oxon. Tel: (0608) 677238.

Eur ● Eureka, 20 Hardacre Street, Ormskirk. Tel: (0695) 579179.

1924 Chenard-Walcker 3 Litre Sports Tourer. Est. £20,000-30,000 *C(A)*

1955 Vincent-HRD Black Prince. £18,000-20,000 *P*

FOR ● Fortescue Garages Ltd, 2A Luther Road, Winton, Bournemouth. Tel: (0202) 529929.

GIL * Gildings, Roman Way, Market Harborough, Leics. Tel: (0858) 410414.

GWC ● Graham White Classic Cars, Old House Farm, Ham Road, Sidlesham, Chichester, W. Sussex. Tel: (0243) 641528.

H * Holloway's, 49 Parsons Street, Banbury, Oxon. Tel: (0295) 253197.

Hu ● Huntsworth, 24/28 Boston Place, London NW1. Tel: 071-724 0269.

Hus * Husseys, Alphin Brook Road, Exeter, Devon. Tel: (0392) 50441.

KSC ● Kent Sports Cars, Nonington, Dover, Kent. Tel: (0304) 840878.

LF * Lambert & Foster, 77 Commercial Road, Paddock Wood, Kent. Tel: (0892) 832325.

Mar ● Marksdanes Classic Cars, Shepton Mallet, Somerset. Tel: (0749) 830862.

MOC Metropolitan Owners' Club, Goat Cottage, Nutbourne Common, Pulborough, W. Sussex. Tel: (0798) 813921.

Mot ● Motospot, North Kilworth, Lutterworth, Leics. Tel: (0455) 552548 or (0831) 120498.

P * Phillips, Son & Neale, 10 Salem Road, Bayswater, London W2. Tel: 071-229 9090.

PJF ● P. J. Fischer Classic Automobiles, Dyers Lane, Upper Richmond Road, Putney, SW15. Tel: 081-785 6633.

PMS ● Paul Matty Sportscars, 12 Old Birmingham Road, Bromsgrove, Worcs. Tel: (0527) 35656.

PT † ● Paris A Traction (Mr R. Rother), Preston House Studio, Preston, Canterbury, Kent. Tel: (0227) 722596.

PWC ● The Pre-war MG Parts Centre, 1A Albany Road, Chislehurst, Kent. Tel: 081-467 7788.

RBB * Russell, Baldwin and Bright, Ryelands Road, Leominster, Herefords. Tel: (0568) 611166.

RCH ● Regency Car Hire, 47 Ash Grove, Moulsham Lodge, Chelmsford, Essex. Tel: (0245) 358028.

Ren * Renaissance, 36-38 London Road, Hazel Grove, Stockport, Cheshire. Tel: 061-483 9427.

RH ● Robert Hughes, Investment House, 28 Queens Road, Weybridge, Surrey. Tel: (0932) 58381/42309.

RSC ● R.S. Coachworks, The Trees, Sulhamstead Abbots, Reading, Berks. Tel: (0734) 832319.

RTC ● Red Triangle Classic Cars, Cherry Street, Warwick. Tel: (0926) 410176.

S * Sotheby's, 34-35 New Bond Street, London W1. Tel: 071-493 8080.

S(A) Sotheby's Australia Pty Ltd., 926 High Street, Armadale, Victoria 3143. Tel: (03) 509 2900.

SCC ● Simon Copsey Classic Cars, Sparrowes Nest, Henley Road, Ipswich, Suffolk. Tel: (0473) 256936.

SEN * Sentries Auctions, Huntworth Manor, Huntworth, Somerset. Tel: (0278) 793100.

S(M) * Sotheby's, B.P. 45 Le Sporting Hiver, Place du Casino, MC98001 Monaco Cedex. Tel: 33 (93) 30 88 80.

SNY * Sotheby's, 1334 York Avenue, New York NY10021. Tel: (212) 606 7000.

S(S) * Sotheby's, Summers Place, Billingshurst, W. Sussex. Tel: (0403) 783933.

SVRe ● S.V. Restorations, Grosvenor Road, Billingborough, Sleaford, Lincs. Tel: (0529) 240339.

Tal ● Talacrest Ltd, Station Road, Egham, Surrey. Tel: (0784) 439797.

T&M ● Thrupp & Maberly Ltd, 3-13A Harriet Walk, Belgravia, London SW1. Tel: 071-235 8016/7.

W ● P. & A. Wood, Great Easton, Dunmow, Essex. Tel: (0371) 84848.

1911 Sizaire-Naudin 12/16hp Two Seater with Dickey, £19,500-20,000 *C*

INDEX TO CAR CLUB ADVERTISERS

INDEX TO ADVERTISERS

Glossary

We have attempted here to define some of the terms that you will come across in this book. Many of them, notably the bodywork terms, are open to interpretation and where there is a different meaning in America we have tried to explain it. If there are any terms or technicalities you would like explained or you feel that should be included in future please let us know.

Berline – See Sedanca de Ville.

Brake – A term from the days of horse drawn vehicles for any form of open carriage, sometimes used for shooting parties, hence shooting brake. If a shooting brake, or estate car was used to ferry passengers to the railway station it became known as a station wagon. Originally the seating was fore and aft, with the passengers facing inwards.

Brougham – A limousine with some or all of its rear windows blanked out to ensure extra privacy.

Cabriolet – A two-door four-seater body with a folding soft top, usually with wind-up windows. A commonly mis-used term.

Chassis – A framework to which the car body, engine, gearbox, and axles are attached.

Chummy – An open top two-door body just about covered by a folding hood.

Cloverleaf – A three-seater open body style usually with a single door, two seats in the front and one at the rear.

Coachbuilt – A car body which is built separately from the rest of the vehicle and attached to the chassis. Usually an aluminium or fabric covering over a wooden frame.

Convertible – A general term (post-war) for any car with a soft top.

Dickey Seat – A passenger seat, usually for two people contained in the boot of the car without a folding hood (the boot lid forms the backrest). Known in America as a rumble seat.

Doctors Coupé – A much abused term; strictly speaking a fixed or folding head coupé without a dickey seat and the passenger seat slightly staggered back from the driver's to accommodate the famous black bag.

1920 Rochet-Schneider Type 2.6 Litre 15000 Dual Cowl Torpedo. £12,000-14,000   B

1930 L29 Cord Golfers Cabriolet. Est. £100,000-120,000   *BLE*

Coupé – Before the war it was a general term applied to a two-door two-seater with a folding hood. There are a number of versions some of which were applied or created at the whim of the manufacturer, see Doctors Coupé, Golfers Coupé, Fixed Head Coupé.

Coupé de Ville – Body type with the rear passenger compartment enclosed and the driver either in the open or with a sliding or folding canvas roof.

Dog Cart – A horse drawn dog cart was originally used to transport beaters and their dogs to a shoot (the dogs were contained in louvred boxes under the seats, the louvres were kept for decoration long after the dogs had gone).

Dos-a-dos – Literally back-to-back, i.e. the passenger seating arrangement.

Drop Head Coupé – Originally a two-door two-seater with a folding roof, see Roadster.

Engine – Engine sizes are given in cubic centimetres (cc) in Europe and cubic inches (cu in) in the USA. 1 cubic inch equals 16.38cc (1 litre = 61.02cu in).

Estate Car – See brake.

Fixed Head Coupé – FHC a coupé with a solid fixed roof.

Golfers Coupé – Usually an open two-seater with a square-doored locker behind the driver's seat to accommodate golf clubs.

Hansom – As with the famous horse drawn cab, an enclosed two-seater with the driver out in the elements either behind or in front.

Landau – An open carriage with a folding hood at each end which would meet in the middle when erected.

Landaulette – Half a Landau, i.e. the rear passenger compartment would fold down.

Limousine – A large enclosed car, usually with a glass sliding door between the passengers and the driver, often with pull down occasional seats, sometimes called a pullman.

Monocoque – A type of construction of car bodies without a chassis as such, the strength being in the stressed panels. Most modern mass produced cars are built this way.

Phaeton – A term from the days of horse drawn vehicles for an open body. If there are two rows of seats it is a double phaeton. Replaced by the term Tourer or Touring in the USA. Normally a folding hood would be provided.

Post Vintage Thoroughbred (PVT) – A British term drawn up by the Vintage Sports Car Club (VSCC) for selected models made in the vintage tradition between 1931 and 1942.

Roadster – An American term for a two-seater sports car. The hood should be able to be removed totally rather than folded down as a drop head coupé.

Rumble Seat – See Dickey Seat.

Runabout – Light open two-seaters from the 1900s

Roi des Belges – A very elaborate open touring car named after King Leopold II of Belgium.

Saloon – A two- or four-door car with four or more seats and a fixed roof.

Sedan – See Saloon.

Sedanca de Ville – Generally a version of a limousine body with the driving compartment covered with a folding or sliding roof section. Sometimes known in America as a Town Car.

Sociable – A cycle car term meaning that the passenger and driver sat side-by-side.

Spyder – An open two-seater sports car, sometimes a 2+2, (a 2+2 means there are two small occasional seats behind the two front seats).

Station Wagon – See Brake.

Surrey – An early 20thC open four-seater with a fringed canopy. A term from the days of horse drawn vehicles.

Stanhope – Originally a term from the days of horse drawn vehicles for a single seat two-wheel carriage with a hook. Later, a four-wheeled two-seater, sometimes with an underfloor engine.

Tandem – A cycle car term, the passengers sat in tadem, with the driver at the front or at the rear.

Targa – A coupé with a removable centre roof section.

Tonneau – A rear entrance tonneau is a four-seater with access through a centrally placed door at the rear. A detachable tonneau meant that the rear seats could be removed to make a two-seater. Tonneau nowadays usually means a waterproof cover over an open car used when the roof is detached.

Torpedo – An open tourer with an unbroken line from the bonnet to the rear of the body.

Tourer – An open four- or five-seater with three or four doors, folding hood, with or without sidescreens, generally replaced the term torpedo.

Veteran – All vehicles manufactured before 31st December 1918, only cars built before 31st March 1904 are eligible for the London to Brighton Commemorative Run.

Victoria – Generally an American term for a two- or four-seater with a very large folding hood, if a four-seater, the hood would only cover the rear seats.

Vantage – Any vehicles manufactured between the end of the veteran period and 31st December 1930. See Post Vintage Thoroughbred.

Vis-a-Vis – Face-to-face, an open car where one or two passengers sit opposite each other.

Voiturette – A French term meaning a very light car, originally used by Léon Bollée.

Weyman – A system of construction employing Rexine fabric panels over a Kapok filling to prevent noise and provide insulation.

THE WAY YOU BUY ANTIQUES IS COSTING YOU TOO MUCH MONEY.

◆

Now there is a way to know precisely what is coming up at auction, within your field

of interest, at over 400 salerooms in the U.K. – from as little as £350 a year.

To find what you are looking for, telephone Thesaurus on 0983 299252 or write to us at

Thesaurus Group Ltd., FREEPOST 6 (WD4 359), London W1E 1JZ.

CONTENTS

AC

The first AC vehicle was a three wheeler, the Sociable, produced in 1909. The company's reputation was founded on high quality sports and saloon cars before 1940. Post-war production was started with saloon cars, but the appearance of the Ace in 1954 inspired the Cobra of the early '60s, probably AC's most copied motor car.

1938 AC 2–4–6 Tourer, mechanics in fair condition, body and interior poor, last in use about 1960.
£14,000-15,000   *CC*

1955 AC Ace, mostly original condition, engine reconditioned.
£57,000-60,000   *ADT*

Introduced in 1947, the 2 litre was the last 4 seater sports saloon to be built by AC.

1951 AC 2 Litre, mechanically sound, but similar engine to the original fitted with various other modifications, upholstery poor, some instrumentation non-original, current MOT.
£4,000-4,500   *ADT*

1955 AC 2 Litre Saloon, completely restored with complete engine rebuild, electrical items overhauled or renewed.
£14,000-15,000   *ADT*

This 2 litre saloon is one of the rare 4 door models produced at the latter end of the model's production.

1960 AC Greyhound 2.2 Litre 6 Cylinder, manual gearbox with overdrive, restored.
£30,000-40,000   *LF*

The Greyhound Sports Saloon was built from 1960 to 1963 and is probably one of the most beautiful cars produced by the Company.

Make: AC
Model: Cobra
Type: 289
Years Manufactured: 1962-69
Quantity: 560
Price when new: Mk III, £2,573
Engine Type: Ford V8, front engine/rear drive
Size: 4260/4727cc
Max Power: 164-197 bhp
Max Torque: 269-314 ft/lb @ 4800/3400 rpm
Transmission: 4 speed
Wheelbase: 90in
Performance: Max speed: 138 mph; 0-60: 5.5 secs. Mpg: 17.

MAKE	ENGINE	DATES	CONDITION		
AC			1	2	3
2-litre	1991/6	1947/55	£5,000	£4,000	£500
Buckland	1991/6	1949/54	£7,000	£5,500	£1,500
Ace	1991/6	1953/63	£45,000	£40,000	£30,000
Ace Bristol	1971/6	1954-63	£55,000	£45,000	£35,000
Ace 2.6	1553/6	1961/62	£70,000	£55,000	£40,000
Aceca	1991/6	1954-63	£43,000	£28,000	£20,000
Aceca Bristol	1971/6	1956-63	£48,000	£32,000	£25,000
Greyhound Bristol	1971/6	1961-63	£19,500	£15,000	£10,000
Cobra Mk II	4727/8	1963-64	£120,000	£98,000	£90,000
Cobra Mk III	6998/8	1965-67	£180,000	£140,000	£100,000
289	4727/8	1965-69	£170,000	£135,000	£95,000
428 Frua Fastback	7014/8	1967-73	£42,000	£30,000	£21,000
428 Frua Convertible	7014/8	1967-73	£65,000	£42,000	£35,000
3000 ME	2994/6	1976-84	£17,000	£13,000	£11,000

Make: AC
Model: Ace-Bristol and Aceca-Bristol
Type: Sports, Coupé
Years Manufactured: 1957-64
Quantity: Ace, 446; Aceca, 169
Price when new: Ace, £1,100; Aceca, £1,585
Engine Type: Overhead valve 6 cyl
Size: 1971cc
Max Power: 105/120/125/130 bhp @ 4750/5750/6200 rpm
Max Torque: 120/122/123/128 ft/lb @ 3750/4250/5000 rpm
Transmission: 4 speed, overdrive optional from 1956
Wheelbase: 90in
Performance: Max speed: (125 bhp models) Ace, 117 mph; Aceca, 116 mph; 0-60: Ace, 9.1 secs; Aceca, 10.3 secs.

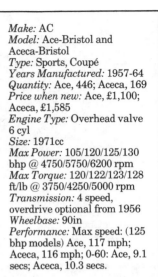

The Ace was available with 3 engine choices, initially AC's own straight six unit, then the Bristol unit and latterly the 2663cc Ford Zephyr as developed by Ruddspeed.

1957 AC ACE Bristol, left-hand drive, mechanically overhauled, and other light restoration work. **£34,000-36,000** *ADT*

Make: AC
Model: Cobra
Type: 427
Years Manufactured: 1965-68
Quantity: 510
Price when new: £2,951
Engine Type: V8, front engine/rear drive
Size: 6998cc
Max Power: 390 bhp @ 5200 rpm
Max Torque: 475 ft/lb @ 3700 rpm
Transmission: 4 speed
Wheelbase: 90in
Performance: Max speed: 143 mph; 0-60: 4.8 secs. Mpg: 12.

1961 A.C. Greyhound, excellent condition. **£25,000-35,000** *BC*

1962 AC Greyhound Two Door Saloon, 6 cylinder in line, water-cooled monobloc engine, overhead valves, 65mm bore x 100mm stroke, 1991cc, 4 speed gearbox with overdrive, Borg & Beck single dry plate clutch, hypoid bevel rear axle; independent coil spring front and rear suspension, wheelbase 100in, tyres 6.4 x 15in. Est. **£25,000-30,000** *S*

1965 A.C. Cobra 289 Mk III, excellent condition. **£120,000-130,000** *BC*

1937 AC Ace 2 Litre Drop Head Coupé with Dickey seat, chassis No. L541, engine No. UMB 495.
£19,000-21,000   *B*

1959 AC Ace 2 Litre Roadster.
Est. £60,000-70,000   *B*

AC Ace Two Seater Sports,
left-hand drive, 6 cylinder in line, water-cooled monobloc engine, overhead valves, 1991cc, Moss 4 speed manual gearbox, Borg & Beck single dry plate clutch, hypoid bevel rear axle, independent transverse leaf spring suspension front and rear, tyres 175 x 16in, 16,000 miles recorded.
Est. £65,000-75,000   *S(M)*

1970 AC 428 Fastback, 7.0 litre V8, 0-100 mph in 14.5 seconds, only 2 owners from new, bare metal respray.
£52,000-55,000   *ADT*

This model is so named as it has a displacement of 428 cubic in. Only 51 Fastbacks were built, mostly automatic.

1968 AC Cobra 4.7 Litre Mk III,
V8 cylinder engine, water-cooled, pushrod-operated overhead valves, 100mm bore x 70mm stroke, 4727cc, 4 speed synchromesh gearbox, limited slip differential, independent front and rear suspension, coil spring and wishbone front with semi-trailing arms rear, wheelbase 100in, tyres 15in.
Est. £200,000-240,000   *S(M)*

The Mk III cars appeared late in 1964 to compete with Ferrari and Porsche in the GT championship. From January 1965 the car had the new 7 litre Ford engine and modifications to the chassis, producing 480bhp at 6,000rpm. This gave the Mk III a top speed of 165mph and 0-60mph acceleration in 4.2 seconds. This car was the last Mk III Cobra to leave the factory.

1989 Replica Cobra 427, by
Cobretti Engineering.
£17,000-18,000 *S*

986 Gravetti Cobra Replica, this
vehicle was built by Gravetti
Engineering in 1986 and has a
Rover SDI V8 engine.
Est. **£12,000-15,000** *LF*

Dax Cobra Replica, based around
a Rover 3½ litre V8 engine,
producing 200bhp.
£11,000-13,000 *ADT*

ABBOT

1938 2 Litre 15-98 Abbot Short,
chassis No. C/N E8819SC, this has
been totally rebuilt with a leather
interior.
£100,000-120,000 *Mar*

Did you know
*MILLER'S Collectors Cars
Price Guide builds up year
by year to form the most
comprehensive photo-
reference system
available*

ADAMS

1907 Adams 10hp Two Seater,
single cylinder horizontal
water-cooled monobloc engine,
120mm bore x 150mm stroke,
2 speed epicyclic gearing with
reverse, leaf springs all round, chain
final drive, wheelbase 82in, tyres
760 x 90.
£14,850-15,250 *S*

AERO

1939 Aero Series 50 2 Litre Two Door Saloon, 4 cylinder, 2 litre engine, 50bhp.
Est. **£6,000-8,000** *P*

AJS

1930 AJS 'Nine' Richmond Saloon.
£2,100-2,500 *ADT*

Manufactured by the motorcycle manufacturer, A J Stevens created and produced small family cars between 1930 and 1931. Using a Coventry-Climax side valve engine of 1018cc both a 2 seater tourer and a 4 door saloon were produced priced between £210 and £240. This was expensive compared with similar Austin and Morris varieties of the same period. The quality and robustness of the cars was undoubted and had the parent company not collapsed in 1931 the marque could well have rivalled Riley and Standard by the mid 1930s.

ALPINE

1965 Alpine A110 GT4, this 4 seater is one of only 112 built.
£9,950-11,000 *GWC*

Make: Alpine-Renault
Model: A110
Type: Sports Coupé/Convertible
Years Manufactured: 1963-77
Quantity: 7,176
Engine Type: Rear engine/rear drive, in-line 4 cyl
Size: 956-1647cc
Max Power: Up to 127 bhp
Transmission: 4 or 5 speed
Performance: Max speed: 1300, 123 mph; 0-60 9.1 secs; Mpg: 28.

1968 Alpine A110 1300S, fully restored in metallic blue.
£15,500-16,500 *GWC*

1965 Alpine, A110 GT4, this car has been fully restored and is one of only 112 built, 4 seater.
£10,500-11,000 *GWC*

Make: Alpine-Renault
Model: A310
Type: Sports Coupé
Years Manufactured: 1971-85
Quantity: 1.6 ltr, 2,334
Engine Type: Rear engine/rear drive, in-line 4 cyl
Size: 1605 or 2664cc
Max Power: 1605cc, 127 bhp @ 6250 rpm; 2664cc, 150 bhp @ 6000 rpm
Max Torque: 1605cc, 108 ft/lb @ 5000 rpm; 2664cc, 150 ft/lb @ 3500 rpm
Transmission: 5 speed
Wheelbase: 89.4in
Performance: Max speed: (4 cyl), 131 mph; (V6 cyl), 137 mph; 0-60: (4 cyl), 8.1 secs; (V6 cyl), 7.5 secs; Mpg: (4 cyl), 24; (V6 cyl), 25.

MAKE Alpine	ENGINE	DATES	CONDITION 1	2	3
A110 1300G	1255/4	1966-70	£19,000	£15,000	£10,000
A110 1300S	1296/4	1966-70	£22,500	£18,500	£12,500
A110 1300V85	1289/4	1970-76	£15,000	£11,000	£8,000
A110 1600S	1565/4	1969/75	£26,000	£19,000	£15,000
A110 1600 High Spec	1596/4	1969/75	£35,000	£28,000	£21,000
A310 1600	1605/4	1972/76	£8,000	£5,000	£3,000
A310 V6	2664/6	1976-85	£12,000	£8,500	£6,000

ALFA ROMEO

Alfa (Anonima Lombardo Fabbrica Automobili) was founded in 1910, being taken over by Nicolo Romeo in 1915. The classic pre-war Alfas are the Jano designed 6C and 8C models and they were extremely successful competition cars. Post-war production featured, amongst other cars, the Giulietta range and the 1750/2000 series, but attempts at the 'mass market' have been reckoned a disappointment.

1930 Alfa Romeo 6C 1750 Tourismo, coachwork by James Young of Bromley, excellent condition.
£60,000-70,000   *BC*

1928 Alfa Romeo 6C 1500 Supercharged Mille Miglia Speciale, excellent condition.
£230,000-260,000   *BC*

1932 Alfa Romeo 8C 2.3 Drophead Coupé, coachwork by Graber.
Est. **£200,000-250,000**   *C(M)*

1930 Alfa Romeo 1.75 Litre Tipo 6C-1750 Gran Turismo Spyder, by Carrozzeria G. Castagna & C., Milan, chassis No. 8613381, engine No. 8613381.
£99,000-105,000   *B*

1958 Alfa Romeo Giulietta Spyder, body painted red with black upholstery.
£16,000-18,000   *Hu*

19

ALFA ROMEO

MAKE	ENGINE	DATES	CONDITION		
Alfa Romeo			1	2	3
24HP	4084/4	1910-11	£25,000	£20,000	£15,000
12HP	2413/4	1910-11	£20,000	£13,000	£9,000
40-60	6028/4	1913-15	£38,000	£25,000	£18,000
RL	2916/6	1921-22	£35,000	£25,000	£18,000
RM	1944/4	1924-25	£33,000	£20,000	£18,000
6C 1500	1487/6	1927-28	£14,000	£10,000	£8,000
6C 1750	1752/6	1923-33	£100,000+		
8C 2300	2336/8	1931-34	£300,000+		
6C 1900	1917/6	1933	£18,000	£15,000	£12,000
6C 2300	2309/6	1934	£22,000	£18,000	£15,000
8C 2900	2905/8	1935-39	£500,000+		
6C 2500 SS	2443/6	1939-45	£30,000+		

The variety of Alfa Romeos is endless! Value is very dependent on sporting history, body style and engine type.

Make: Alfa Romeo
Model: Giulietta
Type: Saloon/Coupé/Sports
Years Manufactured: 1954-63
Quantity: 45,814 all types
Price when new: Saloon, £2,191; Coupé, £2,315
Engine Type: Double overhead camshaft 4 cyl
Size: 1290cc
Max Power: 80 bhp @ 6300 rpm; 90 bhp @ 6500 rpm (Veloce); 115 bhp @ 6500 (Sprint Speciale and Zagato)
Max Torque: 86.8 ft/lb @ 4500 rpm (Veloce)
Transmission: 4 speed, 5 speed on Sprint Speciale and Zagato
Wheelbase: 93.7in; Spider, SS and SZ, 88.6in
Performance: Max speed: 103 mph (Sprint, Spider); 112 mph (Spider Veloce); 124 mph (SS and SZ); 0-60: 11.0 secs (Spider Veloce).

1960 Alfa Romeo Giulietta Spyder (101) Concours.
£22,000-24,000   *Hu*

1962 Alfa Romeo Guilia, Spyder, by Touring of Milan.
£14,000-16,000   *BLE*

Make: Alfa Romeo
Model: Giulia
Years Manufactured: 1962-75
Engine Type: Twin ohc, 4 cyl
Size: 1570/1780/1962cc
Max Power: 82/92/122/131 bhp @ 5500/5500/5500 rpm
Max Torque: 103 ft/lb @ 3000 rpm (Sprint GT)
Transmission: 4 speed, 5 speed
Wheelbase: 92.5in (Sprint)
Performance: Max speed: 102-120 mph; 0-60: 10-14.5 secs; Mpg: 23-30.

1963 Alfa Romeo 2600 Spyder.
£25,000-30,000   *CTC*

Engine Sizes

The R.A.C. Horsepower figure will vary for a given engine capacity as it was a formula based on the bore and number of cylinders; this figure was used to specify the taxation class between 1910 and 1948

750cc =	*7hp*
1000cc =	*8hp*
1300cc =	*10hp*
1500cc =	*12hp*
1800cc =	*14hp*
2000cc =	*16hp*
4000cc =	*30hp*

N.B. These are approximate figures

Locate the source

The source of each illustration in Miller's can be found by checking the code letters below each caption with the list of contributors

1958 Alfa Romeo Giulietta Spring Veloce Zagato Sports Coupé, 4 cylinder in line, water-cooled monobloc engine, overhead valves, 1290cc, 74mm bore x 75mm stroke, 4 speed synchromesh manual transmission, shaft drive to live rear axle, independent spiral coil spring suspension, tyres 155 x 15in, left-hand drive.
Est. £120,000-140,000   *S(M)*

1960 Alfa Romeo 2000 Spyder Veloce Convertible, coachwork by Touring of Milan, 4 cylinder in line, water-cooled monobloc engine, twin overhead camshafts, 84.5mm bore x 88mm stroke, 1975cc, 115bhp, 5 speed manual gearbox with synchromesh, shaft drive to rear axle, independent front, trailing arms rear suspension, tyres 165 x 400, left-hand drive.
£17,000-18,000   *S*

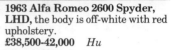

1963 Alfa Romeo 2600 Spyder, LHD, the body is off-white with red upholstery.
£38,500-42,000   *Hu*

1967 Alfa Romeo 1750 Boat-Tail Spyder, with left-hand drive.
£9,500-12,000
BLE

1967 Alfa Romeo Giulia Sprint, some restoration already carried out but more is needed.
£1,000-2,000   *LF*

1970 Alfa Romeo 1750 Spyder Duetto, this car has its original wheels, the bodywork is finished in red with a black hood.
Est. **£6,500-8,500**   *ADT*

1963 Alfa Romeo 2600 Sprint, by Bertone, this car was introduced at the Geneva Motor Show in 1962 and has spent all its life in Naples, recorded mileage 46,000km believed correct.
Est. **£12,000-16,000**   *P*

1972 Alfa Romeo Montreal Coupé.
Est. **£17,000-20,000**   *P*

Styled by Bertone, some 3,925 cars were built, of which the vast majority were left-hand drive.

ALFA ROMEO

MAKE Alfa Romeo	ENGINE	DATES	CONDITION		
			1	2	3
2000 Spyder	1974/4	1958-61	£16,000	£10,000	£4,000
2600 Sprint	2584/6	1962-66	£12,000	£8,000	£4,000
2600 Spyder	2584/6	1962-65	£25,000	£17,000	£12,000
Giulietta Sprint	1290/4	1955-62	£15,000	£8,000	£4,000
Giulietta Spyder	1290/4	1956-62	£13,000	£7,000	£3,500
Giulia Saloon	1570/4	1962-72	£4,000	£2,500	£300
Giulia Sprint (rhd)	1570/4	1962-68	£15,000	£6,500	£2,000
Giulia Spyder (rhd)	1570/4	1962-65	£14,000	£7,500	£2,500
Giulia SS	1570/4	1962-66	£35,000	£25,000	£18,000
GT 1300 Junior	1290/4	1966-72	£7,500	£5,500	£4,000
1300GT Junior	1290/4	1973-75	£4,000	£2,000	£750
Giulia Sprint GT (105)	1570/4	1962-68	£9,500	£5,000	£3,000
1600GT Junior	1570/4	1972-75	£7,500	£4,000	£1,400
1750/2000 Berlina	1779/ 1962/4	1967-77	£2,750	£1,700	£1,000
1750GTV	1779/4	1967-72	£12,000	£7,500	£3,000
2000GTV	1962/4	1971-77	£12,000	£7,500	£3,000
1600/1750 (Duetto)	1570/ 1779/4	1966-67	£14,000	£9,000	£6,000
1750/200 Spyder (Kamm)	1779/ 1962/4	1967-78	£10,000	£7,000	£3,500
Montreal	2593/8	1970-77	£16,000	£12,000	£7,000
Junior Zagato 1290	1290/4	1968-74	£18,000	£15,000	£6,000
Junior Zagato 1600	1570/4	1968-74	£22,000	£17,000	£6,500
Alfetta GT/GTV (chrome)	1962/4	1974-84	£3,000	£1,500	£500
Alfasud	1186/ 1490/4	1972-83	£1,500	£600	£250
Alfasud ti	1186/ 1490/4	1974-81	£2,500	£1,000	£500
Alfasud Sprint	1284/ 1490/4	1976-85	£4,000	£2,000	£500
GTV6	2492/6	1981-	£4,000	£2,000	£500

Make: Alfa Romeo
Model: Disco Volante
Type: Spider/Coupé
Years Manufactured: 1952-60
Quantity: 9
Engine Type: Double overhead camshaft 4 cyl
Size: 1997/2995/3495cc
Max Power: 1997cc, 158 bhp; 2995cc, 230 bhp; 3495cc, 246 bhp @ 6500 rpm
Transmission: 4 speed or 5 speed
Wheelbase: 2 lt, 87.4, 3/3.5 lt, 88.6
Performance: Max speed: 137-159 mph with racing bodywork.

Make: Alfa Romeo
Model: Monteal
Type: Coupé
Years Manufactured: 1972-75
Quantity: 3,925
Engine Type: Double overhead camshaft V8
Size: 2953cc
Max Power: 230 bhp @ 6500 rpm
Transmission: 5 speed
Wheelbase: 92.5in
Performance: Max speed: 132 mph; 0-60: 8.0 secs.

1975 Alfa Romeo Montreal, this vehicle has right-hand drive with mileage of just over 39,000 miles. Est. **£18,000-20,000**   *ADT*

1966 Alfa Romeo Giulia 1600GT Spyder, 4 cylinder in line, water-cooled monobloc engine, overhead camshaft, 72mm bore x 82mm stroke, 1570cc, 5 speed manual, shaft drive, hypoid bevel rear axle, independent coil spring and wishbone front suspension, coil spring, radius arms and A-bracket rear suspension, tyres 155SR 15in, right-hand drive. Est. **£16,000-18,000**   *S*

1973 Alfa Romeo 2000 Spyder Veloce, excellent condition. **£12,000-16,000**   *BC*

1953 Alfa Romeo 1900C Sprint,
this model was designed by
Pininfarina and is left-hand drive.
£18,700-20,000 *C*

Make: Alfa Romeo
Model: 1900
Type: Saloon/Coupé/Sports
Years Manufactured: 1950-58
Engine Type: Double overhead
camshaft 4 cyl
Size: 1952-53, 1884cc; 1954-58,
1975cc
Max Power: 1952-53, 100 bhp;
1954-58, 115 bhp @ 5500 rpm
Transmission: 4 speed, 5 speed
on 1954-58 Super Sprint
Wheelbase: 98.5in
Performance: Max speed: 100
mph (Sprint Cabriolet); 106
mph (Sprint Coupé); 112 mph
(SS).

1959 Alfa Romeo 200 Spyder.
£11,000-13,000 *B*

**1964 Alfa Romeo 1.6 Litre Giulia
Sprint Speciale Coupé.**
Est. £35,000-40,000 *B*

Make: Alfa Romeo
Model: Giulia Spyder
Type: Sports Car
Years Manufactured: 1966-date
Price when new: 1962-65,
1570cc, £1,499
Engine Type: Front engine, rear
drive, 4 cyl
Size: 1290-1962cc
Max Power: 132 bhp @ 5500
rpm
Max Torque: 132 ft/lb @ 2900
rpm
Transmission: 5 speed
Wheelbase: 88.6in
Performance: Max speed: 116
mph (2000 Spider Veloce);
0-60: 9.8 secs; Mpg: 27.

Make the Most of Miller's

*In Miller's we do NOT just
reprint saleroom
estimates. We work from
realised prices either from
an auction house or a
dealer. Our consultants
then work out a realistic
price range for a similar
vehicle. This is to try to
avoid repeating freak
results – either low or
high*

1974 Alfa Romeo GT Junior 1.3,
this car is finished in silver/grey
with a black interior.
£1,450-2,500 *CMA*

Make Alfa Romeo	FRANCE +2%	GERMANY +2%	ITALY +5%	JAPAN +5%	USA —

1975 Alfa Romeo Montreal Sports Saloon, coachwork by Bertone.
Est. **£18,000-20,000** *S*

1974 Alfa Romeo Montreal Sports Saloon, coachwork by Bertone.
Est. **£22,000-24,000** *S*

1977 Alfa Romeo Montreal, 8 cylinder, 90° V8 5-bearing light alloy block engine, light alloy cylinder heads, twin overhead camshafts, 2.6 litre, Spica fuel injection and dry sump lubrication, producing 200bhp at 6,500rpm, torque 173lb/ft at 4,750rpm, 5 speed all synchromesh gearbox, live rear axle with limited slip differential.
£13,500-14,000 *SEN*

1982 Alfa Romeo 2 Litre Spyder, with left-hand drive.
£8,000-9,000 *BLE*

> **Did you know**
> *MILLER'S Collectors Cars Price Guide builds up year by year to form the most comprehensive photo-reference system available*

Make: Alfa Romeo
Model: GTV-6
Type: Coupé
Years Manufactured: 1981-86
Engine Type: Single overhead camshaft V6
Size: 2492cc
Max Power: 154 bhp @ 5500 rpm
Max Torque: 152 ft/lb @ 3200 rpm
Transmission: 5 speed
Wheelbase: 94.5in
Performance: Max speed: 125 mph; 0-60: 8.4 secs.

1981 Alfa Romeo GT V6 2.5, finished in red with a grey interior, in good order throughout.
Est. **£4,000-5,000** *CMA*

ALLARD

Sydney Allard founded the company in 1937, making V8 or V12 Allard Specials. Post-war demand for replicas of his pre-war models coupled with very fast saloon and racing cars ensured the Clapham based company success until the business suffered from the competition from Jaguar and production ceased in 1959.

MAKE	ENGINE	DATES	CONDITION		
Allard			1	2	3
K/K2/L/M/M2X	3622/8	1947-54	£17,000	£9,000	£5,500
K3	var/8	1953-54	£22,000	£13,000	£10,000
P1	3622/8	1949-52	£16,000	£10,000	£5,500
P2	3622/8	1952-54	£25,000	£18,000	£11,000
J2/J2X	var/8	1950-54	£70,000	£60,000	£55,000
Palm Beach	1508/4, 2262/6	1952-55	£10,000	£7,500	£4,500
Palm Beach II	2252/ 3442/6	1956-60	£27,500	£18,000	£13,000

1951 Allard J2 Competition Roadster, V8 cylinder Chrysler Firepower hemi-head engine with high lift camshafts, 5430cc, 3 speed gearbox, single plate clutch, spiral bevel rear axle, independent front suspension by coil springs, swing axles and radius arms, De Dion rear suspension, wheelbase 100in.
Est. **£90,000-100,000** S

Racing driver Sydney Allard produced his first Allard Special in 1936 using a Ford V8 engine and a Bugatti bodyshell. Post-war he produced a range of sports racing cars using his own chassis layout, and a lightweight body designed by Godfrey Imhof, called the K1. The J2X was produced in 1951 and 1952, and was described as a competition 2 seater, with a 100in wheelbase. Various engines were used in the 83 examples produced.

Make: Allard
Model: K1
Type: Convertible
Years Manufactured: 1946-49
Quantity: 151
Price when new: £1,001
Engine Type: Ford V8
Size: 3622cc
Max Power: 85/95 bhp @ 3600 rpm
Transmission: 3 speed
Wheelbase: 106in

1952 Allard J2X Competition Roadster, V8 cylinder Ford engine with Ardun heads, overhead valve, 5.4 litres, 4 speed manual gearbox, spiral bevel final drive, independent transverse leaf spring suspension with swing axles and radius arms and front, transverse leaf spring rear; wheelbase 106in.
£44,000-45,000 S(M)

Make: Allard
Model: K2
Type: Sports
Years Manufactured: 1950-52
Quantity: 119
Engine Type: Ford V8/Mercury V8
Size: 3622/3917cc
Max Power: Mercury, 95/100 bhp @ 3600 rpm
Transmission: 3 speed
Wheelbase: 106in

ARROL-ASTER

1927 Arrol-Aster 17/50 Type SV Saloon.
£11,000-12,500 S

Specification: 6 cylinder in line, water cooled monobloc with single sleeve valves, bore 67.5mm, stroke 110mm, capacity 2361cc, 4 speed right-hand gate change gearbox, single plate clutch, enclosed shaft, sprival bevel drive rear axle, semi-elliptical springs front and rear, wheelbase 10ft 7½in, tyres 21in.

AMILCAR

This famous French company manufactured cars from 1921 until 1939. Most models were offered with a selection of bodies and engines by, among others, Delahaye and Hotchkiss.

1929 Amilcar CGSS Sports Two Seater.
£18,000-19,000   *S*

Specification: four cylinder in line engine, water cooled monobloc, bore 60mm, stroke 105mm, capacity 1187cc, side valve, 3 speed gearbox, multi-plate clutch, spiral bevel rear axle, semi-elliptic leaf front springs, quarter elliptic at the rear, wheelbase 7ft 10in, tyres 4.00 x 19in.

1929 Amilcar GS 2+2 Sports, with twin tonneau covers but no other weather equipment.
Est. £18,500-19,500   *ELD*

AMERICAN

1914 American Underslung Type 666 Six Passenger Tourer, the T-head monobloc engine of massive 573cu in capacity was said to develop 65bhp at 1,000rpm giving the car excellent performance with its massive 38 x 4½in tyres and direct drive on top gear.
£56,500-57,500   *SNY*

Built in Indianapolis by the American Motors Company the American car was produced from 1906 to 1914 and offered a range of quality 4 and 6 cylinder engined cars.

ALVIS

Alvis commenced production with the side-valve 10/30 in 1920. They enjoyed a justified reputation for manufacturing good looking, high quality sporting cars. In 1966 Rover acquired the controlling interest and motor vehicle production stopped. Alvis now make a series of armoured fighting vehicles.

1926 Alvis 12/50 Four Seater Sports Saloon, in excellent original condition.
£24,000-25,000   *SVRe*

1934 Alvis Speed 20 Open Tourer.
£44,500-45,000   *BLE*

1931 Alvis 12/60 Beetleback.
£34,500-37,000 *DB*

**1934 Alvis Speed 20 Sports
Saloon,** by Charlesworth, recently
restored and serviced.
£32,500-33,000 *DJ*

**1934 Alvis Speed 20 Two Door
Saloon,** coachwork by Vanden Plas,
Design 1136 and 6 cylinder engine
capacity.
Est. **£16,000-20,000** *ADT*

**1933 Alvis Firefly Four Seat
Tourer,** 4 cylinder in line,
water-cooled monobloc engine,
pushrod-operated overhead valve,
69mm bore x 100mm stroke, 1496cc,
4 speed pre-selector gearbox, spiral
bevel rear axle, semi-elliptic leaf
springs front and rear, wheelbase
118½in.
Est. **£10,000-12,000** *S*

*The Alvis Firefly was announced in
August 1932 as the successor to the
long running series of 12/50 and
12/60 cars. The Wilson pre-selector
gearbox was offered as an option at a
cost of an additional £15. In saloon
form the Firefly sold for £495, fuel
consumption was 26mpg and it had
a top speed of over 70mph.*

**Miller's is a price
GUIDE not a price
LIST**

ALVIS

1937 Alvis 4.3 Saloon, by Charlesworth, in excellent condition.
£35,000-37,000   *SVRe*

Alvis TA14 Saloon, original and with low mileage.
£10,000-11,000   *SVRe*

1935 Alvis Speed 20 Tourer, body by Vanden Plas, original and in excellent condition.
£65,000-70,000   *SVRe*

1934 Alvis Firefly Open Tourer, by Cross & Ellis.
£24,950-26,950   *BLE*

MAKE	ENGINE	DATES	CONDITION		
Alvis			1	2	3
10/30	1460/4	1920-22	£7,000	£5,000	£3,000
12/50	1496/4	1923-32	£10,000	£7,000	£5,000
Firefly	1496/4	1932-34	£14,000	£10,000	£6,000
Speed 20 (tourer)	2511/6	1932-36	£45,000	£28,000	£18,000
Speed 20 (closed)	2511/6	1932-36	£22,000	£15,000	£11,000
Crested eagle	3571/6	1933-39	£10,000	£7,000	£4,000
Firebird (tourer)	1842/4	1934-39	£14,000	£10,000	£8,000
Firebird (closed)	1842/4	1934-39	£7,000	£5,000	£4,000
Speed 25 (tourer)	3571/6	1936-40	£45,000	£30,000	£20,000
Speed 25 (closed)	3571/6	1936-40	£25,000	£15,000	£12,000
3.5 litre	3571/6	1935-36	£35,000	£25,000	£18,000
4.3 litre	4387/6	1936-40	£44,000	£30,000	£22,000
Silver Crest	2362/6	1936-40	£14,000	£10,000	£7,000
TA	3571/6	1936-39	£18,000	£12,000	£8,000
12/70	1842/4	1937-40	£15,000	£10,000	£7,000

Make the Most of Miller's

Veteran Cars are those manufactured up to 31 December 1918 although only vehicles built before 31 December 1904 are eligible for the London/Brighton Commemorative Run. Vintage Cars are vehicles that were manufactured between 1 January 1919 and 31 December 1930

Make: Alvis
Model: TC/TD/TE/TF
Type: Saloon/Convertible
Years Manufactured: 1953-67
Price when new: TD21 Saloon,
1958-62, £2,827
Engine Type: Overhead valve
6 cyl
Size: 2993cc
Max Power: 115 bhp @ 4000
rpm
Transmission: 4 speed
Performance: Max speed: 104
mph; 0-60: 14 secs; Mpg: 18-20.

1938 Alvis Speed 25 S.C. Sports Saloon, by Charlesworth with knock-on wire wheels, restored.
£56,000-58,000   *DJ*

This was the show car on the Alvis stand at the Earls Court Motor Exhibition, 1938. The Speed 25 represented the state-of-the-art motor car design in 1938.

1948 Alvis TA14 Drop Head Coupé, 4 seater car with new hood, paintwork and mechanical overhaul.
£24,950-26,000   *DJ*

1936 Alvis Speed 20 Drop Head Coupé, with body by Charlesworth, fully restored.
£85,000-87,000   *SVRe*

1948 Alvis TA14 Saloon, by Mulliner with 1892cc, 4 cylinder engine.   **£6,200-7,500**   *LF*

1939 Alvis 4.3 Open Tourer, with body by Vanden Plas.
£124,500-127,000   *BLE*
At one time the 4.3 litre model was one of the fastest saloons on the British market, capable of over 100mph. After the second World War, Alvis adopted a one model policy, the TA14 appearing in 1946 having evolved from the pre-war 12/70. Its 4 cylinder, pushrod engine was of 1892cc, which continued in production until 1950.

1953 Alvis TA21 Three Position Drop Head Coupé, by Tickford and fitted with a TC21 100 engine and still has original red leather upholstery.
£32,950-34,000   *DJ*

1949 Alvis TA14 Drop Head Coupé, 4 cylinder 74 x 110mm, 1892cc, 65bhp at 4,000rpm, overhead valves, single SU carburettor with impact hot spot, 4 speed gearbox driving a hypoid bevel rear axle, half-elliptic springs front and rear with double acting dampers. This model, with Duncan Coachwork, is believed to be the only known survivor of just a handful built. Total body-off restoration 7-8 years ago, complete with handbooks and tools, including spare bulbs.
£20,000-22,000   *SEN*

The TA14 was the first post-war model of the famous Alvis concern. It was largely based on the old 12/70 though it had disc wheels in place of the earlier wires. Some 3,300 TA14s of all body types were produced.

1951 Alvis TA21 Drop Head Coupé 3 Litre Straight Six.
£10,000-14,000   *H*

Only 100 TB14 Roadsters had been produced when production stopped in 1950 and this example is numbered 87. When new the basic price of the car was £998 and this, together with Purchase Tax brought the price up to £1,276, a figure that was quite substantial for the time but reflecting the quality of manufacture. The 14hp model was introduced in 1946 and found great popularity in TA14 saloon form.

1950 Alvis TB14 Roadster, with coachwork by A.P. Metalcraft Ltd., Coventry.
£16,000-17,000   *ADT*

Miller's is a price GUIDE not a price LIST

1947 Alvis TA14 Saloon, by Mulliner with 4 cylinder engine.
Est. **£11,000-12,000**   *LF*

Based upon a pre-war design the TA14 was a very tough and flexible vehicle.

1959 Alvis TD21 Drop Head Coupé, fully restored.
£35,000-40,000   *CTC*

1963 Alvis TD21 II FHC, 5 Speed Manual.
£12,000-15,000   *RTC*

1954 Alvis TC/21/100 Grey Lady.
£10,000-15,000   *RTC*

MAKE	ENGINE	DATES	CONDITION		
Alvis			1	2	3
TA14	1892/4	1946-50	£10,000	£7,000	£3,000
TA14 DHC	1892/4	1946-50	£15,000	£12,000	£5,000
TB14	1892/4	1949-50	£25,000	£15,000	£7,000
TA21/TC21	2993/6	1950-55	£15,500	£9,500	£4,000
TA21/TC21 DHC	2993/6	1950-55	£20,000	£15,000	£11,500
TC21/100	2993/6	1953-56	£17,000	£11,000	£4,500
TC21/100 DHC	2993/6	1954-56	£25,000	£21,000	£14,000
TD21	2993/6	1958-62	£15,000	£12,000	£7,000
TD21 DHC	2993/6	1958-62	£30,000	£20,000	£12,000
TE21	2993/6	1963-67	£18,000	£15,000	£12,000
TE21 DHC	2993/6	1963-67	£30,000	£25,000	£15,000
TF21	2993/6	1966-67	£18,000	£15,000	£10,000
TF21 DHC	2993/6	1966-67	£30,000	£25,000	£15,000

1965 Alvis TE Manual.
£15,000-20,000 *RTC*

1965 Alvis TE21 DHC.
£25,000-30,000 *RTC*

1963 Alvis TD21.
£6,500-7,500 *ADT*

In 1958 Alvis began using their 3 litre production engine in the TD21 saloon and subsequent TE and TF21 series cars which eventually ceased production in 1967 but perhaps the most successful feature of the car was the Park Ward built bodyshell.

1963 Alvis TD21 Series II Two Door Saloon, with coachwork by Park Ward, 6 cylinder engine with overhead valve, water cooled monobloc 2993cc bore 84mm, stroke 00mm, 5 speed all synchromesh gearbox, front suspension by coil and wishbone semi-elliptic rear, hypoid bevel live rear axle and tyres .00 x 15in.
8,500-9,500 *S*

Originally styled by Graber of Switzerland the TD21 was evolved from TC108/G of the mid 1950s. Park Ward successfully produced lighter weight panels and together with minor restyling thus reducing body weight, helped Alvis achieve the height of its post-war reputation in the beginning of the 1960s. The final Alvis car was produced in 1967 following the acquisition of the company by Rover.

1967 Alvis TF21 DHC.
£30,000-45,000 *RTC*

1966 Alvis TF21 FHC Automatic.
£20,000-30,000 *RTC*

ARAB

The ARAB of 1926-28 was an
advanced sports car, chain
driven, and produced by Reid
Railton.

**1929 Arab Super-Sports Low
Chassis,** 4 cylinder in line,
water-cooled monobloc engine,
single overhead camshaft, 72mm
bore x 127mm stroke, 1960cc,
4 speed Moss gearbox, bevel rear
axle, semi-elliptic leaf spring
suspension, wheelbase 113in, tyres
4.75/5.00 x 20in.
Est. **£24,000-26,000**   *S*

ARMSTRONG-SIDDELEY

In 1919 the first Armstrong-
Siddeley, the 30hp 5 litre,
appeared, a product of an
amalgamation between
Armstrong Whitworth (Motor
Cars) and Siddeley-Deasey.
Many quality motor cars were
made before the company failed
in 1960, its motor cars too
expensive compared to its
rivals, mainly Jaguar.

**1929 Armstrong Siddeley Coupé
with Dickey,** engine capacity
2872cc.
Est. **£30,000-35,000**   *ADT*

*Of the four models produced for
1929, the 20hp was the most sporting
with successes in the Alpine Trial
and RAC Rallies. It was produced
with a variety of coachwork and with
the introduction of the Wilson
epicyclic gearbox it became a great
favourite amongst the ladies of the
aristocracy.*

MAKE	ENGINE	DATES	CONDITION		
Armstrong Siddeley			1	2	3
Hurricane	1991/6	1945-53	£9,500	£5,500	£2,500
Typhoon	1991/6	1946-50	£7,000	£3,000	£1,000
Lancaster/Whitley	1991/ 2306/6	1946-53	£7,500	£3,500	£1,250
Sapphire 234/236	2290/4, 2309/6	1955-58	£6,500	£4,000	£2,500
Sapphire 346	3440/6	1953-58	£8,500	£5,000	£2,500
Star Sapphire	3990/6	1958-60	£9,000	£6,000	£2,500

**1947 Armstrong Siddeley
Typhoon Fixed Head Coupé,**
with 2309cc, 6 cylinder engine.
£2,600-3,000   *LF*

*Armstrong Siddeley's post-war
range comprised the Lancaster
6 light Saloon, the Whitley 4 light
Saloon and variations, the
Hurricane Drop Head Coupé and the
Typhoon Fixed Head Coupé. The
Typhoon was only built from 1946 to
1950 whereas the others went on to
1952 or 1953.*

MAKE	ENGINE	DATES	CONDITION		
Armstrong-Siddeley			1	2	3
30HP	4965/6	1919-23	£20,000	£15,000	£12,000
18HP	2385/6	1922-23	£18,000	£12,000	£9,000
15HP	1930/6	1929-34	£16,000	£10,000	£6,000
12HP	1434/6	1933-36	£12,000	£8,000	£5,000
20HP	3190/6	1933-36	£10,000	£8,000	£4,000
15HP	2169/6	1934-35	£10,000	£7,000	£4,000
Special	4960/6	1934-38	£15,000	£9,000	£6,000
Sports 17	2394/6	1934-39	£8,000	£5,000	£3,000
12	1666/6	1936-39	£7,000	£4,500	£2,000

1954 Armstrong Siddeley Sapphire 346, with 3435cc, 6 cylinder engine, this car has had only 3 owners from new and comes with the original registration book. **£3,800-4,200**   *LF*

During the 6 year production of the Sapphire 346, some 7,000 were built with the option of automatic, pre-select or manual gear boxes.

1954 Armstrong Siddeley Sapphire, with 3499cc, 6 cylinder engine. **Est. £8,000-10,000**   *ADT*

Miller's is a price Guide not a price List

The price ranges given reflect the average price a purchaser should pay for similar vehicle. Condition, rarity, provenance, racing history, originality and any restoration are factors that must be taken into account when assessing values. When buying or selling, it must always be remembered that prices can be greatly affected by the condition of any vehicle. Unless otherwise stated, all cars shown in Miller's are of good merchantable quality, and the valuations given reflect this fact. Vehicles offered for sale in exceptionally fine condition or in poor condition may reasonably be expected to be priced considerably higher or lower respectively than the estimates given herein

Make: Armstrong Siddeley
Model: Star Sapphire
Type: Saloon/Limousine
Years Manufactured: 1958-60
Price when new: £2,645
Engine Type: Overhead valve 6 cyl
Size: 3990cc
Max Power: 165 bhp @ 4250 rpm
Transmission: Auto
Performance: Max speed: 100 mph; 0-60: 14 secs; Mpg: 12-18.

1955 Armstrong Siddeley Sapphire. Est. £8,000-10,000   *ADT*

1960 Armstrong Siddeley Star Sapphire 4½ Litre Automatic. Est. £6,500-8,000   *Cen*

Considered the last and best of the Sapphires, the Star used a 3990cc, 6 cylinder engine that with its twin carburettors produced 165bhp. It had servo disc/drum brakes and a Borg-Warner automatic gearbox. Only 980 Star Sapphires were produced during 1959 and 1960.

ASTON MARTIN

Although founded by Lionel Martin and Robert Bamford in 1914, the first vehicle was not produced until 1922. Most of the pre-war cars were 1½ litre models. David Brown, the tractor manufacturer, bought the company in 1947 and produced the DB Series of sports and GT cars, winning at Le Mans and the World Sportscar Championships in 1959.

1933 Aston Martin Le Mans.
£50,000-80,000   *DG*

1930 Aston Martin 1½ Litre International, with coachwork by Bertelli, chassis No. 567 and engine No. 567.
£48,950-52,000   *C*

Engine: 4 cylinder 1495cc, 56bhp at 4,250rpm. Dry sump lubrication. Gearbox: 4 speed and reverse. Brakes: mechanical Perrot-type front. Suspension: ½ elliptic front and rear. Shock absorbers: André Hatford all round. Wheel base: 8ft 6in, track 4ft 4in, tyres 4½ x 19in. Right-hand drive.
In 1926 Aston Martin Ltd. was formed and their new car was ready for the London Motor Show in 1927. It was a completely re-designed car in all ways and some 15 were built, both flat and long chassis versions.

1938 Aston Martin 15/98 2 Litre Short Chassis Sports Tourer, chassis No. B.8-866-SO, engine No. 8-866-SO a 4 cylinder in-line 1949cc engine with 98bhp at 5,000rpm, twin S.U. carburettors, a gearbox with 4 speeds plus reverse, synchromesh on 2nd, 3rd and 4th. Girling brakes, 14in, and hydraulic drum on 4 wheels. Suspension with half elliptic springs with hydraulic shock absorbers, 17in Rudge Whitworth wheels with centre lock wire spoke, overall length 13ft 9in, wheelbase 8ft 3in, track 4ft 6½in.
Est. **£55,000-65,000**   *C*

Two experimental 2 litres were entered for the 1936 Le Mans 24-hour race, unfortunately the race was cancelled at the last moment due to French labour strikes. The 2 litre model was launched as the 15/98 (15hp/98bhp) and was available on either a short or long chassis as a 2 seater, a coupé, open 2/4 seater or a saloon.

Make: Aston Martin
Model: DB1
Type: Sports
Years Manufactured: 1948-50
Quantity: 15
Price when new: £1,914
Engine Type: Overhead valve 4 cyl
Size: 1970cc
Max Power: 90 bhp @ 4750 rpm
Transmission: 4 speed manual
Wheelbase: 108in
Performance: Max speed: 85-95 mph.

The 1949 Works Prepared Aston Martin DB1 Le Mans Three Seater, 6 cylinder in line, water-cooled monobloc engine, twin overhead camshaft, 78mm bore x 90mm stroke, 2580cc, 4 speed gearbox, single dry plate clutch, hypoid bevel rear axle, independent coil spring front suspension, leaf rear springs, wheelbase 108in, chassis No. AMC/49/5, fitted with lightweight aluminium coachwork.
Est. **£120,000-150,000**   *S*

1953 Aston Martin DB2/4, with chrome w/w and has been restored.
£48,000-50,000   *DJ*

1955 DB2/4 Mk I Drop Head, C/N LML955, has been rebuilt.
£125,000-130,000   *Mar*

1953 Aston Martin DB2/4 Mk I Fixed Head Coupé, chassis No. LML515 and engine No. VB6J 286L, 6 cylinder engine with twin overhead camshafts, monobloc, 83mm bore x 90mm stroke, 2922cc, 4 speed syncromesh central change gearbox, hydraulic footbrake on 4 wheels, handbrake on rear wheels, independent coil front and coil rear suspension and right-hand drive.
£50,000-55,000   *C*

1954 Aston Martin DB2/4 Mk I, by Mulliner, with 2580cc, 6 cylinder engine.
Est. **£30,000-35,000**   *ADT*

1955 Aston Martin DB Mk II (2/4) Development Model, chassis No. Am/300/1102 and engine No. VBLJ 623.
Est. **£38,000-42,000**   *P*

In 1947 Aston Martin Ltd was bought by tractor manufacturer and entrepreneur David Brown resulting in the birth of the legendary 'DB' series of cars, starting with the 2 litre Sports (DBI) in 1948 and culminating with the DBS V8 in 1972. In 1953 the 2580cc DB2/4 appeared in coupé and drop head form to world wide acclaim. This was followed by the 2922cc Mk II in '55 and the heavier but more powerful Mk III in '57 with front disc brakes.

1955 DB2/4 RHD C/N LML969,
with rebuilt engine.
£58,000-60,000 *Mar*

**1956 Aston Martin DB2/4 Mk II
Fixed Head Coupé,** chassis No.
AM 300 1168 and engine No.
VB6J 793, 6 cylinder twin overhead
camshaft, monobloc, 83mm x 90mm
stroke, 2922cc, 140bhp and 4 speed
synchromesh gearbox, 4 wheel
hydraulic brakes, independent coil
front and rear suspension and
right-hand drive.
Est. £60,000-80,000 *C*

*The DB2/4 Mk II was released to the
public at the London Motor Show in
October 1955. It was the first Aston
to sport coachwork by the newly
purchased firm of Tickford in
Newport Pagnell, 199 DB2/4 Mk IIs
were made and of these 139 were
saloons.*

**1956 Aston Martin DB2/4 Mk II
Saloon,** 6 cylinder in line,
water-cooled monobloc engine,
overhead valves operated by double
overhead camshafts, 83mm bore x
90mm stroke, 2922cc, single dry
plate clutch, 4 speed gearbox,
hypoid bevel gear drive live rear
axle, front suspension by trailing
links and coil springs, stabilised by
Panhard rod, wheelbase 99in, tyres
16in.
Est. £45,000-55,000 *S(M)*

**1957 Aston Martin DB2/4 Mk III
Drop Head Coupé,** 6 cylinder in
line, water-cooled monobloc engine,
overhead valves operated by double
overhead camshafts, 78mm bore x
90mm stroke, 2580cc, single plate
dry clutch, 4 speed gearbox, hypoid
bevel drive rear axle, independent
front suspension by coil spring, live
rear axle with parallel radius arms
and coil springs, wheelbase 99in,
tyres 16in.
Est. £120,000-150,000 *S*

**1958 Aston Martin DB5 Mk III
Drop Head,** very well restored.
£85,000-98,000 *AUT*

**1959 DB2/4 Mk III LHD C/N
AM300-31674,** this car has been
restored.
£75,000-85,000 *Mar*

MAKE	ENGINE	DATES	CONDITION		
Aston Martin			1	2	3
DB1	1970/4	1948-50	£28,500	£17,000	£13,500
DB2	2580/6	1950-53	£30,000	£22,000	£15,000
DB2 Conv	2580/6	1951-53	£34,000	£26,000	£18,000
DB2/4 Mk I/II	2580/				
	2922/6	1953-57	£32,000	£24,000	£18,000
DB2/4 Mk II Conv	2580/				
	2922/6	1953-57	£35,000	£28,000	£20,000
DB2/4 Mk III	2580/				
	2922/6	1957-59	£29,000	£25,000	£18,000
DB2/4 Mk III Conv	2580/				
	2922/6	1957-59	£38,000	£32,000	£25,000
DB Mk III	2922/6	1957-59	£35,000	£28,000	£22,000
DB Mk III Conv	2922/6	1957-59	£40,000	£36,000	£26,000
DB4	3670/6	1959-63	£38,000	£26,000	£20,000
DB4 Conv	3670/6	1961-63	£55,000	£35,000	£25,000
DB4 GT	3670/6	1961-63	£110,000	£85,000	—
DB5	3995/6	1964-65	£35,000	£28,000	£20,000
DB5 Conv	3995/6	1964-65	£45,000	£32,000	£26,000
DB6 Mk III manual	3995/6	1965-69	£26,000	£24,000	£20,000
DB6 Mk I auto	3995/6	1965-69	£24,000	£20,000	£17,000
DB6 Mk I Volante	3995/6	1965-71	£48,000	£35,000	£28,000
DB6 Mk II Volante	3995/6	1969-70	£50,000	£38,000	£30,000
DBS	3995/6	1967-72	£14,500	£9,500	£6,500
AM Vantage	3995/6	1972-73	£18,500	£12,500	£9,500
DBS V8 (single headlight)	5340/8	1972-73	£17,000	£11,000	£8,500
AM V8 carb	5340/8	1973-78	£20,000	£13,000	£11,000
AM V8 (Oscar India)	5340/8	1978-85	£24,000	£15,000	£12,000
Vantage	5340/8	1977-85	£22,000	£14,000	£12,000
Volante	5340/8	1978-85	£35,000	£30,000	£25,000

Make: Aston Martin
Model: DB2
Type: Sports or Coupé
Years Manufactured: 1950-53
Quantity: 410
Price when new: Coupé, £2,042; Sports, £2,879
Engine Type: Double overhead camshaft 6 cyl
Size: 2580cc
Max Power: 105 bhp @ 5000 rpm; Vantage, 125 bhp @ 5000 rpm
Max Torque: 125 ft/lb @ 3000 rpm; Vantage, 144 ft/lb @ 2400 rpm
Transmission: 4 speed manual
Wheelbase: 99in
Performance: Max speed: 110 mph; 12.4 secs.

Miller's is a price GUIDE not a price LIST

1959 Aston Martin DB4 GT Coupé, chassis No. DB4GT/0110/R and engine No. 370/0110/GT. Est. **£200,000-250,000** *P*

Introduced at the London Motor Show in October 1958, the standard Aston Martin DB4 was an all new Grand Touring machine bodied by Carrozzeria Touring of Milan. Mechanically the car used a detuned version of the superb 3.7 litre twin cam straight six engine designed by Tadek Marek for the racing DBR2. The standard car produced some 240bhp whilst the more sporting Vantage offered 255bhp on the same chassis. The DB4 GT, was introduced in 1959, only 75 examples had been built when production stopped in 1963. The GT was 5in shorter than the standard car and weighed 200lb less and had a 272bhp engine. The DB4 GT was capable of 150mph, had a 0-60mph time of 6.4 seconds and 0-100mph could be reached in 14.2 seconds.

1960 Aston Martin DB4 Mk III Saloon, chassis No. DB4/334/R. Est. **£40,000-50,000** *P*

1958 Aston Martin DB Mk III 3 Litre Drop Head Coupé, coachwork by Tickford. **£58,000-60,000** *B*

1960 DB4 Series 2 RHD C/N DB4383R, with chrome wire wheels. **£59,500-62,000** *Mar*

1960 Aston Martin DB4 Series II, with chassis No. DB4/256/R and engine No. 370/268 with 6 cylinder chain driven twin overhead camshafts, aluminium block and cylinder head, 92mm bore x 92mm stroke, capacity 3670cc, twin SU carburettors, coil ignition, rated to develop 274bhp at 5,500rpm, the chassis is semi unitary platform type, with tubular steel frame members, independent front suspension with wishbone and coil spring/damper units, beam rear axle with coil springs, radius arms, and Watts linkage, 4 speed synchromesh gearbox, 4 wheel disc type brakes with vacuum servo, centre lock wire type wheels carrying 185 x 16 tyres and standard factory 2-4 seater, 2 door GT Coupé bodywork with aluminium panelling, built on Touring 'Superleggera' principles. Est. **£60,000-70,000**   *C(A)*

Make: Aston Martin
Model: DB4
Type: Coupé or Sports
Years Manufactured: 1958-63
Quantity: 1,110
Price when new: Coupé, £3,755; Sports, £4,449
Engine Type: Double overhead camshaft 6 cyl
Size: 3670cc
Max Power: 240 bhp @ 5500 rpm; Vantage, from Sept, 1961, 266 @ 5750 rpm
Max Torque: 240 ft/lb @ 4250 rpm
Transmission: 4 speed manual with optional overdrive or optional Borg-Warner 3 speed auto
Wheelbase: 98in
Performance: Max speed: 240 bhp engine, 141 mph; 0-60: 240 bhp engine, 8.5 secs.

1961 Aston Martin DB4 Mk II Superleggera Grand Touring Coupé, chassis No. DB4/573/R, and engine No. 370/582, 6 cylinder, twin overhead camshaft, 3760cc engine, 4 speed manual gearbox, 4 wheel disc brakes, wishbone front, coil springs rear suspension, and right-hand drive. Est. **£50,000-60,000**   *C*

The DB4 was capable of 140mph and the remarkable feat of accelerating to 100mph and returning to standstill within the timespan of 30 seconds. It was hand-built in small numbers and by the time that it was replaced by the DB5 after five seasons, only 1,202 examples had been built.

1963 Aston Martin DB4 Series V, chassis No. DB4.104.6R and engine No. 3701164. Est. **£25,000-28,000**   *ADT*

1963 Aston Martin DB4 Series V, chassis No. DB4/1019/R and engine No. 370/973. Est. **£35,500-37,500**   *ADT*

1964 DB5 Manual RHD C/N DB5-1495R, with chrome wire wheels and 92,000 miles recorded. **£65,000-70,000**   *Mar*

1965 Aston Martin DB5 Manual, a mechanical overhaul was carried out 30,000 miles ago and a 5 speed gearbox has been fitted. **£44,000-48,000**   *Cen*

MAKE	ENGINE	DATES	CONDITION		
Aston Martin			1	2	3
Lionel Martin Cars	1486/4	1921-25	£30,000	£20,000	£18,000
International	1486/4	1927-32	£33,000	£20,000	£18,000
Le Mans	1486/4	1932-33	£65,000	£45,000	£38,000
Mk II	1486/4	1934-36	£45,000	£35,000	£30,000
Ulster	1486/4	1934-36	£100,000	£80,000	—
2 litre	1950/4	1936-40	£25,000	£18,000	£14,000

Value is dependent upon racing history, originality and completeness. Add 40% if a competition winner.

1965 Aston Martin DB5 Sports Convertible, chassis No. DB5/C/2102R, and engine No. 4002095 with 6 cylinder, twin overhead camshaft, 3997cc, 285bhp, 5 speed synchromesh gearbox, front wheel servo disc brakes, independent front, coil spring live axle rear suspension and right-hand drive.
Est. **£130,000-150,000**   *C*

1965 Aston Martin DB5, excellent original condition.
£35,000-39,000   *AUT*

1967 4 Litre Aston Martin DB6 Coupé.
£32,000-35,000   *B*

Make: Aston Martin
Model: DB5
Type: Saloon/Convertible/Estate
Years Manufactured: 1963-65
Quantity: 1,050
Price when new: £4,248
Engine Type: Front engine, rear drive, in-line 6 cyl
Size: 3995cc
Max Power: 282 bhp @ 5500 rpm; Vantage option, 325 bhp @ 5750 rpm
Max Torque: 288 ft/lb @ 3850 rpm
Transmission: 4 or 5 speed, optional overdrive on 4 speed, or automatic
Wheelbase: 98in
Performance: Max speed: 141 mph; 0-60: 8.1 secs; Mpg: 15.

1965 Aston Martin DB5 Saloon, chassis No. DB5/2052/R and engine No. 400/2047.
Est. **£35,000-45,000**   *P*

The 6 cylinder twin overhead camshaft engine produced 285bhp and was first coupled to a 4 speed Aston Martin gearbox but later to a 5 speed ZF box.

The DB5 was announced in 1963 as a logical follow up to the DB4 which had been much modified over the years. It had an enlarged engine, a 5 in place of a 4 speed gearbox, adjustable dampers, 4 wheel power discs, rack and pinion steering, electric windows and the familiar Touring of Milan styled bodywork constructed from aluminium on a framework of small diameter steel tubes.

Make: Aston Martin
Model: DB6
Type: Saloon/Convertible
Years Manufactured: 1965-71
Quantity: 1,753
Price when new: Mk I, £5,084; Mk II, £5,501
Engine Type: Front engine, rear drive, in-line 6 cyl
Size: 3995cc
Max Power: 282 bhp @ 5500 rpm; Vantage option, 325 bhp @ 5750 rpm
Max Torque: 288 ft/lb @ 3850 rpm
Transmission: 5 speed overdrive or 3 speed auto
Wheelbase: 101.7in
Performance: Max speed: 148 mph; 0-60: 6.5 secs; Mpg: 15.

**1967 Aston Martin DB6 Mk I
Saloon,** chassis No. DB6 3206R and
engine No. 400 3248.
Est. **£35,000-40,000** *P*

1968 Aston Martin DBS.
Est. **£8,000-10,000** *ADT*

1969 Aston Martin DBS, chassis
No. DBS5322/R and engine No.
4003962/S, engine capacity 3995cc,
6 cylinder.
£30,000-33,000 *LF*

**1968 4 Litre Aston Martin DB6
Volante,** chassis No. DBVC 3703R
and engine No. 400 3802 with
6 cylinder, twin overhead camshaft,
triple carburettor, 4 litre, 282bhp,
automatic gearbox, 4 wheel servo
disc brakes, coil spring independent
front, live axle rear suspension and
right-hand drive.
Est. **£150,000-180,000** *C*

*The new Aston Martin DB6 model
was introduced at the 1965 London
Motor Show as a distinctively
restyled development of the
successful DB4 and DB5 model
ranges with the new flat 'Kamm-tail'
integral spoiler. The new bodyshell
was only 17lb heavier than its
predecessor, the DB6.*

Aston Martin DBS V8.

*Only 404 of this model were built
and were the last of the David Brown
cars to be produced. Produced after
David Brown's association with
Aston Martin had ceased, the car
was mechanically similar to the DB5
in most respects. Identifiable by
2 instead of 4 headlamps and a DB3
style grille, these cars, with their 5.3
litre, V8, 350bhp engine gave
150mph performance and superb
handling and comfort.*

**1969 Aston Martin DB6 Mk 2
Automatic.**
Est. **£15,000-20,000** *T&M*

1971 Aston Martin DBS Vantage Grand Touring Four Seater, chassis No. DBS 5665R and engine No. 4004739 SVC with capacity of 3995cc, 6 cylinders and right-hand drive. This particular car is in need of restoration.
Est. **£13,000-15,000**   *C*

Make: Aston Martin
Model: DBS V8
Type: Saloon/Convertible
Years Manufactured: 1969-date
Quantity: Still in production
Price when new: £7,501
Engine Type: Front engine, rear drive, V8
Size: 5340cc
Max Power: 350-375 bhp (estimated)
Transmission: 5 speed auto
Wheelbase: 102.8in
Performance: Max speed: 145 mph; 0-60: 6.2 secs; Mpg: 13.

Aston Martin DBS V8.
£45,000-48,000   *FOR*

1972 Aston Martin DBS V8 Convertible, V8 cylinder water-cooled, 4 overhead camshafts, 100mm bore x 85mm stroke, 5340cc, automatic transmission, single plate clutch, hypoid rear axle, independent coil front suspension, De Dion rear axle with coil springs, wheelbase 102¾in.
Est. **£40,000-50,000**   *S*

1972 Aston Martin DBS Vantage, chassis No. DBS5824/R and engine No. 400/468/4SVC with capacity of 3995cc, 6 cylinder.
Est. **£35,000-45,000**   *LF*

1974 Aston Martin AM V8.
£30,000-35,000   *RTC*

Make: Aston Martin
Model: Lagonda
Type: Saloon
Years Manufactured: 1976-date
Quantity: Still in production
Engine Type: Front engine, rear drive, V8
Size: 5340cc
Transmission: Auto
Performance: Max speed: 143 mph; 0-60: 8.8 secs; Mpg: 14.

1974 Aston Martin Lagonda V8 Four Door, chassis No. L12003 and engine No. V540/2003 with capacity of 5340cc, 8 cylinder.
£39,500-44,000   *ADT*

Some controversy exists as to just how many Lagonda V8s were eventually produced, either seven or eight.

1973 Aston Martin V8, chassis No.
V8/10650/RCA and engine No.
V/540/502 and capacity of 5340cc,
8 cylinder.
Est. **£45,000-47,000**   *ADT*

**1978 AM V8 Manual Volante
RHD C/N V8COR15402,** with
41,000 miles recorded and service
history.
Est. **£105,000-110,000**   *Mar*

1975 Aston Martin DBS V8,
chassis No. V8/11267/RCA, and
engine No. V/5401267 with capacity
of 5340cc V8.
Est. **£30,000-40,000**   *LF*

Miller's is a price Guide not a price List

The price ranges given reflect the average price a purchaser should pay for similar vehicle. Condition, rarity, provenance, racing history, originality and any restoration are factors that must be taken into account when assessing values. When buying or selling, it must always be remembered that prices can be greatly affected by the condition of any vehicle. Unless otherwise stated, all cars shown in Miller's are of good merchantable quality, and the valuations given reflect this fact. Vehicles offered for sale in exceptionally fine condition or in poor condition may reasonably be expected to be priced considerably higher or lower respectively than the estimates given herein

**1978 5.4 Litre Aston Martin V8
Coupé.**
£32,000-35,000   *B*

**1979 Aston Martin AM V8
Vantage.**
Est. **£90,000-100,000**   *S(A)*

1980 Aston Martin V8 Volante,
manual gearbox, low mileage.
£65,000-70,000   *AUT*

1981 Aston Martin Vantage Volante Convertible, 90° V8 cylinder, water-cooled, overhead valve, 5340cc, 3 speed automatic transmission, independent coil spring suspension, wheelbase 103in, tyres Avon 225/70.
Est. **£125,000-135,000** *S(M)*

Make: Aston Martin
Model: Vantage
Type: Saloon/Convertible
Years Manufactured: 1977-date
Quantity: Still in production
Price when new: £6,949
Engine Type: Front engine, rear drive, V8
Size: 5340cc
Max Power: 406 bhp (estimated)
Transmission: 5 speed or auto
Wheelbase: 102.8in
Performance: Max speed: 170 mph; 0-60: 5.4 secs; Mpg: 14.

1987 Aston Martin V8 Vantage Volante, chassis No. SCFCV81C6HTR15565 and engine No. V5805565X, with a capacity of V8, twin overhead camshaft per bank, 5340cc, 408bhp, 5 speed synchromesh gearbox, disc on all wheels servo-assisted brakes, independent front and rear suspension and right-hand drive.
Est. **£180,000-220,000** *C*

Allegedly the world's fastest road going car at the time of its introduction and 50 were built for sale. Production was built around a shortened Vantage chassis, Zagato used hand beaten aluminium for the body panels except for the plastic bootlid and front and rear deformable bumper section, which also house the light clusters. To improve its aerodynamics the glass for the front, rear and side screens was glued to the main pillars providing all round flush fitting and the side windows are split.

1986 Aston Martin Zagato, chassis No. SCFCV81Z7GTR20017 and engine No. V/580/0017/X with a capacity of 5340cc, 8 cylinder.
Est. **£150,000-200,000** *ADT*

1986 Aston Martin V8 Volante Convertible, 90° V8, water-cooled, double overhead camshafts per bank, electronic ignition, twin external oil coolers, 100mm bore x 85mm stroke, 5340cc, 3 speed automatic transmission with torque converter, hypoid final drive with limited slip differential, independent front and rear suspension with De Dion type rear axle, wheelbase 103in, tyres 15in.
£140,000-180,000 *S*

International Price Comparison

Make	FRANCE	GERMANY	ITALY	JAPAN	USA
Aston Martin	+4%	+2%	+2%	—	—

ASTON MARTIN

1986 Aston Martin Vantage Zagato, chassis No. SCFCV81Z3GTR20015 and engine No. V/580/0015/X, V8, 100mm bore, 85mm stroke, 5341cc, aluminium block and heads, 10.5:1 compression, 2 chain driven overhead camshafts per bank, 4 Weber 481DF 3/150 twin body carburettors, 432bhp (DIN) at 6,200rpm. Aluminium body, glass reinforced plastic bootlid. Transmission, ZF 5 speed gearbox, limited slip differential, front independent by wishbones and coil springs, telescopic dampers and anti roll bar suspension, rear De Dion axle with Watts linkage and longitudinal arms, coil springs and adjustable telescopic dampers, ventilated discs with servo brakes, alloy wheels, 255/50VR16 tyres, wheelbase 102¾in, track 59¾/60½in, length 172¾in, width 73¼in, height 51in and weight 3,638lb.
Est. £250,000-300,000   *C*

AUBURN

Auburn had been producing motor vehicles since 1900 with great success when Cord took over in 1924 with a range of cars designed by J. M. Crawford. Auburn went on to produce some wonderful vehicles, representing the best in American design.

1934 Auburn 850 Four Seater Tourer, right-hand drive car originally registered in South Africa, where it was owned by MGM Studios, and was reputedly used by Clark Gable whilst filming in Africa.
Est. £35,000-45,000   *P*

1936 Auburn 851 Supercharged Speedster, 8 cylinder in line, water-cooled side valve monobloc engine, 77.8mm bore x 120.7mm stroke, 4596cc, supercharged, 3 speed synchromesh gearbox with free wheel and dual ratio rear axle, single dry plate clutch, open shaft spiral bevel rear axle, semi-elliptic leaf springs front and rear, wheelbase 126in, tyres 7.00 x 16in, right-hand drive.
£80,000-85,000   *S*

The Auburn took its name from the Indiana town of its birthplace and the first car to bear that name appeared in 1900.

AUSTIN

Austin was founded by Herbert Austin (later Sir) in 1905 and built their reputation on reliable and rugged motor cars, albeit somewhat uninteresting and unglamorous. The ubiquitous Seven was built under licence worldwide, including USA, Japan, Germany and France. It formed the British Motor Corporation in 1952 with Morris, one of the most famous of its products being Alex Issigonis's Mini. BMC merged with Leyland in 1968.

1927 Austin Seven Chummy Two Door Open Tourer, chassis No. A39515 and engine No. M31108 with 4 cylinder, 8hp capacity, this vehicle is an ideal restoration project.
£8,000-8,500   *C*

An output of under 2,000 in 1923 leapt to 7,000 in 1925 and 25,447 in 1929.

1936 Austin 7 Ruby.
£3,000-3,200   *DB*

1928 Austin Seven Chummy Two Door Open Tourer, chassis No. C47612 and engine No. M58553 with 4 cylinder, 747cc capacity and right-hand drive, in need of restoration.
£4,500-5,000   *C*

1931 Austin Seven Box Saloon.
Est. **£3,800-4,200**   *ADT*

1931 Austin Seven Van, chassis No. 123488 and engine No. M124240.
Est. **£3,500-4,500**   *S*

1934 Austin Seven Saloon, chassis No. 195860 and engine No. M195804.
£5,555-6,000   *S*

1937 Austin Seven Ruby Saloon, engine No. M254990 and 747cc, 4 cylinder capacity.
Est. **£1,600-2,000**   *LF*

1928 Austin Seven Two Seater Racing Special, chassis No. KENT 1225 and engine No. AND 1097 with 747cc, 4 cylinder capacity.
£4,000-4,200   *LF*

1928 Austin Seven Taylor Sports.
£4,900-5,200   *ADT*

1928 Austin 12/4 'Open Road' Tourer, with 4 cylinder in-line, water-cooled monobloc, bore 72mm, stroke 114.5, capacity 1861cc, 4 speed gearbox, single dry plate clutch, shaft drive to helical bevel rear axle, semi-elliptic leaf spring suspension, tyres 4.75 x 21.
Est. **£14,000-18,000**   *S*

The Austin '12' appeared in 1922 and was one of the company's most successful models for the entire decade. The cars were well built, robust and reliable, and sold for a reasonable £550.

1933 Austin 10hp De Luxe Saloon, with 4 cylinder in-line water-cooled monobloc, side valve, capacity 1125cc engine, 4 speed gearbox, shaft drive to live rear axle, semi-elliptic leaf springs front and rear.
£6,270-6,500   *S*

1935 Austin Seven Single Seat Racing Car, 4 cylinder in-line, water-cooled monobloc engine, side valve, 56mm bore x 76mm stroke, 747cc, single dry plate clutch, 4 speed close ratio gearbox, torque tube drive sprial bevel drive live rear axle, independent front suspension by transverse leaf spring, rear suspension by quarter elliptic leaf spring, wheelbase 81in. tyres 15in.
£6,000-6,500   *S*

Suitable for 750 Motor Club and other competitive events.

1935 Austin Six Four Seater Tourer, this lovely original car has had two owners with 67,000 miles recorded and believed correct.
£12,950-13,500   *DJ*

Miller's is a price
GUIDE not a price
LIST

MAKE	ENGINE	DATES	CONDITION 1	2	3
Austin					
16	2199/4	1945-49	£3,000	£2,000	£1,000
A40 Devon	1200/4	1947-52	£1,500	£1,000	£750
A40 Sports	1200/4	1950-53	£6,000	£4,000	£2,000
A40 Somerset	1200/4	1952-54	£2,000	£1,500	£750
A40 Somerset DHC	1200/4	1954	£5,000	£4,000	£2,500
A40 Dorset 2 door	1200/4	1947-48	£2,000	£1,500	£1,000
A70 Hampshire	2199/4	1948-50	£1,750	£1,500	£1,000
A70 Hereford	2199/4	1950-54	£1,850	£1,500	£1,000
A90 Atlantic DHC	2660/4	1949-52	£8,000	£6,000	£4,000
A90 Atlantic	2660/4	1949-52	£5,000	£3,000	£2,000
A40/A50 Cambridge	1200/4	1954-57	£1,200	£750	£500
A55 Mk I Cambridge	1489/4	1957-59	£1,000	£750	£500
A55 Mk II	1489/4	1959-61	£1,000	£750	£500
A60 Cambridge	1622/4	1961-69	£1,000	£750	£500
A90/95 Westminster	2639/6	1954-59	£2,000	£1,500	£750
A99 Westminster	2912/6	1959-61	£1,500	£1,000	£500
A105 Westminster	2639/6	1956-59	£2,000	£1,500	£750
A110 Mk I/II	2912/6	1961-68	£2,000	£1,500	£750
Nash Metropolitan	1489/4	1957-61	£2,500	£1,500	£750
Nash Metropolitan DHC	1489/4	1957-61	£4,000	£3,000	£1,500
A30	803/4	1952-56	£1,000	£500	—
A30 Countryman	803/4	1954-56	£1,500	£1,000	—
A35	948/4	1956-59	£1,000	£500	—
A35 Countryman	948/4	1956-62	£1,500	£1,000	—
A40 Farina Mk I	948/4	1958-62	£1,250	£750	£200
A40 Mk I Countryman	948/4	1959-62	£1,500	£1,000	£400
A40 Farina Mk II	1098/4	1962-67	£1,000	£750	—
A40 Mk II Countryman	1098/4	1962-67	£1,200	£750	£300
1100	1098/4	1963-73	£1,000	£750	—
1300 Mk I/II	1275/4	1967-74	£750	£500	—
1300GT	1275/4	1969-74	£1,250	£1,000	£750
1800/2200		1964-75	£1,500	£900	£600
3 litre	2912/6	1968-71	£3,000	£1,500	£500

Make: Austin
Model: A30/A35
Type: Saloon, A35 Van or Commercial also
Years Manufactured: A30, 1951-56; A35 Saloon, 1956-59; A35 Commercials, 1959-62; A35 Van, 1962-66 (1098cc); A35 Van, 1964-68 (848cc)
Price when new: A35 Saloon, £541
Engine Type: Overhead valve 4 cyl
Size: A30, 803cc; A35, 948cc; A35 Vans, 1098/848cc
Max Power: A30, 28 bhp @ 4800 rpm; A35, 948cc, 34 bhp @ 4750 rpm; A35, 1098cc, 45 bhp @ 5100 rpm; A35, 848cc, 34 bhp @ 5100 rpm
Transmission: 4 speed
Performance: Max speed: A30, 65 mph; A35, 848/948cc, 75 mph; A35, 1098cc, 80 mph; 0-60: A30, 38 secs; A35, 848/948cc 29 secs; A35, 1098cc, 80 secs; Mpg: 38-42.

1933 Austin 7hp Two Seater Sports, with chassis No. 176148 and engine No. M 18383, 4 cylinder in-line, water-cooled monobloc, side valve, bore 56mm, stroke 76mm, capacity 747cc, 4 speed gearbox, dry plate clutch, spiral bevel rear axle, transverse semi-elliptic leaf front spring, quarter elliptic leaf rear springs, wheelbase 6ft 9in and tyres 4.75 x 15in.
£4,800-5,200 *S*

1936 Austin Seven Special.
£2,200-2,500 *LF*

1936 Austin Seven Brooklands, chassis No. 255509 and engine No. M288521 with 747cc, 4 cylinder capacity.
£8,000-8,500 *LF*

1936 Austin Six 18hp Saloon, with chassis No. 47461/18 and engine No. IEE S159/18 with 6 cylinder in-line, water-cooled monobloc, capacity 2510cc, side valve, 4 speed manual gearbox, shaft drive to live rear axle, semi-elliptic suspension front and rear.
£3,795-4,250 *S*

1938 Austin 'Big Seven', with chassis No. CRU 10486 and engine No. 1A 714, 4 cylinder, side valve 900cc and right-hand drive.
£1,650-1,800 *C*

The Austin 'Big Seven' range of cars was introduced in 1937 and was the third Seven produced by the company. It was named the Big Seven being of a larger capacity engine than the legendary Seven produced between 1922 and 1932.

1936 Austin Ruby Saloon.
£2,500-3,500 *DB*

1938 Austin 12, the interior being original but bodywork has been restored.
Est. **£3,500-3,750** *CC*

1947 Austin Eight Saloon, powered by a 900cc side valve engine.
Est. **£1,000-1,500** *Cen*

1937 Austin 10hp Cambridge Saloon, 4 cylinder in line, water-cooled monobloc engine, side valve 63.5mm bore x 89mm stroke, 1125cc, 4 speed gearbox, single dry plate clutch, spiral bevel rear axle, semi-elliptic leaf spring suspension front and rear, wheelbase 93¾in.
Est. **£4,200-4,800** *S*

1952 Austin A90 Atlantic Fixed Head Coupé, with chassis No. BE2 122798 and engine No. 1B 136520, 2660cc, 4 cylinder.
Est. **£10,000-12,000** *ADT*

MAKE	ENGINE	DATES	CONDITION		
Austin			1	2	3
25/30	4900/4	1906	£40,000	£30,000	£22,000
20	3600/4	1919-27	£30,000	£20,000	£14,000
12	1661/4	1922-26	£8,000	£5,000	£2,000
7	747/4	1924-39	£8,000	£4,000	£1,500
7 Coachbuilt	747/4	1924-39	£13,000	£9,000	£7,000
12/4	1861/4	1927/35	£5,500	£4,000	£2,000
16	2249/6	1928-36	£9,000	£7,000	£4,000
20/6	3400/6	1928-38	£18,000	£11,000	£8,000
12/6	1496/6	1932-37	£6,000	£4,000	£1,500
12/4	1535/4	1933-39	£5,000	£3,500	£1,500
10/4	1125/4	1933-47	£4,000	£3,000	£1,000
18	2510/6	1934-39	£8,000	£5,000	£3,000
14	1711/6	1937-39	£6,000	£4,000	£2,000
Big Seven	900/4	1938-39	£3,500	£2,500	£1,500
8	900/4	1939-47	£3,000	£2,000	£1,000
28	4016/6	1939	£6,000	£4,000	£2,000

Condition Guide

1. *A vehicle in top class condition but not 'concours' standard, either fully restored or in very good original condition*
2. *A good, clean, roadworthy vehicle, both mechanically and bodily sound*
3. *A runner, but in need of attention, probably both bodywork and mechanically*

1950 Austin A90 Atlantic Convertible, with chassis No. BD278965 and engine No. 1B100961, 4 cylinder water-cooled monobloc, overhead valves, bore 87.3mm stroke 111.1mm, capacity 2660cc, 4 speed gearbox, shaft drive to live rear axle, independent suspension front, semi-elliptic rear.
£7,700-8,000   *S*

Based on the Austin A90 chassis, the Austin Atlantic was intended to find an appropriate export style to capture American imagination. The design was not popular and the model had a very short production run and survivors are rare today.

1952 Austin A40 Somerset, with chassis No. G54712959 and engine No. 1G815673, 1200cc, 4 cylinder.
£800-1,000   *LF*

Austin introduced the A40 Somerset in 1952 to replace the earlier Devon, and they produced the Somerset until 1954.

1951 Austin A40 Devon Saloon, chassis No. GS2599933 and engine No. 19622032 with 4 cylinder water-cooled monobloc, overhead valves, bore 65.5mm, stroke 88.9mm, capacity 1200cc, 4 speed gearbox, shaft drive to live rear axle, independent front suspension, semi-elliptic leaf spring suspension at rear, wheelbase 7ft 8½in and tyres 5.25 x 16in.
£880-1,200   *S*

The A40 Devon Saloon, with 4 doors, was introduced in 1947 with its companion model, the Dorset, a 2 door car. The cars shared several modern features, the passenger doors were hinged from the front, and the gearbox had synchromesh between the 3 upper ratios.

1954 Austin A40 Somerset Saloon, with chassis No. GS4877763 and engine No. FHSRG14RH12674, 4 cylinder water-cooled monobloc, overhead valves, bore 65.5mm, stroke 88.9mm, capacity 1200cc, shaft drive to live rear axle, independent front suspension, leaf spring semi-elliptic suspension, wheelbase 7ft 8½in and tyres 525 x 16in.
£2,035-2,250   *S*

1949 Austin Princess A135, with engine capacity of 3995cc, 6 cylinder.
£3,100-3,500 *LF*

1948 Austin 4 Litre Two Seater Sports, with straight six 3992cc engine, believed Sheerline, a very rare vehicle which is believed to be of Australian origin as Austins were assembled in that country between 1948 and 1951 with some specifically Australian models being evolved at the time, chassis No. DS7 and engine No. 21.
£8,900-9,500 *Cen*

1956 Austin A90 Westminster Saloon, with chassis No. BS425240 and engine No. 1C25240, 6 cylinder water-cooled monobloc, overhead valve, bore 79.4mm, stroke 89mm, capacity 2639cc, 4 speed gearbox, shaft drive to live rear axle, independent coil spring front suspension, semi-elliptic springs at rear, wheelbase 8ft 7¾in and tyres 6.40 x 15in.
£1,760-2,000 *S*

The Austin A90 was a new model designed to provide a large car in the Austin range, and cost £791 when new.

1959 Austin Seven Mini Saloon with 4 cylinder water-cooled monobloc, overhead valves, transversely mounted, front wheel drive, capacity 848cc engine, 4 speed manual transmission and independent front and rear suspension.
Est. **£3,000-4,000** *S*

1960 Austin Seven Mini, chassis No. MA25444233 and engine No. 76900, 848cc, 4 cylinder capacity.
£1,900-2,200 *LF*

Make: BMC
Model: Mini/Clubman/1275GT
Type: Saloon
Years Manufactured: 1959-date
Quantity: 5,000,000+
Price when new: £497-£868
Engine Type: 4 cyl
Size: 848-1275cc
Max Power: 34-41 bhp
Transmission: 4 speed or auto
Performance: Max speed: 848cc, 82 mph; 0-60: 848cc, 18.7 secs; Mpg: 34.

1964 Austin Mini Cooper 'S' 1071cc Saloon, 4 cylinder in line, water-cooled monobloc engine, overhead valve, in unit with clutch, gearbox and final drive, bore 2.5in x stroke 3in, 4 speed manual transmission gearbox, independent front with Hydrolastic displacers suspension, independent rear with trailing arms and 145 x 10 tyres.
Est. **£6,000-8,000** *S*

1971 Austin Hearse. *Based on a London Taxi Cab*
£340-500 *CMA* *Chassis this hearse by coachbuilder Thomas Starting Junior uses a 2 litre petrol engine.*

1970 Austin Mini Cooper 'S', chassis No. XAD129452CA and engine No. 12H610X8154, 1275cc, 4 cylinder.
Est. **£5,000-6,000** *ADT*

AUSTIN METROPOLITAN

The Austin Metropolitan car was made in England by the then British Motor Corporation at their factory in Longbridge, Birmingham. It was an American design by Nash and early Metropolitans were known as either Nash or Hudson Metropolitans. Production of prototypes started in 1952 with mass production following in 1953. Cars were available to the public from March 1954. It was specifically for export until 1957 when, for one reason or another, the model was released to the home market. These cars were known simply as the Metropolitan 1500. Four years later came the end. Sales slowed and ceased in 1961. Hard top and convertible versions were available throughout the production run. Approximately 103,000 cars were produced with 95,000 or so destined for the North American market.

Austin Metropolitan Convertible, in very good condition.
£2,700-3,500 *MOC*

Austin Metropolitan 1500.
£1,800-2,100 *LF*

Austin of Britain and Nash in the USA pooled resources to produce a compact car in the American style which was marketed in the UK as the Austin Metropolitan and in the USA as the Nash Metropolitan and the convertible is more desirable. Convertibles, and particularly prize winning examples, will command a premium over the above prices which are offered only as a guide. Contact the Owners Club if you require further advice.

AUSTIN HEALEY

The Donald Healey Motor Company designed the 100 BNI around the Austin A90 power plant. Austin were keen to adopt the project as a potential rival to the Triumph TR2. The 100/4 developed to the 100/6 and then the famous 3000. The Sprite took the affordable end of the market with the Mk I frogeye becoming one of the best bred sports cars. The Sprite remained in production until 1977. The big Healey ceased in 1968.

1958 Austin Healey 'Speedwell' Sprite Mk I.
£15,000-20,000   *CTC*

1955 Austin Healey 100/4, with chassis No. BN1222872 and engine No. IB222872 with 2660cc, 4 cylinder capacity.
Est. £2,200-2,700   *LF*

Austin Healey Mk I.
Est. £8,000-9,000   *Cen*

1959 Austin Healey Sprite Mk I, chassis No. AN5-L/15445 and engine No. 2C-U-H/15183.
Est. £4,000-6,000   *Cen*

Miller's is a price GUIDE not a price LIST

1959 Austin Healey Sprite 948cc Mk I Roadster.
£6,000-7,000   *B*

The 'Frogeye' Austin Healey Sprite, a twin carburettor, 'A' series engined sports car based on the A35 was introduced in May 1958. The frogeye headlamps came about almost by accident when the original lay flat lamps were too expensive to engineer.

1959 Austin Healey 'Frogeye' Sprite Mk I Sports Roadster, 4 cylinder, water-cooled monobloc engine, pushrod operated overhead valves, 62.9mm bore x 76.2mm stroke, 948cc, 4 speed manual gearbox, shaft drive to live rear axle, independent front suspension, quarter elliptic rear springs with radius arms.
Est. £6,400-7,000   *S(A)*

1957 BN4 100/6, with overdrive and wire wheels.
£18,900-20,000   *Mar*

1956 Austin Healey 100/4.
Est. **£12,000-15,000**   *Cen*

Austin Healey production began in 1953 after Donald Healey introduced his design to the then managing director of B.M.C. The 2660cc engine from the old Austin A90 produced 90bhp and gave a top speed of just 100mph. The original BNI specification included a 4 speed gearbox with top gear blanked off. Electric overdrive on 3rd and 2nd gears effectively gave 5 forward gears.
Various performance options followed including the 100S which featured an all aluminium body and produced 132bhp. Also a BN2 variation, the 100M, in two tone paintwork, 110bhp engine and chassis modifications was produced in slightly greater quantity.

1957 Austin Healey 100/6 BN4.
Est. **£14,000-18,000**   *Cen*

The 100/6 was introduced in 1956, was the first model to be fitted with the 6 cylinder engine. There were 14,436 100/6s produced until it was replaced by the Mk I Austin Healey 3000 in 1959.

1957 Austin Healey 100/6 BN4, with right-hand drive.
£24,000-30,000   *Ren*

1954 BN2, RHD, with wire wheels and has only travelled 4,000 miles since being rebuilt. **£24,900-26,000**   *Mar*

1962 Austin Healey 3000 Mk II.
£11,500-12,000   *ADT*

1959 Austin Healey 3000 Mk I,
LHD and wire wheels.
Est. **£9,000-12,000**   *Cen*

Introduced in 1959, the 3000 Mk I was similar to the 100/6, however, a 6 cylinder, 2912cc, 124bhp engine was fitted along with front disc brakes.

1961 Austin Healey 3000 Mk I Roadster.
£11,500-12,500   *B*

Make: Austin-Healey
Model: 100 Six
Type: Sports
Years Manufactured: 1956-59
Quantity: 14,439
Price when new: £1,223
Engine Type: Overhead valve 6 cyl
Size: 2639cc
Max Power: 102/117 bhp @ 4600/4750 rpm
Max Torque: 142/144 ft/lb @ 2400/3000 rpm
Transmission: 4 speed manual with optional electric overdrive
Wheelbase: 92in
Performance: Max speed: early, 102 mph; late, 111 mph; 0-60: early, 11.2 secs; late, 12.9 secs.

Prompted by the use of triple carburettors in the 1960 competition Healeys, the Mk II 3000 for 1961, adopted a triple carburettor layout. Only the BN7 and the BT7 series were fitted with this format, due to the inadequacies of the servicing garages of the time and subsequently the later models reverted to the twin carburettor layout.

1961 Austin Healey 3000 Mk II,
with engine capacity of 2912cc, 6 cylinder.
Est. **£16,500-18,500**   *ADT*

1963 Austin Healey 3000 Mk II Convertible.
Est. **£13,000-15,000**   *S*

By 1963 the 3 litre engine was developing some 136bhp at 3,750rpm, giving a performance in excess of 100mph.

1962 Austin Healey 3000 Mk II.
£15,100-15,500   *Cen*

Locate the source

The source of each illustration in Miller's can be found by checking the code letters below each caption with the list of contributors

1962 Austin Healey 3000 Mk II Roadster.
£16,000-18,000   *B*

Make Austin Healey	FRANCE —	GERMANY +3%	ITALY +3%	JAPAN +5%	USA −5%

Austin Healey 3000 Mk III
fully restored.
£35,000-40,000   *CTC*

INTERNATIONAL PRICE COMPARISON

The figures below represent a percentage increase or decrease on average condition for middle of the range models. The top models, particularly with a racing history or proven provenance, can be considered in the market place as any other work of art.

— = same price as U.K.

Make	FRANCE	GERMANY	ITALY	JAPAN	USA
Alfa Romeo	+2	+2	+5	+5	—
Aston Martin	+4	+2	+2	—	—
Austin Healey	—	+3	+3	+5	−5
Bentley	+5	+3	—	+10	−3
Bugatti	+5	—	+10	+20	+10
Cadillac	−10	—	−2	—	—
Chevrolet	−10	—	−2	—	+1
Ferrari	+5	—	+2	+15	—
Fiat	—	—	—	+2	+2
Ford	−4	+3	−4	−5	+8
Jaguar	—	+5	—	+3	−3
Lamborghini	+5	—	+2	+5	+6
Land Rover	−20	—	−5	—	−20
Maserati	+5	—	+7	+10	—
Mercedes-Benz	−5	+10	+3	−5	−5
MG	—	+7	−5	+5	+10
Mini (Austin)	+5	+3	—	+10	−15
Morris	−5	−3	−10	−10	−15
Porsche	+5	+5	+3	+7	+5
Rolls-Royce	+5	—	—	+15	+7
Triumph	+2	+5	—	+2	+4
Volkswagen	+5	+5	—	—	−15

1954 Austin Healey 100 LHD, fully restored.
£28,000-30,000   *CTC*

Austin Healey 100/4 BN1 Sports Two Seater LHD, 4 cylinder, overhead valve, twin SU H4 carburettors, 2660cc, 90bhp engine.
£10,000-11,000   *SEN*

The 1954 Austin Healey 100S 2.6 Litre (Stirling Moss) Works Team Car, with 4 cylinder in line, water-cooled monobloc engine, detachable aluminium cylinder head, overhead valve, bore 87.3mm x stroke 111.1mm, 2660cc, 132bhp at 4,700rpm, 4 speed gearbox with manual transmission, shaft drive to live rear axle, independent wishbone and coil spring suspension front, semi-elliptic rear springs.
£176,000-200,000   *S*

Austin Healey 3000 Mk II, this car has been restored and has 4 speed manual with overdrive.
Est. **£14,000-18,000**   *H*

1963 Austin Healey 3000 Mk IIa, with chrome wire wheels.
£18,000-19,000   *Cen*

1966 Austin Healey Mk III, RHD.
£20,000-25,000   *DJ*

MAKE Austin-Healey	ENGINE	DATES	CONDITION 1	2	3
100 BN 1/2	2660/4	1953-56	£25,000	£15,000	£11,000
100/6, BN4/BN6	2639/6	1956-59	£21,000	£15,000	£9,000
3000 Mk I	2912/6	1959-61	£22,000	£14,000	£9,000
3000 Mk II	2912/6	1961-62	£24,000	£15,000	£9,000
3000 Mk IIA	2912/6	1962-64	£23,000	£15,000	£11,000
3000 Mk III	2912/6	1964-68	£23,000	£16,000	£12,000
Sprite Frogeye Mk I	948/4	1958-61	£7,000	£4,000	£2,000
Sprite Mk II	948/4	1961-64	£4,000	£2,000	£500
Sprite Mk III	1098/4	1964-66	£4,000	£2,000	£500
Sprite Mk IV	1275/4	1966-71	£4,000	£2,000	£500

Make: Austin-Healey
Model: Sprite
Type: Sports
Years Manufactured: 1958-71
Quantity: 129,359
Price when new: £612-703
Engine Type: Overhead valve 4 cyl
Size: 948/1098/1275cc
Max Power: 43/56/65 bhp @ 5000 rpm
Max Torque: 948cc, 52 ft/lb @ 3300 rpm
Transmission: 4 speed
Wheelbase: 80in
Performance: Max speed: 85/90/93 mph; 0-60: 23/18/15 secs; Mpg: 35-45.

1959 Austin Healey 100/6 LHD.
£9,000-10,000 *LF*

1963 Austin Healey 3000 Mk II A 2+2 Sports, with 6 cylinder in line, water-cooled monobloc engine, overhead valve, capacity 2912cc, 4 speed manual gearbox with overdrive, shaft drive to live rear axle, spiral bevel rear axle, independent coil springs suspension in front, semi-elliptic leaf rear springs, wheelbase 90in, 15in tyres, right-hand drive, completely restored in 1987.
Est. £24,000-26,000 *S*

Austin Healey 3000 Mk III Phase 2, LHD.
£18,000-20,000 *SEN*

1965 Austin Healey 3000 Mk III.
£3,900-6,000 *ADT*

1964 Austin Healey 3000 Mk III Sports Convertible, LHD.
£22,000-25,000 *S*

1965 Austin Healey 3000 Mk III Sports Convertible, with 6 cylinder engine cast integrally with crankcase, water-cooled monobloc, pushrod operated overhead valves, bore 83.36mm x stroke 89mm, 2912cc, developing 150bhp at 5,250rpm, 3 speed manual gearbox with overdrive, shaft drive to live rear axle, independent front suspension with wishbones, coil springs, shock absorbers and anti-sway bars, semi-elliptic rear with shock absorbers and Panhard rod, wheelbase 92in, 5.90 x 15in tyres, left-hand drive.
£13,500-14,000   *S*

1966 Austin Healey 3000, with engine capacity 2912cc, 6 cylinder.
£36,000-38,000   *LF*

Only 1,038 of the 16,314 produced stayed in Britain, although many have now returned.

1965 Austin Healey 3000 Mk III.
Est. **£17,000-18,000**   *AMR*

1966 Austin Healey 3000 Mk III.
Est. **£22,000-25,000**   *C*

1966 Austin Healey BJ8 Phase 1 RHD.
£35,000-37,000   *Mar*

1966 Austin Healey BJ8 Phase 2 RHD, with overdrive and wire wheels.
£28,500-30,000   *Mar*

Make: Austin-Healey
Model: 3000
Type: Sports
Years Manufactured: 1959-67
Quantity: 42,902
Price when new: Mk I, £1,168; Mk II £1,185
Engine Type: Overhead valve 6 cyl
Size: 2912cc
Max Power: 142 bhp @ 4600 rpm (to May 1961); 132 bhp @ 4750 rpm (from May 1961)
Transmission: 4 speed, optional overdrive
Wheelbase: 92in
Performance: Max speed: 114 mph (to May 1961); 116 mph (from May 1961); 0-60: 9.5-10.5 secs; Mpg: 17-34.

AUTOCAR

Built in Ardmore, Pennsylvania from 1901-1912, the Autocar was the brainchild of the Clark brothers who had previously experimented more or less successfully with the Pittsburgh tricycles and 4 wheelers.

1907 Autocar Type XV 12hp Runabout, twin cylinder horizontally opposed engine, water-cooled, mechanical exhaust valves, atmospheric inlet valves, bore 4in x 4in stroke, 100-6cu in, 3 speed gearbox, shaft drive to live rear axle, semi-elliptic leaf spring front suspension, full elliptic leaf rear springs, wheelbase 80in, 30 x 3½in tyres.
£13,000-14,000   *SNY*

BENTLEY

The first production Bentley was the 1921 3 litre, starting a line of archetypal vintage sports cars. These Bentleys, with many body styles and builders, had many race successes, including a glorious string of Le Mans victories. Rolls-Royce bought the company in 1933 and Bentley continued to make their own version of the parent company's models. The present range, notably the Turbo, are going away from the Rolls-Royce image.

In summary there are three main areas of Bentley motor cars; firstly the Vintage models, produced by W. O. Bentley; the Derby Bentleys, made by what went on to become Rolls-Royce; and lastly the post-war Bentleys, made in Crewe.

Make: Bentley
Model: Continental S2/S3
Type: Saloon/Convertible
Years Manufactured: 1959-66
Quantity: 700
Price when new: £5,661-£8,945
Engine Type: V8
Size: 6230cc
Transmission: Auto
Performance: Max speed: 113 mph; 0-60: 8.9 secs; Mpg: 14.

1926 Bentley 3 Litre 'Speed Model', chassis No. LT1581 and engine No. LT1589, with fabric covered Weymann lightweight saloon body, built by J Gurney Nutting and Co. Ltd, London, body No. A723, 4 cylinder, with single gear driven overhead camshaft, 4 valves per cylinder, twin 'sloper' S.U. carburettors, and twin ML magnetos, bore 80mm x 149mm stroke, capacity 2996cc, channel section side members, with channel section cross members, beam axles front and rear underslung on semi-elliptic springs, with original friction shock absorbers at front, non-original hydraulic shock absorbers at rear, close ratio 4 speed 'A' type sliding mesh gears, 4 wheel rod operated Perrot-type brakes with 16in drums and centre lock wellbase wire type wheels, carrying 6.00 x 20 tyres and twin spare wheels mounted in front mudguards.
£65,000-70,000   *C(A)*

While most short chassis 'Speed Model' 3 litres, popularly known by

the usual colour of the radiator badge as 'Red Label', were fitted with the classic lightweight fabric tourer body produced by Vanden Plas, there were also other standard bodies offered by Bentley Motors, and of course many owners specified their own particular designs which were then executed by various coach builders.

1923 Bentley 3 Litre TT Replica Tourer, with 4 cylinder in-line water-cooled monobloc engine, overhead valve, overhead camshaft, bore 80mm x stroke 149mm, 2996cc, 4 speed gearbox, cone clutch, spiral bevel rear axle, semi-elliptic leaf spring suspension front and rear, wheelbase 118in and 5.00/5.25 x 21in tyres.
Est. **£120,000-150,000**   *S*

1928 Bentley 4½ Litre Sports Tourer, chassis No. KM 3093 and engine No. ES3605 4 cylinder in-line, single overhead camshaft, bore 100mm, stroke 140mm, capacity 4398cc 4 valves per cylinder, 4 speed sliding mesh and reverse, right-hand change, single dry plate clutch, semi-elliptic leaf springs front and rear and right-hand drive.
£145,000-150,000   *C(A)*

BENTLEY

1926 Bentley 3 Litre Speed Model Tourer, coachwork by Jarvis and Sons.
Est. £120,000-140,000   *B*

1928 Bentley 6½ Litre Open Two Seater Replica, coachwork by Richard Moss.
Est. £180,000-220,000   *B*

1931 Bentley 8 Litre Tourer, chassis No. YR 5076 and engine No. YR 5076 6 cylinder in-line, 7983cc bore and stroke 110mm x 140mm, compression ratio 5.5:1, 225bhp at 3,200rpm, single overhead camshaft with 4 valves per cylinder, ignition coil and magneto with 2 sparking plugs per cylinder, twin S.U. HO8 carburettors, 4 speed F type gearbox with right-hand gate gear change, single dry plate clutch, 4 wheel drum servo assisted brakes, deep channel-section chassis with tubular cross members, semi-elliptic front and rear suspension with rear springs outrigged, Bentley-Draper Duplex shock absorbers, Rudge wheels with Whitworth centre-lock wire spoke and 21in x 700 tyres, wheelbase 13ft, track 4ft 8in, overall length 17ft 9in.
Est. £700,000-850,000   *CNY*

1929 Bentley 4½ Litre, with original Thrupp & Maberly coachwork, excellent condition.
£150,000-180,000   *BC*

60

1929 Bentley 4½ Litre Tourer, chassis No. FB 3304 and engine No. FB 3304.
Est. **£180,000-220,000**   *P*

1934 Bentley 3½ Litre Saloon, by Park Ward, with chassis No. B140CR and engine No. M8PB.
Est. **£18,000-22,000**   *LF*

1934 Bentley 3½ Litre Sports Saloon, coachwork by Hooper, chassis No. D16AHO, engine No. H3BN, 6 cylinder, overhead valve, water-cooled monobloc engine, 3669cc, 4 speed gearbox with synchromesh, servo assisted brakes, semi-elliptic front and rear suspension.
£35,000-37,500   *S*

In 1933 a new 3½ litre Bentley (Rolls-Bentley) 'Silent Sports Car' which was powered by an improved version of the Rolls Royce 20/25 engine, with an OHV crossflow head and twin carburettors was announced. The power unit drove to a 4 speed gearbox with synchromesh on 3rd and top gears, the chassis embodied the Hispano power assisted braking system using a gearbox driven servo to aid braking effort.
R.R. improved on the Hispano arrangement, by making the brakes servo assisted also when travelling backwards, which was not the case with Hispano Suiza.
By 1936 some extra power was seen to be needed from the Rolls-Bentley engine, which was therefore bored out to 3½in to make the capacity 4¼ litres, which made the 4¼ the best of the Rolls-Bentleys. The car was in production for just over 3 years and 1,241 examples were built. The 6 cylinder engine has pushrod valve operation, the wheelbase is 10ft 6in and the track 4ft 8in.

MAKE	ENGINE	DATES	CONDITION		
Bentley			1	2	3
Abbreviations: HJM = H J Mulliner; PW = Park Ward; M/PW = Mulliner/Park Ward					
Mk VI Standard Steel	4257/				
	4566/6	1946-52	£24,000	£12,000	£7,000
Mk VI Coachbuilt	4257/				
	4566/6	1946-52	£30,000	£19,000	£15,000
Mk VI Coachbuilt	4566/6	1946-52	£60,000	£46,000	£35,000
R Type Standard Steel	4566/6	1952-55	£26,000	£12,000	£7,000
R Type Coachbuilt	4566/6	1952-55	£32,000	£20,000	£15,000
R Type Coachbuilt	4566/				
	4887/6	1952-55	£65,000	£48,000	£35,000
R Type Cont (HJM)	4887/6	1952-55	£90,000	£60,000	£50,000
S1 Standard Steel	4887/6	1955-59	£28,000	£16,000	£10,000
S1 Cont 2 door (PW)	4877/6	1955-59	£50,000	£40,000	£35,000
S1 Cont Drop Head	4877/6	1955-59	£90,000	£75,000	£50,000
S Cont F"back (HJM)	4877/6	1955-58	£85,000	£65,000	£40,000
S2 Standard Steel	6230/8	1959-62	£24,000	£14,000	£9,000
S2 Cont 2 door (HJM)	6230/8	1959-62	£50,000	£40,000	£30,000
S2 Flying Spur (HJM)	6230/8	1959-62	£45,000	£38,000	£30,000
S2 Conv (PW)	6230/8	1959-62	£85,000	£70,000	£50,000
S3 Standard Steel	6230/8	1962-65	£24,000	£15,000	£12,000
S3 Cont/Flying Spur	6230/8	1962-65	£45,000	£38,000	£30,000
S3 2 door (PW)	6230/8	1962-65	£35,000	£30,000	£22,000
S3 Conv (PW)	6230/8	1962-65	£50,000	£40,000	£32,000
T1	6230/6,				
	6750/8	1965-77	£15,000	£10,000	£6,000
T1 door (M/PW)	6230/6,				
	6750/8	1965-70	£21,000	£18,000	£12,000
T1 Drop Head (M/PW)	6230/6,				
	6750/8	1965-70	£30,000	£25,000	£18,000

Locate the source

The source of each illustration in Miller's can be found by checking the code letters below each caption with the list of contributors

1934 Bentley 3½ Litre Four Door
Sports Saloon.
£25,000-27,000   S

1934 Bentley 3.5 Litre Vanden
Plas Style Open Four Seater
Tourer.
£52,500-53,500   DJ

1935 Bentley 3.5 Litre Sports
Saloon, by Thrupp and Maberly,
this car has been restored.
£30,000-32,500   DJ

1935 Bentley 3½ Litre Saloon, by
Park Ward, for restoration.
£24,500-25,000   DB

1935 Bentley 3½ Litre Sports
Saloon, with coachwork by Park
Ward, chassis No. B85 CW and
engine No. D6BY 6 cylinder OHV,
3669cc, bore and stroke 3¼in and
4½in, 4 speed right-hand change
gearbox and mechanical brake
servo with semi-elliptic leaf spring
front and rear chasses.
£18,150-19,000   S

*This car was supplied to the Earl of
Carnarvon of Highclere Castle, Nr.
Newbury, Berks, in February 1935
through Jack Barclay Ltd. The
invoice shows that he paid an extra
£4.17s.6d. to have his crest painted
on the rear doors. The car passed
from him to H. F. S. Morgan in
1936, the founder of The Morgan
Car Co. who retained it until the
1950s. At the end of the 50s it was
exported to the United States where it
seems to have spent most of the time
in storage.*

1936 Bentley 4¼ Litre Sedanca
De Ville, with coachwork by
Gurney Nutting, chassis No.
B117GP and engine No. JS BY.
Est. £100,000-150,000   C

*After the takeover of Bentley by Rolls
Royce they produced the first of a
new breed of Bentley incorporating a
much modified 20/25 6 cylinder
engine known as the 'silent sports
car'.*

1937 Bentley Four Seater Tourer.
£48,500-50,000   DJ

MAKE	ENGINE	DATES	CONDITION		
Bentley			1	2	3
3 litre	2996/4	1920-27	£90,000	£60,000	£40,000
Speed Six	6597/6	1926-32	£110,000	£75,000	£50,000
4.5 litre	4398/4	1928-32	£100,000	£70,000	£50,000
8 litre	7983/6	1930-32	£500,000	—	£100,000
3.5 litre	3699/6	1934-37	£65,000	£30,000	£15,000
4.25 litre	4257/6	1937-39	£70,000	£35,000	£20,000
Mark V	4257/6	1939-41	£45,000	£25,000	£20,000

Prices are very dependent on engine type, body style and extras like supercharger, gearbox ratio, history and originality.

> **Miller's is a price GUIDE not a price LIST**

1938 Bentley 4¼ Litre MR Barouche De Ville, coachwork by James Young, chassis No. B38 MR, engine No. E4 BK, 6 cylinder in line, water-cooled monobloc engine, pushrod-operated overhead valves, 3½in bore x 4½in stroke, 4257cc, 4 speed, right-hand change gearbox with overdrive top gear, single dry plate clutch, spiral bevel rear axle, semi-elliptic leaf spring suspension front and rear, wheelbase 126in, tyres 17in.
Est. **£75,000-80,000**   *S*

1939 Bentley MX 4¼ Litre Razor Edge Saloon, with coachwork by Mann Egerton, 6 cylinder in line, water-cooled monobloc engine, pushrod operated overhead valves, bore 3½in x stroke 4½in, 4257cc, 4 speed synchromesh gearbox with overdrive top, single dry plate clutch, spiral bevel rear axle, semi-elliptic leaf springs front and rear, wheelbase 126in and 6.50 x 17in tyres.
£30,000-33,000   *S*

1939 Bentley MX 4¼ Litre Continental Sports Saloon, by Park Ward, in original condition, with chassis No. B137 MX and engine No. V8BE, 4257cc, 6 cylinder capacity.
Est. **£29,000-34,000**   *ADT*

1937 Bentley 4¼ Litre Pillarless Saloon, 6 cylinder, water-cooled monobloc engine, overhead valves, 3½in bore x 4½in stroke, 4257cc, 29.4hp RAC, 4 speed gearbox with shaft drive to live rear axle, semi-elliptic springs front and rear, wheelbase 126in.
Est. **£60,000-80,000**   *S(A)*

1939 Bentley 4¼ MR Continental, with coachwork by Park Ward, 6 cylinder in-line engine, bore 3¼in x stroke 4½in, 4257cc, RAC rating 29.4bhp, 4 speed gearbox, synchromesh on 3rd and 4th gear, spiral bevel final drive.
£34,000-37,000   *SEN*

1947 Bentley Mk VI Special Tourer, 6 cylinder in line, water-cooled monobloc engine, pushrod-operated inlet valves, side exhaust valves, 3½in bore x 4½in stroke, 4257cc, single dry plate clutch, 4 speed, right-hand change gearbox, hypoid bevel final drive, independent front suspension by coil springs, semi-elliptic leaf spring rear suspension, wheelbase 120in, tyres 16in.
£23,000-25,000   *S*

1948 Bentley 4.2 Litre Mk VI Saloon.
£22,000-25,000   *B*

1948 Bentley MK IV Two Door Four Seat Tourer, with coachwork by Saoutchik, Neuilly, Paris, 6 cylinder in line, water-cooled monobloc engine, pushrod operated overhead inlet valves, side exhaust valves, bore 3.5in x stroke 4.5in, 4257cc, single dry plate clutch, 4 speed gearbox, hypoid bevel drive live rear axle, independent front suspension by coil springs and wishbones, hydraulic dampers, semi-elliptic leaf spring rear suspension, adjustable lever arm hydraulic dampers, wheelbase 120in, and 16in tyres.
Est. £130,000-160,000   *S(M)*

1948 Bentley Mk VI Coach-built Sedanca De Ville Special, coachwork designed by William Towns.
£16,000-17,000   *ADT*

1949 Bentley Mk VI, James Young, in need of full restoration.
£6,950-8,000   *DB*

1949 Bentley Mk VI Drop Head, chassis No. B126F.V. and engine No. B63F, 4257cc, 6 cylinder capacity and drop head by Abbot of Farnham.
£49,000-50,000   *Ren*

Make	FRANCE	GERMANY	ITALY	JAPAN	USA
Bentley	+5%	+3%	—	+10%	−3%

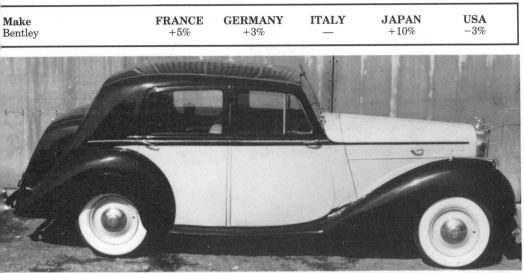

1949 Bentley Mk VI Saloon.
£8,000-12,000   *DB*

1950 Bentley Mk VI.
£18,000-22,000   *DJ*

1950 Bentley Mk VI Saloon,
chassis No. B170 HR and engine
No. B86H, 4257cc, 6 cylinder
capacity and 4 door, steel.
£13,000-14,000   *Ren*

*The car was rebodied in 1984 by
Roger Fry.*

1951 Bentley Mk VI Special,
chassis No. B25KL and engine No.
RE7753, 6 cylinder in-line,
overhead valve, bore 88.9mm,
stroke 114.3mm, 4257cc, 4 speed
transmission with synchromesh on
2nd, 3rd and 4th, mechanical brakes
at rear, hydraulic at front,
semi-elliptic rear spring suspension,
independent open helical front
spring, and right-hand drive.
£32,500-33,500   *C(A)*

1949 Bentley Mk VI Sedanca De Ville, coachwork by James Young, chassis No. B19SEW, engine No. B347E, 6 cylinder in line, water-cooled monobloc engine, pushrod-operated overhead inlet valves, side exhaust valves, 3½in bore x 4½in stroke, 4257cc, 4 speed manual gearbox, single dry plate clutch, semi-floating hypoid bevel rear axle, independent coil spring front suspension, semi-elliptic leaf rear springs, wheelbase 120in, tyres 6.7 x 16in.
Est. **£19,000-22,000**   *S(A)*

1950 Bentley Mk VI Standard Steel Saloon.
Est. **£9,000-14,000**   *Cen*

The Bentley Mk VI was the first Bentley to be produced after World War II. Offered with a choice of special bodies, 80 per cent of production were of Standard Steel coachwork. Production finished in 1952, the model being replaced with the 'R' Type.

1951 Bentley Mk II Roadster, by Lawrence, chassis No. SL01, available with copies of the original sales material and the 'Motor Sport' road test of October '74.
£37,000-42,000   *SEN*

1952 Bentley 4½ Litre Racer, b Donington.
£40,000-41,000   *BLE*

1952 Bentley Razor Edge 'R' Type, by H. J. Mulliner.
Est. **£30,000-40,000**   *CW*

1952 Bentley 4½ Litre Sports Special, chassis No. B42NZ and engine No. B2IN 6 cylinder OHV 4566cc, bore 3⅝in, stroke 4½in, 4 speed gearbox with right-hand change, independent front suspension, semi-elliptic rear suspension and wheelbase 10ft 10in, 4 seater open coachwor by Harry Rose.
Est. **£16,000-18,000**   *S*

The new post-war Bentley was sol primarily with a standard steel bodyshell by the Pressed Steel Company, however it was still possible for customers to buy a rolling chassis and to have coachwork fitted by an approved coachbuilder. The Mk VI was launched in May 1946 and by 195 production was over 1,000 units p year.

1953 Bentley 'R' Type.
£23,000-24,000   *DJ*

1952 Bentley Mk VI Sports Saloon, chassis No. B 145 PU, engine No. B222P, 6 cylinder in line, water-cooled monobloc engine, pushrod-operated overhead valves, side exhaust valves, 3½in bore x 4½in stroke, 4257cc, 4 speed manual gearbox, single dry plate clutch, semi-floating hypoid bevel rear axle, independent coil spring front suspension, semi-elliptic leaf rear springs, wheelbase 120in, tyres 6.7 x 16in.
£17,500-20,000   *S(A)*

1953 Bentley 'R' Type Saloon, with coachwork by H. J. Mulliner, chassis No. B397 SP and engine No. B448 S, 6 cylinder in-line, water-cooled monobloc, overhead inlet valves, side exhaust valves, bore 3⅝in, stroke 4½in, capacity 4566cc, 4 speed manual gearbox, semi-floating hypoid rear axle, independent front suspension, semi-elliptic leaf rear springs, wheelbase 10ft and tyres 16in.
£12,100-12,750   *S*

Launched in 1952 the 'R' Type Bentley featured the 4566cc engine which had been offered in the Mk VI.

1953 Bentley R Type Standard Steel Saloon, chassis No. B198UM, engine No. B224U, 6 cylinder in line, water-cooled monobloc engine, overhead inlet valves, side exhaust valves, 3⅝in bore x 4½in stroke, 4566cc, 4 speed automatic gearbox with manual selection over-ride, semi-floating hypoid rear axle, independent spring front suspension, semi-elliptic leaf spring rear, with adjustable ride, mechanical servo-power brakes, centralised chassis lubrication, wheelbase 120in, tyres 6.7 x 15in, right-hand drive.
Est. £14,000-18,000   *S(A)*

1954 Bentley 'R' Type, manual.
£22,000-23,000   *DJ*

1954 Bentley 'R' Type, automatic.
£9,750-10,000   *DB*

1954 Bentley R Type Standard Steel Saloon.
£16,500-18,000   *S*

1954 Bentley 'R' Type.
£22,000-23,000   *DJ*

1954 Bentley 'R' Type Standard Steel Saloon, chassis No. B65WG and engine No. B182W.
£13,500-14,000   *S*

1954 Bentley 'R' Type Convertible, by Park Ward, 6 cylinder, 4566cc, 192in long, 71in wide and tyre size 6.50 x 16. This car has been restored.
£125,000-128,000   *T&M*

1955 Bentley S2 Flying Spur Continental Saloon, coachwork by James Young & Co., chassis No. BC 80BY, V8 cylinder, water-cooled engine, pushrod-operated overhead valves, 104.14mm bore x 91.44mm stroke, 6230cc, 4 speed automatic gearbox, hypoid bevel rear axle, independent front suspension, semi-elliptic leaf spring rear, wheelbase 123in, tyres 8.00 x 15in.
Est. **£50,000-60,000**   *S*

1954 Bentley 'R' Type Continental.
£225,000-250,000   *PJF*

1954 Bentley 'R' Type.
Est. **£25,000-30,000**   *CW*

1956 Bentley Lightweight Four Door Sports Saloon, by H. J. Mulliner, with service history.
£48,950-50,000   *DJ*

1956 Bentley S1 Standard Steel Saloon, 6 cylinder in-line engine, water-cooled monobloc, overhead inlet valve, side exhaust valve, bore 3¾in, stroke 4½in, capacity 4887cc, 4 speed automatic gearbox, hypoid bevel rear axle, independent front suspension, semi-elliptic leaf rear spring, wheelbase 10ft 3in and tyres 15in.
Est. **£12,000-15,000**   *S*

The new S Type Bentley shared the same standard steel coachwork design as the contemporary Rolls Royce Silver Cloud, a 4 door saloon with an overall length of 12in longer than the predecessor.

1956 Bentley S1, standard steel saloon converted by Harold Radford, chassis No. B110EG and engine No. BE55, 6 cylinder, 4887cc, 212in long, 74½in wide, 64in high and tyre size 820 x 15.
£19,500-20,000   *T&M*

1954 Bentley 'R' Type 4½ Litre Two Door Coupé, chassis No. B401S.P. and engine No. BE 754, with Abbott coachwork, 6 cylinder in-line, 4566cc engine bore and stroke, 92mm x 114.3mm, 2 valves per cylinder, overhead inlet valves, side exhaust valves operated by single camshaft, twin S.U. H6 carburettors, CR 6.4:1, 150bhp, 4 speed gearbox G.M. automatic, deep channel section with cruciform bracing chassis, semi-elliptical rear springs, independent open helical front springs in combination with wishbone arms on hydraulic shock absorbers, drum type hydraulic power assisted brakes, pressed steel disc type wheels 16in with 6.50 x 16 tyres, overall length 16ft 7½in, wheelbase 10ft and track 4ft 10½in. Est. **£45,000-55,000**   *C*

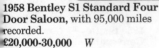

1957 Bentley S1, in good condition. Est. **£13,995-15,000**   *GWC*

1958 Bentley S1 Standard Four Door Saloon, with 95,000 miles recorded. **£20,000-30,000**   *W*

1958 Bentley S1 2 Door 2 Seater Drop Head Coupé, with coachwork by Freestone and Webb, 6 cylinder in-line engine, water-cooled monobloc pushrod operated overhead valves, side exhaust valves, bore 3¾in x 4½in stroke, 4887cc, automatic transmission in unit with engine, hypoid bevel rear axle with semi-floating half shafts, independent wishbone and coil spring front suspension, semi-elliptic, with aeroplane type shocks and sway bar, wheelbase 123in, 15in tyres. **£230,000-250,000**   *SNY*

1957 Bentley S1 Continental Two Door Coupé, coachwork by Park Ward, chassis No. BC 73 BG, engine No. BC 72 B. Est. **£95,000-100,000**   *S*

1958 Bentley S1 Continental Convertible.
£190,000-210,000   *PJF*

1956 Bentley S1 Continental Fastback, by H. J. Mulliner, with chassis No. BC99AF and engine No. BC98A.
£95,000-100,000   *T&M*

1957 Bentley Continental S1 Continental Fastback Coupé, with 6 cylinder water-cooled monobloc engine, 4887cc, 4 speed automatic transmission gearbox, shaft drive to live rear axle, independent coil spring front suspension, semi-elliptic leaf spring rear, and Goodyear whitewall tyres 235 x 15in.
£79,000-85,000   *S*

1957 S1 Continental Two Door Coupé, by H. J. Mulliner.
£165,000-170,000   *PJF*

1958 Bentley S1 Continental Convertible.
£190,000-210,000   *PJF*

Bentley S1 Continental, by James Young, one of 14 made.
£100,000-120,000   *PJF*

1958 Bentley S1 Standard Steel Saloon.
£14,850-15,500   *S*

1959 Bentley S1 Continental Flying Spur.
£100,000-120,000   *PJF*

1960 Bentley S2 Continental Drop Head Coupé, by Park Ward, chassis No. BC20LBY and engine No. B19BC, this car has had only one owner from new.
£85,000-90,000   *T&M*

1960 Bentley S2 Continental Two Door Coupé, by H. J. Mulliner, with chassis No. BC50AR and engine No. A49BC 8 cylinder, 6230cc, 212in long and 75in wide.
£89,000-95,000   *T&M*

This car was the 1960 Geneva Show Car.

1962 Bentley S2 Standard Steel Saloon, chassis No. B373DV and engine No. P4388, V8 cylinder, water-cooled, pushrod operated overhead valve, bore 104.14mm, stroke 91.44mm, capacity 6230cc, 4 speed automatic gearbox, semi-floating hypoid spiral bevel rear axle, independent coil spring front suspension, semi-elliptic leaf rear springs and wheelbase 10ft 3in.
Est. £12,000-15,000   *S*

1960 Bentley S2 Saloon.
Est. £10,000-15,000   *Cen*

The S2 was produced between 1959 and 1962, the outcome amounting to 1,932.

1961 Bentley S2 Flying Spur.
£65,000-70,000   *PJF*

1961 Bentley S2 Flying Spur.
£90,000-110,000   *PJF*

1962 Bentley Continental, by James Young.
£85,000-95,000   *PJF*

Bentley S3 Flying Spur, by H. J. Mulliner.
£125,000-140,000   *PJF*

1962 Bentley Continental Coupé,
by H. J. Mulliner.
£85,000-95,000   *PJF*

**1961 Bentley S2 Continental
Convertible,** by Park Ward.
£65,000-70,000   *DB*

1962 Bentley S2 Continental,
with coachwork by H. J. Mulliner,
V8 cylinder, water-cooled, pushrod
overhead valve, bore 104.14mm x
91.44mm, 6230cc, 4 speed
automatic, hypoid spiral bevel rear
axle, independent front, semi-
elliptic leaf spring rear suspension,
wheelbase 123in, right-hand drive,
requires attention to upholstery,
wood veneer trims and paintwork.
£62,000-65,000   *S*

**1962 Bentley S3 Continental
Convertible,** with coachwork by
Mulliner Park Ward, 90° V8
cylinder, water-cooled engine,
pushrod operated overhead valves,
bore 104.14mm x stroke 91.44mm,
6230cc, 4 speed automatic gearbox,
semi-floating hypoid spiral bevel
rear axle, independent coil spring
and wishbone front suspension,
semi-elliptic leaf rear spring,
wheelbase 123in and 8.20 x 15in
tyres.
£99,000-1,100,000   *S(M)*

**1962 Bentley S2 Continental
Flying Spur Four Door Saloon,**
coachwork by H. J. Mulliner,
chassis No. BC 123CZ, engine No.
C 122 BC.
£90,000-95,000   *S*

**1962 S3 Bentley Continental
Coupé,** by H. J. Mulliner.
£90,000-110,000   *PJF*

**1964 Bentley S3 Drop Head
Coupé,** Mulliner Park Ward with
air conditioning.
Est. **£85,000-90,000**   *CW*

1963 Bentley S3 Drop Head Coupé, 90° V8 cylinder, water-cooled engine, pushrod-operated overhead valve, 104.14mm bore x 91.44mm stroke, 6230cc, 4 speed automatic gearbox, semi-floating hypoid bevel rear axle, independent coil spring and wishbone front suspension, semi-elliptic leaf rear springs, wheelbase 123in, tyres 8.20 x 15in. Est. **£110,000-140,000** *S*

1963 Bentley S3 Continental, Drop Head Coupé, LHD, by Park Ward, this car has been restored. **£110,000-120,000** *PJF*

Bentley S3 Continental, by James Young. **£125,000-140,000** *PJF*

1964 Bentley S3 Standard Steel, with air conditioning and full service history. **£30,000-35,000** *CW*

1964 Bentley S3 Continental Flying Spur. **£90,000-100,000** *PJF*

1965 Bentley S3 Convertible, a Mulliner Park Ward car. **£115,000-120,000** *CW*

1965 Bentley S3 Drop Head Coupé, coachwork by Mulliner Park Ward. Est. **£80,000-100,000** *S*

1968 Bentley T1. **£7,300-8,000** *Cen*

Introduced in 1966 to replace the S3 the T1 had different body styling from its predecessor with all independent self-levelling suspension, monocoque hull and dual circuit servo disc brakes and a 6 litre V8 engine.

1965 Bentley S3 RHD. **£23,500-24,000** *Mar*

BENTLEY

1970 Bentley T Series Saloon, V8 cylinder, water-cooled engine, pushrod-operated overhead valves with hydraulic tappets, 104.1mm bore x 91.4mm stroke, 6230cc, 4 speed automatic gearbox, hypoid bevel rear axle, independent front suspension with coil springs and hydraulic dampers, independent rear suspension by single trailing arms, coil springs and hydraulic dampers, wheelbase 119½in, tyres 235/70.15.
Est. **£15,000-18,000**   *S*

1971 Bentley T Series Corniche, a 2 door fixed head coupé by Mulliner Park Ward with 8 cylinder, 6750cc engine, 302½in long, 72in wide, 59in high and tyre size 235 x 15.
Est. **£38,000-40,000**   *T&M*

One of only 99 2 door coupés produced between 1965 and 1976.

1976 Bentley T1, with OHV V8, 6750cc engine, 3 speed automatic transmission, one of only 50 built with matching body, with 97,000 miles recorded.
£12,000-14,000   *SEN*

Bentley T1.
£22,000-28,000   *PJF*

1978 Bentley T2.
£15,000-18,000   *RH*

BERKELEY

These lightweight sports cars were designed by Lawrie Bond and produced at Charles Panter's caravan manufacturers between 1956 and 1961. Powered by motorcycle engines, the 322, 2 cylinder Anzani, the 2 and 3 cylinder Excelsior and the 2 cylinder 692cc Royal Enfield were built. With good handling and power to weight ratios, the later 40bhp models could reach 100mph. About 2,000 models in all were produced.

1958 Berkeley Four Wheeled Excelsior engine.
£2,000-3,000   *DB*

MAKE	ENGINE	DATES	CONDITION		
Berkeley			1	2	3
B60	322/2	1956-57	£2,000	£1,000	£500
B65	328/2	1957-60	£2,500	£1,500	£850
B90	492/3	1957-59	£2,500	£1,500	£850
B95/105	692/2	1959-61	£3,000	£2,250	£1,000

BIANCHI

1911 Bianchi Type G 16/20hp,
4 cylinder fixed L head type engine,
90mm bore x 115mm stroke, 2928cc,
channel section side members,
beam axles front and rear carried on
semi-elliptic springs, separately
mounted 4 speed sliding mesh type
gearbox with right-hand change,
rod operated drum type brakes on
rear wheels by hand brake, foot
operated transmission brake,
wooden fixed type wheels carrying
815 x 105 beaded edge tyres,
right-hand drive.
Est. £8,000-12,000   C(A)

*Bianchi started building bicycles,
and by 1900 was building a single
cylinder Voiturette of neat design. By
1906 a range of 4 and 6 cylinder cars
was being produced, similar in
design to Mercedes practice of the
period, firstly with chain drive and
then by 1909 with shaft drive. The
16/20hp appeared in 1909, and was
current until 1912.*

BMW

BMW started making aero
engines, their first motor car
was the Dixi, which was an
Austin 7 built under licence.
Pre-war production was very
low, only about 55,000 cars
being built between 1928 and
1939. BMW produced the Isetta
bubble car from 1955, which
nearly resulted in bankruptcy.
The new series, starting from
the 1960s, has given BMW a
highly respected and prestigious
range of motor cars today.

1937 BMW 327 Roadster, chassis
No. 73279 and engine No. 73279
6 cylinder in-line, water-cooled
monobloc, overhead valves, capacity
1971cc, shaft drive to live rear axle,
independent front suspension,
semi-elliptic rear suspension, knock
off disc wheels.
Est. £40,000-60,000   S

*BMW introduced their 6 cylinder
1490cc engine designed by Fritz
Feidler in 1933. The 6 cylinder
engine developed 34bhp and was
also built as a 40bhp sports model.
From 1936 onwards, a 1911cc
6 cylinder version was made and
this was eventually overshadowed by
the superlative 328 of a year later. In
England between 1935 and 1939,
BMWs were marketed as Fraser
Nash-BMW.*

1938 328 BMW Cabriolet, with
coachwork by Weinberger, chassis
No. 85185 and engine No. 85091,
6 cylinder in-line, 1971cc, bore
66mm x 96mm stroke, 4 speed
gearbox with reverse front
suspension, tranverse leaf spring
with wishbones and hydraulic shock
absorbers, semi-elliptic leaf springs
with rigid axle at rear and left-hand
drive.
Est. £100,000-120,000   C(M)

*In 1896 the company of
Fahrzeugfabrik Eisenach
commenced production of
Decauvilles under licence. 1904 saw
the introduction of the Dixi model
and in 1918 the firm became known
as Gothaer Waggonfabrik. However
this title was short lived, after only
one year the name changed to
Dixi-Werke. The Shapiro Group
acquired the company in 1921 and
Austin Sevens were produced there
under licence from 1928.*

BMW

MAKE BMW	ENGINE	DATES	CONDITION 1	2	3
501	2077/6	1952-56	£7,500	£5,500	£2,000
501 V8/502	2580, 3168/8	1955-63	£8,000	£6,000	£3,000
503	3168/8	1956-59	£25,000	£20,000	£15,000
507	3168/8	1956-59	£95,000	£80,000	—
Isetta (4 wheels)	247/1	1955-62	£900	£500	£250
Isetta (3 wheels)	298/1	1958-64	£750	£500	£200
Isetta 600	585/2	1958-59	£1,000	£600	£300
1500/1800/2000	var/4	1962-68	£1,100	£700	£200
2000CS	1990/4	1966-69	£5,500	£4,000	£1,500
1500/1600/1602	1499/ 1573/4	1966-75	£2,000	£1,000	£300
1600 Cabriolet	1573/4	1967-71	£6,000	£4,500	£2,000
2800CS	2788/6	1968-71	£5,000	£4,000	£1,500
1602	1990/4	1968-74	£2,000	£1,500	£600
2002	1990/4	1968-74	£3,000	£2,000	£750
2002 Tii	1990/4	1971-75	£4,500	£2,500	£800
2002 Touring	1990/4	1971-74	£3,000	£2,000	£500
2002 Cabriolet	1990/4	1971-75	£6,000	£4,000	£2,500
2002 Turbo	1990/4	1973-74	£11,000	£7,000	£5,000
3.0 CSa/CSi	2986/6	1972-75	£9,000	£6,000	£4,000
3.0 CSL	3003/ 3153/6	1972-75	£17,000	£12,000	£9,500

Make: BMW
Model: 507
Type: Sports
Years Manufactured: 1956-59
Quantity: 253
Engine Type: Overhead valve V8
Size: 3168cc
Max Power: 150 bhp @ 5000 rpm
Max Torque: 173 ft/lb @ 2000 rpm
Transmission: 4 speed manual
Wheelbase: 97.6in
Performance: Max speed: 124 mph; 0-60: 8.8 secs.

1952 BMW 327-3 Sports Coupé, chassis No. 88113 and engine No. 30375.
£35,000-37,000   *CMA*

The Bayerische Moteren-Werke (BMW) of Eisenach were nationalised in 1945. Production of pre-war BMW motor cars was taken up again in 1945, under the management of a consortium called Awtowelo, mainly for export. The original BMW emblem was used. In 1952 the factory was renamed the Eisenacher Moteren-Werke. The EMW 321 was identicial to, and the 327 only slightly different from, the pre-war 2 litre models. Model 340/2 was based on the 326, but had a new radiator grille. The name Automoblilwerk Eisenach was officially adopted in 1955 and production of BMW cars ceased.

1954 BMW 502 Series A Saloon, chassis No. 60124 and engine No. 8149, 3867cc, with left-hand drive
£1,320-1,500   *C*

1961 BMW Frua V1600 GT Coupé, coachwork by Frua, chassis No. 455 2800, engine No. 347, 4 cylinder water-cooled monobloc engine inclined at 30°, 4 stroke, 84mm bore x 71mm stroke, 1573cc, compression 9.5:1, maximum power (SAE) 118hp at 6,400rpm, maximum torque (DIN) 97lb at 4,500rpm, maximum engine rpm 6,400, 2 Solex 40 PHH horizontal twin barrel carburettors, 4 speed manual gearbox, single dry plate clutch, hypoid bevel final drive, independent front and rear suspension.
£10,000-11,000   *S(A)*

1956 BMW Type 501 Four Door Saloon, chassis No. 54627R and engine No. 12374, V8 cylinder overhead valve water-cooled engine, bore 74mm, stroke 75mm, capacity 2598cc, 4 speed gearbox, all round independent suspension by adjustable torsion bars with upper and lower wishbones, and with telescopic shock absorbers front and rear, hydraulic self-adjusting brakes on all 4 wheels, live rear axle, tyres 6.40 x 15 and wheelbase 9ft 3½in.
£11,000-12,000   *S*

Following the partition of Germany after WWII, the Eisenach plant of BMW was nationalised in Eastern Germany and the company was left with only the Munich plant. Initially only motorcycles were produced, but in 1952 the first Munich-produced model appeared. By 1956, however, the 501 was available with a 2077cc uprated engine, and for the 1957 season could also be had with the 2½ litre V8 engine first offered in the 502.

MAKE	ENGINE	DATES	CONDITION		
BMW			1	2	3
Dixi	747/4	1927-32	£5,000	£3,000	£1,500
303	1175/6	1934-36	£15,000	£8,000	£5,000
309	843/4	1933-34	£6,000	£4,000	£2,000
315	1490/6	1935-36	£12,000	£7,000	£5,000
319	1911/6	1935-37	£15,000	£9,000	£6,000
326	1971/6	1936-37	£18,000	£13,000	£9,000
320 series	1971/6	1937-38	£20,000	£15,000	£10,000
327/328	1971/6	1937-40	£25,000	£18,000	£14,000
328	1971/6	1937-40	50,000+		

Make: BMW
Model: 2000CS
Type: Coupé
Years Manufactured: 1965-68
Quantity: 11,720
Engine Type: 4 cyl
Size: 1990cc
Max Power: 100-120 bhp
Transmission: 4 speed or auto
Performance: Max speed: 110 mph; 0-60: 10.4 secs; Mpg: 22.

1973 BMW CSA, with engine capacity 2985cc, 6 cylinder.
£9,000-9,500 *ADT*

1967 BMW 1600 Alpina Coupé, LHD, chassis No. 158 3237 and engine No. CC297438, 4 cylinder 1980cc, twin Weber carburettors, single overhead camshaft, water-cooled, 5 speed manual gearbox with reverse, McPherson struts and coil springs suspension, disc and drum brakes (dual), and wheelbase 100.4in.
Est. **£12,000-15,000** *C*

First produced in 1966, this model was initially referred to as the 1600-2, the 2 indicating the 2 door body. The original specifications of the 1600 were 1573cc with a bore and stroke of 84 x 71mm. Alpina modification upped the performance quite dramatically.

1973 BMW 2500A Saloon.
Est. **£1,000-1,500** *CMA*

The BMW 2500 used a 6 cylinder engine of 2.5 litres which was derived from the 4 cylinder unit. Top speed was 110mph and 93,363 were produced before production ceased in 1977.

1974 BMW 2002, with 1990cc, 4 cylinder engine capacity.
£2,600-3,000 *ADT*

1974 BMW 2002 Auto Coupé.
Est. **£1,500-2,500** *Cen*

Introduced in 1968 and powered by a 4 cylinder 1990cc engine this series was BMW's best selling vehicle in the 1970s with 339,084 made between the years of 1968 and 1976.

1974 BMW 2002 Touring, 1998cc capacity, limited number imported.
£2,500-4,000 *PC*

1975 BMW 3.0csi RHD, with Alpina alloy wheels, this car has been partially restored and comes with service history.
Est. **£5,400-5,700** *CMa*

1975 BMW 2002 Two Door Automatic.
£2,600-2,800   *Cen*

1975 BMW 2000 Tii LUX.
Est. £2,800-3,000   *Cen*

Make: BMW
Model: 1600/2002
Type: Saloon/Touring Estate/Convertible
Years Manufactured: 1966-75
Price when new: 2002, Saloon, £1,597
Engine Type: Overhead valve 4 cyl
Size: 1573-1990cc
Max Power: 96 bhp @ 5800 rpm; 100 bhp @ 5500 rpm
Transmission: 4 speed, 5 speed or auto optional
Performance: Max speed: 2002, 107 mph; 0-60: 10.6 secs; Mpg: 26.

1980 3.5 Litre BMW MI Mid-Engined Sports Coupé,
6 cylinder double overhead chain driven camshaft, 4 valves per cylinder 93.4mm, bore x 84mm, stroke, 3453cc, iron block canted over to lower the centre of gravity, dry sump lubrication, Bosche fuel injection, 5 speed ZF and transaxle gearbox, all round coil spring suspension, power assisted ventilated disc brakes and left-hand drive.
Est. £110-130,000   *C*

1975 BMW 1602 Saloon, chassis No. 3561743 and engine No. 3561743 with 1573cc, 4 cylinder capacity.
Est. £800-1,000   *LF*

Make: BMW
Model: M1
Type: Sports Coupé
Years Manufactured: 1978-81
Quantity: 450
Engine Type: Twin cam 24 valve 6 cyl
Size: 3453cc
Max Power: 277 bhp @ 6500 rpm
Max Torque: 243 ft/lb @ 5000 rpm
Transmission: 5 speed
Wheelbase: 100.8in
Performance: Max speed: 162 mph; 0-60: 5.5 secs; Mpg: 17.

1980 BMW M1 Biturbo Special.
Est. £100,000-120,000   *C*

1989 BMW ZI.
Est. £27,000-30,000   *P*

BNC

**1928 BNC Type 527 Armenonville
Two Seater Sports Coupé,**
4 cylinder in line, water-cooled
monobloc engine, overhead valve,
60mm bore x 97mm stroke, 1100cc,
3 speed gearbox, live rear axle,
semi-elliptic leaf front and rear
springs, cantilever at rear,
wheelbase 92in, tyres 4.00 x 19in.
Est. **£15,000-20,000** *S*

BNC 1100cc Sport Voiturette,
with 4 cylinder in line, water-cooled
monobloc engine, bore 59mm x
stroke 100mm, 1049cc, 3 speed
gearbox with reverse, shaft drive,
bevel rear axle, leaf spring front and
rear suspension, wheelbase 2.30m
and 3.50/4.00 x 19in tyres.
Est. **£20,000-25,000** *S(M)*

BRISTOL

The Bristol Aeroplane
Company branched out into
motor car manufacture in 1947,
starting with a version of the
pre-war BMW 327, leading to a
series of very attractive,
aerodynamic Bristol bodies
with Frieder BMW engines.
Versions of these 6 cylinder
engines powered several sports
cars including Frazer Nash,
Cooper and AC. In 1962 the
Chrysler V8 engine was
adopted. Bristol still
manufacture fast, luxurious
cars, currently the 140mph
Beanfighter Turbo convertible.

1949 Bristol 400, with 1971cc,
6 cylinder engine capacity.
£19,000-20,000 *ADT*

1948 Bristol 400.
£38,500-39,000 *DJ*

1949 Bristol 400, this car has been extensively restored and successfully competed in the 1989 'Mille Miglia'.
£37,950-40,000   *DJ*

Make: Bristol
Model: 401/402
Type: Sports Saloon
Years Manufactured: 1949-53
Quantity: 401, 650; 402, 24
Price when new: £2,724-£4,244
Engine Type: Overhead valve 6 cyl
Size: 1971cc
Max Power: 85 bhp @ 4500 rpm
Max Torque: 107 ft/lb @ 3500 rpm
Transmission: 4 speed
Wheelbase: 114in
Performance: Max speed: 94 mph; 0-60: 17.4 secs; Mpg: 20-25.

Make: Bristol
Model: 404
Type: Saloon
Years Manufactured: 1953-58
Quantity: 40
Price when new: £3,543
Engine Type: Overhead valve 6 cyl
Size: 1971cc
Max Power: 105/125 bhp @ 4500 rpm
Max Torque: 117 ft/lb @ 3500 rpm
Transmission: 4 speed manual
Wheelbase: 96in
Performance: Max speed: 110+ mph; 0-60: est 13.5 secs.

1951 Bristol 401, with body and mechanics fully restored.
£16,950-18,000   *GWC*

1950 Bristol 400, this car holds RAC Rally log book and F.I.S.A. documents.
£37,000-40,000   *DJ*

1953 Bristol 404 Two Door Sports Coupé.
Est. **£35,000-40,000**   *C*

1951 Bristol 401 Saloon, with 6 cylinder in-line overhead valve, water-cooled monobloc engine, bore 66mm x stroke 96mm, 1917cc, Borg Warner 4 speed gearbox, independent front suspension by transverse leaf spring, torsion bars at rear, live rear axle, wheelbase 114in and 5.50 x 16 tyres.
£12,000-12,750   *S*

MAKE	ENGINE	DATES	CONDITION		
Bristol			1	2	3
400	1971/6	1947-50	£18,000	£13,000	£9,000
401	1971/6	1949-53	£17,000	£12,000	£7,000
402	1971/6	1949-50	£28,000	£20,000	£13,000
403	1971/6	1953-55	£17,500	£12,500	£8,000
404 Coupé	1971/6	1953-57	£26,000	£18,000	£12,000
405	1971/6	1954-58	£16,000	£10,500	£8,000
405 Drop head	1971/6	1954-56	£30,000	£23,000	£15,000
406	2216/6	1958-61	£12,000	£9,000	£6,000
407	5130/8	1962-63	£11,000	£8,000	£5,500
408	5130/8	1964-65	£11,500	£8,000	£5,500
409	5211/8	1966-67	£12,500	£8,500	£6,000
410	5211/8	1969	£15,000	£10,000	£7,000
411 Mk 1-3	6277/8	1970-73	£14,000	£9,000	£7,500
411 Mk 4-5	6556/8	1974-76	£14,500	£10,000	£8,000
412	5900/				
	6556/8	1975-82	£17,000	£9,500	£5,500
603	5211/				
	5900/8	1976-82	£16,000	£9,000	£5,000

Make: Bristol
Model: 403
Type: Coupé
Years Manufactured: 1953-55
Quantity: 300
Price when new: £2,976
Engine Type: Overhead valve 6 cyl
Size: 1971cc
Max Power: 100 bhp @ 4500 rpm
Max Torque: 117 ft/lb @ 3500 rpm
Transmission: 4 speed manual
Wheelbase: 114in
Performance: Max speed: approx 100 mph; 0-60: approx 15 secs.

1956 Bristol 405 Drop Head Coupé, with straight 6 cylinder water-cooled engine, overhead valve, capacity 1971cc, 4 speed gearbox with manual overdrive, shaft drive to live rear axle, front wishbones with transverse leaf spring and live axle radius arms suspension, 'A' bracket torsion bars to the rear, drum brakes front and rear, wheelbase 96in and right-hand drive.
£35,000-40,000   *S*

1953 Bristol 401, 6 cylinder engine, inclined overhead valves with transverse pushrods and rockers, bore 66mm, stroke 96mm, 1971cc, 7.5:1 compression, 3 Solex 32 BI carburettors, 85bhp at 4,500rpm, Borg Warner CR5 gearbox with synchromesh, 4 speeds and reverse with freewheel on 1st, front suspension independent by transverse leaf spring, rear longitudinal torsion bars, Lockheed hydraulic brakes, 11in drum, 2LS on front, perforated steel disc wheels, tyres 5.50 x 16, rack and pinion steering, wheelbase 9ft 6in, track front 4ft 3¾in, rear 4ft 6in, 15ft 11½in long, 5ft 7in wide, 5ft high and 2,700lb approx in weight.
Est. **£18,000-22,000**   *C*

Make the Most of Miller's

CONDITION is absolutely vital when assessing the value of a vehicle. Top class vehicles on the whole appreciate much more than less perfect examples. However a rare, desirable car may command a high price even when in need of restoration

There was never any attempt to conceal the BMW ancestry of the first car, the Type 400, made by the Bristol Aeroplane Company in 1946. Even the famous kidney shaped grille was carried over and when the company announced an additional model in the autumn of 1949, the 401, it still had the distinctive air intake and the brilliant overhead valve conversion of the old BMW 6 cylinder 2 litre engine. 650 examples of the 401 were made between 1949 and 1953 before it gave way to the 403.

1955 Bristol 405 Sports Saloon,
6 cylinder in-line water-cooled
monobloc, overhead valve, bore
66mm, stroke 96mm, capacity
1971cc, 4 speed gearbox with
overdrive, independent front
suspension, beam axle rear, and
wheelbase 9ft 6in.
Est. **£15,000-18,000** *S*

Make: Bristol
Model: 406
Type: Saloon
Years Manufactured: 1958-61
Quantity: 292
Price when new: £4,244
Engine Type: Overhead valve
6 cyl
Size: 2216cc
Max Power: 105 bhp @ 4700
rpm
Max Torque: 120 ft/lb @ 3000
rpm
Transmission: 4 speed manual
with electric overdrive
Wheelbase: 114in
Performance: Max speed:
approx 105 mph.

1973 Bristol 411 Series 3, restored
and upgraded by Bristol Cars.
£49,950-52,000 *BLE*

Make: Bristol
Model: 412
Type: Convertible
Years Manufactured: 1975-82
Price when new: £14,584
Engine Type: V8
Size: 5898/6556cc
Transmission: Auto
Performance: Max speed: 140
mph; 0-60: 7.4 secs; Mpg: 14.

Make: Bristol
Model: 407/408/409/410/411
Type: Saloon
Years Manufactured: 1961-76
Price when new: £4,848-£6,997
Engine Type: V8
Size: 407/408, 5130cc; 409/410,
5211cc; 411, 6277cc
Max Power: 407, 250 bhp @
4400 rpm; 411 (1973-76), 264
bhp @ 4800 rpm
Max Torque: 407, 340 ft/lb @
2800 rpm; 411 (1973-76), 335
ft/lb @ 3600 rpm
Transmission: Auto
Wheelbase: 114in
Performance: Max speed: 407,
122 mph; 411, 138 mph;
0-60: 407, 9.9 secs; 411, 7 secs.

1974 Bristol 411 Mk 4, has
recorded just 6,000 miles since being
completely restored.
£44,500-45,000 *BLE*

Make: Bristol
Model: 603
Type: Saloon
Years Manufactured: 1976-83
Engine Type: V8
Size: 5211-5900cc
Max Power: 147-172 (DIN) bhp
Transmission: Auto
Performance: Max speed: 140
mph; 0-60: 8.6 secs; Mpg: 13.

1968 Bristol 410, with 5211cc V
engine.
£18,000-20,000 *Ren*

BEAN

1925 Bean 14 Four Seat Tourer,
with 2297cc, 4 cylinder engine
capacity.
£16,200-17,000 *ADT*

MAKE	ENGINE	DATES	CONDITION		
Bean			1	2	3
12	1794/4	1920-27	£14,000	£10,000	£7,000
14	2297/4	1924-29	£16,000	£12,000	£9,000
18/50	2692/6	1927-28	£18,000	£13,000	£9,000

BSA

1934 BSA 10HP Coupé.
Est. **£6,000-9,000** *LF*

BSA produced two distinct ranges of cars; the Scout 3 and 4 wheelers were produced by their motorcycle factory whilst Daimler, who they took over in 1910, were building cheaper versions under the Lanchester badge, which they took over in 1931. This car incorporates the renowned Daimler fluid flywheel and pre-select gearbox. The BSA 10 had a side valve engine of 1330cc and could attain some 60mph. The price new was £235.00.

BROUGH

1937 Brough Superior Three Position Drop Head.
Est. **£40,000-50,000** *ADT*

Built by George Brough at Nottingham, the maker of the coloquially named 'Rolls Royce of motorcycles', the car was one of several British makes dating from the mid-30s that utilised American engines. Manufactured between 1935 and 1939 various body styles were available, to include a 4 door saloon and a 2 seater called the Alpine Grand Sport. The last Brough Superior model appeared in 1938.

Miller's is a price Guide not a price List

The price ranges given reflect the average price a purchaser should pay for similar vehicle. Condition, rarity, provenance, racing history, originality and any restoration are factors that must be taken into account when assessing values. When buying or selling, it must always be remembered that prices can be greatly affected by the condition of any vehicle. Unless otherwise stated, all cars shown in Miller's are of good merchantable quality, and the valuations given reflect this fact. Vehicles offered for sale in exceptionally fine condition or in poor condition may reasonably be expected to be priced considerably higher or lower respectively than the estimates given herein

BUICK

The first Buick cars developed by David Buick featured overhead valves and planetary transmission. The first Indianapolis winner was a Buick in 1909 and over 30,000 of these cars were produced by 1910. Buicks were sold in the UK as 'All-British Bedfords' and then 'Bedford Buicks'.

MAKE Buick	ENGINE cu in	DATES	CONDITION 1	2	3
Special/Super 4 door	248/364/8	1950-59	£8,000	£4,000	£2,000
Special/Super Riv	263/332/8	1950-56	£11,000	£6,000	£3,000
Special/Super conv	263/332/8	1950-56	£10,000	£5,500	£3,000
Roadmaster 4 door	320/365/8	1950-58	£18,000	£8,000	£6,000
Roadmaster Riviera	320/364/8	1950-58	£14,000	£7,000	£5,000
Roadmaster conv	320/364/8	1950-58	£20,000	£11,000	£7,000
Special/Super Riv	364/8	1957-59	£14,000	£7,500	£5,000
Special/Super conv	364/8	1957-58	£18,000	£11,000	£6,000

1907 Buick 'F' Touring, 2 cylinder, 2.6 litre engine, planetary transmission driven by a single chain with 2 forward gears and 1 reverse, right-hand drive. **£9,500-10,000** *C*

1907/8 Buick Model 10 Three Seat Roadster, 4 cylinder, 2687cc engine. Est. **£16,000-18,000** *ADT*

1922 Buick Special Six 54 Roadster. Est. **£20,000-25,000** *P*

All 2,562 cars built were painted deep maroon, had red Spanish grain leather upholstery and were powered by a 242ci (4000cc) straight 6 engine.

1918 Buick 6 Cylinder Touring. **£19,500-20,000** *DB*

1930 Buick Four Door Sedan, 6 cylinder, 2575cc engine. **£8,000-8,500** *ADT*

1930 Buick Series 40 Phaeton, 6 cylinder, 4500cc engine. Est. **£22,000-26,000** *LF*

The Series 40 was otherwise known as the Empire Series, only 128 were built in right-hand drive form.

1931 Buick 66S Coupé, 8 cylinder in-line overhead valve, cast iron block engine, 80mm bore x 125mm stroke, 4457cc, giving 90hp at 3,000rpm, 3 speed gearbox, mechanical brakes on 4 wheels.
£12,000-13,000   *SEN*

Scottish plumber, David Dunbar Buick, built his first prototype in 1903 using his own overhead valve flat twin engine. This was the start of the company which from 1919 to 1926 had the largest sales, in dollar terms, in the US car industry. Four-wheel brakes came in 1924 along with a Packard-like radiator with thermostatically controlled shutters.

1931 Buick Straight Eight Sedan, 8 cylinder, 5500cc engine.
£5,600-6,000   *LF*

General Motors acquired the company in 1908 and the name survives today.

MAKE Buick	ENGINE	DATES	CONDITION 1	2	3
Veteran	2600/2	1903-09	£20,000	£12,000	£8,000
18/20	3881/6	1918-22	£12,000	£5,000	£2,000
Series 22	2587/4	1922-24	£9,000	£5,000	£3,000
Series 24/6	3393/6	1923-30	£9,000	£5,000	£3,000
Light 8	3616/8	1931	£18,000	£14,500	£11,000
Straight 8	4467/8	1931	£22,000	£18,000	£10,000
50 Series	3857/8	1931-39	£18,500	£15,000	£10,000
60 Series	5247/8	1936-39	£24,000	£18,500	£12,000
90 Series	5648/8	1934-35	£24,000	£18,000	£10,000
40 Series	4064/8	1936-39	£22,000	£18,000	£12,000
80/90	5247/8	1936-39	£25,000	£20,000	£15,000
McLaughlin	5247/8	1937-40	£30,000	£20,000	£10,000

Various chassis lengths and bodies will affect value. Buick chassis fitted with English bodies previous to 1916 were called Bedford-Buicks. Right hand drive can have an added premium of 25%.

Make the Most of Miller's

Veteran Cars are those manufactured up to 31 December 1918 although only vehicles built before 31 December 1904 are eligible for the London/Brighton Commemorative Run. Vintage Cars are vehicles that were manufactured between 1 January 1919 and 31 December 1930

1937 Buick Series 40 Special Coupé, chassis No. 3073030, engine No. 43252219.
Est. **£6,500-7,500**   *S(A)*

1939 Buick Series 90 Seven Passenger Limousine, 8 cylinder in line, water-cooled monobloc engine, pushrod operated overhead valve, 87.3mm bore x 109.5mm stroke, 5247cc, 3 speed gearbox, single dry plate clutch, hypoid bevel rear axle, independent coil spring suspension front and rear, wheelbase 140in, tyres 7.50 x 16in.
£9,000-10,000   *S*

Buick had been a pioneer of overhead valves from its earliest days and it is notable that while many of its contemporaries stuck doggedly to side valve engines, Buick continued overhead valve engine production in the 30s.

The marque found favour with royalty, the Queen Mother with King George VI using a McLaughlin Buick on the Canadian Tour in 1939, and the car found favour with both King Edward VII and Wallis Simpson.

1938 Buick Series 40 Special Roadster, 8 cylinder in line, water-cooled monobloc engine, overhead valve, coil ignition, 3 speed synchromesh gearbox with centre change, spiral bevel final drive, hydraulic brakes on 4 wheels, mechanical handbrake operating on rear wheels, independent front suspension, semi-elliptic spring suspension rear.
Est. **£7,000-10,000**   *S*

BUGATTI

The history of Bugatti is really the history of Ettore Bugatti. There are two areas to look at, the Racing Cars and the Road Cars. The first Bugatti was produced in 1909, Bugatti himself died in 1947. Beware fake racing cars, some of which date back to the early 1950s.

A Type 49 chassis modified to similar specifications as a Type 43 with Type 44 engine and running gear.

1928 Bugatti Type 49/44 Tourer, with 8 cylinder engine plain bearing, 2991cc, single camshaft, bore 69mm x 100mm stroke, coil ignition, 1 plug per cylinder, multi-plate wet clutch, 4 speed gearbox with reverse, both axles are Type 44 as is the braking system, and right-hand drive.
Est. **£60,000-70,000** *C*

1936 Bugatti Type 57, Corsica 2 Seater Roadster, with 8 cylinder in-line, 3257cc engine, bore and stroke 72mm x 100mm, 135bhp at 5,000rpm, twin overhead camshaft, 2 valves per cylinder, twin choke updraught Stromberg UUE.2 carburettor, coil ignition, 4 speed gearbox with dry single plate clutch, cable operated brakes on 4 wheels, Rudge Whitworth centre lock wire spoke wheels, tyre sizes 18 x 5.50, half elliptic front suspension, reverse quarter elliptic on rear, wheelbase 10ft 10in and track 4ft 5in.
Est. **£125,000-145,000** *CNY*

Make the Most of Miller's

Veteran Cars are those manufactured up to 31 December 1918 although only vehicles built before 31 December 1904 are eligible for the London/Brighton Commemorative Run. Vintage Cars are vehicles that were manufactured between 1 January 1919 and 31 December 1930

Make	FRANCE	GERMANY	ITALY	JAPAN	USA
Bugatti	+5%	—	+10%	+20%	+10%

1933 Bugatti Type 55 Super Sports, with 8 cylinder engine 60mm x 100mm, 2262cc, 130bhp at 5,000rpm, twin overhead camshaft, 2 valves per cylinder, Roots supercharger, 4 speed and reverse gearbox, 4 wheel cable operated brakes, cast alloy integral rim wheels, 500 x 19 tyres, front half-elliptic suspension, rear reversed quarter elliptic and right-hand drive.
£700,000-800,000 *C(Mon)*

The engine was identical, apart from a lower compression ratio, to that of the successful Type 51 Grand Prix car, having a capacity of 2.3 litres supercharged twin overhead camshafts and a roller bearing crankshaft. The adjustable absorbers had cockpit operated controls for the front and rear.

1937 Bugatti Type 57S Drop Head Coupé.
£715,000-800,000 *S*

CADILLAC

Henry M. Leland founded Cadillac in 1903 and proceeded to produce a world famous series of motor cars and a number of world 'firsts', notably the first proper electric lighting system and the first synchromesh gearbox. Cadillac V8, V12 and V16 engines were all world leaders, as was the coachwork and standard of build.

MAKE Cadillac	ENGINE	DATES	CONDITION 1	2	3
4 door sedan	331/8	1949	£8,000	£4,500	£3,000
2 door fastback	331/8	1949	£12,000	£8,000	£5,000
Convertible coupé	331/8	1949	£30,000	£18,000	£7,000
Series 62 4 door	331/ 365/8	1950-55	£7,000	£5,500	£3,000
Sedan de Ville	365/8	1956-58	£8,000	£6,000	£4,000
Coupé de Ville	331/ 365/8	1950-58	£12,500	£9,500	£3,500
Convertible coupé	331/ 365/8	1950-58	£25,000	£20,000	£10,000
Eldorado	331/8	1953-55	£65,000	£35,000	£20,000
Eldorado Seville	365/8	1956/58	£11,500	£9,000	£5,500
Eldorado Biarritz	365/8	1956-58	£45,000	£32,000	£16,000
Sedan de Ville	390/8	1959	£12,000	£9,500	£5,000
Coupé de Ville	390/8	1959	£15,000	£9,000	£5,500
Convertible coupé	390/8	1959	£40,000	£25,000	£9,500
Eldorado Seville	390/8	1959	£13,000	£10,000	£6,000
Eldorado Biarritz	390/8	1959	£45,000	£35,000	£22,000
Sedan de Ville	390/8	1960	£10,000	£8,000	£4,500
Convertible coupé	390/8	1960	£27,000	£14,000	£7,500
Eldorado Biarritz	390/8	1960	£30,000	£17,000	£10,000
Sedan de Ville	390/ 429/8	1961-64	£7,000	£5,000	£3,000
Coupé de Ville	390/ 429/8	1961-64	£8,000	£6,000	£4,000
Convertible coupé	390/ 429/8	1961-64	£15,000	£9,000	£7,000
Eldorado Biarritz	390/ 429/8	1961-64	£26,000	£16,000	£11,000

1903 Cadillac Model A 6½hp Rear Entrance Tonneau, single cylinder water-cooled engine, mechanically operated inlet and exhaust valves, 5in bore x 5in stroke, 98.2cu in capacity, 2 speed forward and reverse planetary transmission, final drive by sprocket and chain to differential, live rear axle, front rear suspension by semi-elliptic leaf springs, wheelbase 70in, tyres 30 x 3½in.
£22,000-25,000   *S*

The Model A was available in 2 or 4 seater forms and had a maximum speed of some 30-35mph returning 25-30mpg. The 2 seater was priced at $750.

1913 Cadillac Model 30 40-50hp 5 Passenger Tourer, 4 cylinder in-line engine, separately cast, water-cooled, side valve, bore 4½in x 5¾in stroke, 365.8cu in, 3 speed gearbox, right-hand change, right-hand drive, cone clutch, shaft drive to bevel rear axle, semi-elliptic leaf springs front and rear suspension with auxiliary transverse rear leaf spring, wheelbase 120in, 36 by 4½in tyres.
Est. **£20,000-30,000**   *SNY*

Locate the source

The source of each illustration in Miller's can be found by checking the code letters below each caption with the list of contributors

1930 Cadillac Series 353 Limousine, 90° V8 cylinder water-cooled bi-bloc engine, 84mm bore x 128mm stroke, 5786cc, 2 disc dry plate clutch, 3 speed gearbox, Delco Remy coil ignition, pump and fan cooling, spiral bevel rear axle, wheelbase 140in, tyres 7.00 x 19in.
Est. **£27,000-30,000**   *S(M)*

Make	FRANCE	GERMANY	ITALY	JAPAN	USA
Cadillac	−10%	—	−2%	—	—

1930 Cadillac Series 353 8 Door 4 Door Town Sedan, 90° V8 cylinder engine, water-cooled, side valve, bore 3½in x 4¹⁵⁄₁₆in stroke, 353cu in, 3 speed gearbox, twin disc clutch, spiral bevel final drive, semi-elliptic leaf spring suspension, wheelbase 140in, 6.00/6.50 x 19in tyres, in need of some restoration.
£16,500-17,500 *SNY*

The first V8 engined Cadillac, a landmark car in the history of the motor car, left the Detroit production line in 1915 and from the very outset this simple side valve unit was to capture a significant slice of the luxury car market.

1962 Cadillac Coupé De Ville.
Est. **£4,500-5,500** *LF*

1975 Cadillac Eldorado, 8 cylinder, 8200cc engine.
Est. **£5,000-6,000** *ADT*

By the mid-70s sales of the General Motors Cadillac were running at just over 250,000 per annum.

CASE

> ## Miller's is a price Guide not a price List
>
> *The price ranges given reflect the average price a purchaser should pay for similar vehicle. Condition, rarity, provenance, racing history, originality and any restoration are factors that must be taken into account when assessing values. When buying or selling, it must always be remembered that prices can be greatly affected by the condition of any vehicle. Unless otherwise stated, all cars shown in Miller's are of good merchantable quality, and the valuations given reflect this fact. Vehicles offered for sale in exceptionally fine condition or in poor condition may reasonably be expected to be priced considerably higher or lower respectively than the estimates given herein*

The Case Threshing Machine Co. of Racine, Wisconsin, produced America's well-known range of agricultural equipment, including tractors, threshing machines and steam traction engines. The company generally only offered one model at a time, although the models were changed annually. Motor car production extended from 1910 or so until 1927, with 6 cylinder cars offered from 1918.

1912 Case Model 'M' 40hp Open Tourer, chassis No. 15096, 4 cylinder in line, water-cooled monobloc engine, side valve, 'L' head, shaft drive to live rear axle, semi-elliptic leaf spring front and rear suspension, wheelbase 120in, detachable rim BE wheels.
£27,500-30,000 *S*

CHEVROLET

The Chevrolet company, founded in 1911, provided the lower end of the General Motors range. The 490 (because it cost $490) was to rival the Model T Ford. The most famous Chevrolet products though are probably the Corvettes, the epitome of the American Sportscar.

1925/26 Chevrolet Superior Series K Tourer, 4 cylinder, 171cu in capacity engine. Est. **£5,500-6,500** *ADT*

1922 Chevrolet FB50 Tourer, 4 cylinder overhead valve engine, 94mm bore x 133.4mm stroke, 3703cc producing 37bhp, 3 speed gearbox with reverse, cone clutch, semi-elliptic leaf spring suspension front and rear, wheelbase 110in, left-hand drive. Est. **£12,000-15,000** *C*

1931 Chevrolet Sports Roadster, with dickey seat, right-hand drive, restored. **£16,000-17,000** *GWC*

1935 Chevrolet Master Town Sedan De Luxe, 6 cylinder, water-cooled, overhead valve engine, 3390cc, 3 speed gearbox with reverse, Dubonnet independent front suspension with conventional leaf rear, left-hand drive. The monobloc engine was known as 'the cast iron wonder'. Est. **£7,000-10,000** *C*

1935 3.8 Litre Chevrolet Coupé. **£6,500-7,500** *B*

1955 Chevrolet Corvette, V8 engine, water-cooled, pushrod operated overhead valves, bore 3.75in x 3in stroke, 265cu in, automatic transmission with floor shift, hypoid bevel live rear axle, independent front suspension by coil springs and stabilisers, semi-elliptic leaf spring rear, wheelbase 102in, 15in tyres. **£60,000-65,000** *SNY*

Make	FRANCE	GERMANY	ITALY	JAPAN	USA
Chevrolet	−10%	—	−2%	—	+1%

MAKE	ENGINE	DATES	CONDITION		
Chevrolet			1	2	3
Bel Air 4 door	235/6	1953-54	£6,000	£4,000	£3,000
Bel Air sports coupé	235/6	1953-54	£7,000	£4,500	£3,500
Bel Air convertible	235/6	1953-54	£12,500	£9,500	£6,000
Bel Air 4 door	283/8	1955-57	£8,000	£4,000	£3,000
Bel Air sports coupé	283/8	1955-56	£11,000	£7,000	£4,000
Bel Air convertible	283/8	1955-56	£16,000	£11,000	£7,000
Bel Air sports coupé	283/8	1957	£11,000	£7,500	£4,500
Bel Air convertible	283/8	1957	£14,500	£10,500	£8,000
Impala sports sedan	235/6, 348/8	1958	£12,500	£9,000	£5,500
Impala convertible	235/6 348/8	1958	£14,500	£11,000	£7,500
Impala sports sedan	235/6 348/8	1959	£8,000	£5,000	£4,000
Impala convertible	235/6 348/8	1959	£14,000	£10,000	£5,000
Corvette roadster	235/6	1953	£28,000	£19,000	£17,000
Corvette roadster	235/6, 283/8	1954-57	£26,000	£17,000	£8,000
Corvette roadster	283, 327/8	1958-62	£22,000	£14,000	£7,000
Corvette Stingray	327, 427/8	1963-67	£20,000	£14,000	£10,000
Corvette Stingray DHC	327, 427/8	1963-66	£26,000	£15,000	£8,000
Corvette Stingray DHC	427/8	1967	£32,000	£25,000	£12,000

Make the Most of Miller's

CONDITION is absolutely vital when assessing the value of a vehicle. Top class vehicles on the whole appreciate much more than less perfect examples. However a rare, desirable car may command a high price even when in need of restoration

The first Chevrolet appeared in 1912. Built by William Durant, it was named after his assistant, Louis Chevrolet, as Durant liked the faintly foreign sound and the association of the name with motor racing. The firm became a division of General Motors in 1917. The FB model was launched in 1919, costing $885. Production ceased in 1922.

1959 Chevrolet Impala V8 Two Door Pillarless Coupé, V8 cylinder, water-cooled engine, overhead valves, 97mm bore x [?]5mm stroke, 283cu in capacity, [?] speed automatic gearbox, bevel [r]ear axle, independent front [s]uspension, wheelbase 119in, tyres [?].50 x 14in.
£8,500-9,500   *S*

[T]he top of the range Chevrolet for [1]959 was the Series 1700 Impala, [o]ffered in 6 cylinder and V8 form [a]nd in 4 different body styles. The [m]aker's claimed 185bhp at [?],600rpm for the V8 engined car.

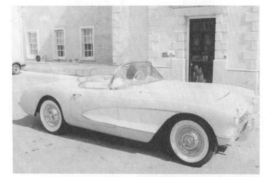

1956 Chevrolet Corvette Roadster.
Est. £25,000-30,000   *P*

[1]958 4.6 Litre Chevrolet Corvette [R]oadster.
[£2]2,000-25,000   *B*

1957 Chevrolet Corvette Roadster, V8 cylinder, water-cooled engine, overhead valve, 283cu in, 4 speed manual gearbox, shaft drive to live rear axle, independent front suspension, semi-elliptic leaf springs at rear.
Est. £25,000-30,000   *S(A)*

1958 Corvette Roadster, V8 cylinder, water-cooled engine, pushrod operated overhead valves, 4in bore x 3¼in stroke, 327cu in capacity, 4 speed floor shift gearbox, hypoid bevel live rear axle, independent coil spring front suspension, semi-elliptic leaf spring rear, wheelbase 102in, tyres 15in.
£20,000-22,000 *S(M)*

Make: Chevrolet
Model: Corvette
Type: Sports
Years Manufactured: 1958-60
Quantity: 1958, 9,168; 1959, 9,670; 1960, 10,261
Engine Type: Overhead valve V8
Size: 4638cc
Max Power: 1958-60, 230 bhp @ 4800 rpm; 1958-59, 250 bhp @ 5000 rpm; 1960, 275 bhp @ 5200 rpm
Max Torque: 1958-60, 300 ft/lb @ 3000 rpm; 1958-59 305 ft/lb @ 3800 rpm; 1960, 290 ft/lb @ 4200 rpm
Transmission: 3/4 speed manual, 2 speed auto
Wheelbase: 102in
Performance: Max speed: 103-128 mph; 0-60: 6.6-9.2 secs.

1964 Corvette XP-819 prototype, V8, 327cu in engine, water-cooled, carburated, 2 speed automatic transmission, rack and pinion steering, independent suspension, coil springs, wheelbase 90in, weight 2,700lb.
£60,000-65,000 *SNY*

1963 Chevrolet Corvette
Est. **£18,000-22,000** *P*

Although this car was a one-off, several of its design features were to appear later on other Corvettes. The car's Coke-bottle shape and unique front section strongly influenced the design of the XP-880/Astro II show car. The 1968 production Corvette, which utilised the Coke-bottle and front end styles, shared the SP-819's roofline and targa-type lift out roof section.

1963 Chevrolet Corvette Stingray Roadster, V8 cylinder, 5359cc engine.
Est. **£31,000-35,000** *ADT*

1964 Chevrolet Corvette Stingray Convertible, 8 cylinder, 7439cc engine.
£15,500-16,000   *ADT*

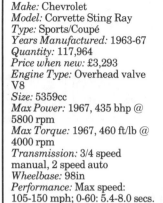

Make: Chevrolet
Model: Corvette Sting Ray
Type: Sports/Coupé
Years Manufactured: 1963-67
Quantity: 117,964
Price when new: £3,293
Engine Type: Overhead valve V8
Size: 5359cc
Max Power: 1967, 435 bhp @ 5800 rpm
Max Torque: 1967, 460 ft/lb @ 4000 rpm
Transmission: 3/4 speed manual, 2 speed auto
Wheelbase: 98in
Performance: Max speed: 105-150 mph; 0-60: 5.4-8.0 secs.

1966 Chevrolet Corvette Stingray Roadster, 8 cylinder, 5360cc engine.
Est. £19,000-23,000   *ADT*

1967 Chevrolet Corvette Stingray Convertible, manual gearbox, with works hard and soft tops.
£24,500-25,000   *BLE*

Introduced in 1963, the Stingray took both its name and general shape from Mitchell's Stingray racer of the late 50s.

1967 Chevrolet Camaro 350SS, 5735cc engine, manual gearbox.
£10,500-11,000   *LF*

1973 Chevrolet Corvette Stingray.
Est. £6,000-8,000   *LF*

Miller's is a price Guide not a price List

The price ranges given reflect the average price a purchaser should pay for similar vehicle. Condition, rarity, provenance, racing history, originality and any restoration are factors that must be taken into account when assessing values. When buying or selling, it must always be remembered that prices can be greatly affected by the condition of any vehicle. Unless otherwise stated, all cars shown in Miller's are of good merchantable quality, and the valuations given reflect this fact. Vehicles offered for sale in exceptionally fine condition or in poor condition may reasonably be expected to be priced considerably higher or lower respectively than the estimates given herein

1971 Chevrolet Corvette Stingray, V8 cylinder, 5735cc engine.
Est. £7,000-10,000   *LF*

CHRYSLER

Chrysler started production of the '70' model in 1923, founded by former Willys and Buick engineer William Chrysler. They acquired Dodge and also manufactured Plymouth and De Soto. Chrysler moved into Europe after the war and acquired Simca and the Rootes Group.

1927 Chrysler Model 72 Five Passenger Tourer, 6 cylinder in line, water-cooled monobloc engine, side valve, 80mm bore x 125mm stroke, 248.9cu in capacity, 3 speed centre change gearbox, single disc clutch, spiral bevel rear axle, semi-elliptic leaf spring suspension front and rear, wheelbase 119¾in, tyres 5.25/5.50 x 18in.
Est. £30,000-40,000   *S*

The Chrysler range for 1928, launched in 1927, included 4 different models, the 4 cylinder Model 52 and the 6 cylinder Models 62, 72 and 80. The 6 cylinder cars were smooth and powerful and most of the 4 door cars were fitted with sedan coachwork.

Locate the source

The source of each illustration in Miller's can be found by checking the code letters below each caption with the list of contributors

1938 Chrysler Royal Four Door Phaeton, 6 cylinder, water-cooled monobloc engine, side valve, 85.73mm bore x 114.3mm stroke, 3970cc, 3 speed manual gearbox, independent front suspension, semi-elliptic rear, single dry plate clutch, hypoid rear axle, wheelbase 119in, tyres 6.25 x 16in.
Est. £16,000-20,000   *S*

Fitted with right-hand drive from new, this car was reputedly built for the Governor of Rhodesia.

1954 Chrysler New Yorker De Luxe Sedan, V8 cylinder engine, water-cooled, overhead valves, bore 3.81in x 3.63in stroke, 331.1cu in, 3 speed automatic gearbox, bevel rear axle, independent coil spring front suspension, leaf rear springs, wheelbase 125½in, 15in tyres.
£2,500-3,000   *SNY*

The De Luxe Sedan sold new in 195 for $3,433 and a further $130 boug the power steering option with whic this example is fitted.

1930 Chrysler 66 Sedan, 6 cylinder, 3205cc engine, artillery wheels, right-hand drive.
Est. £18,000-22,000   *LF*

The 66 was only produced in 1930 and over 22,500 were built. Those for the US market had 3600cc engines developing 70bhp whilst those for the UK had 3.2 litre versions of the 6 cylinder side valve engine.

CITROËN

Andre Citroën, a gear manufacturer, produced the Type A Citroën in 1919. Successive models, notably the 1922 5CV Cloverleaf, the 1934 Traction Avant, the 'cult' 2CV of 1949, and the DS Series of 1955, have ensured Citroën a place in motoring history. In 1926 Citroën started a factory in Slough which manufactured cars until 1966. In 1935 the company was bought out by Michelin and in 1976 joined the Peugeot-Talbot group.

MAKE	ENGINE	DATES	CONDITION		
Citroën			1	2	3
2CV	375, 425, 602/2	1948 on	£3,000	£1,500	£250
Bijou	425/2	1960-62	£2,000	£1,500	£500
Ami 6/8	602/2	1961-78	£1,000	£600	£300
Dyane	425, 602/2	1968-82	£1,300	£900	£350
11BL/11B (Paris)	1911/4	1934/57	£7,000	£4,000	£2,000
Light 15/Big 15 (Slough)	1911/4	1934-55	£9,000	£6,000	£3,000
15/6, 15/6H (Paris)	2866/6	1939-55	£11,000	£8,000	£5,000
Big Six (Slough)	2866/6	1946-55	£11,500	£9,000	£6,000
ID19/DS19/21/23	var/4	1955-75	£6,000	£3,500	£1,500
SM	2670, 2974/6	1970-75	£14,000	£9,000	£5,000

1924 Citroën 5CV 'Type C' Torpedo.
Est. **£9,000-9,250**   *Cen*

Citroën's first mass produced car affectionately known as 'the little lemon'.

1953 Citroën 11B Normale, rust free car requiring repaint, retrim and some chrome.
£5,000-6,000   *PT*

1952 Citroën 11BL, with 1911cc, cylinder engine capacity.
Est. **£8,500-9,500**   *ADT*

1938 Citroën 7C, some restoration required.
£4,000-4,500   *PT*

1939 Citroën 7C, some restoration required.
£6,000-7,000   *PT*

1950 11B Normale.
£4,000-10,500   *PT*

1954 Citroën Traction Avant Light 15.
Est. **£5,000-8,000**   *LF*

1952 Citroën 15/6 Cylinder, mechanics excellent, body badly restored, trim excellent.
£6,000-11,000   *PT*

A much sought after car abroad.

1953 11B Normale, mechanics in good order but requiring some restoration.
£4,000-9,000   *PT*

1956 11B Familiale, marketed as a 9 seater.
£8,500-10,000   *PT*

1952 Citroën Light Fifteen Saloon, with 4 cylinder in-line engine, water-cooled side valve, capacity 1914cc, 4 speed manual transmission, front wheel drive, indepedent suspension front and rear.
£2,800-3,250   *S*

1956 Citroën 15/5 Familiale.
£11,500-12,500   *PT*

1954 Citroën Traction 11B.
Est. **£4,250-4,750**   *GWC*

1956 Citroën 11BL.
£4,000-9,500   *PT*

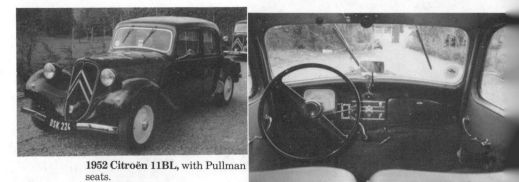

1952 Citroën 11BL, with Pullman seats.
£6,500-7,000   *PT*

1933 AC Ace Drop Head Coupé with Dickey Seat, 2 litre 6 cylinder engine, one of the AC team for the 1933 R.A.C. Rally, unused for 40 years and is in exceptional condition, totally rebuilt engine. **£27,000-29,000** *ELD*

1956 AC Ace Bristol Two Seater Sports, chassis No. BE134, engine No. 100 C2 3288, 6 cylinder in-line capacity 1971cc, 4 speed gearbox; excellent condition. **£40,000-45,000** *S*

1964 AC Cobra 289 Mk II Sports Two Seater, chassis No. COB 6021, engine No. 3187, Ford V8, 289cu in, 4727cc, 280bhp; 4 speed synchromesh gearbox. **£185,000-200,000** *C*

1964 AC Cobra 289 Two Seater Sports, chassis No. CSX 2346, engine Ford V8 cylinder, 4727cc, 280bhp at 5400rpm; Borg-Warner 4 speed manual gearbox; factory extras include hood scoop, full hood and tonneau cover, centre lock chromed wheels, and Cobra radio; this car was completely restored in 1980/81, covering about 200 miles since. **£80,000-85,000** *CNY*

1966 AC Cobra 427 Mk III Two Seater Sports, engine Ford V8 cylinder 6997cc, 425bhp at 5600rpm, in immaculate condition. **£150,000-180,000** *CNY*

1933 Alfa Romeo 8C 2.3 Litre Supercharged, chassis No. 2311205, engine No. 2311205, 8 cylinder, 2336cc, twin overhead camshaft, 142bhp at 5200rpm, 4 speed gearbox with reverse. **£725,000-800,000** *C(M)*

1947 Alfa Romeo 6C 2500SS Coupé, chassis No. 915543, engine No. 923635, 6 cylinder in-line 2443cc twin overhead camshaft, 105bhp at 4800rpm, triple carburettors, 4 speed all synchromesh plus reverse manual gearbox. **£80,000-100,000** *C(M)*

1949-50 2.5 Litre Alfa Romeo 6C-2500 Super Sport Cabriolet, with coachwork by Pininfarina, this model was introduced in 1939 capable of a speed of 102mph and right-hand drive.
£99,000-110,000   *C*

1964 Alfa Romeo Giulia Spyder, with red leather trim in excellent condition, very good bodywork and mechanics, rust free, ex-USA.
£13,000-14,000   *CFC*

1965 Alfa Romeo 2600 Spyder, with 2584cc, 6 cylinder engine, sports roadster coachwork, totally original with only 62,000 miles recorded, complete with log book, road fund

licence and MOT certificate and a competitor in a recent R.A.C. Norwich Union Rally. **£14,000-15,000**   *Ren*

1939 Alvis 'Speed 25' Four Seater Drop Head Coupé, with coachwork by Charlesworth, chassis No. 14639 and engine No. 15123, 6 cylinder, ohv, 3571cc, 25.63hp, 7 bearing crank, triple S.U. carburettors producing 110bhp at 3,800rpm, 4 speed synchromesh gearbox, Luvax ALC shock absorbers, Luvax Bijur lubrication system, 0-30 in 4.7 seconds and 0-50 in 10.4 seconds, right-hand drive, this car holds a current MOT test certificate.
£40,000-42,000   *C*

1933 Alvis 12/50 Drop Head Coupé.
£22,000-23,000   *RTC*

1949 Alvis TA14 Saloon.
£11,000-13,000   *RTC*

1935 Alvis Firebird Saloon.
£15,000-18,000   *RTC*

1936 Alvis Crested Eagle.
£35,000-45,000   *RTC*

1953 Alvis TC21/100 Grey Lady.
£14,000-18,000   *RTC*

1933 Alvis Firefly Saloon.
£14,000-18,000   *RTC*

1961 Alvis TD21 Drop Head Coupé, interior restored
Red Triangle.
£60,000-70,000   *RTC*

1963 Alvis TD21 Saloon.
£14,000-18,000   *RTC*

1961 Alvis TF21 Drop Head Coupé.
£30,000-50,000   *RTC*

1960 Alvis TD21 Drop Head Coupé, chassis No. 26?
engine No. 26392, 6 cylinder, 2993cc, automatic
transmission, fully restored to a very high
standard.
£25,000-27,000   *C*

1966 Alvis TF21 Saloon.
£35,000-40,000   *RTC*

1965 Alvis TE21 Saloon.
£18,000-20,000   *RTC*

Alvis TE21 Drop Head Coupé,
totally restored by Red Triangle.
£65,000+   *RTC*

1929 Amilcar Type G, restored
in France about 15 years ago.
£4,500-5,500   *GWC*

Alvis TA14 Tickford Drop Head Coupé, totally restored
by Red Triangle.
£35,000-45,000   *RTC*

1924 Austin 12/4 Tourer, with excellent interior, good body and mechanics and new upholstery, hood and screens, current MOT.
£23,000-24,000   *Mot*

1929 Austin 16/6 Saloon, with coachwork by Cheetham & Borwick, fully restored in 1979/80, very good body, good mechanics and interior.
£14,750-16,000   *Mot*

1935 Armstrong Siddeley 12HP, with very good body and interior, good mechanics, and sensitively restored.
£7,500-8,500   *CC*

1955 Austin FL1, Hire Car Limousine, restored in 1988, finished in black with brown interior and trim, warranted mileage of 62,000 miles, with V5 logbook and MOT certificate.
£2,300-3,000   *ADT*

1964 ASA 100GT Coupé, with coachwork by Bertone, 4 cylinder in line, 1032cc, bore and stroke 69mm x 69mm, compression ratio 9.1:1, 97bhp at 6,800rpm, 4 speed synchromesh gearbox, tubular frame chassis, Dunlop disc brakes and left-hand drive, the single ohc engine is based on the Testa Rossa giving 1032cc capacity and a claimed 97bhp, and a speed of 113mph.
£16,000-17,500   *C*

1954 Austin Healey 100/4, chassis No. BN1219240, engine No. 1B219240, 2660cc, 6 cylinder, 3 speed gearbox with overdrive on 2nd and 3rd, full restoration and only 100 miles since, complete with hood, tonneau and side screens.
£23,000-25,000 *LF*

1955 Austin Healey 100/4 BN1 Sports Two Seater, chassis No. BN1 224052, engine No. BN1 224052, 4 cylinder, overhead valve, 2 SU carburettors, 2660cc, 90bhp at 4,000rpm, 3 speed synchromesh with overdrive on 2nd and 3rd gears.
£16,000-18,000 *C*

1964 Austin Healey 3000 Mk III Sports Two Seater, chassis No. 26457, engine No. 1545, 6 cylinder in line, 2012cc, giving 148bhp; 4 speed gearbox.
£25,000-27,000 *C*

The dashboard detail of 1964 Austin Healey 3000 Mk III.

1970 Austin Healey Sprite, chassis No. HAN 9771106, engine No. 12CCDAH2373, 4 cylinder, 1275cc.
£4,000-5,000 *Ren*

Austin Healey Sprite, restored but in need of a respray.
£6,000-7,000 *FOR*

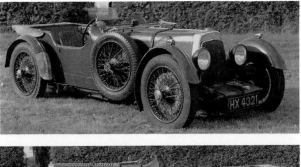

1931 Aston Martin 1½ Litre International Team Car, chassis No. LM5 and engine No. LM5, 4 cylinder in-line engine, water-cooled monobloc, overhead camshaft, overhead valve, bore 69.3mm x stroke 99mm, capacity 1495cc, 4 speed gearbox, final drive by worm and wheel, semi-elliptic leaf springs front and rear, wheelbase 102in and 5.00 x 20in tyres, the present coachwork was fitted in 1932 and this car has competed at Brooklands, Le Mans and the Swedish Grand Prix.
£70,000-80,000   *S*

1965 Aston Martin DB5 Vantage Grand Touring, chassis No. DB5-2245-R, engine No. 400-2513-V, 6 cylinder, twin overhead camshaft 3995cc, 314bhp, 5 speed synchromesh gearbox, 4 wheel servo disc brakes, coil spring suspension independent at front, live rear axle, chrome wire spoked centre lock wheels and right-hand drive, there were only 65 Vantage models produced so this is a rare car in excellent condition.
£88,000-95,000   *C*

1963-65 Aston Martin DB5, to Vantage specification, with 3995cc in line, 6 cylinder engine, the engine converted to Vantage specifications in 1985 including new rings, bearings, valves and guides and ported head, with a DBS6 cam fully and properly balanced, the 3 SU carburettors were replaced by factory Webers, the improvements producing a 230bhp when tested, externally the panelwork is all original and the car was recently resprayed in Aston Martin Royal Claret. **£68,000-70,000**   *ADT*

1966 Aston Martin DB6 Mk I, in very good condition, with original mechanics, interior refurbished in 1987 and body repainted Suffolk Red in 1985, 73,000 miles recorded with original log book and handbook.
£56,000-60,000   *SCC*

1955 Aston Martin DB2/4 Mk I Saloon, chassis No. LML 991, engine No. VB6H/578, 6 cylinder in line, water-cooled monobloc, overhead valves, overhead camshafts, bore 78mm x stroke 90mm, capacity 2580cc, single dry plate clutch, 4 speed gearbox, hypoid bevel rear axle, independent front suspension, live rear axle, wheelbase 99in. **£29,000-32,000**   *S*

1967 Aston Martin DB6 Sports Saloon, chassis No. DB6/3040/R engine No. 4003075, 6 cylinder in line water-cooled monobloc, twin overhead camshafts, bore 96mm x stroke 92mm, capacity 3995cc, 5 speed manual gearbox, shaft drive to hypoid rear axle, independent suspension, wheelbase 102in and tyres 15in, the car is finished in champagne livery with black leather interior, all in excellent condition, with its original green log book, V5 registration document and a number of MOT certificates.
£28,000-30,000   *S*

1969 Aston Martin DB6 Mk II, automatic with power steering, engine No. 400/4326, 3995cc, 6 cylinder, this car has just undergone a complete bare metal repaint with new headlinings and has been thoroughly checked through both mechanically and electrically, finished in dark blue with dark blue leather interior.
£69,500-72,000   *T&M*

1971 Aston Martin Ogle, designed by Ogle and based on the DBS V8 mechanical components, engine No. V/540/318, 8 cylinder, this car was the Embassy cigarette promotion car, 25,075 recorded miles.
£75,000-80,000   *T&M*

1971 Aston Martin DBS Automatic, chassis No. DBS/5697/F1/R, engine N 400/4846/SF1, 3995cc, 6 cylinder, with new chromed wire wheels, Borg-Warner automatic transmission and factory option of triple Weber carburettors, with curren Road Tax and MOT certificate, all in excellent condition.
£23,500-26,000   *Ren*

1976 Aston Martin V8 Convertible, by Banham, all alloy 5340cc V8 engine, all panelwork excellent, all mechanical and ancillary equipment good, the black interior is original and in fair condition and the black canvas hood is excellent. **£28,000-32,000** *ADT*

1977 Aston Martin DBS V8, with 5.3 aluminium 4 camshaft V8 engine, in showroom condition throughout, 2,400 miles recorded, left-hand drive, made for US market and runs on lead-free petrol. **£70,000-80,000** *ADT*

1979 Aston Martin V8 Volante chassis No. V8COR15080, engine No. V/540/50805, twin overhead camshaft, 5340cc, 5 speed synchromesh gearbox, power assisted disc brakes, independent front and rear suspension right-hand drive. **£121,000-123,000** *C*

Part of interior of 1979 Aston Martin V8 Volante Convertible, showing steering wheel and column and gear change stick.

1987 Aston Martin V8 Volante Vantage, chassis No. SCFCV81C6HTR15565, engine No. V/580/5565/X, 5340cc, 8 cylinder, length 183in, the ultimate Aston Martin convertible in showroom condition with less than 8,000 miles recorded from new, finished in red with tan leather upholstery piped in red. **£245,000-250,000** *T&M*

1929 Bentley 4½ Litre Mulliner Tourer, chassis No. FB 3304, engine No. FB 3304, 4 cylinder in line, 4398cc, bore and stroke 100mm x 140mm, CR 5.3:1, 110bhp at 3,500 rpm, 4 tulip shaped valves per cylinder, single overhead camshaft, 5 bearing crankshaft, twin sparking plugs per cylinder with twin ML Magnetos, 2 SU carburettors, 4 gears and reverse type box right-hand gate change, channel section pressed steel chassis, semi-elliptic leaf springs with Bentley and Draper shock absorbers, centre lock Rudge Whitworth wire spoke wheels with 5.25 x 21 tyres, wheelbase 130in, right-hand drive, this car has been completedly restored. **£98,000-250,000** *C*

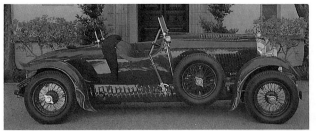

1930 Bentley 4½ Litre Supercharged Two Seater, with coachwork by Gurney Nutting, chassis No. SM 3909, engine No. SM 3910 4 cylinder in line, water-cooled monobloc, single overhead camshaft, overhead valve, bore 100mm x stroke 140mm, capacity 4398cc, 4 speed D type gearbox, single plate clutch, bevel rear axle, semi-elliptic leaf spring suspension front and rear, wheelbase

130in and 6.50 x 19in tyres, a road speed of 105mph is achievable at 3,500rpm, this car was once owned by Woolf Barnato and is now presented in as near to original specification as possible but enjoying the benefits of Ed Swearingen's mechanical

modifications, it has been newly painted to the highest American standards in anthracite grey/green livery and the compact cockpit is upholstered in pleated red leather, the car has been maintained in excellent mechanical order by its distinguished owners, noted motor enthusiasts, and must surely be the most coveted of the 40 or so surviving 'Blower Bentleys'. **£1,100,000-1,250,000**   *S*

1931 Bentley 4½ Litre Supercharged Four Seater Sports Tourer, with coachwork by Vanden Plas, chassis No. MS 3927, engine No. MS 3930 4 cylinder overhead camshaft water-cooled monobloc, bore 100mm x stroke 140mm, capacity 4398cc, roots type supercharger, 4 speed manual C-type gearbox,

twin magneto ignition, pump cooling, single plate clutch, spiral bevel rear axle, wheelbase 130in and 5.50 x 21 tyres, and still wears original coachwork, it underwent extensive restoration work in the 1970s and as a largely original Vanden Plas bodied car, with its original engine and supercharger this is a most sought after vintage sports car which when new was capable of

105mph, the Roots type blower providing 9½lb boost at 3,500rpm, with only 50 cars built, demand for Blower Bentleys will always exceed supply. **£400,000-420,000**   *S*

1934 Bentley 3.5 Litre Airline Two Door Sports Saloon, with Thrupp & Maberly streamline coachwork, this revolutionary design caused a sensation in its day. **£50,000-70,000** *DJ*

The interior of 1936 Bentley 4¼ Litre Sports Coupé, showing dashboard, steering wheel and column.

1938 4½ Litre Bentley Tourer, chassis No. B3LE and engine No. T8BY 6 cylinder push rod overhead valve, 3½in bore x 4½in stroke, capacity 4257cc, twin SU carburettors, coil ignition, rated to develop approximately 125bhp at 4,500rpm, 4 speed gearbox with synchromesh on 2nd, 3rd and top gear, rod and cable operated 4 wheel brakes with Rolls Royce mechanical servo, 18in centre lock wire wheels, and 5.50 x 18 tyres, original body. **£110,000-120,000** *C(A)*

1949 Bentley Mk VI Convertible, chassis No. BD 142A and 6 cylinder overhead valve, 4257cc, 135bhp, 4 speed with synchromesh on 2nd, 3rd and 4th gears, brakes mechanical at rear, hydraulic at front, semi-elliptic rear spring suspension and independent helical front springs. **£35,000-38,000** *C*

...oot and spare wheel of 1936 ...entley 4¼ Litre Sports Coupé.

1936 Bentley 4¼ Litre Sports Coupé, with coachwork by Van Vooren, chassis No. B140 GA, engine No. M6 BU, 6 cylinder in line, water-cooled monobloc, push rod operated overhead valve, bore 89mm x stroke 114mm, capacity 4257cc, 4 speed and reverse gearbox, right-hand change. **£50,000-52,000** *S*

1927 Bentley 3 Litre Speed Model 3 Seater Sports, with coachwork by Martin Walter Ltd., 4 cylinder, 2996cc engine. **£156,500-160,000** *S*

1937 Bentley 4¼ Litre Coupé Cabriolet De Ville, with coachwork by Barker & Co., 6 cylinder, 4257cc engine. **£68,500-70,000** *S*

1937 Bentley 4¼ Litre Saloon, with coachwork by Park Ward, 6 cylinder, 4257cc engine, 4 speed manual gearbox, dry plate clutch, shaft drive to rear axle, semi-elliptic spring suspension. **£28,000-30,000** *S*

1928 Bentley 4½ Litre Vanden Plas Le Mans Replic chassis No. XL3105, engine No. PL3496, 4 cylinder in line, water-cooled monobloc, single overhead camshaft, bore 100mm x stroke 140mm, 4 speed manual gearbox with right-hand change, spiral bevel rear axle, semi-elliptic leaf spring suspension front and rear, wheelbase 130in, 5.00 x 21 tyres. **£182,000-185,000** *S*

1949 Bentley Mk VI Four Door Saloon, 6 cylinder, 4257cc engine, 4 speed gearbox semi-floating hypoid bevel rear axle, independent coil spring front suspension, coachwork by H. J. Mulliner. **£19,000-21,000** *S*

1949 Bentley Mk VI Two Door Drop Head Coupé, with coachwork by E. D. Abbott Ltd., 6 cylinder, 4257cc engine, 4 speed gearbox, right-hand drive. Est. **£60,000-80,000** *S*

1952 Bentley R Type Two Door Lightweight Convertible, with coachwork by H. J. Mulliner, chassis No. B47SP, engine No. B273S, 6 cylinder overhead inlet, side exhaust valve, twin SU carburettors, 4566cc, 4 speed synchromesh gearbox, hydro mechanical servo-assisted brakes, independent front suspension semi-elliptic rear with adjustable dampers, it is capable of over 100mph and 16 to 20mpg, has a current MOT certificate and road fund licence.
£77,000-80,000 *C*

1950 Bentley Mk VI, by Freestone and Webb, this black over beige example has been repainted recently, the steering has been overhauled and the brakes are good, altogether a fine period 50s Bentley with distinctive coachwork.
£7,200-9,000 *ADT*

1955 Bentley R Type Continental Coupé, with coachwork by H. J. Mulliner, chassis No. BC 7E, engine No. BC E7, 6 cylinder in-line overhead valve water-cooled monobloc engine, bore 95.25mm, stroke 114.3mm, capacity 4887cc, 3 speed automatic transmission, independent front suspension by coil spring and wishbone, semi-elliptic rear springs, wheelbase 120in and 8.20 x 15 tyres, is capable of travelling at 120mph,

this example has had only 2 owners since 1982 and for the past 3 years has been exhibited in a private collection, generally good throughout, with dark blue paintwork and red upholstery, 2nd gear slips occasionally and requires attention, the car is MOT'd until October 1991 and has MOT certificate and Swansea V5.
£105,000-110,000 *S*

Part of the interior of 1960 Bentley S2 Continental Two Door Saloon.

1960 Bentley S2 Continental Two Door Saloon, chassis No. BC47AR, engine No. A46 BC, with coachwork by H. J. Mulliner, 6.2 litre V8 engine, with power steering and hydro mechanical power-assisted brakes, the engine being a General Motors design. **£132,000-135,000**   *C*

1985 Bentley Mulsanne Turbo Four Door Sports Saloon, chassis No. H 12473, engine No. 412473, V8, 6750cc, water-cooled, bore 104.1mm x stroke 99.1m Garrett AiResearch turbocharger, transmission G.M. 400, 3 speed automatic, front

suspension independent coil and wishbone, rear coil springs with semi-trailing arms, power-assisted steering, wheelbase 120in and VR rated 235/70 x 15 tyres, it has a top speed of 135mph, the car is finished in Magnolia with Everflex roof and

magnolia leather upholstery, all in good condition, recorded mileage of 48,000 in one ownership from new, with Swansea V5 document and MOT and road tax to March 1991. **£30,000-40,000**   *S*

The radiator grille detail of 1985 Bentley Turbo Four Door Sports Saloon.

1957 BMW 507 Sports, chassis No. 70080, engine No. 001079, V8, capacity 3168cc, 4 speed gearbox, torsion bar suspension and finned Alfin brakes, can reach 125mph with the standard 3:7 final drive, only 507 built over 2½ years, this car is in the original black colour, and has red leather upholstery, the equipment includes a period Becker Brescia radio, the front drum brakes have been replaced by discs, as supplied by the factory on the later cars, the car runs well. **£148,500-150,000** *C*

1973 BMW 3.0 CSL Coupé, chassis No. 2285.275, engine No. 2285.275, 3158cc capacity with 206bhp, aluminium wheels, Recaro seats, electric sun roof, very light with aluminium panels, a rare right-hand drive car in excellent order. **£17,500-19,000** *C*

1949 Bristol 400, in very good condition. **£30,000-35,000** *BLE*

1950 Bristol 401 Two Door Sports Saloon, chassis No. 401298, engine No. 85C1509, 6 cylinder, overhead valve, monobloc, bore 66mm x stroke 96mm, capacity 1971cc, coil ignition, 4 speed synchromesh gearbox, with free wheel on 1st gear, central change, spiral bevel final drive, hydraulic footbrake on 4 wheels, handbrake on rear wheels, independent transverse front suspension, torsion bar rear, one of only 650 produced. **£24,000-25,000** *C*

1925 Bugatti Type 35 Grand Prix, chassis No. 117/BC6, 8 cylinder, 1991cc, tyre size 710 x 90, this car has been assembled in the main from Bugatti manufactured components and was at one time owned by Barrie Price also one time Chairman of the Bugatti Owners Club.
£215,000-230,000   *T&M*

1923 Bugatti Type 13A Brescia Racing Two Seater, chassis No. 2260 and engine No. 667, 4 cylinder in-line water-cooled monobloc, single overhead camshaft, 16 valve engine, this example is listed in the British Bugatti Register and reputed only to have been used for racing,

finished in black livery with burnished copper bolster petrol tank, weather protection, upholstery and instrumentation spartan, the car is well known in both Bugatti Owners Club and VSCC circles and is suitable for all classes of competition organised by these clubs.
£73,000-80,000   *S*

Front of 1927 Type 40 Bugatti Four Cylinder, showing headlamps and wings.

1927 Type 40 Bugatti Four Cylinder, chassis No. 40499, Grand Sport 2/3 body, 4 cylinder, 72mm bore (type 40A Block) x 100mm stroke, capacity 1627cc, 3 valves per cylinder operated by single gear driven overhead camshaft, crankshaft carried in plain bearings, with plain big ends, rated to deliver 50bhp at 4,500rpm, channel section chassis with round section front axle, carried on semi-elliptic leaf springs, rear axle carried on reversed quarter elliptic springs, 4 speed sliding mesh with central gear lever, 4 wheel mechanical cable operated brakes, Bugatti compensator, centre lock wire type wheels carrying 5.00 x 19in tyres a good Type 40 had a maximum speed of 75-80mph, and this car was entered in the first Australian Grand Prix on Phillip Island in 1928, during the mid-1980s the car was extensively re-built and fitted with a replica body, fitted with a new Bugatti Owners Club crankcase casting and a new 72mm bore block, together with new crankshaft, pistons, valves and other necessary engine components.
£55,000-60,000   *C(A)*

Part of interior of 1927 Bugatti Type 40 Four Cylinder, showing dashboard and steering wheel.

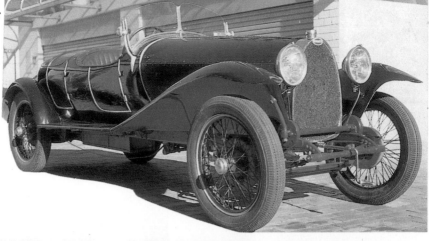

1926 Type 30 Bugatti 8 Cylinder, chassis No. 4724, engine No. 277, straight 8 cylinder, 60mm bore x 88mm stroke, 1991cc, 4 speed sliding mesh with right-hand gear lever.
£90-110,000   *C(A)*

This car was designed by Gianoberto Bugatti for his sisters and was owned by Lidia Bugatti for over 40 years.

1928 Bugatti Type 40 Super-charged Fiacre Drop Head Coupé, chassis No. 40623, engine No. 448, 4 cylinder in line, 69mm bore x 100mm stroke, 1496cc, 4 speed gearbox.
£280,000-300,000   *S*

1932 Bugatti Type 49 Coupé, chassis No. 49474, engine No. L455, 8 cylinders in-line bi-block, single overhead camshaft, 3 valves per cylinder with 72mm bore x 100mm stroke giving a capacity of 3257cc, 4 speed gearbox, the Type 49 was developed from the 3 litre Bugatti Type 44 and first appeared in 1930, the coachwork by Gangloff of Colmar.
£190,000-210,000   *C*

Part of the interior of the 1949 Cisitalia Tipo 202 Coupé, showing the steering wheel and column and dashboard.

1949 Cisitalia Tipo 202 Coupé, with coachwork by Pininfarina and produced by Vignale, chassis No. 129 SC, engine No. 249712522, 4 cylinder, 1089cc, bore 68mm x 75mm stroke, 55bhp at 5,500rpm, compression 7.5:1, single Weber 36 DR 4Sp carburettor, the original competition inlet manifold included with the car but another Weber carburettor is required, independent front suspension with transverse semi-elliptical spring, trailing axle with semi-elliptical springs at rear, hydraulic telescopic shock absorbers all round, right-hand drive, one of only 153 produced and is in excellent condition.
£106,000-110,000   *C(M)*

1924 Citroën 5CV, with excellent bodywork, mechanics and interior, restored in France.
£9,000-10,000   *GWC*

1924 Citroën B14, a totally original and unrestored car with original paintwork and only one owner since 1960, the bodywork, mechanics and interior all in fair condition.
£5,750-7,000   *GWC*

1925 Delage DI, with very good mechanics, and good body and interior, in original condition, this car has had only 2 owners throughout its life and was built originally for a French author.
£19,000-21,000   *GWC*

1954 Citroën Light 15 Leger, in extremely sound and presentable condition throughout, left-hand drive version.
£8,500-9,000   *ELD*

1948 Daimler DB18 Three Position Drop Head, chassis No. 52509, engine No. 43979, 6 cylinder 2522cc, this car has recently been fully restored throughout and has won awards for its pristine condition.
£17,500-19,000 *ADT*

60s Daimler V8 Saloon, automatic, is car was given a bare metal spray in 1987 and has been in regular e ever since, with a recorded ileage of 10,800.
,000-7,000 *ADT*

1968 Daimler V8 250, this is a completely original car in very good condition.
£11,000-12,000 *RH*

73 Daimler Double Six Vanden Plas, e of only 225 produced, this is a e and excellent example with 59,000 les recorded.
000-10,000 *RH*

1921-36 Derby Three Seat Roadster, French built right-hand drive car, with 4 cylinder water-cooled Chapuis-Dornier engine of 939cc, period disc wheels, quarter elliptic rear springs and transverse half-elliptic springs on the front axle.
£7,000-9,000 *ADT*

51 Dellow Mk I Open orts Two Seater, assis No. 161151, engine . RC 890073P Ford 2cc side valve bore 5 x stroke 92.5 31bhp carburettor, 3 speed rbox, 'Fiddle' braking tem, right-hand drive, pletely restored.
000-10,000 *C*

1957 Ferrari 250GT Berlinetta 'Tour de France', with coachwork by Scaglietti, chassis No. 0773 GT, engine No. 0773 V12 cylinder, 2953cc bore and stroke, 73mm x 58.8mm, compression ratio 8.5:1 260bhp at 7,000rpm, 3 Weber DCF carburettors, 4 speed gearbox, rigid axle, front independent Helicoidal springs suspension, rear semi-elliptic leaf springs, hydraulic drum brakes on

each wheel, Borrani wire spoke wheels, centre lock, wheelbase 2,600mm, and 600 x 16 tyres. **£1,150,000-1,300,000** *C(M)*

Rear and side view of 1957 Ferrari 250GT Berlinetta 'Tour de France'.

1958 Ferrari 250GT Series I Cabriolet, chassis No. 0849, engine No. 0849, V12 cylinder, 2953cc bore and stroke 73mm x 58.8mm, compression ratio 8.5:1, 220bhp, at 7,000rpm, 3 Weber DCF carburettors, 4 speed gearbox, rigid axle, hydraulic drum brakes. **£510,000-530,000** *C(M)*

A view of part of interior of 1958 Ferrari 250GT Series I Cabriolet, with coachwork by Pininfarina showing dashboard and steering wheel.

1961 Ferrari 250GT SWB Berlinetta, with coachwork by Pininfarina, chassis No. 3281, engine No. 3281, V12 cylinder, 72.9mm bore x 58.9mm stroke, capacity 2953cc, rated to develop 235bhp at 7,000rpm, aluminium alloy block and cylinder heads with single chain driven overhead camshafts, 3 twin choke Weber carburettors, 4 speed synchromesh gearbox, independent front suspension by coil springs and wishbones, beam rear axle carried on leaf springs, disc brakes on all 4 wheels with vacuum servo, centre lock Borrani wire wheels, with magnesium alloy rims, carrying 185 x 15 tyres, and right-hand drive. **£850,000-950,000** *C(A)*

Views of the engine and part of the interior of 1961 Ferrari 250GT SWB Berlinetta.

1961 Ferrari 250GT Short Wheelbase Berlinetta, with coachwork by Pininfarina, built by Scaglietti, chassis No. 2417, engine No. 2417, V12 60°, 73mm bore x 58.8mm stroke, 2953cc, 180.2cu in, single overhead cam per bank, 2 Marelli distributors, 9.2:1 compression, 280bhp at 7,000rpm, 3 Weber 46DCL/3 carburettors, single dry plate clutch, 4 speed all synchromesh gearbox unit, independent front suspension with double wishbones and coil springs, live rear axle, semi-elliptic springs, trailing arms, disc brakes, Borrani wire centre lock wheels, wheelbase 240cm, and tyres 6.00 x 16.
£1,250,000-1,500,000   *CNY*

1960 Ferrari 196S Dino, V6 cylinder 60° single overhead camshaft on each bank, capacity 1985cc, bore and stroke 77mm x 71mm, compression ratio 9.8:1, 00bhp at 7,600rpm, triple Weber 42 DCN twin choke carburettors, live rear axle, speed gearbox, multi-disc y plate clutch, independent ont suspension 'A-arms' coil ring, rear live axle.
2,600,000-2,800,000   *C(M)*

The dashboard detail and engine of 1960 Ferrari 196S Dino.

64 Ferrari 250GT/Lusso, assis No. 5463 GT, engine . 5463 GT, V12 single erhead camshaft 2953cc, 0bhp, 4 speed synchromesh arbox, disc brakes, lependent front suspension, e axle with semi-elliptic r springs, right-hand drive.
40,000-600,000   *C*

1967 Ferrari 275GTB/4 Berlinetta, chassis No. 0976 engine No. 09767, V12 cylinders, 3286cc, 72mm bore x 58.8mm stroke, giving 300bhp at 8,000rpm, 6 Weber twin choke carburettors, 5 speed gearbox with reverse, coachwork by Pininfarina. The 275GTB/4 was unveiled at the Paris Salon in October 1966, being the first production Ferrari to boast the use of the quadruple camshaft V12 power unit.
£480,000-500,000 *C(M)*

American regulations governing emissions helped to limit production of the 275GTB/4 to only about 280.

1976 Ferrari Dino 308GT4 2+2 Sports Coupé, chassis No. 08756, engine No. 08756, V8 cylinder double overhead cam per block, 81mm bore x 71mm stroke, 2926cc, 5 speed gearbox, power output 256bhp at 7,600rpm, bodywork by Bertone.
£15,000-18,000 *S*

1978 Ferrari 512 Boxer Berlinetta, chassis No. F102BB24927, engine No. 00302, flat 12 cylinders, 4942cc, coachwork by Pininfarina.
£170,000-180,000 *T&M*

1979 Ferrari 308GTS, chassis No. 27295, engine No. 27295, V8, double overhead camshaft per bank, 2962cc, 250bhp, 5 speed synchromesh gearbox.
£50,000-53,000 *C*

1980 Ferrari 400i Convertible, chassis No. 31779, engine No. F101C010-00213, V12, double overhead camshaft, 4823cc, 340bhp, 5 speed synchromesh gearbox. The 400i was introduced at the Paris Salon in October 1976, and was available with an automatic transmission option.
£70,000-73,000 *C*

1982 Ferrari 400i, chassis No. 41425, engine No. 41425, V12, double overhead camshafts, 4823cc, 340bhp, turbo Hydro-matic 3 speed automatic gearbox.
£43,000-46,000 *C*

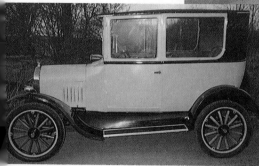

Ford Model T Two Seater Speedster, chassis No. 6871145, 4 cylinder in-line engine, water-cooled monobloc, side valve, 95mm bore x 102mm stroke, Treasury rating 22.4hp, epicyclic 2 speed gearbox with reverse, multi-disc clutch for direct drive top gear, bevel final drive. **£8,000-9,000** *S*

1929 Ford Model A, this car has been restored. **£10,000-12,000** *CC*

1924 Ford Model T Tudor Saloon, restored with new upholstery, repainted but not to a very high standard. **£12,000-15,000** *Mot*

23 Ford Model T Tourer, by Linnaker ght-hand drive, fully restored, th coachbuilt body. 0,000-12,000 *Mot*

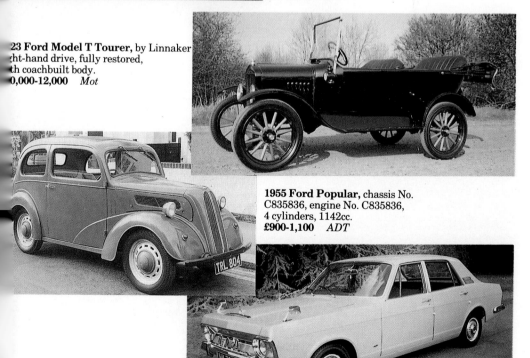

1955 Ford Popular, chassis No. C835836, engine No. C835836, 4 cylinders, 1142cc. **£900-1,100** *ADT*

7 **Ford Zephyr Mk 4,** excellent dition. 000-3,500 *RH*

1914 Ford Model T Two Seater Tourer, well restored.
£13,500-14,500 *DB*

1920 Ford Model T Centre-Door Saloon.
£6,500-7,500 *DB*

1922 Ford Model T Depot Hack.
£5,500-6,500 *DB*

1919 Ford Model T Two Seater, electric start, very good condition.
£8,500-9,500 *DB*

1926 Ford Model T Four Seate twin-speed rear axle.
£9,500-10,000 *DB*

1914 Ford Model T Tourer.
£11,000-13,000 *DB*

1923 Ford Model T Ton Truck, well restored.
£7,500-8,500 *DB*

1937 Ford V8 Saloon, right-hand drive, good condition.
£4,500-5,500 *DB*

1913 Ford Model T Four Seater, twin-speed rear axle, well restored. **£16,500-17,500** *DB*

1972 Citroën SM, with 2670cc,
6 cylinder engine capacity.
Est. £18,000-20,000   *ADT*

1972 Citroën DS 19, with 1985cc,
4 cylinder engine capacity.
Est. £3,000-4,000   *LF*

1971 Citroën Maserati SM. Est. £9,000-12,000 *Cen*

Make: Citroën
Model: SM
Type: Sports Coupé
Years Manufactured: 1971-75
Quantity: 12,920
Price when new: £5,957
Engine Type: Double overhead camshaft V6
Size: 2670/2965cc
Max Power: 2670, 170 bhp (178 bhp with fuel injection) @ 5500 rpm; 2965, 180 bhp @ 4750 rpm
Max Torque: 2670, 172 (164 with fuel injection) ft/lb @ 4000 rpm; 2965, 181 ft/lb @ 4000 rpm
Transmission: 5 speed manual or 3 speed auto
Wheelbase: 116.1in
Performance: Max speed: 2.7 injection, 139 mph; 0-60: 2.7 injection, 9.3 secs.

MAKE	ENGINE	DATES	CONDITION		
Citroën			1	2	3
A	1300/4	1919	£4,000	£3,000	£2,000
5CV	856/4	1922-26	£6,000	£3,000	£2,000
12/24	1538/4	1927-29	£4,000	£2,000	£1,000
Twenty	2650/6	1932-35	£8,000	£6,000	£4,000
Fifteen 11CV	1911/4	1935-55	£8,000	£5,000	£3,000
6	2866/6	1938-56	£6,000	£3,000	£1,500

Value is dependent on left or right hand drive and body type.

121

CLYNO

1926 Clyno 11-9, in storage for 30 years and in need of restoration. Est. **£4,400-4,800** *CC*

CLEVELAND

1920 Cleveland Model 40 Five Passenger Tourer, 6 cylinder in-line engine, water-cooled, overhead valve, bore 3in x 4.49in stroke, maker's rating 45hp, 3 speed gearbox, plate clutch, spiral bevel rear axle, semi-elliptic leaf spring suspension front and rear, wheelbase 112in, 32 x 4in tyres. **£5,700-7,000** *SNY*

The Chandler Motor Company was set up in Cleveland in 1913 by key figures from the Lozier Motor Company, including F. C. Chandler, from whom the company took its name.

COLUMBIA

1906 Columbia Five Seater Experimental Open Touring Car, 4 cylinder L-head engine with cylinders pair-cast on a common aluminium crank case, 3 speed gearbox, with shaft drive to live rear axle, camshaft-driven water pump with cooling fan, exposed valve gear, ¾ elliptic rear suspension, semi-elliptic at front with transverse 'helper' spring. **£14,000-14,500** *S*

1923 Columbia Model Six Tourer, 6 cylinder, 24hp engine, original right-hand drive built in Detroit for the export market. Est. **£9,000-12,000** *LF*

CORD

1936 Cord 810 Beverly Four Door Sedan, Lycoming V8, side valve engine, 4729cc, 125bhp, 4 speed synchromesh gearbox with electro-vacuum shift, front wheel drive, independent, transverse leaf front suspension, 4 wheel hydraulic brakes, left-hand drive. Est. **£35,000-40,000** *C*

CROSSLEY

1919 Crossley 25/30 Sports Coupé with Dickey, 4 cylinder, water-cooled monobloc engine, side valve, 4500cc, 4 speed manual non-synchromesh gearbox, dry plate clutch, shaft drive to live rear axle, semi-elliptic spring suspension, wheelbase 135in, tyres 21in. Est. **£30,000-35,000** *S*

1935 Crossley Regis 4 Door Sports Saloon. **£14,950-16,000** *DJ*

Locate the source

The source of each illustration in Miller's can be found by checking the code letters below each caption with the list of contributors

DAIMLER

Although Daimler imported cars from Germany it is still considered to be the oldest UK manufacturer. The company was bought by BSA in 1910 and by the 1920s these luxury automobiles were the favoured transport of royalty. After the second world war a cheaper, relatively, Conquest range was introduced but the Majestic series and the SP250 sports car failed to save the company from takeover by Jaguar in the 1960s. Daimler still make their own variation of Jaguar models.

1911 Daimler TG15 Five Seat Open Tourer, with 4 cylinder, 3000cc engine.
£23,500-24,000
ADT

1928 Daimler Shooting Brake/Estate.
£14,000-16,000   *DJ*

1932 Daimler 16/20 Saloon, with full service record, this car has been rebuilt.
£24,500-25,000   *BLE*

1930 Delage D8 4 Litre Tourer, coachwork by Vanden Plas.
Est. £60,000-70,000   *B*

1935 Daimler 15HP Light Six, by Mulliner, with 2006cc, 6 cylinder engine capacity, extensively restored.
£5,600-6,000   *LF*

1937 Daimler Straight 8 Light Saloon, in good condition.
£21,750-23,000   *BLE*

1938 Daimler Straight 8 Saloon.
£18,950-20,000   *DJ*

1937 Daimler 4 Litre Straight Eight.
£16,500-17,000   *DB*

1940 Daimler DB18, by Tickford, this car has been extensively restored and is in excellent condition.
Est. £20,000-25,000   *Cen*

MAKE Daimler	ENGINE	DATES	CONDITION 1	2	3
DB18	2522/6	1946-49	£7,500	£4,000	£1,000
DB18 Conv S/S	2522/6	1948-53	£15,000	£8,000	£2,000
Consort	2522/6	1949-53	£4,000	£2,000	£500
Conquest/Con. Century	2433/6	1953-58	£4,000	£2,000	£500
Conquest Roadster	2433/6	1953-56	£8,000	£4,000	£1,000
Majestic 3.8	3794/6	1958-62	£4,000	£2,000	£450
SP250	2547/8	1959-64	£17,000	£10,000	£4,500
Majestic Major	4561/8	1961-64	£5,000	£3,000	£500
2.5 V8	2547/8	1962-67	£8,000	£6,000	£2,500
V8 250	2547/8	1968-69	£7,500	£5,000	£2,000
Sovereign 420	4235/6	1966-69	£6,500	£4,500	£1,500

Make: Daimler
Model: 2½ Litre V8 250
Type: Saloon
Years Manufactured: 1962-69
Quantity: 17,620
Price when new: £1,569
Engine Type: Overhead valve V8
Size: 2548cc
Max Power: 140 bhp @ 5800 rpm
Transmission: 4 speed, optional overdrive or auto
Performance: Max speed: 112 mph; 0-60: 13 secs; Mpg: 18-22.

1951 Daimler DB18 Roadster, by Barker with chassis No. V53967. Est. **£20,000-25,000**   *P*

The 2½ litre DB18 Daimler was available in saloon, drop head coupé and roadster form, most of the bodies were built by Barker of London.

1952 Daimler Empress, with body by Hooper.
£16,500-17,000   *RTC*

1965 Daimler V8, unrestored but good original condition. Est. **£9,750-10,250**   *RH*

1966 Daimler 2½ V8 Saloon, chassis No. 1A116/4BW and engine No. 7A12295, 2548cc, V8 capacity. Est. **£9,000-12,000**   *LF*

1955 Daimler Century Three Position Drop Head.
£15,000-15,500   *Mot*

1957 Daimler 2½ Litre Conquest Century Saloon.
£5,000-6,000   *B*

1962 Daimler SP250.
Est. £15,000-18,000   *CGO*

1960 Daimler SP250 'Dart' Two Plus Two Seater Sports, engine V8 cylinder pushrod operated, bore 76.2mm x 69.85mm, 2548cc, 140bhp, 4 speed gearbox, hypoid bevel final drive, independent front suspension, half elliptic leaf spring rear, disc brakes all round.
Est. £11,000-13,000   *S*

1962 Daimler SP250 'Dart' B Series.
£10,120-12,000   *S*

1966 Daimler V8 2.5 Litre Saloon.
Est. £15,000-18,000   *S*

1963 Daimler SP250 Dart, in need of total restoration.
£7,000-8,000   *AMR*

During April 1963 the SP250 more usually referred to as the Daimler Dart, received further additions to its standard specifications listing. The additions included the provision of an interior heater and demister unit, a cigarette lighter and a trickle charger socket. The SP250's standard equipment also included a petrol reserve unit and switch, front and rear bumpers, adjustable steering column and windscreen washers.

1964 Daimler SP250.
Est. £17,000-18,000   *ADT*

Make: Daimler	
Model: SP250	
Type: Sports	
Years Manufactured: 1959-64	
Quantity: 2,648	
Price when new: £1,395	
Engine Type: Overhead valve V8	
Size: 2548cc	
Max Power: 140 bhp @ 5800 rpm	
Max Torque: 155 ft/lb @ 3600 rpm	
Transmission: 4 speed (auto option from 1961)	
Wheelbase: 92in	
Performance: Max speed: 125 mph; 0-60: 8.8 secs; Mpg: 22-26.	

1966 Daimler V8 250 Sports Saloon, with V8 2548cc engine, driving through Borg Warner 3 speed automatic transmission, independent front suspension, quarter-elliptic rear leaf spring and live rear axle, 42,000 miles recorded.
£8,000-10,000   *SEN*

DAIMLER

MAKE	ENGINE	DATES	CONDITION		
Daimler			1	2	3
Veteran (Coventry built)		1897-1904	£80,000	£60,000	£40,000
Veteran		1904-19	£35,000	£25,000	£15,000
30hp	4962/6	1919-25	£40,000	£25,000	£18,000
45hp	7413/6	1919-25	£45,000	£30,000	£20,000
Double Six 50	7136/12	1927-34	£60,000	£40,000	£30,000
20	2687/6	1934-35	£18,000	£14,000	£12,000
Straight 8	3421/8	1936-38	£20,000	£15,000	£12,000

Value is dependent on body style, coachbuilder and condition of the sleeve valve engine.

Make: Daimler
Model: Conquest
Type: Saloon/Drop Head Coupé
Years Manufactured: 1954-57
Price when new: Saloon, £1,511
Engine Type: Overhead valve 6 cyl
Size: 2433cc
Max Power: 100 bhp @ 4400 rpm
Transmission: 4 speed; pre-selector/fluid flywheel (auto option from 1956)
Performance: Max speed: 85 mph; 0-60: 16.3 secs; Mpg: 16-20.

1967 Daimler 250 V8 Saloon, chassis No. 1K2245BW and engine No. 7K2312 with 2548cc, V8 capacity.
£10,800-12,000 *LF*

1967 Daimler V8 250 Saloon, chassis No. PA13166BW and engine No. 7A13881, 90 degree V8 cylinder, water-cooled, overhead valve, bore 76mm, stroke 70mm, capacity 2548cc, Borg Warner 3 speed automatic transmission, hypoid rear axle, independent coil spring front suspension, cantilever leaf springs at rear with radius arms and Panhard rod, wheelbase 8ft 11½in and tyres 15in.
Est. **£7,000-9,000** *S*

1967 Daimler 420.
Est. **£2,500-3,500** *AMR*

1968 Daimler V8 250 Manual
Est. **£6,000-9,000** *Cen*

1968 Daimler V8 250, rare manual in totally original condition with only 2,600 miles recorded.
Est. **£31,000-32,000** *RH*

1975 Daimler 4.2 Coupé, an excellent unrestored car.
Est. **£9,500-10,000** *RH*

1968 Daimler Sovereign Saloon, chassis No. A32907BW and engine No. A332088, 4235cc capacity and 4 speed automatic transmission.
£3,200-3,500 *GIL*

1969 Daimler 250 V8 Saloon, V8 cylinder, water-cooled, overhead valve engine, 2548cc, 3 speed automatic gearbox, shaft drive to live rear axle, independent coil and leaf spring suspension, right-hand drive.
Est. **£7,000-8,000** *S*

Daimler had been acquired by Jaguar in 1960, and the effects soon showed in the modified product range. The body styling was borrowed from the Jaguar Mk II and other than the mechanical specifications and adoption of Daimler's distinctive fluted grille, the cars were very similar.

1978 Daimler XJ6C Two Door Coupé, with straight 6 cylinder, water-cooled monobloc engine, double overhead camshafts, bore 3.625in x stroke 4.173in, 4235cc, 3 speed gearbox automatic transmission, shaft drive to live rear axle, independent front and rear suspension with coil springs, wishbones and telescopic shock absorbers, and ER70/VR15 tyres.
Est. **£5,000-7,000** *S*

1977 Daimler Sovereign V12 Coupé.
Est. **£2,000-5,000** *LF*

The Coupé is relatively rare as only 370 were made.

DARRACQ

French engineer Alexandre Darracq set up the Gladiator Cycle Company in 1891, developed it over a five year period and sold out in 1896.

CONDITION is absolutely vital when assessing the value of a vehicle. Top class vehicles on the whole appreciate much more than less perfect examples. However a rare, desirable car may command a high price even when in need of restoration

1903 Darracq 8hp Four Seat Entrance Tonneau, with vertical single cylinder engine, water-cooled, atmospheric inlet valve, side mechanical exhaust valve, bore 112mm x stroke 112mm, 1103cc, 3 speed gearbox with reverse, column change, semi-elliptic leaf springs front and rear, wheelbase 1.76m and 760 x 80mm tyres.
£33,000-35,000 *S*

DELAGE

Louis Delage formed the company bearing his name in 1905 and, with a first class design and engineering, standards soon rivalled Rolls-Royce and Hispano-Suiza as a manufacturer of top quality motor vehicles. Delage was bought by Delahaye in 1935. Hotchkiss acquired the company in the 1940s and by 1954 production had ceased.

1931 Delage D8 'Square Type Dandy' body Grand Luxe, coachwork by Henri Chapron, with 8 cylinder in line, water-cooled monobloc engine, pushrod operated overhead valves, bore 77mm x stroke 109mm, 4050cc, single dry plate clutch, 4 speed gearbox, spiral bevel live rear axle, semi-elliptic leaf spring front and rear suspension, wheelbase 3.48m, and 18in tyres.
Est. **£70,000-80,000** *S*

The price ranges given reflect the average price a purchaser should pay for similar vehicle. Condition, rarity, provenance, racing history, originality and any restoration are factors that must be taken into account when assessing values. When buying or selling, it must always be remembered that prices can be greatly affected by the condition of any vehicle. Unless otherwise stated, all cars shown in Miller's are of good merchantable quality, and the valuations given reflect this fact. Vehicles offered for sale in exceptionally fine condition or in poor condition may reasonably be expected to be priced considerably higher or lower respectively than the estimates given herein

DELAGE

1913 Delage 12hp Tourer AB Series 7, with 4 cylinder, side valve engine, bore 75mm x stroke 120mm, 12hp, HT Magneto ignition, water-cooled, 3 speed and reverse gearbox, shaft, bevel geared rear axle, cone clutch, right-hand drive.
Est. £14,000-16,000   *C(A)*

Make the Most of Miller's

CONDITION is absolutely vital when assessing the value of a vehicle. Top class vehicles on the whole appreciate much more than less perfect examples. However a rare, desirable car may command a high price even when in need of restoration

1933 Delage DR70 Saloon with Division, 4 wheels have aluminium covers with wire wheels inside, in overall good condition.
£18,000-22,000   *LF*

DELAHAYE

Emil Delahaye manufactured his first automobile in 1894, producing an ordinary range of cars until he acquired Delage in 1935. They then produced sports cars as well as Grand Prix racing cars. Following a series of mergers and takeovers the company stopped production in 1956.

1952 Delahaye 235 Two Door Drop Head Coupé, coachwork by Chapron, with 6 cylinder in line, water-cooled monobloc engine, pushrod operated overhead valves, bore 84mm x stroke 107mm, capacity 3557cc, single dry plate clutch, electro magnetic 4 speed gearbox, spiral bevel live axle, front suspension by transverse leaf spring and wishbones, rear suspension by semi-elliptic leaf spring, wheelbase 115in, and 17in tyres.
Est. £120,000-140,000   *S*

DEEMSTER

1922 Deemster 10hp Roadster With Dickey, with 4 cylinder in line, water-cooled engine, bore 62mm x stroke 90mm, 10hp, 4 speed gearbox, shaft drive in-line rear axle, semi-elliptic leaf spring suspension front and rear and 25 x 3in tyres, engine produced by Ogston, total restoration required.
Est. £5,000-7,000   *S*

The Wilkinson Touring Motorcycle Company of Acton, London, produced a series of designs for motorcycles and light cars between about 1907 and 1914, and plans were projected for various models using their own design for a 4 cylinder 10hp engine. In 1914 the manufacturing rights were sold to the Ogston Motor Company, who manufactured a light car to the Wilkinson designs as the 'Deemster'

DATSUN

1971/72 Datsun Nissan 240Z Two Seater.
£12,000-12,500 *CZ*
These cars are very rare and much sought after as they are eligible to race in the Historic Sports Car Club races.

MAKE	ENGINE	DATES	CONDITION		
Datsun			1	2	3
240Z	2393/6	1969-71	£9,000	£5,000	£3,000
240Z	2393/6	1972-74	£3,000	£2,500	£1,000
260Z	2565/6	1974-79	£2,000	£1,500	£750
260Z 2+2	2565/6	1974-79	£1,000	£750	—

1978/79 Datsun Nissan 260Z 2+2.
£6,000-6,500 *CZ*
This car is now highly sought after and due to dwindling numbers is rising in value.

Did you know
MILLER'S Collectors Cars Price Guide builds up year by year to form the most comprehensive photo-reference system available

DELLOW

The Register is a small, friendly club, small due to the rareness of the Z models, but big on its welcome to owners via its many social venues. Members receive a quarterly A4 magazine, spares discounts, club insurance, technical back-up and a chance to meet sister clubs worldwide. Nissan supports the Register and its principles wholeheartedly. Nissan has established a special discount for members with its A.F.G dealerships, and produces our beautiful club magazines.

Membership stands at 187
Membership fee £15.00 per year

Chairman: Mrs. Lynne Godber,
'Thistledown', Old Stockbridge Road, Kentsboro,
Wallop, Stockbridge, Hants SO20 8DZ
Telephone: Andover (0264) 781979

954 Dellow Mark II
ompetition/Trials Two Seater,
ith 1172cc (Ford 100E twin
arburettors, high compression –
e normal Dellow unit), in
rooklands green with chassis
o. JW1 1 and engine No. 861226C.
st. **£5,000-8,000** *H*

DE TOMASO

1972 De Tomaso Pantera LHD.
Est. **£15,000-20,000**   *Cen*

INFORMATION SHEET

Make: De Tomaso
Model: Pantera
Type: Sports Coupé
Years Manufactured: 1971-88
Quantity: est 9,500 up to 1987
Engine Type: Overhead valve V8
Size: 5763cc
Max Power: 250-350 bhp @ 5400-6000 rpm
Max Torque: 325-330 ft/lb @ 3600-3800 rpm
Transmission: 5 speed manual
Wheelbase: 99in
Performance: Max speed: 140-160 mph; 0-60: 5.2-7.5 secs.

MAKE	ENGINE	DATES	CONDITION		
De Tomaso			1	2	3
Mangusta	4727/8	1967-72	£30,000	£15,000	£9,000
Pantera	5763/8	1969-89	£24,000	£14,000	£9,000
Deauville	5763/8	1970-88	£8,000	£5,000	£2,000
Longchamps	5763/8	1972-	£9,000	£6,000	£2,000

1983 De Tomaso Longchamps GTS, with 90° V8 cylinder, water-cooled engine, pushrod operated overhead valves, bore 101.6mm x stroke 88.9mm, 5769cc, Ford 3 speed automatic gearbox, hypoid bevel rear axle, independent coil spring and wishbone front and rear suspension, 265 x 14in tyres, with coachwork by Ghia, and left-hand drive.
Est. **£20,000-25,000**   *S*

DE LOREAN

1982 De Lorean, chassis No. SCEDT26 TX BD006122 and engine No. SCEDT26 TX BD006122.
Est. **£16,000-20,000**   *P*

1981 De Lorean.
Est. **£12,000-14,000**   *ADT*

The legacy of this ill-fated company was some 10,000 state of the art sports cars for the 1980s featuring gull wing doors, brushed stainless steel body panels, a Volvo V6 engine and competitive suspension. All but 30 of the production run were left-hand drive cars.

DESOTO

1929 DeSoto Model K Two Seater Roadster with Rumble Seat.
Est. **£25,000-30,000**   *P*

1948 DeSoto S 11 Custom Four Door Sedan, 6 cylinder in-line engine, water-cooled monobloc, side valve, bore 3⁷⁄₁₇in x 4¼in stroke, 236.6cu in, 3 speed gearbox with DeSoto fluid drive transmission, bevel rear axle, wheelbase 121½in, 710 x 15in tyres.
£5,500-6,500   *SNY*

MAKE	ENGINE	DATES	CONDITION		
DeSoto			1	2	3
Firedome/Fireflite	341, 383/8	1957-59	£9,000	£5,000	£3,000
Adventurer	348, 383/8	1957-59	£15,000	£12,000	£8,500

DODGE

In 1928 Walter Chrysler paid $175 million for the Dodge Company, started in 1914 by the Dodge brothers.

1918 Dodge Five Seat Tourer, with 4 cylinder, 3673cc engine. Est. **£13,000-15,000** *ADT*

1939 Dodge 3.6 Litre 'Luxury Liner' Deluxe Coupé. Est. **£8,000-10,000** *P*

DETROIT

1918 Detroit Electric Model 75 Brougham. **£11,000-12,000** *SNY*

1924 Dodge 17/24 HP Two Door Coupé, with 4 cylinder, side valve, 3.5 litre engine, 17/24hp, 3 speed sliding mesh gearbox, rear wheel mechanical brakes, semi-elliptic suspension, detachable artillery wheels and left-hand drive. **£7,700-8,200** *C*

MAKE	ENGINE	DATES	CONDITION		
			1	2	3
Dodge					
Coronet	230/6, 383/8	1957-59	£6,000	£4,000	£2,500
Custom Royal	230/6, 383/8	1957-59	£8,000	£6,500	£4,500

DORIOT

In 1912 DFP cars were being imported into Britain by Bentley and Bentley Ltd who acquired the British Empire concession. The Bentley brothers in England pushed the sporting image of the 2 litre 12/15 DFP tuning it and fitting attractive bodywork.

1910 Doriot Flandrin Parant — DFP, engine No. 1042, 4 cylinders, Doriot and Flandrin had worked for Clement-Bayard and Peugeot, they then started business in 1906 as Doriot and Flandrin making single cylinder voiturettes. Two years later they were joined by Alexandre and Jules-Rene Parant who formed Doriot, Flandrin and Parant, the singles were still being marketed as late as 1910, but the 1908 range included two 4 cylinder cars with SU Chapins Vemier engines of 2.4 litre and 2.8 litre capacity, by 1910 there was a small four, the very successful 10/12 HP of 1.6 litres with megneto ignition, thermo-syphon coding, cone clutch and 3 speed gearbox. **£14,000-15,000** *C*

DUTTON PHAETON

1963 Dutton Phaeton, the Dutton Phaeton is based on Triumph Spitfire mechanic s and running gear. This example is fitted with the 1147cc, 4 cylinder engine.
Est. **£3,000-4,000** *ADT*

DUESENBERG

1930 Duesenberg Model J Dual Cowl Phaeton (Barrel-Side), with coachwork by Le Baron, chassis No. 2270, engine No. J243 straight 8, water-cooled monobloc, double overhead camshafts, 4 valves per cylinder, bore 3¾in x 4¾in stroke, 420cu in, 3 speed gearbox, double disc clutch, hypoid bevel rear axle, semi-elliptic leaf springs front and rear, wheelbase 142½in, 19in tyres.
£825,000-900,000 *SNY*

1934 Duesenberg Model-J, with coachwork by Murphy-Convertible Sedan, 8 cylinder, twin chain driven overhead camshafts, 4 valves per cylinder, 6876cc (418.9cu in), bore 95.25mm x stroke 120.65mm, compression 5.2:1, 5 main bearings, alloy sump 265bhp at 4,200rpm, single 38mm Duplex updraught carburettor, double disc clutch, 3 speed gearbox, hypoid rear axle, alloy steel ladder frame chassis with 7 cross members, semi-elliptic springs front and rear suspension, Duesenberg hydraulic, finned drums brakes, chrome centre lock wire wheels, 7.00 x 17 tyres, wheelbase 142.5in, 56in track front and rear and weight 5,270lb.
Est. **£470,000-500,000** *CNY*

1931 Duesenberg Model J Supercharged Mudd Coupé, with coachwork by Bohman and Schwartz, chassis No. 2234, engine No. J212 (S/C) straight 8, water-cooled monobloc, double overhead camshafts, 4 valves per cylinder, bore 3¾in x 4¾in stroke 420cu in, 3 speed gearbox, double disc clutch, hypoid bevel rear axle, semi-elliptic leaf springs front and rear, wheelbase 142½in, 7.50 x 17 tyres.
£1,200,000-1,500,000 *SNY*

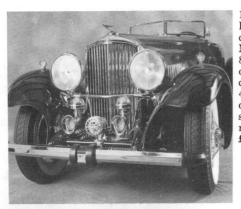

1932 Duesenberg Model J The French Speedster, with coachwork by Figoni, chassis No. 2178, engine No. J153 straight 8, water-cooled monobloc, double overhead camshafts, 4 valves per cylinder, bore 3¾in x 4¾in stroke, 420cu in, 3 speed gearbox, double disc clutch, hypoid bevel rear axle, semi-elliptic leaf springs front and rear, wheelbase 142½in, 19in tyres.
£1,100,000-1,500,000 *SNY*

1935 Duesenberg Model J Convertible Victoria, with coachwork by Anciens Establishments d'Ieteren Freres, S.A., chassis No. 2548, engine No. J519 straight 8, water-cooled monobloc, double overhead camshafts, 4 valves per cylinder, bore 3¾in x 4¾in stroke, 420cu in, 3 speed gearbox, double disc clutch, hypoid bevel rear axle, semi-elliptic leaf springs front and rear, wheelbase 153½in, 19in tyres.
£585,000-600,000 *SNY*

1935 Duesenberg Model J Convertible Victoria, coachwork by Fernandez & Darrin, chassis No. 2516, engine No. J499 straight 8, water-cooled monobloc, double overhead camshafts, 4 valves per cylinder, bore 3¾in x 4¾in stroke, 420cu in, 3 speed gearbox, double disc clutch, hypoid bevel rear axle, semi-elliptic leaf springs front and rear, wheelbase 153½in, 19in tyres.
£620,000-650,000 *SNY*

Locate the source

The source of each illustration in Miller's can be found by checking the code letters below each caption with the list of contributors

FERRARI

The first V12 Ferrari was produced by Enzo Ferrari in 1946 and they have continued to produce a superb range of models ever since, being without doubt among the truly great names in motoring history. Their sports car and Grand Prix racing history is far too long to even highlight here. Fiat acquired the majority shareholding in 1969.

1951 Ferrari 195 Inter, with coachwork by Ghia, chassis No. 0109S and engine No. 0109S, V12 cylinder, 2340cc, bore and stroke 65mm x 58.8mm, compression ratio 7.5:1, 130bhp at 6,000rpm, 1 Weber DCF 32 carburettor, 5 speed gearbox, rigid axle, front independent suspension A arms and transverse leaf spring; rear, rigid axle semi-elliptic springs and torsion bars, hydraulic drum brakes on all wheels, Borrani wire spoke wheels, centre lock, tyres 5.90 x 15 with wheelbase 2,500mm, front track 1,270mm and rear track 1,250mm.
Est. **£750,000+** *C(M)*

Make: Ferrari
Model: 195 and 212
Type: Sports Coupé, Convertible
Years Manufactured: 1950-53
Quantity: approx. 130
Engine Type: Single overhead camshaft V12
Size: 195, 2341cc; 212, 2562cc
Max Power: (1951) 195 130 bhp @ 6000 rpm (Inter); 160-180 bhp @ 6000 rpm (Sport); (1951-53), 130 bhp @ 6000 rpm (Inter); 150-170 bhp @ 6500 rpm (Export)
Transmission: 5 speed manual
Wheelbase: 86.6in, 195 Sport; 88.6in, 212 Export); 98.5in, Inter
Performance: Max speed: (195), 110 mph; (212), 120 mph.

1952 Ferrari 225S Sport, chassis No. 160ED and V12 cylinder engine, 2715cc, bore and stroke 70mm x 58.8mm, compression ratio 8.5:1, 210bhp at 7,200rpm, 3 Weber DCF 36 carburettors, 5 speed gearbox, rigid axle, front independent suspension A arms and transverse leaf spring, rear rigid axle, semi-elliptic springs and torsion bars, hydraulic drum brakes on each wheel, Borrani wire spoke wheels, centre lock, tyres F.5.25 x 16, 6.50 x 16, wheelbase 2,250mm, front track 1,278 and rear track 1,250mm.
Est. **£750,000-900,000**   *C(M)*

The 225S model was then further developed into a 3 litre and was the forerunner of the 250MM marking the beginning of the famous 250 series of road and competition cars.

1958 Ferrari 250GT Series 1 Cabriolet, with 12 cylinders in vee formation, water-cooled, inclined valves operated by single overhead camshaft per bank, bore 73mm x stroke 58.8mm, capacity 2953cc, multiple disc dry clutch, 4 speed gearbox, bevel drive live rear axle, front suspension by wishbones and coil springs, rear suspension by semi-elliptic leaf spring, Houdaille suspension dampers, wheelbase 2,600mm, and 6.00 x 16in tyres.
Est. **£550,000-700,000**   *S(M)*

Make: Ferrari
Model: 250GT long wheelbase
Type: Sports Coupé
Years Manufactured: 1954-62
Quantity: All types, 905
Engine Type: Single overhead camshaft V12
Size: 2953cc
Max Power: 220-260 bhp @ 7000 rpm
Transmission: 4 speed manual, with overdrive from 1960
Wheelbase: 102.3in
Performance: Max speed: 124-155 mph; 0-60: 7.0-8.0 secs.

1958 Ferrari 250GT Berlinetta Coupé, with coachwork by Pininfarina, chassis No. 1409GT and engine No. 1409GT, V12 cylinders 60°, 2953.21cc, bore 73mm x 58.8mm, stroke 235bhp, 4 speed gearbox integral with engine, front independent suspension double wishbone, coil springs, rear rigid axle semi-elliptic springs and left-hand drive.
Est. **£160,000-200,000**   *C*

The 250GT made its debut at the 1956 Geneva Show. Two versions were available, one the Pininfarina coupé and the Boano designed cabriolet. The model continued until 1960 with the production of almost 500 cars.

1962 Ferrari 250GT Short Wheelbase Berlinetta, coachwork by Carrozeria Pininfarina, 60° V12 cylinder, water-cooled engine, single overhead camshaft per bank, 73mm bore x 58.8mm stroke, 2953cc, 4 speed gearbox, single dry plate clutch, rigid axle with limited slip differential, coil spring and wishbone front suspension, semi-elliptic leaf rear springs, wheelbase 94½in.
£900,000-950,000   *S(M)*

1961 Ferrari 250GT Coupé, coachwork by Pininfarina, 60° V12 cylinder, water-cooled engine, single overhead camshaft per bank, 73mm bore x 58.8mm stroke, 2953cc, 4 speed gearbox, spiral bevel rear axle, independent coil spring and wishbone front suspension, semi-elliptic leaf springs and radius arms at rear, wheelbase 102.4in.
Est. **£125,000-130,000**   *S(M)*

The 250GT of 1955 adopted the race bred Colombo V12 engine and a similar design tubular chassis frame to the Europa, which was produced alongside the 250GT for some 4 years.

1959 Ferrari 250 PF Coupé, 60,000km, left-hand drive, good condition.
£85,000-115,000   *Tal*

Make: Ferrari
Model: 250GT short wheelbase
Type: Sports Coupé
Years Manufactured: 1959-64
Quantity: Berlinetta, 175; Spyder California, 57; Berlinetta Lusso, 350
Engine Type: Single overhead camshaft V12
Size: 2953cc
Max Power: 280 bhp @ 7000 rpm
Transmission: 4 speed manual
Wheelbase: 94.5in
Performance: Max speed: 140-150 mph; 0-60: est. 6.5-7.0 secs.

1960 Ferrari 250GTE 2+2 Coupé, with coachwork by Pininfarina, V12 cylinder, water-cooled engine, overhead valve, overhead camshafts, bore 73mm x stroke 58.8mm, capacity 2953cc, 4 speed synchromesh, remote control change, gearbox, single dry plate clutch, spiral bevel rear axle, independent coil spring and wishbone front suspension, semi-elliptic leaf rear springs and radius arms, wheelbase 102in and 16in tyres.
£49,000-52,000   *S*

1962 Ferrari 250GTE 2+2 Sports Coupé, V12 cylinder, water-cooled engine, overhead valve, overhead camshafts, 73mm bore x 58.8mm stroke, 2953cc, 4 speed manual gearbox with synchromesh, remote control change, single dry plate clutch, spiral bevel rear axle, independent coil spring and wishbone front suspension, semi-elliptic leaf rear springs and radius arms, wheelbase 102in, tyres 16in.
£75,000-80,000   *S(M)*

1962 Ferrari 250GTE 2+2 Coupé, coachwork by Pininfarina, 60° V12 water-cooled engine, single overhead camshaft, 73mm bore x 58.8mm stroke, 2953cc, 4 speed manual gearbox with overdrive, single dry plate clutch, independent front suspension, semi-elliptic rear springs, live rear axle, tyres 6.00 x 16in, left-hand drive.
£120,000-125,000   *S*

The 250 Ferrari was one of the fastest production sports cars of its time.

1963 Ferrari 400 Superamerica Coupé, coachwork by Pininfarina, 60° V12 cylinder, water-cooled engine, single overhead camshaft per bank, 77mm bore x 71mm stroke, 3968cc, 4 speed manual gearbox with overdrive, spiral bevel rear axle, independent coil spring and wishbone front suspension, semi-elliptic leaf springs and radius arms at rear, wheelbase 102in, tyres 15in.
£500,000-600,000   *S*

1964 Ferrari 250GT Lusso Berlinetta, by Pininfarina, chassis No. 5567 and engine No. 5567.
Est. **£250,000-300,000**   *P*

The final development was the 250GT Lusso, meaning luxury, or the GTL for short, introduced in 1962.

The 400 Superamerica was the top of the range Ferrari in 1963 and the fastest of the road cars. The V12 Colombo engine displaced 3968cc and developed some 360bhp at 7,000rpm giving the car a top speed in the order of 150mph.

Make: Ferrari
Model: 400 Superamerica
Type: Coupé, Convertible
Years Manufactured: 1960-64
Quantity: Cabrio. (1960) 6;
'Series I' Coupé (1961-62) 29;
Series II Coupé (1963-64) 19
Engine Type: Single overhead camshaft
Size: 3967cc
Max Power: 400 bhp @ 6750 rpm
Transmission: 4 speed manual with overdrive
Wheelbase: Series I, 95.2in;
Series II, 102.3in
Performance: Max speed: 140-160+ mph.

1962 Ferrari 400 Series I Superamerica Aerodynamica, coachwork by Pininfarina, 60° V12 cylinder, single overhead camshaft cylinder heads, water-cooled, 77mm bore x 71mm stroke, 3968cc, 4 speed manual gearbox with overdrive, spiral bevel rear axle, independent coil spring and wishbone front suspension, semi-elliptic leaf springs and radius coms at rear.
Est. **£500,000-550,000**   *S(M)*

The Superamerica and Superfast series of Ferraris were the most expensive, the most powerful and the most exclusive of Maranello's road cars.

1963 Ferrari 250 GT, 32,000 miles,
left-hand drive.
£175,000-225,000 *Tal*

1965 Ferrari 275GTS Spyder,
coachwork by Pininfarina, chassis
No. 07013, engine No. 07013/213
V12 cylinder, water-cooled,
overhead valve, overhead camshaft,
bore 77mm x 58.8mm stroke,
3286cc, 5 speed manual rear
mounted transaxle gearbox with
Borg and Beck diaphragm clutch,
independent front and rear
suspension, wheelbase 94in.
£225,000-250,000   *SNY*

1967 Ferrari 275 GTB/2, 33,000
miles, right-hand drive.
£395,000-425,000 *Tal*

**1966 Ferrari 330GT 2+2 Sports
Coupé,** with V12 cylinder engine,
water-cooled, twin overhead
camshaft per bank, bore 77mm,
stroke 71mm, capacity 3976cc,
5 speed gearbox, bevel final drive,
double wishbone and coil spring
front suspension, coil and leaf
springs at rear and wheelbase
8ft 6in.
Est. £50,000-60,000   *S*

**1966 Ferrari 275 GTB/2 N.A.R.T.
Type Spyder,** 11,000km,
right-hand drive.
£375,000-450,000   *Tal*

1968 Ferrari 206 GT, 50,000km,
left-hand drive.
£75,000-90,000   *Tal*

1967 Ferrari 330GTC Fixed Head Coupé,
by Pininfarina.   Est. **£110,000-130,000**   *P*

**1967 Ferrari 275GTB/4
Berlinetta, 60°** V12 cylinder,
water-cooled engine, 2 overhead
camshafts per cylinder bank, 77mm
bore x 58.8mm stroke, 3286cc,
5 speed rear mounted gearbox,
spiral bevel rear axle, independent
front and rear suspension,
wheelbase 94.4in, tyres 14in.
Est. **£50,000-60,000**   *S(M)*

1968 Ferrari 330 GTC, 31,000
miles, right-hand drive.
£125,000-150,000   *Tal*

1968 Ferrari 275GTB4, the
Pininfarina coachwork design built
by Scaglietti, V12 60°, engine 77mm
bore, 58.8mm stroke, 3285cc,
compression 9.2:1, twin overhead
camshaft per bank, 6 Weber twin
choke downdraught carburettors,
300bhp at 8,000rpm, 5 speed
manual all indirect, all
synchromesh in unit with the
differential gears, independent
front and rear suspension by
unequal length wishbones, coil
springs and telescopic dampers,
welded steel tubular ladder type
chassis, disc brakes, alloy wheels,
tyres 205/70 VR14, wheelbase
94½in, front track 55in, rear track
56in, height 4ft ½in, weight 2,490lb
and right-hand drive.
Est. **£500,000-600,000**   *C*

*Following the 250GT, the next series
production Ferrari was the 1964
275GTB (275cc per cylinder Grand
Turismo Berlinetta).*

**1969 Ferrari 365 GTC Sports
Coupé,** 60° V12 cylinder engine,
water-cooled, double overhead
camshafts per bank, 81mm bore x
71mm stroke, 4390cc, 4 speed
manual gearbox, hypoid bevel final
drive, independent coil spring
suspension front and rear,
wheelbase 94.4in.
Est. **£171,000-176,000**   *S(A)*

1972 Ferrari 365GTC4 Coupé,
chassis No. 16161, engine
No. 16161, V12 60°, twin overhead
camshafts, single outside plug,
4390cc, 81mm bore x 71mm stroke,
2 sets of 3 Weber 38 DCOE
carburettors, 320bhp, wet sump
lubrication, 5 speed mounted in unit
with the V12, hydraulic disc brakes
in 15in cast alloy wheels, right-hand
drive, immaculate condition.
Est. **£150,000-200,000**   *C*

> **Miller's is a price
> GUIDE not a price
> LIST**

Make: Ferrari
Model: 365GT4 2+2/400i/412i
Type: Coupé
Years Manufactured: 1972-88
Quantity: 365GT4 2+2, 470;
400i/400iA, 412
Engine Type: Double overhead
camshaft
Size: 365GT4 2+2, 4390cc;
400i/400iA, 4823cc; 412i, 4942cc
Max Power: 365GT4 2+2, 320
bhp @ 6200 rpm; 400i/400iA,
340 bhp @ 6500 rpm; 412i, 340
bhp @ 6000 rpm
Max Torque: 365GT4 2+2, 319
ft/lb @ 4600 rpm; 400i/400iA,
347 ft/lb @ 3600 rpm; 412i, 333
ft/lb @ 4200 rpm
Transmission: 5 speed overdrive
manual or 3 speed auto
(exc. 365)
Wheelbase: 106.3in
Performance: Max speed:
144-155 mph; 0-60: 7.1 secs.

1968 Ferrari 330GTS Spyder,
with coachwork by Pininfarina,
V12, 3967cc engine, bore 77mm x
71mm stroke producing 300bhp at
7,500rpm, 3 twin choke Weber
carburettors, 5 speed gearbox plus
reverse, double wishbone and coil
with anti-roll bar at front
suspension, live axle with
semi-elliptical leaf springs and coil
at rear, wheelbase 2,400mm and
left-hand drive.
Est. **£140,000-160,000**   *C(M)*

*Based upon the 330GTC model the
Spyder is identical mechanically. At
the end of 1968 the 330GTS was
superseded by the 365GTS.*

**1970 Ferrari 365GTB 4 Daytona
Coupé,** 60° V12 cylinder,
water-cooled engine, double
overhead camshafts per bank,
81mm bore x 71mm stroke, 4390cc,
5 speed gearbox, hypoid bevel final
drive, independent front and rear
suspension by coil springs,
wheelbase 94.4in, 57,000km from
new.
£20,000-225,000   *S(M)*

Make: Ferrari
Model: 365GT 2+2
Type: Sports Coupé
Years Manufactured: 1967-71
Quantity: Approx. 800
Engine Type: Single overhead
camshaft
Size: 4390cc
Max Power: 320 bhp @ 6600
rpm
Transmission: 5 speed manual
Wheelbase: 104.2in
Performance: Max speed:
140-145+ mph; 0-60: 7.1 secs.

1969 Ferrari 365GT 2+2 Coupé,
coachwork by Pininfarina, V12
overhead camshaft water-cooled
bi-bloc engine, 4390cc, 5 speed
manual gearbox, independent
suspension, live rear axle, wheels
Boranni wire 2.00 x 15, wheelbase
104.2in.
Est. **£90,000-100,000**   *S*

1969 Ferrari 365GTC, with
coachwork by Pininfarina, V12 60°
engine, single overhead camshaft
per bank, single plug per cylinder,
coil ignition integral with final
drive, 81mm x 71mm stroke, giving
4390cc producing 320bhp at
6,600rpm front and rear double
wishbone, coil springs suspension,
5 speed synchromesh gearbox, all
round hydraulic disc brakes and
left-hand drive.
Est. **£180,000-200,000**   *C*

*The 365GTC was introduced in
1968 replacing the 330GTC. The
only visible difference being the new
arrangement for venting hot air from
the engine compartment, the 330
having vents in the side of the body
behind the front wheel, the 365GTC
below the windscreen.*

**1971 4.4 Litre Ferrari 365GTB4
Daytona,** with coachwork by
Carrozzeria Pininfarina.
Est. **£85,000-125,000**   *C*

*It appears that a total of some 1,350
Ferrari 356GTB4 Daytona cars were
manufactured between 1968 and
their cessation of production in 1973.*

1972 Ferrari Dino 246GT Coupé,
6 cylinder, water-cooled monobloc
engine, double overhead camshaft,
92.5mm bore x 60mm stroke,
2418cc, 5 speed manual gearbox,
independent coil spring front and
rear suspension with anti-roll bars,
wheelbase 92in, tyres 14in.
Est. **£70,000-90,000** *S*

1972 Ferrari 246 GTS, 15,000
miles, right-hand drive.
£80,000-100,000 *Tal*

**1971 Ferrari Dino 246GT Sports
Coupé,** coachwork by Pininfarina,
built in steel by Scaglietti,
6 cylinder, water-cooled monobloc
engine, double overhead camshafts,
92.5mm bore x 60mm stroke,
2418cc, 5 speed manual
transmission, independent coil
spring front and rear suspension,
with anti-roll bars, wheelbase 92in,
tyres 14in.
Est. **£80,000-85,000** *S(M)*

*Ferrari credited his son with the
inspiration for a series of small
capacity V6 racing engines built by
Ferrari from 1956, and in turn the
name was given to a new line of
mid-engined volume production
Ferrari V7 coupés which first went
on sale in 1968 in 2 litre form.
The 246, with its 2.4 litre V6,
appeared in late 1969, and fewer
than 4,000 were built (about 1,200 o
these were the detachable roof
Spyder version) before the
introduction of the slightly larger,
and completely re-styled, V8 engine
308 Dino in 1973.*

1972 Ferrari 365 GTB/4 Daytona,
15,000 miles, right-hand drive.
£180,000-225,000 *Tal*

**1973 Ferrari GTB/4 Daytona
Coupé Competition,** 68,000 mile
right-hand drive.
£200,000-250,000 *Tal*

**1972 Ferrari Dino 246 GT 2.4
Litre Berlinetta.**
£42,000-44,000 *B*

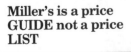

1974 Ferrari Dino 308GT4,
chassis No. 08910, engine
No. 08910, V8, 2926cc.
£25,000-30,000 *Ren*

> **Miller's is a price
> GUIDE not a price
> LIST**

Make	FRANCE	GERMANY	ITALY	JAPAN	USA
Ferrari	+5%	—	+2%	+15%	—

Make: Ferrari
Model: 208/308GT4
Type: Coupé
Years Manufactured: 1973-81
Quantity: 3,666
Price when new: 308GT4, £8,340
Engine Type: Transverse V8 cyl
Size: 1991cc/2928cc
Max Power: 170-250 bhp
Max Torque: 308GT4 209 ft/lb
@ 5000 rpm
Transmission: 5 speed
Wheelbase: 308GT4, 100.4in
Performance: Max speed:
308GT4, 154 mph; 0-60:
308GT4, 6.9 secs; Mpg: 22.

1973 Ferrari 365GTB4 Daytona,
with coachwork by Pininfarina,
LHD, V12, 4390cc engine.
Est. £315,000-318,000   *T&M*

1977 Ferrari Dino 308GT4.
£25,000-26,000   *ADT*

*A rare car with only 2,826 having
been built, it is one of the few to carry
both the 'Dino' and 'Ferrari'
insignias. Only the later cars carried
the Ferrari badge, the Dino name
originating from Enzo Ferrari's son
who died in 1956 at the age of 24.*

1979 Ferrari 308GTS, with engine
capacity of 2926cc, V8.
Est. £60,000-65,000   *Ren*

1977 Ferrari 308GT4.
Est. £18,000-20,000   *ADT*

**1978 Ferrari 308GTB/288GTO
Replica,** 90° V8 cylinder, twin
overhead camshafts per bank,
81mm bore x 71mm stroke, 2926cc,
5 speed manual gearbox in unit
with engine and transaxle, hypoid
bevel final drive, independent coil
spring and wishbone front and rear
suspension, wheelbase 92in.
Est. **£90,000-100,000**   *S*

Make: Ferrari
Model: 308GTB/GTS
Type: Sports Coupé/Convertible
Years Manufactured: 1975-80
Quantity: 6,169
Price when new: Glass fibre,
£11,922; steel, £17,328
Engine Type: Transverse V8 cyl
Size: 2926cc
Max Power: 308GTB, 205 bhp
@ 6600 rpm
Max Torque: 181 ft/lb @ 5000
rpm
Transmission: 5 speed
Wheelbase: 92.1in
Performance: Max speed: 154
mph; 0-60: 6.5 secs; Mpg: 21.

Locate the source

*The source of each
illustration in Miller's can
be found by checking the
code letters below each
caption with the list of
contributors*

*In fact a total of 278 of these twin
turbocharged cars were produced,
all pre-sold. According to 1984 totals
this provided around 60 cars for the
USA, 45 for Italy, 21 for Germany,
15 for France, 14 for Switzerland, 13
for the UK, 7 for Belgium and 25 for
other nations. The 288GTO was
available in only one colour – red.
The proposed total of 200 cars was
exceeded in a production over-run
triggered by special customer
demand, the eventual total of
271-278 being composed essentially
of 41 completed at Maranello during
1984, the bulk of 237 following
during 1985.*

**1979 Ferrari 512 Berlinetta
Boxer,** coachwork designed by
Pininfarina and built by Scaglietti
with engine mid mounted
horizontally opposed (Boxer)
12 cylinder, with twin overhead
camshafts per bank, dry sump
lubrication, 4 triple choke down
draft Weber carburettors, 82mm
bore x 78mm stroke, capacity
4942cc rated to develop 340bhp at
6,200rpm, semi-unitary
construction chassis built from
square section tube and sheet steel,
independent suspension front and
rear by wishbones and coil springs,
right-hand drive, mid mounted
5 speed all synchromesh in unit
with engine gearbox, 4 wheel
ventilated disc brakes and light
alloy 15in diam centre lock wheels.
Est. 120,000-150,000   *C(A)*

*The mid engined Ferrari 'Boxer' was
developed to replace the front
engined V12 Daytona as the top
performance car in the Ferrari
range, and appeared in 1973, as the
365GT4DB, with a flat 12 engine of
the same 4.4 litre capacity as the
Daytona.*

1981 Ferrari Mondial Spyder, by the Daytona Motor Co.
£46,500-47,000   *BLE*

1978 Ferrari 400 Automatic Coupé, coachwork by Pininfarina, V12 cylinder, water-cooled engine, overhead camshaft, 4823cc, 340bhp at 6,500rpm, 3 speed automatic turbo-hydromatic, shaft drive to live rear axle, independent shock absorber suspension, tyres 7.50 x 15in, right-hand drive.
Est. **£40,000-50,000**   *S*

The Ferrari 400 automatic and 400GT 5 speed manual cars were introduced at the 1976 Paris Salon. This was the first time that a 2+2 Ferrari was offered with an automatic gearbox.

1981 Ferrari 400i.
Est. **£30,000-35,000**   *P*

1983 Ferrari Mondial QV, original with 33,000 miles recorded.
£42,000-43,000   *RH*

1984 Ferrari 512 BBi Boxer Berlinetta, horizontally opposed 12 cylinders, water-cooled engine, twin overhead camshafts per head, bore 82mm x 76mm stroke, 4942cc, 5 speed manual gearbox in unit with engine and transaxle, hypoid bevel final drive to rear wheels, independent coil spring and wishbone front and rear suspension, 240/55/VR415 tyres.
£150,000-175,000   *SNY*

1974 Ferrari 365 BB, 30,000 miles, right-hand drive.
£100,000-125,000   *Tal*

Introduced in 1972 as the 365GT4 2+2 the Pininfarina styled Ferrari lasted in its various forms until 1989. With 4.4 litre V12 engine the car was based on the 365GTC4, a derivative of the Daytona.

1978 Ferrari 400 Automatic, V12 cylinder, water-cooled engine, twin overhead camshafts, 81mm bore x 78mm stroke, 4823cc, developing 340bhp at 6,500rpm, twin distributors, six 38 DCOE 50/60 Weber carburettors, 3 speed automatic gearbox, independent front and rear suspension by coil springs, power assisted steering, ventilated disc brakes.
Est. **£36,000-40,000**   *S(A)*

1978 Ferrari 4.9 Litre 512 BB Boxer Berlinetta. Est. £140,000-160,000   *B*

1982 Ferrari 512 BBIi, 25,000 miles, right-hand drive. **£110,000-145,000**   *Tal*

1985 Ferrari 308GTS, with engine capacity 2926cc, V8. Est. **£65,000-70,000**   *Ren*

| MAKE | ENGINE | DATES | CONDITION | | |
Ferrari			1	2	3
166 Inter	1995/12	1948-53	£125,000	£90,000	—
212 Inter	2563/12	1951-53	£140,000	£95,000	—
250 GT	2953/12	1959-63	£75,000	£55,000	£45,000
250 GT SWB (steel)	2953/12	1959-62	£500,000	£350,000	—
250 GT Lusso	2953/12	1962-64	£165,000	£125,000	£95,000
250 GT 2+2	2953/12	1961-64	£65,000	£45,000	£30,000
275 GTB	3286/12	1964-66	£180,000	£145,000	£120,000
275 GTS	3286/12	1965-67	£190,000	£155,000	£125,000
275 GTB 4-cam	3286/12	1966-68	£200,000	£170,000	£135,000
330 GT 2+2	3967/12	1964-67	£65,000	£50,000	£35,000
330 GTC	3967/12	1966-68	£85,000	£65,000	£55,000
330 GTS	3967/12	1966-68	£125,000	£95,000	£85,000
365 GT 2+2	4390/12	1967-71	£35,000	£28,000	£25,000
365 GTC	4390/12	1967-70	£85,000	£65,000	£55,000
365 GTS	4390/12	1968-69	£140,000	£110,000	£95,000
365 GTB (Daytona)	4390/12	1968-74	£125,000	£105,000	£90,000
365 GTC4	4390/12	1971-74	£90,000	£75,000	£65,000
365 GT4 2+2/400GT	4390/				
	4823/12	1972-79	£28,000	£22,000	£19,000
365 BB	4390/12	1974-76	£110,000	£85,000	£80,000
512 BB/BBi	4942/12	1976-81	£85,000	£75,000	£65,000
246 GT Dino	2418/6	1969-74	£40,000	£30,000	£25,000
246 GTS Dino	2418/6	1972-74	£45,000	£35,000	£30,000
308 GT4 2+2	2926/8	1973-80	£25,000	£18,000	£14,000
308 GTB (fireglass)	2926/8	1975-76	£40,000	£35,000	£30,000
308 GTB	2926/8	1977-81	£26,000	£24,000	£18,000
308 GTS	2926/8	1978-81	£35,000	£28,000	£24,000
308 GTBi/GTSi	2926/8	1981-82	£25,000	£22,000	£18,000
308 GTB/GTS QV	2926/8	1983-85	£35,000	£28,000	£24,000
400i manual	4823/12	1981-85	£22,000	£19,000	£16,000
400i auto	4823/12	1981-85	£20,000	£17,500	£14,500

1985 2.8 Litre Twin Turbocharged Ferrari 288GTO Berlinetta, V8 90° engine, twin overhead camshafts, single outside plug, 2855cc, 71mm bore and 80mm stroke, carburation twin turbos and inter-coolers, 400bhp, dry sump lubrication, 5 speed gearbox transaxle V8 and right-hand drive. Est. **£250,000-300,000**   *C(M)*

Make: Ferrari
Model: Mondial 8/3.2 Mondial
Type: Sports Coupé/Convertible
Years Manufactured: 1980-88
Quantity: Mondial 8, 2,500
Engine Type: Double overhead camshaft V8
Size: 2927cc
Max Power: 1980-82, 205 bhp @ 6600 rpm; 1982-84, 230 bhp @ 6800 rpm; 1985-88, 260 bhp @ 7000 rpm
Max Torque: 1980-82, 181 ft/lb @ 5000 rpm; 1982-84, 188 ft/lb @ 5500 rpm; 1985-88, 213 ft/lb @ 5500 rpm
Transmission: 5 speed manual
Wheelbase: 104.2in
Performance: Max speed: 135-145 mph; 0-60: 7.1-9.4 secs.

1985 Ferrari 288 GTO, 6,000km, left-hand drive.
£475,000-575,000 *Tal*

Make: Ferrari
Model: 308GTB/GTS
Type: Sports Coupé/Convertible
Years Manufactured: 1975-80
Quantity: 6,169
Price when new: Glass fibre,
£11,992; steel, £17,328
Engine Type: Transverse V8 cyl
Size: 2926cc
Max Power: 308GTB, 205 bhp
@ 6600 rpm
Max Torque: 181 ft/lb @ 5000
rpm
Transmission: 5 speed
Wheelbase: 92.1in
Performance: Max speed: 154
mph; 0-60: 6.5 secs; Mpg: 21.

1986 Ferrari Testarossa,
coachwork by Pininfarina,
horizontally opposed, mid-mounted,
12 cylinder engine, 82mm bore x
78mm stroke, 4942cc, twin
overhead camshaft, 4 valves per
cylinder, 5 speed manual gearbox,
limited slip differential,
independent front and rear
suspension with double wishbones,
coil springs, telescopic dampers and
anti-roll bar, wheelbase 100in,
wheels 16in.
Est. **£120,000-140,000** *S(M)*

*Few production road cars, the
Porsche 959 and Ferrari's own F40
excluded, can match its 180mph top
speed, 0-60mph acceleration in 5.2
seconds and 0-100mph in 11.4
seconds. The 5 litre, 4 cam engine
has 4 valves per cylinder and
develops a staggering 390bhp at
6,300rpm.*

Make: Ferrari
Model: Testarossa
Type: Sports Coupé
Years Manufactured: 1985-88
Quantity: Still in production
1988
Engine Type: Double overhead
camshaft V12
Size: 4942cc
Max Power: 380 bhp @ 5750
rpm
Max Torque: 354 ft/lb @ 4500
rpm
Transmission: 5 speed manual
Wheelbase: 100.4in
Performance: Max speed: 190
mph; 0-60: 5.3 secs.

1989 Ferrari F40 Berlinetta,
coachwork by Pininfarina, 90° V8,
water-cooled engine, 4 overhead
camshafts, 4 valves per cylinder,
82mm bore x 69.5mm stroke, 2 IHI
water-cooled turbo compressors —
wastegate — 2 heat exchangers,
Weber Marelli IAW electronically
integrated fuel injection, ignition
and turbo-charging system, Ferrari
5 speed gearbox, independent front
and rear — transverse oscillating
wishbones, wheelbase 96½in,
wheels 8in x 17in front, 13in x 17in
rear.
£650,000-700,000 *S(M)*

*This example was first registered to
Nigel Mansell, the British Formula
One racing driver on 23 March 1989
and by August had covered a mere
1,500km. The car was subject to a
track test by Nigel Mansell in
Autocar and Motor at Silverstone
circuit during July 1989 when their
reporter gave a detailed account of
this particular car's performance:
0-112mph in 12 seconds, 200mph
from Abbey to Woodcote!*

Make: Ferrari
Model: F40
Type: Sports Coupé
Years Manufactured: 1987-88
Quantity: 400 announced as
intended
Engine Type: Double overhead
camshaft V8 twin turbocharged
and intercooled
Size: 2936cc
Max Power: 471 bhp @ 7000
rpm
Max Torque: 426 ft/lb @ 4000
rpm
Transmission: 5 speed manual
Wheelbase: 94.5in
Performance: Max speed: 201
mph (manufacturer's data);
0-60: est. 3.0 secs.

**Miller's is a price
GUIDE not a price
LIST**

1989 Ferrari F40, 5,000km,
left-hand drive.
£380,000-410,000 *Tal*

FIAT

Founded by Giovanni Agnelli and Count Carlo Biscaretti, the first Fiat went on sale to the public in 1899. Fiat have always covered all aspects of motor manufacture and every level in the market place. Fiat is now a multi-national industrial giant and owns both Ferrari and Lancia.

1937 Fiat 500 Topolino, with twin cylinder air-cooled 4 stroke engine, capacity 569cc, 4 speed manual gearbox, single dry plate clutch, spiral bevel final drive, independent front and rear suspension.
£1,540-1,700   *S*

1908 Fiat 15/20hp Five Seater Side Entrance Tonneau, with cylinder engine, in line, water-cooled, cast in pairs, side valve, bore 90mm x stroke 120mm, capacity 3054cc, 4 speed gearbox with reverse, multi-disc clutch, shaft drive to bevel rear axle, semi-elliptic leaf front springs, three quarter elliptic springs at rear, wheelbase 121in, and 820 x 120mm tyres.
Est. **£35,000-45,000**   *S*

1955 Fiat 1100 Four Door Saloon, chassis No. 206 132 and engine No. 212 739 with 4 cylinders and left-hand drive.
£825-950   *C*

Fiat recovered from World War II turning out 75,000 vehicles in 1949, nothing new appeared for the first few years apart from a 16.5bhp overhead valve version of the Topolino and revised '1100s' and '1500s' with steering column change. In 1953 the '1100' went over to hypoid rear axle and unitary construction, the standard 35bhp berline being joined shortly afterwards by a 48bhp turismo veloce type.

1937 Fiat Topolino Model A Cabriolet, with 569cc, 4 cylinder engine.
Est. **£3,400-3,800**   *ADT*

Introduced in 1936 the Fiat 500 was the world's smallest production car. It had a side valve 4 cylinder engine 569cc which gave the car a top speed of 53mph. It was nicknamed Topolino (Mickey Mouse) almost immediately. Over 122,000 were made to 1948 when it was briefly replaced by an overhead valve engine version.

1971 Vignale/Fiat Gamine Spyder.
Est. **£4,000-6,000**   *B*

Introduced in 1967, this diminutive 2 seater was produced in small numbers towards the end of Vignale's existence as an independent coachbuilder. It was powered by the Fiat 500's rear mounted 499cc 2 cylinder air-cooled engine and Vignale built an uncomprising open 2 seater body with cutaway doors of appropriately modest proportions.

Fiat Dino 2.4 Coupé, Ferrari power Bertone body.
£19,950-21,000   *Hu*

FIAT

Make: Fiat	
Model: 130 Coupé	
Type: Coupé	
Years Manufactured: 1971-77	
Quantity: 4,491	
Engine Type: Twin overhead camshaft V6	
Size: 3235cc	
Max Power: 165 bhp @ 5600 rpm	
Transmission: Auto, 5 speed manual	
Performance: Max speed: 116 mph; 0-60: 10.6 secs; Mpg 18-24.	

MAKE Fiat	ENGINE	DATES	CONDITION 1	2	3
500B Topolino	569/4	1945-55	£3,000	£1,500	£750
500C	569/4	1948-54	£4,000	£1,700	£1,000
500 Nuova	479, 499/2	1957-75	£3,000	£1,500	£750
600/600D	633, 767/4	1955-70	£4,000	£2,000	£1,000
500F Giardiniera	479, 499/2	1957-75	£3,000	£1,500	£1,000
2300S	2280/6	1961-68	£3,000	£1,700	£1,000
850	843/4	1964-71	£1,000	£750	—
850 Coupé	843, 903/4	1965-73	£1,500	£1,000	—
850 Spyder	843, 903/4	1965-73	£5,000	£3,000	£1,500
128 Sport Coupé 3P	1116/ 1290/4	1971-78	£4,000	£2,500	£1,500
130 Coupé	3235/6	1971-77	£9,000	£6,500	£3,000
131 Mirafiori Sport	1995/4	1974-84	£2,000	£1,000	£750
124 Sport Coupé	1438/ 1608/4	1966-72	£3,500	£2,000	£1,000
124 Sport Spyder	1438/ 1608/4	1966-72	£4,500	£2,500	£1,500
Dino Coupé	1987/ 2418/6	1967-73	£14,000	£10,000	£6,000
Dino Spyder	1987/ 2418/6	1967-73	£32,000	£18,000	£12,500
X1/9	1290/ 1498/4	1972-89	£3,000	£1,500	£750

1967 Fiat Dino 206 Spyder. Est. **£25,000-30,000** *P*

1973 Fiat 130 Coupé, with engine capacity 3200cc, 6 cylinder. Est. **£2,000-3,000** *LF*

Pininfarina designed the 4 seat coupé body for the 130 Coupé. Fiat added the 3235cc V6 double overhead camshaft engine provided by Ferrari which produces 165bhp. Automatic transmission was standard in right-hand drive form but 120mph was attainable.

1967 Fiat Dino Spyder, 2 seater roadster, chassis No. 135AS00028, engine No. 135B0004945, V6, 1987cc, engine overhauled and electrics renewed. Est. **£29,000-32,000** *Ren*

FLANDERS

1910 Flanders 20 Suburban Four Passenger Tourer, 4 cylinder in-line engine, water-cooled, side valve, bore 3⅝in x 3¾in stroke, 154.8cu in, maker's horse power 20, 3 speed gearbox, shaft drive to live rear axle, semi-elliptic leaf suspension front and full elliptic rear, wheelbase 100in, 30 x 3½in tyres. **£11,500-12,000** *SNY*

FORD

The Ford Company was founded by Henry Ford in 1903. The Model T was introduced in 1909 and sold over 16 million cars during an 18 year production run. The Model A followed in 1927 with, amongst other features, 4 wheel brakes. The Model B series stayed in production until 1948. Up until 1932 Ford Great Britain only made right hand drive versions of the American models. Once the plant at Dagenham, Essex, opened a whole new range of British Fords was produced. Ford Germany, started in 1925, producing their versions of American designs and then UK/European models.

1911 Ford Model T, with 4 cylinder, 2400cc engine.
£8,000-9,000   *LF*

Between 1908 when production began and 1927 when the last Model T was built over 15 million examples were sold.

1911 Ford Model T Open Runabout, with 4 cylinder in line, water-cooled monobloc engine, side valve bore 3¼in x stroke 4in, 2895cc, 2 speed Planetary transmission, multi-disc clutch operating in oil, torque tube drive to straight bevel rear axle.
£16,000-18,000   *SEN*

1913 Ford Model T Speedster, chassis No. 1154777, engine No. 1154777, fitted with a 1916 'Roof Sixteen', overhead valve converted engine said to 'allow speeds of up to 60mph for the brave', with original brass quick cool vee radiator which has 20-30% greater cooling capacity than standard Ts.
£10,000-11,000   *SEN*

1913 Model T Ford Three Seater Tourer, with 4 cylinder, side valve, water-cooled monobloc engine, bore 95mm x stroke 102mm, capacity 2900cc, 20hp, 2 speed epicyclic gearbox with foot pedal control, hand throttle, multi-plate clutch, thermo-syphon cooling, shaft drive to spiral bevel rear axle, wheelbase 100in, and 30 x 3½ tyres.
Est. **£9,000-9,500**   *S*

The engine number, which on a Ford T is also the chassis number, indicates that this vehicle was built in 1913, and the brass 'kite shaped' radiator would also indicate pre-1916 manufacture.

1921 Ford Model T Speedster, this car has been imported from the USA all taxes paid, it has original lighting equipment and is fitted with a rare luggage trunk.
Est. **£8,000-11,000**   *LF*

Over 15 million Model Ts were built in a production run which lasted from 1908 to 1927 and used the same basic 2.9 litre engine and 2 speed transmission for the whole period.

1915 Ford Model T, with 4 cylinder, 2900cc engine.
Est. **£11,000-13,000**   *ADT*

**1915 Ford Model T Four Seat
Tourer,** with 4 cylinder, 2900cc
engine.
Est. £11,000-13,000   *ADT*

**1925 Ford Model T Doctors
Coupé.**
£6,000-6,500   *Cen*

*The Model T was in continuous
production from 1909 to 1927, and
during those 18 years over
15,000,000 were produced. In 1909
the first Model T was produced, the
next 8 were then exported to Europe
before it was officially shown at the
Olympia exhibition to the public.
The Model T produced 20bhp from
its 2400cc, 4 cylinder side valve
engine, with a maximum speed of
45mph and 25-30mpg.*

1913 Model T Ford Four Seater.
£16,750-17,500   *DB*

**1918 Ford Model T
7½cwt Light Truck.**
£5,500-6,000   *Cen*

**1926 Ford Model T Four Seat
Tourer,** fully restored in Canada,
left-hand drive.
£15,000-15,500   *ELD*

1924 Ford Model T Tourer, with
4 cylinder in-line water-cooled,
monobloc engine, side valve bore
3¼in x stroke 4in, 2895cc, 2 speed
Planetary Transmission, multi-disc
clutch operating in oil, torque tube
drive to straight bevel axle.
£11,000-12,000   *SEN*

Model T Four Seat Tourer, c1927.
Est. £4,000-6,000   *ADT*

1928 Ford Model A Sports Roadster with Dickey, 4 cylinder, side valve, water-cooled monobloc engine, 90mm bore x 110mm stroke, 40hp, 3 speed manual gearbox, semi-elliptic leaf spring suspension front and rear, 4 wheel mechanical brakes, tyres 21in.
£8,000-8,500   *S*

1929 Ford Model 'A' Tudor Sedan, 4 cylinder in-line engine, water-cooled monobloc, side valve, bore 3⅞in x 4¼in stroke, 200.5cu in, 3 speed centre change gearbox, left-hand drive, dry multi-disc clutch, spiral bevel rear axle, transverse leaf front and rear springs, wheelbase 103½in, 4.50 x 21in tyres.
£12,000-12,500   *SNY*

1930 Ford Model A Roadster, with 4 cylinder, 3285cc engine.
est. **£12,000-14,000**   *ADT*

Make the Most of Miller's

CONDITION is absolutely vital when assessing the value of a vehicle. Top class vehicles on the whole appreciate much more than less perfect examples. However a rare, desirable car may command a high price even when in need of restoration

1930 Ford Model A Tudor Sedan, 4 cylinder in line, water-cooled monobloc engine, side valve, bore 98mm x stroke 108mm, capacity 3283cc, 3 speed gearbox, single disc clutch, spiral bevel rear axle, transverse leaf front and rear suspension and wheelbase 104in.
£4,750-5,000   *S*

Make the Most of Miller's

Veteran Cars are those manufactured up to 31 December 1918 although only vehicles built before 31 December 1904 are eligible for the London/Brighton Commemorative Run. Vintage Cars are vehicles that were manufactured between 1 January 1919 and 31 December 1930

FORD

1930 Ford Model A Two Door Special Coupé, with dickey seat, chassis No. DR 79573, engine No. DR 79573, 4 cylinder, side valve, 3.2 litres, 24hp engine, 3 speed sliding mesh gearbox, transverse leaf front and rear suspension, 4 wheel mechanical brakes, wire spoke wheels, left-hand drive.
Est. **£13,000-15,000** C

1931 Ford Model A Pick-Up LHD.
£15,750-16,250 Mar

1932 Ford Model B Tudor, engine capacity 2043cc, 4 cylinder, in excellent condition.
Est. **£9,500-10,500** ADT

The Model B Ford range followed the A into production in 1932.

1932 Ford Model Y Sports Tourer, with 4 cylinder water-cooled monobloc engine, side valve, capacity 933cc, 3 speed manual transmission, shaft drive to live rear axle, transverse semi-elliptic spring suspension front and rear.
£3,000-3,300 S

Ford's model range post the Model T expanded to include a variety of vehicles beginning with the Model A then the B and C, and smaller economy cars designed for specific markets. The Model Y was introduced in 1932 for the European market, although designed in Dearborn. In Britain it acquired the name Popular and in a saloon version continued in production for some years.

1932 Ford Two Door Saloon, 4 cylinder, water-cooled monobloc engine, side valve, maker's horsepower 15hp, 3300cc, 3 speed manual gearbox, shaft drive to live rear axle, semi-elliptic leaf spring suspension front and rear, right-hand drive.
£17,500-18,000 S

1930 Ford Model A Roadster with Dickey Seat, 4 cylinder, side valve, water-cooled monobloc engine, 3⅞in bore x 4¼in stroke, 200.5cu in, 3 speed gearbox, multi-disc clutch, transverse leaf spring suspension, shaft and spiral bevel final drive, wheelbase 104in, tyres 19 x 4.75.
Est. **£8,200-9,500** S(A)

MAKE Ford	ENGINE	DATES	CONDITION 1	2	3
Model T	2892/4	1908-27	£15,000	£10,000	£5,000
Model A	2033/4	1928-32	£11,000	£7,000	£5,000
Model Y	933/4	1932-37	£7,000	£4,000	£2,000
Model AA	3276/4	1929-32	£10,000	£8,000	£4,000
AB	3285/4	1933-34	£10,000	£8,000	£5,000
V8-60	2227/V8	1936-39	£10,000	£5,000	£2,000
Prefect	1172/4	1935-53	£6,000	£4,000	£1,000
Anglia	933/4	1939-53	£6,000	£4,000	£1,000

There is a premium of 25% for right hand drive vehicles and 50% for coachbuilt vehicles. Drop head coupé cars are the most desirable.

1937 Ford V8 30hp 'Woody' Station Wagon, V8 cylinder, water-cooled monobloc engine, overhead valves, maker's horsepower 30hp, 3 speed manual gearbox, shaft drive to live rear axle, leaf spring front and rear suspension, right-hand drive.
£27,500-32,000 *S*

This particular example was originally the property of the Earl of Grantham, who used it on his estate for shooting parties.

1937 Ford V8 Saloon RHD.
£5,050-5,250 *DB*

1939 Ford V8 Saloon, with engine capacity 4410cc, 8 cylinder.
Est. **£8,000-9,000** *ADT*

1949 Ford V8 Pilot E71A, with 3622cc, 8 cylinder engine.
£7,200-7,500 *ADT*

1936 Ford V8 Roadster.
Est. **£8,000-10,000** *Cen*

The V8 engine fitted into the 1936 model was 3622cc, and developed 65bhp producing 75-80mph. It was the first mass produced popular market V8 car in the world.

1936 Ford V8 Model 62, engine capacity 2227cc, V8.
Est. **£4,000-5,500** *LF*

The Model 62 superseded the 1935 American style Model 60 and was entirely British made. The 2227cc engine developed a useful 62bhp.

Make: Ford
Model: 'Perpendicular' models
Type: Saloon
Years Manufactured: 1953-59
Engine Type: Side valve 4 cyl
Size: 1172cc
Max Power: 30 bhp @ 4000 rpm
Transmission: 3 speed
Performance: Max speed: 60 mph; 0-50: 24 secs; Mpg 30-40.

1953 Ford 103E Popular, with 1172cc, 4 cylinder engine.
Est. **£1,200-1,600** *LF*

The Popular was the cheapest 4 wheeled 4 seater family car on the British market. The 1172cc engine provides 30bhp through the 3 speed gearbox.

1941 Ford V8 Super De Luxe Two Door Convertible.
£10,500-11,000   *SNY*

1955 Ford Fairlane V8 Country Sedan, V8 cylinder engine, water-cooled, overhead valves, bore 3.62in x 3.30in stroke, 272cu in, Ford-o-Matic automatic 3 speed gearbox, bevel rear axle, independent coil spring front suspension, leaf rear springs, 15in tyres.
£4,750-5,250   *SNY*

1965 Ford Thunderbird Coupé, with 8 cylinder, 5500cc engine.
Est. **£13,000-14,000**   *ADT*

The V8 engine with 4 barrel carburettor and dual exhausts developed some 193bhp at 4,400rpm.

MAKE Ford (American built)	ENGINE	DATES	CONDITION 1	2	3
Thunderbird	292/ 312/8	1955-57	£22,000	£13,500	£9,000
Edsel Citation	410/8	1958	£9,000	£4,500	£2,500
Edsel Ranger	223/6- 361/8	1959	£6,000	£3,500	£2,000
Edsel Citation conv	410/8	1958	£12,000	£6,000	£4,000
Edsel Corsair conv	332/ 361/8	1959	£10,500	£7,000	£4,500
Fairlane 2 door	223/6- 352/8	1957-59	£8,000	£4,500	£3,000
Fairlane 500 Sunliner	223/6- 352/8	1957-59	£12,000	£8,000	£6,500
Fairlane 500 Skyliner	223/6- 352/8	1957-59	£16,000	£10,000	£8,000
Mustang hardtop	170/6- 289/8	1965-66	£8,000	£5,000	£4,000
Mustang fastback	170/6- 289/8	1965-66	£9,000	£6,000	£6,000
Mustang conv	170/6- 289/8	1965-66	£12,500	£8,500	£6,000
Mustang hardtop	260/6- 428/8	1967-68	£6,000	£4,000	£3,000
Mustang fastback	260/6- 428/8	1967-68	£6,000	£4,000	£3,000
Mustang convertible	260/6- 428/8	1967-68	£12,000	£6,000	£4,000

Make: Ford
Model: Thunderbird
Type: Hard Top Convertible
Years Manufactured: 1955-57
Quantity: 1955, 16,155; 1956, 15,631; 1957, 21,380
Price when new: £3,497
Engine Type: Overhead valve V8
Size: 4785cc; 5112cc (1956)
Max Power: 4785cc (1955), 193/198 bhp @ 4400 rpm; (1956), 202 @ 4600; (1957), 245 @ 4500 rpm; 5112cc (1956), 215 bhp @ 4600 rpm; (1957), 245 @ 4500 rpm
Max Torque: 4785cc (1955), 280 ft/lb @ 2600 rpm; (1956), 289 ft/lb @ 2600 rpm; (1957), 297 ft/lb @ 2700 rpm; 5112cc (1956), 317 ft/lb @ 2600; (1957), 324 ft/lb @ 2600 rpm; (1957), 332 ft/lb @ 2300
Transmission: 3 speed manual (overdrive optional) or 3 speed auto
Wheelbase: 102in
Performance: Max speed: 105-125 mph; 0-60: 7.0-11.5 secs.

1955 Ford Thunderbird Convertible with Hard Top, V8 cylinder, water-cooled engine, overhead valve, bore 3.75in x stroke 3.3in, capacity 292cu in, 3 speed gearbox with overdrive, semi-centrifugal clutch, bevel rear axle, independent suspension, wheelbase 102in and 6.70 x 15in tyres.
Est. **£19,000-22,000**   *S*

1966 Shelby Mustang GT350 H, with V8, 4736cc engine.
£36,000-40,000   *LF*

Shelby produced a total of 14,368 cars of all types and 2,380 of this particular shape. All of the vehicles are well documented by the SAAC (Shelby American Automobile Club). The suffix 'H' signifies that this was one of the batch of 963 cars built for Hertz Rent-a-car in the USA for use as prestige self-drive cars. So often were the vehicles hired for the weekend and then taken to a racetrack that they became known as 'rent-a-racers'.

1966 Ford Mustang, with cylinder, 5200cc engine.
st. **£7,000-9,000**   *ADT*

The engine number prefix 7R01C decodes as follows:
7 = Year (1967)
R = Plant of Build (San Jose)
01 = indicates 2 door hard top bucket seat luxury model
C = 289cu in 2 valve carburettor engine option.

1967 Ford Mustang 289 Hard op, chassis No. 7R01C231286, ngine No. 31386, V8, 289cu in.
,800-5,200   *LF*

Make: Ford
Model: Mustang
Type: Hardtop, Convertible, Fastback
Years Manufactured: 1964-67
Price when new: £2,044
Engine Type: Overhead valve V8
Size: 289cu in
Max Power: 232 bhp @ 6000 rpm
Transmission: 4 speed (manual)
Performance: Max speed: 115+ mph; 0-60: 8.2 secs; Mpg: 10-15.

**68 Shelby GT350.
5,000-30,000**   *CTC*

1967 Ford Mustang Two Door Hard Top Tour De France Model.
Est. **£35,000-45,000**   *C*

MAKE Ford (British built)	ENGINE	DATES	CONDITION 1	2	3
Anglia E494A	993/4	948-53	£2,000	£850	£250
Prefect E93A	1172/4	1948-49	£3,500	£1,250	£900
Prefect E493A	1172/4	1948-53	£2,500	£1,000	£300
Popular 103E	1172/4	1953-59	£1,875	£825	£300
Anglia/Prefect 100E	1172/4	1953-59	£1,350	£625	£250
Prefect 107E	997/4	1959-62	£1,150	£600	£200
Escort/Squire 100E	1172/4	1955-61	£1,650	£850	£275
Popular 100E	1172/4	1955-61	£1,250	£600	£180
Anglia 105E	997/4	1959-67	£1,400	£500	£75
Anglia 123E	1198/4	1962-67	£1,550	£575	£150
V8 Pilot	3622/8	1947-51	£7,500	£4,000	£1,500
Consul Mk I	1508/4	1951-56	£2,250	£950	£400
Consul Mk I	1508/4	1953-56	£4,750	£3,000	£1,250
Zephyr Mk I	2262/6	1953-56	£3,000	£1,250	£600
Zephyr Mk I	2262/6	1953-56	£6,800	£3,250	£1,500
Zodiac Mk I	2262/6	1953-56	£3,300	£1,500	£700
Consul Mk II/Deluxe	1703/4	1956-62	£2,900	£1,500	£650
Consul Mk II	1703/4	1956-62	£5,000	£3,300	£1,250
Zephyr Mk II	2553/6	1956-62	£3,800	£1,800	£750
Zephyr Mk II	2553/6	1956-62	£8,000	£4,000	£1,500
Zodiac Mk II	2553/6	1956-62	£4,000	£2,250	£750
Zodiac Mk II	2553/6	1956-62	£8,500	£4,250	£1,800
Zephyr 4 Mk III	1703/4	1962-66	£2,100	£1,200	£400
Zephyr 6 Mk III	2552/6	1962-66	£2,300	£1,300	£450
Zodiac Mk III	2553/6	1962-66	£3,000	£1,500	£500
Zephyr 4 Mk IV	1994/4	1966-72	£1,750	£600	£150
Zephyr 6 Mk IV	2553/6	1966-72	£1,800	£700	£150
Zodiac Mk IV	2994/6	1966-72	£2,000	£800	£150
Zodiac Mk IV	2994/6	1966-72	£2,200	£950	£150
Zodiac Mk IV Exec	2994/6	1966-72	£2,300	£950	£150

Locate the source

The source of each illustration in Miller's can be found by checking the code letters below each caption with the list of contributors

Make: Ford
Model: Consul Mk 1
Type: Saloon/Convertible
Years Manufactured: 1950-56
Price when new: Saloon, £667; Convertible £809
Engine Type: 4 cyl
Size: 1508cc
Max Power: 47 bhp @ 4400 rpm
Transmission: 3 speed
Performance: Max speed: 73 mph; 0-60: 26 secs; Mpg 25-32.

1962 Ford Consul 375 Convertible, 4 cylinder in line, water-cooled monobloc engine, pushrod operated overhead valve 82.55mm bore x 79.5mm stroke, 1703cc, single dry plate clutch, 3 speed column change gearbox, hypoid bevel drive live rear axle independent front suspension, semi-elliptic rear, hydraulic dampers, wheelbase 104½in, tyr 155 x 13in.
Est. **£5,000-6,000**   *S*

1957 Ford Anglia 100E.
£1,100-1,500   *CMA*

Make: Ford
Model: 100E Anglia/Popular/ Prefect
Type: Saloon
Years Manufactured: 1953-62
Price when new: Anglia £511
Engine Type: Side valve 4 cyl
Size: 1172cc
Max Power: 36 bhp @ 4500 rpm
Transmission: 3 speed
Performance: Max speed: 71 mph; 0-60: 30 secs; Mpg 25-32.

In 1961 the mid-range Ford model was the Consul 375 priced at just over £873 in saloon de luxe form. Also offered for just over £100 more was a 2 door convertible destined to be sold in far less numbers than the saloon.

1962 Ford Consul Convertible, with 1703cc, 4 cylinder engine.
Est. **£5,000-6,000**   *LF*

1969 Ford Lotus Cortina Mk II.
£2,500-3,000   *CMA*

Contrary to popular belief the Mk II Lotus Cortina was available in a range of body colours other than white. The Lotus modified 1558cc engine produced 109bhp with its twin Weber 40 DCOE carburettors. Introduced in 1967, the Mk II continued in production until 1970.

FORD

1964 Ford Anglia Super Saloon,
with 4 cylinder water-cooled
monobloc engine, overhead valves,
bore 80.96mm x stroke 58.17mm,
capacity 1198cc, 4 speed manual
gearbox, shaft drive to live rear
axle, independent coil spring front
suspension, semi-elliptic leaf spring
suspension at rear, wheelbase
90½in and tyres 5.10 x 13in.
£1,550-1,650 *S*

*The new Ford Anglia arrived on the
English market in September 1959
and was priced at £589 and £610.
The Anglia Super was unveiled in
October 1962, and had a larger
engine. The car cost £575 in 1964,
quite reasonable for the time, and
was built until November 1967 when
it was replaced by the Escort.*

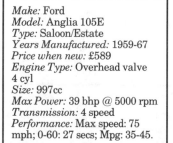

Make: Ford
Model: Anglia 105E
Type: Saloon/Estate
Years Manufactured: 1959-67
Price when new: £589
Engine Type: Overhead valve
4 cyl
Size: 997cc
Max Power: 39 bhp @ 5000 rpm
Transmission: 4 speed
Performance: Max speed: 75
mph; 0-60: 27 secs; Mpg: 35-45.

1967 Lotus Cortina Mk II, all
original interior, repainted and
engine totally rebuilt to a high
specification.
£5,750-6,250 *PMS*

1967 Ford Cortina 1600 Super.
Est. **£1,000-2,000** *CMA*

*The Ford Cortina first appeared in
1962. A Mk II version followed in
1964 and in 1967 the 1600cc version
became available.*

1966 Ford Lotus Cortina Mk I.
Est. **£5,000-7,000** *Cen*

*Built at Ford's Cheshunt factory, the
Lotus Cortina Mk I offered the best of
both worlds. Introduced in 1963 the
Lotus modified 1558cc engine
produced 109bhp.*

**1967 Ford Cortina Lotus Mk II
1.6 Litre Saloon.**
Est. **£12,000-16,000** *B*

*The Mk II Cortina Lotus perpetuated
the concept of its Mk I predecessor, in
being powered by a 1558cc Ford
based twin cam Lotus Elan engine.
But instead of being assembled at
Lotus's Cheshunt factory, the
100mph Mk II was Dagenham built.
Only 4,032 were made between 1967
and 1970 and a mere 1,379 examples
were produced in 1967, which is
when this car was manufactured.*

*The Mk II version of the Ford Lotus
Cortina with the rally proven 1558cc
twin cam 8 valve Lotus engine could
produce 110bhp and a top speed of
105mph.*

1969 Ford Cortina Lotus, with
1558cc, 4 cylinder engine.
Est. **£4,000-6,000** *LF*

155

MAKE	ENGINE	DATES	CONDITION		
			1	2	3
Ford (British built)					
Classic 315	1340/				
	1498/4	1961-63	£1,400	£800	£500
Consul Capri	1340/				
	1498/4	1961-64	£2,100	£1,350	£400
Consul Capri GT	1498/4	1961-64	£2,600	£1,600	£800
Cortina Mk I	1198/4	1963/66	£1,550	£600	£150
Cortina Crayford Mk I	1198/4	1963-66	£3,500	£1,800	£950
Cortina GT	1498/4	1963-66	£1,800	£1,000	£650
Lotus Cortina Mk I	1558/4	1963-66	£12,000	£10,000	£5,000
Cortina Mk II	1599/4	1966-70	£1,000	£500	£100
Cortina GT Mk II	1599/4	1966-70	£1,200	£650	£150
Cortina Crayford Mk II	1599/4	1966-70	£4,000	£2,000	£1,500
Lotus Cortina Mk II	1558/4	1966-70	£5,500	£3,000	£1,800
Cortina 1600E	1599/4	1967-70	£2,800	£1,000	£450
Consul Corsair	1500/4	1963-65	£1,100	£500	£250
Consul Corsair GT	1500/4	1963-65	£1,200	£600	£250
Corsair V4	1664/4	1965-70	£1,150	£600	£250
Corsair V4	1664/4	1965-70	£1,400	£600	£250
Corsair V4GT	1994/4	1965-67	£1,300	£700	£250
Corsair V4GT	1994/4	1965-67	£1,400	£700	£350
Corsair Convertible	1664/				
	1994/4	1965-70	£4,300	£2,500	£1,000
Corsair 2000	1994/4	1967-70	£1,350	£500	£250
Corsair 2000E	1994/4	1967-70	£1,500	£800	£350
Escort 1300E	1298/4	1973-74	£1,900	£1,000	£250
Escort Twin Cam	1558/4	1968-71	£8,000	£5,000	£2,000
Escort GT	1298/4	1968-73	£3,000	£1,500	£350
Escort Sport	1298/4	1971-75	£1,750	£925	£250
Escort Mexico	1601/4	1970-74	£4,000	£2,000	£750
RS1600	1601/4	1970-74	£5,000	£2,500	£1,500
RS2000	1998/4	1973-74	£4,500	£2,200	£1,000
Escort RS Mexico	1953/4	1976-78	£3,500	£2,000	£850
Escort RS2000 Mk II	1993/4	1976-80	£6,000	£3,500	£2,000
Capri Mk I 1300/	1298/				
1600	1599/4	1969-72	£1,500	£1,000	£550
Capri 2000/	1996/4				
3000GT	2994/6	1969-72	£2,000	£1,000	£500
Capri 3000E	2994/6	1970-72	£4,000	£2,000	£1,000
Capri RS3100	3093/6	1973-74	£6,500	£3,500	£2,000
Cortina 2000E	1993/4	1973-76	£2,500	£550	£225
Granada Ghia	1993/4				
	2994/6	1974-77	£4,000	£900	£350

Make: Ford
Model: Lotus Cortina Mk I
Type: Saloon
Years Manufactured: 1963-66
Price when new: £1,100
Engine Type: Twin overhead camshaft 4 cyl
Size: 1558cc
Max Power: 105 bhp @ 5500 rpm
Transmission: 4 speed
Performance: Max speed: 107 mph; 0-60: 9.9 secs; Mpg: 20-25.

Make: Ford
Model: Cortina 1600E
Type: Saloon
Years Manufactured: 1967-70
Quantity: 58,582
Price when new: £1,021
Engine Type: 4 cyl
Size: 1599cc
Max Power: 88 bhp
Transmission: 4 speed
Performance: Max speed: 98 mph; 0-60: 13.1 secs; Mpg: 25.

Lotus modified the 1558cc engine that produced 109bhp with its twin Weber 40DCOE carburettors. Introduced in 1967, the Mk II continued in production until 1970.

1971 Ford Cortina Mk II Savage Replica, with V6 cylinder engine, water-cooled, overhead valves, capacity 3 litres, 4 speed gearbox, bevel rear axle, independent front suspension, semi-elliptic leaf rear springs and 185/60 WR 13 tyres. Est. **£5,000-7,000** *S*

1970 Lotus Cortina Mk II. Est. **£5,000-6,000** *Cen*

1968 Ford Lotus Cortina Mk II Saloon, Rally-Prepared, with 4 cylinder in line, water-cooled monobloc engine, double overhead camshaft, bore 82.55mm x stroke 72.7mm, capacity 1558cc, 4 speed synchromesh gearbox, single dry plate clutch, hypoid bevel rear axle, independent coil spring front suspension, semi-elliptic leaf rear springs, wheelbase 98in, and 185/7 x 13in tyres. Est. **£12,500-15,000** *S*

Make: Ford
Model: Escort RS2000 Mk II
Type: Saloon
Years Manufactured: 1973-74
Price when new: £1,600
Engine Type: 4 cyl
Size: 1993cc
Max Power: 100-110 bhp
Transmission: 4 speed
Performance: Max speed: 109
mph; 0-60: 8.6 secs; Mpg: 25.

1978 Ford Escort RS 2000 Mk II.
Est. £2,000-4,000 *Cen*

Make: Ford
Model: Escort RS Mexico/
RS1800
Type: Saloon
Years Manufactured: 1975-78
Price when new: RS1800 Mk II,
£2,792
Engine Type: 4 cyl
Size: 1593cc/1845cc
Max Power: 95-115 bhp
Transmission: 4 speed
Performance: Max speed:
RS1800, 111 mph; 0-60: 9.0 secs;
Mpg: 28.

1972 Ford Escort Mexico.
£1,700-2,000 *CMA*

**1979 Ford Escort RS 2000
Custom.**
Est. £3,000-5,000 *Cen*

1974 Ford Mexico, with 1600cc,
4 cylinder engine.
Est. £3,000-3,500 *ADT*

Make: Ford
Model: Escort Mk I Mexico
Type: Saloon
Years Manufactured: 1970-74
Price when new: £1,179
Engine Type: Overhead valve
4 cyl
Size: 1599cc
Max Power: 86 bhp @ 5500 rpm
Transmission: 4 speed
Performance: Max speed: 100+
mph; 0-60: 10.5 secs;
Mpg: 25-30.

FORD

1980 Ford Escort RS 2000 Mk II.
£3,800-4,200   *Cen*

1987 Ford Cosworth 500, only 500 produced and this is number 203, the body shell has been seam welded by Aston Martin for strength and for racing, recorded mileage of 39,000. Est. **£18,000-22,000**   *LF*

FRAZER-NASH

1938 Frazer Nash-BMW 328 2 Litre Roadster.
Est. **£90,000-110,000**   *B*

The 328 proved itself to be a versatile 90mph performer and a total of 461 examples were built. The model was imported into Britain by AFN Ltd., the Isleworth, Middlesex based manufacturer of Frazer Nash cars, which had taken up the BMW concession in 1934. The AFN-sold 328s arrived in Britain in right-hand drive form, were badged Frazer Nash-BMWs, and 45 examples were sold between 1937 and 1941.

1935 Frazer Nash 1½ Litre 'Electron', with Meadows model 4ED, 4 cylinder engine, 1½ litre pushrod operated overhead valves, 69mm stroke x 100mm bore, twin SU carburettors, magneto ignition, rated to develop approximately 60bhp at 4,500rpm, straight channel section frame, with tubular front axle suspended on ¼ elliptic springs, and friction type shock absorbers acting as radius arms, solid rear axle suspended on ¼ elliptic springs with torque arms and friction shock absorbers, 4 speed gearbox by individual chain and dog clutch for each ratio, controlled by external gear lever, hydraulically operated brakes in 12in drums, rack and pinion steering with fore and aft drag link, 19in centre lock wire wheels, fitted with 4.50 x 19 tyres, in unrestored condition.
Est. **£62,000-100,000**   *C(A)*

Miller's is a price GUIDE not a price LIST

Make the Most of Miller's

Price ranges in this book reflect what one should expect to pay for a similar example. When selling, however, one should expect to receive a lower figure. This will fluctuate according to a dealer's stock, saleability at a particular time, etc. It is always advisable, when selling, to approach a reputable specialist dealer or an auction house which has specialist sales

1950 Frazer Nash Le Mans Replica, 6 cylinder in line, water-cooled monobloc engine, pushrod operated overhead valves, 66mm bore x 98mm stroke, 1971cc, 4 speed manual remote control gearbox, spiral bevel rear axle, independent front suspension by transverse leaf spring and wishbones, torsion bar and radius arms rear suspension, wheelbase 96in, tyres 5.50 x 16in.
£180,000-200,000 *S*

︎936 Frazer Nash BMW 319/2 ︎wo/Four Seater Cabriolet, ︎achbuilt by Drauz with 4 cylinder ︎verhead valve water-cooled ︎onobloc engine, bore 65mm x ︎roke 96mm, capacity 1911cc, ︎speed gearbox, coil ignition single ︎y plate clutch, transverse ︎dependent front suspension, ︎mi-elliptic leaf rear springs, spiral ︎vel rear axle, 5.25 x 16 tyres and ︎eelbase 96in.
︎7,000-28,000 *S*

︎ 1934 AFN Ltd concluded an ︎greement with BMW for the ︎portation of their car into the ︎nited Kingdom, the eventual ︎tention being licence production by ︎FN if the project went well. Many of ︎e Frazer Nash BMWs were ︎achbuilt — some by English ︎achbuilders and others in ︎rmany.

FREEWAY

1981 Freeway II.
£1,000-1,500 *SNY*

FLINT

Flint was a division of the Locomobile Company of America, and produced motor cars designed for fast touring between 1924 and 1926.

1924 Flint Type 40 Saloon,
6 cylinder in-line 'L' head engine, side valve, water-cooled monobloc, 3⅜in bore x 5in stroke, maker's horsepower 27.3, 3 speed manual gearbox, spiral bevel final drive, lea spring suspension front and rear, wheelbase 114in, tyres 600 x 650 x 20in.
Est. **£8,500-9,500** *S(A)*

1925 Flint Model B-40 Five Passenger Tourer, car No. 3677, engine No. 3822 6 cylinder in line, water-cooled monobloc, side valve, bore 3⅛in x 4¼in stroke, 195.6cu in, 3 speed gearbox, disc clutch, spiral bevel rear axle, semi-elliptic leaf spring suspension front and rear, wheelbase 115in.
£11,500-12,000 *SNY*

GILBERN

Gilbern Invader Mk II.
Est. **£3,000-4,000** *AMR*

Make: Gilbern
Model: GT/Genie/Invader
Type: Coupé/Estate
Years Manufactured: 1966-73
Price when new: £1,995; £2,395 (Invader II)
Engine Type: V6 cyl
Size: 2994cc
Max Power: 141 bhp
Transmission: 4 speed and overdrive or auto
Performance: Max speed: 115 mph; 0-60: 10.7 secs; Mpg: 21.

MAKE	ENGINE	DATES	CONDITION		
Gilbern			1	2	
GTMk/1800	1568/4	1959-66	£3,000	£2,000	£75
Genie/Invader	2994/6	1966-70	£3,500	£3,000	£1,50
Invader II	2994/6	1971/72	£4,500	£3,000	£1,70
Invader III	2994/6	1972-73	£5,000	£3,500	£1,00

GARDNER

R. E. Gardner made the horse-drawn Banner Buggy before turning to motor cars in 1916. At first he assembled Chevrolets, then made his first car in 1919. The original 4 cylinder power unit, especially built for the Gardner by Lycoming, was replaced by a 6 and an 8 for 1924. The make ceased in 1930.

1925 Gardner Town-Coupé,
8 cylinder, 4500cc engine.
£14,000-15,000 *ADT*

GRAHAM

1941 Graham Custom Hollywood Model 113 Supercharged Sedan, 6 cylinder in line, water-cooled monobloc engine, side valve, bore 3¼in x stroke 4⅜in, capacity 218cu in, 3 speed column change gearbox, single dry plate clutch, hypoid bevel final drive, semi-elliptic leaf spring suspension, wheelbase 115in and 6.50 x 16in tyres.
£9,500-10,000 *S*

GORDON KEEBLE

MAKE	ENGINE	DATES	CONDITION		
Gordon Keeble			1	2	3
GKI/GKIT	5395/8	1964-67	£18,000	£10,500	£6,200

1965 Gordon Keeble GT Sports Saloon, V8 cylinder, water-cooled engine, overhead valve, 101mm bore x 82.55mm stroke, 5355cc, speed synchromesh gearbox, independent wishbone and coil spring front suspension, De Dion type rear axle on coil springs, wheelbase 102in, tyres 6.70 x 15in. Est. **£20,000-25,000** *S*

Approximately 100 Gordon Keebles were produced of which a high percentage have survived.

Make: Gordon Keeble
Model: GK1/GT
Type: Fixed Head Coupé
Years Manufactured: 1964-67
Quantity: 99
Price when new: £4,058
Engine Type: V8 cyl
Size: 5355cc
Max Power: 300 bhp
Transmission: 4 speed
Performance: Max speed: 136 mph; 0-60: 7.5 secs; Mpg: 18.

HADFIELD BEAN

1928 Hadfield Bean 14/45.
£26,000-29,000 *DJ*

HART

c1899 Hart Steam Victoria Four Seater Dos-a-Dos, with rear mounted twin cylinder vertical steam engine, full elliptic springing, tiller steering, original lamps, and planetary gear drive live rear axle, rear wheels 41in, front wheels 35in, museum stored from 1946 until c1989 and is reputed to have covered only 200 miles from new, bodywork is original but unrestored and the engine is fitted with a 23in boiler.
Est. **£20,000-22,000** *S*

161

HEALEY

1952 Healey Abbott
Four Seater
Tourer.
£8,500-9,500 *GWC*

Make: Healey
Model: Silverstone
Type: Sports
Years Manufactured: 1946-54
Quantity: 105
Engine Type: Riley 'RM'
overhead valve 4 cyl
Size: 2443cc
Max Power: 104 bhp @ 4500 rpm
Max Torque: 132 ft/lb @ 3000 rpm
Transmission: 4 speed manual
Wheelbase: 96in
Performance: Max speed:
approx. 110 mph; 0-60: 11.0 secs.

*The Lenham
Motor Company
produced competition
and special bodied cars
during the 1950s in
extremely limited numbers.*

**1957 Lenham Healey Two Seater
Sports,** with 6 cylinder water-
cooled monobloc engine, overhead
valves, capacity 2629cc, 4 speed
manual gearbox with overdrive,
shaft drive to live rear axle,
independent front suspension,
semi-elliptic leaf springs rear, the
powerful 6 cylinder engine has a
capacity of 2629cc, and with the
lightweight coachwork fitted, the
car should be capable of some quite
competitive speeds.
£14,300-15,000 *S*

MAKE	ENGINE	DATES	CONDITION		
			1	2	3
Healey					
Westland	2443/4	1946-49	£12,000	£5,500	£2,000
Elliot	2443/4	1946-50	£8,000	£5,000	£2,000
Sportsmobile	2443/4	1949	£12,000	£6,000	£4,000
Silverstone	2443/4	1949-50	£40,000	£32,500	£25,000
Tickford	2443/4	1951-54	£9,000	£5,000	£2,000
Abbott	2443/4	1951-54	£20,000	£15,500	£9,000

HILLMAN

Founded in 1907 the Hillman
Company became part of the
Rootes Group in 1928. By 1964
the Chrysler Corporation had
acquired a controlling interest
and, by the time of the Peugeot
takeover in 1979, the Hillman
name had disappeared.

**1931 Hillman Wizard 65
Foursome Drop Head Coupé,**
with 6 cylinder side valve,
water-cooled monobloc engine, bore
65mm x stroke 106mm, capacity
2110cc (rating 15.72hp), 4 speed
manual gearbox, single dry plate
clutch, coil and battery ignition,
spiral bevel final drive, 5.25 x 19
tyres and wheelbase of 84in.
£5,800-6,500 *S*

1932 Hillman Wizard, with
Cabriolet Coachwork by Salmons &
Sons, with a 2810cc 6 cylinder
engine.
Est. **£12,000-14,000** *ADT*

*William Hillman,
who was born in
1849, began his
career with the
Coventry machinist
company which
later became Swift.*

1935 Hillman Minx 10, with
1185cc, 4 cylinder engine.
Est. **£3,000-4,000** *ADT*

1968 Hillman Super Imp.
£725-900   *CMA*

Introduced in 1965 as Hillman's answer to the Mini. The Imp used an 875cc rear-mounted engine based on a design by Coventry Climax.

Make: Hillman
Model: Imp
Type: Saloon/Estate/Coupé
Years Manufactured: 1963-76
Quantity: 440,032 all types
Price when new: £532
Engine Type: Rear engine 4 cyl
Size: 875cc
Max Power: 39 bhp @ 5000 rpm
Transmission: 4 speed
Performance: Max speed: Imp, 80+; Imp Sport, 90 mph; 0-60: Imp, 23.5 secs; Imp Sport, 16.3 secs; Mpg: Imp, 35-45; Imp Sport, 33.

The Hillman Company produced a range of medium sized vehicles during the 1920s and 1930s, with quite powerful 6 cylinder engines and good quality coachwork.

1968 Hillman Super Imp, this car has one registered owner from new and has recorded only 13,000 miles since 1968, 875cc, 4 cylinder engine.
£1,750-1,900   *ADT*

Make the Most of Miller's

CONDITION is absolutely vital when assessing the value of a vehicle. Top class vehicles on the whole appreciate much more than less perfect examples. However a rare, desirable car may command a high price even when in need of restoration

Make: Hillman
Model: Minx/Super Minx
Type: Saloon/Convertible/Estate
Years Manufactured: 1958-59
Engine Type: Overhead valve 4 cyl
Size: 1494cc
Max Power: 49 bhp @ 4400 rpm
Transmission: 4 speed
Performance: Max speed: 80 mph; 0-60: 26.5 secs; Mpg: 27-32.

MAKE	ENGINE	DATES	CONDITION 1	2	3
Hillman					
Minx Mk I-II	1184/4	1946-48	£1,750	£800	£250
Minx Mk I-II DHC	1184/4	1946-48	£3,500	£1,500	£250
Minx Mk III-VIIIA	1184/4	1948-56	£1,750	£700	£350
Minx Mk III-VIIIA DHC	1184/4	1948-56	£3,750	£1,500	£350
Californian	1390/4	1953-56	£1,500	£750	£200
Minx SI/II	1390/4	1956-58	£1,250	£450	£200
Minx SI/II DHC	1390/4	1956-58	£3,500	£1,500	£500
Minx Ser III	1494/4	1958-59	£1,000	£500	£200
Minx Ser III DHC	1494/4	1958-59	£3,750	£1,500	£400
Minx Ser IIIA/B	1494/4	1959-61	£1,250	£500	£200
Minx Ser IIIA/B DHC	1494/4	1959-61	£3,750	£1,250	£500
Minx Ser IIIC	1592/4	1961-62	£900	£500	£200
Minx Ser IIIC DHC	1592/4	1961-62	£3,000	£1,500	£500
Minx Ser V	1592/4	1962-63	£1,250	£350	£150
Minx Ser VI	1725/4	1964-67	£1,500	£375	£100
Husky Mk I	1265/4	1954-57	£1,000	£600	£200
Husky SI/II/III	1390/4	1958-65	£1,000	£550	£150
Super Minx	1592/4	1961-66	£1,500	£500	£100
Super Minx DHC	1592/4	1962-64	£3,500	£1,250	£450
Imp	875/4	1963-73	£800	£300	£70
Husky	875/4	1966-71	£800	£450	£100
Avenger	var/4	1970-76	£550	£250	£60
Avenger GT	1500/4	1971-76	£950	£500	£100
Tiger	1600/4	1972-73	£1,250	£650	£200

HISPANO-SUIZA

1921 Hispano-Suiza H6 37.2hp Five Seat Tourer, 6 cylinder in line, water-cooled monobloc engine, overhead camshaft, 100mm bore x 140mm stroke, 6597cc, 3 speed gearbox, cone clutch, shaft and bevel final drive, semi-elliptic leaf springs front and rear, servo-assisted 4 wheel brakes, wheelbase 144in, tyres 35 x 5½in.
Est. **£140,000-160,000**   *S*

1923 Hispano Suiza H6B 37.2hp Salamanca, with coachwork by Kellner of Paris, chassis No. 10566, engine No. 300598 6 cylinder in line, water-cooled monobloc, overhead valves, overhead camshaft, bore 100mm x 140mm stroke, 6597cc, 3 speed gearbox, right-hand change, right-hand drive, bevel rear axle, semi-elliptic leaf springs front and rear, wheelbase 144in, 23in tyres.
£95,000-100,000   *SNY*

1935 Hispano-Suiza Model K6 Long Chassis 30/120 HP, with 6 cylinder engine with pushrod operated overhead valves, 100mm bore x 110mm stroke, capacity 5.2 litres, channel section chassis with semi-elliptic leaf springs and beam axles front and rear, 3 speed gearbox with central gear lever, 4 wheel mechanical brakes with Hispano-Suiza servo, centre lock wire wheels and 6.50 x 18 tyres.
Est. **£60,000-80,000**   *C(A)*

The model K6 Hispano was sometimes called 'the ladies Hispano', being a smaller and lighter car than the V12. At the same time the K6 was certainly not inferior in quality or performance since in 1934 a K6 saloon was tested by one of the English motoring magazines, achieving a 0-60mph time of 19.6 seconds and a top speed of 83mph over a timed quarter mile.

HRG

1947 HRG 1100 Sports Roadster, Singer 4 cylinder in line, water-cooled monobloc engine, 68mm bore x 103mm stroke, 1100cc, single overhead camshaft, 4 speed Singer 10/12 synchromesh manual gearbox, dry plate clutch, shaft drive to live rear axle, semi-elliptic spring suspension, wheelbase 100in, tyres 5.00 x 17in, right-hand drive. Est. **£20,000-24,000**   *S(A)*

HORCH

1938 Horch Model 830 BL, with a Horch 3.8 litre engine overhead valves operated by rockers from single camshaft, rated to develop 92bhp, box section chassis independent front suspension by coil springs and wishbones, De Dion rear suspension with chassis mounted differential, 4 speed synchromesh gearbox, 4 wheel hydraulically operated drum type brakes, steel disc wheels and 6.50 x 17 tyres.
Est. **£50,000-75,000**   C(A)

Founded in 1901 by Doctor August Horch, the Company is one of the oldest German car manufacturers. In 1931 it combined with the Saxon car manufacturers, Audi, DKW and Wanderer to form Auto-Union AG. The Horch Marque has continued to maintain its reputation for advanced high quality engineering through the famous Auto-Union racing cars of the 1930s, to the Audi of today. When Dr Horch left the Company carrying his name, he founded a new Company, adopting the name 'Audi', as being the nearest equivalent to the meaning of his own name in Latin, or, in English, 'Hark'.

HUDSON

1915 Hudson Six-40 Seven Seater Open Tourer, 6 cylinder side valve water-cooled monobloc engine, 87mm bore x 125mm stroke, 4725cc, 3 speed gearbox, semi-elliptic front springs, ¾ elliptics at rear, live rear axle, wheelbase 123in, tyres 34 x 4in.
£13,500-14,500   S

1937 Hudson Terraplane Two Door Convertible Coupé, 6 cylinder in line, water-cooled monobloc engine, side valve, 3in bore x 5in stroke, 212cu in capacity, 3 speed gearbox, single disc clutch with cork inserts, shaft drive to semi-floating rear axle, semi-elliptic leaf rear springs, wheelbase 117in, tyres 16in.
Est. **£18,000-22,000**   S

Hudson Motors Ltd of Great West Road, Chiswick were the importers of the Hudson Terraplane, a model with a reputation for high speed motoring, in October 1936 a Terraplane had set a new record at Bonneville of 86.54mph for 24 hours. The Series 72 model, of which this is an example, was the top of the range car.

1935 Hudson Terraplane Convertible Coupé, with 6 cylinder, 2723cc engine and right-hand drive.
£15,000-16,000   ADT

Hudson were well established in England in the 30s with offices and showrooms on the Great West Road at Chiswick.

1934/35 Hudson 'Big Six' Terraplane, 6 cylinder, 3400cc engine, with 44,727 miles recorded.
Est. **£10,000-14,000**   ADT

The 116in wheelbase houses a 6 cylinder L-head, in-line engine, comprising an aluminium block, main bearings, 21.6hp and a 80bhp at 3,800rpm.

Miller's is a price
GUIDE not a price
LIST

HOTCHKISS

1925 Hotchkiss AM2 15.9hp Four Seat Tourer, 4 cylinder in line, water-cooled monobloc engine, overhead valve, 80mm bore x 120mm stroke, 2413cc, 4 speed gearbox, single plate clutch, spiral bevel rear axle, semi-elliptic leaf spring suspension front and rear, wheelbase 121in, tyres 5.50/6.00 x 20in.
Est. £13,000-18,000   *S*

HUMBER

Humber started the manufacture of bicycles in 1868 and by 1898 the first Humber motor car had been produced. By the time of the Rootes takeover in 1930 Thomas Humber's company had two factories, one at Beeston, Nottinghamshire and the other at Coventry.

Rootes-owned coach builders, Thrupp and Maberly, for example, produced some bodies for Humber, these cars obviously being highly sought after. Like Hillman, the Humber name was discontinued following the Peugeot Talbot acquisition of the Chrysler Group in the 1970s.

MAKE	ENGINE	DATES	CONDITION		
Humber			1	2	3
Hawk Mk I-IV	1944/4	1945-52	£2,750	£1,500	£600
Hawk Mk V-VII	2267/4	1952-57	£2,500	£1,500	£400
Hawk Ser I-IVA	2267/4	1957-67	£2,500	£850	£325
Snipe	2731/6	1945/48	£5,000	£2,600	£850
Super Snipe Mk I-III	4086/6	1948-52	£4,700	£2,400	£600
Super Snipe Mk IV-IVA	4138/6	1952-56	£5,500	£2,300	£550
Super Snipe Ser I-II	2651/6	1958/60	£3,800	£1,800	£475
Super Snipe Ser I-II	2651/6	1958-60	£4,000	£1,850	£575
Super Snipe SIII-VA	2965/6	1961-67	£3,500	£1,800	£400
Super Snipe S.III-VA Est.	2965/6	1961-67	£3,950	£1,850	£525
Pullman	4086/6	1946-51	£4,500	£2,350	£800
Pullman Mk IV	4086/6	1952-54	£6,000	£2,850	£1,200
Imperial	2965/6	1965-67	£3,900	£1,600	£450
Sceptre Mk I-II	1592/4	1963-67	£2,050	£900	£300
Sceptre Mk III	1725/4	1967-76	£1,600	£600	£200

1924 Humber 14/40 Open Road Tourer, with completely rebuilt engine, fully restored body and engine capacity of 2050cc, 4 cylinder.
Est. £23,000-25,000   *ADT*

1926 Humber 15/40hp Five Seat Tourer, with 4 cylinder water-cooled monobloc engine, overhead inlet valves, side exhaust valves, bore 80mm x stroke 140mm, capacity 2815cc, 4 speed gearbox, spiral bevel rear axle, semi-elliptic springs front and rear, wheelbase 126in and 820mm x 120mm bead-edge tyres.
£16,500-17,000   *S*

Although the 12/25 and 14/40 Humber of this era are quite common, the 15/40 is rare.

1929 Humber 9/20 Saloon, with 4 cylinder inlet over exhaust water-cooled monobloc engine, bore 58mm x stroke 100mm, capacity 1057cc, 3 speed gearbox in unit with engine, Ferodo lined cone clutch, shaft and bevel drive, semi-elliptic leaf springs, wheelbase 102in and 19 x 3½in tyres.
£5,800-7,000   *S*

1934 Humber Snipe Golfer Coupé, one of only 2 built.
Est. £13,000-16,000   *RTC*

1934 Humber Snipe 80 Drop Head Coupé, with Dickey, 6 cylinder in-line engine, water-cooled monobloc, side valve, bore 80mm x stroke 116mm, capacity 3499cc, 4 speed gearbox with synchromesh on 3rd and top, single dry plate clutch, spiral bevel rear axle, semi-elliptic leaf springs front and rear, wheelbase 124in and 17in tyres, the car is complete but in need of restoration.
£7,700-8,000 *S*

The Snipe 80 introduced for the 1932 Motor Show featured a new 6 cylinder side valve engine, with a cruising speed around 65mph and petrol economy of 17mpg.

Make: Humber
Model: Super Snipe/Imperial
Type: Saloon/Estate
Years Manufactured: 1958-67
Quantity: approx. 32,000;
Imperial approx. 3,032
Price when new: Super Snipe
Series I-III, £1,110
Engine Type: Overhead valve
6 cyl
Size: 2651cc/2965cc
Max Power: 105-129 bhp
Transmission: 4 speed
Performance: Max speed: 100 mph; 0-60: 14.3 secs; Mpg: 20.

1936 Humber Snipe Saloon, with 6 cylinder in line, water-cooled monobloc engine, side valve, capacity 4086cc, 4 speed synchromesh gearbox, single dry plate clutch, bevel rear axle, independent front suspension by transverse leaf spring, semi-elliptic leaf springs rear.
£4,600-5,000 *S*

Humber's excellent reputation was dignified by the performance of their vehicles as staff cars during the Second World War. The Snipe was the company's major model for the main part of the decade to 1939, and was only replaced by the Super Snipe, with a slightly increased capacity in 1939. The cars were favoured by the Police Force and the Military and many have seen service by politicians and heads of state. In 1949 a Humber Super Snipe Convertible was used by HRH Princess Elizabeth and the Duke of Edinburgh on their honeymoon in Kenya.

1966 Humber Imperial, with 2965cc, 6 cylinder engine capacity.
Est. **£1,750-2,750** *ADT*

HUPMOBILE

1914 Hupmobile Model H 15/18hp Coupé, coachwork by Oakley Ltd, London, with 4 cylinder side valve water-cooled engine, bore ¼in x stroke 5½in, rating 15/18hp, 3 speed gearbox, semi-elliptic springing, live rear axle, wheelbase 106in and 815 x 105 tyres.
£8,800-10,000 *S*

1909 Hupmobile Model 20 Two Seat Runabout, 4 cylinder water-cooled monobloc engine, side valve, maker's horsepower 16.9hp, capacity 2800cc, 2 speed and reverse gearbox operated by sliding hand lever, enclosed shaft drive to live rear axle, semi-elliptic leaf springs front and rear suspension, wheelbase 96in.
£12,100-12,500 *S*

ISO GRIFO

Renzo Rivolta of the Iso factory introduced the Grifo in 1963 as a development of the earlier and successful Iso-Rivolta. The Iso-Grifo was engineered by Giotto Bizzarini, late of Ferrari, who was already involved in producing his own very similar car, the Bizzarini GT Strada 5300. The Grifo, like the Rivolta was again styled by Bertone, this time with a Chevrolet V8 engine, capable of over 160mph.

1968 Iso Grifo GL 365 Lusso, with V8, 5359cc, 365bhp engine, 4 speed automatic gearbox, 4 wheel servo disc brakes, wishbone and coil spring front, coil spring and Dion live axle rear suspension and right-hand drive.
Est. **£40,000-60,000**   *C*

ISOTTA FRASCHINI

1928 Isotta Fraschini Type 8A Castagna Roadster Cabriolet, 8 cylinder in line, water-cooled monobloc engine, overhead valves, 95mm bore x 130mm stroke, 7370cc, 3 speed manual transmission, shaft drive to live rear axle, multiple disc clutch, leaf spring front and rear suspension, tyres 155 x 15in.
£144,000-154,000   *S(M)*

INVICTA

This car is the 4th 'S' Type built, since only even numbers starting at S20 were used. During the 1930s 'S' Type Invicta owners formed a Club, and gave names beginning with 'S' to each car, this car's name is Sea Lion.

1930 'S' Type 4½ Litre Invicta, Low Chassis '100 mph' Model, with chassis No. S26 and engine No. 7395, 4½ litre, 6 cylinder engine built by Henry Meadows Ltd, twin ignition, twin SU carburettors, 88.5mm bore x 120.64mm stroke, with pushrod operated overhead valves, rated to develop 140bhp at 3,800rpm, the chassis based on the design of the 1½ litre G.P. Delage, the nickel/chrome steel channel section is of down swept design and passes under the rear axle, beam axles front and rear are carried on trunnion mounted semi-elliptic leaf springs with friction type shock absorbers, 4 speed sliding mesh with right-hand gear lever gearbox, rod operated 4 wheel brakes with 14in diam drums, centre lock 19in wire wheels and 6.00 x 19 tyres.
Est. **£240,000-250,000**   *C(A)*

Use the Index!

Because certain items might fit easily into any of a number of categories, the quickest and surest method of locating any entry is by reference to the index at the back of the book.

This has been fully cross-referenced for absolute simplicity

1932 Invicta 1½ Litre Tourer, one of only 5 of these cars known to still exist, 1600 twin overhead camshaft Blackburn engine, which was the works prototype, exhibited at the 1932 Motor Show.
£34,000-36,000   *DG*

JAGUAR

The SS (Swallow Sidecar) Company had been in business a few years before the first true SS model, the Standard 2 litre engined SS1 was produced. It was not until after the second World War that the name was changed to Jaguar and Sir William Lyon's company produced the first of the XK series sportscars. The XK range finished in 1959 and following many competition successes, especially at Le Mans, the Jaguar company prospered. Many other companies, notably Daimler, were acquired and in 1966 Jaguar merged with BMC before being taken over by Leyland in 1968. Jaguar became a separate company and was floated on the Stock Exchange in 1984.

1932 Invicta 4½ Litre 'S' Type Low Chassis Tourer, coachwork by Carbodies, 6 cylinder in line, water-cooled monobloc engine, pushrod operated overhead valves, 88.5m bore x 120.64mm stroke, 4467cc, 4 speed right-hand gate change gearbox, single dry plate clutch, hypoid bevel rear axle, semi-elliptic leaf springs front and rear, wheelbase 118in, tyres 6.00/6.50 x 19in.
£230,000-250,000 *S*

1936 SS Jaguar 2½ Litre Tourer, with chassis No. 19009, engine No. 250911, 6 cylinder 2½ litre overhead valve, of the 105 models produced only around 10-15 are known to survive and this chassis number makes it the 9th built and possibly the earliest runner, a total restoration project.
£27,000-28,000 *C*

1937 2½ Litre SS Jaguar 100, original car, with 6 cylinder pushrod operated overhead valve engine, 73mm bore x 106mm stroke, capacity 2663cc, rated to develop 104bhp at 4500rpm, twin SE carburettors, coil ignition, boxed channel section chassis with beam axles front and rear, carried on leaf springs, trunnion mounted at front, 4 speed synchromesh gearbox, Girling mechanical 4 wheel drum type rod operated brakes, centre lock wire type wheels and 5.50 x 18 tyres.
£75,000-80,000 *C(A)*

JAGUAR

MAKE	ENGINE	DATES	CONDITION		
Jaguar			1	2	3
Jaguar 1½ Litre	1775/4	1945-49	£8,500	£5,500	£2,000
Jaguar 2½ Litre	2663/6	1946-49	£10,000	£7,500	£2,000
Jaguar 2½ Litre	2663/6	1947-48	£18,000	£10,000	£8,000
Jaguar 3½ Litre	3485/6	1947-49	£12,000	£6,000	£4,000
Jaguar 3½ Litre DHC	3485/6	1947-49	£19,000	£13,500	£5,500
Jaguar Mk V 2½ Litre	2663/6	1949-51	£8,000	£5,000	£1,500
Jaguar Mk V 3½ Litre	3485/6	1949-51	£13,000	£7,000	£1,800
Jaguar Mk V 3½ Litre DHC	3485/6	1949-51	£26,500	£17,000	£8,500
Jaguar Mk VII	3442/6	1951-57	£10,500	£7,500	£2,500
Jaguar Mk VIIM	3442/6	1951-57	£12,000	£8,500	£2,500
Jaguar Mk VIII	3442/6	1956-59	£8,500	£5,500	£2,000
Jaguar Mk IX	3781/6	1958-61	£13,000	£9,000	£2,500
Jaguar Mk X 3.8/4.2	3781/6	1961-64	£8,500	£3,500	£1,500
Jaguar Mx X 420G	4235/6	1964-70	£7,500	£3,000	£1,200
Jaguar Mk I 2.4	2438/6	1955-59	£10,000	£5,500	£2,000
Jaguar Mk I 3.4	3442/6	1957-59	£12,000	£8,000	£2,500
Jaguar Mk II 2.4	2483/6	1959-67	£9,000	£5,000	£2,000
Jaguar Mk II 3.4	3442/6	1959-67	£12,000	£6,500	£3,000
Jaguar Mk II 3.8	3781/6	1959-67	£13,500	£9,000	£4,000
Jaguar S-Type 3.4	3442/6	1963-68	£10,000	£6,500	£2,000
Jaguar S-Type 3.8	3781/6	1963-68	£12,500	£6,500	£2,000
Jaguar 240	2438/6	1967-68	£8,000	£5,000	£2,500
Jaguar 340	3442/6	1967-68	£9,000	£7,000	£3,000
Jaguar 420	4235/6	1966-68	£6,000	£3,000	£2,000

Make: Jaguar
Model: XK120, 140, 150
Type: Drop Head Coupé, Fixed Head Coupé, Sports
Years Manufactured: 1953-61
Price when new: XK150, £2,007
Engine Type: Twin overhead camshaft 6 cyl
Size: 3442cc
Max Power: XK120, 160/180 bhp @ 5000 rpm; XK150, 252 bhp @ 5500 rpm
Max Torque: XK120, 195/203 ft/lb @ 2500/4000 rpm
Transmission: 4 speed, optional overdrive
Wheelbase: 102in
Performance: Max speed: XK150, 130+ mph; 0-60: XK150, 7.5 secs; Mpg: XK150, 18-22.

1936 Jaguar SS Sports Saloon, 6 cylinder in line, water-cooled monobloc engine, 73mm bore x 106mm stroke, 2664cc, overhead valves, 19.84hp developing 97bhp at 4,500rpm, 4 speed manual synchromesh gearbox, Girling brakes, semi-elliptic spring suspension, wheelbase 120in, right-hand drive.
£6,000-8,000   *S(A)*

> **Miller's is a price GUIDE not a price LIST**

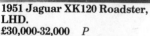

1951 Jaguar XK120 Roadster, LHD.
£30,000-32,000   *P*

1950 Jaguar XK120 Roadster RHD.
Est. **£35,000-45,000**   *P*

1951 Jaguar XK120 Roadster, with 6 cylinder, 3442cc engine and left-hand drive, in need of total restoration.
£9,250-10,000   *C*

1952 Jaguar XK120 Roadster with 3400cc, 6 cylinder engine, 35,900 miles recorded and 'C' type cylinder head.
£44,000-46,000   *T&M*

1952 Jaguar XK120 Roadster, 6 cylinder in line, water-cooled monobloc engine, double overhead camshaft operated overhead valves, 87mm bore x 106mm stroke, 3781cc, single dry plate clutch, 4 speed gearbox, hypoid bevel live rear axle, semi-elliptic rear springs, wheelbase 102in, tyres 16in.
£55,000-60,000   *S*

1953 Jaguar XK120 Roadster, converted to right-hand drive. Est. **£30,000-40,000**   *P*

**1953 Jaguar XK120 M.
£50,000-55,000**   *SEN*

The XK120 M has factory modified suspension as well as fitted wire wheels in order to assist cooling, the drum brakes suffered badly from overheating and fade.

1949 Jaguar XK120 Roadster, LHD, with aluminium body, wheel spats, in original condition with 7,500 miles recorded.
£38,000-42,000   *T&M*

**1951 Jaguar XK120 Roadster 3.4.
£49,000-50,000**   *BLE*

MAKE	ENGINE	DATES	CONDITION		
Jaguar XJ6 2.8 Ser I	2793/6	1968-73	£2,600	£1,500	£1,000
Jaguar XJ6 4.2 Ser I	4235/6	1968-73	£3,000	£2,000	£1,000
Jaguar XJ6 Coupé	4235/6	1974-78	£7,000	£3,000	£2,000
Jaguar XJ6 Ser II	4235/6	1973-79	£3,500	£2,000	£750
Jaguar XJ12 Ser I	5343/12	1972-73	£4,500	£2,250	£1,500
Jaguar XJ12 Coupé	5343/12	1973-77	£8,000	£4,000	£2,000
Jaguar XJ12 Ser II	5343/12	1973-79	£2,000	£1,500	—
Jaguar XK120 DHC	3442/6	1953-54	£28,000	£18,000	£12,000
Jaguar XK120 DHC	3442/6	1949-54	£30,000	£20,000	£13,000
Jaguar XK120 FHC	3442/6	1951-54	£25,000	£17,000	£10,000
Jaguar XK140 DHC	3442/6	1954-57	£30,000	£20,00	£12,000
Jaguar XK140 roadster	3442/6	1954-57	£33,000	£24,000	£14,000
Jaguar XK140 FHC	3442/6	1954-57	£20,000	£15,000	£10,000
Jaguar XK140MC			£35,000	£27,500	£18,00
Jaguar XK150 DHC	3442/6	1957-60	£30,000	£20,000	£15,000
Jaguar XK150 roadster	3442/6	1958-60	£32,000	£22,000	£15,000
Jaguar XK150S			£38,000	£28,000	£18,000
Jaguar XK150 FHC	3442/6	1957-61	£20,000	£15,000	£10,000

Make: Jaguar
Model: XJS
Type: Sports Coupé/Cabriolet/Convertible
Years Manufactured: 1975-date
Quantity: Still in production
Price when new: XJS 1/2, 1975-79, £11,243
Engine Type: V12 cyl
Size: 5343cc
Max Power: 1975-81, 244 bhp @ 5250 rpm; 1982-88, 262 bhp @ 5000 rpm
Max Torque: 1975-81, 269 ft/lb @ 4500 rpm; 1982-88, 290 ft/lb @ 3000 rpm
Transmission: 4 speed or auto
Wheelbase: 102in
Performance: Max speed: 135+ mph; 0-60: 8.5 secs; Mpg: 17.

1954 Jaguar XK120 Roadster, 6 cylinder in-line engine, water-cooled monobloc, twin overhead camshaft, bore 83mm x 106mm stroke, 210cu in, 4 speed synchromesh gearbox, left-hand drive, Borg and Beck single dry plate clutch, bevel rear axle, independent front suspension, semi-elliptic leaf springs at rear, wheelbase 102in, 175 SR 16 tyres.
£23,000-25,000 *SNY*

1954 Jaguar XK120 S/E Model Drop Head Coupé, 6 cylinder twin overhead camshaft, water-cooled monobloc engine, 83mm bore x 106mm stroke, 3442cc, 4 speed gearbox, torsion bar independent front suspension, leaf springs at rear, live rear axle, wheelbase 102in, tyres 6.00 x 16in.
£50,000-55,000 *S(M)*

1957 Jaguar XK140, in need of total restoration, rust free.
£12,500-14,000 *FOR*

1955 Jaguar XK140 Drop Head Coupé, with 6 cylinder water-cooled monobloc engine, twin overhead camshafts, bore 83mm x stroke 106mm, capacity 3442cc, 4 speed manual transmission with overdrive, independent front suspension with torsion bars, semi-elliptic rear springs with telescopic shock absorbers, live rear axle, wheelbase 102in and 16in tyres.
Est. **£30,000-40,000** *S*

Locate the source

The source of each illustration in Miller's can be found by checking the code letters below each caption with the list of contributors

1955 Jaguar XK140 MC Roadster, chassis No. S811439, engine No. G35948-8, twin carburettor 3.4 litre version of the twin overhead camshaft Jaguar XK Series engine, rated to develop 210bhp. Box section frame with torsion bar and wishbone independent front suspension, and beam type rear axle carried on semi-elliptic leaf springs. Four speed synchromesh gearbox, with Laycock overdrive, rack and pinion steering, drum type, hydraulically operated brakes, 16in centre lock wheels, chromium plated, with 6.50 x 16 tyres.
Est. **£85,000-100,000**   *C(A)*

A total of 3,350 XK140s were built in this body style. Most of these were exported to America, with only about 70 being built in right-hand drive.

1953 Jaguar XK120 3.4 Litre Fixed Head Coupé.
£21,000-23,000   *B*

1954 Jaguar XK120 Drop Head Coupé, 6 cylinder in line, water-cooled monobloc engine, double overhead camshaft, overhead valves, 83mm bore x 106mm stroke, 3442cc, Moss 4 speed manual gearbox, dry plate clutch, hypoid bevel live rear axle, independent torsion bar front suspension, semi-elliptic leaf springs at rear, wheelbase 102in tyres 15in CWW.
Est. **£38,000-42,000**   *S(A)*

1957 Jaguar XK140 MC Roadster, LHD, fully restored and UK registered.
£69,000-70,000   *T&M*

1953 Jaguar XK120 Roadster, with 6 cylinder engine in-line water-cooled monobloc, double overhead camshaft, bore 83mm x stroke 106mm, capacity 3442cc single dry plate clutch, 4 speed gearbox, hypoid bevel live rear axle, semi-elliptic rear springs, wheelbase 102in and 16in tyres.
£32,000-35,000   *S*

**1956 Jaguar   XK140 Sports
Coupé.**
Est. £20,000-22,000   *S(A)*

**1956 Jaguar XK140 Roadster,
LHD,** chassis No. S812844, engine
No. E1805-8, 3442cc, 6 cylinder, all
duties paid.
Est. £36,000-40,000   *Ren*

**1959 Jaguar XK150 Drop Head
Coupé 2+2,** excellent condition.
£85,000-87,500   *BLE*

**1959 Jaguar XK150 Drop Head
Coupé, RHD.**
£56,000-57,000   *BLE*

**1958 3.5 Litre Jaguar XK150 SE
Drop Head Coupé, LHD,** chassis
No. S837679, engine No. VS2778-8,
6 cyinder in-line monobloc with
double overhead camshafts, 87mm
bore x 106mm stroke, 3781cc,
4 speed manual gearbox with
overdrive, 4 wheel servo disc
brakes, independent front and
semi-elliptic leaf spring rear
suspension, wire spoked wheels.
Est. £40,000-50,000   *C*

**1959 Jaguar XK150S 3.4 Litre
Roadster,** chassis No.
S8361023 DN, engine No.
VS1265-9.
Est. £50,000-70,000   *P*

**1958 Jaguar XK150 Fixed Head
Coupé,** chassis No. S835466 DN,
engine No. V36058, has been
converted to right-hand drive.
£23,000-26,000   *P*

**1959 Jaguar XK150S 3.4 Litre
Fixed Head Coupé,** chassis No.
S824845 DN, engine No. VS1942-9,
original right-hand drive, totally
restored.
Est. £30,000-40,000   *P*

The Jaguar E-Type was announced at the London Motor Show in 1961. The design was based on the successful sports/racing D-Type, but with the added benefit of independent rear suspension, and powered by a 3 carburettor 3.8 litre version of Jaguar's XK engine. With a selling price far below that of any comparable car and remarkable performance and handling the E-Type was a great success. The design was steadily developed until 1971 when the Series 3 was announced, powered by the new 5.3 litre V12 engine, it endowed the E-Type with even more performance, and a further increase in its high speed cruising capabilties.

1961 Jaguar E Type 3.8 Litre Coupé.
Est. £24,000-36,000   S(A)

964 Jaguar E-Type 3.8 Litre Roadster, chassis No. 879807, ngine No. RA28939.
'20,000-22,500   P

1962 Jaguar E-Type 3.8 Litre Series 1 Flat Floor Roadster, chassis No. 850551, engine No. R6163-9.
Est. £48,000-54,000   P

959 Jaguar XK150 2+2 Fixed Head Coupé, chassis No. 824941 SN, engine No. V70308, cylinder, in-line monobloc with ouble overhead camshaft, 83mm ore x 106mm stroke giving 3442cc, speed synchromesh gearbox with verdrive, servo-assisted 4 wheel isc brakes, torsion bar independent ont suspension, semi-elliptic leaf ring rear, right-hand drive.
st. £35,000-40,000   C

nly 4,400 Fixed Head Coupés were uilt with the great majority having ft-hand drive for export.

he Jaguar XK150 model was erhaps the greatest of Jaguar's open odels until the introduction of the -Type in 1961. Under 10,000 of ese cars were manufactured tween 1957 and 1961. The XK150 arted life with a 190bhp engine though the SE or Special uipment option had a 210bhp gine. The engine also carried a ronger clutch, lightened flywheel d lead-bronze bearings. ntemporary road tests indicated a o speed of 133mph.

1966 Jaguar E-Type 4.2 Litre Fixed Head Coupé, full restoration 18 months ago, 63,000 miles from new, right-hand drive. **£21,000-23,000** *SEN*

1966 Jaguar E-Type Roadster chassis No. IE16235, engine No. 7R13112-9. Est. **£30,000-35,000** *P*

1968 Jaguar E-Type 4.2 Litre Coupé, 6 cylinder in line, water-cooled monobloc engine, twin overhead camshaft, 92mm bore x 106mm stroke, 4235cc, 4 speed gearbox, single dry plate clutch, hypoid bevel rear axle, independent front and rear suspension, wheelbase 96in, tyres 15in. Est. **£30,000-35,000** *S*

1969 Jaguar E-Type Roadster, chassis No. IR10060, engine 4235cc 6 cylinder. Est. **£32,000-36,000** *LF*

1969 Jaguar E-Type 4.2 Litre Roadster. **£16,000-16,500** *ADT*

1973 Jaguar E-Type V12 Roadster, chassis No. 151588, engine No. 757938SA, 5343cc, V12. Est. **£55,000-65,000** *Ren*

1969 Jaguar E-Type Fixed Head Coupé 2+2, engine 4235cc, 4 cylinder. **£10,500-12,000** *LF*

Make: Jaguar
Model: E-Type, Series III
Type: Sports Car/Coupé
Years Manufactured: 1971-74
Quantity: 15,287
Price when new: Fixed Head Coupé, £3,369
Engine Type: V12 cyl
Size: 5343cc
Max Power: 272 bhp @ 5850 rpm
Max Torque: 304 ft/lb @ 3600 rpm
Transmission: 4 speed or auto
Wheelbase: 104.7in
Performance: Max speed: 142 mph; 0-60: 6.8 secs; Mpg: 16.

1969 E-Type Roadster, RHD.
Est. **£26,000-26,500** *Mar*

**1972 Jaguar E-Type 2+2, V12
Fixed Head Coupé, RHD.**
£26,500-27,000 *Mar*

**1973 Jaguar Series III V12
E Type Sports Coupé.**
Est. **£24,000-32,000** *S(A)*

Make the Most of Miller's

CONDITION is absolutely vital when assessing the value of a vehicle. Top class vehicles on the whole appreciate much more than less perfect examples. However a rare, desirable car may command a high price even when in need of restoration

1974 Jaguar XKE V12 Roadster.
£45,000-47,000 *SNY*

**1973 Jaguar E-Type V12 Series
III, 2+2 Coupé,** chassis No.
IS 74278BW, engine No.
7S 5967 SB, capacity 5343cc, 90mm
bore x 70mm stroke, automatic
gearbox with hypoid rear axle,
independent front and rear
suspension, left-hand drive.
Est. **£20,000-25,000** *C(M)*

**1973 Jaguar E-Type V12
Roadster,** chassis No. UD1521813,
engine No. 7S9796LB, capacity
5343cc, 95% original.
£34,500-40,000 *LF*

1973 Jaguar E-Type Roadster,
chassis No. U61S23689BW, engine
capacity 5343cc.
Est. **£20,000-25,000** *ADT*

**1969 Jaguar E-Type Series II, 4.2
Litre Roadster, LHD,** chassis No.
1R7834, engine No. 7R2771/9,
chrome wire wheels.
£39,500-40,000 *T&M*

MAKE	ENGINE	DATES	CONDITION		
E-type 3.8 flat floor roadster		1961	£40,000	£30,000	£21,500
E-type S1 3.8 roadster	3781/6	1961-64	£28,000	£18,000	£13,000
E-type 3.8	3781/6	1961-64	£18,000	£13,000	£9,000
E-type S1 4.2 roadster	4235/6	1964-68	£22,000	£18,000	£12,000
E-type 4.2	4235/6	1964-68	£18,000	£13,000	£9,000
E-type 2+2 manual	4235/6	1966-68	£15,000	£10,000	£8,000
E-type S.1 2+2 auto FHC	4235/6	1966-68	£13,000	£9,000	£7,000
E-type S.II roadster	4235/6	1968-70	£22,000	£18,000	£12,000
E-type S.II FHC	4235/6	1968-70	£18,000	£12,000	£8,000
E-type S.II 2+2 manual FHC	4235/6	1968-70	£15,000	£10,000	£8,000
E-type S.III roadster	5343/12	1971-75	£32,000	£22,000	£15,000
E-type S.III 2+2 manual FHC	5343/12	1971-75	£19,000	£14,000	£10,000
E-type S.III 2+2 auto FHC	5343/12	1971-75	£17,000	£12,000	£9,000
Jaguar XJS manual	5343/12	1975-78	£6,000	£4,500	£2,500
Jaguar XJS auto	5343/12	1975-81	£4,000	£2,200	£1,500

Make: Jaguar
Model: E-Type (6 cyl)
Type: Sports Car/Sports Coupé
Years Manufactured: 1961-71
Quantity: 57,230
Price when new: Series II, 2+2 Fixed Head Coupé, £2,799
Engine Type: 6 cyl
Size: 3781cc/4235cc
Max Power: 3781cc, 265 bhp @ 5500 rpm; 4.2 litre, 265 bhp @ 5400 rpm
Max Torque: 3781cc, 260 ft/lb @ 4000 rpm; 4.2 litre, 283 ft/lb @ 4000 rpm
Transmission: 4 speed, auto option on 2+2 from March 1966
Wheelbase: 2 seater, 96in; 2+2, 105in
Performance: Max speed: 4.2 litre, 153 mph; 0-60: 4.2 litre, 7.6 secs; Mpg: 4.2 litre, 20.

1969 Jaguar E-Type 2+2 Automatic.
£12,500-13,000   *FOR*

1974 Jaguar E-Type V12 Series III Roadster, chassis No. UE1523877BW, engine No. 751504LB, overhead camshafts, capacity 5343cc, 314bhp, 4 speed automatic gearbox, 4 wheel servo disc brakes, all round independent suspension, left-hand drive.
Est. **£50,000-80,000**   *C*

1972 Jaguar E-Type V12 Roadster, chassis No. 151211, engine No. 7551185A, 5343cc.
Est. **£28,000-33,000**   *LF*

1974 Jaguar E-Type V12 Roadster Automatic, engine No. 7S1332058, capacity 5343cc, 36,900 miles from new.
Est. **£55,000-60,000**   *Ren*

1974 Jaguar E-Type Series III V12 Roadster, one owner, 25,00 miles, left-hand drive, original.
£50,000-55,000   *CTC*

1973 Jaguar E-Type Series 3, V12 Open 2 Seater, chassis No. 1S2398, engine No. 7S13393 SB, 60° V12 cylinder engine, 90mm stroke x 70mm bore, 5343cc, aluminium cylinder heads with single overhead chain driven camshafts, rated to develop 272bhp at 5,850rpm, 4 Zenith carburettors. Steel monocoque chassis, with tubular steel sub-frame to carry front suspension and engine/gearbox assembly. Independent suspension by wishbone and torsion bars at front, and coil spring/damper units with locating arms and drive-shaft link at rear; ventilated disc type brakes, in board at rear, with vacuum booster; rack and pinion, power assisted steering; 4 speed, all synchromesh gearbox; ventilated steel disc type wheels, chromium plated, with E70 VR 15 tyres. Est. **£120,000-150,000**   *C(A)*

974 Jaguar E-Type Series III 12 Roadster, 60° V12 cylinder, ater-cooled engine, overhead alve, overhead camshaft, 90mm ore x 70mm stroke, 5343cc, 4 speed utomatic gearbox, hypoid rear xle, independent front and rear uspension, wheelbase 105in, tyres 5in. st. **£65,000-75,000**   *S*

975 Jaguar E-Type V12 oadster Commemorative lodel, chassis No. 1S2853BW, ngine No. 7S16477-SA, 60° V12 linder, water-cooled, overhead lves, overhead camshaft, 90mm re x 70mm stroke, capacity 343cc, Borg Warner 3 speed utomatic transmission, hypoid ar axle, independent front and ar springs, wheelbase 105in, tyres in. st. **£70,000-90,000**   *S*

The last 50 machines built were produced as a commemorative edition, and were painted black and fitted with factory hard tops and soft tops, with various other special details.

1974 Jaguar E-Type V12 Roadster, chassis No. UE1S23942BW, engine No. 7514834LB, capacity 5343cc, chrome wire wheels.
£31,500-32,000 *LF*

Over 77% of the production of the Mk III E-Type (the V12) was produced for export. The Mk III Roadster gave far more room than the earlier Roadsters because it was on the longer chassis which had previously only been used for the hard-top versions.

1978 Jaguar XJS Automatic.
£2,500-3,000 *CMA*

1989 Jaguar D-Type Replica, chassis No. 1B5757DN, engine No. 7B65448, capacity 3442cc, 6 cylinder.
Est. **£36,000-42,000** *LF*

A fine replica example of the legendary racing car of the 1950s professionally built by Peter Thurston at Herne Bay. The chassi is by Reynard.

1981 Lister Jaguar XJS Coupé, V12 cylinder engine, single overhead camshaft per bank, 93mm bore x 70mm stroke, 5707cc, single dry plate clutch, 5 speed manual gearbox, open propellor shaft, hypoid bevel drive rear axle unit, independent front and rear suspension, wheelbase 102in, tyres 225 x 50 VR 16in.
£8,500-9,500 *S*

The XJS introduced in the mid 70s as a replacement for the V12 E-Type Jaguar was conceived as a luxurious fast touring car rather than an out and out sports car.

1955 Jaguar Mk VIIM Sports Saloon, 6 cylinder in-line engine, water-cooled monobloc, twin overhead camshafts, bore 83mm x stroke 106mm, 3442cc, 4 speed gearbox with overdrive, Borg and Beck clutch, hypoid bevel final drive, independent front suspension, leaf springs at rear, wheelbase 120in, 6.70 x 16in tyres.
Est. **£10,000-13,000** *S(A)*

1955 Jaguar Mk VIIM Sports Saloon, 6 cylinder in-line engine, water-cooled monobloc, twin overhead camshafts, bore 83mm x stroke 106mm, 3442cc, 3 speed automatic gearbox, hypoid bevel final drive, independent front suspension, leaf springs rear, wheelbase 120in, 6.50 x 16in tyre:
Est. **£10,000-13,000** *S(A)*

1964 Jaguar Mk II Saloon, 3.4 litre, right-hand drive, manual gearbox with overdrive, restored.
£24,500-25,500 *Mar*

1966 Jaguar Mk II 2.4 Litre Saloon.
Est. **£6,000-8,000** *B*

Make: Jaguar
Model: Mk VII, VIII, IX
Type: Saloon
Years Manufactured: 1951-61
Price when new: Mk IX, £1,948
Engine Type: Mk IX, twin overhead camshaft 6 cyl
Size: 3781cc
Max Power: Mk IX, 220 bhp @ 5500 rpm
Transmission: Auto, 4 speed plus overdrive optional
Performance: Max speed: Mk IX, 115 mph; 0-60: Mk IX, 11 secs; Mpg: Mk IX, 12-18.

1948 Jaguar 3½ Litre Drop Head Coupé.
£36,000-38,000   *DJ*

1947 Jaguar 3½ Litre Saloon, left-hand drive.
£32,000-35,000   *DJ*

1950 Jaguar Mk V Drop Head Coupé, 6 cylinders, 3485cc.
£35,000-40,000   *ADT*

1958 Jaguar Mk I M.O.D., engine XF 3042 8, 6 cylinder, 3442cc, registration number included.
£15,000-16,000   *Ren*

1956 Jaguar Mk VII Automatic, ?,000 miles, original vehicle.
£23,000-24,000   *DJ*

1959 Jaguar Mk I 3.4 Litre Saloon, engine 6 cylinder, 3442cc, 4 speed manual gearbox with overdrive, left-hand drive.
£11,000-13,000   *LF*

The Mk I was the first of the stylish saloons of the late 50s and early 60s, incorporating the proven XK engine.

1961 Jaguar Mk II 3.8 Litre Saloon, in good original condition, converted to right-hand drive, resprayed, engine overhauled.
£25,000-26,000   *RSC*

1961 Jaguar Mk IX Automatic.
£34,500-35,500   *DJ*

Make	FRANCE	GERMANY	ITALY	JAPAN	USA
Jaguar	—	+5%	—	+3%	−3%

1961 Jaguar Mk II 2.4 Litre Automatic.
£7,750-8,250   *Cen*

Make: Jaguar
Model: Mk II
Type: Saloon
Years Manufactured: 1959-69
Quantity: 90,640
Price when new: £1,611
Engine Type: 6 cyl
Size: 2483cc/3781cc
Max Power: 120-220 bhp
Transmission: 4 speed, optional overdrive, auto
Performance: Max speed: 3.8 Mk II, 125 mph; 0-60: 3.8 Mk II, 8.5 secs; Mpg: 3.8 Mk II, 16.

1962 Jaguar Mk II 3.8 Litre Saloon, much restoration, new leather interior, louvred bonnet, chrome wire wheels.
£28,000-30,000   *RSC*

1961 Jaguar Mk II 3.8 Litre Automatic, 6 cylinders, 3781c totally restored.
£16,000-17,000   *ADT*

1963 Jaguar Mk II 2.4 Litre Saloon, recorded mileage 22,00 stored in a barn for many years
£4,600-6,000   *ADT*

1964 Jaguar Mk II 2.4 Litre Saloon, 6 cylinders, 2483cc.
£8,000-12,000   *LF*

Introduced in 1959 to replace the earlier model and amongst the improvements was the increase in width of the rear track by 3.75in. This improved the handling.

1963 Jaguar Mk II Sports Saloon.
Est. **£13,000-16,000**   *S(A)*

1968 Jaguar Mk II 2.4 Lit
6 cylinders, 2483cc.
£9,000-13,000   *ADT*

1964 Jaguar Mk II 3.4 Litre,
6 cylinders, 3400cc.
£7,500-8,500   *ADT*

1968 Jaguar 240 2.4 Litre Manual.
£5,000-6,000   *Cen*

*From 1967, the Jaguar Mk II 2.4
was designated 240 and fitted with
the E-Type's straight port cylinder
head. The model was a derivative of
the luxuriously equipped Mk I with
modifications to include divided
grille, recessed front foglamps,
revised dashboard and seats.*

**1964 Jaguar Mk II 3.4 Litre
Sports Saloon,** 6 cylinder in line,
water-cooled monobloc engine,
overhead valves, 3442cc, 83mm
bore x 106mm stroke, 3 speed
automatic gearbox, shaft drive to
live rear axle, coil and leaf spring
suspension, tyres 600/640 x 15in,
right-hand drive.
£13,500-14,500   *S*

*The Mk II Jaguars were first
produced at Browns Lane in 1955
and fuelled a production run that
continued, with assorted variations,
until 1969.*

1968 Jaguar 240.
£5,000-6,000   *CMA*

*The Jaguar 240 was essentially a
Mk II in its last year of production. It
used SU carburettors and a new
refined all synchromesh gearbox.*

1968 Jaguar 340 Automatic.
£9,000-10,000   *Cen*

*From 1967 the Jaguar Mk II 3.4
Litre was designated the 340.*

1966 Jaguar 420G, 28,000 miles,
original condition.
£9,500-10,000   *RH*

JAGUAR

1967 Jaguar 420S Saloon.
£14,500-15,500 *Cen*

Make: Jaguar
Model: S-Type/420
Type: Saloon
Years Manufactured: 1966-68
Quantity: 24,900
Price when new: 420, £2,054
Engine Type: 420, twin overhead camshaft 6 cyl
Size: 4235cc
Max Power: 420, 245 bhp @ 5400 rpm
Transmission: 4 speed, optional overdrive, or auto
Performance: Max speed: 420, 117 mph; 0-60: 420, 9 secs; Mpg: 420, 15-20.

1968 Jaguar 340 Automatic,
6 cylinders, 3442cc.
£9,000-10,000 *LF*

1968 Jaguar 'S' Type, 60,000 miles, excellent, unrestored condition.
£13,000-13,500 *RH*

1977 Jaguar XJ Coupé,
6 cylinders, 4235cc.
£3,200-4,000 *LF*

1977 was the last year that the XJ6C was built. It was introduced in 1973 with the advent of the Mk II XJ Saloons, but was phased out in 1977 when the short wheelbase saloon, on which it was based, also went. These cars were capable of over 120mph and of producing 245bhp, some 6,500 cars having been built in total.

JENSEN

Richard and Allen Jensen, the firm's founders, moved from coachbuilding into motor car manufacture in 1936 with the Jensen S Type. Jensen have a history of producing stylish sports/GT cars with handbuilt English bodies usually coupled with large American engines. Ronald Healey joined the company in the early '70s and the Jensen Healey was produced. The company is best known for the Interceptor series of the '60s and '70s, the Mark III of which had a 7.2 litre Chrysler V8 engine.

1956 Jensen 541, fully restored.
£9,500-10,500 *GWC*

1958 Jensen 541 R 2+2 Sports Coupé, Austin straight 6 cylinder, water-cooled monobloc engine, overhead valve, 3993cc, 4 speed manual transmission, shaft drive to live rear axle, semi-elliptic leaf spring suspension, part restored condition, requiring further work, most parts are present to complete the car.
£8,250-9,000 *S*

MAKE Jensen	ENGINE	DATES	CONDITION 1	2	3
541/541R/541S	3993/6	1954-63	£8,000	£5,000	£3,500
CV8 Mk I-III	5916/ 6276/8	1962-66	£10,000	£6,000	£4,000
Interceptor	6276/8	1967-76	£10,000	£7,000	£4,500
Interceptor SP	7212/8	1971/76	£15,000	£11,000	£8,500
Interceptor	6276/8	1974-76	£33,000	£20,000	£13,500
FF	6766/8	1967-71	£24,000	£16,000	£11,000
Healey	1973/4	1972-76	£5,000	£3,000	£1,500
Healey GT	1973/4	1975-76	£6,000	£3,000	£2,000

Make: Jensen
Model: Interceptor/FF
Type: Coupé/Convertible
Years Manufactured: 1966-76
Quantity: 5,577/320
Price when new: 6276cc, £3,743
Engine Type: V8 cyl
Size: 6276cc/7210cc
Max Power: 325-385 bhp
Transmission: 4 speed or auto
Performance: Max speed: Mk I, 133 mph; 0-60: Mk I, 7.3 secs; Mpg: Mk I, 14.

968 Jensen Interceptor FF eries 1 Coupé, 90° V8 cylinder ngine, water-cooled, overhead lve, 108mm bore x 86mm stroke, 276cc, Torqueflite 3 speed utomatic transmission with torque nverter, Ferguson Formula wheel drive, independent front spension, semi-elliptic dual rate ar springs, wheelbase 109in, tyres in.
0,000-22,000 *S*

1966 Jensen CV8 Mk III, 25,000 miles.
£25,000-26,000 *DJ*

1968 Jensen Interceptor Mk I Racing Saloon, V8 engine, overhead valve, 6250cc, 450bhp, 4 speed manual gearbox, hydraulic 4 wheel ventilated disc brakes, independent front and semi-elliptic rear suspension, right-hand drive, one of only 11 Mk I manual saloons built, subject to complete rebuild and race preparation.
Est. £25,000-30,000   C

In the post-war period Jensen produced a number of differing models and from 1949-55 produced a 6 cylinder Interceptor followed by the 541 series. In 1961 the CV8 was introduced with a Chrysler V8 engine and was succeeded in 1966 by the re-introduced Interceptor series which was a very stylish Grand Touring car retaining the same engine.

1972 Jensen Interceptor S.P., V8 engine, 110mm bore x 90mm stroke, 7212cc, 6 choke carburettor, 3 speed Torqueflite automatic transmission, independent front suspension by double wishbones, rear semi-elliptic springs and live axle, wheelbase 105in.
£10,000-11,000   S

In 1971 the Mk III version was introduced with a high performance variant which was the S.P., with 7 litres and a claimed 330bhp. This was the most powerful Interceptor ever produced. Some 62 right-hand drive examples were manufactured.

1972 Jensen Interceptor Mk III, J Series.
£25,000-30,000   CTC

1972 Jensen Interceptor Mk III, in immaculate condition, 24,000 miles recorded.
£25,000-26,000   DJ

1974 Jensen Interceptor Mk III
£11,750-12,500   CMA

In April 1973 Autosport tested a Mk III and recorded a 0-60 time of 6.4 seconds with a top speed of 140mph.

1973 Jensen Interceptor Mk III Coupé, V8 cylinder, water-cooled monobloc engine, overhead valve, 4.32in bore x 3.75in stroke, 7212cc, 3 speed automatic transmission, independent coil spring front suspension, semi-elliptic dual rate rear springs, wheelbase 109in, tyres 15in.
£18,000-20,000   S

1974 Jensen Interceptor Mk III.
£5,000-6,000   Cen

JENSEN HEALEY

1975 Jensen Healey GT, fully restored.
£6,950-7,500   *GWC*

1976 Jensen Healey Mk II 5 Sp, fully restored.
£9,250-10,250   *APP*

JOWETT

The first Jowett was produced by Benjamin and William Jowett in 1906, and by 1920 over 100 cars a week were being made. Before the company was wound up in 1954 they had shaken the British motor industry after the second World War with the design and introduction of both the Javelin and Jupiter models. The Jowett Car Club has its own spare parts company.

1939 Jowett Saloon Twin Cylinder.
£12,000-12,500   *DB*

1951 Jowett Javelin Saloon, horizontally opposed flat 4 cylinder, 1486cc engine, 4 speed gearbox, shaft drive to live rear axle, independent torsion bar front suspension, semi-elliptic leaf spring rear suspension.
£3,740-4,500   *S*

1924 Jowett Type C 7hp Two Seater with Dickey, with twin cylinder, horizontally opposed, water-cooled engine, with side valves and non-detachable cylinder heads, bore 75.4mm x stroke 101.5mm, capacity 907cc, thermo-syphon cooling, gravity feed petrol from scuttle tank, 3 speed gearbox, cone clutch, spiral bevel axle, semi-elliptic springs front and rear, Sankey type artillery wheels, 19in tyres.
£7,500-8,500   *S*

Built in Idle, Yorkshire by William and Bejamin Jowett who earned a reputation for reliability and economy, its advertising slogan was 'The little engine with the big pull'. The Edwardian designed engine in only slightly modified form powered Jowett vehicles up to the Bradford vans of the early 1950s with their notable exhaust beat.

1952 Jowett Javelin.
Est. **£2,000-3,000**   *LF*

JOWETT

MAKE	ENGINE	DATES	CONDITION		
Jowett			1	2	3
Javelin	1486/4	1947-54	£4,000	£3,000	£1,000
Jupiter	1486/4	1950-54	£8,000	£5,000	£3,500

Miller's is a price GUIDE not a price LIST

1950 Jowett Jupiter, with 4 cylinder engine and right-hand drive, in need of restoration. Est. **£4,000-6,000**   *C*

After the war the sole model on offer by Jowett was the Javelin, with independent torsion bar suspension front and rear, rigid unitary body chassis construction, good aerodynamic shape, light weight and high gearing with fine handling.

1953 Jowett Jupiter Sports Roadster, horizontally opposed flat 4 cylinder, 1486cc engine, 4 speed gearbox, shaft drive to live rear axle, independent torsion bar front suspension, semi-elliptic leaf spring rear suspension. **£18,000-20,000**   *S*

The car was capable of 90mph but only 1,200 were made before the company's demise in 1954.

JEWETT

The Jewett was one of the sturdy American cars which dominated the NZ car market in the 1920s. They were well sprung, with a high clearance and handled the primitive roads better than European models. Named after H. M. Jewett, the president of the Paige Motor Company, the Jewett was in reality a smaller Paige sold as a make on its own. It was a popular car and more than 40,000 of various models were sold.

1925 Jewett 23/25 Two Door Sedan, 6 cylinder in-line engine, water-cooled monobloc, side valve, bore 3¼in, 3980cc, developing 63hp at 2,800rpm, crash 3 speed gearbox, mechanical clutch, hydraulic brakes, leaf spring suspension, wheelbase 114in. **£11,500-15,500**   *S(A)*

KOUGAR

1988 Kougar Sports, 6 cylinder, 3781cc engine capacity, a 3.8 S-Type Jaguar donor vehicle, built in 1988 with 1,600 miles recorded. **£11,000-11,500**   *LF*

1964/83 Kougar Sports, with a 3.8 Jaguar S-type engine with 24,000 miles recorded. **£9,000-10,000**   *LF*

The Kougar was conceived by Dick Crosthwaite and John Gardiner, restorers specialising in Frazer-Nashes and Bugattis, who were joined by Rick Stevens, an aeronautical engineer, and the Kougar was born.

LAND ROVER

1948 Land Rover Series 1 Station Wagon, with 4 cylinder, 2000cc engine with overhead inlet, side exhaust, 4 speed gearbox with synchromesh 3rd and 4th, transfer gearbox with high and low range, constant 4 wheel drive, right-hand drive.
£5,500-6,000   *C*

The Land Rover first appeared in 1948 using the earlier Rover 60 engine, changing to the later 2 litre unit in 1951.

MAKE	ENGINE	DATES	CONDITION		
Land Rover			1	2	3
Land Rover Ser I	1595/4	1948-51	£2,200	£1,000	£500
Land Rover Ser I	1995/4	1951-53	£2,000	£1,000	£300
Land Rover Ser I	1995/4	1953-58	£2,000	£1,000	£300
Land Rover Ser I	1995/4	1953-58	£2,800	£1,500	£750
Land Rover Ser 2	1995/4	1958-59	£2,000	£950	£500
Land Rover Ser 2	1995/4	1958-59	£2,800	£1,200	£500
Land Rover Ser 2	2286/4	1959-71	£2,000	£950	£500
Land Rover Ser 2	2286/4	1959-71	£2,500	£1,200	£500
Range Rover	3528/V8	1970-	£2,200	£1,200	£600

LAGONDA

Founded by an American, Wilber Gunn, in 1906, Lagonda cars enjoyed much success and indeed founded their famous reputation between 1925 and 1940. David Brown bought the company in 1947 and it became part of Aston Martin. The name is still featured on the luxury Aston Martin range.

1930 Lagonda 3 Litre Special Tourer, 6 cylinder in line, water-cooled monobloc engine, pushrod operated overhead valves, 72mm bore x 120mm stroke, 2931cc, 4 speed gearbox, single plate clutch, enclosed shaft, spiral bevel rear axle, semi-elliptic leaf spring suspension front and rear, wheelbase 129in, tyres 5.20/6.00 x 20in.
£75,000-80,000   *S*

LOMBARD

1928 Lombard Type AL3, with supercharged 4 cylinder engine, with gear driven twin overhead camshafts, 61.5mm bore x 92mm stroke, capacity 1093cc, built up crankshaft carried on ball bearings, with roller bearing big ends, rated to develop approximately 90bhp, channel section side members chassis, with 5 cross members, underslung at rear, front and rear axles carried on semi-elliptic springs with friction type shock absorbers, 4 speed sliding mesh type gearbox, with central charge, Perrot type rod operated brakes, 4 wheel with 12in drums, centre lock wire type wheels carrying 5.00 x 16 racing tyres.
Est. £125,000-130,000   *C(A)*

Lombards were successfully campaigned in the popular 1100cc Classic in Europe and England during the late 20s/early 30s.

LANCHESTER

1933 Lanchester 10hp Romney Coupé, 4 cylinder in line, water-cooled monobloc engine, overhead valves, 63.5mm bore x 95mm stroke, 1203cc, 4 speed self-changing pre-selector gearbox, shaft drive to live rear axle, semi-elliptic leaf spring suspension with hydraulic shock absorbers.
Est. £10,000-12,000   *S*

Locate the source

The source of each illustration in Miller's can be found by checking the code letters below each caption with the list of contributors

1932 Lagonda Two Litre 'Supercharged' T3 Tourer, with 4 cylinder in-line 1954cc engine, bore 72mm x stroke 120mm, twin overhead camshaft overhead valves, Zoller 7lb boost pressure supercharger, single SU carburettor, 75bhp at 4,500rpm, low style pressed steel box section chassis with tubular cross section, semi-elliptic springs front and rear suspension with adjustable shock absorbers, 4 speed gearbox plus reverse, right-hand gear control, 21in Rudge Whitworth wheels with centre lock wire spoke and 4.50-4.75 x 21in tyres, 14in drum brakes on all 4 wheels, handbrake on rear wheels only, wheelbase 120in, track front and rear 54in.
Est. **£80,000-90,000**   *C*

1933 Lagonda 16/80, with T7 4 seater coachwork, used in the BBC series Campion, with 6 cylinder, 1991cc engine capacity.
Est. **£40,000-50,000**   *ADT*

Wilbur Adams Gun named his cars after Lagonda Creek, Ohio, which had been his American home until 1890. Born the second child of the Reverend J. W. Gunn, Wilbur bought a large home in Staines after being apprenticed to the Singer Sewing Machine Company and various ambitions at becoming an opera singer and musician. The greenhouse at Staines was converted into a workshop and with the help of Alfie Cranmer, started to manufacture motorcycles and later tricars. The first 4 wheeled cars appeared in 1907 but the company only became famous in the late 1920s with the advent of the 2 litre model.

1938 Lagonda LG6 4½ Litre Drop Head Coupé.
£71,000-73,000   *B*

1938 Lagonda V12 Saloon, partly restored.
£30,000-32,000   *DB*

1939 Lagonda V12 Four Door Saloon, V12 overhead valve water-cooled bi-bloc engine, 75mm bore x 84.5mm stroke, 4480cc, single dry plate clutch, 4 speed manual gearbox, hypoid rear axle, wheelbase 124in, tyres 6.50 x 18in.
Est. **£38,000-40,000**   *S*

MAKE	ENGINE	DATES	CONDITION		
Lagonda			1	2	3
3 Litre	2922/6	1953-58	£12,000	£7,000	£4,500
3 Litre DHC	2922/6	1953-56	£15,000	£12,000	£8,500
Rapide	3995/6	1961/64	£11,000	£7,000	£4,500

**1953 Lagonda 3 Litre Drop Head
Coupé,** 6 cylinder in line,
water-cooled monobloc engine, twin
overhead camshaft, 83mm bore x
90mm stroke, 2992cc, 4 speed
manual gearbox, single dry plate
clutch, hypoid bevel rear axle,
independent front and rear
suspension, wheelbase 113½in,
tyres 16in.
£33,000-35,000 *S*

**1927 Lagonda 14/60 Two Litre
Sports Tourer,** 4 cylinder in line,
water-cooled monobloc engine, twin
high camshafts, 72mm bore x
120mm stroke, 1954cc, 4 speed
gearbox, single plate clutch, spiral
bevel rear axle, semi-elliptic leaf
springs front and rear, wheelbase
10in, tyres 5.50 x 21in. The car is
complete, in excellent condition.
£33,000-35,000 *S*

The Lagonda 14/60 announced in
August 1925 replaced the somewhat
dated 12/24 model and offered more
performance combined with superior
quality both in engineering and
coachwork. In tourer form the car
was quite expensive, retailing in
1927 at £650, nevertheless some 400
or so examples of the 14/60 and
2 litre cars left the factory each year
during the first 3 years of production.

**1950 Lagonda 2½ Litre Four
Door Saloon,** 6 cylinder in line,
water-cooled monobloc engine,
overhead valves, 78mm bore x
90mm stroke, 2580cc, 4 speed David
Brown synchromesh gearbox, Borg
and Beck single plate clutch, hypoid
bevel rear axle, independent front
and rear suspension, wheelbase
113½in, tyres 6.00 x 16in.
Est. £12,000-15,000 *S*

W. O. Bentley had been working on
the development of the new Lagonda
during the war years and the
injection of cash following the
takeover of Lagonda by David
Brown in 1947 enabled the new car
to be launched. It had a new twin
camshaft engine of 2.6 litre capacity,
which was to go on to greater fame in
the later DB Series Aston Martin.
The Feltham-built cars had the
David Brown gearbox and offered
fast and luxurious motoring.
Courtenay Edwards, writing in The
Daily Mail described the car as
having 'such good manners at
90mph' and this became the
advertising slogan for the model.

LAMBORGHINI

Tractor and air-conditioning manufacturer Ferruccio Lamborghini started the company in 1963. The Muira of 1966 was a sensation, as was the Countach in the early 1980s. Arguably the ultimate dream machine.

1967 Lamborghini 350GT Two Door Coupé, 60° V12 cylinder, water-cooled engine, twin overhead camshafts per bank, 77mm bore x 62mm stroke, 3464cc, 5 speed ZF gearbox, single dry plate clutch, bevel rear axle, independent front and rear suspension with coil springs and telescopic shock absorbers, wheelbase 100½in, tyres 15in.
£130,000-135,000   *S(M)*

1975 Lamborghini Urraco.
Est. **£32,000-40,000**   *LF*

The body was designed by Bertone has the V8 2500cc engine, which produces 220bhp and 140mph and it is thought that only 35 right-hand drive models were built.

1971 Lamborghini P400 Miura S, engine transversely located, mid mounted 60° V12 cylinder, 82mm bore x 62mm stroke, capacity 3929cc, rated to develop 370bhp at 7,000rpm, aluminium alloy block and cylinder heads, 4 chain driven overhead camshafts, 4 3-barrel Weber carburettors, dry sump lubrication, fabricated sheet steel chassis with independent suspension front and rear by wishbones and coil springs, right-hand drive, 5 speed synchromesh gearbox combined as a unit with the engine and final drive gearing, 4 wheel ventilated disc type brakes with vacuum servos, centre lock magnesium alloy wheels carrying 215/70 VR 15 tyres. Est. **£125,000-150,000**   *C(A)*

1969 Lamborghini Muira P400S Coupé, 60°, V12 configuration transversely mid mounted, overhead valve, 82mm bore x 62mm stroke, 3929cc, 5 speed manual, all synchromesh gearbox, 4 wheel disc brakes, independent coil suspension, wheelbase 98½in, tyres 25 x 15in, left-hand drive. Est. **£170,000-190,000**   *S(M)*

The Miura derived its name from the famous and ferocious Spanish fighting bull.

Make: Lamborghini
Model: Miura
Type: Sports Coupé
Years Manufactured: 1966-73
Quantity: 763
Price when new: £8,050
Engine Type: V12 cyl
Size: 3929cc
Max Power: Miura SV, 385 bhp @ 7850 rpm
Max Torque: 294 ft/lb @ 5750 rpm
Transmission: 5 speed
Performance: Max speed: 370 bhp, 172 mph; 0-60: 370bhp, 6.7 secs; Mpg: 370 bhp 14.

Locate the source

The source of each illustration in Miller's can be found by checking the code letters below each caption with the list of contributors

Miller's is a price Guide not a price List

The price ranges given reflect the average price a purchaser should pay for similar vehicle. Condition, rarity, provenance, racing history, originality and any restoration are factors that must be taken into account when assessing values. When buying or selling, it must always be remembered that prices can be greatly affected by the condition of any vehicle. Unless otherwise stated, all cars shown in Miller's are of good merchantable quality, and the valuations given reflect this fact. Vehicles offered for sale in exceptionally fine condition or in poor condition may reasonably be expected to be priced considerably higher or lower respectively than the estimates given herein

Lamborghini Espada Series III Coupé, chassis/engine No. 9448, chassis built by Marchesi, bodywork by Bertone in Grugliasco, 60° V12 cylinder, water-cooled engine, twin overhead camshafts per bank, 82mm bore x 62mm stroke, 3929cc, 5 speed synchromesh gearbox, single dry plate clutch, constant velocity final drive shafts, independent front and rear suspension with double transverse wishbones with coil springs, telescopic Koni dampers and anti-roll bars, wheelbase 104½in, tyres 15in.
Est. **£45,000-55,000**   *S(M)*

The Espada developed over a long production run and some 1,217 cars in total were produced, making it the best selling of Lamborghini models.

Make: Lamborghini
Model: Espada
Type: Sports Saloon
Years Manufactured: 1968-78
Quantity: 1,217
Engine Type: V12 cyl
Size: 3929cc
Max Power: Series III, 365 bhp @ 7500 rpm
Max Torque: Series III, 300 ft/lb @ 5500 rpm
Transmission: 5 speed or auto
Wheelbase: 104.3in
Performance: Max speed: 325 bhp, 150 mph; 0-60: 325 bhp, 7.8 secs; Mpg: 325 bhp, 16.

Make	FRANCE	GERMANY	ITALY	JAPAN	USA
Lamborghini	+5%	—	+2%	+5%	+6%

LANCIA

The 5.2 litre engine delivers 455bhp at 7,000rpm, producing a 0-60mph time under 6 seconds and 100mph in less than 12 seconds.

1975 Lamborghini Urraco P300,
8 cylinder in 90° V formation, single overhead camshaft per bank, 86mm bore x 64.5mm stroke, 2996cc, 5 speed manual gearbox, transaxle and spur gear final drive, independent front and rear suspension by coil springs and wishbone, maximum speed over 150mph.
£39,000-42,000 *S*

1987 Lamborghini Countach QV,
12 cylinder, 5176cc engine.
Est. **£175,000-195,000** *ADT*

LANCIA

Although the company was founded in 1906 by Vincenzo Lancia the Lambda model of the 1920s set the reputation that Lancia enjoy for innovation. Lancia made some very good motor cars but were unable to compete with Fiat or Alfa Romeo. Since 1969 Lancia has been owned by Fiat.

1957 Lancia Aurelia B24 Pininfarina Spyder, 60° V6 cylinder, water-cooled engine, pushrod operated overhead valves, 78mm bore x 85.5mm stroke, 2451cc, 4 speed gearbox, single dry plate clutch, spiral bevel rear axle, sliding pillar independent front suspension, de Dion rear axle with semi-elliptic leaf springs, Panhard rod and telescopic shock absorbers wheelbase 96½in.
Est. **£70,000-80,000** *S(M)*

1915 Lancia Theta 35HP.
£12,000-13,000 *P*

1971 Lancia Fulvia Coupé,
4 cylinders, 1298cc.
£1,700-2,000 *ADT*

1963 Lancia Flaminia Coup
with 6 cylinder, 2458cc engin
Est. **£10,000-12,000** *ADT*

1967 Lancia Flavia 1.8 Injection Sports Coupé, with coachwork by Pininfarina, flat 4 cylinder, water-cooled engine, overhead valves, bore 88mm x stroke 74mm, capacity 1800cc, developing 102bhp, front wheel drive, leaf spring and coil suspension, and 175/70 HR 15 tyres.
Est. **£4,500-5,500** *S*

961 Lancia Flaminia Convertible.
30,000-35,000 *SNY*

1971 Lancia Fulvia Coupé, V4 cylinder engine, water-cooled monobloc, overhead valves, 1298cc, front wheel drive, independent coil spring suspension front and rear.
£3,000-4,000 *S*

ancia Monte Carlo SII ody kit, 8,000 miles.
14,500-15,500 *Hu*

1976 Lancia Fulvia Rallye S3 Coupé, 4 cylinder, narrow V formation, water-cooled monobloc engine, 2 overhead camshafts, overhead valves, 77mm bore x 69.7mm stroke, 1298cc, single dry plate clutch, 5 speed gearbox, front suspension by transverse leaf spring and double wishbones, rear suspension of dead axle by semi-elliptic leaf springs, wheelbase 91½in, tyres 14in.
£5,500-6,000 *S*

The Fulvia 2+2 fixed head coupé was introduced in 1965 and was produced until 1976.

72 Lancia Fulvia 1.3 Zagato, ght-hand drive.
4,000-14,500 *Hu*

1962 Lancia Flaminia 3C Drop Head Coupé, by Touring of Milan, 2458cc V6 Lancia engine, 3 Solex twin choke carburettors developing 140hp at 5,600rpm.
Est. **£16,000-20,000** *P*

LEA-FRANCIS

1948 Lea-Francis Fourteen,
4 cylinder, 1767cc engine.
£2,500-3,000   *ADT*

Early in 1946 Lea-Francis launched its post-war cars using similar engines to those of the pre-war models but with bodies now made by A P Aircraft Ltd. The Fourteen engine was initially 1629cc, being later replaced by a 1.8 litre 4 cylinder unit.

1930 Lea-Francis P Type,
4 cylinder, 1496cc engine.
£19,000-21,000   *ADT*

In 1922 the manufacture of cars took on a new impetus and the 1000cc Coventry Simplex engined car was a great success. During 1928 a wider family market was sought with the introduction of the P-Type. This carried the very successful 4ED Meadows engine of 1496cc which again proved to be most successful. The 4 seater tourer version of this P-Type is the rarest model.

1948 Lea-Francis 1.8 Sports,
4 cylinder, 1767cc engine.
£20,000-22,000   *ADT*

MAKE Lea-Francis	ENGINE	DATES	CONDITION 1	2	3
12/14HP	1496/ 1767/4	1946-54	£8,000	£5,000	£1,500
14HP Sports	1767/4	1947-49	£15,000	£8,000	£3,000
14/7018HP	1767/ 2496/4	1949-53	£9,000	£4,000	£2,000
2½ Litre Sports	2496/4	1950-53	£20,000	£15,000	£7,000

LINCOLN

1946 Lincoln Continental, with 12 cylinder, 4998cc engine.
Est. **£4,000-5,000**   *ADT*

1938 Lincoln Zephyr 4.4 Lit Four Door Convertible.
Est. **£8,000-12,000**   *P*

MAKE Lincoln	ENGINE	DATES	CONDITION 1	2	3
Premiere Coupé	368/8	1956-57	£9,000	£6,000	£4,000
Premier Conv	368/8	1956-57	£19,000	£14,000	£8,000
Continental Mk II	368/8	1956-57	£17,000	£10,000	£6,000
Continental 2 dr	430/8	1958-60	£10,000	£6,000	£4,000
Continental Conv	430/8	1958-60	£23,000	£18,000	£10,000

1966 Lincoln Continental Four door Convertible.
Est. £8,000-10,000   *P*

LOCOMOBILE

1928 Locomobile Model 8/70 Sedan, with 8 cylinder, 3254cc engine.
Est. £20,000-23,000   *ADT*

913 Locomobile Model 30 Type Four Passenger Torpedo.
55,000-60,000   *SNY*

Locate the source

The source of each illustration in Miller's can be found by checking the code letters below each caption with the list of contributors

The Locomobile is possibly the finest quality motor car to be produced in the United States competing as it did with Rolls Royce and Stevens Duryea as the most expensive then available. Their halcyon days were from 1911 to 1929 but their origins go back to the turn of the century, with cars powered by steam.

LOTUS

tarted in a Hornsey lock-up
arage by Colin Chapman,
otus soon gained a reputation
r roadgoing sports cars and
ut and out race cars. As well
s many famous victories and
veral World Championships,
otus have also produced some
f the best British sports cars.

**962 Lotus Elite S2 Sports
oupé,** 4 cylinder in-line Coventry
imax engine, water-cooled
onobloc, single overhead
mshaft, 76.2mm bore x 66.6mm
oke, 1216cc, 95bhp at 7,000rpm,
peed gearbox, hypoid bevel rear
le, independent front and rear
spension, wheelbase 88in, tyres
n.
t. £29,000-32,000   *S*

1965 Lotus Elan S2 Drop Head Coupé.
£10,000-14,000   *KSC*

Lotus Elan S4/SE Fixed Head Coupé.
£8,000-15,000   *KSC*

1972 Lotus Elan Sprint, with new
Lotus chassis, in original condition.
£17,000-18,000 *PMS*

**Lotus Elan Sprint Fixed Head
Coupé,** with new Lotus chassis, in
original condition.
£15,000-16,000 *PMS*

**Lotus Elan S3/SE Fixed Head
Coupé.**
£7,000-15,000 *KSC*

**Lotus Elan S4/SE Fixed Head
Coupé,** with gold leaf colours.
£8,000-15,000 *KSC*

**Lotus Elan Sprint Drop Head
Coupé.**
£14,000-20,000 *KSC*

1973 Lotus Elan Sprint, original
gold leaf team colours, fully restored
£25,000-30,000 *CTC*

INTERNATIONAL PRICE COMPARISON

The figures below represent a percentage increase or decrease on average condition for middle of the range
models. The top models, particularly with a racing history or proven provenance, can be considered in the market
place as any other work of art.
— = same price as U.K.

Make	FRANCE	GERMANY	ITALY	JAPAN	USA
Alfa Romeo	+	+2	+5	+5	—
Aston Martin	+4	+2	+2	—	—
Austin Healey	—	+3	+3	+5	−5
Bentley	+5	+3	—	+10	−3
Bugatti	+5	—	+10	+20	+10
Cadillac	−10	—	−2	—	—
Chevrolet	−10	—	−2	—	+1
Ferrari	+5	—	+2	+15	—
Fiat	—	—	—	+2	+2
Ford	−4	+3	−4	−5	+8
Jaguar	—	+5	—	+3	−3
Lamborghini	+5	—	—	+3	−3
Land Rover	−20	—	−5	—	−20
Maserati	+5	—	+7	+10	—
Mercedes-Benz	−5	+10	+3	−5	−5
MG	—	+7	−5	+5	+10
Mini (Austin)	+5	+3	—	+10	−15
Morris	−5	−3	−10	−10	−15
Porsche	+	+5	+3	+7	+5
Rolls-Royce	+5	—	—	+15	+7
Triumph	+2	+5	—	+2	+4
Volkswagen	+5	+5	—	—	−15

1971 Lotus Elan +2S, with new
Lotus galvanised chassis.
£9,000-10,000 *PMS*

Lotus Elan +2S 130/S.
£10,000-11,000 *KSC*

1972 Lotus Elan +2S 130, rebuilt
with new Lotus chassis, rebuilt
engine, repainted, original interior.
£11,000-12,000 *PMS*

1972 Lotus Elan +2S 130.
Est. **£9,000-10,000** *ADT*

*In 1970 Lotus developed a 'big valve'
version of their twin cam engine.
Both the Elan Sprint and the Elan
+2S received the newly developed
engine giving both cars 126bhp. The
new +2S became the +2S 130
because of this.*

1972 Lotus Europa Twin Cam,
fully restored.
£13,000-15,000 *CTC*

1973 Lotus Elan 2+2, with
4 cylinder, 1558cc engine.
Est. **£8,000-10,000** *LF*

1973 Lotus Elan 2+2 S130/S
Commemorative Model.
Est. **£12,000-15,000** *P*

Lotus Esprit Turbo, HC
Giugiaro Shape.
£22,000-23,000 *KSC*

LOTUS

1973 Lotus Europa Twin Cam
Special.
£15,000-16,000   *KSC*

Lotus Europa SII, with Renault
engine.
£5,000-5,500   *KSC*

Lotus 11, Coventry Climax engine
totally original, some racing history
£70,000-90,000   *PMS*

1981-87 Lotus Esprit Turbo.
£17,000-18,000   *KSC*

1969 Lotus Europa Series 2
Sports Coupé.
Est. £4,000-5,000   *S(A)*

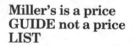

Miller's is a price
GUIDE not a price
LIST

Lotus Esprit Turbo.
£16,000-17,000   *KSC*

MASERATI

There were five Maserati
brothers who founded the
company which was taken over
by the giant Orsi Manufacturing
group in 1938. Their race cars
won fame and fortune but the
first real roadgoing motor cars
were not offered until 1947. As
manufacturers of exotic Italian
sports cars Maserati are
considered to be undervalued in
today's market.

1969 Maserati Ghibli Spyder 4.7
Litre Sports, 90° V8 cylinder,
water-cooled engine, twin overhead
camshaft per bank, 93.9mm bore x
85mm stroke, 4709cc, 5 speed
gearbox, dry single disc clutch, bevel
final drive, coil spring and telescopic
shock absorber front suspension,
semi-elliptic leaf rear springs with
telescopic shock absorbers,
wheelbase 100½in, tyres 15in.
Est. £100,000-120,000   *S(M)*

1967 Maserati Tipo 109 Mistral
Berlinetta, designed by Frua and

built by Vignale.
Est. £38,000-42,000   *P*

200

1963 Maserati 3500GT, by Touring of Milan, original car with right-hand drive.
Est. **£38,000-45,000**   *P*

Designed by Ing. Giulio Alfieri and first shown at the 1957 Geneva Motor Show, the 3500GT was based on the 350S racing engine, detuned from 325bhp to 220. Most bodies were built of aluminium by Carrozzeria Touring of Milan, although other coachbuilders such as Vignale did build a few of the 1981 cars produced between 1957 and 1964. In 1960 the engine was uprated to 260bhp and disc brakes fitted to the front wheels, a 5 speed synchromesh gearbox was available in 1961 and fuel injection as an optional extra in 1962.

1951 Maserati A6 2000 Gran Sport Frua Spyder, straight 6 cylinder, water-cooled monobloc engine, single overhead camshaft, 1954cc, 72mm bore x 80mm stroke, 4 speed manual gearbox, single dry plate clutch, independent coil spring suspension and hydraulic shock absorbers front, leaf spring and hydraulic shock absorbers rear, wheelbase 100½in, tyres 5.50 x 16in.
£228,000-230,000   *S(M)*

Maserati's A6G of 1951 used an upgraded version of the 1½ litre engine, and the 2 litre result, using triple Weber carburettors, enabled the lighter bodied cars to reach speeds approaching 100mph. Only 16 A6G cars were produced, 5 of which carried Frua's open coachwork.

1968 Maserati Mistral Spyder, coachwork by Fura, 6 cylinder in line, water-cooled monobloc engine, twin overhead camshaft, 86mm bore x 106mm stroke, 3692cc, speed gearbox, single dry plate clutch, hypoid bevel final drive, independent coil spring front suspension, semi-elliptic leaf rear springs, wheelbase 94½in, tyres 5in.
Est. **£120,000-140,000**   *S(M)*

Make: Maserati	
Model: A6/1500	
Type: Coupé	
Years Manufactured: 1946-50	
Quantity: 61	
Engine Type: Overhead camshaft 6 cyl	
Size: 1488cc	
Max Power: 65 bhp @ 4700 rpm	
Transmission: 4 speed manual	
Wheelbase: 102in	
Performance: Max speed: 95 (claimed) mph.	

1968 Maserati Ghibli 2+2 Coupé, 90° V8 cylinder, water-cooled engine, twin overhead camshafts per bank, 93.9mm bore x 85mm stroke, 4719cc, 4 speed automatic gearbox, hypoid bevel rear axle, independent coil spring front suspension, semi-elliptic leaf springs at rear, wheelbase 100½in, tyres 15in.
Est. **£75,000-85,000**   *S(M)*

1968 Maserati Ghibli Coupé,
coachwork by Ghia, 90° V8 cylinder,
water-cooled engine, twin overhead
camshafts per bank, 93.9mm bore x
89mm stroke, 4930cc, 5 speed
manual ZF gearbox, single dry plate
clutch, hypoid bevel rear axle,
independent coil spring front
suspension, leaf springs and
hydraulic shock absorbers at rear,
wheelbase 100½in, tyres 15in.
Est. £75,000-85,000   *S(M)*

1968 Maserati Ghibli Spyder, V8
cylinder, water-cooled monobloc
engine, 4 overhead camshafts,
93.9mm bore x 85mm stroke, ZF
5 speed manual gearbox, single dry
plate clutch, independent coil spring
front suspension, semi-elliptic coil
spring rear, hydraulic shock
absorbers front and rear, wheelbase
100½in, tyres 215 x 15in.
£177,500-180,000   *S(M)*

1970 Maserati Ghibli, V8 4719cc
engine, with 13,029 miles recorded.
Est. £60,000-70,000   *ADT*

*Production of the Maserati Ghibli
extended from 1966-73, during
which time only 125 examples were
made in the open version, and 1,149
cars with closed coupé coachwork.*

1974 Maserati Merak, with
6 cylinder 2980cc engine, 14,140km
recorded.
£34,000-35,000   *ADT*

*The V8 Bora prototype introduced at
the 1971 Geneva Motor Show, styled
by Ital Design, was an immediate
success and a year later a smaller V6
powered model was produced — the
Merak. The Merak engine was
already being used in the Citroën SM
and other Citroën components were
employed including the hydraulic
brake circuits, instrument panel and
steering wheel.*

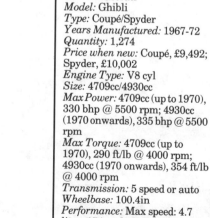

Make: Maserati	
Model: Ghibli	
Type: Coupé/Spyder	
Years Manufactured: 1967-72	
Quantity: 1,274	
Price when new: Coupé, £9,492; Spyder, £10,002	
Engine Type: V8 cyl	
Size: 4709cc/4930cc	
Max Power: 4709cc (up to 1970), 330 bhp @ 5500 rpm; 4930cc (1970 onwards), 335 bhp @ 5500 rpm	
Max Torque: 4709cc (up to 1970), 290 ft/lb @ 4000 rpm; 4930cc (1970 onwards), 354 ft/lb @ 4000 rpm	
Transmission: 5 speed or auto	
Wheelbase: 100.4in	
Performance: Max speed: 4.7 litre, 154 mph; 0-60: 4.7 litre, 7.5 secs; Mpg: 4.7 litre, 15.	

1968 Maserati Mistral, with
6 cylinder, 4012cc engine.
Est. £49,000-53,000   *ADT*

1982 Maserati Merak SS,
6 cylinder, 2965cc engine.
Est. **£29,000-30,000**   *ADT*

1974 Maserati Bora, with mid mounted 90° V8 cylinder, 93.9mm bore x 85mm stroke, capacity 4719cc, aluminium alloy block and cylinder heads with 4 overhead camshafts and 4 Weber twin choke carburettors, rated to develop 310bhp at 6,000rpm, semi-unitary construction chassis with tubular steel frame members, independent front and rear suspension by wishbones and coil springs/damper units, right-hand drive, ZF 5 speed synchromesh gearbox, 4 wheel ventilated disc brakes power operated by Citroën hydraulic system, magnesium alloy disc wheels, carrying 215/70 VR 15 tyres.
Est. **£55,000-60,000**   *C(A)*

1977 Maserati Merak SS.
Est. **£30,000-40,000**   *P*

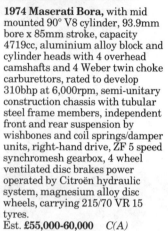

1976 Maserati Merak SS, with 40,000 miles recorded, engine and body totally rebuilt.
Est. **£45,000-47,000**   *FOR*

976 Maserati Khamsin,
cylinder, 4900cc engine capacity,
ne engine has been completely
ebuilt.
28,500-29,500   *ADT*

*he Khamsin first appeared in 1972
nd 3 years later entered production
ith styling by Bertone.*

1972 Maserati Indy America 2+2 Coupé, by Vignale, with V8, 4719cc engine.
Est. **£20,000-25,000**   *Ren*

1981 Maserati Quattroporte Auto, by Frua, engine V8, 4930cc.
Est. **£15,000-17,000**   *Ren*

'82 Maserati Kyalami SS.
t. **£25,000-30,000**   *Ren*

MASERATI

MATHIS EMY

**1933 Mathis Emy Four Door
Saloon,** 4 cylinder in line,
water-cooled monobloc engine, side
valve, 1400cc, 4 speed gearbox,
single dry plate clutch, bevel rear
axle, leaf spring suspension.
£4,000-5,000   *S*

**1988 Maserati 425 Bi-Turbo
Saloon,** 90° V6 cylinder,
water-cooled engine, 2491cc, turbo
charged, 5 speed manual gearbox,
shaft drive to live rear axle,
independent suspension all round,
right-hand drive.
£17,500-18,000   *S*

*The 4 door Bi-turbo was announced
in Modena in December 1983. In 2.5
litre form it was designated 425
(4 door, 2.5 litre). With 90° V6
cylinder power unit, the car can
develop 200hp at 5,500rpm. Top
speed is around 215kph, delivery
commenced in August 1984.*

MAXWELL

1915 Maxwell Four Seat Tourer
in need of total restoration.
Est. **£4,750-5,000**   *DB*

**1910 Maxwell Q3 Four Seat
Tourer,** with 22hp engine.
Est. **£13,000-18,000**   *ADT*

*The Maxwell-Briscoe Motor
Company started in 1904 and
operated until 1913 when later cars
were sold as Flanders. Many
technical features patented by
Jonathon Maxwell include multiple
steel disc clutch, force feed oilers,
universal joint and 'straight
through' exhaust converter.*

MERCEDES-BENZ

Mercedes amalgamated with Benz in 1926 and produced magnificent sports and racing cars up to the start of the war. Post-war sports cars, notably the 300 SL Gullwing and the 300 SC, continued to enhance this enviable reputation. Mercedes-Benz still manufacture very desirable motor cars, most of which, especially the sports cars, will be among the classics of tomorrow. They are also currently the world Sportscar Champions.

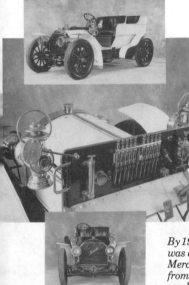

1903 Mercedes Simplex 28/32hp Rear Entrance Tonneau, 4 cylinder in-line engine, water-cooled, side valve T-head, bore 110mm x 140mm stroke, 450cu in, 4 speed gearbox, double chain drive, semi-elliptic leaf springs front and rear, wheelbase 104½in, 34 x 4½in tyres.
400,000-450,000   SNY

By 1901, the shape of the modern car was evolving. The 35hp 5.9 litre Mercedes epitomised the change from horseless carriage to car, combining the modern features of a pressed steel chassis, honeycomb radiator, and gate gearchange and mechanically operated inlet valves. The types 8/11 and 12/16 which followed, and the later 18/22, 28/32, 40/45 and 60/70hp models embodied all these features and set the pattern for a new generation of cars that were to write the history of motoring. To emphasise how easy they would be to drive in an era when cars were often difficult, they were given the name Mercedes-Simplex.

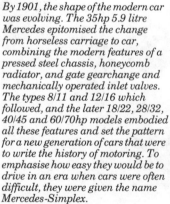

1906 Mercedes Simplex 45HP Seven Passenger Tourer with Separate Sports Body, with coachwork by Sindelfingen, 4 cylinder T-head engine, 120mm bore x 150mm stroke, 5319cc, low tension ignition, 45hp, 4 speed gearbox, double chain drive, semi-elliptic springs suspension, pedal acting on differential countershaft, and rear wheel brakes, wheelbase 96½in, 58in track.
Est. **£330,000-400,000   CNY**

1932 Mercedes-Benz 500 Nurberg 'C' Cabriolet, chassis No. M84785, engine straight eight, 4884cc, 4 speed manual gearbox, bodywork by Voll & Ruhbeck, of Berlin-Charlottenburg, it is believed that this is the only Nurberg to have been bodied by Voll & Ruhrbeck, who were Adolf Hitler's chosen coach workers. Excellent condition.
£100,000-130,000   SEN

This car would not realise the £250,000 plus figure of its similar looking contemporaries because of its somewhat underpowered side valve engine.

1935 Mercedes-Benz 170V Cabriolet Saloon Four Seater Convertible.
£10,000-12,000   *P*

The Mercedes 170 was first introduced in 1931 with a 6 cylinder, 1692cc engine and all round independent suspension. One of the rarest 170Vs was the Cabriolet Saloon, a 2 door, 4 seater convertible with a most attractive body.

1934 Mercedes-Benz 500K Cabriolet 'A'.
£400,000-450,000   *SNY*

1939 Mercedes-Benz 320 Cabriolet B, 6 cylinder, side valve engine, 85mm bore x 100mm stroke, 3405cc, 4 speed manual gearbox, 4 wheel hydraulic operated drum brakes, independent front and rear suspension, left-hand drive.
Est. **£35,000-45,000**   *C*

The 320 was introduced in February 1937 and was the successor of the 290. The 320 had a larger and more powerful engine. In the autumn of 1938 the engine capacity was increased from 3.2 to 3.4 litres.

1935 Mercedes-Benz 500K Cabriolet B, coachwork by Daimler-Benz Sindelfingen, 8 cylinder in line, water-cooled monobloc engine, overhead valves, 86mm bore x 106mm stroke, 5018cc supercharged, 3 speed manual gearbox with overdrive, single dry plate clutch, enclosed shaft spiral bevel rear axle, independent coil spring suspension front and rear, wheelbase 129½in, tyres 7.00 x 17in, right-hand drive.
£198,000-220,000   *S*

Following the merger of Daimler and Benz in 1926, Dr Ferdinand Porsche's 6 cylinder supercharger sports car design was further developed from the successful 33/140 to the 33/180 K, and on to the S Type, SS and SSKs of the late 20s and early 30s.

MAKE Mercedes	ENGINE	DATES	CONDITION 1	2	3
300AD	2996/6	1951-62	£14,000	£12,000	£8,000
220A/S/SE Ponton	2195/6	1952-60	£7,500	£3,500	£1,800
220S/SEB Coupé	2915/6	1956-59	£9,000	£5,000	£3,500
220S/SEB Cabriolet	2195/6	1958-59	£32,000	£18,000	£7,000
190SL	1897/4	1955-63	£18,000	£15,000	£12,000
300SL 'Gullwing'	2996/6	1954-57	£280,000	£250,000	£200,000
300SL Roadster	2996/6	1957-63	£260,000	£170,000	£120,000
230/250SL	2306/				
	2496/6	1963-68	£14,000	£9,000	£7,000
280SL	2778/6	1967-71	£16,000	£14,000	£8,000
220/250SE	2195/				
	2496/6	1960-68	£8,000	£6,000	£3,000
300SE	2996/6	1961-65	£12,000	£8,000	£5,000
280SE Conv	2778/6	1965-69	£30,000	£22,000	£12,000
280SE V8 Conv	3499/8	1969-71	£41,000	£20,000	£16,000
280SE Coupé	2496/6	1965-72	£9,000	£7,500	£3,000
300SEL 6.3	6330/8	1968-72	£14,000	£7,500	£3,500

1953 Mercedes-Benz Type 220 Cabriolet 'A', 6 cylinder, 2200cc engine, excellent condition, extensive history and photographs of restoration.
£57,000-58,000   *T&M*

1951 Mercedes-Benz 170S, 4 cylinder, 1697cc engine.
Est. **£4,500-5,500**   *ADT*

1952 Mercedes-Benz 300S D Convertible Sedan, 6 cylinder in-line engine water-cooled monobloc, overhead valve overhead camshaft, bore 85mm x 88mm stroke, 2996cc, manual gearbox, independent wishbone and coil spring front suspension, single jointed swing rear axle with low slung pivot and additional torsion bar springing, hypoid rear axle, wheelbase 120in, 15in tyres.
£32,000-35,000   *SNY*

1954 Mercedes-Benz Type 220A Cabriolet, 6 cylinder in-line engine, water-cooled monobloc, single overhead camshaft, overhead valve, bore 80mm x 72.8mm stroke, 2195cc, single dry plate clutch, 4 speed gearbox, hypoid bevel final drive, independent front and rear suspension, wheelbase 111in, 15in tyres.
£39,000-42,000   *SNY*

1960 Mercedes-Benz 300SL Roadster with Factory Hard Top, 6 cylinder in line, water-cooled engine, overhead camshaft, overhead valve, 85mm bore x 88mm stroke, 4 speed gearbox, single dry plate clutch, hypoid bevel rear axle, independent front suspension with coil springs and parallel wishbone arms, single joint swing axle, coil springs, shock absorbers with compensating springs at rear, wheelbase 94½in, tyres 15in.
Est. **£240,000-250,000**   *S(M)*

1957 Mercedes-Benz 190SL, excellent original condition, right-hand drive.
£27,000-28,000   *CMa*

When the 190SL was discontinued in February 1963 to be replaced by the 230SL, 26,000 examples had been sold.

1956 Mercedes-Benz 190SL Roadster, 4 cylinder, overhead camshaft engine, 1897cc, 2 horizontally-mounted 2 barrel Solex carburettors, 4 speed synchromesh gearbox, independent front and rear suspension, 4 wheel servo-assisted drum type brakes, left-hand drive.
Est. **£16,000-18,000**   *C*

1961 Mercedes-Benz 190SL Roadster, 4 cylinder in line, water-cooled monobloc engine, overhead valve, overhead camshaft, 85mm bore x 83.6mm stroke, 1897cc, 4 speed synchromesh gearbox, independent coil spring front and rear suspension, hypoid rear axle, wheelbase 106½in, tyres 13in.
Est. **£16,000-18,000**   *S*

Make: Mercedes-Benz
Model: 190SL
Type: Sports
Years Manufactured: 1954-63
Quantity: 25,881
Engine Type: Overhead camshaft 4 cyl
Size: 1897cc
Max Power: 105 bhp @ 5700 rpm
Max Torque: 105 ft/lb @ 3200 rpm
Transmission: 4 speed
Wheelbase: 94.5in
Performance: Max speed: 105+ mph; 0-60: 13.3-14.5 secs.

1961 Mercedes-Benz 190SL Roadster.
Est. **£20,000-22,000**   *S*

c1960 Mercedes-Benz 190SL Roadster, 4 cylinder in-line engine, water-cooled monobloc, overhead camshaft, bore 85mm x stroke 83.6mm, 1897cc, 4 speed manual gearbox, single plate clutch, 4 wheel mechanical brakes, independent coil spring suspension front and rear.
Est. **£36,000-40,000**   *S(A)*

Mercedes-Benz 280SL.
£44,000-46,000   *FOR*

1960 Mercedes-Benz 300SL Roadster with Hard Top, 6 cylinder in-line engine, water-cooled monobloc, overhead camshaft, bore 85mm x 88mm stroke, 2996cc, 4 speed gearbox, single dry plate clutch, bevel rear axle, independent coil spring front and rear suspension, wheelbase 94½in, 15in tyres.
Est. **£140,000-160,000**   *SNY*

1970 Mercedes-Benz 280SL Convertible Sports Two Seater, 6 cylinder, overhead camshaft engine, fuel injection, 2778cc, 170bhp, 4 speed automatic gearbox, 4 wheel servo disc brakes, all-round independent suspension, right-hand drive.
Est. **£16,000-18,000**   *C*

23,885 examples of the 280SL were built.

1971 Mercedes-Benz 280SL, 62,000 miles from new.
Est. **£20,000-25,000**   *P*

The SL range of cars started in 1954 and the Mercedes 280SL was introduced in 1968, with a 2.8 litre straight six engine.

1969 Mercedes-Benz 280SL.
£21,000-22,000   *ELD*

1973 Mercedes-Benz 350SL, type M116 V8 iron block engine, alloy head, 3499cc, 5 main bearing, Bosch electronic injection, 9.5:1 compression ratio, 200bhp, 211 lb/ft torque at 4,000rpm, this car was a special factory order with manual transmission.
£10,000-11,000   *SEN*

969 Mercedes-Benz 280SL, ight-hand drive, excellent, original ondition.
25,000-26,000   *CMa*

Make: Mercedes-Benz
Model: 230SL/250SL/280SL
Type: Coupé/Convertible
Years Manufactured: 1963-71
Quantity: 19,831
Price when new: 250SL, £3,414
Engine Type: 6 cyl
Size: 2306cc/2496cc/2778cc
Max Power: 150-170 bhp
Transmission: 4 speed, 5 speed or auto
Wheelbase: 94.5in
Performance: Max speed: 280SL, 121 mph; 0-60: 280SL, 9.3 secs; Mpg: 280SL, 19.

Locate the source

The source of each illustration in Miller's can be found by checking the code letters below each caption with the list of contributors

1965 Mercedes-Benz 230SL Roadster, 6 cylinder in line, water-cooled monobloc, single overhead camshaft engine, 82mm bore x 87.28mm stroke, 2308cc, 4 speed manual gearbox, hypoid bevel rear axle, independent front and rear suspension, wheelbase 94½in, tyres 14in.
£13,500-14,000   *S*

1964 Mercedes-Benz 230SL,
extensive restoration in 1987.
£15,500-16,500   *GWC*

**1968 Mercedes-Benz 280SL
Coupé Convertible,** 6 cylinder in
line, water-cooled monobloc engine,
single overhead camshaft, 86.5mm
bore x 78.8mm stroke, 2778cc,
hypoid bevel rear axle, independent
front and rear suspension,
wheelbase 94½in, tyres 14in.
£14,000-15,000   *S*

**1959 Mercedes-Benz 300D Four
Door Saloon,** 6 cylinder, overhead
camshaft engine, water-cooled
monobloc, 85mm bore x 88mm
stroke, 2996cc, 4 speed automatic
transmission, tubular cruciform
frame, independent suspension, live
rear axle, tyres 7.60 x 15, wheelbase
124in.
Est. **£10,000-12,000**   *S*

Make: Mercedes-Benz
Model: 300SEL 6.3
Type: Saloon
Years Manufactured: 1967-72
Quantity: 6,526
Price when new: £7,729
Engine Type: V8 cyl
Size: 6332cc
Max Power: 250 bhp
Transmission: Auto
Performance: Max speed: 134
mph; 0-60: 7.1 secs; Mpg: 16.

**1961 Mercedes-Benz 300D
Pillarless Saloon.**
Est. **£12,000-13,000**   *S(A)*

**1964 Mercedes-Benz 220SEB
Saloon,** 6 cylinder, 2195cc engine.
£3,000-4,000   *LF*

**1959 Mercedes-Benz 220S
Saloon,** 6 cylinder, 2195cc engine,
requiring total restoration.
Est. **£100-200**   *LF*

**1970 Mercedes-Benz 300SEL 6.3
Sedan.**
£13,000-14,000   *CMA*

*This performance, luxury saloon
was introduced in 1968 and fitted
with the 6.3 litre V8 engine from the
600 series limousine, top speed was
137mph and 0-60 time about 6.5
seconds.*

1964 Mercedes-Benz 220SEB Cabriolet, fully restored.
£25,000-35,000 *CTC*

1970 Mercedes-Benz 220 Four Door Sedan, 6 cylinder engine, automatic transmission, right-hand drive.
£900-1,100 *C*

1971 Mercedes-Benz 280SE, 8 cylinders, 3499cc.
£2,200-2,500 *ADT*

1973 Mercedes-Benz 350SE, V8, 3499cc engine.
£3,000-3,600 *LF*

1971 Mercedes-Benz 300SEL 6.3, cylinder, 6300cc engine.
Est. **£26,000-27,000** *Ren*

1977 Mercedes-Benz Condor, by Crayford, the Mercedes-Benz 450SLC (Sports Light Coupé) was authentically similar to the 350 version but has the natural benefit of the 4.5 litre V8 engine, this one-off estate version of the 450SLC was built by Crayford Auto Development Ltd, the base model is a 1977 2 door left-hand drive coupé with automatic transmission.
Est. **£11,000-13,000** *ADT*

1971 Mercedes-Benz 280CE Saloon, stacked headlight model.
£4,000-5,000 *Cen*

The S Type was introduced in 1965 with the 250s to be replaced by the 280s in 1968 powered by a 2778cc straight 6 engine.

1972 Mercedes-Benz 280SE automatic, power steering, electric sunroof and aerial, white-wall tyres, stacked headlamps, 83,380 miles.
£2,800-3,500 *Cen*

1986 Replica Mercedes-Benz 300SLR, 2 seater open sports bodywork made of GRP, box section chassis, Chevrolet V8 engine, displacement of 302ci.
£32,000-34,000 *ADT*

MARMON

1924 Marmon 34-B 5.5 Litre Seven Seater Sedan.
£16,000-18,000 *B*

MARCOS

The Marcos 3 and 2.5 litre series were produced between 1969 and 1971 with 3 variations of engine. Either a Ford V6, a Triumph 2500 or a Volvo 3 litre straight 6.

MAKE	ENGINE	DATES	CONDITION		
Marcos			1	2	3
1800	1780	1964-66	£7,500	£4,500	£2,000
1500/1600	1499/4	1966-69	£7,500	£4,000	£2,000
3 litre V6 (Ford)	2994/6	1969-70	£8,000	£6,000	£2,500
3 litre (Volvo)	2978	1970-72	£7,000	£5,000	£2,500
Mini Marcos	var	1965-72	£2,000	£1,500	—
Mantis	2499/6	1971-72	£7,000	£4,000	£1,000

1970 Marcos 3 litre V6, Ford
£8,000-10,000 *Cen*

Make: Marcos
Model: V6 3 litre
Type: Fixed Head Coupé
Years Manufactured: 1969-71
Price when new: Approx. £2,026
Engine Type: Overhead valve V6
Size: 2994cc
Max Power: 128 bhp @ 4750 rpm
Transmission: 4 speed plus overdrive
Performance: Max speed: 125 mph; 0-60: 7.5 secs; Mpg: 20-25.

MAZDA

Mazda Cosmo Sport, Mazda's first production rotary engine model, released for sale on 30 May 1967, one of only 2 Cosmos known in the UK today.
£2,800-3,200 *C*

MITCHELL

1910 Mitchell Model 'S' 50hp Seven Passenger Tourer,
6 cylinder in-line engine, water-cooled, cast in pairs, pushrod operated overhead exhaust valves, side inlet valves, bore 4¼in x 5in stroke, 425.6cu in, 4 speed gearbox, shaft drive to live rear axle, semi-elliptic leaf springs at front and rear with additional transverse leaf rear spring, wheelbase 130in, 36 x 4½in front tyres and 37 x 5in rear.
£40,000-42,000 *SNY*

MESSERSCHMITT BUBBLETOP

The Fend design of 3 wheel bubble car was taken over by Regensburger Stahl- und Metallbau GmbH (Messerschmitt, the former aircraft manufacturer), in 1953. The KR 175 was the first model produced. It is believed that only 13 vehicles still exist. The design of the car makes it handle particularly well on corners and the cars were originally capable of 85km/h.

1954 KR 175 Messerschmitt Bubbletop Two Seater Town Car, rear mounted single cylinder Sachs 2 stroke engine, 175cc, 4 speed forward and reverse gearbox, cork clutch, chain drive, rubber suspension, handlebar steering, wheelbase 80in, 4 x 8in tyres.
Est. **£5,500-6,500**   *S(A)*

MERCER

1910 Mercer Model 30 Five Passenger Tourer.
Est. **£40,000-45,000**   *SNY*

METZ

1918 Metz, with variable transmission.
£9,500-10,000   *DB*

Miller's is a price Guide not a price List

The price ranges given reflect the average price a purchaser should pay for similar vehicle. Condition, rarity, provenance, racing history, originality and any restoration are factors that must be taken into account when assessing values. When buying or selling, it must always be remembered that prices can be greatly affected by the condition of any vehicle. Unless otherwise stated, all cars shown in Miller's are of good merchantable quality, and the valuations given reflect this fact. Vehicles offered for sale in exceptionally fine condition or in poor condition may reasonably be expected to be priced considerably higher or lower respectively than the estimates given herein

MINERVA

The Belgian firm of Minerva commenced car production in 1900 after a period of producing bicycles and motorcycles. They initially manufactured very fine, low priced chain driven voiturettes and from 1905 developed engines with increased horse power leading to many race successes, e.g. winning the 1907 Circuit des Ardennes for Kaiserpreis cars (8 litre limit).

1909/10 Minerva 38HP Tourer, with Knight Patent double sleeve valve design with full hemispherical combustion chambers, 5 bearing crankshaft, 4 speed sliding mesh gearbox, straight cut bevel differential, rear wheel drum brakes, right-hand drive.
£20,000-21,000   *C(A)*

MORGAN

MONTEVERDI

1974 Monteverdi 375/4 L Four Door Saloon, V8 cylinder engine, water-cooled monobloc, 7.2 litres, developing 375bhp at 4,600rpm, 3 speed automatic gearbox, independent front suspension with helical coil springs and parallel wishbones, full De Dion rear with coil springs and trailing arms, transverse Watts linkage to a Z.F. light alloy rear axle centre unit, inboard disc brakes, wheelbase 125in.
Est. **£11,000-15,000**   *S(A)*

Automobile Monteverdi Ltd, was founded by the Swiss Formula One driver Peter Monteverdi. The first luxury car was exhibited at the Frankfurt Motor Show in 1967. The car had been styled with some assistance from Frua, and the 2+2 coupé was powered by a 7.2 litre V8 Chrysler engine. The bodies were built by Fissore in Italy.

MERLIN

1984 Merlin Thoroughbred Sports Convertible, Ford mechanical parts, 2000cc engine, steel spoke radial wheels, 9,538 miles.
£4,000-4,250   *Cen*

MORGAN

HFS founded the Morgan Motor Company at Malvern, offering the first Morgans for sale in 1910. The three-wheeled pre-war Morgans, well proven in competition, sold well and by the late 1930s the first 4-wheelers were produced. Today Morgans still make hand-made, traditional sports cars and there is a long waiting list. The top of the range Plus 8 has 1990s supercar performance with the charm of pre-war motoring. Morgan is the longest running independent motor manufacturer in the UK and is still family owned and run.

H.F.S. Morgan produced the first of his three wheeler cars in 1910, aimed pretty much directly at the economy market, for the cars were little more than overbodied motorcycles, but they proved highly suitable for competition and general sports use. A variety of engines were used including Aero, Matchless and JAP, in both side valve and overhead valve forms, and these cars provided some exciting motoring at modest cost for many enthusiasts before the Second World War.

1930 Morgan Family Four, JAP air-cooled V-twin.
£9,000-10,000   *DB*

1949 Morgan 'F' Super Three Wheeled Sports, complete but partly disassembled, exact model not known.   **£2,500-2,750**

936 Morgan 4+4 Two Seater Sports.
10,000-11,000 *LF*

1936 Morgan 4+4, supplied to the Redhill Motor Works in September 1936.
£14,000-15,000 *DJ*

Sales of Morgan 3 wheeler cars were on the decline by the mid 1930s as a result of competition from 4 wheel sporting cars produced by other manufacturers. Consequently, in 1935 Morgan introduced the 4+4 — 4 wheels and 4 cylinders — powered by an 1122cc Coventry Climax engine. Morgans of that period gave their chassis the same number as the engine used.

Make: Morgan
Model: Plus 8
Type: Sports
Years Manufactured: 1968 to date
Quantity: Still in production
Price when new: £1,510
Engine Type: Overhead valve V8
Size: 3528cc
Max Power: 143 bhp @ 5000 rpm to 190 bhp @ 5200 rpm; injection, Sept 1984 on, 190 bhp @ 5280 rpm
Max Torque: 202 ft/lb @ 4700 rpm to 220 ft/lb @ 4000 rpm
Transmission: 4 speed, 5 speed from Oct 1976
Wheelbase: 98in
Performance: Max speed: 124 mph; Injection, 126 mph; 0-60: 5.7 secs; Injection, 6.0 secs; Mpg: 19-25.

1958 Morgan 4+4 Series II, extensive restoration, chrome wire wheels, right-hand drive.
£8,000-10,000 *Cen*

Produced between 1956 and 1960, the 4+4 Series II was Morgan's re-entry into car production after a 5 year lapse. Given a 36bhp 100E Ford engine and hydraulic brakes initially, it was available with a 40bhp Aqua-plane-head engine from 1958.

Make: Morgan
Model: 4/4
Type: Drop head Coupé, Sports
Years Manufactured: 1946-63
Price when new: Drop head Coupé (1956), £684
Engine Type: Overhead valve 4 cyl
Size: 1267cc, 1340cc and other engines used
Max Power: 1267cc, 39 bhp @ 4300 rpm
Transmission: 3 speed manual to 1960, then 4 speed
Wheelbase: 96in
Performance: Max speed: 1267cc, 75 mph; 1340cc, 80+ mph; 0-60: 1267cc, 25.0 secs; 1340cc, 18.5 secs; Mpg: 25-32.

MAKE	ENGINE	DATES	CONDITION		
Morgan			1	2	3
4/4 Series I	1098/4	1936-50	£11,000	£9,000	£6,000
Plus 4	2088/4	1950-53	£12,000	£9,000	£7,000
Plus 4	1991/4	1954-68	£12,000	£10,000	£8,000
4/4 Series II/III/IV	997/4	1954-68	£8,000	£6,000	£3,000
4/4 1600	1599/4	1960 on	£11,000	£9,000	£6,000
Plus 8	3528/8	1969 on	£18,000	£13,500	£10,000

1976 Morgan Plus Eight, with Rover V8 engine and 4 speed gearbox, in excellent original condition.
£18,000-20,000 *PC*

MORRIS

William Morris was initially a bicycle manufacturer who had started to assemble and then produce his own motor cars by 1914. The mid twenties saw Morris as the largest car producer in the UK, acquiring many competitors including the Wolseley company in 1926. One of the best selling post war cars was the 1948 Issigonis designed Morris Minor, but despite this success, Austin was a stronger company at the time of the BMC merger in 1952. The Morris name soon vanished from the motoring scene.

MAKE	ENGINE	DATES	CONDITION		
Morris			1	2	3
Prices given are for saloons					
Cowley Tourer	1550/4	1913-26	£11,000	£8,000	£6,000
Cowley	1550/4	1927-39	£9,000	£6,000	£4,000
14/28 Oxford	1803/4	1924-33	£10,000	£5,000	£4,000
16/40	2513/4	1928-33	£9,000	£7,000	£6,000
18	2468/6	1928-35	£9,000	£7,000	£5,000
8 Minor	847/4	1929-34	£6,000	£4,000	£2,000
10/4	1292/4	1933-35	£5,000	£3,000	£1,500
25	3485/6	1933-39	£11,000	£8,000	£5,000
Eight	918/4	1935-39	£4,000	£3,000	£1,500
10hp	1140/4	1939-47	£4,500	£3,000	£1,500
16hp	2062/6	1936-38	£5,000	£3,500	£2,000
18hp	2288/6	1935-37	£5,000	£3,500	£2,500
21hp	2916/6	1935-36	£6,000	£4,000	£2,500

A touring version of the above is worth approximately 65% more.

1913 Morris 10HP Oxford.
£12,000-13,000   *P*

1925 Morris Cowley Occasional Four Door Tourer, with chassis No. 88336, engine No. 101191, 4 cylinder, right-hand drive.
£10,500-11,000   *C*

1925 was the Bullnose Morris's peak year with 54,151 units delivered.

1930 Morris Cowley 11.9hp Roadster with Dickey, 4 cylinder, side valve, water-cooled monobloc engine, 69.5mm bore x 102mm stroke, rating 11.9hp, 3 speed gearbox, multiplate clutch with cork inserts, spiral bevel rear axle, tyres 750 x 19, wheelbase 105in.
£7,300-8,000   *S*

1930 Morris Minor CMS Special Sports Boat Tail Two Seater, coachwork by Coventry Motor & Sundries Co. Ltd., 4 cylinder, overhead camshaft water-cooled monobloc engine, 57mm bore x 83mm stroke, 847cc, 3 speed gearbox, single plate clutch, coil ignition, thermo-syphon cooling, shaft drive to spiral bevel rear axle, tyres 4.00 x 19, wheelbase 78in.
Est. **£7,500-8,000**   *S*

1931 Morris Cowley 'Flatnose
4 cylinder, 1479cc engine.
£6,800-7,200   *LF*

The successor to the Bullnose Cowley, the Flatnose has the Hotchkiss derived 11.9hp engine.

The 11.9hp model was the mainstay of the Morris Company's range, and the chassis was used as the basis for a great number of private and commercial vehicles.

1934 Morris Minor Saloon
in need of total restoration
£1,300-1,500   *DB*

928 Hadfield Bean 14/45 Open Five Seater Tourer, ith full weather equipment, side mounted spare, completely restored concours winner, the only nown survivor in Europe.
29,000-35,000 *DJ*

70 Ford Escort RS 1600, once owned by r Leonard Crossland, chassis No. 349 KD22444, engine No. KL22444/HE1008 cylinder, 1600cc, resprayed red in 87, in excellent condition with many tras, including a large history file.
,500-10,500 *ADT*

73 Gilbern Invader Mk III, unregistered, assis No. M111/0198, 6 cylinder, 00cc engine capacity, this is lieved to be the last car ever built the factory and most probably the best ample of a Gilbern available.
,000-10,000 *ADT*

1931 Ford Tudor Coupé, chassis No. A4384523, engine capacity 3 litre, 4 cylinder, this car was restored in 1986 and in the 1940s hydraulic brakes were fitted.
£15,000-18,000 *Ren*

1974 Ford Capri 3.0 Ghia, chassis No. GAECPJO1599, engine No. PJO1599 6 cylinder, 2994cc, with 9,900 miles recorded, in excellent condition throughout, spare wheel, tyre and tools all unused.
£4,500-5,500 *ADT*

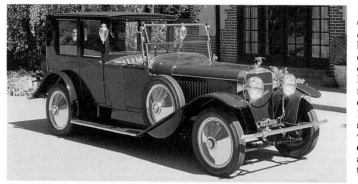

**1922 Hispano-Suiza H6B Rothsch
Coupé Limousine,** chassis No. 104?
engine No. 300521 6 cylinder, 100m
bore 140mm stroke, 6.5 litres, shaft
driven overhead camshaft with non-
detachable head and nitrided steel
liners, Birkigt patent valve adjustin
mechanism, dual ignition with twin
distributors, two barrel carburettor,
135bhp at 2,800rpm, Birkigt patent
single plate clutch adjustable for
wear, 3 speed gearbox, long semi-
elliptic leaf springs, hydraulic shock
absorbers, Birkigt patent servo syste
to all 4 wheels. **£210,000-250,000**

An external view from the side of
the Hispano-Suiza showing one of the
wind wings.

A view of part of the engine of the 1922 Hispano-Suiza.

A view of the interior of the 1922 Hispano-Suiza H6B, showing
the fine mahogany garnish mouldings with metal inlay.

A view of the 1922 Hispano-Suiza
showing another area of the inter

The dashboard
and steering wheel of
the 1922 Hispano-Suiza
H6B.

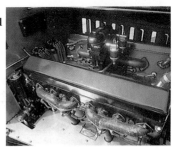

Hispano-Suiza V12, Model J12, 54-220hp, probably made in 1933, previously owned by Midland Motor Museum who renovated it to a high standard. 60°, V12, 9½ litre engine, aluminium alloy cylinder block and fixed heads, twin ignition by Scintilla magnetos, 2 twin choke Hispano-Suiza carburettors, rated to develop approx 220bhp at 3,000rpm, currently had 4 speed synchromesh Bentley gearbox, original 3 speed gearbox with car.
£250,000-270,000   *C(A)*

A side view of the Hispano-Suiza V12, Model J12, Type 68, 54-220hp, showing o full advantage his very elegant ar.

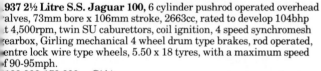

937 2½ Litre S.S. Jaguar 100, 6 cylinder pushrod operated overhead alves, 73mm bore x 106mm stroke, 2663cc, rated to develop 104bhp t 4,500rpm, twin SU caburettors, coil ignition, 4 speed synchromesh earbox, Girling mechanical 4 wheel drum type brakes, rod operated, entre lock wire type wheels, 5.50 x 18 tyres, with a maximum speed f 90-95mph.
100,000-150,000   *C(A)*

1951 Jaguar XK150.
£37,000-40,000   *BLE*

A view of the Jaguar XK140 radiator grille and badge.

1955 Jaguar XK140 Drop Head Coupé, with twin-cam engine by Bill Heynes, this car is one of only 480 right-hand drive models manufactured and has undergone a professional restoration. **£90,000-95,000** *ADT*

1956 3.4 Litre Jaguar XK140 Roadster, chassis No. A311499, engine No. G 39278, with 190bhp, Alford & Alder rack and pinion steering and a top speed of 120mph, this left-hand drive example has 65,987 miles recorded. **£31,000-35,000** *C*

A view of part of the interior of the 1956 3.4 litre Jaguar.

1959 Jaguar XK150 2+2 Fixed Head Coupé, chassis No. S824903 DN, engine No. V6892/8 6 cylinder in-line monobloc with double overhead camshaft 83mm bore x 160mm stroke giving 3442cc, 4 speed synchromesh gearbox with overdrive, servo assisted 4 wheel disc brakes. **£37,500-40,000** *C*

1958 Jaguar XK150S Roadster, 6 cylinder, 3442cc engine, left-hand drive, this car is one of only 147 examples manufactured, and has been restored. **£30,000-32,000** *ADT*

1960 Jaguar XK150 Fixed Head Coupé, chassis No. 5836529, engine No. VA11719 6 cylinder, twin overhead camshaft, 83mm bore x 106mm stroke, 3442cc. **£22,000-25,000** *C*

A view of part of the interior of the 1960 Jaguar XK150, showing the steering wheel and dashboard.

1968 Jaguar 340 Mk II Saloon, chassis No. 1J50916BW, engine No. 7J51203-8 6 cylinder in-line monobloc with double overhead camshaft, 83mm bore x 106mm stroke giving 3442cc, automatic gearbox transmission, Dunlop servo assisted disc brakes, independent front suspension, live axle cantilever spring rear and right-hand drive, ths car has been extensively restored.
£13,500-14,000   *C*

1970 Jaguar D-Type Replica, chassis No. 1R-27576, engine No. 7R13755-9 4.2 litre with Weber carburettors, independent rear wheel suspension, aluminium body panels finished in silver with red interior.
£46,000-47,000   *C*

Part of the interior of the 1970 Jaguar E-Type Series II Roadster, showing the dashboard and steering wheel.

1970 Jaguar E-Type Series II Roadster, chassis No. 1R 1445, engine No. 7R 9221-9, 92.07mm bore x 106mm stroke, 4235cc, twin overhead camshafts 265bhp gross at 5,400rpm, compression 9:1 (8:1 optional) straight port cylinder head, 3 x 2in SU HD8 carburettors, 4 speed manual transmission, independent front suspension, wishbones, torsion bars, anti-roll bar. **£37,500-38,500**   *C*

Jaguar XJ6 4.2, 2 door, with 4.2 litre engine and gearbox, steering and suspension are in good running order as are the brakes, wheels, tyres and exhaust system, the original leather interior is in excellent condition.
£4,500-5,500   *ADT*

1956 Jensen 541, chassis No. 541/485206, engine No. 1D10649M JEN cylinder, 3993cc, fibre glass body, optional wire wheels, green hide interior and a recent quality respray.
£16,500-17,500   *Ren*

1933 Lagonda 16/80 Sports, in excellent mechanical condition with very good bodywork and interior, this car has undergone full restoration in 1980/81.
£50,000-55,000   *Mot*

1969-71 Lotus Elan S4/SE Drop Head Coupé.
£10,000-14,000   *KSC*

1964 Lotus Elan S1.
£15,000-20,000   *KSC*

1962 Lotus Elite Climax SII, with Coventry Climax engine, and ZF gearbox.
£25,000-45,000   *KSC*

Lotus Elan Sprint Drop Head Coupé, in gold leaf colours.
£14,000-20,000   *KSC*

1972-75 Lotus Europa Twin Cam Special.
£8,000-15,000   *KSC*

Lotus Europa Twin Cam Special.
£8,000-15,000   *KSC*

Lotus Elan +2 130/S.
£5,000-14,000   *KSC*

Lotus Esprit Turbo.
£8,000-25,000   *KSC*

1962 Maserati 3500GTI Vignale Spyder, with chassis No. 101/1439, engine No. 101/1439, 6 cylinder, 3485cc, between 1958 and 1964 only 242 Spyders were produced of which only 6 of these were built in right-hand drive form, this car has undergone complete restoration and has Borrani disc wheels, the car has covered only a few hundred miles since restoration. £50,000-55,000 *ADT*

1964 Maserati Mistral Spyder 4 Litre, with coachwork by Frua, chassis No. 109.021 and engine No. 109.021, 6 cylinder in line 4014cc, bore 88mm x stroke 110mm, 255bhp at 5,500rpm, 5 speed gearbox plus reverse, coil spring, telescopic shock absorbers and semi-elliptical leaf spring suspension and left-hand drive. £140,500-142,000 *C(M)*

Part of interior of 1964 Maserati Mistral Spyder 4 Litre, showing steering wheel and dashboard.

1971/72 Maserati Ghibli SS Coupé, with chassis No. AM 115.49.1440 and engine No. AM 115938, 8 cylinder, 4930cc, coil spring with telescopic shock absorbers front suspension, 4 Weber carburettors, 90° V8 double overhead camshaft engine, bore 93.9mm x stroke 89mm, producing 335bhp at 5,500rpm, this car has a manual gearbox and has been fully restored throughout. Est. £70,000-90,000 *ADT*

Side view of bonnet of Maserati Merak, this model was introduced in 1972, the new 6 cylinder engine was initially designed for the Citroën SM and produced around 190hp, the V6 was developed from V8 and gave rise to a much shorter engine, extensive work has been carried out.

Front view of 1974 Maserati Merak, showing bonnet with badge, this car has been extensively restored.

1974 Maserati Merak Sports Coupé, chassis No. 122-207, engine No. 500-342, 6 cylinder, double overhead camshaft per block, 91.6mm bore x 75mm stroke giving 2965cc, 5 speed synchromesh gearbox, servo assisted 4 wheel disc brakes, independent front and rear coil springs and wishbone suspension and right-hand drive. **£30,000-32,000**   *C*

1976 Maserati Type 117 'Bora', coachwork by Ital Design, chassis No. AM 117798, engine No. AM 117798, 8 cylinder 90° V configuration, 4719cc, producing 310bhp at 6,000rpm, bore 93.9mm x 85mm stroke, 5 speed manual gearbox with reverse, dry single cone clutch, 4 Weber carburettors, suspension by coil springs and telescopic shock absorbers front and rear. **£64,500-66,000**   *C(M)*

A view of part of the 1976 Maserati, showing the steering wheel and dashboard, this is a left-hand drive vehicle capable of 168mph, features include air conditioning, electronic ignition, electric windows, heated rear window, power assisted brakes, adjustable steering wheel, head rests and seats, iodine lamps, anti-theft device and a Blaupunkt sound system, it has 49,000 kilometres recorded.

1965 Matra D Jet 5, with excellent bodywork and very good mechanics and interior, this car has been restored to a very high standard and this model was the world's first mid-engine sports car. **£7,500-8,500**   *GWC*

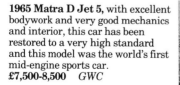

1929 Mercedes-Benz SSK (Specification), with chassis No. 35342, engine No. 66543
6 cylinder, overhead camshaft, 100mm bore x 150mm stroke, 7065cc, 170bhp, or 220bhp
with supercharger engaged at 3,300rpm, compression 5.75:1, twin carburettor and
Roots-type supercharger, 5 gallon cooling system, 2 gallon oil system, 11mpg on
petrol 35 miles per pint of oil. **£618,000-620,000** *CNY*

Above is a view of the
left-hand drive steering
wheel and dashboard of the
1929 Mercedes-Benz and
Below part of the engine,
this car has 4 speed
sliding mesh gearbox,
semi-elliptic front and
rear, Houdaille hydraulic
Hartford friction dampers,
finned 4 wheel mechanical
drum brakes.

...urther view of the 1929 Mercedes-Benz, showing spare
...eel with centre lock wire spokes, wheelbase 116in, track
...in, this vehicle has a top speed of 115mph, blowing
...ough the carburettors instead of sucking through them,
... SSK emits a distinctive siren wail.

1929 Mercedes-Benz 'Nurburg' Four Door Convertible, with chassis No. 4592, engine No. M51220 8 side valve of 4.6 litres, designed by Hans Nibel, the hood was replaced in 1936 but otherwise the car remains in excellent original condition, it has an interesting history having been to Afghanistan, India and the USA.
£77,000-80,000   *C*

1958 Mercedes-Benz 300SL Roadster, with chassis No. 850 0144, 6 cylinder, overhead camshaft engine, 2996cc, 215bhp, 4 speed synchromesh gearbox, servo assisted hydraulic drum type 4 wheel brakes, all round independent suspension, left-hand drive.
£148,500-150,000   *C*

1958 Mercedes-Benz 300SL Roadster, with chassis No. 7500591, 6 cylinder, 2995cc engine, factory fitted hard top, and extensively restored, finished in ivory with red leather interior.
£195,000-200,000   *T&M*

1962 Mercedes 190SL, with excellent mechanics and very good bodywork and interior.
£20,000-22,000   *GWC*

1963 Mercedez-Benz 190SL Two Door Coupé, with chassis No. 12104420025832, engine No. 12192820003825, 4 cylinder, single overhead camshaft. **£20,500-21,000**   *C*

A view of the 1963 Mercedes showing steering wheel and dashboard.

1964 Mercedes 230SL LHD, with 6 cylinder 2306cc, complete with hard and soft tops, finished in beige with red hide interior.
£26,500-28,000 *Ren*

1965 Mercedes-Benz 230SL Convertible Sports Two Seater, with chassis No. 11304222011530, engine No. 12798122002349, 6 cylinder, overhead camshaft, 2306cc, 150bhp, 4 speed automatic gearbox, disc front, drum rear brakes, fully independent suspension, right-hand drive.
£10,500-11,500 *C*

1954 MG TF, with chassis No. HDA 164097, engine No. XPAG/TF/33455 4 cylinder, 1250cc, finished in black with biscuit coloured interior, hood and tonneau.
£32,000-34,000 *Ren*

1959 MGA 1600 Roadster, LHD, with chassis No. GHNL/70271, 4 cylinder, 1588cc engine, 2 seater sports has been recently overhauled and finished in red with tan interior.
£6,000-8,000 *Ren*

1934 MG NE Ulster Magnette (Works Team Car), with chassis No. NA 516, engine No. 66A 134N 6 cylinder in line, 1271cc, bore 57mm x stroke 83mm.
£165,000-170,000   *C*

1946 MG TC Open Sports Two Seater, with chassis No. TC 1293, engine No. X PAG 1972, 4 cylinder overhead valve 1250cc, 4 speed synchromesh gearbox, 4 wheel hydraulic brakes, all round semi-elliptic suspension, wire wheels and right-hand drive.
£22,000-24,000   *C*

1951 MG TD Sports Two Seater, with chassis No. 11055, engine No. C99536 4 cylinder, twin carburettors overhead valve, 1250cc, 4 speed synchromesh gearbox, 4 wheel hydraulic brakes, independent front suspension, semi-elliptic rear, right-hand drive.
£19,000-20,000   *C*

1952 MG TD, LHD, with chassis No. TD15417, engine No XPAG/TDZ/15917 4 cylinder, 1250cc, finished in white with red interior and recently overhauled. **£8,000-10,000**   *Ren*

1960 MGA FHC, with chassis No. GHO85204, engine No. 16GAO116327 4 cylinder, 1622cc this car is in good order throughout.
£3,500-4,500 *ADT*

1962 MGA, in concours condition.
£28,000-30,000 *BEE*

1960 MGA 1600 Series I, with chassis No. GHN83456, engine No. 16GA-U12719 4 cylinder, 1588cc, 79.5bhp and 103mph.
£20,500-21,500 *LF*

1962 Morgan 4/4 2 Seater, with chassis No. B818, engine No. S 271876 4 cylinder, 1172cc, some restoration has been carried out and this car could be good.
£6,500-7,500 *ADT*

1947 Morgan 4/4 2 Seater, with 1267cc overhead valve engine, 4 speed gearbox, spiral bevel back axle, independent front wheel suspension and Girling brakes, this car is in very good condition.
£10,500-11,500 *ADT*

1925 Bullnose Morris Cowley, with good bodywork, very good mechanics and interior, original fabric roof.
£12,500-13,500 *CC*

1927 Morris Cowley 11.9hp 2 Seater, with very good bodywork, excellent mechanics and interior, fully restored in 1987.
£12,000-12,500 *Mot*

1929 Morris Oxford Empire Saloon, an impressive motor car with Morris Commercial running chassis and 4 speed gearbox. **£15,500-16,500** *ELD*

1929 Morris Oxford Empire Four Seat Tourer, with Morris Commercial running chassis and 4 speed gearbox, rear auster screen, full weather equipment. **£18,000-19,000** *ELD*

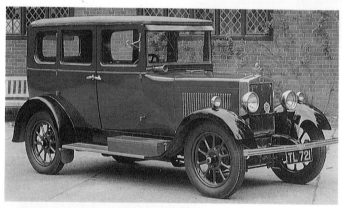

1929 Morris Cowley 11.9hp Saloon, with chassis No. 316113, engine No. 338773 4 cylinder side valve, water-cooled monobloc, bore 69.5mm x stroke 102mm, rating 11.9hp, 3 speed gearbox, multiplate clutch with cork inserts, spiral bevel rear axle, wheelbase 105in and 19 x 5in tyres, generally in good condition. **£8,000-9,000** *S*

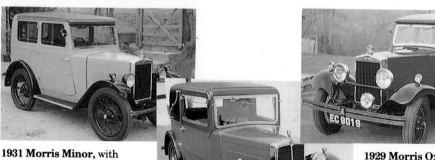

1931 Morris Minor, with chassis No. M34334, engine No. U35013B 4 cylinder, 885cc, with half folding roof and in good running order. **£7,000-7,500** *LF*

1932 Morris Minor Sports Coupé, with chassis No. 36859, engine No. 37375 4 cylinder. **£4,000-5,000** *ADT*

1929 Morris Oxford Sportsman's Coupé, with chassis No. LA722, engine No. 1187, 6 cylinder, 1928cc, fitted with a sliding roof, the engine has been rebuilt, and the car comes with a number of spare parts. Est. **£8,000-12,000** *LF*

Mini Cooper S Mk I.
£3,000-5,000   *KSC*

1962 Morris Mini Minor, with chassis No.
M1A254141186, engine No. 8AMSH385696
4 cylinder, 848cc, the shell is in
good condition with 28,370 miles
recorded.
£1,500-2,000   *ADT*

**1965 Morris Mini Cooper
1275 ex works Rally Car,**
with chassis No.
KA2S4/799887, engine No.
XSP 3068-2, 4 cylinder,
pushrod, BMC 4 speed and
reverse gearbox, full
works competition
specification, competition
dampers suspension,
hydraulic brakes with
servo, disc and drum,
Minilite magnesium wheels,
homologated extras and
right-hand drive, this
car won the 1967 1,000
Lakes Rally, driven
by Timo Makinen.
£71,000-73,000   *C*

1965 Porsche 356C Coupé, this car has always been kept in California and as a result
has an excellent body, mechanics and interior.
£17,000-18,000   *CFC*

1972 Porsche 911S 2.4 Litre RHD,
with excellent bodywork, mechanics,
and interior, a few new panels,
stereo, electric windows and roof.
£28,500-30,000   *CMa*

231

1973 Porsche 911 Carrera RS 2.7 2+2 Sports Coupé, with chassis No. 9113600893, engine No. 9011061015R flat 6 cylinder, rear mounted overhead camshaft, 2687cc, 210bhp, 5 speed synchromesh gearbox, 4 wheel servo disc brakes. **£44,000-50,000** *C*

1977 Porsche 935, with chassis No. 9307700901, engine No. 6772903 2.8 litre air cooled with single turbocharger, developing in excess of 600bhp, a virtually unused car. **£484,000-490,000** *C*

1973 Porsche Carrera 911 RS Touring, with chassis No. 9113601331, engine No. 6631308 flat 6 cylinder, 2687cc, completely rebuilt in 1987 and fitted with electric sun roof and windows. **£85,000-90,000** *T&M*

A view of the 1914 Rolls-Royce Silver Ghost showing the dashboard and steering wheel.

A further view of the engine of the 1914 Rolls-Royce Silver Ghost Tourer.

1925 Renault NT, with good bodywork, mechanics and interior. **£7,500-8,500** *CC*

1914 Rolls-Royce Silver Ghost Tourer, wi coachwork by Van Den Plas, chassis No. 34 LB, engine No. 19H 6 side valved cylinders, 7 litres, dual ignition and three quarter elliptic rear springs, 4 speed gearbox. **£165,000-170,000** *C*

1922 Rolls-Royce Silver Ghost Tourer, with chassis No. 42 ZG, engine No. K 130 6 cylinder with side valves, water cooled, 4 speed gearbox, 4 wheel brakes, twin side mounted spare wheels. **£50,000-55,000** *C*

1924 Rolls-Royce Twenty, with chassis No. GAK33, engine No. G867 6 cylinder pushrod overhead valve, 76mm bore x 114mm stroke, 3127cc, channel section chassis with semi-elliptic leaf springs front and rear, friction type shock absorbers, 3 speed with central gear lever, drum type brakes on rear wheels with separate shoes operated by hand brake, centre lock wire wheels. **£30,000-40,000** *C(A)*

A view of the 1924 Rolls-Royce, showing steering wheel and dashboard.

1927 Rolls-Royce 20hp Barker-style open 4/5 Seater Tourer, this car was recently used by Oliver Reed in a film, now requires minor tidying, finished in ivory with buttoned red leather interior. **£40,000-45,000** *DJ*

A view of the rear of the 1930 Rolls-Royce Phantom II.

1930 Rolls-Royce Phantom II 4 Door Tourer, with coachwork by Gaston Grummer of Paris, 7.7 litre, 6 cylinder, bore 4¼in x stroke 5½in, speed gearbox with synchromesh on 3rd and top, the solid rear axle bodies a Hotchkiss drive and is located on a pair of semi-elliptic springs, 7.00 x 20in tyres and a side mounted spare wheel, the engine is capable of 4,000rpm and has been restored. **£110,000-120,000** *C*

1930 Rolls-Royce Phantom II open 4 Door Sports Tourer, with Barker style coachwork, recent service and new tyres, finished in Wedgwood blue with royal blue interior. **£60,000-70,000** *DJ*

1931 Rolls-Royce Phantom 1 Marlborough Town Car, with coachwork by Brewster, chassis No. S449MR, engine No. 22499, 6 cylinder, 107.95mm bore x 139.7mm stroke, 7668cc, pushrod operated overhead valves. **£192,000-200,000** *CNY*

Rear view of the 1931 Rolls-Royce Phantom 1.

A view of the 1931 Rolls-Royce Phantom 1 showing to its best advantage the 3 position top, this car has a 4 speed gearbox with central change lever, spiral bevel final drive, spur-type differential, semi-elliptic springs front suspension, rear cantilever leaf springs, servo assisted drum brakes on all 4 wheels, 20in wire wheels, 700 x 20 tyres.

A view of the interior of the 1931 Rolls-Royce Phantom 1 showing the ornate wood inlay and gold fittings.

A part of the engine of the 1931 Rolls-Royce Phantom 1.

This view of the 1931 Rolls-Royce Phantom 1, shows the plate of the coachbuilders Brewster.

1934 Rolls-Royce Phantom II Continental Sports Saloon, with coachwork by James Young, chassis No. BXM 91, engine No. BN 45, 6 cylinder in line, water cooled, pushrod operated overhead valves, bore 4¼in x stroke 5½in, 7668cc, 4 speed gearbox, single dry plate clutch, hypoid bevel rear axle, semi-elliptic leaf spring suspension front and rear, 21in tyres.
£50,000-55,000   *S*

34 Rolls-Royce 20/25hp Three sition Drop Head Coupé, with achwork by Mulliner, chassis . AXW 194, engine No. Y8S, ylinder in-line water-cooled nobloc, pushrod operated overhead ves, bore 3¼in x stroke 4½in, 9cc, 4 speed gearbox, single dry te clutch, spiral bevel final ve, semi-elliptic leaf spring pension front and rear, eelbase 122in, 6.50 x 19in tyres. ,000-65,000   *S*

1935 Rolls-Royce Phantom II Continental Sports Saloon, with coachwork by Barker, chassis No. 42UK, engine No. SW65, 6 cylinder, 7668cc, 700 x 19 tyres, finished in black with beige insert, and black leather interior.
£95,000-100,000   *T&M*

1935 Rolls-Royce Phantom II Continental Saloon, Long Chassis, with coachwork by Park Ward, chassis No. 190SK, engine No. XQ-55-X, 6 cylinder, 7.7 litre, synchromesh 3rd and 4th gears, 150in chassis and 19in wheels, all in good working condition.
£66,000-70,000   *C*

1912 Rolls-Royce Silver Ghost 40/50hp Pullman Limousine, with coachwork by Barker & Co. Ltd., 6 cylinder, 7428cc engine, 4 speed gearbox.
£1,500,000-2,000,000 *S*

1927 Rolls-Royce Phantom I Sedanca De Ville, with coachwork by Hooper, 6 cylinder, 7668cc engine, 4 speed gearbox.
£50,000-55,000 *S*

1927 Rolls-Royce Twenty Open Tourer, with coachwork by Hooper, 6 cylinder, 3127cc engine, 4 speed gearbox.
£66,000-70,000 *S*

1927 Rolls-Royce 20hp Cabriolet De Ville, with coachwork by Barker, 6 cylinder, 3103cc, 4 speed gearbox.
£46,500-50,000 *S*

1930 Rolls-Royce Phantom II 40-50hp Two Door Drop Head Coupé, 6 cylinder in-line engine, cast in threes, overhead valve, water-cooled, bore 108mm x stroke 139.7mm, 7668cc, 4 speed gearbox in unit with engine, single plate clutch, open propeller shaft to hypoid rear axle, semi-elliptic suspension front and rear.
£91,000-95,000 *S*

1930 Rolls-Royce 20/25hp Sedanca De Ville, with coachwork by Frederick R. Wood & Co., 6 cylinder engine, water-cooled monobloc, with detachable head, bore 3¼in x stroke 4½in, 3699cc, 4 speed manual gearbox, internal expanding brakes with servo assist on all 4 wheels, independent handbrake on rear wheels.
£83,000-85,000 *S*

1953 Rolls-Royce Silver Wraith Gulbenkian Sedanca De Ville, with coachwork by Hooper & Co. Ltd., 6 cylinder in-line engine, water-cooled monobloc, bore 3⅝in x stroke 4½in, 4566cc, 4 speed manual gearbox, with synchromesh on 2nd, 3rd and 4th, independent front suspension, semi-elliptic leaf rear.
Est. **£125,000-150,000** *S*

A view of the lizard skin dashboard of the 1953 Rolls-Royce Silver Wraith.

1954 Rolls-Royce Silver Dawn Saloon, chassis No. S engine No. SW 20, 6 cylinder in line, 4 speed automatic gearbox, right-hand drive.
£21,000-25,000 *S*

1926 Rolls-Royce 20hp Three Quarter Fixed Head Coupé, with coachwork by Windovers Ltd, chassis No. GZK 34, engine No. G1666, 6 cylinder in line, water-cooled monobloc, overhead valve, bore 3in x stroke 4½in, 3103cc, single dry plate clutch, 4 speed gearbox, with right-hand change, spiral bevel rear axle, semi-elliptic leaf springs front and rear, wheelbase 129in and 19in tyres. £24,000-26,000   *S*

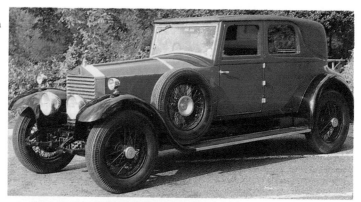

1938 Rolls-Royce Phantom III, with coachwork by H. J. Mulliner, chassis No. 3DL104, engine No. E48Z V12 cylinder, 82.5mm x 114.3mm stroke, 7340cc, pushrod operated overhead valves, with synchromesh 2nd, 3rd, and top gear, right-hand gear lever. £70,000-75,000   *C(A)*

1939 Rolls-Royce Wraith Sedanca De Ville, with coachwork by Thrupp and Maberly, chassis No. WLB 11, engine No. S2WF, 6 cylinder in line, water-cooled monobloc, pushrod operated overhead valves, bore 3½in x stroke 4½in, 4257cc, 4 speed gearbox with synchromesh on 2nd, 3rd and top, single dry plate clutch. £15,500-18,000   *S*

1955 Rolls-Royce Silver Dawn, finished in velvet green with pale grey leather interior, very good car. £37,500-38,500   *DJ*

1931 Rolls-Royce Phantom II Open Tourer, this 6 seater limousine was restored a few years ago and has full weather equipment, including side-mount and trunk covers, and comes complete with a cocktail cabinet of cut glass and crystal.
£84,500-86,000 *BLE*

1948 Riley RMA, chassis No. 38515900, engine No. 15900, 4 cylinder, 1496cc, the engine was rebuilt in 1985 and the bodywork was restored.
£10,000-11,000 *LF*

1930 Riley 4 Seater 4 Door Tour with black wings and red leather interior, all recently restored to a high standard.
£17,000-18,000 *DJ*

1933 Rolls-Royce 20/25hp Cabriolet De Ville, with coachwork by James Young, chassis No. GWX68, engine No. V3R, 6 cylinder in line, water-cooled monobloc, pushrod operated overhead valves, bore 3¼in x stroke 4½in, 3699cc, 4 speed gearbox, single dry plate clutch, spiral bevel rear axle, semi-elliptic leaf spring suspension front and rear, wheelbase 132in, 6.40 x 19in tyres.
£47,000-50,000 *S*

1964 Rolls-Royce Silver Cloud III Four Door Continental Saloon, chassis No. SFU127, engine No. SU63F, 8 cylinder in V formation, water-cooled, pushrod operated overhead valves with hydraulic tappets, bore 4.1in stroke 3.6in, 6230cc, automatic transmission, hypoid bevel final drive, independent coil spring front suspension, wheelbase 123in and 15in tyres.
£27,500-30,000 *S*

1970 Rolls-Royce Phantom VI Limousine, with coachwork by Mulliner, Park Ward Ltd, chassis No. PRH 4575, engine No. 4575 90° V8 cylinder, water-cooled, pushrod operated overhead valves, bore 4.1in stroke 3.6in, 6230cc, 4 speed automatic gearbox, hypoid bevel final drive, independent coil spring and wishbone front suspension, semi-elliptic leaf rear springs with piston-type dampers, wheelbase 145in, and 15in tyres, the engine has been modified to use unleaded fuel.
£34,500-40,000 *S*

1969 Rolls-Royce Phantom VI Limousine, with coachwork by Mulliner Park Ward, chassis No. PRH4573, engine No. 4573 V8 cylinder, set at 90° bore 4.1in stroke 3.6in, 6230cc, overhead pushrods and rockers, 4 speed automatic gearbox, shaft drive to live rear axle, independent coil spring front suspension, asymetric semi-elliptic leaf springs rear, wheelbase 145in.
£42,500-45,000 *S*

1973 Rolls-Royce Silver Shadow I, restored but excellent condition, ,000 miles recorded.
£14,000-16,000 *RH*

1938 Rover 16hp, with good bodywork mechanics and interior.
£4,400-5,400 *CC*

1963 Singer Vogue, with chassis No. B7208442H50, engine No. B7208442H50 4 cylinder, 1592cc, in very good condition throughout having had only one owner and 49,000 miles recorded. **£1,500-2,000** *ADT*

1932 Star Comet, a luxury 6 seater car, with black coachwork and hide interior.
£20,000-21,000 *DJ*

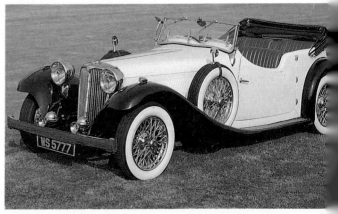

1935 SS1 Four Seat Sports Tourer, with chassis No. 248952, engine No. 248952 6 cylinder, overhead valves, 2.5 litre, 20hp, 4 speed synchromesh gearbox, 4 wheel mechanical brakes, semi-elliptic suspension, right-hand drive, is capable of 75mph and in excellent condition, finished in white with red leather interior.
£50,000-55,000 *C*

1932 SSII Two Door Coupé, this car has been extensively restored and is now in good condition. **£16,000-17,000** *ADT*

Side view of the 1932 SSII which has a 2 litre 6 cylinder side valve engine, finished in primrose yellow with black wings.

1932 Morris Eight Special Coupé, 4 cylinder, 885cc engine, totally rebuilt.
Est. **£8,000-9,000**   *ADT*

1936 Morris Eight Four Seat Tourer, 4 cylinder, 918cc engine.
£4,000-4,500   *ADT*

1934 Morris Minor Two Seater Tourer, 4 cylinder in line, water-cooled engine, side valve, 57mm bore x 83mm stroke, 847cc, 4 speed gearbox, single plate clutch, open shaft, spiral bevel final drive, semi-elliptic leaf springs at front and rear, wheelbase 78in, tyres 4.00 x 18in.
£6,000-6,500   *S*

In 1934, its final year of production, the Minor had a facelift, including the fitting of a synchromesh 4 speed gearbox, new Lockheed hydraulic brakes and smaller but wider section tyres. The 847cc, 4 cylinder side valve engine gave 20bhp at 4,000rpm, giving the car a top speed of around 50mph with a fuel consumption of about 45mpg.

1934 Morris Minor Two Seat Tourer.
£3,000-3,500   *CMA*

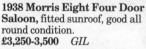

!939 Morris !eries E. !,800-5,000 !C

1938 Morris Eight Four Door Saloon, fitted sunroof, good all round condition.
£3,250-3,500   *GIL*

1937 Morris 8hp Series I Four Seat Tourer, 4 cylinder in line, water-cooled monobloc engine, side valve, 57mm bore x 90mm stroke, 918cc, 3 speed gearbox, single dry plate clutch, spiral bevel final drive, semi-elliptic leaf springs front and rear, wheelbase 90in, tyres 17in. **£5,000-6,000**   *S*

MORRIS

Make	FRANCE	GERMANY	ITALY	JAPAN	USA
Morris	−5%	−3%	−10%	−10%	−15%

1927 Morris Cowley 11.9hp Two Seater and Dickey, 4 cylinder side valve engine, water-cooled monobloc, bore 69.5mm x stroke 102mm, 1548cc, 3 speed gearbox, multi-plate clutch with cork inserts, semi-elliptic leaf springs, high tension magneto ignition, thermo-syphon cooling, shaft drive to special bevel rear axle, wheelbase 105in, 27 x 4.4 tyres.
Est. **£8,000-9,000** S(A)

MAKE Morris	ENGINE	DATES	1	2	3
Minor Series MM	918/4	1948-52	£1,800	£1,000	£300
Minor Series MM Conv	918/4	1948-52	£3,250	£1,500	£650
Minor Series II	803/4	1953-56	£1,500	£850	£300
Minor Series II Conv	803/4	1953-56	£3,000	£2,000	£650
Minor Series II Est	803/4	1953-56	£2,500	£1,000	£350
Minor 1000	948/4	1956-63	£1,750	£925	£250
Minor 1000 Conv	948/4	1956-63	£3,000	£2,000	£750
Minor 1000 Est	948/4	1956-63	£2,000	£1,200	£350
Minor 1000	1098/4	1963-71	£2,000	£950	£250
Minor 1000 Conv	1098/4	1963-71	£4,000	£2,250	£750
Minor 1000 Est	1098/4	1963-71	£3,000	£1,200	£400
Cowley 1200	1200/4	1954-56	£1,675	£1,000	£300
Cowley 1500	1489/4	1956-59	£1,750	£950	£350
Oxford MO	1476/4	1948-54	£2,000	£850	£250
Oxford MO Est	1476/4	1952-54	£3,000	£1,500	£350
Series II/III	1489/4	1954-59	£2,000	£1,200	£300
Series II/III/IV Est	1489/4	1954-60	£2,250	£1,350	£250
Oxford Series V Farina	1489/4	1959-61	£1,800	£800	£250
Oxford Series VI Farina	1622/4	1961-71	£1,750	£750	£200
Six Series MS	2215/6	1948-54	£2,500	£1,500	£500
Isis Series I/II	2639/6	1955-58	£2,500	£1,300	£450
Isis Series I/II Est	2639/6	1956-57	£2,600	£1,350	£500

Condition Guide

1. *A vehicle in top class condition but not 'concours' standard, either fully restored or in very good original condition*
2. *A good, clean, roadworthy vehicle, both mechanically and bodily sound*
3. *A runner, but in need of attention, probably both bodywork and mechanically*

Make: Morris
Model: Oxford
Type: Saloon
Years Manufactured: 1954-58 (Series II, III, IV)
Price when new: £745
Engine Type: Overhead valve 4 cyl
Size: 1489cc
Max Power: 50 bhp @ 4200 rpm; Series III (from 1956), 53 bhp @ 4350 rpm
Transmission: 4 speed
Performance: Max speed: 75 mph; Series III, 80 mph; 0-60: 25.0+ secs; Mpg: 28-32.

The Oxford was announced at the same time as the Minor, in October 1948.

1937 Morris 12-4 Saloon, 4 cylinder in line, water-cooled monobloc engine, side valves, 12hp, manual 3 speed gearbox, mechanical clutch, leaf springs.
Est. **£3,000-4,000** S(A)

1953 Morris Oxford Series I Saloon, 4 cylinder in line, water-cooled monobloc engine, side valve, 73.5mm bore x 87mm stroke, 1476cc, 4 speed manual gearbox, shaft drive to live rear axle, semi-elliptic leaf spring suspension rear, independent front.
£700-850 S

1948 Morris Eight Series E Four Door Saloon, 4 cylinder, 918cc engine.
£1,600-1,900 *ADT*

1953 Morris Minor Series II Convertible, 4 cylinder side valve, water-cooled engine, 803cc, 3 speed manual gearbox, shaft drive to live rear axle, semi-elliptic leaf spring suspension front and rear.
£4,500-5,500 *S*

Make: Morris
Model: Minor 1000
Type: Saloon
Years Manufactured: 1948-71
Price when new: 1956, 948cc, £628
Engine Type: Side valve 4 cyl, overhead valve 4 cyl
Size: 918cc/803cc/948cc/1098cc
Max Power: 918cc, 28 bhp @ 4400 rpm; 803cc, 30 bhp @ 4800 rpm; 948cc, 37 bhp @ 4750 rpm; 1098cc, 48 @ 5100 rpm
Transmission: 4 speed
Performance: Max speed: 918cc, 60 mph; 803cc, 62mph; 948cc, 75 mph; 1098cc, 80 mph; 0-60: 803c, 50.0+ secs; 948cc, 26.0 secs; 1098cc, 24.0 secs; Mpg: 38-43

1946 Morris Eight Series E Saloon, 4 cylinder, 918cc engine, original interior.
£3,250-3,500 *LF*

1961 Morris Minor 1000 Convertible, 4 cylinder in line, water-cooled monobloc engine, overhead valve, 64.58 bore x 83.72mm stroke, 1098cc, 4 speed gearbox, single dry plate clutch, floating hypoid rear axle, independent front suspension, semi-elliptic leaf rear springs, wheelbase 86in, tyres 14in.
est. **£3,000-3,500** *S*

1954 Morris Minor Four door Saloon, 4 cylinder, 919cc engine.
£1,500-2,000 *ADT*

1963 Morris 1000 Saloon, 4 cylinder, 1098cc engine.
£1,000-1,400 *LF*

1968 Morris Minor Saloon,
4 cylinder, 1098cc engine.
£1,000-1,200 *LF*

1969 Morris Minor Convertible,
4 cylinder, 1098cc engine.
£2,000-2,500 *LF*

INTERNATIONAL PRICE COMPARISON

The figures below represent a percentage increase or decrease on average condition for middle of the range models. The top models, particularly with a racing history or proven provenance, can be considered in the market place as any other work of art.

— = same price as U.K.

Make	FRANCE	GERMANY	ITALY	JAPAN	USA
Alfa Romeo	+2	+2	+5	+5	—
Aston Martin	+4	+2	+2	—	—
Austin Healey	—	+3	+3	+5	−5
Bentley	+5	+3	—	+10	−3
Bugatti	+5	—	+10	+20	+10
Cadillac	−10	—	−2	—	—
Chevrolet	−10	—	−2	—	+1
Ferrari	+5	—	+2	+15	—
Fiat	—	—	—	+2	+2
Ford	−4	+3	−4	−5	+8
Jaguar	—	+5	—	+3	−3
Lamborghini	+5	—	+2	+5	+6
Land Rover	−20	—	−5	—	−20
Maserati	+5	—	+7	+10	—
Mercedes-Benz	−5	+10	+3	−5	−5
MG	—	+7	−5	+5	+10
Mini (Austin)	+5	+3	—	+10	−15
Morris	−5	−3	−10	−10	−15
Porsche	+5	+5	+3	+7	+5
Rolls-Royce	+5	—	—	+15	+7
Triumph	+2	+5	—	+2	+4
Volkswagen	+5	+5	—	—	−15

1969 Morris Minor Traveller, Series V, 4 cylinder, 1098cc engine. **£2,600-2,900** *LF*

There was not a Series IV, this place having been taken by the Minor Million.

1964 Morris Mini Cooper 1275S, re-bodied and original mechanics refitted, new subframes, re-upholstered. **£1,800-2,200** *Cen*

The most famous of the Coopers is the 1275S which was introduced in 1964, with a 76bhp engine capable of 100mph.

INFORMATION SHEET

Make: BMC
Model: Mini Cooper/Cooper S
Type: Saloon
Years Manufactured: 1961-71
Quantity: Cooper, 101,242; Cooper S, 45,438
Price when new: £640-£756
Engine Type: Overhead valve 4 cyl
Size: 970S/997/998/1071S/1275Scc
Max Power: 970S, 64 bhp @ 6500 rpm; 997, 55 bhp @ 6000 rpm; 998, 54 bhp @ 5800 rpm; 1071S, 68 bhp @ 6500 rpm; 1275S, 76 bhp @ 6000 rpm
Transmission: 4 speed
Performance: Max speed: 970S, 92 mph; 997/998, 90 mph; 1071S, 93 mph; 1275S, 100 mph; 0-60: 970S, 13 secs; 997/998, 15 secs; 1071S, 14 secs; 1275S, 11.5 secs; Mpg: 35-40.

1971 Morris Mini Cooper S Mk 3.
£3,100-3,400 *Cen*

1971 Mini Cooper S 1275 Mk III Saloon, 4 cylinder in line, transverse mounted, water-cooled monobloc engine, overhead valve, 70.6mm bore x 81.33mm stroke, 1275cc, 4 speed manual gearbox with synchromesh, single dry plate clutch, front wheel drive, independent coil spring suspension front and rear, wheelbase 80in, tyres 10in.
Est. £6,000-8,000 *S*

1969 Mini Cooper, 4 cylinder, 998cc engine.
£2,000-2,250 *ADT*

MAKE Mini	ENGINE	DATES	CONDITION 1	2	3
Mini	848/4	1959-67	£2,000	£900	—
Mini Countryman	848/4	1961-67	£1,800	£900	—
Cooper Mk I	997/4	1961-67	£5,000	£3,000	£1,500
Cooper Mk II	998/4	1967-69	£3,500	£3,000	£1,500
Cooper S Mk I	var/4	1963-67	£6,000	£4,000	£2,000
Cooper S Mk II	1275/4	1967-71	£5,000	£4,000	£2,000
Innocenti Mini Cooper	998/4	1966-75	£3,000	£1,500	—

MG

The Morris Garage, founded by Cecil Kimber, first produced a tuned Morris Cowley. By the 1930s the company was producing a range of vehicles to make the MG name synonymous with sports cars. From the pre-war M J and P series, the famous T series through to the MGAs and MGBs, most MGs have enjoyed success on the race track and earned valuable foreign currency with incredible numbers exported, notably to the USA. MG appeared to survive the BMC years but development virtually ceased with the 1970 Leyland takeover.

1929 MG M Type, restored in the 1960s, body, mechanics and interior all in fair condition, has been with the last owner for 30 years.
£7,500-8,000 *CC*

1931 MC 'M' Type Sports Two Seater, 4 cylinder, water-cooled monobloc engine, overhead camshaft, 847cc, rated at 8hp, 4 speed manual gearbox (special order), shaft drive to live rear axle, semi-elliptic leaf spring front and rear suspension.
£18,000-19,000 *S*

1929 MG 'M' Type Midget Two Seater Sports, 4 cylinder in line, water-cooled monobloc engine, overhead valves, overhead camshaft, 57mm bore x 83mm stroke, 847cc, 3 speed gearbox, multi-plate clutch, open shaft, spiral bevel drive, semi-elliptic leaf spring suspension front and rear, wheelbase 78in, tyres 4.00 x 19in.
£9,000-10,000 *S*

1929 MG Midget Two Seater Special, 4 cylinder in line, water-cooled monobloc engine, side valve, 3 speed gearbox, multi-plate clutch, open drive shaft, spiral bevel drive, semi-elliptic leaf spring suspension front and rear, 4.00 x 19in tyres, constructed over several years using mainly original parts this car is still registered as an MG M Type.
£3,200-3,500 *S*

Make: MG
Model: Magnette ZA/ZB
Type: Saloon
Years Manufactured: ZA, 1953-56; ZB, 1956-58
Price when new: £914
Engine Type: Overhead valve 4 cyl
Size: 1489cc
Max Power: ZA, 60 bhp @ 4600 rpm; ZB, 68 bhp @ 5250 rpm
Transmission: 4 speed
Performance: Max speed: ZA, 85 mph; ZB, 90 mph; 0-60: ZA, 22.5 secs; ZB, 18.5 secs; Mpg: 28-32.

1933 MG L1 Magna Four Seater Open Sports, 6 cylinder in line, water-cooled monobloc engine, overhead valve, overhead camshaft, 57mm bore x 71mm stroke, 1086cc, 4 speed manual gearbox, twin dry plate clutch, spiral bevel rear axle, semi-elliptic leaf spring suspension, underslung at rear, wheelbase 94in, tyres 4.50 x 19in.
Est. **£28,000-32,000** *S*

Make: MG
Model: Midget
Type: Sports
Years Manufactured: 1961-79
Quantity: 226,526
Price when new: Mk I, £669; Mk II, £598; Mk III, £699; Mk III (1972-74), £969
Engine Type: Overhead valve 4 cyl
Size: Mk I, 948cc; Mk II, 1098cc; Mk III, 1275cc; 1500, 1493cc
Max Power: 47 bhp @ 5000 rpm to 65 bhp @ 5500 rpm
Max Torque: 52 ft/lb @ 3300 rpm to 77 ft/lb @ 3000 rpm
Transmission: 4 speed
Wheelbase: 80in
Performance: Max speed: 948cc 85 mph; 1098cc, 90 mph; 1275cc, 93 mph; 1500cc, 101 mph; 0-60: 948cc, 20.0 secs; 1098cc, 18.0 secs; 1275, 13.0+; 1500cc, 12.0+; Mpg: A Series engines, 35-45; 1500cc, 28-35.

933 MG 'L' Supercharged Sports Racing Two Seater, cylinder in line, water-cooled monobloc engine, overhead valves, 7mm bore x 71mm stroke, 1087cc, oller MG supercharger, 4 speed manual gearbox, shaft drive to live ear axle, semi-elliptic leaf spring uspension front and rear, tyres 50 x 19in.
st. **£45,000-50,000**   *S*

Make: MG
Model: A
Type: Sports, later also Coupé
Years Manufactured: 1489cc, 1955-59; 1588cc, 1959-61; 1622cc, 1961-62; twin cam, 1958-60
Price when new: 1489cc Sports, £844; twin cam Coupé, £1,357
Engine Type: Overhead valve 4 cyl, or twin cam 4 cyl
Size: 1489cc, 1588cc, 1622cc and 1588cc twin cam
Max Power: 1489cc, 72 bhp @ 5500 rpm; 1588cc, 80 bhp @ 5500 rpm; 1622cc, 86 bhp @ 5500 rpm; twin cam, 108 bhp @ 6700 rpm
Max Torque: 1489cc, 77 ft/lb @ 3500 rpm; 1588cc, 87 ft/lb @ 3800 rpm; 1622cc, 97 ft/lb @ 4000; twin cam, 104 ft/lb @ 4500 rpm
Transmission: 4 speed
Wheelbase: 94in
Performance: Max speed: 1489cc, 98 mph; 1588cc, 101 mph; 1622cc, 105 mph; twin cam, 114 mph; 0-60: 1489cc, 15.5 secs; 1588cc, 14.0 secs; 1622cc, 13.5 secs; twin cam, 13.0 secs; Mpg: 20-30.

Miller's is a price GUIDE not a price LIST

934 MG KN Magnette Four eater Tourer, chassis No. N 0427, engine No. 679 BKN. st. **£40,000-50,000**   *P*

e first small 6 cylinder MG was e F Type Magna of 1931/2, which d a 57 x 83mm 1271cc Wolseley rnet power unit disguised to make ook like an MG engine, giving .2bhp. From 1932-34 the F Type s replaced by the K Type agnettes with shorter stroke 57 x mm 1087cc engines developing .8bhp in the KA engine to 54.5bhp the KD, with pre-selector rboxes. From 1933-34 there was a re expensive Magna, the L Type, th the K2 wheelbase of 94in (the was 108in), the KB engine veloping 41bhp, and a pre-selector rbox. The K3, of which only just r 30 were made, from 1932-34 th supercharged 1087cc engines. rer still is the KN Tourer, it is ieved that only 25 open cars were duced, 8 in 1934 and the nainder in 1935. Powered by a 87cc, 6 cylinder overhead nshaft engine.

Did you know

MILLER'S Collectors Cars Price Guide builds up year by year to form the most comprehensive photo-reference system available

MAKE MG	ENGINE	DATES	CONDITION 1	2	3
TC	1250/4	1946-49	£17,000	£11,000	£7,000
TD	1250/4	1950-52	£13,000	£9,000	£5,000
TF	1250/4	1953-55	£19,000	£15,000	£8,000
TF 1500	1466/4	1954-55	£21,500	£14,500	£9,000
Ser. YA/YB	1250/4	1947-53	£5,500	£2,750	£1,500
Magnette ZA/ZB	1489/4	1953-58	£3,000	£2,000	£500
Magnette Mk III/IV	1489/4	1958-68	£2,500	£850	£350
MGA 1500	1489/4	1955-59	£10,000	£7,500	£3,500
MGA 1500 FHC	1489/4	1956-59	£8,500	£5,500	£3,000
MGA 1600	1588/4	1959-61	£11,000	£9,000	£4,500
MGA 1600 FHC	1588/4	1959-61	£9,000	£8,000	£3,000
MGA Twin Cam	1588/4	1958-60	£20,000	£17,000	£12,000
MGA Twin Cam FHC	1588/4	1958-60	£17,000	£13,000	£10,500
MGA 1600 Mk II	1622/4	1961-62	£12,000	£10,000	£4,000
MGA 1600 Mk II FHC	1622/4	1961-62	£9,000	£7,000	£3,000
MGB Mk I	1798/4	1962-69	£8,000	£4,000	£1,200
MGB GT Mk I	1798/4	1965-69	£5,000	£3,500	£1,000
MGB Mk II	1798/4	1967-71	£9,000	£4,000	£1,500
MGB GT Mk II	1798/4	1969-71	£5,000	£3,000	£850
MGB Mk III	1798/4	1971-74	£9,000	£4,000	£1,100
MGB GT Mk III	1798/4	1971-74	£5,000	£3,000	£1,000
MGB Roadster (rubber)	1798/4	1975-80	£6,000	£4,500	£1,200
MGB GT	1798/4	1975-80	£4,000	£3,000	£1,000
MGB Jubilee	1798/4	1975	£6,000	£3,000	£1,200
MGB LE	1798/4	1980	£8,500	£4,750	£2,250
MGB LE FHC	1798/4	1980	£6,000	£3,750	£2,000
MGC	2912/6	1967-69	£9,000	£7,500	£4,000
MGC GT	2912/6	1967-69	£7,000	£5,500	£2,000
MGB GT V8	3528/8	1973-76	£9,500	£6,000	£3,000
Midget Mk I	948/4	1961-62	£4,000	£2,000	£850
Midget Mk II	1098/4	1962-66	£3,000	£2,000	£850
Midget Mk III	1275/4	1966-74	£3,200	£2,000	£850
Midget 1500	1491/4	1975-79	£3,000	£2,000	£850

1934 MG 'P' Type Special, with 4 cylinder, pushrod overhead valve from MG 'TB', 66.5mm bore x 90mm stroke, twin SU carburettors, originally rated to develop 54bhp at 5,200rpm, channel section side members chassis with tubular cross members, beam axles front and rear carried on underslung semi-elliptic springs with sliding trunion rear location, MG 'TC' 4 speed gearbox with synchromesh on 2nd, 3rd and top, hydraulically operated 12in drum type brakes on all 4 wheels, centre lock wire type 16in diam wheels, with Engelbert racing tyres.
£25,000-30,000   *C(A)*

The MG 'PA' was introduced in 1934 as an improved version of the successful 'J2' midget. The first racing derivitive of the 'P' type was the supercharged 'Q' type, of basically similar chassis design, while the supercharged engine of the 'Q' type was used in further developed form in the all independently sprung 'R' type. All these models were powered by the Wolseley inspired overhead camshaft 4 cylinder engine.

1934 MG PA Airline Coupé, 4 cylinder in line, water-cooled monobloc engine, single overhead camshaft, overhead valves, 57mm bore x 83mm stroke, 847cc, single dry plate clutch, 4 speed gearbox, spiral bevel rear axle, semi-elliptic leaf spring front and rear suspension, wheelbase 87½in, tyres 19in, this car has won major class honours in MG Car Club concours events.
£55,000-60,000   *S*

Only 19 examples of this striking fastback bodied car were sold in 1934, though approximately the same number were available the following year on the PB Midget.

1934/35 MG Q Type Midget Replica, with 4 cylinder, 847cc engine.
Est. **£34,000-38,000**   *ADT*

Only 8 Q Types were ever produced so it is not surprising that replicas using the same component parts available in 1934 are fabricated.

1934 MG PA Roadster, registered 25th March 1934 as a demonstrator for J Cockshoot & Co., Manchester, chassis No. 0417 was the 166th PA Midget to be built.
Est. **£13,000-18,000**   *P*

The last ohc Midget was the P Type of 1934-36, the PA having a 34.9bhp 847cc engine and the PB a 43.3bhp, 939cc.

Miller's is a price **GUIDE** not a price **LIST**

1935 MG PA, with 4 cylinder, 885cc engine, in good condition.
Est. **£10,000-14,000** *LF*

1937 MG TA Midget Open Sports Two Seater, with 4 cylinder overhead valve monobloc engine, bore 63.5mm x stroke 102mm, capacity 1292cc, coil ignition, 4 speed synchromesh gearbox, central change, spiral bevel final drive, footbrake hydraulic on 4 wheels, handbrake on rear wheels, semi-elliptic front and rear suspension, wheelbase 94in, right-hand drive.
£23,000-24,000 *C*

First of the pushrod Midgets, the TA was announced in June 1936 and produced until the spring of 1939. Its engine was a derivative of the contemporary 10/40 Wolseley. The total deliveries of 3,003 units make it the rarest of the Ts apart from the short lived TB.

1937 MG TA.
£5,800-6,200 *P*

1939 MG TA Sports Roadster.
Est. **£10,000-14,000** *S(A)*

Make: MG	
Model: B GT V8	
Type: Fixed Head Coupé	
Years Manufactured: 1973-76	
Quantity: 2,591	
Price when new: 1973-74, £2,294	
Engine Type: Overhead valve V8	
Size: 3528cc	
Max Power: 137 bhp @ 5000 rpm	
Transmission: 4 speed plus overdrive	
Performance: Max speed: 125 mph; 0-60: 8.6 secs; Mpg: 20-27.	

1938 MG TA.
£16,000-17,000 *SEN*

1946 MG TC Sports.
£11,000-12,000 *CMA*

1946 MG TC Roadster, with cylinder, water-cooled monobloc engine, overhead valve, maker's horsepower 10.97hp, capacity 1250cc, 4 speed manual gearbox, wheel mechanical brakes, semi-elliptic spring suspension with dampers, 4.50 x 19in tyres.
Est. **£10,000-12,000** *S*

1949 MG TC Sports Roadster.
Est. **£16,000-18,000** *S*

1949 MG TC Sports Roadster,
with 34,000 miles recorded.
Est. £16,000-18,000   *S*

1950 MG TD, with 1250cc engine,
pushrod OHV, 54bhp at 5,200rpm,
right-hand drive, returned from
South Africa in very sound
condition.
£12,000-14,000   *SEN*

1953 MG TD, with 4 cylinder,
1250cc engine.
£13,000-13,500   *ADT*

**1954 MG TF 1¼ Litre Two Seater
Sports.**
Est. £18,000-21,000   *S(A)*

1954 MG Mk II Sports Roadster,
chassis No. TD 017220 and engine
No. EPAG/TD3 17560.
Est. £13,500-15,000   *S*

*The MG TD was preceded by the
highly successful TA, TB and TC
series of sports cars, and became one
of the most popular versions with it's
improved chassis, steering and
suspension details.*

1954 MG TF Midget, with
4 cylinder, 1250cc engine.
Est. £26,000-29,000   *ADT*

**1954 MG TF 1250 Two Seater
Sports,** 4 cylinder in line,
water-cooled monobloc engine,
pushrod operated overhead valves,
66.5mm bore x 90mm stroke,
1250cc, 4 speed gearbox, single dry
plate clutch, hypoid bevel live rear
axle, wishbone and coil spring front
suspension, semi-elliptic leaf spring
rear, wheelbase 94in, tyres 15in.
£18,500-19,500   *S*

MAKE	ENGINE	DATES	CONDITION		
MG			1	2	3
14/28	1802/4	1924-26	£30,000	£25,000	£20,000
18/80 Mk I/Mk II	2468/4	1927-33	£45,000	£28,000	£20,000
M Type Midget	847/4	1928-32	£14,000	£10,000	£8,000
J Type Midget	847/4	1932-34	£15,000	£13,000	£10,000
J3 Midget	847/4	1932-33	£20,000	£14,000	£12,000
PA Midget	847/4	1934-46	£13,000	£10,000	£8,000
PB Midget	936/4	1935-36	£14,000	£10,000	£8,000
F Type Magna	1271/6	1931-33	£35,000	£28,000	£20,000
L Type Magna	1087/6	1933-34	£35,000	£28,000	£20,000
K1/K2 Magnette	1087/6	1932-33	£50,000	£40,000	£35,000
N Series Magnette	1271/6	1934-36	£40,000	£30,000	£20,000
TA Midget	1292/4	1936-39	£15,000	£12,000	£9,000
SA 2 litre	2288/6	1936-39	£28,000	£18,000	£15,000
VA	1548/4	1936-39	£12,000	£8,000	£5,000
TB	1250/4	1939-40	£15,000	£11,000	£9,000

Value will depend on body style, history, completeness, racing history, the addition of a supercharger and originality.

Make: MG
Model: T Type
Type: Sports
Years Manufactured: TC, 1945-49; TD, 1949-53; TF, 1953-55
Quantity: TC, 10,000; TD, 29,664; TF, 6,200; TF1500, 3,400
Price when new: TC, £479; TD, £569; TF, £644; TF1500, £780
Engine Type: Overhead valve 4 cyl
Size: TC/TD/TF, 1250cc; TF1500, 1466cc
Max Power: TC/TD, 54.4 bhp @ 5200 rpm; TD Mk II, TF, 57 bhp @ 5500 rpm; TF1500, 63 bhp @ 5000 rpm
Max Torque: TC, TD, 64 ft/lb @ 2600 rpm; TF, 57 ft/lb @ 5500 rpm; TF1500, 63 ft/lb @ 5000 rpm
Transmission: 4 speed
Wheelbase: 94in
Performance: Max speed: TC/TD, 78 mph; TD Mk II, 80+ mph; TF1250, 85+ mph; TF1500, 90 mph; 0-60: TC/TD, 22.0 secs; TD Mk II/TF1250, 20.0 secs; TF1500, 19.0; Mpg: 25-30.

1968 MG C Roadster, with 6 cylinder in line, 2912cc, 145bhp engine. **£8,500-9,000** *SEN*

1967 MG TF Replica, this won the National Kit Car show in 1989. **£12,000-13,000** *CMA*

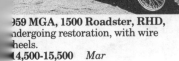

1954 MG TF. Est. **£18,000-25,000** *P*

The TF was the most advanced T-Type, with a more aerodynamic body, and was available with the 1250cc engine, or a 1461cc unit.

1959 MGA, 1500 Roadster, RHD, undergoing restoration, with wire wheels. **£14,500-15,500** *Mar*

1959 MGA Twin Cam Roadster, 4 cylinder in-line engine, water-cooled monobloc, twin overhead camshafts, bore 75.39mm x stroke 88.9mm, 1588cc, 4 speed gearbox, shaft drive to live rear axle, independent front suspension, semi-elliptic leaf springs rear, centre lock vented steel disc wheels with 5.90 x 15in tyres. Est. **£25,000-26,000** *S(A)*

1951 MG 'Y' A Type 1¼ Litre Four Door Saloon, 4 cylinder overhead valve, water-cooled monobloc engine, 66.7mm bore x 90mm stroke, 1250cc, 4 speed gearbox, independent front suspension, leaf springs at rear, live rear axle, wheelbase 99in, tyres 5.25 x 16in. **£2,000-2,250** *S*

1959 MGA Roadster, LHD, with 4 cylinder, 1588cc engine.
£9,000-10,000   *Ren*

1960 MGA 1600 Roadster.
£14,750-15,250   *SEN*

1960 MGA 1600, left-hand drive, body and mechanics in very good condition and the interior in good condition.
£5,500-6,000   *CC*

1959 MGA Roadster Mk I 1600, this car was first registered with Tommy Steele Productions and was used by Tommy Steele, with a letter of confirmation.
£12,750-13,500   *Cen*

31,000 examples of the Mk I 1588cc car were built in its 2 year production run.

1960 MGA Twin Cam 1588cc Two Seater Sports Coupé, with 4 cylinder, twin overhead camshaft water-cooled monobloc engine, bore 75.41mm x stroke 89mm, capacity 1588cc, 4 speed gearbox, live rear axle, wheelbase 94in and 5.90 x 15 tyres.
£11,000-12,000   *S*

1960 MGA 1600 Fixed Head Coupé, with 4 cylinder, 1588cc engine.
£9,000-10,000   *ADT*

1960 MGA 1500, with 4 cylinder, 1500cc engine.
Est. **£9,000-12,000**   *LF*

Introduced in 1955, the MGA was the last MG sports car with a separate chassis. It proved very successful in competitions and these cars handle extremely well, reaching 100mph and 25-30mpg.

Make	FRANCE	GERMANY	ITALY	JAPAN	USA
MG	—	+7%	−5%	+5%	+10%

MGA Roadster, LHD.
£6,750-7,250 *FOR*

1950 MG YT Tourer.
£11,000-12,000 *DB*

1961 MGA Mk II 1600cc Roadster,
4 cylinder in line, water-cooled
monobloc engine, pushrod operated
overhead valves, 76.2mm bore x
88.9mm stroke, 1622cc, 4 speed
gearbox, hypoid bevel final drive,
independent coil spring front
suspension, semi-elliptic leaf rear
springs, wheelbase 94in, tyres 15in.
£21,500-22,000 *S*

1962 MGA Mk II Roadster RHD,
with wire wheels, extensive
restoration.
£16,500-17,000 *Mar*

1962 MGA Mk II FHC, with
4 cylinder, 1622cc engine and
76,000 miles recorded.
£6,500-7,250 *ADT*

1967 MG Midget.
£5,500-7,250 *FOR*

1978 MG ZA Magnette, with
4 cylinder, 1622cc engine.
Est. £3,500-4,500 *ADT*

1973 MG Midget, with 4 cylinder,
1275cc engine.
£4,000-4,500   *LF*

1974 MG Midget, with 4 cylinder,
1275cc engine.
£2,000-2,500   *LF*

1978 MG Midget, with 4 cylinder,
1500cc engine.
£2,000-2,500   *ADT*

1964 MGB Roadster.
£3,500-4,000   *LF*

1967 MGB Roadster, with
4 cylinder, 1798cc engine, this car
has been totally rebuilt.
£3,600-4,200   *LF*

1974 MG Midget, this car has been
restored but not rebodied.
Est. £4,750-5,750   *ADT*

1964 MGB Roadster Mk I.
Est. £10,000-14,000   *LF*

1966 MGB Roadster.
£6,750-7,250   *Cen*

1970 MGB Roadster, with
4 cylinder, 1798cc engine.
£1,500-1,600   *LF*

1975 MGB Roadster.
Est. £6,000-6,250   *PC*

1971 MGB Roadster, rebuilt with
a Heritage body shell by Snowdens
of Harrogate, lightened and
balanced 1950cc engine, uprated
suspension chrome wire wheels,
new hood and tonneau, walnut door
cappings and dashboard and has
travelled only 1,900 miles since the
rebuild.
£12,000-12,500   *Cen*

1971 MGB Roadster.
Est. £4,000-6,000   *LF*

1971 MGB LHD, in original
condition with 50,000 miles
recorded.
£8,500-8,750   *FOR*

Make the Most of Miller's

*CONDITION is absolutely
vital when assessing the
value of a vehicle. Top
class vehicles on the whole
appreciate much more
than less perfect examples.
However a rare, desirable
car may command a high
price even when in need of
restoration*

1973 MGB Roadster, with
4 cylinder, 1800cc engine,
completely rebuilt with a British
Motor Heritage body shell and an
engine rebuild.
£8,000-8,500 *LF*

1976 MGB Roadster, with only
26,475 miles recorded.
£7,750-8,000 *Cen*

*Successor to the MGA the MGB
Roadster was introduced in 1962.*

1980 MGB Roadster, a totally
original car with only 5,317 miles
recorded and has been featured in
the MGOC magazine.
Est **£11,500-11,750** *Cen*

1972 MGB GT 2+2 Sports Coupé,
4 cylinder, water-cooled monobloc
engine, overhead valve, 76mm bore
x 85mm stroke, 1798cc, 4 speed
gearbox, coil spring independent
suspension at front, leaf springs at
rear, live rear axle, wheelbase 91in,
tyres 165R14.
£3,600-4,000 *S*

1973 MGB GT Coupé, with 4 speed
manual gearbox with overdrive.
£5,500-5,850 *GIL*

1973 MGB GT V8,
3528cc engine.
Est. **£10,000-11,000**
Ren

Make the Most of Miller's

*Price ranges in this book
reflect what one should
expect to pay for a similar
example. When selling,
however, one should
expect to receive a lower
figure. This will fluctuate
according to a dealer's
stock, saleability at a
particular time, etc. It is
always advisable, when
selling, to approach a
reputable specialist dealer
or an auction house which
has specialist sales*

Make: MG
Model: C
Type: Sports
Years Manufactured: 1967-69
Quantity: 8,999
Price when new: £1,257
Engine Type: Overhead valve
6 cyl
Size: 2912cc
Max Power: 145 bhp @ 5250
rpm
Max Torque: 170 ft/lb @ 3400
rpm
Transmission: 4 speed or auto,
overdrive optional from 1968
Wheelbase: 91in
Performance: Max speed: 120+
mph; 0-60: 10.0 secs; Mpg: 20-27.

1974 MGB GT V8, with 8 cylinder.
3528cc engine, extensively restored
98,000 miles recorded.
Est. **£7,000-8,000** *ADT*

1978 MGB GT.
£2,500-2,750
CMA

Make: MG
Model: B
Type: Sports
Years Manufactured: 1962-80
Price when new: 1962-64, £950; 1964-67, £870
Engine Type: Overhead valve 4 cyl
Size: 1798cc
Max Power: 62-95 bhp @ 5400 rpm
Max Torque: 87-110 ft/lb @ 3000 rpm
Transmission: 4 speed (auto option 1967-73, overdrive option 1963 on, standard 1975 on)
Wheelbase: 91in
Performance: Max speed: 105 mph; 0-60: 13.0 secs; Mpg: 26-30.

1976 MGB GT.
£4,000-4,500   *Cen*

1975 MGB GT V8, 3528cc Rover engine and capable of 125mph.
Est. **£12,000-16,000**   *LF*

1979 MGB GT, with only 23,000 miles recorded.
Est. **£5,500-5,800**   *Cen*

1980 MGB GT, with 3,000 miles recorded since restoration and a genuine 67,167 miles from new.
£3,000-3,300   *Cen*

1968 MGC GT, with wire wheels and overdrive.
£6,600-7,200   *LF*

Introduced in 1968 the MGC had a reworked version of the Austin Healey 3000 engine though BMC dropped plans to market a version as the Austin Healey 3000 Mk IV. 8,999 were built.

1968/69 MGC GT, with triple Dellorto carburettors, provides in excess of 200bhp and 7,000rpm, 6 cylinder, 2996cc engine.
£6,000-6,500   *ADT*

NASH

Charles Nash founded his company after he left General Motors in 1916 and the Nash Motor Company remained independent until 1954 when it became part of American Motor Corporation. That company subsequently produced such popular models as the Nash Metropolitan and the Rambler Rebel.

1930 Nash Series 480 Twin Ignition Six Five Passenger Sedan, 6 cylinder in-line engine, water-cooled monobloc, overhead valve, bore 3⅜in x stroke 4½in, 242cu in, 3 speed gearbox, single dry plate clutch, spiral bevel rear axle, semi-elliptic leaf spring suspension, wheelbase 118in, 20 x 5.50in tyres.
Est. **£8,500-9,500**   *S(A)*

1939 Nash 400 Six Seater Sedan, Lafayette 6 cylinder in-line engine, water-cooled monobloc, side valve, 234.8cu in, bore 3⅜in x stroke 4⅜in, 3 speed manual gearbox, wheelbase 116in, standard suspension.
Est. **£5,000-7,000**   *S(A)*

Nash Five Seat Tourer, c1917, 6 cylinder, 248cu in engine.
£2,300-2,600   *ADT*

Make: Nash-Healey
Type: Convertible and Coupé
Years Manufactured: 1951-54
Quantity: 506
Engine Type: Overhead valve 6 cyl
Size: 1951, 3848cc; 1952-54, 4140cc
Max Power: 1951, 125 bhp @ 4000 rpm; 1952-54, 135 bhp @ 4000 rpm
Max Torque: 1951, 215 ft/lb @ 2500 rpm; 1952-54, 230 ft/lb @ 2000 rpm
Transmission: 3 speed manual with overdrive
Wheelbase: 102in
Performance: Max speed: 102-104 mph; 0-60: 11.5-12.0 secs.

OAKMAN-TYPE

Oakman-Type Two Seater Stanhope, c1900, V-twin, air-cooled side mounted 4 stroke engine, capacity unknown, 2 speed gearbox, chain-cum-belt final drive, wheelbase 58in, tyres 26 x 2.125.
Est. **£18,000-18,500**   *ADT*

OLDSMOBILE

Arguably the Oldsmobile Curved Dash Runabout was the world's first mass-produced automobile. Founded by a brilliant engineer, Ranson Eli Olds, the company was taken over by General Motors. Oldsmobile has always been in the technical forefront of automobile development and styling.

MAKE	ENGINE	DATES	CONDITION		
Oldsmobile			1	2	3
Curved Dash	1600/1	1901-04	£20,000	£18,000	£14,000
30	2771/6	1925-26	£9,000	£7,000	£4,000
Straight Eight	4213/8	1937-38	£12,000	£8,000	£6,000

1936 Oldsmobile Straight 8, 8 cylinder, 3940cc engine, Australian Holden bodied versic the Oldsmobile Straight 8, origi condition, right-hand drive.
Est. **£9,000-12,000**   *LF*

1902 Oldsmobile Curved Dash.
£17,750-18,250
DB

1903 Oldsmobile 1.6 Litre Curved Dash.
£23,000-25,000   *B*

1952 Oldsmobile Rocket 88, 303.7cu in engine, 65,800 miles.
£15,000-16,000   *LF*

The 303.7cu in 'Rocket' engine was originally designed for the larger 98 series car but Oldsmobile hit on the idea of putting the engine in the 88.

1973 Owen Sedanca Two Door Coupé, 6 cylinder in line, water-cooled monobloc engine, twin overhead camshaft, 92.07mm bore x 106mm stroke, 4235cc, 3 speed automatic gearbox, hypoid bevel rear axle, independent front and rear suspension with coil springs, wheelbase 108in, tyres 15in.
Est. £18,000-22,000   *S*

OWEN

The Gurney Nutting Owen Sedanca originally appeared in the early 1930s and was generally based upon Rolls-Royce or Bentley chassis. The 1970s saw a new interpretation of bespoke car manufacture with the introduction of the Owen Sedanca built by SAC Design, a member of the SAC Group, like H. R. Owen. The wedge shaped car was shown at H. R. Owen's London showrooms and then at the Scottish Motor Show of 1978.

PACKARD

The first Packard was produced in 1899 by the Packard brothers. They made the first 'double six' engine but by 1929 only 8 cylinder engines were in use. During the 1950s Packard almost had a dual production, half making economy models and half the workforce producing the top range, which only represented less than 10% of the total production. Packard merged with Studebaker in 1954.

1916 Packard Twin 6, Seven Seater Tourer.
Est. £60,000-80,000   *P*

1923 Packard Six Series 1-26 Tourer, fully restored, Rudge wire wheels, right-hand drive.
£27,500-28,000   *Mot*

1927 Packard Model 443 Custom Fourth Series 5 Passenger Phaeton, 8 cylinder in-line engine, water-cooled monobloc, side valve, bore 3½in x 5in stroke, 384.8cu in, 3 speed gearbox, 2 plate clutch, hypoid rear axle, semi-elliptic leaf spring suspension, wheelbase 143in.
£24,500-25,500   *SNY*

1930 Packard 734 Speedster, with coachwork by Packard Custom, engine No. 184008, chassis No. 184005, frame No. 184006, steering box No. 184001, straight 8 engine, water-cooled, side valve, bore 3½in x 5in stroke, 384cu in, 4 speed transmission, hypoid bevel rear axle, semi-elliptic leaf spring suspension, wheelbase 134½in, 7 x 19in tyres.
£159,000-165,000 *SNY*

1930 Packard Custom Eight 740 Convertible Coupé, 8 cylinder in-line engine, water-cooled monobloc, side valve, bore 3½in x 5in stroke, 384.8cu in, 4 speed gearbox, 2 plate clutch, hypoid bevel rear axle, semi-elliptic leaf spring suspension, wheelbase 140½in, 19in tyres.
£45,000-45,500 *SNY*

1933 Packard Super 8 Convertible Victoria, coachwork by Dietrich, 8 cylinder in line, 6306cc engine, 88mm bore x 127mm stroke (384.8cu in), detachable cylinder head, 2 side valves per cylinder, single Detroit lubricator carburettor, 145bhp at 3,200rpm, single dry plate clutch and 3 speed synchromesh manual gearbox, separate pressed steel chassis frame with channel section side members and tubular cross bracings, Bijur automatic chassis lubrication, semi-elliptic leaf spring suspension front and rear with lever type hydraulic dampers, 4 wheel cable operated drum brakes, wheelbase 141in, 17in wire spoke wheels with 7.00 x 17in tyres.
Est. **£150,000-180,000** *CNY*

James Ward Packard, an electric lamp manufacturer of Warren, Ohio and his brother William Doud bought their first car, a Winton, in 1898. Dissatisfied with it they decided to design and build their own car and in 1903 opened their new factory in Detroit, becoming within a few years one of America's leading car manufacturers.

MAKE	ENGINE	DATES	CONDITION		
Packard			1	2	3
Twin Six	6946/12	1916-23	£30,000	£25,000	£18,000
6	3973/6	1921-24	£20,000	£15,000	£12,000
6, 7, 8 Series	5231/8	1929-39	£45,000	£30,000	£22,000
12	7300/12	1936-39	£45,000	£30,000	£18,000

1933 Packard Dual-Cowl Custom Sport Phaeton, with coachwork by Dietrich, engine No. 901139, Dietrich body No. 20695488, Firewall No. 174354, V12 engine, water-cooled, side valve, bore 3⁷⁄₁₆in x 4in stroke, 445.5cu in, 160bhp at 3,200rpm, 3 speed transmission, semi-elliptic leaf springs front and rear, wheelbase 147in, 7.50 x 17in tyres.
£585,000-600,000   *SNY*

1935 Packard Fourteenth Series Twelve 1407 Club Sedan, 67° V12 cylinder, water-cooled, side valve engine, 3⁷⁄₁₆in bore x 4½in stroke, 473.3cu in capacity, 3 speed synchromesh gearbox, single plate clutch, bevel rear axle, wheelbase 139¼in, tyres 17in.
£35,200-36,500   *S*

The V12 Series 1407 was Packard's flagship car in 1935/36 and was offered in 9 body styles.

1936 Packard Series 1407 V12 Coupé, chassis No. 938219, engine No. 904577, V12 cylinder, side valve, water-cooled, bore 3⁷⁄₁₆in x 4in stroke, 473.3cu in, 3 speed floor shift gearbox, single plate clutch, bevel rear axle, wheelbase 139in, 7.50 x 17in tyres.
35,000-40,000   *SNY*

1936 Packard V12 Speedster.
£195,000-200,000   *BLE*

1937 Packard 120 Four Door Convertible Sedan, serial No. 1097-1114, 8 cylinder in-line engine, water-cooled monobloc, side valve, bore 3¼in x 4½in stroke, 282cu in, 3 speed synchromesh gearbox, single dry plate clutch, hypoid bevel final drive, independent coil spring front suspension, semi-elliptic leaf rear springs, wheelbase 120in, 16in tyres.
£30,000-35,000   *SNY*

1937 Packard Model 1507 V12 Convertible Coupé, chassis No. 1139210, 67° V12 cylinder, side valve, water-cooled, bore 3⁷⁄₁₆in x 4in stroke, 473.3cu in, 3 speed gearbox, single plate vacuum assisted clutch, bevel rear axle, wheelbase 139in, 7.50 x 16in tyres, in need of restoration.
35,000-40,000   *SNY*

1938 Packard Super Eight Coupé, 8 cylinder, water-cooled monobloc engine, side valve, 5232cc, shaft drive to live rear axle, 3 speed synchromesh gearbox, single plate clutch, semi-elliptic leaf spring suspension.
Est. **£3,000-5,000**   *S*

1946 Packard Custom Super Clipper Seven Passenger Limousine, 8 cylinder, 5838cc engine, left-hand drive.
3,000-4,500   *C*

PALMER-SINGER

1911 Palmer-Singer 6-40 Five Passenger Touring Car, chassis No. 4021, engine No. 106 LOKJHE, 6 cylinder in line, cast in blocks of 3, water-cooled, side valve, T-head, bore 4in x 4¾in stroke, 358cu in, 4 speed gearbox, shaft drive to live bevel rear axle, semi-elliptic leaf springs to front and rear, wheelbase 125in, 36 x 4in front tyres, 37 x 5in rear.
£42,000-45,000   *SNY*

PANHARD LEVASSOR

1914 Panhard Levassor 28hp Four Seater Tourer, by Driguet.
Est. **£40,000-60,000**   *P*

1897 Panhard Levassor Phoenix Twin Cylinder.
£50,000-52,000   *DB*

1928 Panhard   Levassor 1.8 Litre 16/45 X59 Weymann Faux Cabriolet.
£14,700-17,000   *B*

PEUGEOT

Founded in 1889 by Robert Peugeot, Peugeot are one of the oldest manufacturers of automobiles. They probably introduced the 'small car' concept with the Bugatti designed Bebe of 1913. Through a long and distinguished history including some very successful racing cars, Peugeot, controlling Talbot and Citroën, are amongst the giants of motor manufacturing.

MAKE	ENGINE	DATES	CONDITION		
Panhard			1	2	3
Dyna	610/745/				
	851/2	1947-53	£4,000	£2,000	£1,000
PL 17	851/2	1959-65	£3,000	£2,000	£1,000
24 CT	851/2	1963-67	£4,000	£3,000	£2,000

1911 Peugeot Tourer Type 135, 4 cylinder, side valve (T-head) engine, 100mm bore x 160mm stroke, 22hp, magneto ignition, 4 speed and reverse transmission by 2 concentric shafts and 2 pairs of bevel-gears on live axle, cone clutch, right-hand drive.
£31,000-33,000   *C(A)*

MAKE	ENGINE	DATES	CONDITION		
Peugeot			1	2	3
153	2951/4	1913-26	£5,000	£4,000	£2,000
163	1490/4	1920-24	£5,000	£4,000	£2,000
Bebe	676/4	1920-25	£7,000	£6,000	£3,000
156	5700/6	1922-24	£7,000	£5,000	£3,000
174	3828/4	1922-28	£6,000	£4,000	£2,000
172	714/4	1926-28	£4,000	£3,000	£1,500
183	1990/6	1929-30	£4,000	£3,000	£1,500
201	996/4	1930-36	£4,000	£3,000	£1,500
402	2140/4	1938-40	£4,000	£3,000	£1,000

Locate the source

The source of each illustration in Miller's can be found by checking the code letters below each caption with the list of contributors

PHILOS

1913 Philos Type 4M 1.2 Litre Tourer, in need of total restoration.
£6,500-7,500   *B*

1913 Philos Tourer.
£9,500-10,000   *DB*

PIERCE ARROW

The George N. Pierce Co. was founded in 1901. A manufacturer of bicycles and bird cages, the cars were immediately successful. In 1904 a 28hp 'Great Arrow' was to win The Glidden Tour, a reliability test, making the Pierce Great Arrow. In 1909 the Pierce-Arrow was introduced and the limited production seldom met the high demand for the vehicle. In 1913 the first Pierce-Arrows appeared with the headlamp cowls attached to the top of the front wings.

1934 Pierce-Arrow Straight Eight Sedan, 6000cc engine.
£18,000-20,000   *SEN*

PONTIAC

1985 Pontiac Firebird Trans-Am, V8, 305cu in, 5 litre engine, tuned port fuel injected.
Est. **£8,000-10,000**   *LF*

1987 Pontiac Firebird Trans-Am, V8, 305cu in, 5 litre carburettor engine.
£9,500-10,000   *LF*

MAKE	ENGINE	DATES	CONDITION		
Pontiac			1	2	3
Six-27	3048/6	1926-29	£10,000	£8,000	£5,000
Silver Streak	3654/8	1935-37	£12,000	£9,000	£5,500
	3638/6	1937-49	£7,000	£4,000	£3,500
	4078/8	1937-49	£7,000	£4,000	£3,500

Make: Pontiac
Model: Firebird
Type: Coupé/Convertible
Years Manufactured: 1966-81
Engine Type: various 6 cyl, V6 cyl, V8 cyl
Size: 3.8-7.5 litre
Max Power: 165-375 bhp
Transmission: 4 speed or auto

POPE WAVERLEY

Originally known as the Waverley, and built initially by the Indiana Bicycle Company of Indianapolis from 1898, the Waverley electric became the Pope Waverley when the company became the Waverley Department of the Pope Motor Car Co. in 1903.

1904 Pope Waverley Model 22 Two Seater Electric, 3hp electric motor mounted on rear axle, 2 forward speeds and reverse, tiller steering, shaft final drive, 8 x 12 volt storage batteries providing power and in-built recharging unit, full elliptic springs all round, mechanical brakes acting on the rear wheels, and electric brakes connected to the motor.
£12,000-13,000 *S*

PORSCHE

By 1939 Dr. Ferdinand Porsche had designed the immortal Volkswagen as well as being involved in the SS Mercedes and the world beating Auto Union racing cars. Besides the world championship winning sports cars both the 356 series and the 911s combine to make Porsche one of the most successful post war specialist car manufacturers.

1985 Replica Porsche GP Spyder RSK 718, replica of the rally car of the late 1950s based on a VW floor pan and a twin bore engine.
Est. **£4,000-5,000** *LF*

1960 Porsche 356B Sports Coupé.
Est. **£20,000-25,000** *S(A)*

1958 Porsche 356 A Coupé, rear mounted engine, 4 cylinder horizontally opposed, air-cooled, pushrod operated overhead valve, 82.5mm bore x 74mm stroke, 1582cc, 4 speed manual gearbox in unit with engine and transaxle, spiral bevel final drive, independent front and rear suspension, wheelbase 83in.
Est. **£25,000-30,000** *S*

Ferdinand Porsche, a distinguished engineer, set up his own design bureau, and was responsible for the first Volkswagens and the mid-engined Grand Prix car for Auto Union. The first 356 Porsche car relied on the VW Beetle chassis and components from 1948, but as the years progressed, more and more specialised Porsche components were developed. The 356 A model was introduced in 1955, and was the fastest production car in Germany at the time.

Make: Porsche
Model: 356A
Type: Coupé/Convertible
Years Manufactured: 1955-59
Quantity: 20,626 all models
Engine Type: Overhead valve flat 4 cyl; double overhead camshaft flat 4 cyl
Size: 1300 (1955-57), 1290cc to 1600GS/GT Carrera (1958-59), 1588cc
Max Power: 1300 (1955-57), 44 bhp @ 4200 rpm; 1600GS/GT Carrera (1958-59), 105/110 bhp @ 6500 rpm
Max Torque: 1600GS/GT Carrera (1958-59), 86 ft/lb @ 5000 rpm
Transmission: 4 speed manual
Wheelbase: 82.7in
Performance: Max speed: 98-125 mph; 0-60: 10.5-14.4 secs.

1962 Porsche 356B T6 Sports Coupé.
Est. **£13,000-16,000** *S(A)*

1962 Porsche 356B Fixed Head Coupé.
Est. **£14,000-15,000** *S*

The first 356 cars were built in Stuttgart in 1950, and the model was in production for 15 years.

Make	FRANCE	GERMANY	ITALY	JAPAN	USA
Porsche	+5%	+5%	+3%	+7%	+5%

1964 Porsche 356SC Coupé, left-hand drive.
Est. £13,000-15,000   *C*

The 356C was visually little changed from the previous B series except that it had a new wheel and hubcap design, which covered the all new 4 wheel disc brakes, a larger rear window and twin air vents on the engine cover.

1967 Porsche 912 Coupé.
£5,700-6,200   *Cen*

1967 Porsche 912, 4 cylinder, 1582cc engine.
Est. £5,500-6,500   *ADT*

To fill the gap left between the 356 and the 911, Porsche introduced the 912 which effectively was the 356 flat 4 engine in the 911 coupé bodyshell.

1965 Porsche 356C Coupé, left-hand drive.
Est. £10,000-12,000   *S*

The 'C' specification cars developed some 75bhp at 5,200rpm.

Dr Ferdinand Porsche, third of four children of a Reichenberg tinsmith, must go down as one of the greatest motor car designers, having been involved in the design of the mighty supercharged Mercedes-Benz cars of the 20s, at the other extreme Hitler's people's car, the Volkswagen, and finally the sports car which bore his own name and which was to carve out an enviable reputation in motor sport and also became a plaything of the rich. The first Porsche cars were based on the Volkswagen and the flat 4, air-cooled engine was used throughout the 356 range. The impressive performance of the 356 was not always matched by the driving abilities of its owners, the car having distinctive handling characteristics, however once mastered there are few cars more sure footed than the 356.

Make: Porsche
Model: 912
Type: Sports Coupé/Targa Carbiolet
Years Manufactured: 1965-69
Quantity: 30,745
Price when new: £2,467
Engine Type: Flat 4 cyl
Size: 1582cc
Max Power: 90 bhp @ 5800 rpm
Max Torque: 87 ft/lb @ 3500 rpm
Transmission: 4 speed or 5 speed
Wheelbase: 1965-68, 87.1in; 1969, 89.3in
Performance: Max speed: 119 mph; 0-60: 11.9 secs; Mpg: 25.

1964 Porsche 356SC Cabriolet 100C, 4 cylinder, horizontally opposed in pairs, air-cooled by fan, single camshaft operating inclined overhead valves through pushrods, 82.5mm bore x 74mm stroke, 1582cc, single dry plate clutch, 4 speed synchromesh manual gearbox, hypoid bevel final drive, trailing arm and torsion bar front suspension, independent rear by swing axles and torsion bars, wheelbase 83in, tyres 5.60 x 15in, right-hand drive.
£65,000-70,000   *S*

PORSCHE

1968 Porsche 911S Coupé,
6 cylinder, horizontally opposed,
air-cooled engine, single overhead
camshaft cylinder heads, 80mm
bore x 66mm stroke, 1991cc, 5 speed
synchromesh gearbox in unit with
transaxle, spiral bevel final drive,
independent front and rear
suspension,
tyres 15in.
£14,300-15,000   *S*

*The Frankfurt Motor Show in
September 1963 saw the unveiling of
the Porsche 901, to replace the long
lived 356 and using many of the
features of that car. It was different
in that it had a 6 cylinder engine of
2 litre capacity which developed
some 130bhp at 6,200rpm. It was
developed into the 911 in 1964. The
911S, introduced in August 1966,
had modified camshafts, bigger
valves and 9.1:1 compression ratio
and developed 160bhp at 6,600rpm,
giving the car a top speed of around
140mph.*

1969 Porsche 911E Coupé,
left-hand drive, 95,000 miles.
£8,600-9,000   *Cen*

*Originally designated the 901, it was
changed to 911 following protests
from Peugeot.*

1971 Porsche 914, in need of major
restoration.
£1,100-1,250   *C*

*The majority of vehicles built were
powered by the Volkswagen 411 type
air-cooled engine. In its 6 year
production run, a little over 115,000
vehicles were built.*

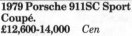

**1979 Porsche 911SC Sport
Coupé.**
£12,600-14,000   *Cen*

**1989 Porsche 911 Turbo
Cabriolet,** 6 cylinder horizontally
opposed, air-cooled, turbo charged
engine, 97mm bore x 74.4mm
stroke, 3299cc, dry plate clutch,
5 speed manual gearbox, hypoid
bevel rear axle, independent front
and rear suspension, wheelbase
89in, tyres 16in, delivery mileage
only.
£73,000-75,000   *S*

*The turbo charged version became
available in 1975, and this car, the
latest model from Porsche, produces
300bhp (DIN).*

MAKE	ENGINE	DATES	CONDITION		
Porsche			1	2	3
356	var/4	1949-51	£20,000	£15,000	£10,000
356 Cabriolet	var/4	1951-53	£25,000	£17,000	£12,000
356A	1582/4	1955-59	£12,000	£7,000	£3,000
356A Cabriolet	1582/4	1956-59	£18,000	£11,000	£8,000
356A Speedster	1582/4	1956-58	£28,000	£20,000	£15,000
356 Carrera	1582/				
	1966/4	1960-65	£30,000	£25,000	£18,000
356C	1582/4	1963-65	£12,000	£9,000	£4,000
356C Cabriolet	1582/4	1963-64	£18,000	£14,000	£8,000
911/911L/T/E	1991/6	1964-68	£10,500	£6,500	£4,500
912	1582/4	1965-68	£9,000	£6,000	£2,500
911S	1991/6	1966-69	£12,000	£9,000	£6,000
911S	2195/6	1969-71	£14,000	£10,500	£6,500
911T	2341/6	1971-73	£13,000	£9,000	£6,500
911E	2341/6	1971-73	£15,000	£11,500	£7,000
914/4	1679/4	1969-75	£4,000	£3,000	£1,000
914/6	1991/6	1969-71	£5,000	£3,500	£1,500
911S	2341/6	1971-73	£17,000	£14,000	£9,500
Carrera RS lightweight	2687/6	1973	£60,000	£40,000	£25,000
Carrera RS Touring	2687/6	1973	£45,000	£30,000	£20,000
Carrera 3	2994/6	1976-77	£15,000	£10,000	£7,000
924 Turbo	1984/4	1978-83	£8,500	£6,500	£4,500

Make: Porsche
Model: 911
Type: Sports Coupé
Years Manufactured: 1974-77
Quantity: 37,737 all models
Engine Type: Single overhead
camshaft flat 6
Size: 2687cc
Max Power: 911 (1974), 150 bhp
@ 5700 rpm; 911S/Carrera
(1975-77), 165 bhp @ 5800 rpm
Max Torque: 911 (1974), 168
ft/lb @ 3800 rpm; 911S/Carrera
(1975-77), 161/168 ft/lb @ 4000
rpm
Transmission: 4/5 speed manual
Wheelbase: 89.4in
Performance: Max speed:
130-145 mph; 0-60: 7.5-8.5 secs.

1965 Porsche 356SC Cabriolet.
£25,000-30,000   *AUT*

1973 Porsche 911 Carrera RS 2.7 Litre Touring Coupé.
Est. £45,000-55,000   *B*

1989 Porsche 959, flat 6 cylinder engine, water-cooled heads, double overhead camshafts, 4 valves per cylinder, 2850cc, 6 speed gearbox, hydraulic clutch, rear differential and Porsche control clutch, 4 wheel drive, coil spring and wishbone suspension front and rear, tyres 17in, Kevlar and aluminium body.
Est. **£480,000-500,000**   *S(M)*

The first of the Porsche 959s left the production line in 1988. A limited edition of 250 or so cars were produced in the short production run ending in 1989. The flat 6 engine has twin turbochargers and intercoolers and develops 450bhp at 7,500rpm and the 959 adopts the Bosch Motronic injection and ignition system as used in the 956 Group C racers. The car has 4 wheel drive and ABS.

1973 Porsche 911 2.7 Litre Carrera RS Touring Coupé.
Est. £50,000-60,000   *P*

The 911 Carrera RS of 1973 was ostensibly a competition car but was also available, in limited numbers, as a road car. The engine produced 210bhp at 6,300rpm, the 911S having produced 190bhp at 6,500rpm. Performance was 0-60mph in 5.5 seconds, 0-100mph in 13.0 seconds, and a maximum speed of 149mph.

73 Porsche Carrera ST, 2.7 litre, flat ngine and manual earbox.
t. £45,000-50,000   *ADT*

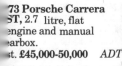

RELIANT

RAILTON

1935 Railton Terraplane Straight 8, 4.1 Litre, aluminium body by Coachcraft.
£18,000-22,000   *Cen*

1935 Railton Straight 8 with Coachcraft bodywork.
£30,000-32,000   *DB*

The owners of the failed Invicta company invited Reid Railton to produce a car which would make use of American power in a typically British chassis and body. Thus, the Terraplane was 'born' and in 1935 using the Hudson straight 8 engine on the Essex Terraplane chassis, the Railton quickly became popular on account of its classic British appearance, excellent acceleration and reasonable price.

RELIANT

Although Reliant was founded as early as 1935 by T. L. Williams, the first public offering was in 1952, an Austin powered three wheeler. Despite a series of three wheelers Reliant are most famous for the GTE models.

1970 Reliant Scimitar Grand Touring Estate (GTE), Ford 3.0 litre V6 engine.
£1,000-1,500   *Cen*

1965 Reliant Sabre Six, fully restored, an excellent example.
£7,500-8,500   *GWC*

1983 Reliant Scimitar GTC, original car, low mileage.
£11,750-12,500   *GWC*

1972 Reliant Scimitar GTE, restored condition.
£5,000-7,000   *CTC*

Make: Reliant
Model: Sabre
Type: Sports
Years Manufactured: 1961-64
Quantity: 6 cyl, 77
Price when new: 4 cyl, £1,064; 6 cyl, £1,016
Engine Type: 4 cyl or 6 cyl
Size: 1703cc/2553cc
Max Power: 57-109 bhp
Transmission: 4 speed
Performance: Max speed: 6 cyl, 111 mph; 0-60: 6 cyl, 12.2 secs; Mpg: 6 cyl, 21.

MAKE	ENGINE	DATES	CONDITION		
Reliant			1	2	3
Sabre	1703/4	1961-63	£4,000	£2,000	£1,000
Sabre Six	2553/8	1962-64	£4,500	£2,000	£1,000
Scimitar GT	2553/8	1964-70	£2,500	£1,000	—
Scimitar GTE	2994/8	1969-86	£4,000	£1,500	£1,000
Scimitar GTC	2792/8	1980-86	£6,000	£3,500	£2,000

RENAULT

The Renault brothers, particularly Louis Renault, started the giant Renault company in 1898. By the first World War they were producing nearly 25% of all French motor cars. Renault was nationalised in 1945 and continues to produce mass market automobiles, but there are several very collectable models.

1909 Renault 20/30hp Limousine, coachwork by Million-Guiet, engine No. 3176, 4 cylinder, 20/30hp, air compressor impulse starter, 4 speed and reverse transmission, right-hand drive.
£45,500-48,000   *C(A)*

Louis Renault produced his first car with a 1¾hp air-cooled De Dion engine in 1898. Within 6 months the small firm founded by Louis and his brothers Marcel and Fernand delivered 60 cars.

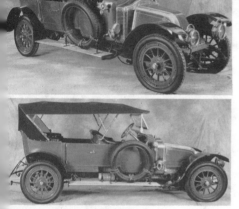

1912 Renault 14/20hp Tourer, with 4 cylinder in-line engine, cast in pairs, water-cooled, side valve, bore 3⁹⁄₁₆in x 5½in stroke, 219.28cu in, 4 speed gearbox, shaft drive to bevel rear axle, right-hand drive, semi-elliptic leaf front springs, three-quarter elliptic leaf rear springs, wheelbase 134in, 880 x 120mm tyres.
£28,000-32,000   *SNY*

1929 Renault KZ3 4/5 Seat Tourer, original and in good condition throughout, right-hand drive.
£13,500-14,000   *ELD*

Condition Guide

1. *A vehicle in top class condition but not 'concours' standard, either fully restored or in very good original condition*
2. *A good, clean, roadworthy vehicle, both mechanically and bodily sound*
3. *A runner, but in need of attention, probably both bodywork and mechanically*

Make: Renault
Model: 8 Gordini
Type: Saloon
Years Manufactured: 1965-70
Price when new: £984
Engine Type: 4 cyl
Size: 1108cc/1255cc
Max Power: 95-103 bhp
Transmission: 4 speed or 5 speed
Performance: Max speed: 1300, 108 mph; 0-60: 1300, 10.9 secs; Mpg: 1300, 25.

1929 Renault Monasix 12.5hp Saloon.
£5,300-6,000   *S*

MAKE Renault	ENGINE	DATES	CONDITION 1	2	3
4CV	747/ 760/4	1947-61	£3,500	£2,000	£850
Fregate	1997/4	1952-60	£3,000	£2,000	£1,000
Dauphine	845/4	1956-66	£1,500	£1,000	£350
Dauphine Gordini	845/4	1961-66	£2,000	£1,000	£450
Floride	845/4	1959-62	£3,000	£2,000	£600
Caravelle	956/ 1108/4	1962-68	£4,500	£2,800	£750
R4	747/ 845/4	1961-86	£2,000	£1,500	£350
R8/R10	1108/4	1962-71	£1,800	£750	£200
R8 Gordini	1108/4	1965-66	£8,000	£5,000	£2,000
R8 Gordini	1255/4	1966-70	£8,000	£5,500	£2,500
R8S	1108/4	1968-71	£2,000	£1,200	£400

RENAULT

**1975 Renault Alpine A110 Two
Door Coupé,** rear engine,
4 cylinder, bore 73mm x 77mm
stroke, 1289cc, 9.5:1 compression,
85bhp (DIN) at 6,000rpm, pushrod
overhead valve, twin choke Weber
32DIR carburettor, 4 speed gearbox,
tubular backbone frame with
outriggers and glass reinforced
plastic bodywork, independent front
suspension with coil springs and
wishbones, rear by swing axles and
coil springs, disc brakes all round
with servo, alloy wheels 4½J rims,
145-15 or 165-13 tyres, wheelbase
83in, 1,200lb in weight.
£10,000-11,000   *C*

**1982 Renault 5 Turbo I
Convertible.**
Est. **£11,000-12,000**   *P*

1983 Renault 5 Turbo 2, resprayed
and converted to right-hand drive.
£11,000-12,000   *GWC*

1981 Renault 5 Turbo I, resprayed.
£17,000-18,000   *GWC*

RICHARD

**1902 Georges Richard Rear
Entrance Tonneau,** chassis No.
490.
Est. **£30,000-40,000**   *C*

1902 Georges Richard 10hp Rea
Entrance Tonneau, vertical twin
cylinder engine, monobloc,
water-cooled, overhead atmospher:
inlet valves, side exhaust valves,
bore 100mm x 100mm stroke,
1571cc, 3 speed gearbox with
reverse, live rear axle, semi-ellipti
front and rear suspension,
wheelbase 76in.
£42,000-44,000   *S*

REO

1905 Reo 16hp Model 'A' Four Seater with Detachable Tonneau, horizontally opposed engine underfloor twin cylinder side valve, water-cooled, bore 4¾in x 6in, rating 16hp (capacity 3.6 litres), 2 speed epicyclic gear with reverse, full elliptic springing all round, chain final drive, wheelbase 85in, 30 x 3½ tyres.
£19,250-20,000   *S*

Built by the company formed by Ransom E. Olds, following his departure from Oldsmobile.

ROESCH TALBOT

1934 Roesch Talbot AV 105 Sports Tourer.
Est. **£110,000-130,000**   *P*

1934 Riley 9hp Monaco Saloon, 4 cylinder in-line engine, water-cooled monobloc, pushrod operated overhead valves, bore 60.3mm x 95.2mm stroke, 1089cc, 4 speed gearbox, enclosed shaft spiral bevel rear axle, semi-elliptic leaf springs front and rear, wheelbase 106in, 19in tyres, ideal project for restoration.
Est. **£3,000-4,000**   *S*

RILEY

Riley was founded in 1898 and became part of the Nuffield empire in 1938. After the second World War Riley were really only 'badge-engineered' BMC models. The Riley name ceased to be used after 1969.

1936 Riley Lynx 12hp Four Seater Tourer, 4 cylinder in-line engine, water-cooled monobloc, overhead valves, 1496cc, Wilson 4 speed pre-selector gearbox, shaft drive to live rear axle, semi-elliptic leaf spring suspension front and rear, in need of total restoration.
£7,700-9,000   *S*

The 1935 Riley 1½ litre car quickly became famous for its superb handling ability and quick acceleration. Derivatives of this car included the Sprite, Kestrel and Lynx.

1930 Riley 9hp Brooklands Two Seater, 4 cylinder in-line engine, water-cooled monobloc, pushrod operated overhead valves, bore 60.3mm x 95.2mm stroke, 1089cc, 4 speed gearbox, single plate clutch, spiral bevel rear axle, semi-elliptic leaf springs front and rear, wheelbase 96in, 19in tyres.
Est. **£65,000-85,000**   *S*

MAKE	ENGINE	DATES	CONDITION		
Riley			1	2	3
hp	1034/2	1906-07	£9,000	£6,000	£3,000
Speed 10	1390/2	1909-10	£10,000	£6,000	£3,000
1	1498/4	1922-27	£7,000	£4,000	£2,000
	1098/4	1928-32	£10,000	£7,000	£4,000
Gamecock	1098/4	1932	£15,000	£10,000	£6,000
incock	1458/6	1933-36	£9,000	£7,000	£5,000
mp	1089/4	1934-35	£32,000	£28,000	£20,000
Kestral	1496/4	1936-38	£8,000	£5,000	£2,000
prite	1496/4	1936-38	£40,000	£35,000	£20,000

1929 Riley Tourer.
£16,500-18,500 *DJ*

1929 Riley Nine Four Seat Tourer, 4 cylinder engine with 2 camshafts operating overhead valves via pushrods, bore 60.3mm x 95.2mm stroke, 1087cc, 4 speed gearbox, semi-elliptic leaf springs front and rear.
£12,500-14,000 *S*

Introduced in 1926 the Riley Nine was a technically innovative and high performance 1100cc light car. A development of its engine went on to power the ERA, one of the most successful racing cars ever produced in England.

Make: Riley
Model: Pathfinder and Two-Point-Six
Type: Saloon
Years Manufactured: Pathfinder, 1953-57; Two-Point-Six, 1957-59
Price when new: Pathfinder, £1,241; Two-Point-Six, £1,411
Engine Type: Pathfinder, overhead valve 4 cyl; Two-Point-Six, overhead valve 6 cyl
Size: Pathfinder, 2443cc; Two-Point-Six, 2639cc
Max Power: Pathfinder, 110 bhp @ 4500 rpm; Two-Point-Six, 102 bhp @ 4500 rpm
Transmission: 4 speed, overdrive and auto option on Two-Point-Six
Performance: Max speed: 100 mph; 0-60: 16.0 secs; Mpg: 20-25.

Make: Riley
Model: 1.5
Type: Saloon
Years Manufactured: 1955-65
Price when new: £864
Engine Type: Overhead valve 4 cyl
Size: 1489cc
Max Power: 64 bhp @ 4800 rpm
Transmission: 4 speed
Performance: Max speed: 90 mph; 0-60: 19.0 secs; Mpg: 26-32.

1958 Riley 2600 Saloon.
£3,200-4,000 *Cen*

1937 Riley 'Victor' Four Door Saloon, 4 cylinder, 1496cc engine, the engine, pre-selector gearbox, steering and wheels are in good condition, 97,909 recorded miles. **£4,400-5,200** *ADT*

1969 Riley Elf Mk II, 29,000 miles recorded.
Est. **£2,000-3,000** *ADT*

1953 Riley 1½ Litre Sportsman Saloon, 4 cylinder in-line engine, water-cooled monobloc, overhead valves, 1496cc, 4 speed gearbox, shaft drive to live rear axle, independent torsion bar front suspension, semi-elliptic leaf spring rear.
£4,200-5,250 *S*

Miller's is a price GUIDE not a price LIST

MAKE Riley	ENGINE	DATES	CONDITION 1	2	
1½ litre RMA	1496/4	1945-52	£5,000	£3,500	£1,50
1½ litre RME	1496/4	1952-55	£5,000	£3,500	£1,50
2½ litre RMB/F	2443/4	1946-53	£11,000	£8,500	£3,00
2½ litre Roadster	2443/4	1948-50	£20,000	£15,000	£9,00
2½ litre Drop head	2443/4	1948-51	£22,000	£18,000	£10,00
Pathfinder	2443/4	1953-57	£3,500	£2,000	£75
2.6	2639/6	1957-59	£3,000	£1,800	£75
1.5	1489/4	1957-65	£4,000	£2,000	£85
4/68	1489/4	1959-61	£1,500	£700	£30
4/72	1622/4	1961-69	£1,600	£800	£30
Elf I/II/III	848/4	1961-66	£1,500	£850	£40
Kestrel I/II	1098/4	1965-67	£1,500	£850	£40

ROLLS-ROYCE

Although always considered the best in the world, during the 1930s both Bentley and Hispano-Suiza were arguably better machines. However, Rolls-Royce will always be the most prestigious of all motor cars. The company was founded in 1904 after the merger of Rolls and Royce. During the first World War both ambulances and armoured cars were produced on Rolls-Royce chassis. Some fake bodies are known, and chassis records are held by both the Rolls-Royce Enthusiasts Club and the Rolls-Royce Owners Club. At present most post World War II cars represent excellent value for money.

1912 Rolls-Royce 40/50hp Silver Ghost Barker Cabriolet, chassis No. 1861, engine No. 84. Est. **£200,000-300,000** *C*

The British armoured cars of 1914-18 were based on the 40/50hp Rolls-Royce chassis.

1923 Rolls-Royce 20hp Doctor's Drop Head Coupé with Dickey. £50,000-52,000 *BLE*

1922 Rolls-Royce Silver Ghost, 6 cylinder, 7695cc engine, rebodied as a Tourer believed to be by Wilkinson's of Derby. Est. **£55,000-65,000** *LF*

1911 Rolls-Royce Silver Ghost Landaulet, with coachwork by Windovers of London, chassis No. 1547, 6 cylinder set in line in blocks of 3 cylinders with water cooling and side valves, bore 114mm x 121mm stroke, 7,428 litres, 3 speed and reverse, cone clutch, hypoid bevel and live axle, semi-elliptic front springs suspension, three-quarter elliptic rear, right-hand drive. **£235,000-240,000** *C(A)*

1907 Rolls-Royce Silver Ghost 40/50hp Tourer, chassis No. 60-565, 6 cylinder in-line engine, in 2 groups of 3, water-cooled, side valve, bore 4½in x 4½in stroke, 7036cc, 4 speed gearbox with direct drive in 3rd, cone clutch, bevel rear axle, semi-elliptic leaf spring front suspension, 880mm x 120mm tyres. **£2,000,000-2,250,000** *SNY*

1907 Rolls-Royce Silver Ghost 40/50hp Tourer **£1,500,000-1,750,000** *SNY*

1914 Rolls-Royce Silver Ghost 40/50hp Tourer, with coachwork by Brewster & Co., chassis No. 20 TB, engine No. G 113, 6 cylinder in line, in 2 groups of 3, water-cooled, side valves, bore 4½in x 4¾in stroke, 7428cc, 4 speed right-hand change gearbox, cone clutch, bevel rear axle, semi-elliptic leaf spring front suspension, cantilevered leaf spring rear, wheelbase 143½in, 895 x 135mm tyres. **£230,000-250,000** *SNY*

1912 Rolls-Royce Silver Ghost 40/50hp London-Edinburgh Tourer, The Mystery, with coachwork by Holmes, chassis No. 1826 E, registration No. in UK R 1265, 6 cylinder in-line engine, cast in 2 groups of 3, water-cooled, side valve, bore 4½in x 4¾in stroke, 7428cc, 3 speed gearbox, clone clutch, bevel rear axle, semi-elliptic leaf spring suspension, underslung cantilever at rear, wheelbase 143½in, 880 x 120mm tyres. **£975,000-1,000,000** *SNY*

**1922 Rolls-Royce Silver Ghost
40/50hp Pall Mall Tourer.
£125,000-130,000** *SNY*

**926 Rolls-Royce Silver Ghost
0/50hp Piccadilly Roadster,**
ith Rolls-Royce Custom
achwork, chassis No. S 315 RK,
ngine No. 22154, 6 cylinder in line,
2 blocks of 3, side valve,
ater-cooled, bore 4½in x 4¾in
roke, 7428cc, 3 speed centre
ange gearbox, cone clutch,
closed torque tube to live rear
le, semi-elliptic leaf front springs,
ntilever rear springs, wheelbase
44in, 33 x 5in tyres.
50,000-175,000 *SNY*

**1924 Rolls-Royce Silver Ghost
40/50hp Piccadilly Roadster,**
chassis No. 300 K, 6 cylinder in-line
engine, in blocks of 3, side valve,
water-cooled, bore 4½in x 4¾in
stroke, 7428cc, 4 speed gearbox,
cone clutch, enclosed torque tube to
live rear axle, semi-elliptic leaf front
springs, cantilever rear springs,
wheelbase 144in, 33 x 5in tyres.
£75,000-80,000 *SNY*

Make the Most of Miller's

Price ranges in this book reflect what one should expect to pay for a similar example. When selling, however, one should expect to receive a lower figure. This will fluctuate according to a dealer's stock, saleability at a particular time, etc. It is always advisable, when selling, to approach a reputable specialist dealer or an auction house which has specialist sales

MAKE Rolls-Royce	ENGINE	DATES	CONDITION 1	2	3
40/50	7035/6	pre-WWI	£1 million	→	£50,000
40/50	7428/6	post-WWI	£100,000	£68,000	£35,000
20hp	3127/6	1922-25	£45,000	£30,000	£22,000
20hp	3127/6	1925-29	£50,000	£32,000	£24,000
Phantom I	7668/6	1925-29	£45,000	£28,000	£22,000
20/25	3669/6	1925-26	£25,000	£18,000	£15,000
Phantom II	7668/6	1929-35	£50,000	£30,000	£22,000
Phantom II Continental	7668/6	1930-35	£75,000	£40,000	£28,000
25/30	4257/6	1936-38	£25,000	£18,000	£12,000
Phantom III	7340/12	1936-39	£55,000	£28,000	£16,000
Wraith	4257/6	1938-39	£48,000	£32,000	£25,000

Prices will vary considerably depending on heritage, originality, coachbuilder, completeness and body style.

Make Rolls-Royce	FRANCE +5%	GERMANY —	ITALY —	JAPAN +15%	USA +7%

1924 Rolls-Royce Silver Ghost 40/50 Shooting Brake, chassis No. 89 RM, engine No. S 281, 6 cylinder in 2 blocks of 3, bore 4½in x 4¾in stroke, 7428cc, aluminium alloy pistons, non-detachable head, side valve, single camshaft, 4 speed gearbox and reverse, cone type clutch, footbrake externally contracting on the propshaft, handbrake internally expanding within the rear brake drums on to the rear hubs, front braking system by means of mechanical servo, semi-elliptic front springs suspension with cantilever at the rear, telecontrol shock absorbers were fitted as special equipment, right-hand drive.
Est. **£55,000-60,000**   *C*

1924 Rolls-Royce Silver Ghost, fully restored, some history, and in excellent condition.
£165,000-167,000   *BLE*

1926 Rolls-Royce 20hp Saloon.
£26,500-27,500   *DB*

1926 Rolls-Royce 20hp, with Litchfield bodywork.
£22,500-23,000   *DB*

1927 Rolls-Royce 20hp Barrel-Sided Tourer, chassis No. GCK 44, engine No. G1571, coachwork by Horsefield of Halifax, 6 cylinder in line, water-cooled monobloc, pushrod operated overhead valves, bore 3in x 4in stroke, R.A.C. rating 21.6hp, 4 speed gearbox, spiral bevel rear axle, semi-elliptic leaf spring suspension front and rear.
£38,000-40,000   *DJ*

1926 Rolls-Royce 20hp Three Quarter Fixed Head Coupé, with 6 cylinder in-line engine, water-cooled monobloc, overhead valve, bore 3in x 4½in stroke, 3103cc, single dry plate clutch, 4 speed gearbox with right-hand change, spiral bevel floating live rear axle, semi-elliptic leaf springs front and rear, wheelbase 129in, tyres 19in.
£34,000-35,000   *S*

1928 Rolls-Royce Phantom I Brougham De Ville, with coachwork by Wilkinson, chassis No. 63 RF, engine No. FV 35, 6 cylinder in 2 blocks of 3, overhead valve, water-cooled, bore 108mm x 139.7mm stroke, 7668cc, producing 85bhp, 4 speed gearbox with reverse and single dry plate clutch, semi-elliptic spring suspension at front and cantilever leaf spring at rear, wheelbase 133in, servo assisted braking system, right-hand drive.
Est. **£50,000-60,000**   *C*

1922 Rolls-Royce 20hp Open Tourer, with coachwork by Clyde Auto Company, chassis No. 42 G5, engine No. G143, 6 cylinder in line, water-cooled monobloc, pushrod operated overhead valves, bore 3in x 4½in stroke, 3103cc, single dry plate clutch, 3 speed gearbox, spiral bevel drive, fully floating live axle, semi-elliptic leaf spring front and rear suspension, wheelbase 129in, tyres 21in.
£55,000-57,000   *S*

1927 Rolls-Royce 20hp, now fitted with coachwork by Gordon, with wire wheels, sun roof and Boa horn.
£27,000-28,000   *DJ*

1928 Rolls-Royce Phantom I Open Four Door Sports Tourer, with Barker style coachwork.
£73,000-75,000   *DJ*

1927 Rolls-Royce Phantom I Limousine, chassis No. 40EH, engine No. HU65, 6 cylinder in line in blocks of 3, overhead valve, bore 108mm x 139.7mm stroke, 7668cc, 4 speed sliding mesh transmission, right-hand change, single plate clutch and spiral bevel rear axle, semi-elliptic front suspension, cantilever rear, right-hand drive, British manufacture and carries 4 door, 6 light, 7 seater limousine, coachwork by Park Ward.
£38,000-40,000   *C(A)*

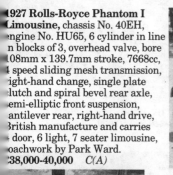

Condition Guide

1. *A vehicle in top class condition but not 'concours' standard, either fully restored or in very good original condition*
2. *A good, clean, roadworthy vehicle, both mechanically and bodily sound*
3. *A runner, but in need of attention, probably both bodywork and mechanically*

MAKE	ENGINE	DATES	CONDITION		
Rolls-Royce			1	2	3
Silver Wraith LWB	4566/				
	4887/6	1951-59	£22,000	£15,000	£9,000
Silver Wraith SWB	4257/				
	4566/6	1947-59	£20,000	£12,000	£9,000
Silver Wraith drop head	4257/				
	4566/6	1947-59	£60,000	£35,000	£25,000
Silver Dawn St'd Steel	4257/				
	4566/6	1949-52	£30,000	£15,000	£10,000
Silver Dawn St'd Steel	4566/6	1952-55	£30,000	£20,000	£15,000
Silver Dawn Coachbuilt	4257/				
	4566/6	1949-55	£35,000	£25,000	£18,000
Silver Dawn drop head	4257/				
	4566/6	1949-55	£70,000	£50,000	£35,000
Silver Cloud I	4887/6	1955-59	£20,000	£10,000	£8,000
SCI Coupé Coachbuilt	4887/6	1955-59	£30,000	£20,000	£15,000
SCI Conv (HJM)	4887/6	1955-59	£80,000	£60,000	£40,000
Silver Cloud II	6230/8	1959-62	£19,000	£10,000	£8,000
SCII Conv (HJM)	6230/8	1959-62	£80,000	£75,000	£40,000
SCII Conv (MPW)	6230/8	1959-62	£60,000	£40,000	£32,000
Silver Cloud III	6230/8	1962-65	£25,000	£12,000	£10,000
SCIII Conv (MPW)	6230/8	1962-65	£75,000	£45,000	£35,000
Silver Shadow	6230/				
	6750/8	1965-76	£11,000	£8,000	£6,000
S Shadow I Coupé (MPW)	6230/				
	6750/8	1965-70	£15,000	£10,000	£8,000
SSI drop head (MPW)	6230/				
	6750/8	1965-70	£33,000	£25,000	£18,000

1928 Rolls-Royce 20hp Doctor's Coupé, with 6 cylinder in-line engine, water-cooled monobloc, pushrod operated overhead valves, bore 3in x 4½in stroke, 3103cc, single dry plate clutch, 4 speed gearbox, spiral bevel drive, fully floating live rear axle, semi-elliptic leaf spring front and rear suspension wheelbase 129in, 21in tyres.
£38,000-40,000 *S*

The 40/50hp Rolls-Royce was generally considered to be the best car available in its class, and the company felt that a smaller car would satisfy the demand created by the less affluent or for town driving. Thus in 1922 the company announced their 20hp model, and some 3,000 were sold during the 8 year production run.

1929 Rolls-Royce Phantom I Open Tourer.
£75,000-80,000 *BLE*

1929 Rolls-Royce 20hp Open Tourer, 6 cylinder, 3127cc engine.
£27,500-30,000 *ADT*

1930 Rolls-Royce 20/25.
£48,500-50,000 *DJ*

1931 Rolls-Royce Phantom II Piccadilly Speedster.
£87,000-88,000 *BLE*

1931 Rolls-Royce Phantom II Open Tourer.
£84,000-85,000 *BLE*

1930 Rolls-Royce Phantom I Open Tourer.
£74,500-76,000 *BLE*

1930 Rolls-Royce Phantom I Tourer, in Barker style.
£65,000-68,000 *DJ*

1932 Rolls-Royce 20/25 Three Position Drop Head Coupé, in good mechanical order.
£52,500-53,500 *ELD*

1932 Rolls-Royce Phantom II Rolling Chassis.
£17,500-18,500   *C*

1928 Rolls-Royce 20hp, with 6 cylinder in-line engine, water-cooled monobloc, pushrod operated overhead valves, bore 3in x 4in stroke, R.A.C. rating 21.6bhp, 4 speed gearbox, spiral bevel rear axle, semi-elliptic leaf spring suspension front and rear, fitted with a 20/25 radiator shell and a late 30s style saloon body, needs restoration.
£9,000-10,000   *SEN*

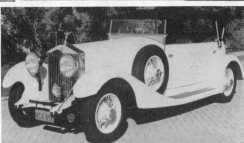

1932 Rolls-Royce Phantom II Continental Tourer.
Est. £100,000-125,000   *C(A)*

1932 Rolls-Royce 20/25 Mayfair Saloon.
£14,000-15,000   *DB*

1934 Rolls-Royce Phantom II Series R2 Four Door Sports Saloon, with coachwork replica in style of Kellner.
Est. £50,000-53,000   *S(A)*

1933 Rolls-Royce 20/25 Convertible, with coachwork by Thrupp & Maberly.
£65,000-66,000   *DB*

1933 Rolls-Royce Phantom II, with coachwork by Mulliner.
£47,500-48,500   *DB*

1933 Rolls-Royce 20/25 Sports Saloon, by James Young.
£29,000-30,000   *BLE*

1930 Rolls-Royce 20/25hp Sedanca De Ville Town Car, with coachwork by Fred K. R. Wood and Son of New York, chassis No. GWP 37, engine No. G42, 6 cylinder in line, water-cooled monobloc, pushrod operated overhead valves, bore 3¼in x 4½in stroke, 3699cc, 4 speed right-hand change gearbox, single dry plate clutch, open shaft, spiral bevel rear axle, semi-elliptic leaf springs front and rear, wheelbase 132in, 19in tyres.
£27,000-30,000 *SNY*

1933 Rolls-Royce Phantom II 40/50hp Henley Roadster, with coachwork by Brewster & Co., chassis No. 291 AJS, engine No. A 95J, 6 cylinder in line, water-cooled, cast in 3s with one-piece detachable cylinder head, pushrod operated overhead valves, bore 4¼in x 5½in stroke, 7668cc, 4 speed gearbox, single dry plate clutch, hypoid bevel fully floating rear axle, semi-elliptic leaf spring suspension front and rear, wheelbase 144in, 20in tyres.
£410,000-430,000 *SNY*

1933 Rolls-Royce 20/25hp Fixed Head Coupé, with coachwork by Gurney Nutting, chassis No. GSY 20, engine No. L3C, 6 cylinder in line, water-cooled monobloc, pushrod operated overhead valves, bore 3¼in x 4½in stroke, 3699cc, 4 speed gearbox, single dry clutch plate, spiral bevel final drive, semi-elliptic leaf spring suspension front and rear, wheelbase 132in, 19in tyres.
£41,000-44,000 *SNY*

1937 Rolls-Royce Phantom III 40/50hp Limousine, coachwork by Rippon Bros. Ltd., Huddersfield, Yorks., chassis No. 3 BT 71, engine No. W 78 F, 12 cylinders in 60° V formation, water-cooled pushrod operated overhead valves from single central camshaft, 3¼in bore x 4½in stroke, 7340cc, 4 speed synchromesh gearbox with right-hand change, single dry plate clutch, hypoid bevel fully floating rear axle, independent coil spring front suspension, semi-elliptic leaf rear springs with automatic hydraulic dampers, wheelbase 142in, tyres 18in.
£32,000-35,000 *SNY*

1926 Rolls-Royce Phantom I, by Hibbard & Darren.
£38,000-39,000 *DB*

1932 Rolls-Royce 20/25 Saloon, with coachwork by Park Ward.
£13,500-14,500 *DB*

1955 Rolls-Royce 20/25 Two Door Drop Head Coupé, with coachwork by Windover.
£55,000-60,000 *DB*

1933 Rolls-Royce Phantom II Continental.
£65,000-66,000 *DB*

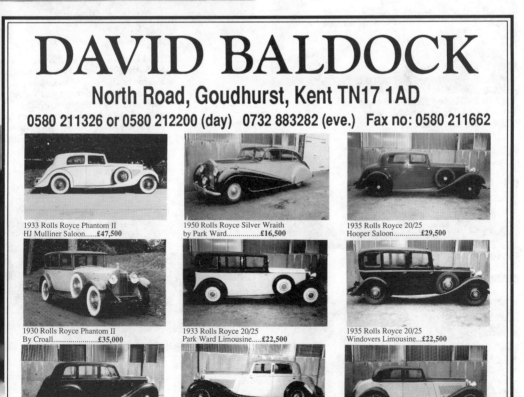

1933 Rolls-Royce 20/25 Two Door Saloon.
£22,500-23,500   *DB*

1933 Rolls-Royce 20/25 Saloon, by Freestone & Webb, 6 cylinder, 3128cc engine.
Est. £22,000-25,000   *LF*

1933 Rolls-Royce 20/25 Limousine, by Park Ward
£22,500-23,500   *DB*

1934 Rolls-Royce 20/25, by Thrupp & Maberly.
£21,500-22,500   *DB*

1934 Rolls-Royce 20/25 Sedanca De Ville, by Thrupp and Maberly.
£28,750-29,750   *BLE*

1934 Rolls-Royce 20/25hp Shooting Brake, 6 cylinder in-line engine, water-cooled monobloc, pushrod operated overhead valves, bore 3¼in x 4½in stroke, 3699cc, 4 speed right-hand change gearbox, single dry plate clutch, spiral bevel, fully floating rear axle, semi-elliptic leaf springs front and rear, wheelbase 132in, tyres 19in.
£30,000-32,000   *BLE*

1934 Rolls-Royce 20/25 Hooper Saloon with Division.
£16,500-17,500   *DB*

1934 Rolls-Royce Phantom II Hooper Limousine.
£21,000-22,000   *DB*

1934 Rolls-Royce 20/25 Hooper Saloon.
£26,500-27,500   *DB*

> **Miller's is a price GUIDE not a price LIST**

1934 Rolls-Royce Phanton II Continental Saloon, by Park Ward.
Est. £55,000-65,000 *LF*

1934 Rolls-Royce 20/25 Saloon, with coachwork by H. J. Mulliner.
£28,500-30,000 *DB*

1934 Rolls-Royce 20/25 Airline, by Lanefield, the only one in the world.
£34,500-35,500 *BLE*

1935 Rolls-Royce 20/25 Baker Saloon.
£26,500-27,500 *DB*

1935 Rolls-Royce 20/25 Sports Saloon, with coachwork by Barker, 6 cylinder, 3669cc engine.
Est. £24,000-28,000 *ADT*

1935 Rolls-Royce Phantom II Continental Sports Saloon, with coachwork by Barker, chassis No. 42UK, engine No. SW65, 6 cylinder water-cooled unit with the cylinders in line in 2 groups of 3, the overhead valves are operated by pushrods, bore 4¼in x 5½in stroke, 7668cc, 4 speed gearbox in unit with the engine, synchromesh on 3rd and top gears, wheelbase 144in, top speed in excess of 90mph, semi-elliptic springs all round.
Est. £70,000-100,000 *C*

1936 Rolls-Royce 25/30, with three position drop head by Freestone and Webb.
£60,000-62,000 *BLE*

Make the Most of Miller's

CONDITION is absolutely vital when assessing the value of a vehicle. Top class vehicles on the whole appreciate much more than less perfect examples. However a rare, desirable car may command a high price even when in need of restoration

---

1936 Rolls-Royce 25/30 Sedanca Coupé, by Barker.
£50,000-55,000 *DB*

1935 Rolls-Royce 20/25 Limousine, by Hooper.
£29,500-30,500 *DB*

ROLLS-ROYCE

**1936 Rolls-Royce Phantom III
Sedanca,** by H. J. Mulliner.
£100,000-110,000 *PJF*

1935 Rolls-Royce 20/25 Sedanca,
by Windovers.
£31,500-32,500 *DB*

**1935 Rolls-Royce
20/25 Landaulette,**
by Thrupp & Maberly.
£32,000-33,000 *DB*

1937 Rolls-Royce Phantom III,
by Hooper.
£30,000-32,000 *BLE*

1936 Rolls-Royce 20/25 Saloon,
with coachwork by Park Ward,
chassis No. GC J27, engine No.
G24X, 6 cylinder, 3669cc.
Est. **£25,000-30,000** *ADT*

1935 Rolls-Royce 20/25, by Thrupp
& Maberly.
£21,000-22,000 *DB*

**1936 Rolls-Royce 20/25 Hooper
Saloon.
£30,000-32,000** *DB*

**1936 Rolls-Royce 20/25 Windover
Convertible.
£67,000-68,000** *DB*

**1936 Rolls-Royce 20/2
Cockshoot Saloon.
£16,500-17,500** *DB*

284

1936 Rolls-Royce Hooper Sports Saloon.
£25,000-30,000   *DB*

1937 Rolls-Royce Phantom III Touring Limousine, with coachwork by Barker, engine No. N58N, V12 cylinder, overhead valve, bore 82.5mm x stroke 114mm, 7.34 litre, 50.7hp, 4 speed synchromesh gearbox, right-hand change, hypoid final drive, 4 wheel servo assisted brakes, handbrake on rear wheels, independent coil front suspension, semi-elliptic rear, right-hand drive.
£35,000-36,000   *C(A)*

1937 Rolls-Royce Phantom III Touring Limousine, with coachwork by Barker & Co, chassis No. 3 CP 94, engine No. H 68 U, 12 cylinder, in 60° V formation, water-cooled pushrod operated overhead valves from single central camshaft, bore 3¼in x stroke 4½in, 7340cc, 4 speed synchromesh gearbox with right-hand change, single dry clutch plate, hypoid bevel fully floating rear axle, independent coil spring front suspension, semi-elliptic leaf rear springs with automatic hydraulic dampers, wheelbase 142in and 18in tyres.
Est. £28,000-32,000   *S*

1937 Rolls-Royce 25/30 Windovers Landaulette.
£17,500-18,500   *DB*

1938 Rolls-Royce Wraith, by Thrupp & Maberly.
£12,000-13,000   *DB*

1937 Rolls-Royce 25/30, with coachwork by H. J. Mulliner.
£32,500-35,000   *DB*

1937 Rolls-Royce 25/30, with coachwork by H. J. Mulliner.
£26,500-27,500   *DB*

1937 Rolls-Royce 25/30, by Thrupp & Maberly, this car's engine has seized.
£14,000-15,000   *DB*

Rolls-Royce Phantom III Landaulette, by Barker.
£25,000-27,000   *DB*

1951 Rolls-Royce Silver Wraith, chassis No. WLE23, engine No. W22E, 4 cylinder, 4566cc.
Est. £14,000-16,000   *LF*

1954 Rolls-Royce Silver Dawn Standard Steel Saloon, chassis No. LSPG63, engine No. S81G, 6 cylinder, 4566cc, this car has been completely rebuilt.
£69,500-72,000   *T&M*

1948 Rolls-Royce Silver Wraith Limousine, by Park Ward.
£11,750-12,500   *DB*

1951 Rolls-Royce Silver Wraith Sedanca De Ville, with coachwork by H. J. Mulliner.
£37,000-40,000   *DJ*

1950 Rolls-Royce Silver Wraith 'Monte Carlo Rally' Saloon, with coachwork by Park Ward, chassis No. WHD 40, engine No. W 39 D, 6 cylinder in line, water-cooled monobloc, pushrod operated overhead inlet valves, side exhaust valves, bore 89mm x stroke 114mm 4257cc, 4 speed gearbox with synchromesh on 2nd, 3rd and top, single dry plate clutch, semi-floating hypoid bevel rear axle, independent coil spring front suspension, semi-elliptic leaf rear springs, 6.00/6.50 x 17in tyres.
Est. £15,000-20,000   *S*

1955 Rolls-Royce Silver Wraith, with coachwork by Park Ward, chassis No. DLW 136, engine No. L/135/D, 6 cylinder, 4566cc, 4 speed automatic gearbox, independent front suspension, semi-elliptic rear, front brakes servo assisted, rear mechanical.
£18,000-20,000 *GIL*

1955/56 Rolls-Royce Wraith Touring Limousine, with coachwork by H. J. Mulliner, chassis No. ELW79, engine No. L78E.
Est. £30,000-35,000 *C*

The Wraith was announced in 1946, in company with the Mk VI Bentley, each car using an engine similar to the pre-war 4¼ litre unit, but with overhead inlet valves. The Bentley and later on the Rolls-Royce Silver Dawn, used a 4 door body by Pressed Steel, which was later finished in the Rolls-Royce works at Crewe. The Wraith was offered only as a chassis, and thus was considered very much a cut above its mass-produced cousins, with the coachbuilt bodies giving a much more solid feel to the cars on the road.

1961 Rolls-Royce Phantom V, 6230cc, V8 engine.
£37,000-38,000 *LF*

1958 Rolls-Royce Silver Cloud I Limousine, chassis No. ALC 10, engine No. C 10A, 6 cylinder in line, water-cooled, pushrod operated overhead valves, side exhaust valves, bore 3¾in x stroke 4½in, 4887cc, 4 speed automatic gearbox in unit with engine, hypoid bevel rear axle with semi-floating half shafts, independent wishbone and coil spring front suspension, semi-elliptic rear, with piston dampers and anti-roll bar, wheelbase 127in, and 15in tyres.
Est. £18,000-22,000 *S*

1959 Rolls-Royce Silver Cloud I Drop Head Coupé, by H. J. Mulliner, chassis No. SKG33, 6 cylinder, 4887cc engine, and only 45,000 miles recorded.
£150,000-155,000 *T&M*

1958 Rolls-Royce Silver Cloud Two Door Drop Head Coupé, coachwork by Freestone and Webb.
£215,000-218,000 *SNY*

1960 Rolls-Royce Silver Cloud II, with good bodywork, mechanics and interior.
£16,000-18,000 *GWC*

1961 Rolls-Royce Silver Cloud II Standard Steel Saloon, chassis No. 5ZD85, engine No. 317DS, V8 with overhead valves, hydraulic tappets, cast aluminium block and heads, 6230cc, compression rate 8:1, 4 speed automatic transmission, independent front suspension, semi-elliptic rear.
£11,500-14,000 *GIL*

1961 Rolls-Royce Silver Cloud II Standard Steel Saloon, V8 cylinder engine, water-cooled, overhead valve, bore 4.1in x stroke 3.6in, 6230cc, 4 speed automatic gearbox, hypoid bevel rear axle, independent front suspension, semi-elliptic leaf rear springs, wheelbase 123in and 8.20 x 15in tyres.
£20,000-21,000 *S*

Rolls-Royce Silver Cloud II 7504 Model Convertible, with coachwork by H. J. Mulliner.
£195,000-200,000 *PJF*

1960 Rolls-Royce Silver Cloud II 6.2 Litre Saloon.
£13,500-15,000 *B*

Rolls-Royce Silver Cloud III Flying Spur.
£130,000-135,000 *PJF*

Make: Rolls-Royce
Model: Silver Shadow
Type: Saloon
Years Manufactured: 1965-80
Quantity: 32,339 inc. Bentley-badged cars
Price when new: Mk 1, £6,557
Engine Type: V8 cyl
Size: 6230cc/6750cc
Transmission: Auto
Performance: Max speed: 117 mph; 0-60: 10.2 secs; Mpg: 25.

1966 Rolls-Royce Silver Shadow Two Door Fixed Head Coupé, with coachwork by H. J. Mulliner, Park Ward, chassis No. CRH 1442.
Est. **£17,000-19,000** *P*

Rolls-Royce Silver Cloud III.
£25,000-40,000 *PJF*

1964 Rolls-Royce Silver Cloud III, with 8 cylinder, 90° V formation, pushrod operated overhead valves, bore 4.1in x stroke 3.6in, 6230cc, 4 speed automatic gearbox to a hypoid bevel final drive, independent wishbones and coil springs front suspension, semi-elliptic rear, 108,000 miles recorded.
£19,000-20,000 *SEN*

1964 Rolls-Royce Silver Cloud III Drop Head Coupé, by H. J. Mulliner, Park Ward Ltd., chassis No. LSFU 515, engine No. SU 257F.
Est. £60,000-80,000 *P*

1967 Rolls-Royce Silver Shadow, with coachwork by H. J. Mulliner/Park Ward, 8 cylinder, 6230cc engine.
Est. £15,000-18,000 *ADT*

1967 Rolls-Royce Four Seat Convertible, with coachwork by Mulliner Park Ward, chassis No. CRH 3641, engine No. 3641, V8 cylinder, water-cooled, pushrod operated overhead valves with hydraulic tappets, bore 4.1in x stroke 4in, capacity 6750cc, 3 speed automatic gearbox, hypoid bevel rear axle, independent front suspension with coil springs and hydraulic dampers, independent rear with single trailing arms, coil springs and hydraulic dampers, wheelbase 119½in, and 235/70 HR 15 tyres.
18,000-19,000 *S*

1971 Rolls-Royce Corniche Convertible, chassis No. DRH11750, engine No. 11750, 90° V8 cylinder, with pushrod operated valves and hydraulic tappets, aluminium block and cylinder heads, 104mm bore x 99mm stroke, 6750cc, 3 speed automatic gearbox with electrical selector lever, 4 wheel hydraulic power operated ventilated disc type brakes, 15in steel disc wheels and 205 x 15 radial tyres.
Est. £60,000-70,000 *C(A)*

1972 Rolls-Royce Silver Shadow I, in original condition, with only 32,000 miles recorded.
£17,000-18,000 *RH*

1973 Rolls-Royce Corniche Convertible, chassis No. DRX 15 111, engine No. 15111, V8 in 90° V with 4.1in bore x 3.9in stroke, 6750cc, 3 speed automatic gearbox torque converter with over-riding hand control and range selection from steering column lever, 4 wheel independent suspension, front double wishbones, coil springs and hydraulic telescopic dampers, rear trailing arms, coil springs and hydraulic telescopic dampers, hydraulic operated discs all round, left-hand drive.
Est. **£40,000-45,000**   *C*

1973 Rolls-Royce Corniche Convertible.
£36,000-37,000   *BLE*

1976 Rolls-Royce Shadow I, with 6750cc, V8 engine and only 43,000 miles recorded.
Est. **£14,000-17,000**   *LF*

1985 Rolls-Royce Corniche II.
£50,000-65,000   *PJF*

Miller's is a price GUIDE not a price LIST

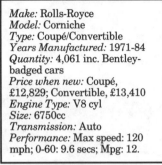

Make: Rolls-Royce
Model: Corniche
Type: Coupé/Convertible
Years Manufactured: 1971-84
Quantity: 4,061 inc. Bentley-badged cars
Price when new: Coupé, £12,829; Convertible, £13,410
Engine Type: V8 cyl
Size: 6750cc
Transmission: Auto
Performance: Max speed: 120 mph; 0-60: 9.6 secs; Mpg: 12.

1975 Rolls-Royce Corniche Convertible, V8 cylinder engine, water-cooled, pushrod operated overhead valves with hydraulic tappets, bore 4.1in x stroke 3.9in, 6750cc, 3 speed automatic gearbox, hypoid bevel rear axle, independen front suspension with coil springs and hydraulic dampers, independent rear with single trailing arms, coil springs and hydraulic dampers, wheelbase 119½in, 235/70 HR 15 tyres.
£33,000-35,000   *S*

The Rolls-Royce Corniche and its Bentley equivalent were developed from the Silver Shadow specification coachwork designed and constructec by Mulliner/Park Ward.

1985 Rolls-Royce Silver Spu
£40,000-41,000   *BLE*

Make: Rolls-Royce
Model: Camargue
Type: Coupé
Years Manufactured: 1975-86
Quantity: 526
Engine Type: V8 cyl
Size: 6750cc
Transmission: Auto
Performance: Max speed: 120 mph; 0-60: 10.0 secs; Mpg: 13.

ROSENGART

1937 Rosengart, 4 cylinder, 750cc engine, right-hand drive.
£2,600-3,000   *LF*

Basically an Austin 7 built under licence in France, but with a few alterations. Rosengart built Austin 7s under licence from 1928 until the outbreak of World War II, originally at Neuilly-Sur-Seine but moving production to Paris in 1937.

ROVER

The Rover Company, founded in 1904, have always enjoyed the reputation and image of the motor car for the professional and middle classes. The post war 'P' series models represent very good value as collectable cars. In 1966 Rover became part of the British Leyland organisation.

1932 Rover 10 Special Saloon.
£10,500-11,500   *LF*

When Captain Wilks was appointed Managing Director of Rover, he brought with him some ideas from his previous employers Hillman, the Rover 10 Special Saloon shared a number of panels in common with the Hillman models. The body was basically the same as the earlier 10/25, but had greatly improved mechanics and chassis.

1933 Rover 10 Hastings Coupé, this car is an original example with one owner from 1933-70 and a documented history.
£6,500-7,500   *GWC*

MAKE Rover	ENGINE	DATES	CONDITION 1	2	3
10hp	998/2	1920-25	£5,000	£3,000	£1,500
9/20	1074/4	1925-27	£6,000	£4,000	£2,000
10/25	1185/4	1928-33	£6,000	£4,000	£2,500
12	1496/4	1934-37	£4,000	£3,000	£1,000
20 Sports	2512/6	1937-39	£5,000	£4,000	£2,500

1948 Rover 60 Four Door Saloon, 6 cylinder in-line engine, water-cooled monobloc, overhead inlet valve, side exhaust valve, bore 65.5mm x stroke 105mm, 1595cc, 4 speed gearbox with Rover freewheel, single plate clutch, spiral bevel final drive, independent front suspension, semi-elliptic leaf rear springs, wheelbase 110½in, and 5.25/5.50 x 17in tyres.
£4,000-5,000   *S*

1960 Rover 80, 4 cylinder, 2286cc engine.
Est. **£500-1,200**   *ADT*

ROVER

1960 Rover P4 100, with
6 cylinder, 2625cc engine, this car
was restored in 1986/87 and given a
complete respray and is now in good
condition.
Est. **£750-1,750**   *ADT*

1962 Rover 3 Litre Saloon, with
6 cylinder, 2995cc engine, with
chauffeur partition by Harold
Radford, 34,750 miles recorded.
£4,500-5,000   *LF*

**1948 Rover 12hp Four Seat
Tourer,** 4 cylinder in-line engine,
overhead valve, water-cooled
monobloc, bore 69mm x stroke
100mm, 1496cc, 4 speed gearbox
with freewheel, single dry plate
clutch, open propellor shaft to spiral
bevel drive rear axle, semi-elliptic
leaf springs to front and rear
controlled by hydraulic dampers,
wheelbase 112in and 4.75 x 17in
tyres.
£9,570-10,000   *S*

*In the 2nd half of the 30s the
company introduced a range of car
in 10, 12, 14 and 16 horse power
variants. The same cars, with minor
changes were the company's offerin
for the immediate post-war period
and continued in production until
the entirely new Rover 60 and 75
models were introduced.*

MAKE	ENGINE	DATES	CONDITION		
Rover			1	2	3
P2 10	1389/4	1946-47	£2,900	£2,000	£500
P2 12	1496/4	1946-47	£3,200	£2,300	£600
P2 12 Tour	1496/4	1947	£6,500	£3,000	£1,000
P2 14/16	1901/6	1946-47	£4,000	£2,800	£700
P2 14/16 Sal	1901/6	1946-47	£3,700	£2,500	£700
P3 60	1595/4	1948-49	£2,900	£2,000	£500
P3 75	2103/6	1948-49	£3,800	£2,700	£600
P3 75 Sal	2103/6	1948-49	£3,500	£2,400	£600
P4 75	2103/6	1950-51	£2,800	£1,000	—
P4 75	2103/6	1952-64	£2,500	£900	—
P4 60	1997/4	1954-59	£2,300	£750	—
P4 90	2638/6	1954-59	£2,900	£1,100	—
P4 75	2230/6	1955-59	£2,500	£900	—
P4 105R	2638/6	1957-58	£3,000	£1,600	—
P4 105S	2638/6	1957-59	£3,000	£1,600	£250
P4 80	2286/4	1960-62	£2,500	£900	—
P4 95	2625/6	1963-64	£2,800	£1,600	—
P4 100	2625/6	1960-62	£3,200	£1,500	—
P4 110	2625/6	1963-64	£3,250	£1,600	—
P5 3 litre	2995/6	1959-67	£3,500	£2,000	£550
P5 3 litre Coupé	2995/6	1959-67	£5,500	£3,500	£750
P5B (V8)	3528/8	1967-74	£7,000	£4,000	£900
P5B (V8) Coupé	3528/8	1967-73	£7,500	£4,250	£1,250
P6 2000 SC Series 1	1980/4	1963-65	£2,200	£800	—
P6 2000 SC Series 1	1980/4	1966-70	£2,000	£800	—
2000 SC Auto Series 1	1980/4	1966-70	£1,500	£600	—
P6 2000 TC Series 1	1980/4	1966-70	£2,000	£900	—
P6 2000 SC Series 2	1980/4	1970-73	£2,000	£900	—
P6 2000 SC Auto Series 2	1980/4	1970-73	£1,500	£800	—
P6 2000 TC Series 2	1980/4	1970-73	£1,750	£900	—
P6 3500 Series 1	3500/8	1968-70	£2,500	£1,400	—
P6 2200 SC	2200/4	1974-77	£1,750	£850	—
P6 2200 SC Auto	2200/4	1974-77	£2,250	£900	—
P6 2200 TC	2200/4	1974-77	£2,000	£950	—
P6 3500 Series 2	3500/8	1971-77	£2,800	£1,700	—
P6 3500 S Series 2	3500/8	1971-77	£26,000	£15,000	—

Make: Rover
Model: P4 90
Type: Saloon
Years Manufactured: 1954-59
Price when new: £1,297
Engine Type: Inlet over exhaust
6 cyl
Size: 2638cc
Max Power: 93 bhp @ 4500 rpm
Transmission: 4 speed with
freewheel/overdrive
Performance: Max speed: 90
mph; 0-60: 19.0 secs; Mpg: 17-25

1961 Rover 100 Saloon, with 79,819 miles recorded.
£575-750   *Cen*

With many derivatives the P4 range was reduced to only 2 models in 1959, one of these being the Rover 100. This model used a 2625cc development of the Rover 3.0 litre P5's straight 6 engine producing 100bhp.

1966 Rover P5 3.0 Litre Saloon, with 34,300 miles recorded.
£3,000-3,500   *Cen*

Make: Rover
Model: P5/P5B
Type: Saloon/Fixed Head Coupé
Years Manufactured: P5, 1958-67; P5B, 1967-73
Price when new: P5 Saloon, £1,734; P5 Coupé, £1,857; P5B Saloon, £2,174; P5B Coupé, £2,270
Engine Type: P5, inlet over exhaust 6 cyl; P5B, overhead valve V8
Size: P5, 2995cc; P5B, 3528cc
Max Power: P5, 115 bhp @ 4500 rpm; P5B, 161 bhp @ 5200 rpm
Transmission: P5, 4 speed, optional overdrive; standard from Feb 1960; or auto; P5B, auto
Performance: Max speed: P5, 97 mph; P5B, 108 mph; 0-60: P5, 16.0 secs; P5B, 11.0 secs; Mpg: 16-24.

The Rover 3½ litre P5B used the specially developed General Motors V8 engine and Borg Warner 3 speed automatic transmission. There was no manual option. Top speed 110mph with a 0-60 time of around 10 seconds.

1966 Rover P3 3 Litre Saloon, chassis No. 77004045, engine No. 77006619, 6 cylinder, water-cooled monobloc, overhead valve, bore 77.8mm x stroke 105mm, 2995cc, 4 speed manual gearbox with overdrive, shaft drive to live rear axle, leaf spring and coil suspension, wheelbase 2.81m and 6.70 x 15in tyres.
Est. **£5,000-6,000**   *S*

1968 Rover 3.5 P5B Saloon.
£290-500   *CMA*

77 Rover 2200TC Manual P6, th 52,500 miles recorded.
,650-2,000   *Cen*

1966 Rover 2000SC, 4 cylinder, 1978cc engine and 56,000 miles recorded.
Est. **£1,000-1,500**   *LF*

SIMCA

ROYAL

1905 Royal Tourist Model F 32/38hp Touring Car No. 514, 4 cylinder in line, water-cooled, cast in pairs, T-head side vale, 5in bore x 5½in stroke, 432cu in, 3 speed gearbox, shaft final drive, semi-elliptic leaf springs front and rear, wheelbase 108in, tyres 33 x 4in.
£32,000-35,000   *SNY*

SALMSON

1927 Salmson Grand Sport Type VAL3, Series 6, chassis No. 20665, engine No. 20665, 4 cylinder with gear driven twin overhead camshafts, 62mm bore x 90mm stroke, 1098cc, rated to develop 27bhp at 3,330rpm, channel section chassis with tubular front axle carried on semi-elliptic leaf springs, rear axle carried on quarter elliptic leaf springs, special 4 speed close ratio racing gearbox with sliding mesh type gears, cable and rod operated 4 wheel drum type brakes, 19in centre lock wire type wheels with Salmson patented key type hub, and 4.40 x 19 tyres.
Est. £25,000-30,000   *C(A)*

SIMCA

1951 Simca 8 Sport Two Door Coupé, with coachwork by Facel to Pininfarina design, with 4 cylinder in-line engine, water-cooled monobloc, overhead valve, bore 72mm x stroke 75mm, 1221cc, 4 speed gearbox, single dry plate clutch, bevel rear axle, independent coil spring front suspension, leaf rear springs, 15in tyres.
£6,800-7,000   *S*

Simca's own 1221cc engine developed some 50bhp at 4,800rpm and a top speed of 84mph.

SINGER

Singer was started in 1905 and enjoyed much success during the 20s and 30s, at one stage being third to Morris and Austin as the UKs largest car manufacturer. Like many companies they were unable to compete against the BMC organisation after the war and were bought by Rootes in 1956. The Singer name was used on top of the range Hillman models until Chrysler acquired Rootes in 1965 and the name was lost.

MAKE Singer	ENGINE	DATES	CONDITION 1	2	3
Roadster 4A/4AB	1074/4	1948-53	£5,500	£2,850	£1,500
Roadster 4AD	1500/4	1951-55	£6,000	£3,500	£1,700
Hunter/SM1500	1479/4	1948-56	£1,200	£600	£100
Gazelle I-II (OHC)	1497/4	1956-58	£1,000	£550	£100
Gazelle I-II (OHC) DHC	1497/4	1956-58	£2,000	£1,300	£400
Gazelle IIa-IIIc	1494/4	1958-62	£2,000	£1,300	£400
Gazelle IIA-V	1600/4	1958-66	£1,200	£500	£200
Chamois I	875/4	1964-65	£700	£400	£100
Vogue III	1592/4	1964-65	£900	£600	£150

1927 Singer 14hp Six Cylinder Two Seater with Dickey, 6 cylinder in-line engine, water-cooled monobloc, overhead valve, bore 63mm x stroke 95mm, 1776cc, treasury rating 14.76hp, 4 speed gearbox, single plate clutch, spiral bevel rear axle, semi-elliptic leaf springs, cantilever at rear, wheelbase 114in, and 5.00 x 20in tyres.
£9,000-10,500 *S*

Singer commenced business producing bicycles, graduated to motorcycles and produced their first car in 1905. Pre-war production focused around White and Poppe engined cars, however in post-war years their own engines were used.

1929 Singer Junior.
£6,000-6,500 *Cen*

Produced between 1927 and 1932 the Singer Junior was powered by a 4 cylinder, 848cc engine and was the first cheap British car with an overhead cam engine, about 25,000 Juniors were sold from 1927 to 1930.

1934 Singer Le Mans 1 Litre Team Racing Car, chassis No. 10327, engine No. 55238, 4 cylinder water-cooled monobloc, detachable one-piece cylinder head, overhead valves, bore 60mm x stroke 86mm, 972cc, 4 speed manual transmission with reverse, open shaft drive to live rear axle, semi-elliptic leaf spring front and rear suspension with Hartford shock absorbers, self locking knock on wire wheels with 18 x 450 tyres. This 1 litre car is AV9245, one of 4 Singer team cars entered in the 1934 Le Mans race. Carrying number 47, the car was driven by J. D. Barnes and T. H. Wisdom, and came 18th overall.
£22,000-24,000 *S*

The Le Mans 24 hour race of 1934 saw 6 cars fielded by Singer, keen to improve their increasingly successful competition history. Two litre 6 cylinder cars were run and four 1 litre 2 seaters.

1930 Singer Junior 8hp Boat Tail Two Seater, 4 cylinder engine, water-cooled monobloc, overhead valve, overhead camshaft, bore 56mm x stroke 86mm, 847cc, 4 speed gearbox, dry plate clutch, spiral bevel rear axle, semi-elliptic leaf springs front and rear, wheelbase 90in, 4.00 x 19in tyres.
Est. **£4,500-6,000** *S(A)*

MAKE	ENGINE	DATES	CONDITION		
Singer			1	2	3
10	1097/4	1918-24	£4,000	£2,000	£1,000
15	1991/6	1922-25	£6,000	£3,000	£1,500
14/34	1776/6	1926-27	£7,000	£4,000	£2,000
Junior	848/4	1927-32	£6,000	£3,000	£1,500
Senior	1571/4	1928-29	£7,000	£4,000	£2,000
Super 6	1920/6	1928-31	£7,000	£4,000	£2,000
9 Le Mans	972/4	1932-37	£12,000	£8,000	£5,000
Twelve	1440/4	1932-34	£10,000	£7,000	£6,000
1.5 litre	1493/6	1934-36	£3,000	£2,000	£1,000
2 litre	1993/6	1934-37	£4,000	£2,000	£1,000
11	1459/4	1935-36	£3,000	£2,000	£1,000
12	1525/4	1937-39	£3,000	£2,000	£1,000

Make: Singer
Model: Vogue
Type: Saloon
Years Manufactured: Series I, II and III, 1961-67
Price when new: £902
Engine Type: Overhead valve 4 cyl
Size: Series I/II/III, 1592cc; Series IV, c1725cc
Max Power: Series I, 62 bhp @ 4800 rpm; Series II, 58 bhp @ 4400 rpm; Series III, 78 bhp @ 5000 rpm; Series IV, 85 bhp @ 5500 rpm
Transmission: 4 speed, overdrive and auto optional
Performance: Max speed: Series I/II, 85 mph; Series III, 90+ mph; Series IV, 98 mph; 0-60: Series I/II, 22.0 secs; Series III, 15.0 secs; Series IV, 13.0 secs; Mpg: 22-32.

Make: Singer
Model: Gazelle
Type: Saloon
Years Manufactured: Series V, 1963-65; Series VI, 1965-67
Engine Type: Overhead valve 4 cyl (Series VI)
Size: Series V, 1592cc; Series VI, 1725cc
Max Power: Series V, 53 bhp @ 4100 rpm; Series VI, 59 bhp @ 4200 rpm
Transmission: 4 speed, overdrive and auto option
Performance: Max speed: Series V, 80 mph; Series VI, 85 mph; 0-60: Series V, 26.0 secs; Series VI, 19.5 secs; Mpg: 24-32.

1962 Singer Vogue Saloon, 4 cylinder engine, water-cooled monobloc, overhead valve, bore 81.5mm x stroke 76mm, capacity 1592cc, 4 speed gearbox, shaft drive to live rear axle, independent coil spring and wishbone front suspension, semi-elliptic leaf spring at rear, wheelbase 101in and 5.90/6.00 x 13 tyres, 44,297 miles recorded.
£1,100-1,500 *S*

1949 Singer Roadster, with 4 cylinder, 1074cc engine.
£7,500-8,250 *ADT*

1953 Singer Roadster, wit 4 cylinder, 1497cc engine.
£6,000-7,000 *LF*

SIZAIRE-NAUDIN

1909 Sizaire-Naudin 12hp Two Seater, chassis type F No. 1503 Series 9, engine No. 1083, single cylinder, overhead valve, 9hp, direct drive on 3 forward speeds by means of a propellor shaft that shifts to engage corresponding rings of teeth on the crown wheel, transverse leaf spring and sliding pillars suspension, right-hand drive, Scharlach headlamps, Dreadnought sidelamps and a bugle horn.
Est. **£5,000-8,000** *C(A)*

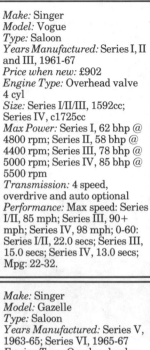

c1907 Sizaire-Naudin, in need total restoration.
Est. **£5,000-8,000** *P*

SCHACHT

1906 Schacht Motor Buggy, twin cylinder, side valve, 12hp, mid-mounted engine, chain drive transmission, steering wheel, wheelbase 84in.
Est. £11,000-13,000 *S(A)*

STANDARD

Founded by Mr. R. W. Maudsley in 1903, the Standard Motor Company of Coventry was producing 6 cylinder motor cars as early as 1906. The SL04 sold well in the 1920s but the Standard Nine was the real money maker for the company. Standard acquired Triumph in 1945 and the most famous post war model was the Standard Vanguard, which provided the engine for the Triumph TR2 sports car. Standard Triumph was taken over by Leyland in 1961 and the Standard name disappeared.

MAKE	ENGINE	DATES	CONDITION		
Standard			1	2	3
12	1609/4	1945-48	£2,000	£950	£250
12 DHC	1509/4	1945-48	£3,200	£2,000	£500
14	1776/4	1945-48	£2,100	£950	£250
Vanguard I/II	2088/4	1948-55	£1,800	£750	£150
Vanguard III	2088/4	1955-61	£1,500	£750	£150
Vanguard III Est	2088/4	1955-61	£2,000	£800	£150
Vanguard III Sportsman	2088/4	1955-58	£2,000	£800	£200
Vanguard Six	1998/6	1961-63	£1,500	£700	—
Eight	803/4	1952-59	£1,250	£500	—
Ten	948/4	1955-59	£1,400	£800	—
Ensign I/II	1670/4	1957-63	£1,000	£800	—
Ensign I/II Est	1670/4	1962-63	£1,000	£850	—
Pennant Companion	948/4	1955-61	£1,800	£850	£300
Pennant	948/4	1955-59	£1,650	£825	£250

1933 Standard 10hp Avon Two Door Closed Sporting Coupé, chassis No. 159801, engine No. 159801, 4 cylinder water-cooled, side valve monobloc, bore 63.5mm x stroke 106mm, 1343cc, 4 speed gearbox, single dry plate clutch, coil ignition pump and fan cooling, shaft drive to spiral bevel rear axle, wheelbase 94in, 4.50 x 18 tyres.
£11,500-12,500 *S*

Make: Standard
Model: Vanguard Phase I/II
Type: Saloon
Years Manufactured: 1947-55
Price when new: £543
Engine Type: Overhead valve 4 cyl
Size: 2088cc
Max Power: 68 bhp @ 4200 rpm
Transmission: 3 speed, overdrive optional
Performance: Max speed: 78 mph; 0-60: 24.0 secs; Mpg: 26-32.

Make: Standard
Model: Vanguard Sportsman
Type: Saloon
Years Manufactured: 1956-58
Price when new: £1,231
Engine Type: Overhead valve 4 cyl
Size: 2088cc
Max Power: 90 bhp @ 4500 rpm
Transmission: 3 speed or 4 speed optional
Performance: Max speed: 90 mph; 0-60: 17.5 secs; Mpg: 18-30.

The first owner is reputed to have been Amy Johnson, the pioneer aviator, and the chassis number indicates that this is the very first Standard 10hp.

1935 Standard 12 Four Door Saloon, fully restored 5 years ago and has 67,000 miles recorded.
£4,200-4,600 *DDM*

STANDARD

MAKE	ENGINE	DATES	CONDITION		
Standard			1	2	3
SLS	1328/4	1919-20	£5,000	£4,000	£1,000
VI	1307/4	1922	£5,000	£4,000	£1,000
SLO4/4v	1944/4	1922-28	£5,000	£4,000	£1,000
V3	1307/4	1923-26	£4,000	£3,000	£1,000
Little 9	1006/4	1923-33	£4,000	£2,000	£1,000
9	1155/4	1928-29	£4,000	£3,000	£1,000
15	1930/6	1929-30	£6,000	£4,000	£2,000
12	1337/6	1933-34	£4,000	£3,000	£1,500
10hp	1343/4	1933-37	£4,000	£2,500	£1,000
9	1052/4	1934-36	£4,000	£2,500	£1,000
Flying 9	1131/4	1937-39	£3,000	£1,800	£750
Flying 10	1267/4	1937-39	£3,000	£1,800	£750
Flying 14	1776/4	1937-48	£4,000	£2,000	£1,000
Flying 8	1021/4	1939-48	£3,000	£1,800	£750

Make: Standard
Model: Eight/Ten/Pennant
Type: Saloon
Years Manufactured: 1953-61
Price when new: Eight, £481;
Ten, £624; Pennant, £729
Engine Type: Overhead valve
4 cyl
Size: Eight, 803cc; Ten 948cc
Max Power: Eight, 26 bhp @
4500 rpm; Ten, 33 bhp @ 4500
rpm
Transmission: 4 speed, 2 pedal
control or optional on Gold Star
models from April 1957
Performance: Max speed: Eight,
65 mph; Ten, 68 mph; 0-60:
Eight, 50.0+ secs; Ten, 38.0
secs; Mpg: 38-45.

1946 Standard 8, by Fisher and
Lunlow, with 4 cylinder, 800cc
engine.
Est. **£3,000-5,000**   *ADT*

STAR

*Edward Lisle Srs Star Motor Co.
produced its first car in 1898, and
offered it for sale the following year.
For its first few years the company
relied on other people's designs, from
1898 to 1902 they were based on the
3½hp belt driven Benz, and were
sometimes known as Star Benzes,
although from the beginning Star
was a manufacturer rather than an
assembler. Production was running
at one car a week from October 1899.*

1898/99 Star 3½hp Vis-a-Vis,
single cylinder water-cooled engine,
belt primary drive and chain final
drive transmission, centre steering
operated from the left.
£81,000-83,000   *C(A)*

1932 Star Comet.
£22,500-25,000   *DJ*

STEYR

1934 Steyr 120S Sports Tourer,
6 cylinder in line, water-cooled,
pushrod operated overhead valve,
bore 68.5mm x stroke 90mm,
1976cc, 4 speed gearbox, 2 plate
clutch, open shaft, spiral bevel final
drive, transverse leaf front springs,
quarter elliptic leaf rear springs,
wheelbase 111½in, and 17in tyres,
this car underwent a major
restoration 8 years ago.
Est. **£18,000-22,000**   *S*

*The 6 cylinder Type 120 had an
overhead valve engine of almost
2 litre capacity which gave the car a
top speed of about 75mph.*

STUDEBAKER

c1913 Studebaker 15/20hp Four Seater Open Tourer, chassis No. W 300 29625, engine No. W 300 29625, 4 cylinder monobloc, water-cooled with side valves, bore 92mm x stroke 96mm, 3153cc, 3 speed manual gearbox, leather lined cone clutch, shaft and bevel drive, leaf springs front and rear fixed wooden wheels, with detachable rims, 30 x 3½ tyres, acetylene headlamps and oil sidelights.
Est. £13,000-14,000   S

928 Studebaker 'President' 'our Door Saloon, with cylinder, 3959cc engine. 6,500-7,000   ADT

1929 Studebaker Straight 8 Commander Four Door Tourer.
Est. £15,000-20,000   P

947 Studebaker Champion Starlight Coupé.
Est. £3,500-4,500   C

The brothers Henry and Clem Studebaker opened a blacksmiths and wagon building shop in South Bend, Indiana, in 1852, giving Studebaker the longest history of any American car. In 1897 they started experiments with electric cars and by 1904 they started to produce the Model C petrol car. Studebaker cars became very popular and in 1911 they were the second largest car producer in the USA. During the 20s their fortunes were quite variable in terms of market position, being 4th in 1921, its worst was 12th in 1929.

956 Studebaker Hawk Two oor Coupé, with only 50,000 iles recorded and left-hand drive. st. £8,000-12,000   C

1959 Studebaker Silver Hawk.
Est. £6,000-8,000   P

Restyling and development of the Starliner produced the sporting Hawk coupé powered Packard's V8 4¼ litre engine and Ultramatic transmission.

Miller's is a price GUIDE not a price LIST

STUDEBAKER

1962 Studebaker Hawk Gran Turismo.
£3,500-4,000   *ADT*

STEPHENS

The Stephens is a relatively rare make of car, even in its native America, and started life in 1916 being built by the Stephens Motor branch of the Moline Plow Company of Moline, Illinois. Up until 1918 it used mainly engines of Continental (Detroit) manufacture, and was a well made product built by a respected and well established maker of farm implements. The factory was located at Freeport, Illinois.

1922 Stephens Model 96 Three Seater Roadster
Est. £15,000-16,000   *S(A)*

STUTZ

1928 Stutz Model M Eight Cylinder Sedan, 8 cylinder in-line engine, water-cooled monobloc, overhead valves and camshaft, bore 82.5mm x stroke 114.3mm, 4811cc, 3 speed gearbox, single dry plate clutch, underslung worm drive rear axle, semi-elliptic leaf spring suspension front and rear, wheelbase 134½in, 6.00/6.50 x 20in tyres.
Est. £17,000-20,000   *S(A)*

1974 Stutz Blackhawk Coupé, V8 cylinder, water-cooled, overhead valve engine, 4.15in bore x 4.21in stroke, 455cu in, Turbo-Hydramatic 3 speed transmission, independent front and rear suspension, wheelbase 118in, tyres 17in.
£12,000-15,000   *SNY*

SUNBEAM

The first Sunbeam was the Mabley, a De Dion engined machine built under licence. Sunbeam produced a series of sports/racing cars and achieved the first Grand Prix victory for Great Britain in 1923 at the French Grand Prix. Sunbeam merged with Talbot/Darracq to form STD Motors Ltd. but this arrangement failed and Sunbeam was bought by Rootes. Sunbeam did not produce motor cars between 1937 and 1953, and then the company was acquired by Chrysler. Sunbeam as a marque disappeared in 1974.

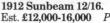

MAKE	ENGINE	DATES	CONDITION		
Sunbeam			1	2	3
12/16	2412/4	1909/11	£20,000	£14,000	£9,500
16/20	4070/4	1912-15	£32,000	£22,000	£15,000
24	4524/6	1919-22	£28,000	£18,000	£10,000
3 litre	2916/6	1925-30	£48,000	£30,000	£20,000
16	2040/6	1927-30	£16,000	£12,500	£10,000
20	2916/6	1927-30	£22,000	£15,000	£10,500
Speed 20	2916/6	1932-35	£15,000	£10,000	£8,000
Dawn	1627/4	1934-35	£8,000	£5,000	£3,500
25	3317/6	1934	£10,000	£8,000	£4,000

Prices can vary depending on replica bodies, provenance, coachbuilder, drop head, etc.

1912 Sunbeam 12/16.
Est. £12,000-16,000   *P*

The Sunbeam Motor Car Co Ltd was started in 1905, making an all British 16/20 designed by Angus Shaw. In 1909 Louis Coatalen arrived as a designer. By 1910 pressure lubrication, OHVs and an overdrive gearbox had been introduced. During World War I, Sunbeam concentrated on aero engines and in 1919 upon returning to car production, introduced the 4/16.

1919 Sunbeam 4/16 Open Tourer, 3016cc, 4 cylinder engine.
£25,000-27,000   *Cen*

1921 Sunbeam 16hp Five Seat Tourer, 4 cylinder in-line engine, water-cooled monobloc, side valve, bore 80mm x stroke 150mm, 3016cc, 4 speed gate change gearbox, cone clutch, shaft and spiral bevel final drive, semi-elliptic leaf spring suspension front and rear, wheelbase 124in, 820 x 120mm beaded edge tyres.
Est. **£32,000-35,000**   *S*

1924 Sunbeam 16/50 Tourer, 6 cylinder engine, water-cooled, overhead valves, bore 70mm x stroke 110mm, 2540cc (18.13hp RAC), 4 speed gearbox, shaft drive to live rear axle, 4 wheel brakes, suspension semi-elliptic springs at front, cantilever springs at rear, wheelbase 129½in.
Est. **£19,000-21,000**   *S(A)*

1939 Sunbeam-Talbot 10hp Tourer.
Est. **£10,000-15,000**   *P*

1939 Sunbeam Talbot 10 Sports Saloon, 4 cylinder, 1185cc engine.
£6,500-7,000   *ADT*

MAKE	ENGINE	DATES	CONDITION		
Sunbeam-Talbot/Sunbeam			1	2	3
Talbot 80	1185/4	1948-50	£4,000	£2,250	£750
Talbot 80 DHC	1185/4	1948-50	£6,000	£4,500	£2,000
Talbot 90 Mk I	1944/4	1949-50	£4,000	£2,100	£750
Talbot 90 Mk I DHC	1944/4	1949-50	£7,000	£4,750	£2,000
Talbot 90 II/IIa/III	2267/4	1950-56	£5,000	£3,000	£1,500
Talbot 90 II/IIa/III DHC	2267/4	1950-56	£8,000	£4,500	£2,250
Talbot Alpine I/III	2267/4	1953-55	£9,000	£7,500	£3,750
Talbot Ten	1197/4	1946-48	£3,500	£2,000	£750
Talbot Ten Tourer	1197/4	1946-48	£7,000	£4,000	£2,000
Talbot Ten DHC	1197/4	1946-48	£6,500	£4,000	£2,000
Talbot 2 litre	1997/4	1946-48	£4,000	£2,500	£1,000
Talbot 2 litre Tourer	1997/4	1946-48	£7,500	£4,000	£2,250
Rapier I	1392/4	1955-57	£1,200	£700	£300
Rapier II	1494/4	1957-59	£1,800	£900	£300
Rapier II Conv	1494/4	1957-59	£3,000	£1,500	£450
Rapier III	1494/4	1959-61	£2,000	£1,200	£400
Rapier III Conv	1494/4	1959-61	£3,500	£1,600	£600
Rapier IIIA	1592/4	1961-63	£2,000	£1,200	£400
Rapier IIIA Conv	1592/4	1961-63	£3,600	£1,700	£650
Rapier IV/V	1592/1725/4	1963-67	£2,000	£700	£250
Alpine I-II	1494/4	1959-62	£6,000	£3,500	£1,800
Alpine III	1592/4	1963	£6,500	£4,000	£1,250
Alpine IV	1592/4	1964	£6,500	£4,000	£1,250
Alpine V	1725/4	1965-68	£7,000	£4,000	£1,250
Harrington Alpine	1592/4	1961	£8,000	£4,750	—
Harrington Le Mans	1592/4	1962-63	£10,000	£6,500	—
Tiger Mk 1	4261/8	1964-67	£15,000	£10,000	£5,000
Tiger Mk 2	4700/8	1967	£18,000	£13,000	£5,000
Rapier Fastback	1725/4	1967-76	£1,100	£700	£250
Rapier H120	1725/4	1968-76	£1,500	£800	£300

Make: Sunbeam-Talbot
Type: Saloon, Convertible
Years Manufactured: 1954-57
Price when new: Saloon, £1,127;
Convertible, £1,198
Engine Type: Overhead valve
4 cyl
Size: 2267cc
Max Power: 80 bhp @ 4400 rpm
Transmission: 4 speed,
overdrive optional
Performance: Max speed: 100
mph; 0-60: 18.0 secs; Mpg: 20-30.

Make the Most of Miller's

Price ranges in this book reflect what one should expect to pay for a similar example. When selling, however, one should expect to receive a lower figure. This will fluctuate according to a dealer's stock, saleability at a particular time, etc. It is always advisable, when selling, to approach a reputable specialist dealer or an auction house which has specialist sales

**1952 Sunbeam Alpine Sports
Two Seater Prototype.
£22,000-25,000** *S*

1954 Sunbeam Talbot 90,
4 cylinder, 2267cc engine, 'Supreme'
drop head variant produced in late
1954, mechanically sound.
Est. £4,000-5,000   *ADT*

1954 Sunbeam Talbot Mk III.
Est. £2,000-4,000   *P*

*Between 1951 and 1957 some 19,000
Sunbeam Talbot 90s were produced.
They had a sturdy chassis fitted with
the 2.3 litre OHV 4 cylinder engine
used in other Rootes Group vehicles.*

1965 Sunbeam Tiger Mk I, one
owner and in good original
condition.
£18,000-20,000   *CTC*

1965 Sunbeam Tiger Mk I.
£14,000-15,000   *AMR*

*The Tiger Mk I was produced
between 1964 and 1966 and was
fitted with the American Ford 260
engine, as fitted to the early AC
Cobras. This V8 engine produced
164bhp and offered 120mph and
0-60mph in 9 seconds.*

Did you know
**MILLER'S Collectors Cars
Price Guide builds up year
by year to form the most
comprehensive photo-
reference system
available**

Make: Sunbeam
Model: Tiger
Type: Sports
Years Manufactured: 1964-67
Quantity: Mk I, 6,495; Mk II, 571
Price when new: Mk I, £1,446;
Mk II, £1,691
Engine Type: Overhead valve
V8
Size: Mk I, 4261cc; Mk II,
4737ccc
Max Power: Mk I, 164 bhp @
4400 rpm
Max Torque: Mk I, 258 ft/lb @
2200 rpm
Transmission: 4 speed
Wheelbase: 86in
Performance: Max speed: Mk I,
116 mph; 0-60: Mk I, 9.0 secs;
Mpg: Mk I, 20-26.

SUNBEAM

**1966 Sunbeam Alpine Series V
2+2 Convertible,** 4 cylinder
engine, overhead valve, water-
cooled monobloc, 1760cc, 4 speed
gearbox with overdrive, double
wishbone front suspension,
semi-elliptic leaf springs at rear,
live rear axle, 175/70 x 15 tyres,
fitted with the Holbay 1760cc
engine and twin 40 Dellorto
carburettors, and 2,000 miles
recorded since new engine.
£5,750-6,000 *S*

Make: Sunbeam
Model: Alpine
Type: Sports
Years Manufactured: 1959-68
Quantity: 69,251
Price when new: 1491cc, £1,032
Engine Type: Overhead valve
4 cyl
Size: 1494cc/1592cc/1725cc
Max Power: Series II, 80 bhp @
5000 rpm
Max Torque: Series II, 94 ft/lb @
3800 rpm
Transmission: 4 speed,
overdrive optional
Performance: Max speed: Series
II, 103 mph; 0-60: Series II, 13.5
secs; Mpg: Series II, 25-30.

1970 Sunbeam Alpine Series 5.
£3,500-4,500 *AMR*

1970 Sunbeam Imp Sport
£1,200-2,000 *AMR*

SWIFT

1927 Swift P Type Tourer.
£12,000-13,000 *LF*

*The Swift Cycle Company was
formed in 1896 and in 1898 started
to build motor tricycles and
motorcycles. Motor quads started in
1900 and true call entered
production in 1902.*

TALBOT

Clement Talbot Ltd. was
founded in 1903 to import the
French Clement automobile
into England. A Talbot driven
by Percy Lambert was the first
car to travel 100 miles in one
hour, at Brooklands in 1913.
Talbot was part of the Sunbeam,
Talbot, Darracq combine but
this was not a great success and
was taken over by Rootes in
1935.

1916 12hp Talbot, 4 cylinder
engine, fixed head side valve, 80mm
x 120mm stroke, 2409cc, channel
section chassis with beam axles
carried on semi-elliptic leaf springs,
4 speed gearbox with right-hand
change, rear wheel drum type
brakes, separate shoes for foot and
hand operation, steel Sankey type
wheels, 815 x 105 beaded edge tyres.
Est. **£35,000-40,000** *C(A)*

1926 Talbot 10/23 Two Seater and Dickey, 4 cylinder pushrod operated overhead valve, water-cooled monobloc, bore 60mm x stroke 95mm, 1073cc, RAC rating 9hp, 3 speed gearbox, single dry plate clutch, shaft and spiral bevel drive, wheelbase 108in, and 4.50 x 19 tyres.
£10,000-10,500 *S*

1935 Talbot BD75 Sports Tourer, 6 cylinder engine, pushrod operated overhead valves, 69.5mm bore x 100mm stroke, 2276cc, rated to develop approximately 76bhp at 4,500rpm, channel section chassis side members with semi-elliptic leaf springs front and rear, right hand drive, 4 speed synchromesh gearbox with central gear change lever, cable operated mechanical type brakes on all 4 wheels in large ribbed drums, centre lock wire type wheels.
Est. £22,000-25,000 *C(A)*

1936 Talbot 105 Tourer, cylinder, 2969cc engine.
£36,000-40,000 *ADT*

> *Make:* Talbot
> *Model:* Sunbeam Lotus
> *Type:* Hatchback
> *Years Manufactured:* 1979-82
> *Quantity:* 2,308
> *Engine Type:* 16 valve, overhead camshaft 4 cyl
> *Size:* 2172cc
> *Max Power:* 150 bhp @ 5600 rpm
> *Transmission:* 5 speed
> *Performance:* Max speed: 122 mph; 0-60: 7.8 secs; Mpg: 16-25.

MAKE	ENGINE	DATES	CONDITION		
Talbot			1	2	3
25hp and 25/30	4155/4	1907-16	£40,000	£30,000	£15,000
12hp	2409/4	1909-15	£25,000	£15,000	£9,000
8/18	960/4	1922-25	£8,000	£5,000	£2,000
14/45	1666/6	1926-35	£16,000	£10,000	£5,000
75	2276/6	1930-37	£22,000	£12,000	£7,000
105	2969/6	1935-37	£28,000	£20,000	£15,000

Higher value for tourers and coachbuilders.

Locate the source

The source of each illustration in Miller's can be found by checking the code letters below each caption with the list of contributors

TRIUMPH

The Triumph Company, makers of famous motorcycles, did not produce their first motor car until 1923. After the second World War it became part of Sir John Black's Standard Triumph organisation. During the 1950s and 60s a good range of sports and saloon cars was produced, notably the TR sports car series. Sadly the Triumph name was dropped by Austin Rover in 1984.

1929 Triumph Super Seven, named 'sixpence', its last tax disc being 1941 issue, a current MOT, and V5 come together with a 1929 sixpence, its original cost.
£7,500-8,500 *ADT*

In 1929 a Mr Alfred Bennett of St Austell, Cornwall, entered a competition—the entry fee for which was sixpence. Much to Mr Bennett's surprise, he won first prize, a Triumph Super Seven Tourer. Prior to being delivered to Mr Bennett in Cornwall, the car was registered by the Triumph Motor Company (VC 2318) and was delivered to his home in December 1929. Mr Bennett used the car regularly until the end of 1941 in which time he had covered less than 46,000 miles.

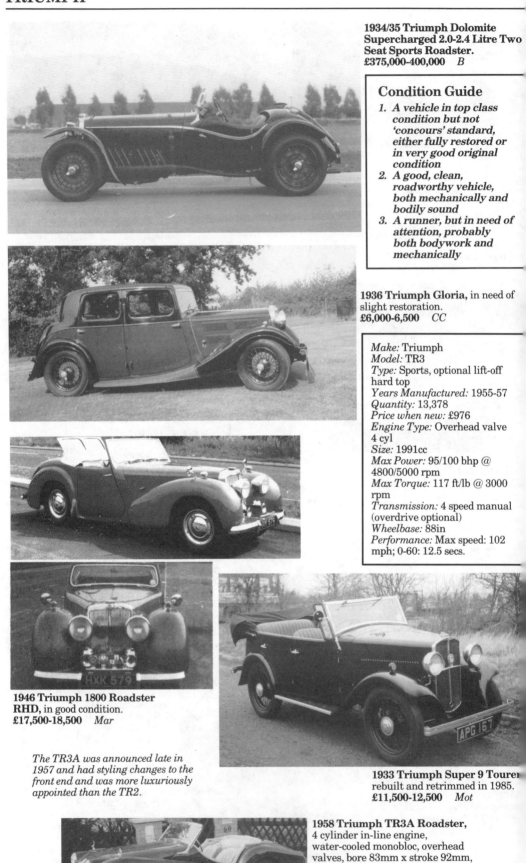

1934/35 Triumph Dolomite Supercharged 2.0-2.4 Litre Two Seat Sports Roadster.
£375,000-400,000   *B*

Condition Guide

1. *A vehicle in top class condition but not 'concours' standard, either fully restored or in very good original condition*
2. *A good, clean, roadworthy vehicle, both mechanically and bodily sound*
3. *A runner, but in need of attention, probably both bodywork and mechanically*

1936 Triumph Gloria, in need of slight restoration.
£6,000-6,500   *CC*

Make: Triumph
Model: TR3
Type: Sports, optional lift-off hard top
Years Manufactured: 1955-57
Quantity: 13,378
Price when new: £976
Engine Type: Overhead valve 4 cyl
Size: 1991cc
Max Power: 95/100 bhp @ 4800/5000 rpm
Max Torque: 117 ft/lb @ 3000 rpm
Transmission: 4 speed manual (overdrive optional)
Wheelbase: 88in
Performance: Max speed: 102 mph; 0-60: 12.5 secs.

1946 Triumph 1800 Roadster RHD, in good condition.
£17,500-18,500   *Mar*

The TR3A was announced late in 1957 and had styling changes to the front end and was more luxuriously appointed than the TR2.

1933 Triumph Super 9 Tourer rebuilt and retrimmed in 1985.
£11,500-12,500   *Mot*

1958 Triumph TR3A Roadster, 4 cylinder in-line engine, water-cooled monobloc, overhead valves, bore 83mm x stroke 92mm, 1991cc, 4 speed gearbox, single dry plate clutch, hypoid bevel rear axle, independent coil spring front suspension, semi-elliptic leaf rear springs, wheelbase 88in, 15in tyres, restored and 92,000km recorded.
£14,000-14,500   *S(M)*

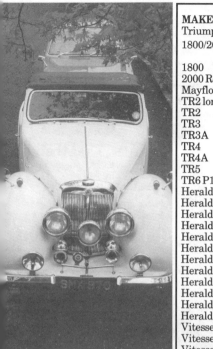

1948 Triumph 1.8 Litre Roadster.
£12,500-13,000 *B*

Make: Triumph
Model: 1800/2000 Roadster
Type: Roadster
Years Manufactured: 1946-49
Quantity: 1800 (1946-48), 2,501;
2000 (1949), 2,000
Price when new: £799
Engine Type: Standard
overhead valve 4 cyl
Size: 1946-48, 1776cc; 1949,
2088cc
Max Power: 1776cc, 65 bhp @
4500 rpm; 2088cc, 68 bhp @
4200 rpm
Max Torque: 1776cc, 92 ft/lb @
2000 rpm; 2088cc, 108 ft/lb @
2000 rpm
Transmission: 1946-48, 4 speed
manual; 1949, 3 speed manual
Wheelbase: 108in
Performance: Max speed: 70-77
mph; 0-60: 27.9-34.4 secs.

MAKE Triumph	ENGINE	DATES	CONDITION 1	2	3
1800/2000 Roadster	1776/ 2088/4	1946-49	£12,000	£7,500	£2,500
1800	1776/4	1946-49	£4,200	£2,000	£950
2000 Renown	2088/4	1949-54	£4,200	£2,000	£950
Mayflower	1247/4	1949-53	£1,700	£750	£350
TR2 long door	1247/4	1953	£14,000	£10,000	£8,000
TR2	1247/4	1953-55	£12,000	£9,000	£5,000
TR3	1991/4	1955-57	£9,000	£8,500	£3,500
TR3A	1991/4	1958-62	£9,000	£8,500	£3,500
TR4	2138/4	1961-65	£10,000	£7,000	£3,000
TR4A	2138/4	1965-67	£11,000	£6,500	£3,000
TR5	2498/6	1967-68	£14,500	£8,500	£4,000
TR6 P1	2498/6	1969-74	£12,500	£7,500	£3,500
Herald	948/4	1959-61	£800	£400	£150
Herald FHC	948/4	1959-61	£1,200	£550	£300
Herald DHC	948/4	1960-61	£1,500	£800	£350
Herald 'S'	948/4	1961-64	£800	£400	£150
Herald 1200	1147/4	1961-70	£1,100	£500	£200
Herald 1200 FHC	1147/4	1961-64	£1,400	£800	£300
Herald 1200 DHC	1147/4	1961-67	£1,700	£900	£350
Herald 1200 Est	1147/4	1961-67	£1,300	£700	£300
Herald 12/50	1147/4	1963-67	£1,250	£600	£250
Herald 13/60	1296/4	1967-71	£1,300	£600	£200
Herald 13/60 DHC	1296/4	1967-71	£2,000	£1,200	£400
Herald 13/60 Est	1296/4	1967-71	£1,500	£650	£300
Vitesse 1600	1596/6	1962-66	£2,000	£1,250	£550
Vitesse 1600 Conv	1596/6	1962-66	£2,800	£1,350	£600
Vitesse 2 litre Mk I	1998/6	1966-68	£1,800	£800	£300
Vitesse 2 litre Mk I Conv	1998/6	1966-68	£3,000	£1,500	£650
Vitesse 2 litre Mk II	1998/6	1968-71	£2,000	£1,500	£300
Vitesse 2 litre Mk II Conv	1998/6	1968-71	£4,000	£1,750	£650
Spitfire Mk I	1147/4	1962-64	£2,000	£1,750	£300
Spitfire Mk II	1147/4	1965-67	£2,500	£2,000	£350
Spitfire Mk III	1296/4	1967-70	£3,500	£2,500	£450
Spitfire Mk IV	1296/4	1970-74	£2,500	£2,000	£350
Spitfire 1500	1493/4	1975-78	£3,500	£2,500	£750
Spitfire 1500	1493/4	1979-81	£4,500	£3,000	£1,200
GT6 Mk I	1998/6	1966-68	£6,000	£4,000	£1,200
GT6 Mk II	1998/6	1968-70	£7,000	£4,500	£1,400
GT6 Mk III	1998/6	1970-73	£8,000	£5,000	£1,500
2000 Mk I	1998/6	1964-69	£2,500	£1,000	£250
2000 Mk II	1998/6	1969-77	£1,750	£700	£100
2.5 PI	2498/6	1968-74	£2,000	£800	£200
2500 TC/S	2498/6	1974-77	£1,750	£700	£150
2500S	2498/6	1975-77	£2,500	£1,000	£150
1300 (FWD)	1296/4	1965-70	£800	£400	£150
1300TC (FWD)	1296/4	1967-70	£900	£450	£150
1500 (FWD)	1493/4	1970-73	£700	£450	£125
1500TC (RWD)	1296/4	1973-76	£850	£500	£100
Toledo	1296/4	1970-76	£850	£450	£100
Dolomite 1500	1493/4	1976-80	£1,350	£750	£125
Dolomite 1850	1854/4	1972-80	£1,450	£850	£150
Dolomite Sprint	1998/4	1976-81	£8,000	£5,500	£1,000
Stag	2997/8	1970-77	£11,000	£6,000	£2,000
TR7	1998/4	1975-82	£3,000	£1,200	£500
TR7 DHC	1998/4	1980-82	£4,500	£3,500	£1,500

'59 TR3A, recently restored.
5,000-15,500 *DJ*

1959 Triumph TR3A, with
4 cylinder, 1991cc engine.
£12,000-13,500 *ADT*

1961 TR3A LHD.
£14,500-15,000 *FOR*

1962 Triumph TR3B LHD, with
4 cylinder, 2198cc engine and
chromed wire wheels.
Est. **£15,000-18,000** *Ren*

*Introduced to satisfy the demand
from America, the TR3B was only
produced in left-hand drive form
and fitted with the larger 2.2 litre
engine and the new all synchromesh
gearbox with overdrive, it was
produced alongside the new TR4.*

**1963 Triumph TR4 Dove 2+2
Coupé,** 4 cylinder in line,
water-cooled monobloc engine,
overhead valve, bore 86mm x stroke
92mm, 2138cc, 4 speed synchromesh
gearbox with overdrive, single dry
plate clutch, hypoid bevel rear axle,
independent coil spring and
wishbone front suspension,
semi-elliptic leaf rear springs,
wheelbase 88in, tyres 15in, this is a
Dove conversion, fixed head 2+2 car
with hatchback rear window.
£8,800-9,200 *S*

1963 Triumph Spitfire Mk I, fully
restored.
£5,000-6,000 *CTC*

Make: Triumph
Model: TR3A and TR3B
Type: Sports
Years Manufactured: 1958-62
Quantity: TR3A, 58,236; TR3B,
3,331
Price when new: TR3A, £1,050
Engine Type: Overhead valve
4 cyl
Size: 1958-62, 1991cc; 1962,
2138cc
Max Power: 1991cc, 100 bhp @
5000 rpm; 2138cc, 100 bhp @
4600 rpm
Max Torque: 1991cc, 117 ft/lb @
3000 rpm; 2138cc, 127 ft/lb @
3350 rpm
Transmission: 4 speed manual
(overdrive optional)
Wheelbase: 88in
Performance: Max speed: 102
mph; 0-60: 12.5 secs.

1962 Triumph TR4.
£5,000-5,500 *LF*

*By the early 1960s the TR2 and 3
had been in production for nearly
10 years, and 1961 saw the arrival of
the TR4 which was really an
improved TR3 chassis with modern
wind-up window body by Michelotti.*

Make: Triumph
Model: TR2
Type: Sports, optional lift-off
hard top
Years Manufactured: 1953-55
Quantity: 8,628
Price when new: £887
Engine Type: Overhead valve
4 cyl
Size: 1991cc
Max Power: 90 bhp @ 4800 rpm
Max Torque: 117 ft/lb @ 3000
rpm
Transmission: 4 speed manual
(overdrive optional)
Wheelbase: 88in
Performance: Max speed: 103
mph; 0-60: 11.9 secs.

1962 Triumph TR4, with
4 cylinder, 2138cc engine.
£6,000-6,500 *ADT*

1964 Triumph TR4 Sports Two Seater, 4 cylinder in-line engine, water-cooled monobloc, overhead valve, bore 86mm x stroke 92mm, 2138cc, 4 speed manual transmission, single dry plate clutch, hypoid bevel rear axle, independent coil and wishbone front suspension, semi-elliptic rear springs, wheelbase 88in.
£6,050-6,500 *S*

The TR4 has 105bhp at 4,750rpm.

Make: Triumph
Model: TR4/4A
Type: Sports
Years Manufactured: 1961-67
Quantity: 68,718
Price when new: 1961-65, £1,106
Engine Type: Overhead valve 4 cyl
Size: 2138cc (1991cc optional)
Max Power: TR4, 100 bhp @ 4600 rpm; TR4A, 104 bhp @ 4700 rpm
Transmission: 4 speed, overdrive optional
Performance: Max speed: 109 mph; 0-60: 11.0 secs; Mpg: 24-26.

Triumph TR4, 4 cylinder overhead valve engine, 104bhp, bore 86mm x stroke 92mm, 4 speed synchromesh gearbox.
£6,500-7,000 *SEN*

1967 Triumph TR4A.
£10,500-11,000 *ADT*

1967 TR4A, manual with overdrive and wire wheels.
£7,000-7,500 *BLE*

Triumph TR4A, totally rebuilt.
£12,000-15,000 *FOR*

Condition Guide

1. *A vehicle in top class condition but not 'concours' standard, either fully restored or in very good original condition*
2. *A good, clean, roadworthy vehicle, both mechanically and bodily sound*
3. *A runner, but in need of attention, probably both bodywork and mechanically*

1967 Triumph TR4A IRS.
£8,000-8,500 *LF*

1971 Triumph TR6, has undergone a chassis up rebuild and now in 'as new' condition with chrome wire wheels.
£13,000-13,500   *GWC*

1973 Triumph TR6 Two Seater Sports, 6 cylinder in-line engine, water-cooled monobloc, pushrod operated overhead valves, bore 74.7mm x stroke 95mm, 2498cc, single dry plate clutch, 4 speed gearbox with overdrive, hypoid bevel drive live rear axle, independent front suspension by coil springs and wishbones, independent rear by coil springs and semi-trailing wishbones, wheelbase 88in, tyres 15in.
£7,000-7,500   *S*

The TR6 had a 6 cylinder engine, independent suspension all round and a body shell styled by Karmann of Germany. The TR6 had a top speed of around 120mph.

1973 Triumph TR6, converted to right-hand drive.
£7,000-7,750   *GWC*

Make: Triumph
Model: TR5/TR6
Type: Sports
Years Manufactured: 1967-75
Quantity: 106,050
Price when new: TR5, (1967-69), £1,321; TR6PI, £1,396
Engine Type: In line 6 cyl
Size: 2498cc
Max Power: TR5, 150 bhp @ 5500 rpm; TR6, 150 bhp @ 5500 rpm
Transmission: 4 speed, overdrive optional, overdrive standard from 1973
Performance: Max speed: 120 mph; 0-60: 8.8 secs; Mpg: 22-27.

1974 Triumph TR6
£6,000-6,500   *CMA*

1974 Triumph TR6, with 48,000 miles recorded, imported 1990, left-hand drive.
£6,000-6,500   *RCH*

1974 Triumph TR6
Est. **£5,000-6,000**

Triumph TR6, totally rebuilt and restored.
£17,000-18,000   *FOR*

Make: Triumph
Model: 2000/2500
Type: Saloon
Years Manufactured: 1963-77
Price when new: 2500, £1,481
Engine Type: Overhead valve 6 cyl
Size: 1998cc/2498cc
Max Power: 2000, 90 bhp @ 5000 rpm; 2.5PI, 132 bhp @ 5450 rpm; 2500TC, 106 bhp @ 4700 rpm
Transmission: 4 speed, overdrive optional, standard on 2.5PI from Oct 1972, auto optional
Performance: Max speed: 2000, 96 mph; 2.5PI, 111 mph; 2500TC, 103 mph; 0-60: 2000, 14.0 secs; 2.5PI, 9.8 secs; 2500TC, 11.2 secs; Mpg: 19-30.

1975 TR6, overdrive, one owner from new, service history, hard top.
£10,000-10,500   *BLE*

1977 Triumph 2500TC, with 88,000 miles recorded.
£800-1,000   *CMA*

The Triumph 2500TC saloon used the Triumph Mk II chassis and a 106bhp 2498cc engine. Produced from 1974-77.

**976 Triumph 2.5S Automatic
state.**
st. **£2,000-3,000**   *P*

1974 Triumph Stag.
£12,500-13,500   *CMA*

The Triumph Stag was conceived in the late 60s as a high performance luxury sports car. Available from 1970 until 1977 it was powered by a 3 litre V8 engine which gave the car a top speed of 120mph.

MAKE	ENGINE	DATES	CONDITION		
Triumph			1	2	3
TLC	1393/4	1923-25	£6,000	£4,000	£1,500
TPC	2169/4	1926-30	£6,000	£4,000	£2,000
K	832/4	1928-34	£4,000	£2,000	£1,000
S	1203/6	1931-33	£5,000	£3,000	£1,500
G12 Gloria	1232/4	1935-37	£6,000	£4,000	£2,000
G16 Gloria 6	1991/6	1935-39	£7,000	£4,500	£2,000
Vitesse/Dolomite	1767/4	1937-39	£14,000	£10,000	£6,000
Dolomite	1496/4	1938-39	£7,000	£4,000	£2,000

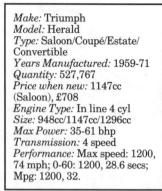

Make: Triumph
Model: Herald
Type: Saloon/Coupé/Estate/
Convertible
Years Manufactured: 1959-71
Quantity: 527,767
Price when new: 1147cc
(Saloon), £708
Engine Type: In line 4 cyl
Size: 948cc/1147cc/1296cc
Max Power: 35-61 bhp
Transmission: 4 speed
Performance: Max speed: 1200,
74 mph; 0-60: 1200, 28.6 secs;
Mpg: 1200, 32.

Triumph Vitesse Mk II.
£8,000-10,000   *FOR*

Make: Triumph
Model: Vitesse
Type: Saloon/Convertible
Years Manufactured: 1962-71
Quantity: 51,212
Price when new: 1596cc
(Saloon), £837; (Convertible)
£893
Engine Type: Overhead valve
6 cyl
Size: 1596cc/1998cc
Max Power: 1600, 70 bhp @
5000 rpm; 2000 Mk II, 104 bhp
@ 5300 rpm
Transmission: 4 speed,
overdrive optional
Performance: Max speed: 1600,
90 mph; 2000 Mk II, 100+ mph;
0-60: 1600, 16.0 secs; 2000
Mk II, 12.0 secs; Mpg: 24-30.

1968 Triumph Herald 120
Saloon.
Est. **£5,000-7,000**   *P*

1966 Triumph Herald, only 4,00
miles recorded.
Est. **£6,000-8,000**   *Cen*

1973 Triumph GT6 Mk II
restored.
£8,000-8,500   *BLE*

1969 Triumph GT6 Mk II, with
23,000 miles recorded, this car was a
Benson & Hedges Concours winner.
£8,500-9,500   *Cen*

Make	FRANCE	GERMANY	ITALY	JAPAN	USA
Triumph	+2%	+5%	—	+2%	+4%

Make: Triumph
Model: GT6
Type: Sports Coupé
Years Manufactured: 1963-73
Quantity: 40,926
Price when new: Mk I/II, £985; Mk III, £1,340
Engine Type: Overhead valve 6 cyl
Size: 1998cc
Max Power: Mk I, 95 bhp @ 5000 rpm; Mk II/III, 104 bhp @ 5300 rpm
Transmission: 4 speed, overdrive optional
Performance: Max speed: Mk I, 107 mph; Mk II/III, 110 mph; 0-60: Mk I, 11.0 secs; Mk II/III, 10.0 secs; Mpg: 24-30.

1970 Triumph GT6, 6 cylinder, 1998cc engine with 20,500 miles recorded, this car won 1st prize at the Motor Sport Concours, Silverstone.
Est. **£12,500-14,000**   *Ren*

1974 Triumph GT6.
£7,000-7,500   *BLE*

1970 Triumph Spitfire Two Seater Sports Coupé.
Est. **£11,000-13,000**   *S(A)*

Make: Triumph
Model: Spitfire
Type: Sports
Years Manufactured: 1962-80
Quantity: 314,342
Price when new: Mk III, 1296cc, £717
Engine Type: Overhead valve 4 cyl
Size: 1146cc/1296cc/1493cc
Max Power: Mk IV, 63 bhp @ 6000 rpm
Transmission: 4 speed, overdrive optional
Performance: Max speed: Mk IV, 90+ mph; 0-60: Mk IV, 16.0 secs; Mpg: Mk IV, 36-40.

1979 Triumph Spitfire 1500.
£3,300-3,600   *Cen*

Introduced in 1962 the Spitfire used the same chassis as the Triumph Herald. In 1975 the Mk V 1500 was introduced using the 1493cc engine that had been fitted for the American market since 1970. This engine produced 71bhp and gave a 100mph top speed.

Make the Most of Miller's

Price ranges in this book reflect what one should expect to pay for a similar example. When selling, however, one should expect to receive a lower figure. This will fluctuate according to a dealer's stock, saleability at a particular time, etc. It is always advisable, when selling, to approach a reputable specialist dealer or an auction house which has specialist sales

1970 Triumph Stag Sports Convertible, 90° V8 cylinder engine, water-cooled, single overhead camshaft, bore 86mm x stroke 64.5mm, 2998cc, 4 speed gearbox, hypoid bevel rear axle, independent front and rear suspension, 15in tyres.
Est. £5,000-6,000   *S*

The Triumph Stag came out of Coventry in 1970 developed from a Michelotti styling exercise based on the Triumph 2000 saloon, with 4 seat passenger accommodation, hard and soft tops.

1973 Triumph Stag, with 3 litre V8 engine, extensively rebuilt with reconditioned automatic gearbox, a replacement back axle and 50,000 miles recorded.
£5,775-6,500   *ADT*

1972 Triumph Stag, with V8 2997cc engine.
£5,700-6,200   *LF*

Make: Triumph
Model: Stag
Type: Convertible
Years Manufactured: 1970-77
Quantity: 25,877
Price when new: £2,061
Engine Type: Overhead camshaft V8
Size: 2997cc
Max Power: 145 bhp @ 5500 rpm
Transmission: 4 speed, auto optional, overdrive optional, standard from Oct 1972
Performance: Max speed: 117 mph; 0-60: 9.8 secs; Mpg: 22-29.

1976 Triumph Stag Mk II Automatic, with hard and soft top
£8,600-9,400   *Cen*

1976 Triumph Stag Automatic, with V8, 2997cc engine, 13,000 miles since undergoing major restoration.
£12,000-13,000   *Ren*

Make: Triumph
Model: Dolomite Sprint
Type: Saloon
Years Manufactured: 1973-80
Quantity: 22,941
Price when new: £1,740
Engine Type: Overhead camshaft 16 valve 4 cyl
Size: 1998cc
Max Power: 127 bhp @ 5700 rpm
Transmission: 4 speed, auto optional, overdrive optional, standard from April 1975
Performance: Max speed: 113 mph; 0-60: 8.0+ secs; Mpg: 22-30.

1977 Triumph Stag.
£11,000-13,000   *LF*

Triumph TR7 Drop Head Coupé.
£6,500-7,000 *FOR*

1981 Triumph TR8, ex British
Leyland demonstration car.
£11,750-12,500 *BLE*

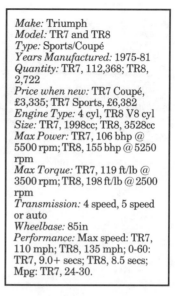

Make: Triumph
Model: TR7 and TR8
Type: Sports/Coupé
Years Manufactured: 1975-81
Quantity: TR7, 112,368; TR8,
2,722
Price when new: TR7 Coupé,
£3,335; TR7 Sports, £6,382
Engine Type: 4 cyl, TR8 V8 cyl
Size: TR7, 1998cc; TR8, 3528cc
Max Power: TR7, 106 bhp @
5500 rpm; TR8, 155 bhp @ 5250
rpm
Max Torque: TR7, 119 ft/lb @
3500 rpm; TR8, 198 ft/lb @ 2500
rpm
Transmission: 4 speed, 5 speed
or auto
Wheelbase: 85in
Performance: Max speed: TR7,
110 mph; TR8, 135 mph; 0-60:
TR7, 9.0+ secs; TR8, 8.5 secs;
Mpg: TR7, 24-30.

1977 Triumph TR8, 8 cylinder,
3528cc engine, with body No. 00002,
engine block stamped EXP 255
(experimental?), left-hand drive
Californian specification the car
was UK registered on 9.5.78 and has
a heated front screen.
Est. **£8,000-12,000** *ADT*

TVR

1978 TVR 3000M.
£7,000-7,500 *GWC*

Make: TVR
Model: M-class
Type: Sports Coupé
Years Manufactured: 1972-79
Quantity: 1,749
Engine Type: 4 cyl, 6 cyl, V6 cyl
Size: 1599cc/2498cc/2994cc
Max Power: 86-138 bhp
Transmission: 4 speed, optional
overdrive on 2500M and 3000M
Performance: Max speed: 121
mph; 0-60: 7.7 secs; Mpg: 22.

Make: TVR
Model: Turbo
Type: Sports Car/Sports
Coupé/Sports Hatchback
Years Manufactured: 1976-80
Quantity: 63
Engine Type: V6 cyl
Size: 2994cc
Max Power: 230 bhp
Transmission: 4 speed, optional
overdrive
Performance: Max speed: 139
mph; 0-60: 5.8 secs; Mpg: 18.

MAKE	ENGINE	DATES	CONDITION		
TVR			1	2	3
Grantura I	1172/4	1957-62	£4,000	£3,000	£2,000
Grantura II	1558/4	1957-62	£4,300	£3,000	£2,000
Grantura III/1800S	1798/4	1963-67	£5,000	£3,000	£2,200
Vixen S2/3	1599/4	1968-72	£5,000	£3,000	£1,500

Did you know

*MILLER'S Collectors Cars
Price Guide builds up year
by year to form the most
comprehensive photo-
reference system
available*

VANDEN PLAS

**1965 Vanden Plas Princess 1100
Saloon.
£850-1,000   *CMA***

> *Make:* Vanden Plas
> *Model:* 3 litre
> *Type:* Saloon
> *Years Manufactured:* 1959-64
> *Price when new:* £1,397
> *Engine Type:* Overhead valve
> 6 cyl
> *Size:* 2912cc
> *Max Power:* Mk I, 112 bhp @
> 4750 rpm; Mk II, 120 bhp @
> 4500 rpm
> *Transmission:* 3 speed +
> overdrive, auto optional
> *Performance:* Max speed: 100
> mph; 0-60: 15.0 secs; Mpg: 20-25.

**1973 Vanden Plas Princess 1300
Saloon,** 4 cylinder in-line engine,
water-cooled monobloc, overhead
valves, bore 2.78in x stroke 3.2in,
78cu in, 4 speed manual gearbox,
front wheel drive, hydrolastic
suspension, wheelbase 93in, 145 x
12in tyres, right-hand drive.
Est. **£2,000-3,000**   *S(A)*

**1966 Vanden Plas Princess
4 Litre R,** with 6 cylinder, 3909cc
engine.
Est. **£5,000-6,000**   *ADT*

> *Make:* Vanden Plas
> *Model:* Princess 4 litre
> *Type:* Saloon
> *Years Manufactured:* 1964-68
> *Quantity:* 6,555
> *Price when new:* £1,995
> *Engine Type:* 6 cyl
> *Size:* 3909cc
> *Max Power:* 175 bhp @ 4800
> rpm
> *Transmission:* Auto
> *Performance:* Max speed: 106
> mph; 0-60: 12.7 secs; Mpg: 15.

1968 Vanden Plas 4 Litre R, with
6 cylinder, 3909cc engine.
Est. **£5,500-7,500**   *ADT*

*Conceived and developed by the
engineers at Crewe pursuing the idea
of a smaller, sporty but well
appointed saloon within a relatively
inexpensive body. Code named
'JAVA' the VDP 4 litre R project
first saw the light of day wearing a
Bentley style grille on the almost
standard Austin Westminster/
Wolseley 3 litre body but with the
Rolls-Royce straight 6 and Crewe
inspired running gear. Factory
archive photographs clearly show
the distinctive 'capped' rear wings on
prototypes — a feature carried
through to production models. The
project was eventually cancelled by
Rolls-Royce and passed back to
Austin who were handed a virtually
completed project, ready for
production.*

**Vanden Plas 1300 Princess.
£1,000-3,000**   *KSC*

MAKE	ENGINE	DATES	CONDITION		
Vanden Plas			1	2	3
3 litre I/II	2912/6	1959-64	£4,000	£2,000	£700
4 litre R	3909/6	1964-67	£4,300	£2,500	£700
1100 Princess	1098/4	1964-67	£2,000	£1,000	—
1300 Princess	1275/4	1967-74	£2,200	£1,500	£500

VAUXHALL

Vauxhall was an engineering company which built its first automobile in 1903. Despite producing good vehicles, including the famous 30/98 Prince Henry sports cars, the company was in financial trouble when taken over by General Motors in 1925. Since the second World War Vauxhall have been greatly influenced by Opel (G M Germany) but are very successful in the volume car market.

1924 Vauxhall 14/40, with coachwork by Mulliner, 4 cylinder, 2297cc engine.
£17,500-18,000   *ADT*

1924 Vauxhall 23/60hp 4 Litre OD Kington Tourer.
Est. **£40,000-50,000**   *B*

1925 Vauxhall 30/98 OE Tourer, 4 cylinder OHV engine, bore 98mm x stroke 140mm, developing 112bhp at 3,400rpm, compression ratio 5.2:1, torque 175ft/lb at 3,400rpm, 4224cc, counterbalanced crankshaft, 23.8hp, semi-elliptic spring suspension, front and rear, Hartford shock absorbers, wheelbase 118in.
Est. **£90,000-100,000**   *S(A)*

Prior to 1925, when Vauxhall was taken over by General Motors, the firm was renowned for its handsome, finely engineered cars which put it on a par with Bentley or Sunbeam. Production of the original D Type was maintained during the First World War when the model was used as an army staff car. After hostilities, D Type manufacture continued, though Pomeroy departed and his place was taken by C. E. King.

VAUXHALL

MAKE	ENGINE	DATES	CONDITION		
Vauxhall			1	2	3
Wyvern LIX	1500/4	1948-51	£3,000	£1,000	£500
Velox LIP	2200/6	1948-51	£3,000	£1,000	£500
Wyvern EIX	1500/4	1951-57	£3,000	£1,320	£400
Velox EIPV	2200/6	1951-57	£3,000	£1,650	£400
Cresta EIPC	2200/6	1954-57	£3,000	£1,650	£400
Velox/Cresta PAS/PAD	2262/6	1957-59	£2,850	£1,300	£300
Velox/Cresta PASY/PADY	2262/6	1959-60	£2,700	£1,500	£300
Velox/Cresta PASX/PADX	2651/6	1960-62	£2,700	£1,300	£300
Velox/Cresta PASX/PADX Est	2651/6	1960-62	£2,700	£1,300	£300
Velox/Cresta PB	2651/6	1962-65	£1,600	£800	£100
Velox/Cresta PB Est	2651/6	1962-65	£1,600	£800	£100
Cresta/Deluxe PC	3294/6	1964-72	£1,500	£800	£100
Cresta PC Est	3294/6	1964-72	£1,500	£800	£100
Viscount	3294/6	1964-72	£1,700	£900	£100
Victor I/II	1507/4	1957-61	£2,000	£1,000	£250
Victor I/II Est	1507/4	1957-61	£2,100	£1,100	£300
Victor FB	1507/4	1961-64	£1,500	£900	£200
Victor FB Est	1507/4	1961-64	£1,600	£1,000	£300
VX4/90	1507/4	1961-64	£2,000	£900	£150
Victor FC101	1594/4	1964-67	£1,600	£900	£150
Victor FC101 Est	1594/4	1964-67	£1,800	£1,000	£200
101 VX4/90	1594/4	1964-67	£2,000	£1,500	£250
VX4/90	1975/4	1969-71	£700	£600	—
Ventora I/II	3294/6	1968-71	£500	£375	—
Viva HA	1057/4	1963-66	£500	£350	—
Viva SL90	1159/4	1966-70	£500	£350	—
Viva Brabham	1159/4	1967-70	£1,200	£500	—
Viva	1600/4	1968-70	£500	£350	—
Viva Est	1159/4	1967-70	£500	£400	—
D/OD	3969/4	1914-26	£35,000	£30,000	£25,000
E/OE	4224/4	1919-28	£40,000	£33,000	£25,000
Eighty	3317/6	1931-33	£10,000	£8,000	£5,000
Cadet	2048/6	1931-33	£7,000	£5,000	£3,000
Lt Six	1531/6	1934-38	£5,000	£4,000	£1,500
14	1781/4	1934-39	£4,000	£3,000	£1,500
25	3215/6	1937-39	£5,000	£4,000	£1,500
10	1203/4	1938-39	£4,000	£3,000	£1,500

Make: Vauxhall
Model: Victor F/FB
Type: Saloon
Years Manufactured: F, 1957-61; FB, 1961-64
Price when new: F, Series I, £729
Engine Type: Overhead valve 4 cyl
Size: 1508cc, 1594cc from Sept 1963
Max Power: 1508, 50 bhp @ 4600 rpm; 1594cc, 59 bhp @ 4600 rpm
Transmission: 3 speed/4 speed
Performance: Max speed: 1508, 75+ mph; 1594, 80+ mph; 0-60: 1508, 24.0 secs; 1594, 18.0 secs; Mpg: 24-30.

Make: Vauxhall
Model: Viva HB
Type: Saloon
Years Manufactured: 1966-70
Engine Type: Overhead valve 4 cyl, Overhead camshaft 4 cyl
Size: 1159cc/1599cc/1975cc (GT)
Max Power: 1159, 56 bhp @ 5400 rpm; 1159cc, 90 bhp @ 5800 rpm; 1599, 72 bhp @ 5600 rpm; GT, 112 bhp @ 5500 rpm
Transmission: 4 speed, auto optional from Feb 1967
Performance: Max speed: 1159, 80 mph; 1159 '90', 85+ mph; 1599, 90+ mph; GT, 102 mph; 0-60: 1159, 19.5 secs; 1159 '90', 16.0 secs; 1599, 90.0+ secs; GT, 10.5 secs; Mpg: 1159, 35-40+; 1159/GT, 25-30.

The OE type Vauxhall succeeded the sturdy E type in 1922, the new engine came in overhead valve form with a shorter stroke and developed about 112bhp at 3,300rpm. In racing trim the model was capable of 100mph and approximately 312 OE types were produced by 1927.

1925 Vauxhall 30/98 Model OE Two Seater Tourer, chassis No. OE 184, engine No. OE 249, 4 cylinder pushrod operated overhead valve, water-cooled monobloc bore 98mm x 140mm stroke, 4224cc, multi-plate Borg & Beck clutch, 4 speed gearbox, spiral bevel final drive, semi-elliptic suspension front and inverted spring rear, wheelbase 117in. Est. **£120,000-140,000** *S*

1934 Vauxhall 12/6 Saloon, with 6 cylinder, 1531cc engine. Est. **£4,500-5,500** *ADT*

1937 Vauxhall 25 Saloon.
£4,500-5,000   *Cen*

Produced between 1937 and 1939 it was the last of the big 6 cylinder Vauxhalls and the last to have a separate chassis and was made in saloon, drop head coupé , cabriolet and limousine style. Having an all synchromesh gearbox, a total of 6,822 Twenty Fives were produced with a large number being exported to Australia where they received Holden bodies.

1967 Vauxhall Viva, in well above above average original condition with only 6,000 miles recorded from new.
£3,000-3,400   *Cen*

1938 Vauxhall 14/6 Four Door Tourer, with 6 cylinder, 1701cc engine, a restoration project.
£3,000-3,500   *ADT*

Make: Vauxhall
Model: Velox/Cresta PA/PB
Type: Saloon
Years Manufactured: 1957-65
Price when new: Velox PA, £984; Cresta PA £1,074
Engine Type: Overhead valve 6 cyl
Size: 2262cc/2651cc/3293cc
Max Power: 2.3, 76 bhp @ 4400 rpm; 2.6, 95 bhp @ 4600 rpm; 3.3, 115 bhp @ 4200 rpm
Transmission: 3 speed, overdrive and auto optional from mid 1960; 4 speed optional from Oct 1964
Performance: Max speed: 2.3, 90 mph; 2.6, 95 mph; 3.3, 100 mph; 0-60: 2.3, 17.5 secs; 2.6, 16.3 secs; 3.3, 14.0 secs; Mpg: 19-24.

1959 Vauxhall Victor Saloon, 4 cylinder engine, water-cooled monobloc, overhead valve, bore 79.3mm x 76.2mm stroke, 1508cc, 3 speed transmission, shaft drive to live rear axle, independent front suspension, semi-elliptic leaf spring rear, wheelbase 98in, 5.60 x 13in tyres, in original condition, this car has had only 3 owners from new.
£1,600-2,000   *S*

VINOT & DEGUINGAND

1911 Vinot & Deguingand 12hp Special Torpedo, 4 cylinder engine, water-cooled monobloc, 12hp, 3 speed gearbox in separate unit with right-hand change outside body, open cone clutch, bevel pinion rear axle, 24in wheels.
Est. £12,000-16,000   *S(A)*

Miller's is a price GUIDE not a price LIST

VOLKSWAGEN

Make	FRANCE	GERMANY	ITALY	JAPAN	USA
Volkswagen	+5%	+5%	—	—	−15%

1967 Volkswagen Karmann-Ghia 1600 Coupé, with 4 cylinder horizontally opposed engine, thermostatically controlled air cooling by fan on crankshaft, bore 3⅓in x 2⁷/₁₀in stroke, 1584cc, 4 speed manual gearbox, single plate dry clutch, twin cranked trailing arms front suspension with torsion bars and telescopic shock absorbers, swing axles on trailing arms at rear, perforated steel disc wheels with 15 x 600 tyres.
Est. £12,000-14,000   S

In 1949 the Volkswagen plant was released from British control and German administration took over control. After the war more than 1,000 vehicles were produced for the British Army and then for private sale, but from 1949 only the saloon version of 'the people's car' was manufactured.

Make: Volkswagen
Model: Karmann-Ghia 1500
Type: Coupé/Convertible
Years Manufactured: 1962-69
Engine Type: 4 cyl
Size: 1493cc
Max Power: 44 bhp @ 4200 rpm
Transmission: 4 speed
Performance: Max speed: 80+ mph; 0-60: 20.0 secs; Mpg: 26-32.

Make: Volkswagen
Model: Beetle 1500
Type: Saloon
Years Manufactured: 1961-70
Price when new: 1500, £697
Engine Type: Overhead valve flat 4 cyl
Size: 1493cc
Max Power: 44 bhp @ 4000 rpm
Transmission: 4 speed
Performance: Max speed: 80+ mph; 0-60: 22.0 secs; Mpg: 26-32.

MAKE	ENGINE	DATES	CONDITION		
Volkswagen			1	2	3
Beetle (split)	1131/4	1946-53	£5,500	£3,500	£2,000
Beetle (oval)	1192/4	1953-57	£4,000	£2,000	£1,000
Beetle slope h'lamps	1192/4	1957-68	£2,500	£1,000	£600
Beetle	1192/4	1953-66	£7,000	£4,500	£2,000
Beetle 1500	1493/4	1966-70	£6,000	£4,000	£2,000
Beetle 1302 LS	1600/4	1970-72	£6,000	£4,000	£2,000
Beetle 1303	1600/4	1973-79	£6,500	£4,000	£1,800
1500 Variant/1600	1493/				
	1584/4	1961-73	£2,000	£1,500	£650
1500/1600 notchback	1493/				
	1584/4	1961-73	£3,000	£2,000	£800
Karmann Ghia/I	1192/4	1955-59	£4,000	£3,000	£1,000
Karmann Ghia/I DHC	1192/4	1957-59	£8,000	£5,000	£2,500
Karmann Ghia/I	1192/4	1960-74	£4,000	£3,000	£1,800
Karmann Ghia/I DHC	1192/4	1960-74	£6,000	£4,500	£2,000
Karmann Ghia/3	1493/4	1962-69	£3,000	£2,500	£1,250

1974 Volkswagen 'Jeans' Beetle Limited Edition, with original 'Jeans' tool pouch and service history, 1200cc engine.
£1,500-2,000   Cen

Condition Guide

1. *A vehicle in top class condition but not 'concours' standard, either fully restored or in very good original condition*
2. *A good, clean, roadworthy vehicle, both mechanically and bodily sound*
3. *A runner, but in need of attention, probably both bodywork and mechanically*

VOLVO

Make: Volvo
Model: Amazon
Type: Saloon
Years Manufactured: 1961-68
Engine Type: Overhead valve
4 cyl
Size: 1778cc
Max Power: 121, 75 bhp @ 4500
rpm; 122S, 90 bhp @ 5000 rpm
Transmission: 4 speed,
overdrive optional; auto
optional from Sept 1965
Performance: Max speed: 121,
95 mph; 122S, 100 mph; 0-60:
121, 14.0+ secs; 122S, 12.0 secs;
Mpg: 25-30.

MAKE	ENGINE	DATES	CONDITION		
Volvo			1	2	3
PV444	1800/4	1958-67	£4,000	£1,750	£800
PV544	1800/4	1962-64	£4,000	£1,750	£800
120(B16)	1583/4	1956-59	£3,000	£1,000	£300
121	1780/4	1960-67	£3,500	£1,500	£350
122S	1780/4	1960-67	£4,500	£1,500	£250
131	1780/4	1962-69	£4,000	£1,500	£350
221/222	1780/4	1962-69	£2,500	£1,500	£300
123Gt	1986/4	1967-69	£3,000	£2,500	£750
P1800	1986/4	1960-70	£3,500	£2,000	£1,000
P1800E	1986/4	1970-71	£4,000	£2,500	£1,000
P1800ES	1986/4	1971-73	£5,000	£3,000	£1,000

*Founded by Assar Gabrielson the
first Volvo production car was
offered in April 1927. By 1929 the
company expanded quite rapidly
producing various models and had a
large commercial involvement. By
1939 Volvo was the best selling car in
Sweden with car production
continuing today and supplemented
by sales of commercial and military
vehicles.*

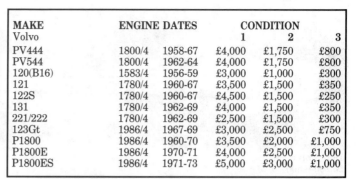

1964 Volvo PV544, with
4 cylinder, 1798cc engine.
Est. **£3,000-4,000** *ADT*

**1963 Volvo PV544 B-18 Two
Door Coupé,** 4 cylinder overhead
valve engine, bore 3.31 x 3.15in
stroke, 1780cc, 4 speed synchromesh
gearbox, 4 wheel drum brakes, all
round springs and telescopic
dampers suspension, left-hand
drive.
Est. **£7,000-10,000** *C*

1963 Volvo 1800S Sports Coupé,
4 cylinder engine, water-cooled
monobloc, overhead valve, bore
84.14mm x 80mm stroke, 1780cc,
4 speed manual gearbox with
overdrive, shaft drive to live rear
axle, independent coil spring
suspension, wheelbase 96½in, 6.5 x
15in tyres, right-hand drive.
Est. **£7,000-8,000** *S*

1966 Volvo 1800S, 4 cylinder,
1778cc engine.
Est. **£6,500-7,500** *ADT*

Make: Volvo
Model: P1800
Type: Coupé/Sports Hatchback
Years Manufactured: 1963-68
Engine Type: Overhead valve
4 cyl
Size: 1778cc
Max Power: 103 bhp @ 5600
rpm
Transmission: 4 speed plus
overdrive
Performance: Max speed: 107
mph; 0-60: 11.9 secs; Mpg: 22-28.

VOLVO

1967 Volvo 1800S.
£6,200-6,600 *CMA*

1973 Volvo 1800 ES, 4 cylinder,
1986cc engine.
£6,000-6,250 *ADT*

1970 Volvo P1800 E.
£6,000-8,000 *Cen*

Make: Volvo
Model: 1800ES
Type: Coupé
Years Manufactured: 1971-73
Engine Type: Overhead valve
4 cyl
Size: 1986cc
Max Power: 120 bhp @ 6000
rpm
Max Torque: 124 ft/lb @ 3500
rpm
Transmission: 4 speed manual
with overdrive, optional 3 speed
auto
Wheelbase: 96.5in
Performance: Max speed:
110-115+ mph; 0-60: 9.7-11.3
secs.

1972 Volvo 1800 ES Sports
Hatchback, 4 cylinder, 1986cc
engine.
£3,500-4,000 *ADT*

1973 Volvo 1800 ES, 4 cylinder,
1986cc engine.
Est. **£4,000-5,000** *ADT*

VULCAN

Vulcan began building cars in
Southport, Lancashire, in 1903
and was originally under the
control of the Hampson family,
who were enthusiastic pioneer
motorists. Car production
continued until 1928 though
the firm is perhaps better
known for its commercial
vehicles.

1908 Vulcan 25hp Roi Des Belges
Style Tourer.
Est. **£45,000-55,000** *B*

WHITE

1907 White Steamer Model H 20hp Runabout, engine No. H316, 2 cylinder, high pressure bore and stroke 3in x 3½in low pressure bore and stroke 5in x 3½in, displacement 93.6cu in, semi-elliptic leaf springs front and rear, wheelbase 104in, tyres 34 x 4in.
£23,000-25,000 *SNY*

WILLYS

1915 Willys Overland 83 Tourer, chassis No. 584, engine No. 83980, 4 cylinder, separate blocks, side valve 16-20hp, 3 speed gearbox with cone clutch, Stromberg carburettor, Dixie Magneto, the rear wheel only brakes are expanding on the drum via the footbrake and contracting on the hub off the handbrake, right-hand drive.
Est. **£10,000-12,000** *C*

1924 Willys Knight Four Door Tourer, 4 cylinder, 21hp.
£6,000-6,500 *ADT*

WINTON

1916 Winton 6 Model 22-A Seven Passenger Tourer, 6 cylinder in-line engine, water-cooled, cast in pairs, side valve, bore 3¾in x 5¼in stroke, 348cu in, 4 speed gearbox, multi-disc dry plate clutch, spiral bevel rear axle, semi-elliptic leaf front springs, three-quarter elliptic underslung rear springs, wheelbase 128in, 37 x 5in tyres.
Est. **£40,000-50,000** *S*

WOLSELEY

From as early as 1896 Wolseley produced motor cars, between 1904 and 1910 known as Wolseley-Siddeley. In 1927 they were absorbed by Morris and increased its range of luxury model Morris cars until the Austin Morris (BMC) merger in 1952. Badge Engineering kept Wolseley alive until the late 1960s.

MAKE Wolseley	ENGINE	DATES	CONDITION 1	2	3
16/38	2567/4	1920-27	£12,000	£10,000	£8,000
E3 Viper	2025/6	1927-34	£18,000	£15,000	£10,000
Hornet	1271/4	1931-35	£10,000	£8,000	£4,000
Hornet Sport	1604/6	1935-36	£12,000	£8,000	£6,000
Wasp	1069/4	1936	£7,000	£5,000	£3,000
Hornet	1378/6	1936	£8,000	£6,000	£3,000
16	2062/6	1936-39	£6,000	£4,000	£2,000
21	2916/6	1936-38	£7,000	£4,000	£2,000
25	3485/6	1936-39	£7,000	£4,000	£2,000
12/48	1547/4	1937-39	£4,000	£3,000	£1,500
18/80	2322/6	1938-39	£5,000	£3,000	£2,000

'Special' built cars are the most sought after. Add a premium of 25% with racing history.

1904 Wolseley 6hp Two Seater, chassis No. 8182, engine No. 86, single cylinder, bore 4½in x 5in stroke, 1296cc, atmospheric inlet and mechanical exhaust valve, 3 speed quadrant change gearbox and reverse, cone clutch, semi-elliptic leaf front springs, three-quarter elliptic rear, wheelbase 111in, 810 x 90mm tyres.
£17,000-17,500 *S*

1912 Wolseley 16/20hp
£34,500-35,000 *BLE*

Make: Wolseley
Model: 6/80
Type: Saloon
Years Manufactured: 1948-54
Engine Type: Overhead camshaft 6 cyl
Size: 2215cc
Max Power: 70 bhp @ 4400 rpm
Transmission: 4 speed
Performance: Max speed: 85 mph; 0-60: 20.0+ secs; Mpg: 19-25.

1934 Wolseley Hornet Saloon.
Est. **£5,000-7,000** *P*

1934 Wolseley Hornet Special, 6 cylinder, 1378cc engine, right-hand drive.
£12,100-12,750 *C*

1935 Eustace Watkins Daytona Special Wolseley Hornet.
Est. **£10,000-15,000** *P*

Make: Wolseley
Model: 6/90
Type: Saloon
Years Manufactured: 1954-59
Price when new: £850
Engine Type: Overhead valve 6 cyl
Size: 2639cc
Max Power: 102 bhp @ 4500 rpm
Transmission: 4 speed, overdrive optional from Oct 1955; auto optional from Oct 1956
Performance: Max speed: 100 mph; 0-60: 16.0 secs; Mpg: 20-25.

1935 Wolseley Wasp 1069 9.3hp. £4,400-5,000   *Cen*

1937 Wolseley Four Door Saloon, chassis No. 2145DU6605, engine No. 7074, 6 cylinder in line, water-cooled monobloc, overhead valve, 1791cc, shaft drive to live rear axle, semi-elliptic spring suspension front and rear. **£2,250-2,750**   *S*

Make the Most of Miller's

Veteran Cars are those manufactured up to 31 December 1918 although only vehicles built before 31 December 1904 are eligible for the London/Brighton Commemorative Run. Vintage Cars are vehicles that were manufactured between 1 January 1919 and 31 December 1930

Miller's is a price Guide not a price List

The price ranges given reflect the average price a purchaser should pay for similar vehicle. Condition, rarity, provenance, racing history, originality and any restoration are factors that must be taken into account when assessing values. When buying or selling, it must always be remembered that prices can be greatly affected by the condition of any vehicle. Unless otherwise stated, all cars shown in Miller's are of good merchantable quality, and the valuations given reflect this fact. Vehicles offered for sale in exceptionally fine condition or in poor condition may reasonably be expected to be priced considerably higher or lower respectively than the estimates given herein

MAKE	ENGINE	DATES	CONDITION		
Wolseley			1	2	3
8	918/4	1946-48	£1,800	£1,000	£500
10	1140/4	1939-48	£2,500	£1,000	£500
12	1548/4	1939-48	£2,500	£1,000	£500
14	1818/6	1946-48	£2,500	£1,200	£500
18	2321/6	1946-48	£3,000	£1,200	£500
25	3485/6	1946-48	£2,500	£1,000	£500
4/50	1476/4	1948-53	£1,900	£600	£300
6/80	2215/6	1948-54	£2,000	£1,000	£400
4/44	1250/4	1952-56	£1,850	£850	£350
15/50	1489/4	1956-58	£1,850	£850	£350
1500	1489/4	1958-65	£3,000	£1,000	£500
15/60	1489/4	1958-61	£1,500	£700	£300
16/60	1622/4	1961-71	£1,600	£800	£300
6/90	2639/6	1954-57	£2,000	£1,000	£500
6/99	2912/6	1959-61	£2,000	£1,000	£500
6/110 Mk I/II	2912/6	1961-68	£1,500	£800	£400
Hornet (Mini)	848/4	1961-70	£1,250	£450	£250
1300	1275/4	1967-74	£1,250	£750	£200
18/85	1798/4	1967-72	£950	£400	£150

COMMERCIAL VEHICLES

1904 Albion 16hp, in need of complete restoration, comprising a chassis, radiator, gearbox, axles and wheels.
£5,000-5,250   *LF*

1910 Autocar Twin Cylinder Truck.
£4,250-4,500   *DB*

1936 Bedford Type WS Dropside Truck, 6 cylinder in line, water-cooled monobloc engine, overhead valve, maker's horsepower 27hp, 4 speed gearbox, shaft drive to live rear axle, semi-elliptic leaf spring suspension, wheelbase 131in, tyres 21in.
£7,200-8,000   *S*

1931 Bedford Type WLG Long Wheelbase Horse Box, chassis No. 103085, engine No. 410299, 6 cylinder water-cooled monobloc engine, overhead valve, 26.3hp rated as 27hp, $3^{5}/_{16}$in bore x $3^{3}/_{4}$in stroke, 4 speed manual gearbox, multi-plate clutch, shaft drive to rear axle, semi-elliptic leaf spring suspension front and rear, detachable pressed steel disc wheels fitted with balloon tyres, horse box body by Vincents of Reading.
£10,000-11,000   *S*

1924 Citroën B2 Camionette, this van has been partly restored in France and was a traditional French baker's van.
£5,950-7,000   *GWC*

1929 Citroën 19.3hp Camionette,
straight 6 cylinder, water-cooled
monobloc engine, side valve, 72mm
bore x 100mm stroke, 2442cc,
3 speed manual gearbox, single dry
plate clutch, shaft drive to live rear
axle, semi-elliptic leaf spring
suspension, disc wheels with 28 x
4.95in tyres, Marchal electric lamps.
£4,100-4,800   *S*

1948 Commer Superpoise
Q4.4 x 4, 289.87cu in engine, only
2,700 miles from new, built to
Ministry of Defence specifications
and powered by the Rootes
6 cylinder OHV engine which was
just over 4.6 litres, served with the
Auxiliary Fire Service.
£1,800-2,000   *LF*

1941 Foden STDG/5 Timber
Tractor.
£18,000-19,000   *SEN*

*Some 70 Foden DG timber tractors
were built in the early 40s, mostly
fitted with Gardener 5LW engines.
The cabs were coachbuilt and heavy
duty 2 speed 25 ton Foden winch
built into the back of the chassis,
complete with integral ground
anchors. There is a tractor-like
swinging front axle, but it is sprung,
and hydraulic brakes on the rear
axle only, with vacuum facilities for
trailer towing.*

1920 Ford Model TT Tabletop
Truck, 4 cylinder side valve,
water-cooled monobloc engine,
95mm bore x 102mm stroke, 2896cc,
maker's horsepower 22.4hp, 2 speed
epicyclic gearbox, multi-plate
clutch, shaft drive to live rear axle,
worm final drive, wheelbase 100in,
tyres 30 x 3½in beaded edge,
left-hand drive.
£7,700-8,200   *S*

1921 Ford Model T Light Van,
4 cylinder, 2900cc.
£4,000-4,400   *ADT*

1923 Ford Model T Dropside Truck.
Est. £13,000-18,000   *ADT*

1924 Ford Model T Huckster.
£2,800-3,000   *Cen*

1925 Ford Model T Ton Truck,
4 cylinder, 2890cc engine.
Est. £7,500-8,500   *ADT*

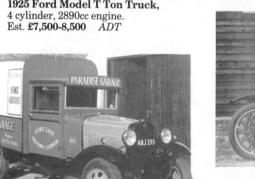

1926 Ford Model T Pickup,
4 cylinder, 2900cc engine, a flatbed pickup with polished wooden bench seat and side supports, oil side lamps and horn.
£4,000-4,400   *ADT*

1933 Ford Model AA One Ton Delivery Van, bodywork by Toler's Garage Ltd., Lothian Road, London SW9, 4 cylinder, side valve, water-cooled monobloc engine, 3.3 litres capacity (24hp), 3 speed gearbox, transverse leaf front springs, cantilever rear, live axle.
£6,000-6,500   *S*

1956 Ford Thames 10 cwt. Van,
total body restoration, chassis restoration, rebuilt engine, gearbox, axle, suspension and steering.
£4,400-4,600   *Cen*

1932 Ford Model B Groundsman's Tractor, tipping body, built for Municipality work such as for golf courses, parks and sports grounds.
Est. £2,500-3,500   *ADT*

**1936 Fordson (25 cwt.) 7V
Dropside Truck,** 8 cylinder,
2600cc engine, restoration in 1972,
wheelbase 106in, overall length
164in.
Est. **£7,000-8,000** *ADT*

**1928 Morris ½ Ton Van.
£10,500-11,000** *DB*

**1960 Ford Thames Light
Delivery Van,** 4 cylinder, side
valve, water-cooled monobloc
engine, 1172cc 63.5mm bore x
92.5mm stroke, 3 speed manual
gearbox, shaft drive to live rear
axle, independent front suspension,
semi-elliptic leaf spring suspension
rear, wheelbase 87in, tyres 5.60
x 13in.
£950-1,050 *S*

**1961 Karrier Bantam
Breakdown Truck,** originally
owned by British Railways,
Southern Region and was an
articulated tractor unit used for
parcels delivery, Perkins diesel
engine.
£300-400 *LF*

1924 Morris Light Van, 4 cylinder,
1934cc engine.
£4,300-4,600 *ADT*

FIRE ENGINES

1928-32 Skoda 2-3 Ton Truck Cab and Chassis, in need of restoration.
£1,400-1,600 *LF*

1911 Reo One-Ton Truck.
Est. **£8,000-10,000** *ADT*

1930 Morris Cowley ½ Ton Truck.
£6,750-7,000 *DB*

FIRE ENGINES

1939 Leyland Cub Fire Appliance, engine No. 4504, 6 cylinder, overhead valve, 29.4bhp, 4 speed constant mesh gearbox, 4 wheel servo mechanical brakes, semi-elliptic front and rear suspension, right-hand drive.
Est. **£7,000-9,000** *C*

Leyland had been at the forefront of fire appliance design and had established a factory at Chorley specifically for this work in 1913. By the 1930s its designs were based on either its highly successful large capacity passenger chassis or else on the smaller Cub/Lynx. This later model had commenced in the early 1930s as a direct answer to the new breed of the American inspired easy to drive and refined 6 cylinder commercial vehicles as typified by the ubiquitous Bedford. The Leyland was a higher grade and a more expensive product that sold in much smaller numbers and yet was extremely successful.

1954 Austin A40 Fire Engine, the vehicle was factory converted to a fire engine for Standard Telephone Company on manufacture in 1954.
£1,300-1,500   *LF*

> **Miller's is a price GUIDE not a price LIST**

MILITARY VEHICLES

1942 Ford/Willys World War II Jeep, 4 cylinder, 2200cc engine, mechanically sound, 15,000 miles.
£6,400-6,600   *ADT*

1952 Austin Champ, 4 cylinder, 2700cc engine, ex-military vehicle.
Est. **£6,000-7,500**   *ADT*

OMNIBUSES

The 34 seat B-Type was in London service from 1910-27 and proved to be both reliable and easy to maintain. No less than 2,500 had been built by 1913. It was quieter than most previous types thanks to enclosed worm drive, a chain gearbox, a wood and steel flitched chassis and low unladen weight of 3 tons.

The B-Type is one of the most significant bus designs of all time. After the Vanguard, London General and London Road Car merged in 1908 to create a massive London Bus Fleet and pooled ideas to create the ideal vehicle for London use.

1911 London General Omnibus Co B-Type Bus, with 4 cylinder, 5.8 litre engine.
£16,500-17,500   *C*

1905 Milnes-Daimler (Marienfelden) Double Decker Omnibus, 4 cylinder, 5315cc engine, 110mm bore x 140mm stroke, 28bhp at 800rpm, steel ladder type chassis, 4 speed sliding mesh gearbox, chain-driven final drive, leaf spring suspension, mechanical brakes to rear wheels only, steel spoke wheels with solid rubber tyres, wheelbase 156in, coachwork by Milnes Coachworks, Hadley, Wellington, Shropshire, double deck, open top, rear stairway, 34 seater.
£152,000-155,000   *CNY*

OMNIBUSES

1947 Leyland Tiger, 35 Seat Bus,
with coachwork by Walter
Alexander, 6 cylinder, 7400cc
engine.
Est. £7,000-9,000   *ADT*

*Alexander & Co. Ltd., operated
about 240 of these 35 seat buses just
after World War II. They purchased
chassis from Leyland Motors and
built to their own specification,
coachwork to suit the needs of the
Highlands and Lowlands of the
North.*

**1920 Rolls-Royce 40/50hp Silver
Ghost 12 Seater Omnibus,** with
6 cylinder in-line engine, cast in
blocks of 3, water-cooled, side valve,
bore 4½in x 4¾in stroke, 7428cc,
4 speed right-hand change gearbox,
cone clutch, enclosed shaft spiral
bevel rear axle, semi-elliptic leaf
spring front suspension, cantilever
rear springs, wheelbase 143½in,
7.00 x 21in tyres.
Est. £60,000-75,000   *S*

*The omnibus coachwork is well
constructed with mahogany
mouldings and aluminium
panelling. The wings, running
boards and body base are believed to
be original.*

TAXIS

**1907 Unic 12/14hp London
Taxicab,** with 4 cylinder L-head
engine, water-cooled monobloc, 1.9
litres, 3 speed gearbox, cone clutch,
shaft drive to live rear axle.
£37,000-38,000   *S*

*The United Motor Cab Company of
London bought 224 Unics between
1907 and 1908, later amalgamating
with the General Cab Company to
form the London General Cab
Company.*

1937 Austin 'Low Loader' 12/4 London Taxicab, 4 cylinder engine, side valve, water-cooled monobloc, bore 69.35mm x 101.6mm stroke, 1535cc, 4 speed gearbox, worm final drive.
£22,500-23,000   S

Austins were relatively late on the taxicab scene, their first purpose-built taxi based on the 12/4 chassis and introduced in October 1929. It was not until April 1930, however, and after consultation with Mann & Overton, that the design was modified to be suitable for London use. Scotland Yard initially refused it a licence because the turning circle was too great. Once that obstacle was overcome, however, the Austin quickly became the most popular taxicab in London, and in 1934 the adoption of a worm drive rear axle enabled a lower body to be fitted, whilst still keeping a flat floor in the passenger compartment. This model became known as the 'Low Loader' or 'LL' model, and this vehicle is a good example of the type, made from 1934-38.

1932 Beardmore Hyper Mk III London Taxicab, 4 cylinder engine, side valve, water-cooled monobloc, 1954cc (12.8hp RAC rating), 4 speed gearbox, live rear axle, 4 wheel brakes.
£21,000-22,000   S

Introduced in May 1929 Beardmore's Hyper model set the standard for London taxicab design for some years and was the first to have front wheel braking. Smaller than earlier 15.9hp models, it was lighter in operation, particularly so far as steering, de-clutching, and braking were concerned, and it was popular with operators.

Make the Most of Miller's

CONDITION is absolutely vital when assessing the value of a vehicle. Top class vehicles on the whole appreciate much more than less perfect examples. However a rare, desirable car may command a high price even when in need of restoration

1957 Beardmore Paramount Mk VII London Taxicab, 4 cylinder Ford Consul engine, water-cooled monobloc, 1508cc, 4 speed gearbox, live rear axle.
£2,800-3,100   S

During the immediate post-war period, Beardmore's Hendon works did not produce any cabs under their own name, acting instead as selling agents for the Wolseley-built Nuffield Oxford cab. When production of this came to an end in 1953 a new Beardmore Paramount model was developed, and this was launched as the Mk VII in 1954.

Beardmore Motors Ltd., of Glasgow, were motor car producers from 1920-28, a small venture when compared to their activities in marine and heavy engineering fields, though perhaps noteworthy as also producing the diesel engines for the early and ill-fated British airships.

The Company took over the old Arrol-Johnston works in Paisley and produced strong, reliable, well engineered machines as one would expect from such a company.

1966 Beardmore Mk VII Hackney Carriage, 4 cylinder in-line engine, water-cooled monobloc, overhead valves, bore 72.55mm x stroke 79.5mm, 1703cc, single dry plate clutch, 4 speed gearbox with column change, spiral bevel drive live rear axle, semi-elliptic leaf spring front and rear suspension, wheelbase 104in, 16in tyres, fitted with a proprietary Ford Zephyr engine the vehicle served as a Hackney, initially in London, and then in Edinburgh, before retirement from active service, when it was stored by a relation of the last commercial driver.
£3,500-4,000   C

1955 Austin FX3 Diesel 2.2 Litre London Taxicab, 4 cylinder engine, water-cooled monobloc diesel, 2.2 litres, 4 speed gearbox, live rear axle.
£6,000-7,000   *S*

Introduced at Mann & Overton's Wandsworth Bridge premises in London in June 1948, Austin's FX3 model was their first post-war production model taxi and was initially powered by their 2199cc 16 engine. Coachwork was in pressed steel by Carbodies of Coventry. By the mid 50s, however, Birch Brothers were offering a diesel conversion using a Standard-built 2 litre engine based on that used in the Ferguson tractor, and in September 1954 Austin introduced their own 2.2 litre diesel model, of which this is an example.
The FX3 remained in production until the end of 1958, by which time diesel engined types were outselling petrol engined cabs by 9 to 1.

The Metrocab was an attempt to break into the London taxicab market by Metropolitan-Cammell-Weymann Ltd. of Birmingham, the well-known makers of passenger vehicle bodywork responsible for the building of many of London's tube trains. They are a subsidiary of the Cammell-Laird shipbuilding group.

1969 Metro-Cammell 'Metrocab' London Taxicab, with Perkins diesel 4 cylinder engine, water-cooled monobloc, 1760cc, 4 speed gearbox, live rear axle.
£3,500-6,000   *S*

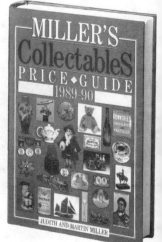

MOTORCYCLES

1966 Aermacchi 350TT Solo Motorcycle.
Est. £4,000-6,000   *P*

Aermacchi switched production after the war from aeroplanes to scooters and 3 wheel trucks and then motorcycles.

1967 Aermacchi 350cc Ala D'Oro Solo Motorcycle.
Est. £14,000-18,000   *P*

Macchi of Varese, in Italy north of Milan, were famous aircraft makers. In 1948 Macchi turned to making motorcycles, the first flat single cylinder 2 stroke 123cc example looked like a cross between a motorcycle and a scooter.

1966 AJS Rickman Type 7.R 350cc Motorcycle, single vertical cylinder engine, air cooled, overhead camshaft, 350cc, 4 speed transmission, chain final drive, telescopic front fork suspension, rear swinging arm.
Est. £11,000-13,000   *S*

1966 AJS 14.
£600-700   *LF*

A. J. Stevens and his sons produced the first AJS machine in 1909. In 1931 the company was sold to the Collier brothers who produced the Matchless Motorcycles. The combined companies became known as Associated Motor Cycles Limited, and eventually that group absorbed James, Francis-Barnett and later Norton. A.M.C. collapsed in 1966 and subsequently were absorbed into Norton-Villiers-Triumph.

1928 Ariel Motorcycle Model A, 557cc engine.
Est. £2,600-3,200   *LF*

Ariel built motorcycles from 1902 until 1970. In 1927 the chief designer, Val Page, produced a new 557cc side valve. Ariel was one of the last of the British makes to adopt saddle tanks the common form of petrol tank which sits over the frame and hides a portion of the frame.

1958 Ambassador 197cc Solo, inclined single cylinder engine, air cooled, 2 stroke, bore 59mm x 72mm stroke, 197cc, 4 speed gearbox, chain final drive, telescopic front fork suspension, rear swinging arm, twin tyres.
£460-520   *S*

The 1958 Ambassador offered the 73cc Popular, the 197cc Envoy and the Super S Villiers engines and was to continue in production until 1964.

c1933 BMW R12 Solo Motorcycle, horizontally opposed engine, air cooled side valve, twin cylinder, 4 stroke, bore 78mm x 78mm stroke, 745cc, 4 speed hand change gearbox, shaft final drive, rigid rear end, hydraulically damped telescopic front forks.
£2,200-2,500   *S*

Benelli 900cc Solo Motorcycle, inclined 6 cylinder in-line engine, overhead valve, overhead camshaft, 906cc, 5 speed gearbox, chain final drive, telescopic front fork suspension, rear swinging arm.
£2,600-2,800 *S*

> **Miller's is a price GUIDE not a price LIST**

1960 BMW R60 594cc Solo Motorcycle, horizontally opposed transverse twin cylinder engine, overhead valve, air cooled, 4 stroke, 594cc, 4 speed gearbox, hydraulic forks with sprung frame at rear, shaft final drive.
£2,200-2,500 *S*

1959 BMW R60 590cc Solo Motorcycle, vertical twin cylinder engine, overhead valve, air cooled 4 stroke, 590cc, 4 speed gearbox, telescopic forks, plunger rear suspension, shaft drive.
£2,200-2,500 *S*

1927 Brough Superior 680cc Solo Motorcycle, V-twin cylinder engine, air cooled, overhead valve 4 stroke, 680cc, 3 speed gearbox, chain final drive, girder fork and coil spring front suspension, rigid rear, 19in wheels.
£14,000-15,000 *S*

1936 Brough Superior SS80 680cc, Solo Motorcycle, V twin cylinder engine, a cooled, overhead valve, 4 stroke, 680cc, gearbox, chain final drive, Brampton front forks and and D spring frame, 3.50 x 21in tyres.
£11,500-12,000 *S*

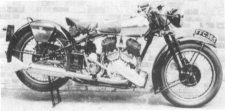

1937 Brough Superior SS80 Solo Motorcycle.
Est. **£15,000-17,000** *P*

1939 Brough Superior SS80 980cc Solo Motorcycle, Matchless V twin cylinder engine, side valve, air cooled, 4 stroke, bore 85.5mm x 85.5mm stroke, 980cc, Norton 4 speed gearbox, girder forks with coil spring front suspension, sprung rear wheel, chain final drive, 26 x 3.50 and 27 x 4.00 tyres.
£8,000-9,000 *S*

1935 Sunbeam Sports Twenty-Five Tourer, chassis No. 2524T, 6 cylinder in-line engine, water-cooled monobloc, pushrod operated overhead valves, bore 80mm, stroke 110mm, 3318cc, 4 speed gearbox, single plate clutch, enclosed shaft spiral bevel rear axle, semi-elliptic leaf spring suspension front and rear, wheelbase 120in and 20in tyres. **£26,500-28,000** *S*

Rear view of the 1934 SS1 Faux Cabriolet.

1934 SS1 Faux Cabriolet Two Door Sports Coupé, chassis No. 210317, engine No. 210317, 6 cylinder in line, water-cooled monobloc, side valve, 2663.7cc, 4 speed manual gearbox, shaft drive to live rear axle, leaf spring suspension front and rear. **£47,000-50,000** *S*

view of the 1934 Talbot 105 showing the steering wheel and dashboard.

1934 Talbot 105 Vanden Plas Tourer, with chassis No. 35349, engine No. AV188, 6 cylinder in line, 2969cc, bore 75mm x stroke 112mm, pushrod operated vertical overhead valves, single Zenith 48mm downdraught carburettor, ratio 6.7:1, 105bhp at 4,500rpm. **£82,500-85,000** *C*

1933 Talbot AV 105, dual racer. **£36,000-40,000** *BLE*

1947 Triumph Roadster, chassis No. TRD 727, engine No. TRD 7HOE 4 cylinder, 1800cc, this car has been completely restored and has won many awards in the past 4 years.
£27,500-30,000   *ADT*

A rear view of the 1947 Triumph Roadster.

1954/55 Swallow Doretti Roadster, only 276 of these cars were built, most being left-hand drive, so this car is rare, Triumph TR2 components were used in building this model but the overall price was slightly more than the TR2 making sales difficult, this car has been completely restored.
£12,500-14,000   *ADT*

Triumph TR5, fully restored to the highest standard. £18,000-20,000 *FOR*

Triumph TR6, 150bhp, body off chassis rebuilt recently. £12,000-14,000 *FOR*

1973 Triumph TR6 PI, 150bhp, rebuilt in 1984, only 18,000 recorded since, wheels and roll bar non standard but 'period'. £11,000-13,000 *RH*

Triumph TR6, 150bhp and recently body off chassis rebuilt. £12,000-14,000 *FOR*

1980 Triumph TR8, chassis No. TPZDV8T211151, 8 cylinder, 3528cc engine, some restoration work has been carried out resulting in air conditioning and power assisted steering and brakes. £6,600-9,000 *ADT*

1968 Volvo Amazon 122S, chassis No. 3011388, engine No. B18B/4603 4 cylinder 1998cc, with a 1957 bodyshell this car has undergone extensive restoration and only 33,140 miles recorded. **£1,000-1,500** *ADT*

1964 TVR Grantura, with very good bodywork, mechanics and interior, found derelict but now fully restored. **£4,500-5,500** *CC*

1924 Vauxhall OD 23/60 H.P. Four Seater Tourer, chassis No. OD 1137, engine No. 1137 4 cylinder overhead valve 3869cc, 23hp stroke 140mm x 95mm bore, 4 speed & reverse, multiplate clutch, footbrake operating on the transmission, handbrake via rear wheels, wheelbase 130in, right-hand drive. **£42,000-45,000** *C*

1924 Vauxhall OD 23/60 Kington Touring Car, chassis No. OD1008, engine No. OD 1073, 3969cc. **£42,000-45,000** *T&M*

1970 Vanden Plas 1300 Princess, chassis No. VAS226558M, engine No. 8308 4 cylinder, 1275cc, this car has undergone a ground up restoration, 57,000 miles recorded. **£2,500-3,500** *ADT*

A view of the interior of the 1970 Vanden Plas, showing the biscuit shade leather interior.

1971 Alpine A110 1600S Rally Car, fully prepared for rallying, with many extras, believed to have taken part in Monte Carlo and San Remo Rallies, condition typical of a used rally car. **£28,000-30,000** *GWC*

1964 3.8 litre Competition 'E' Type Jaguar, raced for the last 10 years, and fully race prepared, engine rebuilt, comprehensive racing history. **£24,000-26,000** *Ren*

GTD Ford GT40 Replica, small block Ford V8 4.9 engine, with gas flowed heads, mild steel comp camshaft, 4 Weber carburettors, giving 325bhp, 5 speed transaxle Renault turbo gearbox, 10in ventilated front brakes. **£21,000-23,000** *ADT*

The GTD Ford GT40 was the result of Ford's intention to win Le Mans, the bodywork of this replica being a Mark 1 shape by KVA, chassis in box section steel, zinc coated and aluminium panelled with aluminium floorpan.

1976-77 McLaren M23 Formula 1 Single-Seater Racing Car, 8 cylinder Cosworth DFV engine, 4 overhead camshafts, bore 85.7mm x stroke 64.8mm, 2993cc, transistorised ignition, 460bhp at 10,000rpm, 6 speed gearbox, transaxle, 4 wheel disc brakes, independent wishbone front suspension, independent wishbone and trailing arms rear, wheelbase 81in. **£460,000-480,000**   *C(M)*

1986 Ferrari T.186 Formula 1 Grand Prix Car, developed from the 1980 Turbo engined Grand Prix car. **£700,000-720,000**   *C(M)*

The engine is a 120° V6 cylinder, 1496cc, bore 81mm x stroke 48.4mm, 950bhp at 11,500rpm 4 valves per cylinder overhead camshaft, twin turbocharged by Garrett with Weber-Marelli indirect fuel injection with digital electronic control.

The V6 Turbo engine developed over 1,000bhp, giving race-winning performance and victories in Canada and Germany to the 1985 engine. The chassis and aerodynamics were improved, and fuel consumption reduced for this 1986 model. Driven by Michele Alboreto, the car was well placed in several Grand Prix. In original condition and race prepared.

1974/75 Alfa Romeo Type 33TT 1? 180° 12 cylinder engine, 2995cc, bore 77mm x stroke 53.6mm 500bhp at 11,000rpm, Bosch fuel injection, 5 speed gearbox, double wishbone and coil spring damper suspension all round. One of the 1975 World Championship Team ca completely renovated to full racing specification. **£550,000-600,000**   *C(M)*

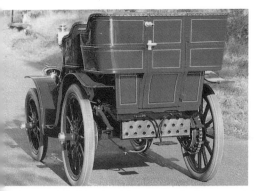

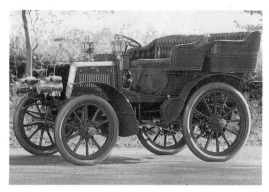

Rear view of 1899 Panhard Levassor 12hp Tonneau, this is one of the earliest 12hp cars known to survive.

1899 Panhard Levassor 12hp Tonneau, 4 cylinder water-cooled Phoenix type engine, bore 90mm x stroke 130mm, 3308cc, 4 speed gearbox, chain final drive, automatic inlet valves, mechanical exhaust valves, leaf spring suspension.
£80,000-90,000   *S*

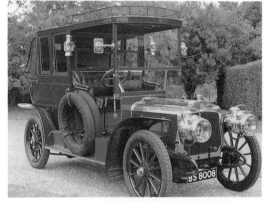

1902 'Baby' Peugeot 5½hp Tourer, engine No. 5133L, 89cc, front mounted AIV single cylinder, the chassis is tubular and it has a 3 speed gearbox.
30,000-35,000   *C*

1904 Société Manufacturière d'Armes, St Etienne 24/30hp Open Drive Landaulette, body No. 5063, engine No. 9869, Aster 4 cylinder T-head side valve water-cooled, Type 46NS, bore 105mm x stroke 140mm, 4 speed gearbox with right-hand gate change.
£100,000-150,000   *S*

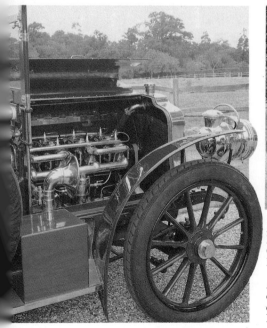

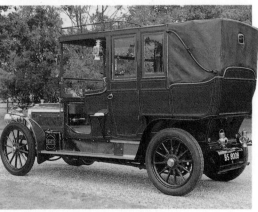

A further view of the 1904 Société Manufacturière d'Armes, coachwork by Carrozeria Italiana Cesare Sala, Milano, Italy.

A view of the Aster Type 46NS engine of the 1904 Société Manufacturière d'Armes, St Etienne, 24/30hp Landaulette.

1907 White Steamer 15hp Rear Entrance Tonneau, with coachwork by Cann Ltd, car No. 1975, engine No. E.160, 2 cylinder with high and low pressure steam chests, forward and reverse gears, rear wheel brakes, semi-elliptic leaf spring suspension front and rear, 875mm x 105mm tyres.
£50,000-70,000   *S*

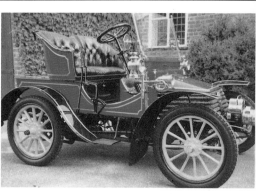

1904 Wolseley 6hp Two Seater, chassis No. 8197, engine No. 107 front mounted horizontal single cylinder, bore 4½in stroke 5in, 1296cc, atmospheric inlet valve, mechanical exhaust valve, 3 speed gearbox with reverse, quadrant change, cone clutch, chain drive to differential live axle, semi-elliptic leaf front springs, three quarter elliptic rear, wheelbase 111in, 810 x 90mm tyres.
£19,500-25,000   *S*

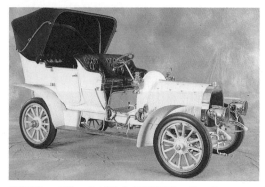

1905 Royal Tourist Model F 32/38hp Touring, car No. 514, 4 cylinder in line, water-cooled, cast in pairs, T-head side valve, bore 5in stroke 5½in, 432cu in capacity, 3 speed gearbox, shaft final drive, semi-elliptic leaf springs front and rear, wheelbase 108in, 33 x 4in tyres.
£22,000-25,000   *S*

1903 Winton, chassis No. 3150, engine No. E 12224 2 cylinder, 20hp, 2 speed gearbox with reverse and central chain final drive, this car has been restored.
£45,000-50,000   *ADT*

1904 De Dion Bouton Model V 8hp Victoria, engine No. 16029, forward mounted vertical single cylinder, water-cooled, atmospheric inlet valve, side exhaust valve. **£24,000-30,000**   *S*

A further view of the 1904 De Dion Bouton, with hood raised.

1908 Jackson 30hp Model K Five Passenger Touri car No. 5484H, engine No. 1401, 4 cylinder in line, cast in pairs, water-cooled, side valve, maker's horsepower 30hp, 3 speed gearbox with reverse, shaft drive to bevel rear axle, semi-elliptic leaf front springs, full elliptic rear springs, wheelbase 110½in, 32 x 4in tyres.
£19,250-21,000   *S*

1904 Rochet-Schneider 16/22hp Side Entrance Tonneau, chassis No. 2545, engine No. 2546, 4 cylinder in line, water-cooled cast in pairs, 4 speed gearbox, chain final drive, semi-elliptic leaf spring front and rear suspension, 880 x 120mm tyres. Est. **£90,000-110,000**   *S*

1910 Napier 4 Litre 6 Cylinder Tourer, chassis No. 7190, engine No. 05783, 6 cylinder in-line engine, water-cooled, cast in pairs, side valve 4 litres, 3 speed gearbox, shaft drive to live rear axle, semi-elliptic leaf spring suspension, 41 x 4½in tyres. Est. **£70,000-90,000**   *S*

1908 E.M.F. Model 3 Gentleman's Roadster, chassis No. A 30575, engine No. 456, 4 cylinder monobloc, water-cooled, side valve, 30hp, 3 speed transaxle, semi-elliptic front suspension, full elliptic rear, wheelbase 106in. **£20,000-25,000**   *SEN*

1902 Georges Richard Rear Entrance Tonneau, chassis No. 490, with twin cylinder engine on an Arbel steel frame, right-hand drive, a transmission brake and external contracting brakes on rear wheels, the paint and varnish work are in excellent condition and the car recently completed the London to Brighton run. **£30,000-40,000**   *C*

1907 Reliable Dayton Model C 'High Wheeler', chassis No. 114, 15hp, horizontally opposed twin cylinder engine, 2 speed planetary gearbox, through countershaft to double chains, solid tyres. **£9,500-12,000**   *SEN*

1898 Mors 6hp Dogcart with Dos-a-Dos Seating for Six, engine No. 6054, front mounted transverse V-4 water-cooled, 2 speed and reverse belt gearing with belt cum chain drive to rear wheels via countershaft, pneumatic tyres. Est. **£40,000-50,000**   *S*

1914 Daimler 20hp Landaulette, engine No. 13241, 4 cylinder, in 2 pairs, engine bore 90 x stroke 130mm, 36bhp at 1,500rpm, 4 speed gearbox, mounted at front of rear axle which is worm driven, cantilever springs front and rear, right-hand drive. Est. **£50,000-60,000**   *C*

1907 Minerva 28hp Type M Side Entrance Tourer, chassis No. M 4118, engine No. 4135, 4 cylinder in line, water-cooled, monobloc, side valve, maker's rating 28hp, 4 speed gearbox, shaft drive to live rear axle, semi-elliptic leaf spring front suspension, three quarter elliptic at rear, 820mm x 120mm tyres.
£34,000-40,000 *S*

1909 Keystone Six-Sixty 7.8 Litre Two P **Roadster,** chassis No. 0024, engine No. 002 6 cylinder in line, water-cooled, separately cast cylinders, side valve, T-head, 7.8 litres, 3 speed gearbox with reverse, disc clutch, shaft drive to bevel rear axle, semi-elliptic leaf spring suspension front and rear, wheelbase 122in 36 x 4in tyres.
£23,000-30,000 *S*

1910 De Tamble Model G 30hp Torpedo Roadster, chassis No. 1147, engine No. 3149, 4 cylinder in line, cast in pairs, water-cooled, side valve, maker's horse power 30hp, 4 speed gearbox with reverse, shaft drive to bevel rear axle, semi-elliptic front springs, three quarter elliptic rear spring, wheelbase 113in, 875 x 105mm tyres.
£26,000-30,000 *S*

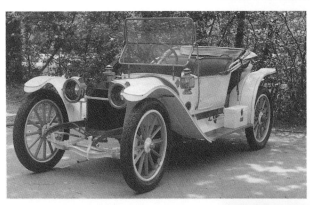

1910 Otto 30/35hp Speedster, chassis No. 210, engine No. CB 601, 4 cylinder in line, side valve, water-cooled monobloc, Bosch ignition, cone clutch, 3 forward and reverse transaxle, semi-elliptic front springs, three quarter elliptic rear, 2 wheel brakes and handbrake, wheelbase 123in, 4½ x 36in tyres.
£20,000-25,000 *S*

1912 Wolseley 16/20hp C5 Two Seater Convertible, chassis No. 16780, engine No. 172839, 4 cylinder, cast in pairs, L-head, 3069cc, bore 90mm x 120.7mm, magneto and coil ignition, 4 speed gearbox, multi-plate clutch, footbrake on transmission, handbrake on rear wheels, semi-elliptic springs at front and three quarter elliptic at rear, wheelbase 117½in, right-hand drive.
£24,000-30,000 *C*

1913 Philos Four Seater Tourer, chassis No. 14081, Ballot 4 cylinder in-line monobloc, 1131cc, 8hp, bore and stroke 60mm x 100mm, Bosch Magneto, Zenith carburettor, single camshaft with valves on left-hand side of monobloc, 2 bearing crankshaft pressure fed by oil pump in sump, Thermo syphon radiator, electric lighting and starter from dynamo, metal Hele-Shaw clutch with 3 speed plus reverse gearbox. **£6,500-8,000**   *C*

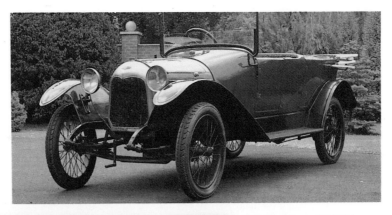

1913 Sunbeam 12/16 Five Passenger Touring Car, chassis No. 6224, engine No. 6750, 4 cylinder in-line water-cooled monobloc, side valve, bore 80mm x stroke 150mm, 3017cc, 4 speed gearbox, cone clutch, bevel final drive, semi-elliptic leaf front springs, three quarter elliptic rear springs, wheelbase 117in and 815 x 105mm tyres. **£34,000-35,500**   *S*

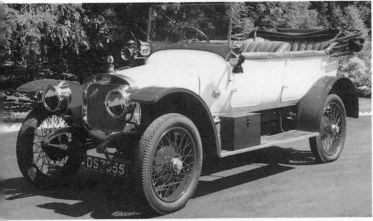

1914 Napier Model T67 30/35hp Torpedo Tourer, chassis No. 15002, engine No. 20438, 6 cylinder in line, water-cooled, side valve, bore 3½in x stroke 5in, 4740cc, 4 speed gearbox, disc clutch, live rear axle, semi-elliptic leaf spring suspension front and rear, detachable wire wheels with beaded edge tyres. **65,000-70,000**   *S*

1913 Sunbeam 12/16hp, chassis No. 7038, engine No. 6488, 4 cylinder side valve fixed head, bore 80mm x 150mm, 3017cc, 4 speed sliding mesh gearbox, semi-elliptic front springs suspension, three quarter elliptic rear, drum type brakes on 2 rear wheels. **£37,000-40,000**   *C(A)*

1950 AEC/Merryweather Fire Engine, 100ft steel turntable ladder, with a Leyland 'Power Plus' diesel engine.
£4,500-5,500   *C*

1935 Ford Model BB Box Van, as used in the BBC series 'Dad's Army', chassis No. BB530774, engine No. R57332, 4 cylinder, 3285cc, this vehicle is in good condition throughout.
£11,500-12,500   *ADT*

1942 Willys Jeep, chassis No. 51850, engine No. 51850, 4 cylinder water-cooled monobloc, side valve, bore 3⅛in x stroke 2⅜in, 2.2 litre, 3 speed synchromesh gearbox, high and low ratios, 2 and 4 wheel drive, single plate clutch, hypoid rear axle. **£5,000-6,000**   *S*

1913 Standard Rhyl Convertible, chassis No. 10151, engine No. 10151 4 cylinder, 1087cc, 3 speed gearbox, worm drive, rear wheel brakes bulb horn, oil side lamps and acetylene head lamps, Oldfield oil rear lamp, 710 x 90mm beaded edge tyres and Smith's speedo tachometer with normal cable drive to the offside front wheel.
£8,000-10,000   *ADT*

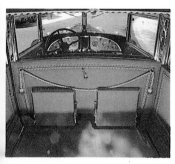

A view of the luxurious interior of the 1930 Cadillac V-16 Madame X Imperial Landaulette.

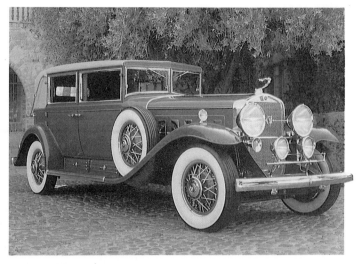

A further view of the 1930 Cadillac V-16 Madame X showing the V-shaped dashboard, chrome trimmed windows and German silver inlays.

1930 Cadillac V-16 Madame X Imperial Landaulette, with coachwork by Fleetwood, a car in grand style, capable of 100mph. **£328,000-450,000** *CNY*

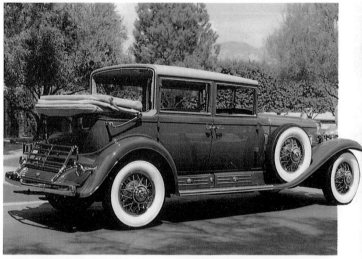

A view of the bonnet mascot of the 1930 Cadillac V-16 Madame X.

A rear view of the 1930 Cadillac showing the hood down and also the wire spoke wheels, tyres 7.50 x 19.

A view showing the fitted interior clock in the 1930 Cadillac V-16 Madame X.

Left. **1930 L 29 Cord Golfers Cabriolet,** with 8 cylinder in-line engine, Lycoming water-cooled, 'L-Head' with separate crankcase, bore 3in x stroke 4in, 4900cc, 3 speed gearbox driving through front wheels, semi-elliptic rear suspension, with double quarter elliptic front springs, this model was driven by such stars as Clark Gable, Greta Garbo and Errol Flynn. **£125,000-130,000** *BLE*

1916 Dodge Brothers Four Seat Tourer, these cars were used in the Campaign against the Mexican bandit Pancho Villa, with a 17/24 horse power engine, HT magneto, multi-plate clutch, 3 speed gearbox, wooden detachable rims, finished in black with black buttoned upholstery.
£8,800-10,000 *ADT*

Buick Two Door Coupé, by Fisher, with unusual 3 seat or opera style seating, with wooden spoked wheels and 525 x 21 white wall tyres, wooden steering wheel, wind down rear windows, folding passenger seat, rear drinks storage area, 'Tilt Ray' drum headlamps, with no glare lens and Delco Remy electrics, the upholstery finished in blue brushed West of England type cloth.
£12,700-14,000 *ADT*

Ford Model A Roadster with Dickey, with L shaped cylinder head, semi-elliptic transverse springing and 4 cylinder engines, coil ignition, 3 speed sliding gear unit, Houdaille hydraulic shock absorbers and 4 wheel brakes, finished in beige and chocolate this example has optional side mounted spare wheel and fold down rear rack.
£7,600-9,000 *ADT*

c1926 Studebaker Two Door Saloon, with 6 cylinder engine and 4 seats, the upholstery is in grey velour, solid wooden steering wheel, the windscreen folds out and it has split run disc wheels.
£4,000-5,000 *ADT*

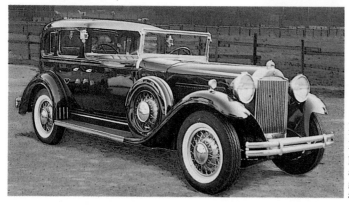

1930 Packard De Luxe 8 Sedanca De Ville, chassis No. 150481, engine No. MDA 23698 6.3 litre, straight 8, with 106bhp, 3 speed gearbox, hypoid rear axle, wheelbase 135in and 700 x 19in wire wheels, it is in generally good order.
£31,000-35,000 *C*

COLOUR REVIEW

1951 Cadillac Fleetwood, chassis No. 516284681, engine No. 51684681 V8, 5147cc, this car has been totally restored, 38,000 miles recorded, complete with original bill of sale, handbook and warranties.
£10,800-12,000 *Ren*

A rear view of the 1951 Cadillac Fleetwood, showing rear fins and spare wheel.

1932 Chevrolet Sports Roadster Two Door Convertible, chassis No. M101710, with synchromesh gearbox with free wheel, right-hand drive.
£13,500-15,000 *C*

1928 Buick 30, ex South Africa, excellent bodywork, very good interior and good mechanics.
£30,000-35,000 *CC*

1936 Cord 812 Speedster, this car has been completely restored and has excellent bodywork, mechanics and interior.
£74,500-78,000 *BLE*

1935 Chevrolet, with good bodywork and interior, and very good mechanics.
£8,000-9,000 *CC*

1938 Buick Model 4, 8 cylinder, 4517cc engine, chassis No. B44193208, engine No. 3419206, 141hp at 3,600rpm, coil spring suspension, manual gearbox, the engine and brakes were rebuilt 2 years ago but has original brown leather interior.
£5,700-8,000 *ADT*

Auburn Four Seat Speedster Replica, formerly of the Galveston Automobile Collection, only 1,000 miles recorded, with pointed tail bodywork, external exhaust pipes, stylised wings and bumpers, heater radio and side screens, finished in ice white with red lining and chromed wire wheels, interior finished in red leather.
£16,500-17,500   *ADT*

Zimmer Golden Spirit, formerly of the Galveston Automobile Collection, 4.2 litre V8 engine and automatic gearbox, coil spring chassis, wheelbase 142in, air conditioning, power steering, electric seats and windows, brown leather upholstery, gold plated mascot, deep pile carpet and rear flower vase.
£19,000-20,000   *ADT*

Ford Model A Police Wagon, built for the specific use of the local police department, well restored and finished in black, it is in running condition with typical wing mounted siren, police blue glass lamps and ankle restrainers.
£11,600-14,000   *ADT*

A close-up view of the silver art work of the Ford Model A Police Wagon.

Ford Model A Roadster Pickup, with 'L' shaped cylinder head, semi-elliptic transverse springing and 4 cylinder engines, coil ignition, 3 speed sliding gear unit, Houdaille hydraulic shock absorbers and 4 wheel brakes, electric horn, side mounted spare wheel and cover.
£8,000-9,000   *ADT*

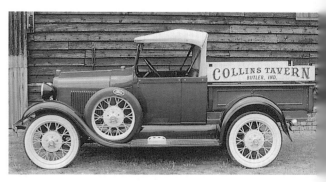

1940 Studebaker Commander, with very good bodywork and mechanics, large roof mounted sun visor, extensively restored apart from the interior.
£4,650-6,000   *GWC*

1961 Chevrolet Corvette, chassis No. 10867S104024, engine No. 10867S104024, with V8, 4638cc engine, this car had a complete engine overhaul in 1989. **£22,500-25,000** *LF*

1967 Chevrolet Corvette Sting Ray, with 8 cylinder, 5359cc engine, disc brakes, 560bhp, this car has been rebuilt with all original parts and is now immaculate winning numerous 'best car' awards. Est. **£14,000-15,000** *ADT*

1968 Chevrolet Corvette, chassis No. 1946785424467, engine No. 1852467-T 6191M, 427cu in, 7.5 litres, 400hp, this car has been rebuilt to absolutely original specificiton, with a manual gearbox and apparently low mileage. Est. **£18,000-22,000** *LF*

1962 Chevrolet Corvette, with very good bodywork, mechanics and interior, this is a good example, some restoration work having been carried out. **£16,500-17,500** *GWC*

1969 Shelby Mustang GT500 KR, 8 cylinder 428cu in Cobra engine, with ram air system and Holley 4 barrel carburettor matched to C6 locking automatic transmission and single pot ventilated front disc brakes, it has a tilt away steering wheel with original paintwork, glass fibre bonnet, wings and boot lid, BF Goodrich radial tyres with original chrome Cobra wheels, 53,400 miles recorded. Est. **£30,000-35,000** *ADT*

1966 Ford Galaxie 390 Convertible RHD, with excellent bodywork and interior, fair mechanical order, power top alloy wheels. **£8,000-9,000** *Mot*

1955 Ford Thunderbird, 8 cylinder, 4786cc engine, 3 speed manual transmission, and electric seats, the chrome brightwork is good, lift-off hard top with black soft top, removable rear wheel spats, and 81,000 recorded miles. **£19,000-20,000** *ADT*

1951 Sunbeam S8 Motorcycle, 500cc en
shaft rear wheel drive, only 3,371 miles
recorded, this motorcycle has been
totally restored and comes with
a number of spares.
£2,700-3,700 *LF*

**1952 Vincent Series C Rapide, 1000cc Solo
Motorcycle,** frame No. RC9808/C, engine
No. F10/AB/1/7908, 4 stroke 50° overhead
valve V twin cylinder, air-cooled, bore
84 x stroke 90mm, 4 speed posi stop
gearbox, chain final drive, Girdraulic
front forks, cantilever rear
suspension, 39,930 miles recorded.
£9,500-11,000 *S*

**1940 Brough Superior SS100 1000cc Solo
Motorcycle,** frame No. MLS/2202, engine
No. BS/X2/1104, 50° V twin cylinder,
air-cooled, overhead valve, 4 stroke,
bore 85.5 x stroke 85.5mm, 4 speed
foot change gearbox, chain final drive,
Castle forks, plunger rear suspension,
this motorcycle has undergone restoration
by Weedon Classics and is now in very
good condition and has its original
buff log book.
£20,000-25,000 *S*

**1951 Vincent Black Shadow Series C
1000cc Solo Motorcycle,** frame No. RC
5410 B, engine No. F10AB/1B/3510, V twin
cylinder, air-cooled, high camshaft overhead
valve, 4 stroke, bore 84 x stroke 90mm, 4 speed
posi-stop gearbox chain final drive, hydraulic
front forks. Est. **£16,000-18,000** *S*

**1958 Velocette Venom 500cc Solo
Motorcycle,** frame No. RS10079, engine No.
VM1879, single cylinder, this motorcycle
has been completely rebuilt and is in
good condition throughout, it comes
complete with old style logbook.
£3,400-5,000 *ADT*

1925 Henderson Motorcycle,
1300cc, 4 cylinder engine.
£6,500-7,500 *LF*

**1923 BSA Model H 557cc So
Motorcycle,** engine No.
R 4741, single vertical
cylinder engine, air-
cooled, 4 stroke, side valve,
4¼hp, 3 speed hand change
gearbox, chain final drive,
Girder fork and coil spring
front suspension, rigid rear.
£4,000-5,000 *S*

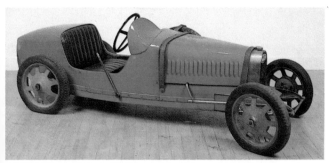

1927/28 Bugatti Type 52 'Electric', with coachwork by Bugatti Automobiles, Molsheim, half scale Type 35 Grand Prix Car, electric starter motor driven by 12 volt battery, mechanical brakes, knock off alloy style wheels with ½ scale 710 x 90 tyres, semi-elliptic front springs enclosed rear axle, worm and sector steering, right-hand drive, top speed 12-15mph. Est. **£28,000-44,000** *CNY*

c1955 Austin J40, chassis No. 10252, dummy OHV engine, battery operated headlamps, leather upholstery and handbrake, this car has been restored to a very high standard.
£850-1,000 *ADT*

Three Austin J40 Children's Pedal Cars, coloured royal blue, maroon and red, all in good condition but the maroon one has some rust to chrome and marks to paintwork, the red one has winged A mascot missing, all 58in (147cm) long.
£550-1,500 each *S*

c1925 Coachbuilt Pedal Car, with hardwood frame, aluminium panels and steel wings, chain drive, opening doors, English, 42½in (108cm) long. **£11,250-12,000** *S(S)*

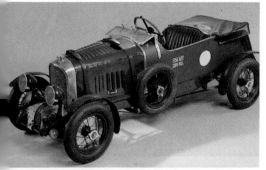

1980 Scratch Built 4½ Litre Supercharged Bentley, aluminium body and chassis, treadle drive, imitation supercharger, engine and detailed dashboard, cord bound leaf springs and steering wheel, English, 68in (173cm) long. **£4,500-5,000** *S(S)*

c1965 Phillips 4½ Litre Supercharged Bentley Electric Sports Racing Car, with steel chassis, fibreglass body and mudguards, 12 volt electric motor, with belt drive to lay shaft, chain drive to back axle, 4 wheel cable brakes, dummy supercharger electric lights, English, 76in (193cm) long.
£2,200-3,000 *S(S)*

1980 Scratch Built 1912 Peugeot G.P. Pedal Racing Car, with aluminium chassis and body, working handbrake, bulb horn, imitation lamps, English, 48in (122cm) long. **£5,000-6,000** *S(S)*

c1923 National of Toledo Packard Phaeton Pedal Car, of pressed steel, with treadle drive, adjustable windscreen, folding hood, imitation handbrake, American, 60in (152cm) long. **£13,500-14,000** *S(S)*

A Post-War 3 Litre 'Speed Model' Bentley Pedal Car, all metal, treadle drive, framed p.v.c. body, aluminium bonnet. **£3,300-4,000**   *S(S)*

c1988 Motorima Ford Model T Runabout, sheet metal body, imitation starting handle, 48½in (123cm) long. **£2,000-3,000**   *S(S)*

A Lines Bros. Type 1928 Rolls-Royce Pedal Car, wooden body and chassis, chain drive, English, 56in (142cm) long. **£4,000-5,000**   *S(S)*

A Scratch Built Aston Martin LM18 Sports Racing Pedal Car, aluminium body, treadle drive, English, 69in (175cm). **£5,500-6,000**   *S(S)*

c1955 Austin J40 Pedal Car, heavy guage pressed steel, adjustable treadle drive, English, 60in (152cm) long. **£1,650-2,000**   *S(S)*

1970s Wendover Bugatti Style Pedal Car, steel body and chassis, treadle drive, English, 66in (168cm) long. **£2,000-3,000**   *S(S)*

c1990 Bugatti Type 52 Replica Half Scale Electric Car, steel chassis, aluminium body, 73in (185cm) long. **£3,000-4,000**   *S(S)*

A Post-War Maserati Style Pedal Racing Car, pressed steel body, treadle drive, 63½in (161cm) long. **£2,000-3,000**   *S(S)*

c1988 Motorima 3 Litre Bentley Pedal Car, sheet metal, treadle drive, folding hood, English, 59in (150cm) long. **£2,600-3,000**   *S(S)*

c1935 Lines Bros. M.G. Pedal Car, coach-built wood and sheet metal, treadle drive, English, 54½in (138cm) long. **£3,600-4,000**   *S(S*

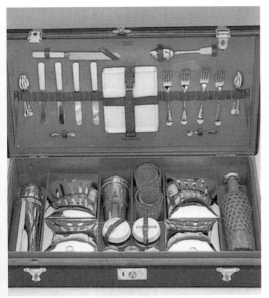

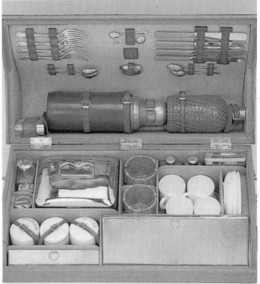

A Stewart Dawson & Co. Ltd., travelling picnic set, the wooden case with brass carrying handles, leather cover and oak interior lining, fitted with 4 place settings, 4 food containers, flask, cocktail shaker and wicker covered bottle, English, 1920s, 28in (71cm) wide. **£600-800** *S*

An unusual combined picnic set and footrest, the shaped lid with tread inset and brass surround, engraved R. A. Walker Sloan Troon, green/grey leatherette cover and fitted with ceramic cups, plates, jars, glass flasks, tumblers, bottle and food containers, 22in (57cm) wide. **£1,200-2,000** *S*

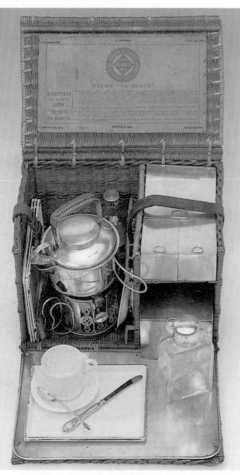

A silver fitted Drew & Sons En Route motoring tea set, in wicker case with leather securing strap, hinged lid and fall front, with silver kettle, 4 silver food containers, 2 silver mounted glass bottles, a flask, 4 enamel plates and other accessories, hallmarked London 1895, 13½in (34cm) wide. **£1,800-2,500** *S*

A Drew motoring picnic set, with brown leather covered case with hinged lid and fall front, with metal kettle and stove, 2 place settings, ceramic plates, cups and saucers and other accessories, 13½in (34cm) wide. **£1,000-2,000** *S*

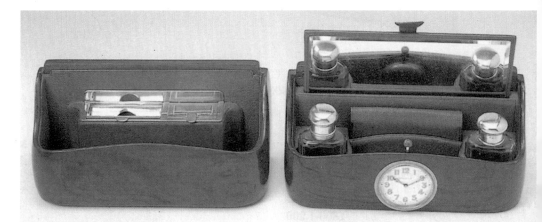

A pair of motoring interior vanity and smoking sets, the shaped walnut case fitted with vesta and ashtray, the other fitted with 2 silver mounted scent bottles, hand mirror and inset with 8 day timepiece, c1921, 9in (23cm) wide. **£900-1,000** *S*

Alfa Romeo Alfetta Tipo 158, a diecast ashtray inscribed Alfa Romeo Campione del Monde 1950, Gran Premi — 11 Vittorie, and mounted with a model of the Alfetta, 7in (18cm) wide. **£660-750** *CNY*

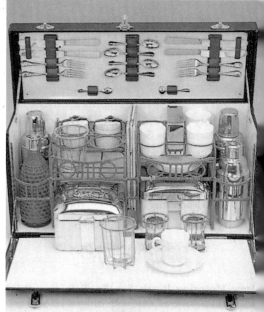

A Coracle picnic set, the black leathercloth covered case with carrying handles at the sides, fitted with 4 place settings, 2 thermos flasks, ceramic preserve jars, cups and saucers, English 1920s, 24in (61cm) wide. **£1,800-2,500** *S*

A Rolls-Royce silver ashtray, the circular dish mounted with miniature Spirit of Ecstasy mascot, hallmarked London 1926, 4in (10cm) high. **£1,050-2,000** *S*

Left. A Rolls-Royce silver cigarette box, the lid inset with image of the Spirit of Ecstasy and shadow, hinged lid and lined interior, hallmarked London 1928, 7in (17cm) wide. **£1,000-1,500**
Centre. A Rolls-Royce silver inkwell, the shaped radiator top mounted with red enamel badge and miniature Spirit of Ecstasy mascot, hallmarked London 1929, 6in (15cm) wide. **£1,200-1,800**
Right. A Rolls-Royce silver desk timepiece, with 8 day movement, hallmarked London 1927, 5in (13cm) high. **£2,000-3,000** *S*

A 1:10 detailed scale model of a 1976 Ferrari
512BB, in brass and aluminium, on a wooden plinth,
with a case, 21in (53cm) long.
£7,000-7,500 *CNY*

A 1:8 detailed scale model of the 1967 Ferrari
330P4, P4s were 1st and 2nd in the 1967
Daytona 24-Hours, helping to give Ferrari
his 12th Constructors' World Championship title.
£11,500-12,000 *CNY*

A pair of BRC 10in acetylene
headlamps, No. 437, each with large
bull's-eye condenser, silvered
reflector, loop carrying handle, oval
section chimney and fork mounting
flanges, French, c1908, 14in (36cm),
together with a complete acetylene
generator with handle, tap and
cylinder.
£3,800-4,200 *S*

A pair of Ducellier brass opera lamps, each
polished brass lamp with 2 bevel windows,
silvered reflector and fitted with later
electric illuminant, French, c1905, 13½in
(35cm) high.
£880-920 *S*

A rare Bosch triple lens rear lamp, shaped,
with 2 red glass lenses and 1 clear lens,
German, 1930s, 7in (18cm) wide.
£800-900 *S*

A German Automobile Club 10,000
Kilometer Race enamel badge, dated
1931, gilt brass shaped badge with
outline of the route through Europe
and inset with the 9 international
motoring club badges in coloured
enamels, and lettered around the
edge, 4½ by 3¼in (11 by 8.5cm).
£550-600 *S*

A Lalique 'Cinq Chevaux' glass car
mascot, with light amethyst tint,
engraved on the base No. 1122,
embossed R.Lalique, wheelcut
France, 4 small air bubbles, slight
chips to flat edge, chip to base,
in ring mount, French, 1930s.
£1,200-1,500 *S*

An Automobile Club de Cannes silver
and enamel plaque, the shaped
plaque mounted with club enamel
badge and cast in relief with
allegorical female figure before a
scene of the city and supercharged
saloon car, c1930, 3in (7.5cm) wide,
in shaped leather case.
£400-450 *S*

Bright Young Things, a nickel plated car mascot, the base signed Ruffony, and mounted on a radiator cap. **£750-800**   *CNY*

A white enamelled SS Jaguar mascot, the base stamped Gordon Crosby, and mounted on a radiator cap, 8in (20cm) long. **£250-500**   *C*

A nickel plated aeroplane mounted on a radiator cap. **£700-800**   *CNY*

Thoni, Grosser Preis der Schweiz für automobile, Bern 22 u. 23 August 1936, lithograph, 39 by 27½in (99 by 70cm). Est. **£4,000-4,500**   *CNY*

B Minne, Monaco, 1er et 2 Juin 1952, lithograph, 48 by 31in (122 by 79cm). **£5,500-6,000**   *CNY*

SA Scuderia Ferrari Yearbook 1930/31/32/33, Italian text, 1933. **£2,700-3,000**   *CNY*

Roy Nockolds, 1931 Targa Florio, Achille Varzi in the Type 33 Bugatti, signed, oil on canvas. **£1,250-2,000**   *S*

Lionel Rouse, Mercedes and Auto Union Duel, signed and dated 1974, oil on board, 23½ by 31½in (60 by 80cm). **£1,250-2,000**   *S*

Graham Turner, Racing The Blue Train, signed, gouache, mounted, framed and glazed. **£3,300-4,000**   *S*

Michael Wright, 1951 French Grande Prix, Chiron in the Largo Talbot and Ascari in the 4.5 Ferrari approach the right hander, signed and inscribed. **£2,000-4,000**   *S*

1937 Brough Superior 11.50 1096cc Solo Motorcycle, J.A.P. V twin engine, side valve, air cooled, 4 stroke, 1096cc, Norton 4 speed gearbox, girder forks with coil spring front suspension, rigid frame at rear, chain final drive, 3.25 x 19 tyres.
£10,000-10,500   *S*

1937 Brough Superior 1150cc Solo Motorcycle, 50° V twin engine, air cooled, side valve, 4 stroke, bore 85.7mm x 95mm stroke, 1096cc, foot change gearbox, chain final drive, Monarch front forks, rigid rear end.
£10,200-10,700   *S*

The largest of the Brough Superior model range during the 1930s was the 1150cc side valve primarily intended for use with a sidecar, although it was equally successful as a high performance solo mount. As with all Broughs, the 1150 was built to the highest standards, utilising the best possible components, its high gearing and long stroke V twin JAP engine endowing the machine with the ability to cover long distances with great ease.

Advertised, with 'Derby's blessing', as The Rolls-Royce of Motorcycles, George Brough's Superior machines enjoyed a reputation as the ultimate rider's bike during the 20s and 30s, and that following is stronger than ever before, today.

1934 B.S.A. Blue Star 500cc Solo Motorcycle. Est. **£4,000-5,000**   *P*

1937 Brough Superior SS80 1000cc Solo Motorcycle, Matchless V twin engine, side valve, air cooled, 4 stroke, 999cc, 3 speed gearbox, coil spring with girder forks, rigid frame at rear, chain final drive.
Est. **£12,000-14,000**   *S*

1937 B.S.A. B23 348cc Solo Motorcycle, single vertical cylinder engine, air cooled, 348cc, 4 speed gearbox, chain final drive, girder front forks, rigid rear.
£2,200-2,500   *S*

1936 B.S.A. 249cc Solo Motorcycle, single vertical cylinder engine, overhead valve, 249cc, 3 speed gearbox, chain final drive, girder fork suspension front, rigid rear.
£2,420-2,800   *S*

1949 B.S.A. ZB 350cc Gold Star.
£4,000-4,500   *P*

1957 B.S.A. 650cc Rocket Gold Star Solo Motorcycle. Est. **£7,500-8,500**   *P*

1958 B.S.A. Gold Star 500cc Solo Motorcycle, vertical twin cylinder engine, overhead valve, air cooled, 4 stroke, 500cc, 4 speed posi-stop gearbox, telescopic forks, swinging arm rear suspension, chain final drive.
£8,250-9,000 *S*

1972 B.S.A. Rocket Three Mk I 750cc Solo Motorcycle, inclined triple cylinder engine, air cooled, overhead valve, 4 stroke, 750cc, 4 speed gearbox, telescopic forks, sprung frame at rear, chain final drive, 19in tyres.
Est. **£6,000-6,500** *S*

1961 B.S.A. DBD34 Clubmans Gold Star 500cc Solo Motorcycle, vertical single cylinder engine, air cooled, overhead valve, 4 stroke, bore 85mm x 88mm stroke, 499cc, 4 speed posi-stop gearbox, chain final drive, telescopic front forks, swinging arm rear suspension controlled by coil spring and hydraulic dampers.
Est. **£6,000-8,000** *S*

1962 B.S.A. Gold Star Clubman, 499cc engine.
Est. **£6,000-8,000** *LF*

1903 Chater-Lea 350cc Solo Motorcycle, vertical single cylinder engine, air cooled, side valve, 350cc, 2 speed gear with 'coffee grinder' lever, belt drive with pedal assistance, girder fork and coil spring front suspension, rigid rear, beaded edge wheels.
£5,500-6,000 *S*

The first Chater-Lea motorcycle made its appearance in London in 1900 from a company established in 1890 which, like many early manufacturers, were to graduate from bicycle to motorcycle and finally to car manufacture.

1966 B.S.A. Bantam 175, 174cc engine.
£275-350 *LF*

The Bantam was the most widely sold of all B.S.A.s and was made in various guises from 1948 until 197

c1913 Connaught 250cc Motorcycle, single cylinder, 250cc engine.
£3,500-4,000 *LF*

1974 Cheney/Triumph 500cc Enduro Solo Motorcycle.
£8,000-8,500 *P*

The Eric Cheney/Triumph Enduros of the mid 1970s were powered by a 500cc Triumph engine.

Connaughts were built from 1910 until 1947 by Bawdsley Engineering Birmingham.

1948 Corgi 98cc Folding Scooter, single cylinder engine, air cooled, 2 stroke, bore 50mm x 50mm stroke, 98cc, single plate clutch, chain final drive, wheels 8¾ x 1¾in. £750-1,000 *S*

Originally built as a paratroopers bike for use in World War II, the Spryt engined Corgi was adapted for civilian use and enjoyed considerable popularity in the post-war period. Known as 'Britain's Pocket Prodigy' it weighed only 95lb, with a top speed of 30mph and economy of 120 miles per gallon.

The Dot Cycle and Manufacturing Company of Arundel St., Manchester, began manufacturing cycles and motorcycle components in 1903. The company's motto was 'Devoid of Trouble'. Dot Motorcycles were also made with Villiers 2 stroke, JAP and Anzani engines. The company is still running from their original premises in Arundel St., Manchester.

1924 Dot Bradshaw 2¾hp Solo Motorcycle, single vertical cylinder engine, oil and air cooled, bore 60mm x 90mm stroke, 254cc, 3 speed gearbox, kick start and single plate clutch, chain final drive, 26 x 3in rear tyres, 26 x 2½in front. £3,300-3,800 *S*

1947 Douglas T35, 350cc engine, this particular 350 has one of the few remaining original engines and is the oldest post-war Douglas recorded on the Douglas register. £3,500-4,000 *LF*

Douglas of Bristol had built motorcycles since 1907 until their demise in 1956 and were better known in later years for the 'Dragonfly' and for the assembly of Vespa scooters.

1918 Douglas 2¾hp Solo Motorcycle. £3,000-3,500 *P*

1974 Dresda Triton 650cc Solo Motorcycle, pre-unit twin cylinder engine, air cooled, 650cc, 4 speed gearbox, chain final drive, telescopic forks with coil spring dampers, front and rear. £2,500-3,000 *S*

1979 Ducatti 900cc Mike Hailwood Replica Solo Motorcycle. Est. £4,000-6,000 *P*

Within six weeks of the late Mike Hailwood winning the Manx T.T. in 1979 Ducatti designed and produced the first series of Hailwood Replicas. Basically a 900 SS there were only 200 examples of the first series produced.

1950 Douglas Mk V 350cc Solo Motorcycle, horizontally opposed
twin cylinder engine, air cooled, overhead valve, bore 60.8mm x
60mm stroke, 349cc, radiadraulic bottom link front fork with
hydraulic damping, torsion bar controlled pivoting fork rear
suspension, 19in tyres.
£3,000-3,500 *S*

**1937 Excelsior 250cc Manxman
Solo Motorcycle.**
£22,600-23,000 *P*

*Fabrique Nationale produced a high
quality range of motorcycles, and
then cars, before World War I.*

1912 FN 2½hp Solo Motorcycle
single cylinder engine, air cooled,
side valve, bore 65mm x 85mm
stroke, 285cc, rated at 2½hp,
2 speed shaft final drive, girder
spring forks, 26in tyres, in
unrestored condition.
£2,500-3,000 *S*

Gnome Rhone.
£2,000-2,300 *LF*

*Although their motorcycles were not
particularly well known in this
country, they were produced from
1919 until 1959 in France, although
the post-war machines have
basically been small 2 strokes.*

1962 Greeves Trials 250cc, in
restored condition.
£1,000-1,250 *LF*

1927 Grindlay Peerless JAP Lacey Short Stroke Racing Replica Solo Motorcycle, JAP KOR single cylinder, overhead valve, air cooled, 4 stroke racing engine, bore 85mm x 85mm stroke, 500cc, 3 speed Sturmey Archer H/W gearbox, girder forks with coil spring front suspension, rigid frame at rear, chain final drive, 28 x 3in tired tyres.
£8,500-9,000 *S*

1962 Harley Davidson XLCH 900 Sportster Solo Motorcycle.
Est. £5,000-5,500   *P*

1967 Honda Monkey Bike, horizontally inclined single cylinder engine, air cooled, 4 stroke, 49cc, 3 speed gearbox, chain final drive, rigid front forks and rigid rear, 4.00 x 5in tyres.
£1,100-1,300   *S*

1921 Harley Davidson 750cc Solo Motorcycle, V twin cylinder engine, air cooled, side valve, 750cc, 3 speed gearbox, hand change, Castle type front forks, rigid rear.
£2,640-3,000   *S*

1942 Indian 500cc Military Motorcycle, V twin cylinder engine, air cooled, side valve, 500cc, 3 speed gearbox, hand change, girder front fork suspension, rigid rear, 6 volt electric system.
£3,300-3,600   *S*

1971 Indian Velo 500cc Solo Motorcycle, Velocette Thruxton single cylinder engine, air cooled, stroke, overhead valve, 500cc, speed gearbox, telescopic forks, sprung frame at rear, chain final drive.
Est. £6,000-6,500   *S*

Make the Most of Miller's

The value of coachbuilt cars is almost entirely dependent on the following factors:
history and provenance
completeness and
originality
racing or competition
history
engine specification,
e.g. supercharger

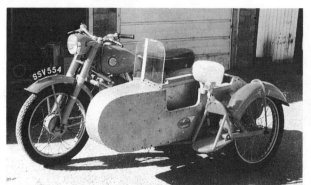

1956 James 197cc Motorcycle Combination, Villiers single vertical cylinder engine, air cooled, 2 stroke, 197cc, 3 speed gearbox telescopic forks, sprung frame, chain final drive.
£720-850   *S*

1962 James Commodore 250, 249cc engine.
£800-1,000   *LF*

James, who subsequently have been taken over by Associated Motor Cycles, built machines from 1902 until 1966. The Commodore range was introduced in 1937 and has AMC's own 250cc engine.

1961 Matchless Model 14 CSR 250cc Solo Motorcycle, vertical single cylinder engine, air cooled, 4 stroke, overhead valve, bore 69.85mm x 64.85mm stroke, 248.5cc, 4 speed gearbox, chain final drive, telescopic front forks, swinging arm rear suspension, 17in tyres.
£385-500   *S*

The overhead valve Model 14 offered performance in excess of 70mph and the designation CSR, although according to the factory stood for Competition, Sports and Roadster, soon became dubbed the Coffee Shop Racer.

1952 Motobi 125cc Racing Motorcycle.
Est. **£8,000-9,000**   *P*

1976 MV Agusta 750S America Solo Motorcycle, 790cc engine, twin cam all alloy four with split roller bearing crank and four 26m choke Delorto carburettors, 75bhp at 8,500rpm.
Est. **£25,000-30,000**   *P*

1941 Moto Guzzi 'Alce' Moose 500cc Solo Motorcycle, horizontal single cylinder engine, air cooled, overhead valve, 500cc, 4 speed gearbox, outside flywheel, chain final drive, girder front forks, swinging arm rear suspension with friction damping.
£1,650-2,000   *S*

1976 MV Agusta 750S America Solo Motorcycle.
Est. **£18,000-22,000**   *P*

1973 MV Agusta.
£22,000-27,000 *AUT*

**1944 New Hudson 98cc
Autocycle,** horizontal single
cylinder engine, air cooled, 2 stroke,
bore 50mm x 50mm stroke, 98cc,
single speed, chain final drive, rigid
frame, 21in tyres.
£300-350 *S*

**1956 Noriel Special 997cc Solo
Motorcycle,** Ariel Square Four
engine, overhead valve, air cooled,
4 stroke, 997cc, 4 speed gearbox,
Norton featherbed frame, chain
final drive.
£2,200-2,500 *S*

**1939 Norton International Solo
Motorcycle.**
Est. £8,000-10,000 *P*

*The single overhead camshaft
Norton engine which appeared in
1928 was Norton's first, they having
used pushrods before and was
known as the single knocker. This
engine was used for racing up until
the 1950s through various stages of
development.*

**1939 Norton International/Manx
Solo Motorcycle,** single vertical
cylinder engine, air cooled,
overhead camshaft, 4 stroke, bore
mm x 88mm stroke, 350cc,
speed gearbox, chain final drive,
girder front forks, plunger rear
suspension.
£8,500-9,000 *S*

1949 Norton ES2 500cc Motorcycle Combination with Swallow Jet 80 Single Seater Sports Sidecar, single cylinder engine, overhead valve, air cooled, 4 stroke, 500cc, 4 speed gearbox, 'garden gate' frame sprung at rear, chain final drive.
Est. £5,500-6,500 *S*

1952 Norton Model 18 500cc Solo Motorcycle, vertical single cylinder engine, air cooled, overhead valve, bore 79mm x 100mm stroke, 490cc, 4 speed foot change gearbox, chain final drive, telescopic front fork suspension, rigid rear, 18in tyres.
£2,200-2,500 *S*

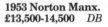

1953 Norton Manx.
£13,500-14,500 *DB*

1953 Norton 500T Solo Motorcycle, vertical single cylinder engine, air cooled, overhead valve, 4 stroke, bore 79mm x 100mm stroke, 490cc, 4 speed gearbox, chain final drive.
£3,520-4,000 *S*

Introduced in the early post-war years for off-road trials work, the 500T used the Model 18 engine in the 16H frame and fitted it with Norton Roadholder forks.

Miller's is a price **GUIDE** not a price **LIST**

1932 OEC 500cc Solo Motorcycle, single vertical cylinder engine, air cooled, 4 stroke, overhead valve, bore 85.7mm x 85mm stroke, 500cc Burman gearbox, chain final drive, dry sump lubrication, OEC duplex steering and front forks, rigid rear suspension, 19in tyres.
£1,100-1,300 *S*

1972 Norton Commando 750cc.
Est. £3,000-4,000 *LF*

1939 O/K Supreme Motorcycle.
Est. £3,000-5,000 *Ren*

1923 Raleigh 3hp Solo Motorcycle, single vertical cylinder engine, air cooled, side valve, bore 76mm x 88mm stroke, 398cc, Sturmey Archer 3 speed gearbox, hand change, chain final drive, Brampton Biflex front forks, rigid rear suspension, 26in tyres.
£2,200-2,500 *S*

1967 Raleigh Wisp Moped 49cc.
£100-120 *LF*

1936 Red Panther 250cc Solo Motorcycle, inclined overhead valve, air cooled single cylinder, 4 stroke engine, bore 60mm x 88mm stroke, 249cc, 3 speed hand change gearbox, chain final drive, rigid rear end, girder front forks.
£950-1,100 *S*

Sold exclusively through Pride and Clarke (a large London dealer) the 250cc Model 20 Red Panther was introduced in 1933 and remained in production until 1939.

1913 Royal Ruby 2¼hp Solo Motorcycle.
Est. £5,000-6,000 *P*

Royal Ruby motorcycles appeared in Manchester in 1909, manufacturing complete machines with single cylinder 2 stroke engines built at the factory.

1939 Royal Enfield 250cc Solo Motorcycle, vertical single cylinder engine, air cooled, 4 stroke, side valve, 250cc, 4 speed hand change gearbox, chain final drive, girder fork and coil spring front suspension, rigid rear.
Est. £800-1,200 *S*

1960 Royal Enfield 350 Bullet.
Est. £2,400-3,000   *LF*

1937 Rudge Special 500cc Solo Motorcycle, vertical single cylinder engine, air cooled, overhead valve, 4 stroke, 85mm bore x 88mm stroke, 499cc, 4 speed gearbox, chain final drive, girder fork front suspension, rigid rear.
£2,800-3,200   *S*

1957 Scott Flying Squirrel 596cc Solo Motorcycle, inclined twin cylinder, water cooled, 2 stroke, 73mm bore x 71.4mm stroke, 596cc, 3 speed gearbox, chain final drive, telescopic front forks, hydraulic dampers rear, tyres 3¼/3½ x 50 x 19in.
£4,300-4,750   *S*

c1907 Simplex 500cc Solo Racing Motorcycle, V twin cylinder engine, air cooled, side valve, approx. 500cc, single speed, belt final drive, girder fork and coil spring front suspension, rigid rear.
£7,000-7,500   *S*

The Dutch manufacturer Simplex was amongst the pioneers of motorcycle manufacturers in Europe, commencing production in 1902. They adopted proprietary engines from Minerva, Fafnir and M.A.G.

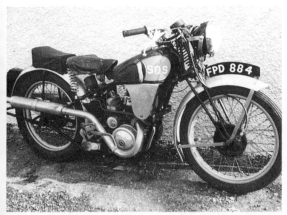

1939 Sunbeam Model HC 350cc Sport Solo Motorcycle, vertical single cylinder engine, air cooled, overhead valve 4 stroke, 350cc, 4 speed foot change gearbox, chain final drive, girder fork and coil spring front suspension, rigid rear. Est. **£3,500-4,500** *S*

c1937 SOS 250cc Solo Motorcycle, Villiers vertical single cylinder, twin port air cooled, 2 stroke engine, 250cc, 3 speed gearbox, girder forks with coil spring front suspension, rigid frame at rear, chain final drive. **£1,400-1,750** *S*

The SOS was built from 1927 until 1939 in Worcester and later Birmingham.

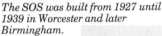

1929 Sunbeam Model 8. **£3,700-4,000** *LF*

1951 Sunbeam S7 489cc Solo Motorcycle, in-line vertical twin, air cooled engine, overhead cam, 4 stroke, 489cc, 70mm bore x 63.5mm stroke, 4 speed gearbox, shaft final drive, telescopic forks, plunger rear suspension, complete and in need of some renovation. **£1,500-2,000** *S*

c1974 Suzuki RG 500 Mk 4 T.T. Solo Motorcycle. **£3,200-3,700** *P*

1951 Sunbeam S7 497cc Solo Motorcycle, in-line twin cylinder, air cooled engine, overhead valve, 4 stroke, 497cc, 4 speed gearbox, telescopic forks with sprung frame at rear, shaft and bevel final drive, good condition. **£2,300-2,750** *S*

c1958 Triton Classic Road Racer. Est. **£2,000-2,600** *LF*

1911 Triumph 3½hp 500cc Solo Motorcycle, single vertical cylinder engine, air cooled, side valve 4 stroke, 499cc, 2 speed gearbox, belt final drive, girder fork and coil spring front suspension, rigid rear, tyres 26 x 2½in. Est. **£6,000-7,000** *S*

This motorcycle saw service with the Royal Flying Corps in the Great War.

1960 Triton 650cc Solo Motorcycle, vertical twin cylinder, air cooled engine, overhead valve, 4 stroke, 71mm bore x 82mm stroke, 649cc, 4 speed gearbox, chain final drive, telescopic front forks, swinging arm rear suspension. **£1,200-1,700**   *S*

The Norton frame and Triumph 650cc engine were commonly married up in the 1960s to produce extremely fast road going or racing machines, with all the excellent handling characteristics for which Norton is noted.

1919 Triumph Model 'H' 4hp Solo Motorcycle, vertical single cylinder engine, side valve 4 stroke, air cooled, 550cc, 3 speed countershaft gearbox, chain primary drive and belt final drive to rear wheel rim, girder forks with coil spring front suspension, rigid at rear.
£5,300-5,800   *S*

The Model 'H' Triumph was perhaps the most famous motorcycles of the Great War, having been supplied in large numbers to the allied armies.

1921 Triumph Model 'H' Motorcycle Combination, in need of restoration. **£1,500-2,000**   *P*

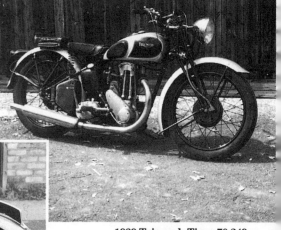

1939 Triumph Tiger 70 249cc Solo Motorcycle, single cylinder overhead valve air cooled engine, 249cc, 4 speed gearbox, girder forks with coil spring front suspension, rigid frame at rear, chain final drive, tyres, front 20 x 3in, rear 19 x 3½in. **£2,500-3,000**   *S*

1939 Triumph T100 500cc Solo Motorcycle, vertical twin cylinder engine, air cooled overhead valve, 4 stroke, 63mm bore x 80mm stroke, 498cc, 4 speed foot change gearbox, chain final drive, girder fork and coil spring front suspension, rigid rear, tyres 19/20in. **£4,000-4,800**   *S*

Miller's is a price GUIDE not a price LIST

1948 Triumph Tiger 100 500cc Solo Motorcycle, fully restored. Est. **£5,000-5,500**   *P*

1950 Triumph TR5 Trophy Solo Motorcycle.
Est. £5,000-7,000   *P*

1952 Triumph 6T Thunderbird 650cc Solo Motorcycle.
£2,200-2,500   *P*

1956 Triumph Speed Twin 500cc Solo Motorcycle.
Est. £3,000-5,000   *P*

1960 Triumph Tiger 110 650cc Solo Motorcycle.
Est. £3,500-4,500   *P*

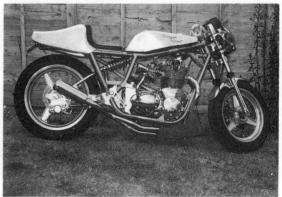

1962 Triumph Model 21 350cc Solo Motorcycle, vertical twin cylinder, air cooled engine, overhead valve, 58.25mm bore x 65.5mm stroke, 349cc, 4 speed foot change gearbox, chain final drive, telescopic front fork suspension, swinging arm rear, tyres 17in.
£1,500-2,000   *S*

Triumph's mainstay production in the post-war years centred around developments of Edward Turner's immortal Speed Twin of 1937. These were to include the Tiger 100s, Bonnevilles and Thunderbirds and at the smaller end of the scale the 3TA Model 21.

1970 Triumph Bonneville (Export Version) T 120R 650cc Solo Motorcycle, vertical twin cylinder, air cooled overhead valve 4 stroke engine, 650cc, 4 speed gearbox, telescopic forks, sprung frame at rear, chain final drive, tyres 19in, fully restored.
Est. £4,000-4,500   *S*

1971 Triumph TR6 Trophy Solo Motorcycle.
£3,000-3,500   *P*

1972 Triumph Trident Rickman Special 750cc Solo Motorcycle, 3 cylinder, air cooled, overhead valve engine, 67mm bore x 70mm stroke, 740cc, 5 speed foot change gearbox, chain final drive.
Est. £4,000-5,000   *S*

c1972 Triumph Trident TI 50 T.
£5,000-6,000 *PC*

1973 Triumph x 75 Hurricane 750cc Solo Motorcycle, 3 cylinder, overhead valve air cooled, 4 stroke engine, 750cc, 5 speed gearbox, telescopic forks, sprung frame at rear, chain final drive, tyres 18in.
Est. £6,000-6,500 *S*

1975 Triumph Trident 'Slippery Sam' Replica, 750cc Solo Motorcycle, 3 cylinder, air cooled engine, overhead valves, 67mm bore x 70mm stroke, 740cc, 5 speed gearbox, chain final drive, telescopic front forks, swinging arm rear suspension, tyres 19in.
Est. £4,000-4,500 *S*

c1977 Triumph Bonneville Silver Jubilee.
£3,000-5,000 *PC*

1,000 of these motorcycles were made for collection, for the U.S. market.

1982 Triumph TSS 750cc Solo Motorcycle, vertical twin cylinder, air cooled engine, overhead valve, 4 valves per cylinder, 750cc, 5 speed foot change gearbox, chain final drive, teledraulic fork front suspension, swinging arm rear.
Est. £2,300-2,800 *S*

Bernard Hooper's 8 valve engine appeared in the spring of 1981 and in 1982 it was fitted in production form in Triumph's new TSS model, effectively an 8 valve Bonneville.

1949 Velocette LE Mk I 149cc Solo Motorcycle, horizontally opposed twin cylinder engine, water cooled, 6 volt electric system, 149cc, 3 speed gearbox with hand change, shaft final drive, telescopic front forks with swinging arm rear end, fully adjustable damping.
£1,000-1,200 *S*

The Mk I Velocette LE was introduced in the winter of 1948.

1949 Velocette MAC 350cc Solo Motorcycle, single vertical cylinder, overhead valve, water cooled engine, 350cc, 3 speed foot change gearbox, chain final drive, telescopic front forks, rigid rear end.
£2,200-2,500 *S*

1964 Velocette 350cc Viper Clubman Solo Motorcycle.
Est. £3,800-4,200 *P*

1954 Velocette MSS 500cc Solo Motorcycle, single vertical cylinder, air cooled, overhead valve engine, 4 stroke, 86mm bore x 86mm stroke, 499cc, 4 speed posi-stop gearbox, chain final drive, telescopic front forks, swinging arm rear suspension.
£3,800-4,200   *S*

1966 Velocette Thruxton 500cc Solo Motorcycle, vertical single cylinder, air cooled, overhead valve engine, 4 stroke, 86mm bore x 86mm stroke, 499cc, 4 speed close ratio gearbox, chain primary and final drives, telescopic front forks, swinging arm rear suspension.
£7,700-8,200   *S*

The Velocette Thruxton represented the final development of the M series overhead valve singles, originally introduced in the pre-war years.

1966 Velocette LE Mk III 200cc Solo Motorcycle, horizontally opposed twin cylinder engine, water cooled, side valve, 200cc, 4 speed foot change gearbox, 12 volt electric system, telescopic front forks, swinging arm rear, with fully adjustable damping.
£950-1,200   *S*

1967 Velocette 500cc Endurance Solo Motorcycle.
£18,000-20,000   *P*

1935 Vincent-HRD Series 'A' Comet 500cc Solo Motorcycle, single vertical cylinder engine, overhead valves, air cooled, 500cc, 4 speed gearbox, girder forks with coil spring suspension at front, sprung frame at rear, chain final drive, tyres 26 x 3¼in.
Est. **£6,500-7,000**   *S*

1938 Vincent-HRD Series 'A' 1000cc Solo Motorcycle, V twin cylinder engine, overhead valve, 4 stroke, 84mm bore x 90mm stroke, 4 speed gearbox, chain final drive, Brampton front forks, pivoted fork at rear, tyres 3½ x 19in.
£20,000-21,000   *S*

1947 Vincent-HRD Black Shadow Model B to C Specification Solo Motorcycle. £15,000-17,000   *P*

1949 Vincent Rapide Series B 1000cc Solo Motorcycle, V twin cylinder, air cooled, overhead valve engine, 84mm bore, 998cc, 4 speed posi-stop gearbox, chain final drive, Girdraulic front forks, cantilever rear suspension.
£8,300-8,500   *S*

1948 Vincent-HRD Rapide Series B 1000cc Solo Motorcycle, V twin cylinder, air cooled overhead valve engine, 84mm bore x 90mm stroke, 998cc, 4 speed posi-stop gearbox, chain final drive, Girdraulic front forks, cantilever rear suspension.
£8,000-10,000 *S*

Announced in 1946, the Vincent Series B Rapide represented the culmination of the efforts of Irving and Vincent to produce a motorcycle worthy of carrying on the traditions set by the pre-war Series A machines.

The epitome of the British Classic bike of the 50s, the Black Shadow followed a distinguished line of Phil Irving designed V twins from the Vincent factory in Hertfordshire.

1951 Vincent 500cc Comet Solo Motorcycle.
£16,000-18,000 *P*

1950 Vincent-HRD Black Shadow Model C Solo Motorcycle.
Est. **£16,000-20,000** *P*

1951 Vincent Rapide Series C 1000cc Solo Motorcycle, V twin cylinder, air cooled engine, overhead valve, 4 stroke, 84mm bore x 90mm stroke, 998cc, 4 speed foot change gearbox, chain final drive, Vincent Girdraulic front forks, pivoted fork rear suspension, tyres 19 x 3¼in front, 19 x 4in rear.
£10,000-11,000 *S*

1952 Vincent Black Shadow 1000cc Motorcycle Combination, V twin cylinder, air cooled engine, overhead valve, 4 stroke, 84mm bore x 90mm stroke, 998cc, 4 speed foot change gearbox, chain final drive, Girdraulic front forks, pivoted fork rear suspension.
Est. **£20,000-23,000** *S*

Philip Vincent designed and marketed the Black Shadow, a sports version of the Rapide, with the distinctive black engine producing some 55bhp at 5,700rpm compared with 45bhp at 5,300rpm from the standard Rapide.

1950 Vincent Rapide Series C 998cc Solo Motorcycle, V twin cylinder, air cooled engine, overhead valve, 4 stroke, 84mm bore x 90mm stroke, 998cc, 4 speed posi-stop gearbox, chain final drive, Girdraulic front forks, pivoted fork rear suspension, tyres 19in.
£8,000-10,000 *S*

1968 Yamaha TD1C 250cc Racing Motorcycle.
£4,600-5,000 *P*

1952 Vincent Series C Comet 500cc Solo Motorcycle, single vertical cylinder air cooled engine, overhead valves, 4 stroke, 500cc, 4 speed gearbox, Girdraulic forks with sprung frame at rear, chain final drive.
£4,700-5,000 *S*

Introduced for the 1973 racing season the TZ 350 featured water cooling but otherwise was a very similar machine to the successful TR3, its predecessor. The TZ 350 dominated the 350, 500 and open classes on circuit.

c1980 Yamaha TZ 350G Solo Racing Motorcycle, inclined twin cylinder engine, water cooled, 2 stroke, 64mm bore x 54mm stroke, 347cc, 6 speed gearbox, chain final drive, telescopic front fork suspension, swinging arm monoshock rear suspension, tyres 18in.
Est. £1,700-2,000 *S*

1955 Vincent Black Shadow Series D 1000cc Motorcycle, 70° V twin cylinder, air cooled engine, overhead valve, 84mm bore x 90mm stroke, 1000cc, 4 speed gearbox, chain final drive, telescopic front forks, pivoted rear suspension.
£22,000-25,000 *S*

1920 Zenith Gradua 1000cc Solo Motorcycle, V twin cylinder engine, air cooled, side valve, 1000cc, Zenith Gradua adjustable pulley gear, girder fork and coil spring front suspension, rigid rear suspension.
£9,000-10,000 *S*

PEDAL CARS

A Scratch-built Alvis 12.50, English, post-war model car, sheet metal with aluminium and steel construction, treadle drive, detailed imitation engine, shock absorbers, honeycombed radiator, mascot, leather-covered steering wheel, dummy instruments, rear mounted spare wheel, polished aluminium finish, blue upholstery, length 60in, width 27½in, wire spoked wheels, pneumatic tyres 12½in x 2¼in, excellent condition.
£4,500-4,750   *S(S)*

An Atco 98cc Two Seat Trainer, c1947, not registered, single cylinder, 2 stroke engine.
£4,500-5,500   *S*

Charles H. Pugh Ltd. commenced production of the Atco Trainer for use in schools for basic training in car handling following the introduction of the Driving Test in 1935.

An Austin Pathfinder Racing Pedal Car, English, c1948, pressed steel construction, treadle drive, bonnet with leather straps, dummy engine, handbrake, original Austin transfers, cream with red wheels and upholstery, length 61in, width 26in, pressed steel wheels, pneumatic rubber tyres 12½in x 2¼in, very good, original condition.
£2,000-2,500   *S(S)*

A Bugatti Type 52 Replica Half-Scale Electric Car, c1989, steel chassis and aluminium body construction, 24 volt electric motor, gearbox driving 2 forward and 2 reverse speeds, cable operated handbrake to all 4 wheels, instrument panel, side-mounted spare wheel, etc, black leather upholstery, French blue finish, length 73in, cast polished alloy wheels with integral brake drums, pneumatic tyres, excellent condition.
£3,000-3,300   *S(S)*

A Eureka Bugatti (based on Type 35) Pedal Car, French, c1931, pressed steel chassis and body, treadle drive, red finish, length 44in, width 19½in, pressed steel disc wheels, solid rubber tyres, good unrestored condition, replacement tyres.
£400-450   *S(S)*

A Post-War Bentley Pedal Car, dark green, leather covered body with leather bonnet strap over polished metal body, Lucas 'headlamps', radiator finished with number 4, length 52in.
£3,300-3,500   *S*

A Child's Ford Pedal Car, English, 1950s, with handbrake, wing mirror and indicator level, length 43in.
£250-300 *S*

A Triang Racing Pedal Car, English, c1950, pressed steel construction, adjustable treadle drive, dark green, repainted finish, length 47¼in, width 18½in, wire spoked wheels, pneumatic tyres 12½in x 2¼in, good condition.
£1,100-1,200 *S(S)*

A Triang Child's Pedal Car, English, c1935, repainted black and navy blue with levered steering and folding windscreen, length 34in.
£300-350 *S*

A child's pedal sports car, the wooden body painted in British racing green and with twin headlamps, bulb horn, hinged windscreen and side door, wire wheels with pneumatic tyres, renovated. **£1,750-2,500** *S*

A Scratch-built 1920s Aero Morgan, English model car, c1980, tubular chassis, sheet metal body, chain to rear wheel drive, detailed dummy engine and suspension, twin external exhausts, lights, etc, red with yellow and black lining, length 65in, width 28in, wire spoked wheels, pneumatic tyres 16 x 3in, very good condition.
£3,000-3,300 *S(S)*

An Austin J40 pedal car, the pressed metal coachwork painted red, with hinged bonnet opening to show a simulated engine bay, with electric headlamps, and printed dashboard instruments. **£720-800** *S*

COMPETITION CARS

1965 Alfa Romeo Giulia TZ1 1.6 Litre Tubolare Zagato Two Seat Competition Berlinetta.
Est. £220,000-280,000   *B*

1974/75 Alfa Romeo Tipo 33 TT-12.
Est. £530,000-600,000   *CNY*

Miller's is a price GUIDE not a price LIST

1982/83 Arrows A.6 Formula One Grand Prix Car.
Est. £125,000-150,000   *C*

The 1984 season saw the much awaited BMW turbo engine installed.

1956 Aston Martin DB3S 3 Litre Sports Racing Two Seater Ex-Works Team Le Mans 24-Hour Race Car, the pair of brand new team DB3S's built for 1956 were the last to be built, chassis '9 and '10, they were intended primarily for Le Mans and featured improved aerodynamic shape with Ferrari like nose intakes, fared-in headlights and a large headrest behind the driver. Est. **£900,000-1,200,000** *B*

Amongst all competition Aston Martins the series of DB3S factory team cars built and campaigned during 1953-56 is widely regarded as being the most attractive. This actual car finished second in the 1956 Le Mans 24-Hour race driven by Stirling Moss and Peter Collins, winning its 3 litre class and being beaten only by the larger engined Jaguar D-Type of Ron Flockhart and Ninian Sanderson.

1967 Austin Healey 1.3 Litre Le Mans Sprite Two Seat Competition Coupé. Est. **£40,000-60,000** *B*

1960 Austin Healey 3000 Mk I Competition Coupé, Ex-Sebring 12 Hours Works Team. Est. **£100,000-130,000** *B*

In preparation for the Sebring 12 Hours World Championship qualifying race, the Donald Healey Motor Car Company's experimental workshop at The Cape, Warwick, had initially taken delivery of 5 brand new HBN7 series Mk I cars during December 1959. After race-preparation and testing at Silverstone, they were shipped to Newark, New Jersey. Four of them, British registered UJB140, 141, 142 and 143, were then transported to the team's Sebring base at Murphy's Garage, Avon Park, Florida. The fifth car, UJB144, was dispatched to the Austin Motor Company, Toronto, for a Canadian competition programme. As built at Abingdon, these 3000 Mk Is were listed as follows 'RHD, British Racing Green, black trim, no overdrive, wire wheels, no heater and hardtops'.

The first open-bodied Le Mans Sprite of 1960 finished 16th at 85.63mph. Two Sprites ran in 1961, neither finishing, one in 1963 again retired, one in 1964 finished 24th at 89.5mph, two entries in 1965 saw one finish 12th at 96.4mph and in 1966 neither of the two entries finished. Initially it appeared in 1965 but it was then prepared specifically for Le Mans in 1967 as a works entry and finished 15th overall at an average speed of 100.8mph. It was entered for the second time at Le Mans the following year and it again finished 15th, after averaging 94.8mph. This won 'The Motor' Trophy for the first British car to finish.

1971 Biota 1.3 Litre Hill Climb Two Seater. Est. £5,000-8,000 *B*

This is thought to be the car which Chris Seaman drove to first overall placing in the Castrol BARC 1972 hill climb championship.

1964 Brabham F2 BT, 2 new racing formulae started in 1964, Formula 2 and Formula 3, and Jack Brabham who was now building cars since striking out on his own from the Cooper team, built much the same chassis for both. A light simple space frame with outboard brakes and wishbone suspension at the front and radius arms at the back, the car was easy to maintain and predictable to drive. In spite of rumours that BMC and Renault would build 1000cc engines for the new Formula 2, only Cosworth produced their single camshaft S.C.A., based on the standard Ford 4 cylinder 109E block, and this engine won every race, apart from a problem with tappets breaking. Est. £80,000-120,000 *C*

1962 Brabham BT2 Formula Junior Racing Car, with mid-mounted Cosworth/Ford 105E 4 cylinder engine, 1100cc, with pushrod operated overhead valves, 2 twin choke Weber carburettors, rated to develop approximate 105bhp at 7,400rpm, tubular space frame chassis, with independent front and rear suspension by tubular arms and coil springs/damper units, rear mounted Hewland 5 speed transaxle gearbox, rack and pinion steering, outboard mounted disc type brakes front and rear, cast magnesium alloy wheels, bolt on type, 13in diam. Est. £36,000-44,000 *C(A)*

1967 Brabham BT21A Formula 2 Racing Car, with mid-mounted Ford 4 cylinder engine, twin overhead camshaft, 1600cc, 2 Weber twin choke carburettors, rated to develop approximately 160bhp at 8,000rpm, tubular space frame chassis, with independent front and rear suspension by tubular arms and coil spring/damper units, rear mounted Hewland 5 speed transaxle gearbox, rack and pinion steering, outboard mounted disc type brakes front and rear, cast magnesium alloy bolt-on type wheels, 13in diam. Est. £32,000-40,000 *C(A)*

1962 BRM P578 1½ Litre Formula 1 Single Seater. £450,000-500,000 *B*

Christened 'Old Faithful' by its British Racing Motors team mechanics, this particular car, 5781, was used by Graham Hill for the majority of the 1962 season races in which he eventually won the Drivers' World Championship title and brought BRM their long awaited victory in the Formula 1 Constructors' Cup.

Did you know

MILLER'S Collectors Cars Price Guide builds up year by year to form the most comprehensive photo-reference system available

1974/75 BRM P.201 Formula 1 Grand Prix Car, with V12 engine, bore 74.6mm x stroke 57.2mm, 2995cc, compression 11.5:1, 2 chain driven overhead camshafts per bank, 4 valves per cylinder, Lucas fuel injection, 450bhp at 11,000rpm, Marelli Dinoplex ignition, BRMP-161 gearbox, Borg & Beck clutch, double wishbones and outboard springs front suspension, lower wishbones, single top links twin radius rods and outboard springs rear, Koni shock absorbers, Lockheed brakes, wheelbase 101½in, Marston Excelsior fuel cells, 47 gallon capacity, weight of engine 360lb, gearbox 108lb, and tub 85lb.
£150,000-180,000   *C*

The 3 litre Grand Prix formula which began in 1966 was less kind to BRM than the 1½ litre one that preceded it. The team had won the World Championship and remained in contention throughout the preceding 5 years, but the search for a powerful and reliable 3 litre engine was to prove elusive.

The Brescia Bugatti was the model with which Ettore Bugatti established himself as a successful racing car designer and builder. The Type 13 Bugatti, the design of which had been completed just before the 1914-18 War, became known as the Brescia Bugatti after its resounding 1, 2, 3, 4 victory in the Voiturette race for the Italian Grand Prix, at Brescia in 1921. The racing Brescia model, with its efficient overhead camshaft 16 valve engine, twin magneto ignition, light and fast gear change, and excellent handling characteristics proved extremely successful in all types of motoring competition during the early 1920s, and was the popular choice for many amateur and semi-professional drivers.

1922 Bugatti Type 13 'Brescia', with 4 cylinder engine, single gear driven overhead camshaft, 4 valves per cylinder, bore 69mm x stroke 100mm, 1496cc, rated to develop approximately 50bhp at 4,500rpm, ignition by twin dashboard mounted magnetos, crankshaft carried on ball bearings with plain big ends, channel section side members with channel and tubular cross members chassis, front axle carried on semi-elliptic leaf springs, rear axle on reversed quarter elliptic leaf springs with friction type shock absorbers, 4 speed sliding mesh gearbox with external right-hand change lever, cable operated brakes on rear wheels, centre lock wire type wheels carrying beaded edge tyres.
Est. **£80,000-100,000**   *C(A)*

1953-63 Cooper Bristol 2 Litre Two Seat Sports Roadster. Est. £40,000-60,000 *B*

1949 Cisitalia Tipo 202 Sporting Coupé, with 4 cylinder in-line engine, water-cooled monobloc, bore 68mm x stroke 75mm, 1089cc, developing 55bhp at 5,500rpm, compression ratio 7.5:1, dual Weber 36 DR 4Sp carburettors, independent front suspension with transverse semi-elliptic leaf springs, trailing axle with semi-elliptic springs at rear, hydraulic shock absorbers all round. Est. **£48,000-64,000** *S(A)*

Designed by Dante Giancosa and Giovanni Savonuzzi, the Cisitalia was the venture of industrialist Piero Dusio into motor racing in the mid-1940s. Pininfarina was commissioned to design the bodywork for the 202 Sports Coupé.

Miller's is a price
GUIDE not a price
LIST

1959/60 Cooper Type 51 Mk IV Grand Prix Single Seater. £95,000-110,000 *B*

In 1955 the Cooper Car Company of Hollyfield Road, Surbiton, south west of London, introduced a successful central seat sports racing car with a Coventry-Climax, fire pump derived, water-cooled engine mounted in the rear and driving through a reversed Citroën 'traction-avant' gearbox. The following year saw a slipper bodied, open wheeled single seater developed from this design for newly announced 1500cc Formula 2. Cooper-Climax came to dominate this division in 1957, and a 1960cc variant was driven in the Monaco Grand Prix by Jack Brabham, finishing 6th. In 1958 Cooper's 'Rear Engined Revolution' really gathered pace.

1964/65 Cooper T72/73 1.5 Litre Formula 2 Single Seater. Est. £40,000-60,000 *B*

1977 Elfin MRSA 'Can-Am' Sports Racing Car, mid-mounted Chevrolet '302' small black V8 engine, pushrod operated valves, 5.0 litres, Scintilla magneto ignition, Lucas fuel injection, rated to develop approx. 505bhp at 8,000rpm, Monococque 'Tub' construction chassis with independent front and rear suspension by tubular arms and coil spring/damper units, Hewland model DG 300 transaxle gearbox, outboard mounted ventilated disc type brakes front and rear, aluminium alloy wheels with central bolt mounting, 13in diam. Est. **£40,000-60,000** *C(A)*

1964 Cooper King Cobra by Shelby, chassis No. CM/2/63, with Traco-Ford V8 engine, 4272cc, bore 101.6mm x stroke 73mm, 10:1 compression ratio 390bhp at 7,000rpm, 4 Weber carburettors dual choke 481DA, 4 speed manual gearbox transaxle McKee, production cars had 5 speed Colotti, unequal length wishbones, coil springs and dampers suspension front and rear, Dunlop disc brakes on all 4 wheels, Cooper cast magnesium 4 stud 8 spoke wheels, 4.50 x 15 front, 5.50 x 15 rear, wheelbase 91in.
Est. **£200,000-250,000**   *CNY*

Hoping to repeat the success of his front engined Cobras, Carroll Shelby looked for a racing car to meet the challenge of the mid-engined 2 seaters that were winning races on the American West Coast in 1962. A batch of 6 cars was laid down by John and Charles Cooper in Surbiton which were basically Cooper Monacos modified to take the 289cu in (4.3 litre) Ford V8 engine which had accomplished so much in the Cobra.

1968 Costin-Nathan Sports Racing GT, chassis No. GT2-698-030, new Lester Owen BMW 2 litre dry sump engine with twin DCOE Weber carburettors, producing 208bhp.
Est. **£80,000-100,000**   *C*

Designed by Frank Costin, who was also responsible for the beautiful Vanwall, this car was one of the most successful of the limited number of sports racing cars produced by Roger Nathan Racing between 1966 and 1970.

Make the Most of Miller's

CONDITION is absolutely vital when assessing the value of a vehicle. Top class vehicles on the whole appreciate much more than less perfect examples. However a rare, desirable car may command a high price even when in need of restoration

1949 Ferrari 166 Short Chassis/Formula Libre (ex Juan Fangio/Benedicto Campos, Froilan Gonzalez), chassis No. 011-F, engine No. 013-F, Type 166 supercharged Formula Libre, 60° V12, bore 60mm x stroke 58.8mm, 1992cc, max. 310bhp at 7,000rpm, single overhead camshaft per bank, 1-30 DCF Weber carburettor on petrol, 1-40 DO3C on mixture, 5 speed gearbox, unequal length 'A' arms-transverse leaf spring and Houdaille vane-type shock absorbers front suspension, swing-axle halfshafts, single radius arms, torsion bars (replaced by transverse leaf springs in 1949) Houdaille vane-type shock absorbers rear, finned alloy drum brakes, 16in centre lock Borrani wire spoke wheels, 5.50 x 16 front tyres, 7.00 x 16 rear, wheelbase 85.04in. The first 166, the cycle-winged Turin Grand Prix car, chassis 002C, was the first Ferrari ever sold, in January 1948 and the second identical car 004C is the oldest surviving original Ferrari which makes this example chassis No. 011, awaiting restoration, one of the most important and earliest short chassis, single seater, Ferrari racing cars.
Est. **£600,000-800,000**   *C*

The third of the 60° V12 engines designed for Ferrari by Giocchino Colombo was the Type 166, in which the cylinder bores of the Type 159 were enlarged to 60mm, the stroke kept at 58mm, giving each cylinder a capacity of 166.25cc. Colombo carried out the development work in the autumn of 1947-48 effectively ending the career of the original 1½ litre V12, Type 125.

1975 Ferrari T1, ex Niki Lauda.
£750,000+   *DHA*

1964/65 Ferrari Tipo 1512 1.5 Litre Flat 12 Formula 1 Grand Prix Single Seater. £1,500,000-1,750,000 *B*

Arguably the most sophisticated and complex car ever built to the 1½ litre Formula 1 of 1961 to 1965. It is the actual car in which works driver Lorenzo Bandini finished 2nd in the 1965 Monaco Grand Prix, and which was driven later by 1964 World Champion Driver John Surtees, and was later owned by him.

1965 Ferrari 4 Litre V12 Engine and Gearbox, engine No. 3638 11407, type No. TIPO 209, Ferrari V12 cylinder at 60° formation in seven-bearing light alloy block/crankcase, 3967cc, bore 77mm x stroke 71mm, 2 detachable light alloy cylinder heads, 2 overhead valves per cylinder, opposed to each other in part-spherical combustion chambers and operated by rockers from single overhead chain driven camshaft per cylinder head, 3 Weber twin choke 40 DCZ6 carburettors, compression ratio 8.8:1, maximum power 300bhp at 6,600rpm, maximum torque 299lb/ft at 5,000rpm, ZF 5 speed all synchromesh gearbox with 8.87in clutch plate, gear ratios, 1st 3.08, 2nd 2.12, 3rd 1.57, 4th 1.25, 5th 1.04. Est. **£25,000-35,000** *C*

1985 Ferrari 156/8S Turbo Grand Prix Car. £750,000+ *DHA*

1967 Ford GT40 Mk I Road GT Coupé, with coachwork by J.W. Automotive Engineering, Slough, with Ford V8 cylinder engine, 4728cc, bore 102mm x stroke 73mm, 335bhp at 6,500rpm, Holley 4 choke carburettor, ZF 5 speed manual gearbox, clutch twin plate Borg and Beck, sheet steel semi-monocoque chassis with square steel stiffening and glass fibre body panels, front suspension double wishbones coil/damper units, anti roll bar, rear twin trailing arms, transverse top links, lower wishbones coil spring/damper units, 15in BRM magnesium alloy wheels, solid disc brakes all round, wheelbase 95in, performance 165mph. Est. **£550,000-650,000** *CNY*

1986 Ford RS200, 350bhp Rally Specification Coupé, with 1.8 litre, 16 valve twin overhead camshaft mid-engine with Garrett turbocharger and intercooler located on roof, permanent 4 wheel drive, FF Development transmission, 5 speed with 3 viscous coupling differentials, ventilated disc brakes all round.
Est. **£100,000-130,000** *P*

1949 Healey Silverstone 2.4 Litre D-Type Two Seat Sports Roadster, completely restored.
£60,000-62,000 *B*

1970 World Cup Rally Hillman GT Saloon 1.7 Litre, this car lay 13th overall at Lisbon but the propshaft broke when running 10th overall and became one of the Rally's last retirements.
£3,520-4,000 *B*

This historic works prepared Hillman GT Saloon was sponsored and entered by the J. C. Bamford (Excavators) Limited company (for the 1970 World Cup Rally). It covered 16,000 miles throughout Europe and South America in 2 major sectors — London to Lisbon via Yugoslavia and Spain, and from Rio de Janeiro to Buenos Aires, Santiago, then to Colombia and another sea trip to Panama for a final 51 hour 'sprint' to Mexico City.

1953 Jaguar C-Type 3.4 Litre Sports Racing Two Seater, this car was originally dispatched new on January 2, 1953, to the Belgian Motor Company run by Jaguar importeuse, Mme Joska Bourgeois, she exhibited it at the 1953 Brussels Salon, and it was then sold to 1950 World Champion Driver, Dr. Giuseppe Farina, whose coachbuilding company was building special bodies for the Belgians.
£900,000-1,000,000 *B*

1955 Jaguar D-Type Sports Racing Car, the D-Type competition engine was developed from Jaguar's classic 6 cylinder twin overhead camshaft production engine, but incorporates many special features, including dry sump lubrication system, 3 Weber twin choke carburettors, rubber fuel tank and competition valve timing, with the capacity of 3.4 litres, it is rated to develop 275bhp at 5,750rpm, light alloy monocoque central 'tub' chassis, with tubular front sub frame, independent front suspension by torsion bars and unequal length wishbones, beam type rear axle, suspended on trailing links and torsion bar, 4 speed special competition all synchromesh gearbox, mated to triple plate racing clutch, rack and pinion steering, disc type brakes, 3 pad calipers at front, 2 pad at rear, power operated by gearbox driven hydraulic pump, 16in magnesium alloy wheels, centre lock disc type, with peg drive.
Est. **£80,000-120,000**   *C(A)*

1962-64 Jaguar 3.8 Litre E-Type Lightweight Sayer Low-Drag Coupé, Ex Dick Protheroe.
£900,000-1,000,000   *B*

Jaguar Mk II 3.8 Litre Competition Saloon, specially developed version of Jaguar's twin overhead camshaft 6 cylinder, bored to 3.95 litre capacity, recent dynamometer tests recorded 348bhp and 317ft/lb torque, semi-monocoque pressed steel chassis, independent front suspension by coil springs and wishbones, beam type rear axle mounted on quarter elliptic leaf springs with upper torque arms, 4 speed synchromesh gearbox, close ratio type with overdrive, high ratio re-circulating ball steering box, Dunlop disc type brakes front and rear, triple laced centre lock wire type wheels, 15in diam.
Est. **£48,000-60,000** C(A)

1972 KMW Interserie Porsche, with 2.4 litre Porsche engine, 5 speed gearbox mounted behind the rear axle.
Est. **£30,000-40,000** C

1975 Lancia Stratos, with V6 engine, 2418cc, 4 overhead camshaft mid-engine transversely mounted 9:1 C.R. 240bhp, bore 92.5mm x stroke 60mm, multi-plate dry plate clutch, ZF Limited Slip Differential 5 speed close ratio Ferrari competition gearbox, 2 door unitory steel construction chassis with fibreglass bodywork, front double unequal length wishbones with heavy duty coil springs, anti-roll bar and telescopic shock absorbers suspension, rear lower wishbones with vertical struts, heavy duty coil springs and telescopic shock absorbers, all suspension rose jointed and of competition specification, competition ventilated disc brakes, wheelbase 86in, left-hand drive.
Est. **£80,000-100,000** C

The story of 'Stratos' goes back to the 1970 Turin motor show where Bertone the Italian coachbuilder exhibited a futuristic wedge-shaped concept car with a mid-engined Fulvia 1600 HF engine and called Stratos, after an employee suggested this new car looked as though it had arrived from the Stratosphere.

1984 Lancia Rally '037' Competition Coupé, with coachwork by Pininfarina.
Est. **£50,000-80,000** C

Billed as the successor to the wonderful Lancia Stratos, the winner of no fewer than 62 World and European Championship events, the Lancia Rally '037' was derived from the Monte Carlo design which itself had been developed for the 1979 Giro d'Italia from the series winning Group 5 Monte Carlo Turbo circuit racing cars.

1960/61 Lotus Coventry Climax FPF Type 18 2.5 Litre Formula 1 Grand Prix Single Seater.
£77,000-80,000   *B*

Lotus S1 Formula Ford, totally restored.
£15,000-20,000   *PMS*

**961 Lotus Formula Junior
Racing Car,** with mid-mounted
cylinder engine, Ford 105E based,
100cc, with pushrod operated
verhead valves, 2 twin choke
Veber carburettors, rated to
evelop approx. 108bhp at
,000rpm, tubular space frame
hassis with independent front and
ear suspension by tubular arms,
rive shaft, and coil spring/damper
nits, rear mounted 4 speed
ansaxle gearbox, outboard
nounted disc type front brakes and
board drums at rear, Lotus
vobbly' cast light alloy bolt on disc
pe wheels, 13in diam front and
5in rear.
st. £24,000-32,000   *C(A)*

*he Lotus 20 was a development of
e original Formula Junior of 1960,
hich in turn was virtually identical
ith the brilliantly successful Lotus
8 Formula One car.*

**1965/66 Lotus Ford V8 Type 30
5.8 Litre Group 7 Sports Racing
Roadster.**
£165,000-170,000   *B*

**1970/71 Lotus Cosworth Type 72
3 Litre Formula 1 Single Seater.**
Est. £250,000-350,000   *B*

1967 Mallock U2 Mark 6B 1.6 Litre Formula 2 Single Seater, this is one of the famous series developed and manufactured over many years by Major Arthur Mallock who worked latterly with his son Ray of Formula 2 and Le Mans Group C racing frame, recently rebuilt, and exactly as raced in 1967.
Est. £10,000-14,000   B

At Zandvoort the car qualified faster than 2 of the true single seat F2 Brabhams, lapping at 1:39.8.

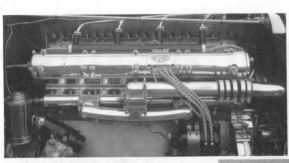

1933 Maserati Tipo 8CM 2.9 Litre Grand Prix Single Seater, the ex-Sommer, ex-Nuvolari, ex-Taruffi.
Est. £800,000-1,100,000   B

1967 McLaren-Ford Formula 2 Racing Car, with mid-mounted Ford-Cosworth FVA 4 cylinder engine, twin overhead camshaft, 1600cc, 2 Weber twin choke carburettors, rated to develop approx. 160bhp at 7,000rpm, monocoque 'tub' construction chassis, independent front and rear suspension by tubular arms and coil springs/damper units, rear mounted Hewland 5 speed transaxle gearbox, rack and pinion steering, outboard mounted disc type brakes front and rear, cast magnesium alloy bolt on type wheels, 13in diam.
Est. £60,000-80,000   C(A)

Bruce McLaren was only 20 years old when he won the New Zealand 'Drivers to Europe' Award which sent him to England. He was immediately associated with the Cooper Car Company, and in 1959 he joined the Cooper Formula 1 Team under the wing of Jack Brabham, taking over the No. 1 position in the Cooper Team in 1962 when Brabham left to found his own company. McLaren followed the same line in 1963, forming his own Racing Team, initially with specially built Coopers, but eventually developing his own very successful series of racing cars, based on the general design layout, and use of components similar to those employed by other racing car manufacturers in England at the time.

1961 Mercedes-Benz 300SL Engine, engine No. 198.980.1000310, 6 cylinder in line, water-cooled in 7 bearing cast iron block, 2996cc, bore 85mm x stroke 88mm, compression ratio 8.55:1, max. power 240bhp (SAE) at 6,100rpm, max. torque 217lb/ft (SAE) at 4,800rpm, detachable light alloy cylinder head with joint not perpendicular to cylinder bores, combustion chamber formed in top of piston and top of cylinder block, 2 overhead valves per cylinder staggered with inlet valves in one line and exhaust valves in other line and operated by rockers from chain driven single overhead camshaft, dry sump lubrication, fuel supply, Bosch mechanical direct fuel injection, ignition, coil and distributor.
Est. £20,000-25,000   C

1969 McLaren M6GT Prototype OBH 500H, chassis No. BMR M6GT-1, engine No. 8932386, Chevrolet Corvette LT1, bore 101.6mm x stroke 88.39mm, 5740cc, 11.0:1 compression, 4 barrel Holley carburettor, 370bhp at 6,000rpm, ZF Type 25, 5 speed 5DS-26 No. 209 gearbox, full monocoque with aluminium panelling chassis, bonded and riveted to steel bulkheads, unequal length upper and lower wishbones, anti-roll bar, and coil spring shock absorber units front suspension, wishbones and twin radius arms, anti-roll bar and coil spring shock absorber units rear, Girling brakes ventilated discs 12in diam with 16-3-LA calipers and dual hydraulic circuits, reinforced polyester resin panelling body, 15 x 10.5 wheels front, 15 x 14 rear, cast magnesium, Goodyear tyres, wheelbase 93.5in, front track 52in, rear 52in, length 155in approx., width 68in, height 41in, weight less fuel approx. 1,500lb, 40% front, 60% rear, recorded mileage 1,918.
Est. **£700,000-900,000**   *CNY*

Bruce McLaren's plans to produce a road car, which would have been made by an offshoot of Bruce McLaren Motor Racing, were cut short by his death in a testing accident in 1970. He had however completed a prototype which was going through an exhaustive programme of testing and development.

1974 McLaren M16C Indianapolis 500 Race Winner, McLaren built the car for the Indianapolis 500 in 1969, using the new turbo-charged Offenhauser 4 cylinder engine coupled with the Hewland LG 500 4 speed gearbox, the M15 was to be a good prototype for McLaren's Indy involvement, but for 1971, the new M16 was announced with its new wedge shape, incorporating many lessons learned in Formula 1, Donahue's M16B was to bring a race victory to the Penske-McLaren camp in 1972.
Est. **£310,000-325,000**   *SNY*

1976 McLaren M23 World Champion Winner, driven by James Hunt.
Est. **£470,000-530,000**   *DHA*

1933 MG L-Type Magna 1.1 Litre, to supercharged racing specification. Est. **£20,000-30,000** *B*

Based on the chassis and 1087cc 6 cylinder single overhead camshaft engine of the L-Type Magna model, this car was one of 486 examples of the L1 line built in 1933/34. Fitted with a 4 seater touring body, it was supplied new in 1933 by the marque's famous London distributors, University Motors, and its numberplate therefore bears the distinctive MG prefix. It is thought to have been transformed into an open 2 seater racing car in 1934.

1961 MGA Mk II BMC Competitions Department Works 1.6 Litre Rally Two Seater Coupé. Est. **£30,000-40,000** *B*

c1925 Phoenix GN Single Seat Racing Car, V twin cylinder engine, air-cooled, overhead valve, bore 85.7mm x stroke 85mm, capacity 1000cc, double chain drive to solid rear axle, quarter elliptic leaf spring suspension front and rear. Est. **£23,000-26,000** *S*

1934 MG K3 Supercharged Sports Racing Car, first registered 28th March 1934, chassis No. K3015 (original), engine No. 1170K, 6 cylinder in line, water-cooled monobloc, bore 57mm x stroke 71mm, 1086cc, single overhead camshaft, Roots-Marshall supercharger, approx. 120bhp at 6,500rpm, ENV-Wilson preselector gearbox, wheelbase 94in. Est. **£200,000-250,000** *S*

The MG K3 was first produced for the 1933 season and the first prototype took part in the Monte Carlo Rally and recorded fastest time in The Mont de Mules hillclimb which formed part of the event. The second prototype was used in preparation for the Mille Miglia and subsequently the next 3 production K3s took part in the event finishing 1st and 2nd in 1100cc class. The MG K3 could well be considered to be the most successful 1100c racing car of all time having overcome the 1100cc Maserati opposition in the Mille Miglia and there were plenty of customers for these sports/racing cars which could be used readily as pure racing cars having easily removable road equipment.

1968 Piper GTR Le Mans, race prepared Lotus twin cam engine, power output approx. 185bhp, Hewland Mk 8 5 speed gearbox with limited slip differential. **£40,000-50,000** *ADT*

A rare Piper GTR Le Mans, this is an original Works car of only 4 made and it was entered for the 1969 24 Hour Le Mans Race. Sponsored by Harper Cars Ltd., it was No. 48 to be driven by T. J. Lalonde.

1955 Porsche Typ 550-1500 1.5 Litre Rennsport Sports Racing Spyder.
£450,000-500,000   *B*

Miller's is a price GUIDE not a price LIST

1965 Porsche 906, with 6 cylinder engine, air-cooled twin valve, 2 chain driven overhead camshafts, displacement 2300cc, 5 speed gearbox, steel tube spaceframe, plastic body, independent suspension, dual circuit disc brakes, wheelbase 2200mm, weight 675kg, top speed approx. 280km/hr.
Est. **£280,000-360,000**   *S(A)*

1964 Porsche 904/6 Carrera GTS, 2 Litre mid-engined Two Seat Competition Coupé.
£410,000-420,000   *B*

1969 Porsche 908-02, chassis No. 02-018, engine No. 903-03013-1, flat 8 cylinder, original 2996cc, bore 85mm x stroke 66mm, 10.4:1 compression ratio, 350bhp, Porsche factory uprated to 3.3 litres with 90mm pistons and cylinders, air-cooled twin overhead camshaft 2 plugs per cylinder, dry sump lubrication, Bosch fuel injection and belt driven cooling fan, aluminium tube frame chassis with fuel cell and fibreglass 'Flounder' style open bodywork with front and rear spoilers, Porsche type 916, 5 speed gearbox, aluminium caliper brakes with cast iron ventilated discs, wheels 15in centre lock magnesium 5 spoke with 9in wide fronts and 12in rears.
Est. **£750,000-900,000**   *CNY*

The first examples of the Porsche 908 were raced in 1968 but several developmental problems were encountered. These were soon resolved so that by 1969 the 908/02 Spyders with improved engines, reduced weight, new transmission, and better visibility dominated most races and brought Porsche their first overall World Championship title. Although 917s were being introduced, factory drivers usually preferred the more reliable, predictable and nimble 908.

**1972/73 Porsche Kremer RS/RSR
2.8 Litre, Competition Coupé,
RHD.
£72,000-75,000**   *B*

*Possibly only 2 right-hand drive
Porsche RSRs or Kremer built RSRs
are known to have been built.*

**1981 Porsche 924 GTR/944 Turbo
'Le Mans',** basic Porsche 944
engine, bore 100mm x stroke
78.9mm, 2500cc.
Est. **£88,000-104,000**   *S(A)*

*This car started life as the Porsche
Cars Australia entry for the Le Mans
24 Hour Race. Unfortunately it was
plagued by a variety of mechanical
problems and failed to qualify.*

**1973/74 Shadow DN3A Formula
1 Grand Prix Car,** chassis No. 3,
8 cylinder 90° V Formation
Cosworth DFV engine, 4 overhead
camshafts, 4 valves per cylinder,
2993cc, bore 85.7mm x stroke
64.8mm, transistorised ignition
460bhp at 10,000rpm, 5 speed
Hewland gearbox with transaxle,
4 wheel disc brakes, independent
wishbone and coil spring dampers
front suspension, independent
wishbones and radius rods with
outboard coil damper units rear,
wheelbase 108in, front track 62in,
rear 64in.
Est. **£100,000-120,000**   *C*

> ## Make the Most of
> ## Miller's
> *CONDITION is absolutely
> vital when assessing the
> value of a vehicle. Top
> class vehicles on the whole
> appreciate much more
> than less perfect examples.
> However a rare, desirable
> car may command a high
> price even when in need of
> restoration*

1988 017 Tyrrell, driven by
Jonathan Palmer.
£120,000-130,000   *DHA*

1931 Talbot 105 (Fox and Nicholl) Team Car, GO54, chassis No. 31054, engine No. AV33, 6 cylinder in line, 2969cc, bore 75mm x stroke 112mm, 132bhp at 4,800rpm, 10.0:1 C.R. (Benzole Fuel), overhead valves with Roesch pushrods and rockers, 4 speed close ratio gearbox, Zenith 48mm down draught carburettor, wheelbase 114in, track front and rear 56in, semi-elliptic front suspension, rear quarter elliptic, drive by torque tube, wheels 19in, centre lock wire, 35 gallon fuel tank.
Est. **£220,000-300,000**   *C*

The epic dual between Bentley and Mercedes in the 1930 Le Mans 24 Hour race overshadowed the remarkable performance of the 2 Talbot 90s that finished 3rd and 4th overall. These new cars were designed and built by George Roesch of Clement Talbot Ltd., Barlbey Road, North Kensington, London. They were only 2.3 litre capacity and of quite simple design being pushrod overhead valve and not the more popular overhead camshaft, and used only a single Zenith down draught carburettor. Their

performance and reliability was truly amazing and to add to their true production touring body design were almost silent in operation. In addition to 3rd and 4th overall, they won the coveted Index of performance award and their class, this was the beginning of a complete domination in the 3 litre class of endurance racing by the London Talbots.

1969 Triumph 2.5 PI 2.5 Litre Works Rally Saloon.
Est. **£20,000-30,000**   *B*

NUMBER PLATES

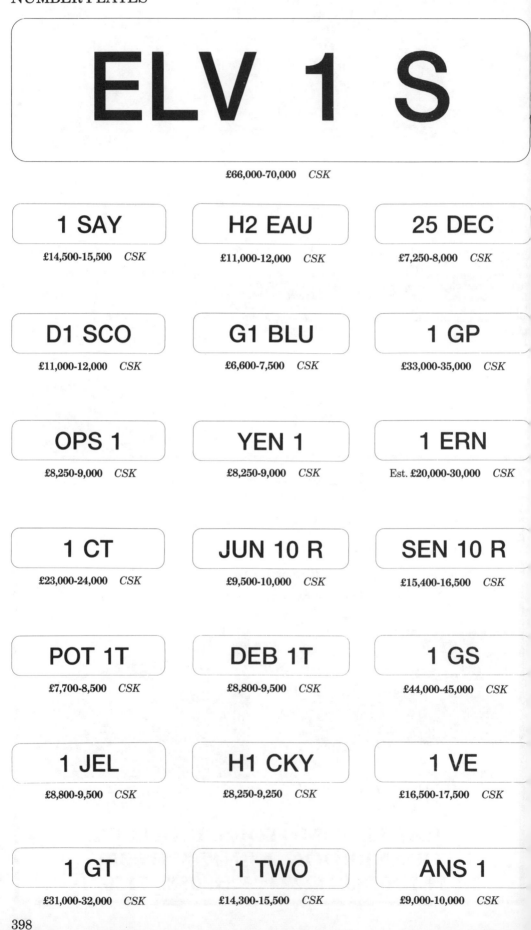

ELV 1 S

£66,000-70,000 *CSK*

1 SAY

£14,500-15,500 *CSK*

H2 EAU

£11,000-12,000 *CSK*

25 DEC

£7,250-8,000 *CSK*

D1 SCO

£11,000-12,000 *CSK*

G1 BLU

£6,600-7,500 *CSK*

1 GP

£33,000-35,000 *CSK*

OPS 1

£8,250-9,000 *CSK*

YEN 1

£8,250-9,000 *CSK*

1 ERN

Est. £20,000-30,000 *CSK*

1 CT

£23,000-24,000 *CSK*

JUN 10 R

£9,500-10,000 *CSK*

SEN 10 R

£15,400-16,500 *CSK*

POT 1T

£7,700-8,500 *CSK*

DEB 1T

£8,800-9,500 *CSK*

1 GS

£44,000-45,000 *CSK*

1 JEL

£8,800-9,500 *CSK*

H1 CKY

£8,250-9,250 *CSK*

1 VE

£16,500-17,500 *CSK*

1 GT

£31,000-32,000 *CSK*

1 TWO

£14,300-15,500 *CSK*

ANS 1

£9,000-10,000 *CSK*

DEN 1M	**1 BEB**	**1 NKS**
£25,500-26,500 *CSK*	£7,700-8,500 *CSK*	£27,500-30,000 *CSK*
1 FT	**15 VAT**	**1 VEG**
£17,600-18,500 *CSK*	Est. £10,000-15,000 *CSK*	£12,650-13,500 *CSK*
TAX 1T	**H1 PPY**	**1 SPY**
£8,250-9,250 *CSK*	£10,000-11,000 *CSK*	£17,600-18,500 *CSK*
1 CES	**944 POR**	**1 MAM**
£24,000-25,000 *CSK*	£11,000-12,000 *CSK*	£15,400-16,500 *CSK*
1 S	**MAJ 1D**	**1 BR**
£88,000-90,000 *CSK*	£24,200-25,000 *CSK*	£55,000-58,000 *CSK*
1 TAJ	**H1 LDA**	**TSB 1**
£17,600-19,000 *CSK*	£29,700-31,000 *CSK*	£12,100-13,000 *CSK*
B1 NGO	**G1 LES**	**PAS 1**
£26,400-27,500 *CSK*	£31,000-33,000 *CSK*	£17,600-19,000 *CSK*
1 DJ	**1 ANA**	Miller's is a price GUIDE not a price LIST
£30,000-32,000 *CSK*	£10,000-11,000 *CSK*	

399

NUMBER PLATES

POP 1T £5,000-6,000 *CSK*	**1 JES** £11,000-13,000 *CSK*	**1 SA** £27,000-29,000 *CSK*
UFO 1 £13,200-14,500 *CSK*	**1 NFO** £8,250-10,000 *CSK*	**1 OTA** £7,150-8,000 *CSK*
1 JT £33,000-35,000 *CSK*	**1 GG** £23,100-25,000 *CSK*	**ROS 1** £10,450-11,500 *CSK*
H1 LLS £14,300-15,500 *CSK*	**1 MAY** £14,300-15,500 *CSK*	**49 ERS** £6,050-7,000 *CSK*
HOB 1T £9,000-10,000 *CSK*	**1 JJ** £18,000-20,000 *CSK*	**FLA 1R** £13,500-14,500 *CSK*
1 VAN £27,000-28,000 *CSK*	**1 DR** £27,500-30,000 *CSK*	**MER 1T** £6,000-7,000 *CSK*
1 DES £20,000-22,000 *CSK*	**Miller's is a price GUIDE not a price LIST**	**H1 PPO** £16,500-18,000 *CSK*
300 SL £62,000-65,000 *CSK*	**1 DB** £32,000-35,000 *CSK*	**SUS 1E** £35,000-38,000 *CSK*

AUTO ART

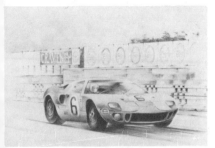

Bob Murray, GT40 1969 winner of
Le Mans, framed and glazed.
£300-400 *S*

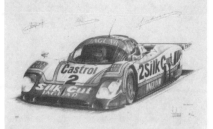

Alan Stammers, 1988 Silk Cut
Jaguar Le Mans Champions, a
limited edition print of a pencil
drawing of the Silk Cut Jaguar
No. 2, numbered 45/100, signed and
dated by the artist and signed by
J. Dumfries, J. Lammers and
A. Wallace, 18 by 28½in (46 by
72cm).
£720-800 *S*

Make the Most of Miller's

*Price ranges in this book
reflect what one should
expect to pay for a similar
example. When selling,
however, one should
expect to receive a lower
figure. This will fluctuate
according to a dealer's
stock, saleability at a
particular time, etc. It is
always advisable, when
selling, to approach a
reputable specialist dealer
or an auction house which
has specialist sales*

Michael Turner, French Grand Prix
Record breakers 1925-34, pencil
drawings of 1925 Renault 40cv,
1925 Citroën 'Rosalie' 8cv and the
Renault 'Nerasport' signed in
pencil, 12½ by 8in (32 by 20cm).
£120-150 *S*

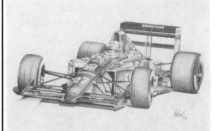

Alan Stammers, 1989 Ferrari 640
Nigel Mansell GB, a limited edition
print numbered 24/250, signed and
dated by the artist and Nigel
Mansell, framed and glazed, 21½ by
33in (54 by 84cm).
£720-800 *S*

Dion Pears, BOAC 500, acrylic on
canvas, signed by the artist, framed,
29 by 38in (74 by 97cm).
£500-600 *S*

Peter Robertson-Rodger, portrait of
Morley and wife in the 'Birkin'
Bentley 1946, an initialled and
dated watercolour, mounted,
framed and glazed together with
several associated monochrome
pictures, various sizes.
770-900 *S*

Michael Turner, 1936 Monte Carlo
Rally, a signed pencil drawing of the
winning Ford V8 Special of Christea
and Zamfires-Cou at the finish, 10
by 7in (25 by 18cm).
£600-700 *S*

Roy Nockolds, 1931 Monaco Grand
Prix, the winner, Chiron, in works
Bugatti, charcoal, 13 by 17in (34 by
43cm).
£450-600 *S*

Robin Lawrie, Midnight in Moscow,
signed, dated 1985, acrylic on
canvas, framed, 25 by 35in (63.5 by
89.5cm).
£800-1,000   *S*

Phil May, Silver Arrows,
watercolour and gouache, signed, 11
by 15in (28 by 38cm).
£350-400   *S*

Bob Murray, 1955 Grand Prix
d'Europe, signed, watercolour and
gouache heightened with white,
13½ by 17½in (34.5 by 44.5cm),
framed and glazed.
£250-350   *S*

Gordon Horner, World Champion
Redman on the works Honda, Isle of
Man, unsigned, black wash,
stamped with Motorcycle copyright,
16½ by 24in (42 by 61.5cm), framed
and glazed.
£100-200   *S*

Bryan de Grineau, 1931 Le Mans,
Leading Bentley at Speed, signed,
watercolour, grey wash and
charcoal, heightened with white, 19
by 25in (48 by 64cm).
£2,000-2,500   *S*

Phil May, The Blue Boys Era,
signed, watercolour and chalks
heightened with white, 9 by 12in
(22.5 by 30.5cm), mounted, framed
and glazed.
£200-250   *S*

Hans A Muth, Alpha 1750, 1930,
unsigned, gouache and ink
heightened with white, reverse of
paper with studio stamp, 15½ by
23in (39.5 by 59cm), mounted,
framed and glazed.
£300-400   *S*

Alain Mirgalet, Ferrari and Bugatti, colour lithograph, signed and dated '86, 172/175, 22 by 29½in (55.5 by 75cm).
£500-600 *C*

Gordon Horner, Les Graham World 500cc Champion 1949, signed and dated 1949, monochrome wash heightened in white, 17 by 11in (43 by 28cm), mounted, framed and glazed.
£500-600 *S*

Bob Murray, 1934 Monaco Grand Prix, signed, watercolour and gouache heightened white, 13½ by 17½in (34.5 by 44.5cm), framed and glazed.
£200-300 *S*

Phil May, The Hon. Dorothy Paget's 4½ litre Bentley, signed, watercolour and chalks heightened with white, mounted, framed and glazed, 11 by 15in (28 by 38cm).
£350-450 *S*

Francesco Scianna, 1987 Mille Miglia, signed, charcoal and gouache, 27 by 39in (69 by 99cm), with a print of the Mille Miglia poster.
£300-400 *S*

Roy Nockolds, Louis Chiron, Bugatti Type 35, signed, airbrush and inks, mounted, framed and glazed.
£250-350 *S*

Roy Nockolds, The First Ford GT40S at Le Mans 1965, unsigned, watercolour and gouache, 12 by 15½in (30.5 by 39.5cm), mounted, framed and glazed.
£150-250 *S*

Roy Nockolds, Isle of Man Tourist Trophy – Retrospective View 1927, signed and dated 1927, charcoal, pencil and gouache, 19½ by 30in (50 by 76cm), framed and glazed.
£400-500 *S*

Roy Nockolds, Duesenburg on Banking at Brooklands, unsigned, pencil heightened with white, 9½ by 14½in (24 by 37cm).
£120-180 *S*

Michael Turner, Mercedes Grand Prix Car 1903, signed, gouache, 5 by 10in (12.5 by 25cm), mounted, framed and glazed.
£150-200 *S*

Michael Turner, Brands Hatch 1967, acrylic on board, signed by the artist, mounted, framed and glazed, 28 by 19in (71 by 49cm).
£3,500-5,000 *S*

This work was originally commissioned by the owners of Brands Hatch, Motor Racing Developments, in 1967 for use as an original for the World Championship Sportscar meeting posters and is one of Turner's best-known works.

Charles Crombie, Motoritis or Other Interpretations of the Motor Act, 12 colour prints, oblong quarto.
£1,100-1,500 *S*

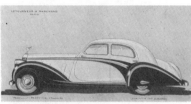

A Letourneur and Marchand Coachwork Design for a Rolls-Royce Phantom III, design No. 5690, gouache heightened with white, mounted and framed, 8 by 16in (20 by 41cm).
£400-500 *S*

John Dixon, Chauffeur-Driven Car at the Hunt, signed watercolour on board, 14 by 19in (36 by 49cm).
£720-800 *S*

This picture was used as the artwork for the front cover of Autocar, c1930.

G. Richardson, Bira in the E.R.A., signed G. Richardson '37 and Bira '37, watercolour and gouache, 8 by 10in (20 by 25cm).
£1,250-1,500 *S*

Michael Turner, 3 coloured lithographs, signed in ink, Scuderia Ferrari P3, Ferrari Alfa Romeo P2, Alfa Romeo Racing at Monza, Campari Alfa Romeo victory celebrations, 4 by 8in (10 by 20cm).
£150-250 *S*

> **Miller's is a price GUIDE not a price LIST**

Michael Turner, Bentley pit stop Le Mans 1927, colour lithograph, signed in ink, 10½ by 8in (26 by 20cm).
£270-350 *S*

Roy Nockolds, Lord Howe in the Bugatti Type 51 at Shelsley Walsh, signed gouache, 19 by 13½in (48 by 35cm).
£5,650-6,000 *B*

George Bishop, Brooklands, Battle of the Giants, charcoal drawing, signed, 16 by 34in (41 by 86cm).
£220-300 *S*

N. A. Watts, Gilles Villeneuve's Ferrari in the pits, signed gouache heightened with white, framed, 28 by 21in (71 by 53cm).
£1,200-1,500 *S*

G. Rosethorne, Le Mans start 1959, signed, oil on canvas, framed, 18 by 26in (46 by 66cm).
£250-350 *S*

Ernest Montaut, Circuit des Ardennes Belges 1906, coloured lithograph, 17 by 35½in (43 by 90cm).
£350-550 *S*

R. J. Lawrie, The Boxing Day Bentley Hunt, signed watercolour, 16 by 21in (41 by 53cm).
£550-650 *S*

Ernest Montaut, En Reconnaissance, coloured lithograph, 35½ by 18in (90 by 46cm).
£450-550 *S*

James Neave, Bluebird breaking world land speed record, Lake Eyre, Australia, 1964, charcoal with grey wash, heightened in white, signed and dated, mounted, framed and glazed, 15½ by 25in (39 by 64cm).
£2,200-3,000 *S*

R. J. Lawrie, Bugatti on the ski slopes, signed watercolour, 15 by 20½in (38 by 52cm).
£720-800 *S*

Michael Turner, 1924 Le Mans, Clement in the winning Bentley at Pontlieve Corner, signed, gouache, 18 by 23in (46 by 59cm).
£900-1,000   *S*

Dion Pears, Racing Jaguar XK120 Leading, signed, charcoal and grey wash heightened in white, 23 by 27½in (59 by 70cm).
£250-300   *S*

Michael Turner, Pit Stop, signed, watercolour and gouache, 10 by 14½in (25 by 37cm).
£500-600   *S*

F. Wood, Sorry No Petrol, signed, blue wash, pen and ink cartoon, 9 by 11in (23 by 28cm), framed and glazed.
£40-80   *S*

Michael Wright, 1908 Grand Prix, Courtade (Motobloc 36) and Lancia (Fiat 7), watercolour, signed, 18½ by 26½in (47 by 67cm).
£1,200-2,000   *C*

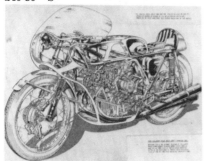

A cut-away drawing of Mike Hailwood's Honda 250/4 world championship motorcycle, published in Motorcycle magazine, February-March 1961, pen and ink, 17 by 27in (43 by 69cm), mounted, framed and glazed.
£300-350   *S*

C. Nevil, Torpedo Mont de Capote Janko, hand coloured lithograph, depicting 3 different positions of the hood to suit different weather conditions, 14 by 34in (35.5 by 86cm), framed and glazed.
£250-300   *S*

Michael Turner, Ferrari 312T at Monte Carlo Pit Stop 1975, signed, pencil drawing of Reutemann in the pits, framed and glazed.
£80-120   *S*

Michael Turner, Bugatti Type 51 in the Workshops, signed, watercolour and gouache, 9 by 12in (23 by 31cm).
£350-450   *S*

Bugatti Type 38, oil on canvas, slight crazing, unsigned.
£150-200   *S*

Carlo Demand, 1914 French Grand Prix, Lautenschlager in the Mercedes cornering at speed, signed, charcoal and grey wash, 19½ by 33in (49 by 84cm).
£800-1,000 *S*

George Bishop, Aston Martin at Le Mans, gouache on board, signed, 16½ by 22½in (42 by 57cm).
£3,200-4,000 *S*

James Dugdale, Bugatti and Mercedes in duel at the station hairpin at Monaco, signed, watercolour and gouache with white, 17 by 20½in (43 by 52cm).
£300-500 *S*

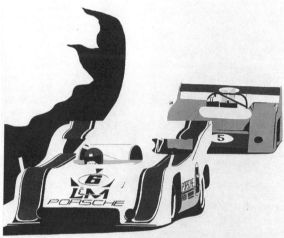

Benjamins, Porsche 917, Can-Am 1972, signed and dated '73, oil on canvas and framed, 40 by 40in (101.5 by 101.5cm).
£150-200 *S*

D. G. Mackay, 1932 Morgan three-wheeler, signed, watercolour heightened with white, 16 by 23½in (40.5 by 60cm).
£400-500 *S*

D. G. Mackay, 1930 4½ litre supercharged Bentley, watercolour heightened with white, signed, 16 by 23½in (40.5 by 60cm).
£500-600 *S*

Peko, Early Motoring, 2 hand coloured lithographs, signed Peko, some foxing, 9 by 15in (23 by 38cm), framed.
£300-400 *S*

Gamy, L'equipe 'La Licorne' dans le Tour de France 1913, Magneto Bosch, Carburateur Claudel, Roues Rudge Whitworth, colour lithograph, unframed, 18 by 59½in (46 by 150cm).
£400-500 *C*

Roy Nockolds, Dick Seaman,
Mercedes 2, a signed print,
mounted, framed and glazed, 12 by
15½in (31 by 40cm).
£375-450   *S*

Bryan de Grineau, Brooklands
Double Twelve Hour Race, 9-10
May 1930, signed watercolour,
heightened with white, Lurani in
the Alfa Romeo 1500, with Kenyon
Thom, 1st in class at 119.5kph, 18½
by 28in (47 by 71cm).
£7,750-8,000   *B*

Bryan de Grineau, Pescara Double
Twelve Hour Race, 12-13 August
1934, Lurani in the Bugatti Type
35, with Luigi Castelbarco, 1st in
class at 89.662kph, signed
watercolour, heightened with
white, 19 by 28½in (47.5 by 71.5cm).
£15,250-16,000   *B*

Bryan de Grineau, Eibsee
(Garmisch Partenkirchen),
7 February 1932, Lurani in his
special Alfa Romeo 6C-1750, 1st in
class at 91.80kph (record), signed
watercolour, heightened with
white, 19 by 28½in (47.5 by 71.5cm).
£10,500-11,500   *B*

Bryan de Grineau, Vermicino –
Rocca di Papa, 19 March 1933,
Lurani in the Maserati 4CS, 1st in
class at 97.70kph (record), signed
watercolour, heightened with
white, 18½ by 28½in (47 by 71.5cm).
£8,250-9,000   *B*

Bryan de Grineau, Crystal Palace,
London Grand Prix, 23 June 1938,
Lurani with the Maserati 1100cc,
4 cylinder, during practice, signed
watercolour, heightened with
white, 19 by 28½in (47.5 by 71.5cm).
£6,000-7,000   *B*

Nicholas Watts, 1934 Monaco
Grand Prix, Guy Moll in the
winning Alfa Romeo P3, leading
team mate Chiron to Casino Square
signed gouache, 29 by 43in (74 by
109cm).
£6,000-7,000   *B*

F. GORDON CROSBY

Bluebird, a signed charcoal, the reverse bearing the inscription 'Sir M. Campbell's Bluebird, a rough sketch, No. 64', 8 by 17in (20 by 43cm).
£1,750-2,500 *B*

Gordon Crosby, 1914 French Grand Prix, Lyons, Lautenschlager in the Mercedes, signed and dated 1914, charcoal and grey wash heightened with white, 17½ by 13in (45 by 33cm).
£4,000-5,000 *S*

Mannin Moar, Isle of Man 1933, the winning Alfa Romeo Monza, No. 6, of the Hon. Brian Lewis leads the Bugatti T51, No. 9, of T. Rose Richards, a signed and dated 1933 charcoal, heightened with white, 27 by 20in (69 by 51cm).
£5,500-6,500 *B*

Austin Seven on the Brooklands banking at night, signed charcoal, heightened with white, 18 by 28in (46 by 71cm).
£3,500-4,500 *B*

French Grand Prix 1913, Dieppe, Boillot in the winning Peugeot No. 8, signed charcoal, heightened with white, 20 by 29in (51 by 74cm).
£7,200-8,000 *B*

Supercharged 4½ litre Bentley, No. 10 at speed, signed oil on canvas, 23½ by 20in (60 by 51cm).
£31,000-35,000 *B*

La Jamais Contente, Jenatzy achieves a new land speed record of 62.85mph over the flying kilometre near Acheres, in France on April 29, 1899, signed and dated 1926, watercolour and charcoal, heightened with white, 16 by 26in (41 by 66cm).
£10,500-12,000 *B*

Busy Days on the Banking at
Brooklands, signed pen, ink and
crayon, 17½ by 13in (44 by 34cm).
£2,000-3,000   *B*

Bluebird at Daytona Beach, signed
and dated 1931, watercolour and
charcoal, heightened with white, 27
by 50½in (69 by 128cm).
£14,300-15,000   *B*

Gwenda Stewart in the record
breaking supercharged 2 litre
Derby-Miller at Montlhery in 1930,
signed watercolour and charcoal,
heightened with white, 27½ by 20in
(70 by 51cm).
£15,500-18,000   *B*

French Grand Prix 1924, Ascari's
riding mechanic failing to re-start
the Alfa Romeo P2, Divo's 12
cylinder Delage passes to gain 2nd
place, signed and dated 1929,
watercolour and charcoal, 18 by
28in (46 by 71cm).
£15,700-18,000   *B*

Alpine Rally 1933, the SS Jaguar,
No. 19, of Needham and Monroe
followed by an MG, signed charcoal,
heightened with white, 18 by 28½in
(46 by 72cm).
£6,600-7,600   *B*

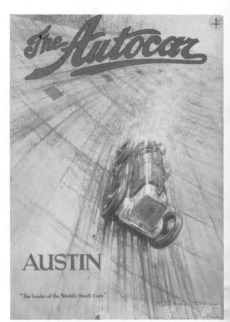

Original front cover artwork for an
Austin advertisement, signed and
dated 1931, watercolour and
charcoal, 30 by 21in (76 by 53cm).
£6,000-8,000   *B*

Nuffield Trophy Race Donington,
June 12, 1937, Dobson's ERA, R7B,
No. 12 leads May's ERA, R4D,
No. 18, signed and inscribed
'Donington 1937', charcoal
heightened with white, 20 by 26in
(50 by 67cm).
£7,200-9,000 *B*

Original front cover artwork for an
MG advertisement, signed
watercolour and charcoal, 24 by
20in (61 by 51cm).
£6,000-8,000 *B*

Panoramic view of Brooklands from
the Club House cocktail bar, signed
and dated 1939, charcoal and wash
heightened with white, 18 by 29½in
(46 by 75cm).
£10,000-12,000 *B*

Luis Fontes and John Hindmarsh in
the 1935 Le Mans winning Lagonda
M45 Rapide, caricature study,
signed, dated and inscribed on
mount, watercolour and charcoal
heightened with white, 14 by 10in
(36 by 25cm).
£5,300-8,000 *B*

Tourist Trophy Donington 1937,
signed, inscribed 'Donington 4/9/37'
with applied label bearing the
inscription '1937 T.T. Donington
Park', Comotti (Darracq 10) and Le
Begue (Darracq 9), original drawing
from the Autocar, charcoal
heightened with white, 19 by 26½in
(49 by 67cm).
£5,500-7,000 *B*

RAC International Trophy, Douglas, Isle of Man, 1937, ERA
leads Maserati, signed, inscribed Douglas and dated 1937, charcoal
heightened with white, 19½ by 26in (49 by 66cm).
£7,000-7,500 *B*

Kaye Don's Silver Bullet, engine
tests on the dynamometer, signed
and dated 1930, charcoal and wash
heightened with white, 18 by 29in
(46 by 74cm).
£4,500-5,000   *B*

Whitney Straight on the Maserati
8CM 2900, caricature study, signed
and dated 1935, inscribed on mount,
watercolour and pencil heightened
with white, 14 by 10in (36 by 25cm).
£2,700-3,200   *B*

MG Factory, signed and dated 1931,
the reverse with IPC archive stamp
and inscribed P1212-1213, 30 12 32
MG factory heading to SCHD article
The Human Element, charcoal
heightened with white, 19 by 30in
(49 by 76cm).
£5,000-5,500   *B*

Gordon Crosby, The White House
Corner Crash, Le Mans 1927, signed
and dated 1930, watercolour and
charcoal, 18 by 29in (46 by 73cm).
£46,000-48,000   *B*

Gordon Crosby, The French Grand
Prix 1921, Jimmy Murphy on his
winning 3 litre Duesenberg, No. 12,
at Mulsanne Corner, signed and
dated 1928, watercolour and
charcoal, 17 by 27in (43 by 69cm).
£13,000-14,000   *B*

Frederick Gordon Crosby, George
Eyston with his 1.1 litre MG Magic
Magnette, initialled, date 1935 and
inscribed George, pencil and
watercolour heightened with white,
7½ by 7in (19 by 17cm).
£1,000-1,500   *B*

Frederick Gordon Crosby, Freddie Dixon with his 2 litre Riley, signed and inscribed Freddie!, pencil and watercolour heightened with white, 10½ by 7in (27 by 18.5cm).
£1,200-2,500 *B*

Emancipation Day Anniversary 1928, The London to Brighton Run, signed, the reverse with The Autocar archive stamp, pen, ink and charcoal heightened with white, 15 by 26½in (38 by 68cm).
£9,000-10,000 *B*

EPHEMERA

A collection of 60 Iota Magazines, the official organ of the 500 Club, the near complete run of magazines for the years 1948 to 1953.
£800-900 *S*

Three Ferrari Yearbooks: l. 1953, red and black lithographic cover with photographic inset, c. 1956, blue lithographed cover, r. 1954, green, yellow and purple lithographic cover with chequer flag design.
£400-500 each *S*

> **Did you know**
> *MILLER'S Collectors Cars Price Guide builds up year by year to form the most comprehensive photo-reference system available*

A collection of 39 motoring interest postcards, including examples by 'Mike', D. Tempest and A. Taylor, from the 1930s.
£100-150 *S*

Posters

De Bax, Renault,
chromolithographic poster, laid
down on linen, 45 by 61in (115 by
155cm).
£1,000-1,300   *S*

Gerber, 1959 Grosser Preis von
Deutschland, chromolithographic
poster of Dino Ferrari and Peter
Collins on Avus Banking, 33 by 23in
(84 by 59cm).
£770-900   *S*

Targa Florio, Alfa Romeo, Palermo
10-13 Maggio 1973,
chromolithographic, 38 by 27in (96
by 69cm).
£170-200   *S*

An ADAC 1000 Kilometre
Nurburgring poster, 1959,
lithographed in yellow and black, 33
by 23in (84 by 59cm).
£280-350   *S*

Motor City Magic, Detroit,
Michigan, June 3-5, 1983, coloured
lithograph, laid down on linen, 36 by
24in (92 by 61cm).
£200-250   *S*

A Nurburgring Photographic
poster, Clay Regazzoni in the
Ferrari 312 B3, 35 by 24in (89 by
61cm).
£90-150   *S*

B. K. Bull, Racing Car Show,
Olympia, coloured lithograph, 30 by
20in (76 by 51cm).
£150-200   *S*

P Calla, XVI 1000 Miglia, Coppa Franco Mazzotti, Brescia 24 Aprile 1949, lithograph in colours on card, 13 by 9½in (33 by 24cm).
£770-800   *CNY*

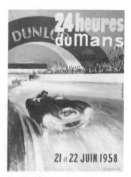

Beligond, Le Mans 1958, mounted and framed.
£250-300   *S*

An RAC British Grand Prix Silverstone 1965 poster, lettered in red and white on blue, with picture of a Ferrari, dated 10 July 1965, creases and adhesive tape marks, framed and glazed, 30 by 20in (76 by 51cm), and a press armband for the British Grand Prix Silverstone 1958, mounted in a frame.
£150-200   *S*

Dennis Simon, XXII Mille Miglia, Brescia 1 Maggio 1955, colour poster showing the Moss and Jenkinson Mercedes 300SLR, signed and autographed by Stirling Moss, 29 by 23½in (74 by 60cm).
£700-750   *C*

Guy Leygnac, 15 et 16 juin 1963, original colour poster, unframed, 22½ by 15½in (57 by 39.5cm).
£500-600   *C*

24 Heures du Mans, a collection of official programmes from 1949 to 1964 inclusive, the 1959 programme autographed by Carroll Shelby and Roy Salvadori who won the race that year for Aston Martin.
£2,500-3,000   *CNY*

Beligond, Le Mans 24 Hour Race, Shell lithographed advertising poster, 26 by 17in (66 by 43cm), framed and glazed.
£250-350   *S*

A Swiss Grand Prix poster, 1966, Sierre Montana Crans, coloured lithographic poster, 25 by 17½in (64 by 45cm).
£200-250   *S*

24 Heures du Mans, a collection of original posters from 1959 to 1971, including both posters produced for 1968 when the race was postponed from June to September due to a student uprising in France, unframed, 23½ by 16in (60 by 41cm).
£2,500-3,000   *CNY*

Photographs

Three colour photographic prints of Jaguar XK150s, racing at Silverstone, 1951, including Stirling Moss and Peter Walker.
£250-350 *S*

A rare album of 37 Le Mans photographs, 1952-56, including Aston Martin DB3S, Mercedes SLRs, Lotus Climax IX, Austin Healey 100s, Maseratis, Bristols, Triumph TR2s, Frazer Nash, Jaguar C-Type, Mercedes Gullwing, in album, 5 by 7in (13 by 18cm).
£1,100-1,500 *S*

Five colour photographic prints of Ferraris racing at Silverstone and Aintree, 1952-57, including Fischer, Ascari and Farina, 7½ by 9½in (19 by 24cm).
£200-300 *S*

Three D-Type Jaguar colour racing prints, Silverstone 1955, including Mike Hawthorne and Tony Rolt, 7½ by 9½in (19 by 24cm).
£120-150 *S*

A photograph of Guyot and Parsy at Le Mans in 1957, seated on their Maserati 200S on their finishing parade lap, mounted, framed and glazed, 18 by 23in (46 by 49cm).
£300-400 *S*

A photograph of Stirling Moss at Le Mans in 1957, with American driver Harry Schell, talking about their Maserati 450S Coupé before the race, mounted, framed and glazed, 23 by 18in (59 by 46cm).
£300-400 *S*

An original photograph of a Mercedes 300SL Gullwing at Le Mans 1956, showing the only privately owned 300SL to race at Le Mans, mounted, framed and glazed, 17 by 23in (43 by 59cm).
£170-300 *S*

An original photograph of Briggs Cunningham at Le Mans 1955, in his D-Type Jaguar, mounted, framed and glazed, 18 by 23in (46 by 59cm).
£200-300 *S*

A collection of photographs of
D-Type Jaguars at Le Mans,
including drivers Sanderson and
Flockhart, mounted, framed and
glazed, in various sizes.
£420-500 *S*

Ninteen photographs of Ferrari 365
GBT/4 Daytona competiton Coupés,
that raced in the Le Mans 24-hour
race between 1972-75, contained in
9 frames, various sizes.
£530-600 *S*

A pair of photographs of Ferraris at
Le Mans in 1956, showing Ferrari
625 LM of De Portago and Hamilton
and the Ferrari 195s of Tavano and
Meyat, both mounted, framed and
glazed, 18 by 23in (46 by 59cm).
£450-550 *S*

Six photographs of Ferrari GTO Le
Mans in the early 1960s, including
Gregory/Piper GTO LMB,
Sear/Salmon 330 LMB, Ireland/
Gregory GTO plus 3 others, all
framed, 19 by 23½in (49 by 60cm).
£800-850 *S*

A photograph of a D-Type Jaguar,
showing Swaters in his Ecurie Belge
ex-works D-Type Jaguar at Le Mans
in 1956, mounted, framed and
glazed, 18 by 23in (46 by 59cm).
£170-300 *S*

An original photograph of Maglioli
at Le Mans 1957, with the rare
Porsche 718 RSK, mounted, framed
and glazed, 15 by 25in (38 by 64cm).
£200-300 *S*

Fourteen Le Mans photographs
1950-58, 24 by 28in (61 by 71cm).
£2,000-2,500 *S*

A portrait of Enzo Ferrari at his
desk in Moderno, signed in purple
ink, with original Ferrari
compliments slip and photograph of
Grand Prix Ferrari, mounted, 16 by
13in (40.5 by 33cm).
£900-1,000 *S*

Le Mans 1951, 5 black and white photographs depicting the start and shots of MG TD, Talbot Lago, Ferrari 340, Allard J2 and Cunningham C-2R, 11 by 19in (28 by 48cm).
£300-350   *CNY*

A collection of 14 original factory photographs by Millander, depicting the famous Jaguar D-types, of the Ecurie Ecosse and Works teams, all framed and glazed.
£350-500   *S*

AUTOMOBILIA
Advertising

A Power Petrol forecourt clock, with double sided clock face and painted blue metal surround, English, 1930s, 36in (92cm) wide.
£400-450   *S*

A Michelin red forecourt trolly compressor, No. 9001.
£700-800   *S*

A Holdtite Motor Accessories advertising figure, base repaired and worn, 18in (45.5cm) high.
£250-300   *S*

A Champion Dependable Spark Plugs counter display, racked at the back to store spark plugs, 29in (73.5cm) wide.
£150-200   *S*

A Lodge advertising spark plug, together with a cast metal Lodge display stand with 4 spark plugs, spark plug 30in (76cm) high, stand 18in (45.5cm) wide.
£150-200   *S*

A cast brass winged wheel wall display, 1930s, 31½in (80cm) wide
Est **£250-350**   *S*

Badges

A replica bronze Spirit of Ecstasy
showroom display, on marble base,
signed on base Charles Sykes, 21in
(53cm) high.
£850-900 *S*

An A.A. Committee Club badge,
No. OC135, 6in (15cm) high.
£500-550 *C*

An Automobile Association Light
Car badge, No. 150328, in chromed
metal with integral radiator cap
mount, 5in (13cm) high.
£550-600 *S*

An RAC Full Member's badge,
No. D5770, the brass badge with
enamel union flag, 5in (13cm) high.
£270-300 *S*

A collection of 10 American enamel
motoring badges, including badges
for Kaiser, Dodge, Paige,
Oldsmobile, Chevrolet and Marmon.
£280-320 *S*

A Brooklands B.A.R.C. enamel
badge, No. 798, enamel chipped and
scratched, English, 1930s, 4in
(10cm) high.
£540-580 *S*

A rare, original Associate Member's
badge for the Automobile Racing
Association Ltd, No. 610, enamelled
in 4 colours, some enamel missing,
3½in (9cm) wide.
£280-350 *S*

A rare Rolls-Royce Ltd badge, in
chromed metal and black enamel,
5in (13cm) wide.
£120-150 *S*

A Motor Union brass badge, lettered
The Mark of the Considerate
Driver, No. 2536, 6in (15cm) high.
£300-350 *S*

An enamelled lapel badge for the
South African Grand Prix, 1938,
finished in red, 1in (2.5cm) wide,
together with 1 mascot and 5 other
badges.
£350-400 *S*

A Mercedes Benz radiator fitted with the following club badges: Canadian Automobile Association, Touring Club de France, Royal Automobile Club Victoria, Automovil Club Argentino, Kuwait Automobile and Touring Club, Automobile Club du Grand Duche de Luxembourg, Light Car Club Australia, Touring Club Switzerland, Royal Automobile Thailand, Automobile Club der Schweiz, Touring Y Automovil Club del Peru, Automobile Club Portugal.
£400-500   *C(A)*

A German Imperial Eagle mascot, on ceramic display stand, 9in (23cm) high, and a D.D.A.C. enamel badge, German, 1930s.
£250-300   *S*

An early B.A.R.C. Brooklands enamel badge, No. 166, enamel chipped in 5 places, wings bent, 3½in (9cm) high.
£400-450   *S*

Brochures

The Allard Special V-8 V-12 sales catalogue, English text, the back cover with envelope containing further information and 6 loose prints.
Est. **£400-500**   *CNY*

A Jaguar XK120 C Type sales brochure, with specification details and an illustration of the racing car, 1951.
£600-650   *CNY*

Les 24 heures du Mans 1954 and 1965 official programmes, with illustrations by Geo Ham.
£250-300   *C*

A Porsche 917 sales catalogue, German, English and French text, 1969.
£450-500 *CNY*

TYP 904

A Porsche Carrera GTS Type 904 sales catalogue, German text, 1964.
Est. **£200-300** *CNY*

A Delahaye, Model 136, V12 and Competition Chassis album, produced with brief specification details and 9 black and white photographs of the styles of coachwork designed by Figoni et Falaschi.
£500-550 *CNY*

Création: Figoni - Falaschi Geo Ham

Clocks & Instruments

A brass dashboard timepiece, with blued steel hands and rim wind, English, 1920s, 3½in (9cm) diam.
£160-200 *S*

A rare 1903 Gordon Bennett Cup Race timepiece, with white painted face and brass drum case, signed by the maker S. Smith & Son Ltd, hour, minute and seconds hands missing, 12in (30cm) diam.
£1,400-1,800 *S*

An A. W. Gamage Ltd 8 day dashboard timepiece, with white enamel dial and bevelled glass in angled brass case, Swiss, 1920s, 3½in (9cm) diam.
£200-250 *S*

An 8 day dashboard timepiece, with white enamel dial and subsidiary seconds dial, in angled brass case, 1920s, 3in (8cm) diam.
£200-250 *S*

An Elliott speed indicator, the nickel plated dial case with triple scale and white enamel dish, in original carrying case, English, c1910, 3in (7.5cm) diam.
£200-250 *S*

A Smith & Son dashboard timepiece, with white enamel dial and angled brass case, 1920s, 3in (8cm) diam.
£270-300 *S*

A Harrods Ltd. 8-day dashboard timepiece, with blued steel hands, the white enamel dial with hairline cracks, bezel 2in (5cm).
Est. **£250-350** *S*

A Doxa dashboard timepiece, contained in a nickel plated angled case, 4in (10cm) diam.
£250-350 *S*

AUTOMOBILIA

A Jones speedometer, American, with miles per hour scale 0-50, glass chipped, c1912, bezel 3in (7.5cm), a Jaeger 8-day dashboard timepiece and a Smiths clock in dashboard mount with replaced glass.
£300-400   *S*

A Rotax Leitner volts/amps dashboard instrument, in brass case, 4in (10cm) wide.
Est. **£200-300**   *S*

A New Haven Clock Co. 8-day dashboard timepiece, in heavy brass case, white enamel dial cracked, bezel 2½in (6.5cm).
Est. **£150-220**   *S*

An S. Smith & Son combined speedometer and trip odometer, with bevel glass displays and brass casing, English, c1910, 7in (17.5cm) wide.
£200-300   *S*

> **Miller's is a price GUIDE not a price LIST**

A silver Bristol radiator mantel piece clock, the 8-day clock with luminous numerals, hallmarked London 1929, 5in (12.5cm) high overall.
£300-350   *S*

An American silver motoring pocket watch, the back cast in relief with 4 seat open tourer, c1910, 2in (5cm) diam.
£300-400   *S*

An unusual silver car side lamp combination deskpiece and clock, with an inkwell under the chimney and a stamp drawer in the base, hallmarked Birmingham 1910, 6in (15cm) high.
£750-800   *S*

Clothing

A green leather motorist's foul weather hat, with peak front and detachable neck cape, with a long green leather jerkin and a brush leather peaked driving cap.
£500-550   *S*

A pair of Gamages foul weather leg shrouds, both with waterproofed outer and blanket lining, the driver's with shaped shoe covers, the passenger's in form of wrap around bag, some repairs to lining and elastic fasteners, English, c1905.
£450-500   *S*

Garage Equipment

A Michelin garage compressor, with pressure gauge and seated figure of Mr Bibendum holding a pipe to his mouth, 1930s, 11in (28cm) long.
£380-420 *S*

A Gilbert and Parker petrol pump, the cylindrical cast iron stand painted bright blue, with hand pump, 5 gallon capacity, and Fina glass petrol pump globe, 1920s.
£700-750 *S*

A bowser garage forecourt oil pump, 1920s, finished in scarlet, with Shell transfer, well restored, 49in (124cm) high.
£450-550 *S*

A bowser garage forecourt petrol pump, 1920s, finished in scarlet, with plaque for Shell-Mex Ltd, with hand crank, quantity indicator, sight glass, Shell shaped price card advertising Summer Shell 1/8 per gallon, brass delivery nozzle and rubber hose, with fat Shell globe repaired, well restored.
£750-800 *S*

Horns

A pair of Lucas short trumpet horns, suitable for Bentley 3½ litre and Rolls-Royce 20/25HP, 7½in (19cm) long.
£240-280 *S*

A pair of Lucas Windtone long trumpet horns, restored, 12in (30cm) long.
£380-420 *S*

An unused and boxed L'Autovox motoring horn, maker's No. 2820, the nickelled horn with original instruction label, cable and horn button, trumpet mesh, filter and mounting bracket, French, c1910, 13in (33cm) high.
£1,600-1,700 *S*

A boa constrictor brass motoring horn, with cast brass snake's head and trembling tongue, English, 1920s, 79in (200cm) long.
£980-1,200 *S*

A baby boa constrictor horn, with mounting bracket and rubber bulb, English, 1920s, 48in (122cm) long.
£900-1,100 *S*

A boa constrictor motoring horn, the chromed metal articulated body with 2 mounting brackets and rubber bulb, English, c1910, 60in (152cm) long.
£400-450 *S*

A Bosch U II-12 electric car horn, with mounting bracket, mouth 4½in (11.5cm) high.
£120-150 *S*

A L'Autovox electric motoring horn with fly-mesh, operating switch, original cable, instructions, in original wooden packing case, with 'important' label, French, 14in (35.5cm) long.
£700-750 *S*

An Accin brass motoring horn, the double coiled horn with mounting bracket, oval shaped trumpet with mesh cover and with rubber bulb, French, c1910, 20in (50.5cm) high.
£450-500 *S*

A pair of Bosch 12 volt electrical horns, each with curved trumpet with mounting bracket, 5½in (14cm) high.
£200-250 *S*

A boa constrictor motoring horn, with pressed brass head, trembling tongue and glass eyes, on display board, 1920s, 69in (175cm) long.
£750-800 *S*

Lighting

A pair of Marchal electric bull's-eye type 43 headlamps, each with triple bulb bar mounted with bull's-eye lens and applied with trade shield flat glass lens and chromed brass outer case, French, 1930s, 8in (20.5cm).
£300-350 *S*

A Lucas 'owl-eye' tail lamp, type 311-L.
£200-250 *S*

A pair of brass Lucas King of the Road rear lamps, restored.
£50-60 *P*

A pair of Marchal rear lamps, with ribbed glass lenses, 1930s, 4in (10cm) long.
Est. **£500-600**   *C*

A pair of Lucas Type 236 spotlamps, each with reverse mounted electric illuminant and chromed metal case, lens 6in (15cm).
£450-500   *S*

Three Marchal electrically illuminated headlamps, French, 1930s, comprising a pair of 9in (22cm) headlamps, the bulb carrier applied with Sunburst trade shields, together with an 8in (20cm) bull's-eye headlamp, bulb arm damaged, all 3 with black painted cases and mirrored reflectors, slight dents to rims and cases.
£650-750   *S*

A pair of Lucas P80 headlamps, each with triple bar electric illuminant support, in chromed metal case, lens 9in (22cm) diam.
£1,000-1,100   *S*

A pair of Bosch 10in (25cm) headlamps, each of the restored lamps with correct style lenses and black painted metal cases, 1930s.
£930-980   *S*

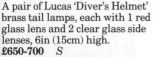

A pair of Lucas 'Diver's Helmet' brass tail lamps, each with 1 red glass lens and 2 clear glass side lenses, 6in (15cm) high.
£650-700   *S*

A pair of Lucas 9in (22cm) headlamps, 1936-39, suitable for SS100 Jaguar 2½ and 3½ litres, the restored lamps with original lenses moulded with U-shaped design, with stoneguards and solenoid dipping units.
£3,000-4,000   *S*

A pair of Brown Bros. 'Duco' diver's helmet rear lamps, the small brass electrically illuminated lamps with flange mounts, red glasses, clear sight lens, clear glass lens 2in (5cm) diam, together with a pair of Cibie headlamps, electrically illuminated with black painted casing, pillar mounts, 2 bulbs, mirrored reflector and clear glass lens, 7in (18cm) diam.
£280-320   *S*

A pair of Lucas Type 676 acetylene headlamps, suitable for Rolls-Royce Silver Ghost, each with polished brass case, shaped chimney, side mounting flanges and mirrored reflector, applied with plaque Lucas King of the Road Projector, English, c1910, lens 9in (22cm) diam.
£1,000-1,100   *S*

A Dependance rear lamp, with
bevelled glazed side lenses and red
glass rear lens, English, c1912,
9½in (24cm) high.
£250-300 *S*

A pair of Bleriot side lamps, each
with candle illuminant, shaped
chimney and red glass rear lens,
c1905, 11½in (29.5cm) high.
£350-450 *S*

A pair of unused Lucas King of the
Road headlamps, each with oil
illuminant, No. 742, with a set of
instructions and complaints slip,
14in (36cm) high.
£150-250 *S*

A pair of brass side lamps, each with
oil illuminant and red glass rear
lens, English, c1910, 9in (22.5cm)
high.
£300-350 *S*

A Butler's Atlantic hand spotlamp,
with shaped handle and mounting
bracket, lens 5in (12.5cm).
£120-150 *S*

A pair of Smiths electrically
illuminated opera lamps, brass
bodied lamps with 2 clear glass
windows, 2 acid etched windows,
red door glass, and electric lead
point at base, 9½in (24cm) high.
£250-300 *S*

A Butler's Atlantic combined
spotlamp and side mirror, restored
chrome metal case, lens 4in (10cm).
£400-500 *S*

A Butler's Atlantic combined
spotlamp and side mirror, in
restored case with green glass side
lens, on mounting bracket, lens 5in
(12.5cm).
£250-350 *S*

A Raydyot hand spotlamp,
restored lamp with chromed
metal case and mounting
bracket, lens 5in (12.5cm).
£100-150 *S*

A Lucas King of the Road rear lamp,
with red glass lens and clear glass
side lenses, loop handle and 2 tier
chimney, No. 432, 12in (30.5cm)
high.
£200-250 *S*

A pair of Lucidus opera side lamps, the nickel plated lamps with bevel glazed windows, oil illuminant, English, c1905, 10½in (26.5cm) high.
£650-700 *S*

A pair of Lucas FT37 spotlights, electrically illuminated, each with clear flat glass lens, bulb hood, split mirrored reflector with rear focus access panel, 6in (15cm) diam.
£400-450 *S*

A Lucas King of the Road rear lamp, with oil illuminant, clear glass large lens and red glass rear lens, loop handle, No. 631, 10in (25cm) high.
£300-350 *S*

A pair of Marchal 9in headlamps, each with rear-mounted electric illuminant and central Marchal shield, on pillar mount, 1930s.
£350-400 *S*

A pair of Carl Zeiss headlamps, each with Zeiss lens, electric illuminant and pillar mount, German, 1930s, 9in (23cm).
£350-400 *S*

A pair of Marchal electric headlamps, each with pillar mounting, twin bulb bar applied with trade shield, flat glass lens and brass outer case, mirrored reflector cracked in places, French, 1930s, 8in (20.5cm).
£250-300 *S*

A pair of Lucas 'owl-eye' tail lamps, type 311-L, with orange, clear and ruby lenses, chrome and black painted finish, reconditioned, 6in (15cm) wide.
£800-850 *S*

A pair of Lucas torpedo side lamps, each with bull's-eye front lens and red glass rear lens, in streamlined brass case, English, 1930s, 5½in (14cm) long.
£700-800 *S*

A Lucas No. 623 oil illuminated brass tail lamp, clear sight lens, loop handle, side flange mount, 2in (5cm) ruby glass lens, 3in (7.5cm) clear glass lens.
£150-200 *S*

A pair of nickel plated Ducellier acetylene headlamps, original condition, 8in (20.5cm) diam.
£250-300 *P*

AUTOMOBILIA

A pair of Lucas 236 side lamps, electrically illuminated, each with ribbed clear glass lens, bulb hood, and mirrored reflector, 6in (15cm) diam.
£250-300   *S*

A pair of Lucas No. 624 oil illuminated brass side lamps, each with loop handle, side flange mount, chimney, and reservoir, one with original ruby sight glass, the other with clear sight glass cracked, 3in (7.5cm) clear glass lens.
£200-300   *S*

A pair of Scintilla rear lamps, each with chromed metal case, red and orange rear lens and clear glass side lens, Swiss, 1930s, 4in (10cm) wide.
£700-800   *S*

A pair of Powell & Hanmer nickel plated oil illuminated side lamps, each with ruby sight glass, oil reservoir, stamped underneath 736R, 4in (10cm) glass lens.
£250-300   *S*

A pair of Lucas No. 791 Duplex acetylene headlamps, each with loop handles, forkmounts, twin self-contained generators, flow regulator, numbered 4325V and 4356V, brass pitted and with minor repairs in places, 6in (15cm) diam concave lens.
£750-800   *S*

A rare Autoroche mechanical spotlamp, the lamp with 4½in (12cm) lens, mounted on windscreen bracket and operated via a flexible tube by a turned mahogany handle, French, 1930s.
£730-780   *S*

A pair of Marchal 10in (25cm) bull's-eye headlamps, suitable for Hispano-Suiza, Isotta Fraschini, the restored lamps with fork mounts, French, 1930s.
£1,100-2,000   *S*

A Lucas 'owl-eye' tail lamp, type 312 L.
£250-300   *S*

Luggage

An Asprey's leather picnic set, the brown leather case fitted with kettle, stove, 2 plates, cups and saucers and plated metal food container, English, 1920s, 11in (28cm) wide.
£1,300-1,500   *S*

A Coracle 4 person picnic set, with black rexine covered case fitted with 4 place settings, a preserve jar and 3 plated metal food containers, English, 1920s, 23in (58cm) wide.
£550-700   *S*

Mascots

A Bregeon brass golfer on a radiator cap, signed on base, French, 1920s, 18in (46cm) high.
£400-500 *S*

A Ch. Soudant speed goddess mascot, marked Susse Fres Edts Paris S, 1930s, 5½in (14cm) long, mounted on wooden base.
£250-300 *S*

A bronze monkey in wheel mascot, the cast figure on shaped base and marble stand, French, 1920s, 6in (15cm) high.
£500-600 *S*

A Guiraud Rivière pierrot mascot, French, 1920s, 4½in (11cm) high.
£120-200 *S*

A Ballot le Renommee trumpeter mascot, the naked female figure standing beside an engine, on dome shaped base, 5in (13cm) high.
£1,000-1,500 *S*

A Ruffony cast white metal dancing couple mascot, signed on the base, French, 1920s, 5½in (14cm) high.
£550-650 *S*

A Sabino embossed glass dragonfly mascot, 6in (15cm) high.
£150-200 *S*

A red Ashay type glass mascot, 4½in (11cm) high.
£350-400 *S*

A Straker-Squire kneeling girl mascot, the naked figure chrome plated, on radiator cap, English, c1921, 6½in (16cm) high.
£400-500 *S*

A nickel plated aeroplane radial engine with mobile propeller, 3½in (9cm) high.
£150-200 *C*

A Joko spelter monkey mascot, the monkey seated on a steering wheel and wearing goggles, on radiator cap, 5in (13cm) high.
£300-400 *S*

Lalique Mascots

A Lalique glass 'Chrysis' mascot with etched glass signature R. Lalique, French, 5in (13cm) high.
£1,100-2,000   *S*

A Lalique glass mascot 'Victoire', with amethyst tint, raised moulded signature R. Lalique France, some damage, 1930s, 10in (25cm) long.
£5,750-6,500   *S*

A Lalique 'Archer' glass mascot, impressed R. Lalique, and engraved France, on brass base, 6½in (16cm) high.
£600-700   *S*

Model Cars

Stanley Wanlass, 'Fast Company', a hand painted bronze study of the ex-works 4.5 litre 1953-54 Ferrari 375 MM Vignale Spyder driven by Phil Hill and Richie Ginther in the 1954 Carrera Pan American road race, Mexico, limited edition, mounted on marble base, 23½in (60cm) long.
£14,700-16,000   *B*

A silver scale model of a 1931 Rolls-Royce Henley Coupé, with dickey seat, hinged side door, removable hood, 2 hinged side doors and opening bonnet, on silver mounted black marble base, hallmarked London 1986, 9in (23cm) long.
£1,650-2,500   *S*

A detailed Pocher ⅛th scale model of a 1933 Bugatti Type 50T, constructed of 1,664 parts in plastic, brass and stainless steel, complete with original box and instruction booklet.
£550-800   *S*

A silver scale model of a Bugatti Royale Berline de Voyage, with removable hood, opening bonnet and gilded upholstered interior, on black marble base, hallmarked London 1987, 9½in (24cm) long.
£1,650-2,500   *S*

A Pocher ⅛th scale model of a 1934 Alfa Romeo Mille-Miglia 8c 2600, finished to a very high standard of detail in maroon, in glazed mahogany display case, 27in (69cm) long. **£720-800**   *S(S)*

A Pocher ⅛th scale model of a 1933 Jean Bugatti Coupé Bugatti Type 50, high standard of detail and finished in yellow and black, in glazed mahogany display case, 34in (86cm) long.
£1,500-2,000   *S(S)*

Radiators

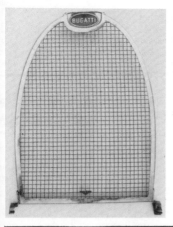

A Bugatti radiator grille, in chrome metal with red, black and white enamel Bugatti badge, 22½ by 17½in (57 by 44cm).
£450-500   *S*

A Rolls-Royce Phantom II radiator grille, complete with correct cap, mascot, movable grille slats and water pipes.
£1,600-2,000   *S*

Trophies & Plaques

A Chevrolet Quota trophy, a die cast zinc model of the Spirit of St Louis, on display stand, American, 1927, wingspan 6in (15cm).
£770-900   *S*

A Monte Carlo Rally enamel plaque, in 8 colours, signed Fraisse-Demo, 1932, 3½in (9cm) wide, in fitted presentation case.
£1,400-2,000   *S*

A Spelter motoring trophy, of a veteran car swathed in laurels, with brass plaque on turned wooden base, signed Moreau France, c1910, 11½in (29cm) high.
£600-700   *S*

General

A nickel plated side mirror, in adjustable mounting bracket and clamp, c1910, mirror 7 by 5in (18 by 13cm).
£385-500   *S*

A fairground ride painted pediment board, English, 1930s, 91in (231cm) long.
£70-150   *S*

A Morris Commercial cigarette case, the front applied with enamel plaque.
£187-200   *S*

A silver motoring card case, the back engraved 'To Miny from Jack Xmas 1925', the inside fitted in green leather, hallmarked, 4 by 3in (10 by 8cm).
£385-450   *S*

A silver cigarette case, in the form of a Lanchester radiator, 1927, 4in (10cm) high.
£440-600   *S*

FURTHER READING

Available from: Albion Scott Ltd (Connoisseur Motobooks), 51 York Road, Brentford, Middx TW8 0QP. Tel: 081-560 3404/5, 081-569 9991. Fax: 081-847 2543. P&P UK £3.00. Overseas £6.00. Credit card sales accepted.

A-Z of Cars of the 1930s
C & SC Magazine. 200pp 1000 ill 195 x 270 Hb
Encyclopedic coverage of every make and model of European and American car sold in Britain during the 30s. Outstanding reference work which was originally published in parts in Classic & Sportscar Magazine. Companion to A-Z of Cars 1945-70.
£19.95

A-Z of Cars of the 1970s
Robson, G. 180pp 700+ ill 260 x 190 Hb
Descriptions, specifications and photos of over 700 models sold in Britain in the 1970s – British, European, American and Japanese. Compiled from the archives of Classic & Sportscar.
£17.95

Abarth – King of Small Cars
Cosentino, A.
£24.95

Carroll Shelby's Racing Cobra
Friedman, D. 208pp 407 ill 270 x 210 Hb
Superb photographic history of the legendary competition Cobra. Reprint of 'Racing Cobras', and highly recommended by Shelby himself!
£29.95

Original AC, Ace and Cobra (Restoration Guide to Authenticity)
Mills, R. 96pp 150+ col 295 x 225 Hb
Excellent guide to restoration and authenticity.
£15.95

Alfa Romeo Catalogue Raisonne (2nd edition 1910-89)
Puttini/Fusi. 550pp 1000+ b/w & col 2 vol slc
Most comprehensive reference work on Alfa. English, French and Italian.
£110.00

Alfa Romeo Tradition
Borgeson, G. 208pp 250 b/w 120 ill 230 x 300 Hb
Meticulously researched history of Alfa Romeo, including such classic models as the Merosi and Satta.
£35.00

Alvis – The Story of the Red Triangle (2nd Edition)
Day, L.
£24.95

Illustrated Aston Martin Buyer's Guide
Woudenberg, P.
£12.80

Aston Martin – The Post-War Road Cars
Rasmussen, H.
£24.95

Austin Seven
Harvey, C.
£15.95

Austin Seven Companion
750 Motor Club
£9.95

Austin Seven Source Book
Purves, B.
£75.00

Original Austin Healey: Restorer's Guide to 100-3000
Clausager, D. 96pp 150 col 295 x 225 Hb
The definitive full-colour restoration guide to the 100, 100/6 and 3000 two-seater, four-seater and convertible models. Essential book for owners!
£15.95

Bentley Specials and Special Bentleys
Roberts, R. 496pp 60 col 1030 b/w 270 x 210 Hb
History of privately built special Bentleys.
£75.00

Bentley: The Cars from Crewe
Steel, R.
£39.95

Bentley: The Silent Sports Car 1931-1942
Ellman-Brown, M.
£39.99

BMW: A Celebration
Dymock, E. 192pp 150 col 150 b/w 254 x 258 Hb
A tribute to BMW, covering its automobiles, motorcycles and aero engines. Written with the full co-operation of BMW's archivists, with contemporary photos and adverts, and specially commissioned colour photography.
£20.00

Bristol: An Illustrated History
Oxley, C. 352pp 250 col & b/w 276 x 219 Hb
History of the marque written by the co-founder of the Bristol Owners' Club, containing many archive photographs never before published. Comprehensive descriptions of every model, Bristol's racing history and the car's engineering.
£35.00

Bugatti Magnum
Conway, H. 540pp 873 b/w & col 330 x 250 Hb
Magnificent work. Only 2,000 in print!
£150.00

Illustrated Cadillac Buyer's Guide
Langworth, R. 162pp 160 ill 198 x 230 Pb
Essential reference book for all Cadillac buffs.
£10.95

Cars: Early and Vintage 1886-1930
Georgano, G. 232pp 200+ col/ill 300 x 265 Hb
Follows the changes and trends of the early years.
£14.95

Chevrolet 1912-1990
Standard Catalogue. c400pp 1000+ ill 275 x 215 Pb
Complete reference guide, covering production to standard features, engine options and body styles, encyclopedia.
£19.95

Chrysler 1924-1990
Standard Catalouge Series. c400pp 1000+ ill 275 x 215 Pb
Complete encyclopedia for the Chrysler, including production, standard features, engine options and body styles.
£19.95

Citroën Traction Avant Gold Portfolio 1934-57
Brooklands. 280 x 200 Pb
Collection of period articles covering road tests, new model introductions, performance data, historical profiles and more for the Six, Twelve and Big and Little Fifteen.
£10.95

Errett Lobban Cord: His Empire, His Motorcars
Borgeson, G. 14½ x 17, autographed by author
After years of research, now comes the full A-C-D story. Strictly limited edition, bound in genuine leather, large landscape size and printed to the highest standard. 'Unquestionably the greatest automobile book ever' – R. A. Wolff, Duesenberg historian.
£395.00

Corvette: Portrait of a Legend
Burton, Jones. 288pp 120 col & b/w 235 x 265 Hb
A massive, beautifully designed and produced book, covering the entire Corvette range. Must be the most exclusive and spectacular Corvette book published so far – a superb present for the Corvette enthusiast.
£50.00

Daimler and Lanchester: An Illustrated History
Freeman, T. 140pp 100+ b/w 300 x 215 Hb
Full history of the two marques.
£19.95

Daimler Anthology: DB 18 and Conquest Ranges 1945-55
Joung, D.
£9.95

How to Restore Your Datsun Z – Car
Humble, W. 240pp 250+ ill 278 x 215 Pb
Rust repairs, body preparation and painting. Suspensions, brakes, engines and more. What tools are needed, how to buy parts. Step by step details with over 500 photos.
£19.95

Delage 3 Litres – La Grand Aventure
Jolly, F.
£35.00

Dodge Muscle Cars 1967-70
Brooklands (ed).
£7.95

E.R.A. – The History of English Racing Automobiles Ltd
Weguelin, D.
£45.00

Complete Ferrari
Eaton, G.
£21.95

Anteprima Ferrari
Varisco, F. 95pp well ill 250 x 290 Hb
Illustrated history of the Ferrari 815, the first car completely built by Enzo Ferrari, released to celebrate its 50th anniversary. Includes many original documents. Italian text.
£39.95

Guide to Ferrari Cars since 1959 (8th Edition 1989)
Maranello.
£6.50

Ferrari Opera Omnia (three volumes in slip case)
Borgeson/Morett. 3 vol 1050pp 700 col 300 b/w Hb
Most comprehensive reference ever published. Limited
£150.00

Ford: The Racing History
Wilson/Stahl. 319pp c300 col & b/w 295 x 220 Hb
Complete history of Australian Ford racing cars. Covers, chapter by chapter, each individual model and its track record, including both race and rally cars. With good photography and a complete listing of Ford competition successes.
£22.95

Ford 1903-1990
Standard Catalogue Series. c400pp 1000+ ill
275 x 215 Pb
Complete guide to all US models. Covers details of production, engine options, body styles, VINS and standard features.
£19.95

Capri: Development and Competition History (3rd edition)
Walton, J. 320pp 260 b/w ill 244 x 177 Hb
New edition of this authoritative, and best-selling, Capri history. Includes coverage of the Capri 280, totally revised appendices and more photos.
£15.95

Ginetta: The Illustrated History 2nd Edition
Rose, J.
£12.95

Healey: The Handsome Brute
Harvey, C. 239pp 210 ill 20 col Hb
Handsome car, handsome book! Covers all aspects of 100, 100/6 and 3000 models including history, competition, restoration, etc.
£15.95

Holden The Official Racing History
Wilson, S. 367pp c400 col & b/w 290 x 220 Hb
Complete history of Holden cars' successes and track record in races and rallies. With individual coverage of models, good photography, contemporary advertisements and a complete competition rundown.
£22.95

HRG: The Sportsman's Ideal
Dussek, I.
£14.95

Humber Story 1868-1932
Demaus/Tarring.
£14.95

Humber Motor Cars: An Illustrated History to 1976
Freeman, T. 128pp 200 b/w 300 x 215 Hb
History of marque, including military vehicles.
£14.95

Jaguar Driver's Book
Ruppert, J. 160pp 200 ill 232 x 171 Hb
A totally new kind of motoring book. Contains a large accumulation of articles – serious and hilarious – reports and features which make good bedside reading for owner and enthusiast alike.
£9.95

Jaguar: A Touch of History (Complete Model Identity Guide)
Kelsey (Editor). 150pp 259 b/w 295 x 210 Pb
Only book of its kind. Compiled from Jaguar Enthusiast.
£10.95

Jaguar E-Type: The Definitive History
Porter, P. 712pp 800+ col & b/w 215 x 275 Hb
The ultimate book on the E-Type Jaguar. A documentary masterpiece of the highest calibre presenting the true, complete history of this legendary British sports car. Packed with a large number of illustrations, many never published before.
£55.00

Jaguar: The Definitive History (New Edition)
Whyte, A. 272pp 200 b/w 240 x 170 Hb
The re-release of THE classic book on Jaguar cars, written by one of the company executives, with the full co-operation of the factory. This is an indispensable history for any Jaguar enthusiast.
£17.50

Jaguar Saloon Cars (2nd Edition)
Skilleter, P. 656pp 865 ill 270 x 210 Hb
Updated edition of the book that has become accepted as
the definitive work on the subject. A comprehensive
record of all Jaguar saloon cars, including information
on the ultimate Series III cars, the XJ-S cabriolet, AJ6
engine and the new XJ6.
£35.00

Jensen
Anderson, K.
£15.95

Lamborghini Catalogue Raisonne (2nd Edition)
Pasini, S. 250pp 24 col 400 b/w 250 x 280 Hb
Updated edition issued to commemorate 25 years of
Lamborghini. Issued in highest quality, with slip-case.
Covers all models ever produced in greatest detail.
Superb illustrations, many published for the first time.
Text in English, Italian and French.
£79.95

Complete Book of Lamborghini
Lyons, P.
£14.95

Lancia Corse
Manganaro/Vinai. 300pp 70 col 300 b/w 280 x 250 Hb
A lavishly illustrated history of Lancia racing and
rallying, from their origins to the present day. Full
details of all competiton cars. English, Italian and
French text.
£59.95

History of Lancia 1906-1989
Lancia (Ed)
£9.95

Lotus Elan: The Complete Story
Taylor, M. 208pp 114 col 55 b/w 258 x 195 Hb
The complete history of this classic car, from conception
to its launch in 1962, and its development since.
Includes details on the new relaunched Elan, buying,
maintenance and addresses of owners' clubs and outlets.
£15.95

Lotus: All the Cars
Pritchard, A. 256pp 200+ col & b/w 270 x 200 Hb
A complete guide book of every Lotus model produced,
from the Mk 1 Special to the current Formula 1 and the
new edition Elan. Full histories and descriptions and
colour illustrations.
£19.95

Colin Chapman's Lotus: Origins of the Elite and Elan
Read, R. 336pp 150 b/w ill 270 x 210 Hb
As Lotus Sales Manager during 1951-62 Read analyses
Chapman's personality and design qualities, looks back
at the cars built and describes the company's developing
technical and commercial activities. A genuine inside
view, with much new source material.
£24.95

Marcos Cars 1960-1988
Brooklands (Ed).
£7.95

Maserati – The Complete History
Orsini and Zagari.
£29.95

Mercedes-Benz: Portrait of a Legend
Seiff, I. 288pp 120 col & b/w 335 x 265 Hb
Massive, beautifully designed and illustrated history of
the company. Fullest coverage of models and
achievements. The ideal present for the Mercedes
enthusiast, as this is the most spectacular book so far
published on the marque.
£50.00

Mercedes-Benz Production Models 1946-1990
Nitzke, R. 263pp 450 b/w 285 x 228 Hb
Photos, brief history, specs, prices and production
figures of each Mercedes model built since WW2.
Separate tables cover annual production totals, engine
design, convesion tables of engine power and torque,
identifications, etc. Completely revised and updated
edition.
£29.95

Racing The Silver Arrows: Mercedes-Benz vs Auto Union
Nixon, C. 350pp c250 b/w 285 x 225 Hb
The story of Mercedez-Benz and Auto Union's
domination of the 'Golden Age' of Grand Prix motor
racing, 1934-39. Chronicled year-by-year, with two
memoirs from each season, profiles of major
personalities, the relationship with the Nazis, etc.
£29.95

MG by McComb (New Edition)
McComb/Nye. 240pp well ill Hb
At last the long-awaited revised and updated history of
the marque, originally compiled by the late Wilson
McComb, the former works historian. This has always
been the most comprehensive MG history, and the new
edition will continue this tradition.
£19.95

Maintaining The Breed: The Saga of MG Racing Cars
Thornley, J. 248pp 70 b/w 214 x 135 Hb
A re-released edition of this classic history of the MG
Racers. Written from an insider's point of view, this is a
fascinating and gripping account. Comes only in a 2,250
copy limited edition, so a genuine collector's item.
£16.95

MG: The Magic of the Marque
Allison, M. 352pp 58 col 412 b/w 235 x 210
Pictorial history of MG, issued as a follow-on to
Magic of MG published by Dalton Watson many years
ago. Similar style and quality, but larger format and
now with colour photos and new material.
£19.95

Mighty Mini
Harvey, C. 256pp 400 b/w 16pp col 216 x 205
Undoubtedly the most thorough and practical book for
Mini owners, published in the renowned Oxford Classic
Car Series. Fullest history and coverage of Minis and
Mini Coopers and their derivatives. A book every Mini
owner will want to have.
£15.95

Four-Wheeled Morgan Volume 2 (Cowled-Radiator Models)
Hill, K.
£12.95

Illustrated Morgan Buyer's Guide
Hill.
£12.50

Morgan: The Last Survivor
Harvey, C.
£15.95

Magnificent Morris Minor
Horvat, M. 112pp 246 x 189 Hb
A complete personal account of the author's 1957 Morris
Minor. Every journey and event the car has taken on
has been logged, detailed and photographed. The
ultimate Minor enthusiast's guide.
£14.95

Metropolitan 1954-1962
Brooklands (Ed)
£7.95

There is no mistaking a Pierce-Arrow
Brierley, B. T.
£29.95

Complete Book of the Ford Mustang
Consumer Guide. 320pp 100s col 230 x 275 Hb
Celebrates 25 years from the original Pony Car to the latest models. Highly detailed model histories, packed with colour photos, specifications, data and more.
£14.95

Plymouth Muscle Cars 1966-1971
Brooklands (Ed)
£7.95

Porsche: Excellence Was Expected
Ludvigsen, K. 888pp 100 col 1000 b/w 275 x 205 Hb
This book has always been regarded as the most comprehensive Porschen history in print – a massive volume with over 1000 illustrations and expert text. Published by Automobile Quarterly.
£49.95

Porsche – Portrait of a Legend
Seiff, I. 288pp 100s col & b/w 275 x 345 Hb
Re-issue of this magnificent tome. A massive book with superb, large colour plates and a detailed history of the marque. Definitely THE coffee table book on Porsche.
£50.00

Porsche Speedster
Moesch/Gratz. 144pp 100 col 80 b/w 240 x 302 Hb
History of the Porsche 911 sports car.
£39.95

Porsche: The Fine Art of the Sports Car
Lewis, L. 312pp 200 col 120 b/w 355 x 280 Hb
This stylish book captures more than 40 models in colour and black and white photographs. Also includes history and descriptions, chronology and specifications, all adding up to a superb volume!
£100.00

Classic Porsche Racing Cars
Cotton, M.
£12.95

Post-War Standard Cars
Freeman/Long. 94pp 100+ b/w 295 x 210 Pb
Complete history of Standard cars, 1946-63. Includes introduction and much reprinted contemporary and archive material. No other book available.
£9.95

Renault in the Thirties
Doisneau, R. 97pp 67 b/w 250 x 225 Hb
Excellent photographic collection from the Renault works at Billancourt, where the author worked. An affectionate and nostalgic account.
£12.95

Rolls-Royce Cars and Bentley from 1931 – Complete History
Schrader/Norb. 304pp 550 col & b/w 255 x 282 Hb
This is the most magnificent Rolls-Royce book to be published for several years. Compiled to the highest standards and produced in brilliant colour and duo-tone black and white. Fullest details of every car. A magnificent gift. Leatherbound and signed 175 pounds!
£74.95

Those Elegant Rolls-Royce (Revised Edition 1978)
Dalton, L. 320pp 5 col 1000 b/w 250 x 190 Hb
A superb Dalton Watson title – the essential guide to Rolls-Royce cars from 1907-39. Organised by the 55 different coachbuilders used, covering every model produced. Excellent photographs, and also a detailed index with types and chassis numbers.
£29.95

Road and Track on Toyota Sports and GT Cars 1966-86
Brooklands.
£7.95

Cars of the Rootes Group
Robson, G. 192pp 300+ ill 273 x 215 Hb
Very important contribution to the motoring library – the first full history of these fascinating cars – every model detailed and described, with much previously unpublished material. Companion to highly acclaimed **Cars from BMC.**
£29.95

Land Rover: The Unbeatable 4x4 (3rd Edition)
Slavin and Mackie. 328pp 216 b/w 30 col 244 x 177 Hb
The evolution, development, success and failures of the world's most successful 4x4 vehicle. Written with full co-operation of Land Rover, this most authoritative history has now been updated and revised to include the latest developments to 1989.
£14.95

Scimitar and its Forebears (2nd Edition)
Pither, D.
The complete account of the Reliant Scimitar range, allied models and the company's fortunes over the decades, richly illustrated. The first and long awaited title on the Reliant marque, and as such, an invaluable reference.
£19.95

Triumph Cars: The Complete Story
Robson/Langwort. 352pp 500+ ill Hb
New, revised and updated edition of what has always been accepted as the most comprehensive and authoritative history of this marque. Traces all developments and models from beginning to the end of production. Superbly written and presented.
£19.95

Triumph TR2-TR8 1953-81 (Schiffer Automotive Series)
Zeichner, W. 96pp 265 x 195 Hb
Profile of the TR series Triumphs. Beautifully produced, with a wealth of photographs and period advertisements. English vesion of Schrader-Motor-Chronik edition.
£14.95

Triumph TRs: A Collector's Guide
Robson, G.
£12.95

TVRs: A Collector's Guide (2nd Edition)
Robson, G.
£12.95

Vanden Plas Coachbuilders
Smith, B. 302pp 1 col 500 b/w 250 x 190 Hb
Available once more, this comprehensively illustrated history from Dalton Watson, of the cars produced by the famous coachbuilders. From the pre-war Bentley sports cars to the Austin Princess.
£29.95

World Sports Cars – Series built from 1945-80
Oleski/Lehbrink. 470pp 500+ col 310 x 278 Hb
Finest book on all models AC-TVR available!
£99.50

435

CAR CLUBS DIRECTORY

If you wish to be included in next year's directory or if you have a change of address or telephone number, please could you inform us by December 31st 1991. Entries will be repeated in subsequent editions unless we are requested otherwise.

ABC Owners Club, D. A. Hales, Registrar, ABC Owners Club, 20 Langbourne Way, Claygate, Esher, Surrey

A.C. Owners Club, Brian Gilbert Smith, The Coach House, Waltham St Lawrence, Berks. Tel: (0734) 343479

Alexis Racing and Trials Car Register, Duncan Rabagliati, 4 Wool Road, Wimbledon, London SW20

Alfa Romeo Section (VSCC Ltd), Allan & Angela Cherrett, Old Forge, Quarr, Nr Gillingham, Dorset

Alfa Romeo 1900 Register, Peter Marshall, Mariners, Courtlands Avenue, Esher, Surrey. Tel: (0223) 894300

Alfa Romeo 2600/2000 Register, Roger Monk, Knighton, Church Close, West Runton, Cromer, Norfolk

Alfa Romeo Owners Club, Michael Lindsay, 97 High Street, Linton, Cambs

Allard Owners Club, Miss P. Hulse, 1 Dalmeny Avenue, Tufnell Park, London N7

The Alvis 12/50 Register, Mr J. Willis, The Vinery, Wanborough Manor, Nr Guildford, Surrey. Tel: (0483) 810308

Alvis Owners Club, 1 Forge Cottages, Bayham Road, Little Bayham, Nr Lamberhurst, Kent

American Auto Club, G. Harris, PO Box 56, Redditch

Pre '50 American Auto Club, Alan Murphy, 41 Eastham Rake, Eastham, S. Wirral. Tel: 051-327 1392

American MGB Association, PO Box 53, Chesterfield, Derbys

The Amilcar Salmson Register, R. A. F. King, The Apple House, Wilmoor Lane, Sherfield on Lodden, Hants

Armstrong Siddeley Owners Club Ltd, Peter Sheppard, 57 Berberry Close, Bournville, Birmingham

Aston Martin Owners Club Ltd, Jim Whyman, AMOC Ltd, 1A High Street, Sutton, Nr Ely, Cambs. Tel: (0353) 777353

Atlas Register, 38 Ridgeway, Southwell, Notts

Austin J 40 Car Club, Mrs K. Vowles, 71 Meadowland Road, Henbury, Bristol

Austin Atlantic Owners Club, Den Barlow, 10 Jennings Way, Diss, Norfolk. Tel: (0379) 642460

A40 Farina Club, Membership Secretary, 113 Chastilian Road, Dartford, Kent

The 1100 Club, Paul Vincent, 32 Medgbury Road, Swindon, Wilts

Austin Cambridge/Westminster Car Club, Mr J. Curtis, 4 Russell Close, East Budleigh, Budleigh Salterton, Devon

Austin Big 7 Register, R. E. Taylor, 101 Derby Road, Chellaston, Derby

Austin Counties Car Club, David Stoves, 32 Vernolds Common, Craven Arms, Shropshire. Tel: (058 47) 7459

Austin Gipsy Register 1958-1968, Mike Gilbert, 24 Green Close, Rixon, Sturminster Newton, Dorset

Austin Healey Club, Mrs P. C. Marks, 171 Coldharbour Road, Bristol

750 Motor Club, 16 Woodstock Road, Witney, Oxon. Tel: (0993) 702285

Austin Seven Mulliner Register, Mike Tebbett, Little Wyche, Walwyn Road, Upper Colwall, Nr Malvern, Worcs

Austin Seven Owners Club (London), Mr and Mrs Simpkins, 5 Brook Cottages, Riding Lane, Hildenborough, Kent

The Austin Seven Sports Register, C. J. Taylor, 222 Prescot Road, Aughton, Ormskirk, Lancs

Austin Seven Van Register, 1923-29, N. B. Baldry, 32 Wentborough Road, Maidenhead, Berks

Austin Swallow Register, G. L. Walker, School House, Great Haseley, Oxford

Austin Healey Club, Midland Centre, Mike Ward, 9 Stag Walk, Sutton Coldfield. Tel: 021-382 3223

Austin A30-35 Owners Club, Andy Levis, 26 White Barn Lane, Dagenham, Essex. Tel: 081-517 0198

Austin Maxi Club, Mr I. Botting, 144 Village Way, Beckenham, Kent

Pre-War Austin Seven Club Ltd, Mr J. Tantum, 90 Dovedale Avenue, Long Eaton, Nottingham. Tel: (0602) 727626

Austin Ten Drivers Club Ltd, Mrs Patricia East, Brambledene, 53 Oxted Green, Milford, Godalming, Surrey

Bristol Austin Seven Club Ltd, 1 Silsbury Cottages, West Kennett, Marlborough, Wilts

Vintage Austin Register, Frank Smith, The Briars, Four Lane Ends, Oakerthorpe, Alfreton, Derbyshire. Tel: (0773) 831646

Scottish Austin Seven Club, 16 Victoria Gardens, Victoria Park, Kilmalcolm, Renfrew

Solent Austin Seven Club Ltd, F. Claxton, 185 Warsash Road, Warsash, Hants

South Wales Austin Seven Club, Mr and Mrs J. Neill, 302 Peniel Green Road, Llansamlet, Swansea

The Wanderers (Pre-War Austin Sevens), D. Tedham, Newhouse Farm, Baveney Wood, Cleobury Mortimer, Kidderminster, Worcs

436

Autovia Car Club, Alan Williams, Birchanger Hall, Birchanger, Nr Bishops Stortford, Herts

Battery Vehicle Society, Keith Roberts, 29 Ambergate Drive, North Pentwyn, Cardiff

Bean Car Club, G. Harris, Villa Rosa, Templewood Lane, Farnham Common, Bucks

Old Bean Society, P. P. Cole, 165 Denbigh Drive, Hately Heath, West Bromwich, W. Midlands

Bentley Drivers Club, 16 Chearsley Road, Long Crendon, Bucks

Berkeley Enthusiasts Club, Paul Fitness, 9 Hellards Road, Stevenage, Herts. Tel: (0438) 724164

Biggin Hill Car Club, Peter Adams, Jasmine House, Jasmine Grove, Anerley, London SE20. Tel: 081-778 3537

The BMW Car Club (Club Office), 'Dracaena', Old Road, Shotover Hill, Headington, Oxford. Tel: (0865) 741229

BMW Drivers Club, Sue Hicks, Bavaria House, PO Box 8, Dereham, Norfolk. Tel: (0362) 694459

Bond Owners Club, Stan Cornock, 42 Beaufort Avenue, Hodge Hill, Birmingham

Borgward Drivers Club, David Stride, 81 Stanway Road, Earlsdon, Coventry

Brabham Register, E. D. Walker, The Old Bull, 5 Woodmancote, Dursley, Glos. Tel: (0453) 543243

Bristol Owners Club, John Emery, Uesutor, Marringden Road, Billingshurst, West Sussex

British Ambulance Preservation Society, Roger Leonard, 21 Victoria Road, Horley, Surrey

British Automobile Racing Club Ltd, Miss T. Milton, Thruxton Circuit, Andover, Hants

British Racing and Sports Car Club Ltd, Brands Hatch, Fawkham, Dartford, Kent

The Brooklands Society Ltd, 38 Windmill Way, Reigate, Surrey

Brough Superior Club, P. Staughton (Secretary), 4 Summerfields, Northampton

Bugatti Owners Club Ltd, Sue Ward, Prescott Hill, Gotherington, Cheltenham, Glos

U.K. Buick Club, Alf Gascoine, 47 Higham Road, Woodford Green, Essex. Tel: 081-505 7347

Buckler Car Register, Stan Hibberd, 52 Greenacres, Woolton Hill, Newbury, Berks. Tel: (0635) 254162

Bullnose Morris Club, Richard Harris, PO Box 383, Hove, East Sussex

C.A. Bedford Owners Club, G. W. Seller, 7 Grasmere Road, Benfleet, Essex

Cambridge-Oxford Owners Club, COOC Membership, 6 Hurst Road, Slough

Citroën Car Club, D. C. Saville, 49 Mungo Park Way, Orpington, Kent. Tel: (0689) 823639

Traction Owners Club, Peter Riggs, 2 Appleby Gardens, Dunstable, Beds

Traction Enthusiasts Club, Preston House Studio, Preston, Canterbury, Kent

2CVGB Deux Chevaux Club of GB, PO Box 602, Crick, Northampton

(Citroën) The Traction Owners Club, Steve Reed, 1 Terwick Cottage, Rogate, Nr Petersfield, Hants

Clan Owners Club, Chris Clay, 48 Valley Road, Littleover, Derby. Tel: (0332) 767410

Classic Corvette Club (UK), Ashley Pickering, The Gables, Christchurch Road, Tring, Herts

The Classic Crossbred Club, 29 Parry Close, Stanford Le Hope, Essex. Tel: (0375) 671843

Classic and Historic Motor Club Ltd, Tricia Burridge, The Smithy, High Street, Ston Easton, Bath

Classic Saloon Car Club, 7 Dunstable Road, Caddington, Luton. Tel: (0582) 31642

Classic Z Register, Lynne Godber, Thistledown, Old Stockbridge Road, Kentsboro, Wallop, Stockbridge, Hants. Tel: (0264) 781979

Clyno Register, J. J. Salt, New Farm, Startley, Chippenham, Wilts. Tel: (0249) 720271

Friends of The British Commercial Vehicle Museum, c/o B.C.V.M., King Street, Leyland, Preston

Commercial Vehicle and Road Transport Club, Steven Wimbush, 8 Tachbrook Road, Uxbridge, Middx

Connaught Register, Duncan Rabagliati, 4 Wool Road, Wimbledon, London SW20

Cougar Club of America, Barrie S. Dixon, 11 Dean Close, Partington, Manchester

The Crayford Convertible Car Club, Rory Cronin, 68 Manor Road, Worthing, West Sussex. Tel: (0903) 212828

Crossley Climax Register, Mr G. Harvey, 7 Meadow Road, Basingstoke, Hants

Crossley Register, Geoff Lee, 'Arlyn', Brickwall Lane, Ruislip, Middx, and M. Jenner, 244 Odessa Road, Forest Gate, London E7

DAF Owners Club, S. K. Bidwell (Club Secretary), 56 Ridgedate Road, Bolsover, Chesterfield, Derbyshire

The Daimler and Lanchester Owners Club, John Ridley, The Manor House, Trewyn, Abergavenny, Gwent. Tel: (0873) 890737

Datsun Z Club, Mark or Margaret Bukowska. Tel: 081-998 9616

Delage Section VSCC Ltd, Douglas Macmillan, Brook Farm, Broadway-on-Teme, Worcs

Delahaye Club GB, A. F. Harrison, 34 Marine Parade, Hythe, Kent. Tel: (0303) 261016

Dellow Register, Douglas Temple Design Group, 4 Roumella Lane, Bournemouth, Dorset. Tel: (0202) 304641

De Tomaso Drivers Club, Chris Statham, 2-4 Bank Road, Bredbury, Stockport. Tel: 061-430 5052

The Diva Register, Steve Pethybridge, 8 Wait End Road, Waterlooville, Hants. Tel: (0705) 251485

DKW Owners Club, C. P. Nixon, Rose Cottage, Rodford, Westerleigh, Bristol

Dutton Owners Club, Rob Powell, 20 Burford Road, Baswich, Stafford, Staffs. Tel: (0785) 56835

Elva Owners Club, R. A. Dunbar, Mapel Tree Lodge, The Hawthorns, Smock Alley, West Alley, West Chiltington, West Sussex

E.R.A. Club, Guy Spollon, Arden Grange, Tanworth-in-Arden, Warks

Facel Vega Owners Club, Roy Scandrett, 'Windrush', 16 Paddock Gardens, East Grinstead, Sussex

Fairthorpe Sports Car Club, Tony Hill, 9 Lynhurst Crescent, Hillingdon, Middx

Ferrari Owners Club, 231 Station Road, Balsall Common, Warks. Tel: (0676) 34862

Fiat 130 Owners Club, Michael Reid, 28 Warwick Mansions, Cromwell Crescent, London SW5. Tel: 071-373 9740

Fiat Dino Register, Mr Morris, 59 Sandown Park, Tunbridge Wells, Kent

Fiat Motor Club (GB), H. A. Collyer, Barnside, Chikwell Street, Glastonbury, Somerset. Tel: (0458) 31443

Fiat Osca Register, Mr M. Elliott, 36 Maypole Drive, Chigwell, Essex. Tel: 081-500 7127

Fiat Twin-Cam Register, Graham Morrish, 19 Oakley Wood Road, Bishops Tachbrook, Leamington Spa, Warks

X/19 Owners club, Sally Shearman, 86 Mill Lane, Dorridge, Solihull

Fire Service Preservation Group, Andrew Scott, 50 Old Slade Lane, Iver, Bucks

Pre-67 Ford Owners Club, Mrs A. Miller, 100 Main Street, Cairneyhill, Fife

Five Hundred Owners Club Association, David Docherty, 'Oakley', 68 Upton Park, Upton-by-Chester, Chester, Cheshire. Tel: (0244) 382789

Ford 105E Owners Club, Sally Harris, 30 Gower Road, Sedgley, Dudley. Tel: (0902) 671071

Ford Mk III Zephyr and Zodiac Owners Club, John Wilding, 10 Waltondale, Woodside, Telford, Salop. Tel: (0952) 580746

The Zephyr and Zodiac Mk IV Owners Club, Richard Cordle, 29 Ruskin Drive, Worcester Park, Surrey. Tel: 081-330 2159

Model A Ford Club of Great Britain, R. Phillippo, The Bakehouse, Church Street, Harston, Cambs

Ford Avo Owners Club, D. Hibbin, 53 Hallsfield Road, Bridgewood, Chatham, Kent

Ford Classic and Capri Owners Club, Roy Lawrence, 15 Tom Davies House, Coronation Avenue, Braintree, Essex. Tel: (0376) 43934

Ford Corsair Owners Club, Mrs E. Checkley, 7 Barnfield, New Malden, Surrey

Capri Club International, Field House, Redditch, Worcs. Tel: (0527) 502066

Ford Capri Enthusiasts Register, Liz Barnes, 46 Manningtree Road, South Ruislip, Middx. Tel: 081-842 0102

Capri Drivers Association, Mrs M Farrelly (Secretary), 9 Lyndhurst Road, Coulsdon, Surrey

Mk I Consul Zephyr and Zodiac Club, 180 Gipsy Road, Welling, Kent. Tel: 081-301 3709

Mk II Consul, Zephyr, Zodiac Club, 170 Conisborough Crescent, Catford

Mk I Cortina Owners Club, R. J. Raisey, 51 Studley Rise, Trowbridge, Wilts

The Cortina Mk II Register, Mark Blows, 78 Church Avenue, Broomfield, Chelmsford, Essex

Ford GT Owners, c/o Riverside School, Ferry Road, Hullbridge, Hockley, Essex

Ford Cortina 1600E Owners Club, Dave Marson, 23 Cumberland Road, Bilston, West Midlands. Tel: Bilston 405055

Ford Cortina 1600E Enthusiasts Club, D. Wright, 32 St Leonards Avenue, Hove

The Savage Register, Trevor Smith, Hillcrest, Top Road, Little Cawthorpe, Louth, Lincs

The Sporting Escort Owners Club, 26 Huntingdon Crescent, off Madresfield Drive, Halesowen, West Midlands

Ford Escort 1300E Owners Club, Robert Watt, 55 Lindley Road, Walton-on-Thames, Surrey

Ford Executive Owners Register, Jenny Whitehouse, 3 Shanklin Road, Stonehouse Estate, Coventry

Ford Granada Mk I Owners Club, Paul Bussey, Bay Tree House, 15 Thornbera Road, Bishops Stortford, Herts

The Ford RS Owners Club, Ford RSOC, 18 Downsview Road, Sevenoaks, Kent. Tel: (0732) 450539

Ford Sidevalve Owners Club, Membership Secretary, 30 Earls Close, Bishopstoke, Eastleigh, Hants

Ford Model 'T' Ford Register of G.B., Mrs Julia Armer, 3 Riverside, Strong Close, Keighley, W. Yorks. Tel: (0535) 607978

Mk II Independent O/C, 173 Sparrow Farm Drive, Feltham, Middx

XR Owners Club, Paul Townend, 50 Wood Street, Castleford, W. Yorks

The Ford Y and C Model Register, Bob Wilkinson, Castle Farm, Main Street, Pollington, Nr Goole, Humberside. Tel: (0405) 860836

Frazer-Nash Section of the VSCC, Mrs J. Blake, Daisy Head Farm, Caulcott, Oxford

The Gentry Register, Frank Tuck, 1 Kinross Avenue, South Ascot, Berks. Tel: (0990) 24637

Gilbern Owners Club, P. C. Fawkes, 24 Mayfield, Buckden, Huntingdon, Cambs. Tel: (0480) 812066

Ginetta Owners Club, Dave Baker, 24 Wallace Mill Gardens, Mid Calder, West Lothian. Tel: (0506) 8883129

Gordon Keeble Owners Club, Ann Knott, Westminster Road, Brackley, Northants. Tel: (0280) 702311

The Gwynne Register, K. Good, 9 Lancaster Avenue, Hadley Wood, Barnet, Herts

The Association of Healey Owners, Don Griffiths, The White House, Hill Pound, Swan More, Hants. Tel: (0489) 895813

Heinkel Trojan Owners and Enthusiasts Club, Y. Luty, Carisbrooke, Wood End Lane, Fillongley, Coventry

Hillman Owners Club, PO Box 94B, East Molesey, Surrey. Tel: 081-941 0604

Historic Commercial Vehicle Society, H.C.V.S., Iden Grange, Cranbrook Road, Staplehurst, Kent

Historic Rally Car Register RAC, Alison Woolley, Tibberton Court, Tibberton, Glos. Tel: (0452) 79648

Historic Sports Car Club, Cold Harbour, Kington Langley, Wiltshire

HRG Association, I. J. Dussek, Little Allens, Allens Lane, Plaxtol, Sevenoaks, Kent

The Holden U.K. Register, G. R. C. Hardy, Clun Felin, Woll's Castle, Haverfordwest, Pembrokeshire, Dyfed, Wales

Honda S800 Sports Car Club, Chris Wallwork, 23a High Street, Steeton, W. Yorks. Tel: (0535) 53845

Humber Register, Hugh Gregory, 176 London Road, St Albans, Herts

Post Vintage Humber Car Club, T. Bayliss, 30 Norbury Road, Fallings Park, Wolverhampton

The Imp Club, Jackie Clark, Cossington Field Farm, Bell Lane, Boxley, Kent. Tel: (0634) 201807

Isetta Owners Club, Brian Orriss, 30 Durham Road, Sidcup, Kent

Jaguar Car Club, R. Pugh, 19 Eldorado Crescent, Cheltenham, Glos

Jaguar Drivers Club, JDC, Jaguar House, 18 Stuart Street, Luton, Beds. Tel: (0582) 419332

Jaguar Enthusiasts Club, G. G. Searle, Sherborne, Mead Road, Stoke Gifford, Bristol. Tel: (0272) 698186

The Jensen Owners Club, Florence, 45 Station Road, Stoke Mandeville, Bucks. Tel: (0296) 612605

Jowett Car Club, Frank Cooke, 152 Leicester Road, Loughborough, Leics. Tel: (0509) 212473

Jupiter Owners Auto Club, Steve Keil, 16 Empress Avenue, Woodford Green, Essex. Tel: 081-505 2215

Karmann Ghia Owners Club (GB), Eliza Conway, 269 Woodborough Road, Nottingham

Kieft Racing and Sports Car Club, Duncan Rabagliati, 4 Wool Road, Wimbledon, London SW20

The Lagonda Club, Mrs Valerie May, 68 Saville Road, Lindfield, Haywards Heath, Sussex

Lancia Motor Club, The Old Shire House, Aylton, Ledbury, Herefordshire

Landcrab Owners Club International, Bill Frazer, PO Box 218, Cardiff

Land Rover Register (1947-1951), Membership Secretary, High House, Ladbrooke, Nr Leamington Spa

The Land Rover Series One Club, David Bowyer, East Foldhay, Zeal Monachorum, Crediton, Devon. Tel: (0363) 82666

Land Rover Series Two Club, PO Box 1609, Yatton, Bristol

Lea Franics Owners Club, R. Sawers, French's, Long Wittenham, Abingdon, Oxon

Lincoln-Zephyr Owners Club, Colin Spong, 22 New North Road, Hainault, Ilford, Essex

London Bus Preservation Trust, Cobham Bus Museum, Redhill Road, Cobham, Surrey

London Vintage Taxi Association, Keith White, 6 Alterton Close, Woking, Surrey

Lotus Cortina Register, 'Fernleigh', Homash Lane, Shadoxhurst, Ashford, Kent

Lotus Drivers Club, Lee Barton, 15 Pleasant Way, Leamington Spa. Tel: (0926) 313514

Lotus Seven Owners Club, David Miryless, 18 St James, Beaminster, Dorset

Club Lotus, PO Box 8, Dereham, Norfolk. Tel: (0362) 694459

Historic Lotus Register, Mike Marsden, Orchard House, Wotton Road, Rangeworthy, Bristol

Marcos Owners Club, 62 Culverley Road, Catford, London SE6. Tel: 081-697 2988

Club Marcos International, Mrs I. Chivers, Membership Secretary, 8 Ludmead Road, Corsham, Wilts. Tel: (0249) 713769

Marendaz Special Car Register, John Shaw, 107 Old Bath Road, Cheltenham. Tel: (0242) 526310

The Marina/Ital Drivers Club, Mr J. G. Lawson, 12 Nithsdale Road, Liverpool

Marlin Owners Club, Mrs J. Cordrey, 14 Farthings West, Capel St Mary, Ipswich

Maserati Club, Michael Miles, The Paddock, Old Salisbury Road, Abbotts Ann, Andover, Hants. Tel: (0264) 710312

Masters Club, Barry Knight, 2 Ranmore Avenue, East Croydon

Matra Enthusiasts Club, M.E.C., 19 Abbotsbury, Orton Goldhay, Peterborough, Cambs. Tel: (0733) 234555

The Mercedes-Benz Club Ltd, P. Bellamy, 75 Theydon Grove, Epping, Essex. Tel: Epping 73304

The Messerschmitt Owners Club, Mrs Eileen Hallam, The Birches, Ashmores Lane, Rusper, West Sussex

Messerchmitt Enthusiasts Club, Graham Taylor, 5 The Green, Highworth, Swindon, Wiltshire

Metropolitan Owners Club, Mr N. Savage, Goat Cottage, Nutbourne Common, Pulborough, Sussex. Tel: (07981) 3921

The MG Car Club, PO Box 251, Abingdon, Berks. Tel: (0235) 555552

MG Octagon Car Club, Harry Crutchley, 36 Queensville Avenue, Stafford. Tel: (0785) 51014

MG Owners Club, R. S. Bentley, 2/4 Station Road, Swavesey, Cambs. Tel: (0954) 31125

The MG 'Y' Type Register, Mr J. G. Lawson, 12 Nithsdale Road, Liverpool

Register of Unusual Micro-Cars, Jean Hammond, School House Farm, Hawkenbury, Staplehurst, Kent

Midget and Sprite Club, Nigel Williams, 15 Foxcote, Kingswood, Bristol. Tel: (0272) 612759

The Military Vehicle Trust, Nigel Gudfrey, 8 Selborne Close, Blackwater, Camberley, Surrey

Mini Cooper Club, Joyce Holman, 1 Weavers Cottages, Church Hill, West Hoathly, Sussex

Mini Cooper Register, Lisa Thornton, 1 Rich Close, Warwick. Tel: (0926) 496934

Mini Marcos Owners Club, Roger Garland, 28 Meadow Road, Claines, Worcester. Tel: (0905) 58533

Mini Moke Club, Paul Beard, 13 Ashdene Close, Hartlebury, Worcs

Mini Owners Club, 15 Birchwood Road, Lichfield

Morgan Sports Car Club, Mrs Christin Healey, 41 Cordwell Close, Castle Donington, Derby

Morgan Three-Wheeler Club Ltd, K. Robinson, Correction Farm, Middlewood, Poynton, Cheshire

Morris Cowley and Oxford Club, Derek Andrews, 202 Chantry Gardens, Southwick, Trowbridge, Wilts

Morris 12 Club, D. Hedge, Crossways, Potton Road, Hilton, Huntingdon

Morris Marina Owners Club, Nigel Butler, 'Llys-Aled', 63 Junction Road, Stourbridge, West Midlands

Morris Minor Owners Club, Jane White, 127-129 Green Lane, Derbyshire

Morris Register, 171 Levita House, Chalton Street, London

Moss Owners Club, David Pegler, Pinewood, Weston Lane, Bath. Tel: (0225) 331509

Norton Owners Club, Shirley Fenner, 18 Wren Crescent, Addlestone, Surrey

Nova Owners Club, Ray Nicholls, 19 Bute Avenue, Hathershaw, Oldham, Lancs

NSU Owners Club, Rosemarie Crowley, 58 Tadorne Road, Tadworth, Surrey. Tel: (073781) 2412

The Ogle Register, Chris Gow, 108 Potters Lane, Burgess Hill. Tel: (0444) 248439

Opel GT UK Owners Club, Martyn and Karen, PO Box 171, Derby. Tel: (0773) 45086

The Opel Manta Club, 14 Rockstowes Way, Westbury-on-Trym, Bristol

The Opel Vauxhall Drivers Club, The Old Mill, Borrow Hall, Dereham, Norfolk. Tel: (0362) 694459

Manta A Series Register, Mark Kinnon, 87 Village Way, Beckenham, Kent

Les Amis de Panhard et Levassor GB, Denise Polley, 11 Arterial Avenue, Rainham, Essex. Tel: (04027) 24425

Panther Car Club Ltd, 35 York Road, Farnborough, Hants. Tel: (0252) 540217

Club Peugeot UK, Dick Kitchingman, Pelham, Chideock, Bridport, Dorset

The Piper (Sports and Racing Car) Club, Clive Davies, Pipers Oak, Lopham Road, East Harling, Norfolk. Tel: (0953) 717813

Porsche Club Great Britain, Ayton House, West End, Northleach, Glos. Tel: (0451) 60792

Post Office Vehicle Club, 7 Bignal Rand Drive, Wells, Somerset

Post 45 Group, Mr R. Cox, 6 Nile Street, Norwich, Norfolk

Potteries Vintage and Classic Car Club, B. Theobold, 78 Reeves Avenue, Cross Heath, Newcastle, Staffs

The Post-War Thoroughbred Car Club, 87 London Street, Chertsey, Surrey

The Radford Register, Chris Gow, 108 Potters Lane, Burgess Hill, West Sussex. Tel: (0444) 248439

Railton Owners Club, 'Fairmiles', Barnes Hall Road, Burncross, Sheffield. Tel: (0742) 468357

Raleigh Safety Seven and Early Reliant Owners Club, Mick Sleap, 17 Courtland Avenue, London E4

Range Rover Register, Chris Tomley, Cwm/Cochen, Bettws, Newtown, Powys

Rapier Register, D. C. H. Williams, 'Smithy', Tregynon, Newton, Powys. Tel: (068687) 396

Reliant Owners Club, Graham Close, 19 Smithey Close, High Green, Sheffield

Reliant Rebel Register, M. Bentley, 70 Woodhall Lane, Calverley, Pudsey, West Yorks. Tel: (0532) 570512

Reliant Sabre and Scimitar Owners Club, RSSOC, PO Box 67, Northampton NN2 6EE. Tel: (0604) 791148

Rear Engine Renault Club, R. Woodall, 346 Crewe Road, Cresty, Crewe

Renault Frères, J. G. Kemsley, Yew Tree House, Jubilee Road, Chelsfield, Kent

Renault Owners Club, C. Marsden, Chevin House, Main Street, Burley-in-Wharfedale, Ilkley, West Yorks. Tel: (0943) 862700

Riley Motor Club Ltd, A. J. Draper, 99 Farmer Ward Road, Kenilworth, Warks. Tel: (0926) 57275

Riley R.M. Club, Bill Harris, 57 Cluny Gardens, Edinburgh

Riley Register, J. A. Clarke, 56 Cheltenham Road, Bishops Cleeve, Cheltenham, Glos

Ro80 Club GB, Simon Kremer, Mill Stone Cottage, Woodside Road, Windsor Forest, Windsor, Berks. Tel: (0344) 890411

Rochdale Owners Club, Brian Tomlinson, 57 West Avenue, Birmingham

Rolls-Royce Enthusiasts, Lt-Col Eric Barrass, The Hunt House, Paulersbury, Northants

Rootes Easidrive Register, M. Molley, 35 Glenesk Road, London SE9

Rover P4 Drivers Guild, Colin Blowers (PC), 32 Arundel Road, Luton, Beds

Rover P5 Owners Club, G. Moorshead, 13 Glen Avenue, Ashford, Middx. Tel: (0784) 258166

P6 Rover Owners Club, PO Box 11, Heanor, Derbyshire

Rover Sports Register, A. Mitchell, 42 Cecil Road, Ilford, Essex

British Saab Enthusiasts, Mr M. Hodges, 75 Upper Road, Parkstone, Poole, Dorset

The Saab Owners Club of GB Ltd, Mrs K. E. Piper, 16 Denewood Close, Watford, Herts. Tel: (0923) 229945

British Salmson Owners Club, John Maddison, 86 Broadway North, Walsall, West Midlands. Tel: (0922) 29677

Salmons Tickford Enthusiasts Club, Keith Griggs, 40 Duffins Orchard, Ottershaw, Surrey

Scootacar Register, Stephen Boyd, 'Pamanste', 18 Holman Close, Aylsham, Norwich, Norfolk

Scimitar Drivers Club, c/o Mick Frost, Pegasus, Main Road, Woodham Ferrers, Essex. Tel: (0245) 320734

Simca Owners Register, David Chapman, 18 Cavendish Gardens, Redhill, Surrey

Singer O.C., Martyn Wray, 11 Ermine Rise, Great Casterton, Stamford, Lincs. Tel: (0780) 62740

Association of Singer Car Owners (A.S.C.O.), Paul Stockwell, 119 Camelot Close, King Arthurs Way, Andover, Hants

Skoda Owners Club of Great Britain, Ray White, 78 Montague Road, Leytonstone E11

South Devon Commercial Vehicle Club, Bob Gale, Avonwick Station, Diptford, Totnes, Devon. Tel: (0364) 73130

South Hants Model Auto Club, C. Derbyshire, 21 Aintree Road, Calmore, Southampton

Spartan Owners Club, Steve Andrews, 28 Ashford Drive, Ravenhead, Notts. Tel: (0623) 793742

Stag Owners Club, John Ramsden, Cedar Cottage, Melplash, Bridport, Dorset. Tel: (030 888) 413

Standard Motor Club, Tony Pingriff, 57 Main Road, Meriden, Coventry. Tel: (0675) 22181

Star, Starling, Stuart and Briton Register, D. E. A. Evans, New Woodlodge, Hyperion Road, Stourton, Stourbridge

Sunbeam Rapier Owners Club, Peter Meech, 12 Greenacres, Downton, Salisbury, Wilts. Tel: (0725) 21140

Sunbeam Alpine Owners Club, Pauline Leese, 53 Wood Street, Mow Cop, Stoke-on-Trent. Tel: (0782) 519865

Sunbeam Talbot Alpine Register, Peter Shimmell, 183 Needlers End Lane, Balsall Common, West Midlands. Tel: (0676) 33304

Sunbeam Talbot Darracq Register, R. Lawson, West Emlett Cottage, Black Dog, Crediton

Sunbeam Tigers Owners Club, Brian Postle, Beechwood, 8 Villa Real Estate, Consett, Co Durham

The Swift Club and Swift Register, John Harrison, 70 Eastwick Drive, Great Bookham, Leatherhead, Surrey. Tel: (0372) 52120

Tornado Register, Dave Malins, 48 St Monicas Avenue, Luton, Beds. Tel: (0582) 37641

TR Drivers Club, Bryan Harber, 19 Irene Road, Orpington, Kent. Tel: (0689) 73776

The TR Register, Rosy Good, 271 High Street, Berkhamsted, Herts. Tel: (0442) 870471

Trident Car Club, Ken Morgan, Rose Cottage, 45 Newtown Road, Verwood, Nr Wimborne, Dorset. Tel: (0202) 822697

Triumph 1300 Register, 39 Winding Way, Leeds

Club Triumph Eastern, Mrs S. Hurrell, 7 Weavers Drive, Glemsford, Suffolk. Tel: (0787) 282176

Club Triumph North London, D. Pollock, 86 Waggon Road, Hadley Wood, Herts

Triumph Mayflower Club, T. Gordon, 12 Manor Close, Hoghton, Preston, Lancs

Pre-1940 Triumph Owners Club, Alan Davis, 33 Blenheim Place, Aylesbury, Bucks

Triumph Razoredge Owners Club, Stewart Langton, 62 Seaward Avenue, Barton-on-Sea, Hants. Tel: (0425) 618074

The Triumph Roadster Club, Paul Hawkins, 186 Mawney Road, Romford, Essex. Tel: (0708) 760745

Triumph Spitfire Club, Johan Hendricksen, Begijnenakker 49, 4241 CK Prinsenbeek, The Netherlands

Triumph Sports Six Club Ltd, 121B St Mary's Road, Market Harborough, Leics. Tel: (0858) 34424

Triumph Sporting Owners Club, G. R. King, 16 Windsor Road, Hazel Grove, Stockport, Cheshire

Triumph 2000/2500/2.5 Register, G. Aldous, 42 Hall Orchards, Middleton, Kings Lynn. Tel: (0553) 841700

Dolomite Sprint Register, DSR, 39 Mill Lane, Arncott, Bicester, Oxon. Tel: (0869) 242847

The Trojan Owners Club, Mrs Christine Potter (Secretary), 64 Old Turnpike, Fareham, Hants. Tel: (0329) 231073

Turner Register, Dave Scott, 21 Ellsworth Road, High Wycombe, Bucks

TVR Car Club, c/o David Gerald, TVR Sports Cars, The Green, Inkberrow, Worcs. Tel: (0386) 793239

United States Army Vehicle Club, Dave Boocock, 31 Valley View Close, Bogthorn, Oakworth Road, Keighley, Yorkshire

Vanden Plas Owners Club, Nigel Stephens, The Briars, Lawson Leas, Barrowby, Grantham, Lincs

Vanguard 1 and 2 Owners Club, R. Jones, The Villa, 11 The Down, Alviston, Avon. Tel: (0454) 419232

Droop Snoot Group, 41 Horsham Avenue, Finchley, London N12. Tel: 081-368 1884

'F' and 'F.B' Victor Owners Club, Wayne Parkhouse, 5 Farnell Road, Staines, Middx

Victor 101 FC (1964-1967), 12 Cliff Crescent, Ellerdine, Telford, Shropshire

The F-Victor Owners Club, Alan Victor Pope, 34 Hawkesbury Drive, Mill Lane, Calcot, Reading, Berks. Tel: (0635) 43532

Vauxhall Cavalier Convertible Club, Ron Goddard, 47 Brooklands Close, Luton, Beds

Vauxhall Owners Club, Brian J. Mundell, 2 Flaxton Court, St Leonards Road, Ayr

Vauxhall PA/PB/PC/E Owners Club, G. Lonsdale, 77 Pilling Lane, Preesall, Lancs. Tel: (0253) 810866

Vauxhall VX4/90 Drivers Club, c/o 43 Stroudwater Park, Weybridge, Surrey

The Viva Owners Club, Adrian Miller, The Thatches, Snetterton North End, Snetterton, Norwich

Veteran Car Club of Great Britain, Jessamine House, High Street, Ashwell, Herts

Vintage Sports Car Club Ltd, The Secretary, 121 Russell Road, Newbury, Berks. Tel: (0635) 44411

The Association of British Volkswagen Clubs, Dept PC, 66 Pinewood Green, Iver Heath, Bucks

Volkswagen Cabriolet Owners Club (GB), Emma Palfreyman (Secretary), Dishley Mill, Derby Road, Loughborough

Historic Volkswagen Clubs, 11A Thornbury Lane, Church Hill, Redditch, Worcs. Tel: (0527) 591883

Volkswagen Owners Club GB, R. Houghton, 49 Addington Road, Irthlingborough, Northants

Volkswagen Owners Caravan Club (GB), Mrs Shirley Oxley, 18 Willow Walk, Hockley, Essex

Volkswagen Split Screen Van Club, Brian Hobson, 12 Kirkfield Crescent, Thorner, Leeds

Volkswagen '50-67' Transporter Club, Peter Nicholson, 11 Lowton Road, Lytham St Annes, Lancs. Tel: (0253) 720023

VW Type 3 and 4 Club, Jane Terry, Pear Tree Bungalow, Exted, Elham, Canterbury, Kent

Volvo Enthusiasts Club, Kevin Price, 4 Goonbell, St Agnes, Cornwall

Volvo Owners Club, Mrs Suzanne Groves, 90 Down Road, Merrow, Guildford, Surrey. Tel: (0483) 37624

Vulcan Register, D. Hales, 20 Langbourne Way, Claygate, Esher, Surrey

The Wartburg Owners Club, Bernard Trevena, 56 Spiceall Estate, Compton, Guildford. Tel: (0483) 810493

Wolseley 6/80 and Morris Oxford Club, John Billinger, 67 Fleetgate, Barton-on-Humber, North Lincs. Tel: (0652) 635138

The Wolseley Hornet-Special Club, Mrs P. Eames, Jasmin Cottage, Weston, Nr Sidmouth, Devon

Wolseley Register, B. Eley, 60 Garfield Avenue, Dorchester, Dorset

XR Owners Club, 20A Swithland Lane, Rothley, Leics

A motorist's map reading aid, c1930, 5in (13cm) long.
£10-15 *RTT*

DIRECTORY OF SPECIALISTS

If you wish to be included in next year's directory or if you have a change of address or telephone number, please could you inform us by December 31st 1991. Entries will be repeated in subsequent editions unless we are requested otherwise. Finally we would advise readers to make contact by telephone before a visit, therefore avoiding a wasted journey, which nowadays is both time consuming and expensive.

Air Conditioning

Airstream, Unit 13, Stonehouse Commercial Centre, Stonehouse, Glos. Tel: (045 382) 8781

Alfa Romeo Specialists

Alfatune, Merton Bank Road, St Helens, Merseyside. Tel: (0744) 21929

Automatic Gearboxes

G. Whitehouse Autos Ltd, Haden Hill Road, Halesowen, West Midlands. Tel: 021-550 7630

Axles

The Axle Centre, 78 Fishponds Road, Eastville, Bristol 5, Avon. Tel: (081 364) 0988

Supertorque Transmissions, Derby. Tel: (0332) 45080/365993

Ball and Roller Bearings

Burton Engineering Supplies, Hawkins Lane, Burton-on-Trent, Staffs. Tel: (0283) 36088

BMW Specialists

Paul or Peter, Aylsham, Norfolk. Tel: (0263) 733621

Brakes

J.E.M., Leicestershire. Tel: (0455) 230626

Carburettors

Southern Carburettors, Unit 6, Nelson Trading Estate, Morden Road, Wimbledon. Tel: 081-540 2723/8128 and
13 Cobham Way, Gatwick Road, Crawley, West Sussex. Tel: (0293) 29502/3

Gower & Lee, 24 Brook Mews North, Paddington, London W2. Tel: 071-262 0300

Burlem Fuel Systems, Spitfire House, Castle Road, Salisbury, Wilts. Tel: (0722) 412500

Carburettor Centre, 105-107 St Leonards Road, Far Cotton, Northampton. Tel: (0604) 766624

Chris Montague, 380/2 Finchley Road, London NW2. Tel: 071-794 7766/7

Dellorto Carburettors, 13 Boult Street, Reading, Berks

Car Radio

Mr A. C. James, 10 Westview, Poulton, Nr Bristol, Avon. Tel: (0761) 413933

Chroming

Q.B. Chroming & Polishing, 91 High Street, Quarry Bank, Brierly Hill, West Midlands. Tel: (0384) 637168

The Standard Chrome Co., Unit 2A/B, 31-41 Cross Road, Foleshill, Coventry. Tel: (0203) 683624

London Chroming Company, 735 Old Kent Road, London SE15. Tel: 071-639 6434

Cleveland Chroming Co., 115, 7d Riverside Park Industrial Estate, Middlesbrough, Cleveland. Tel: (0642) 244911

Kingsley Chrome, Unit 6, Kingsley Business Park, Kingsley, Nr Bordon, Hants. Tel: (0420) 489676

Vintage Chrome Restoration, Unit 6, Parnall Road, Fishponds, Bristol, Avon. Tel: (0272) 653408

S & T Electro-Plate Limited, Unit 15, The Alpha Centre, Great Western Business Park, Armstrong Way, Yate, North Avon. Tel: (0454) 313162

Citroën

Dee Ess Conversions, Unit 12, Link Industrial Estate, Howsell Road, Malvern. Tel: (0684) 892826

Hypertronics, 50 Sapcote Trading Estate, 374 High Road, Willesden, London NW10. Tel: 081-459 3725

Coach Trimming

David Beswick, Unit 17, Robinson Ind. Estate, Shaftesbury Street, Derby. Tel: (0332) 43252

Derek Stilton, The Oast House, Maynards Green, Heathfield, East Sussex. Tel: (04353) 2044

Woolies CC, Blenheim Way, Northfields Industrial Estate, Market Deeping, Nr Peterborough. Tel: (0778) 347347

Gary H. Wright, 126 Tanners Drive, Blakelands, Milton Keynes. Tel: (0908) 617774

R & J Coachtrimming, Ion Bridge Farm, Lower Gravenhurst, Bedford. Tel: (0462) 711036

R & S Coachbuilt's, 123A Old Dover Road, Blackheath, London SE3. Tel: 081-858 4312

J. P. Bevan, Unit 1, Great Western Road, Gloucester. Tel: (0452) 308379

Cliff Barford, Unit 2, Drury Lane Ind. Estate, Drury Lane, Buckley, Clwyd. Tel: (024 454) 8847

The Creech Coachtrimming Centre, 45 Anerley Road, Crystal Palace, London SE19. Tel: 081-659 4136

Covers

Adrian Sacks Textiles, Unit B, Hillam Road Industrial Estate, Off Canal Road, Bradford, Yorks. Tel: (0274) 394147/391758

Classic Additions Ltd. Tel: (0380) 720419/723761

Stainless Systems (AC), 46 Little Street, Rushden, Northants. Tel: (0933) 410851

Engines

Coventry Boring & Metalling Co. Ltd., 3 Coniston Road, Earlsdon, Coventry. Tel: (0203) 672372

Flotec, Accessory and Motor Supplies, Unit A8, Faraday Road, Newbury, Berks. Tel: (0635) 44669

Exhausts

Mike Randall, 128 Stanley Park Road, Wallington, Surrey. Tel: 081-669 1719

P. D. Gough & Associate, Nottingham. Tel: (0602) 382241

SM International, 9 Rostherne Road, Wilmslow, Cheshire. Tel: (0831) 309599

JP Exhausts, Old School House, Brook Street, Macclesfield, Cheshire. Tel: (0625) 619916

Fastenings

D. Middleton, Unit 5, Lady Ann Mills, Batley, West Yorks. Tel: (0924) 470807

Fasteners by Intasprint, Unit 12, Aldridge Depot Industrial Estate, Brickyard Road, Aldridge, Walsall. Tel: (0922] 52466

Bernard F. Wade Ltd., Unit L3, Meltham Mill Industrial Estate, Meltham, Huddersfield. Tel: (0484) 851585

John Worrall Exclusives, 12 Burntoak Drive, Parkfield Road, Stourbridge, West Midlands. Tel: (0384) 375189

Mr Fast'ner Ltd., Unit 2, Warwick House Industrial Park, Banbury Road, Southam, Warwicks. Tel: (0926) 817207

Gaskets

Johnson Gaskets, Verity Street, East Brierley, Bradford, West Yorks. Tel: (0274) 682298

Gearboxes

Hanover Transmissions, 134H North Lane, Aldershot, Hants. Tel: (0252) 310413

Auto-Tech Transmissions, Dept AC, Mona Works, Manor Road, Manchester. Tel: 061-224 4113

General Restorers

Alfa Beta Racing Ltd., 69-75 Newtown Street, Luton, Beds. Tel: (0582) 414941

Alfacenta, Turgis Green, Basingstoke, Hants. Tel: (0256) 882831

Alpine Autos Ltd., Comfortable Place, Upper Bristol Road, Bath. Tel: (0225) 448690

David Alston, Chelsea Reach, 79-89 Lots Road, London SW10

American Auto Specialists, Rutland Street, Ashton-under-Lyne, Lancs. Tel: (061 308) 3410

Aston Martin Lagonda, Tickford Street, Newport Pagnell. Tel: (0908) 610620

Autobahn Motorsport, Unit 5, Thorpe Way Industrial Estate, Banbury, Oxon. Tel: (0295) 61196

Autodelta, Unit 10, Ealing Car Repair Centre, 253A Ealing Road, Alperton, Wembley. Tel: 081-991 5046

Autofarm, Cow Roast, London Road, Nr Tring, Herts. Tel: (0442) 89091

Autoskil, Fisher Lane, Chiddingfold, Surrey. Tel: (0428) 683054

Avant Classic Restorations, Arch 124, Cornwall Road, London SE1. Tel: 071-928 6613

Batheaston Artefactors, Comfortable Place, Upper Bristol Road, Bath. Tel: (0225) 482737

BC Classic American Autos. Tel: 081-958 1756.

Benalfa, Washington Road, West Wiltshire Trading Estate, Westbury, Wilts. Tel: (0373) 864333

Betacars, Unit 12B, Manywells Industrial Estate, Cullingworth, Bradford, W. Yorks. Tel: (0535) 275560

E. Bertelli, 22 Stile Brook Road, Yardley Road West, Olney, Bucks. Tel: (0234) 240024

Birkdale Classics, 6A Kew Road, Birkdale, Southport, Merseyside. Tel: (0704) 64877

BL Autos, Fiddlebridge Industrial Estate, Lemsford Road, Hatfield, Herts. Tel: (0707) 741379

Blue Diamond, Bow House, Bow Street, Langport, Somerset. Tel: (0458) 251147

Bristol Cars, 368-370 Kensington High Street, London W14. Tel: 071-603 5554

C. J. Boon, Unit One, Orchard Court, Orchard Road, Finedon, Northants. Tel: (0933) 681172

Cambrian Classic Car Company, Jubilee Road, Barmouth, Gwynedd. Tel: (0341) 280917

Canal Classic Car Renovations, Lenton Lane, Lenton Lane Industrial Estate, Nottingham. Tel: (0602) 866321

Cartell Motors (Louth) Ltd., Unit 16, Louth Station Estates, off Newbridge Hill, Louth, Lincs. Tel: (0507) 600390

Car Bodies, 14 Scott Street, Bognor Regis, Sussex. Tel: (0243) 862611

C.B. Classics, Unit B, Hollybush Farm, Rattlesden Road, Buxhall, Stowmarket, Suffolk. Tel: (04493) 7897

Chapman Spooner, Middlemore Lane, Aldridge, Walsall, West Midlands. Tel: (0922) 743443

Chelsea Workshop, Nell Gwynn House, Draycott Avenue, London SW3. Tel: (071-584 8363

Classic Autos, 10 High Street, Kings Langley, Herts. Tel: (09277) 62994

Classic Components, Ickornshaw Mill, Cowling, Nr Keighley. Tel: (0535) 35829

Classico, 247 Acton Lane, London NW10. Tel: 081-965 6315/6

G.J. Coachworks Inc., 5 Stanhope Street, Liverpool. Tel: 051-708 5225

Colbornes Restoration Services, Liss, Hants. Tel: (0730) 894180

Country Classic Cars, Unit 5, Westfield Road, Kington Road Industrial Estate, Southam, Warwicks. Tel: (092681) 4327

Frank Dale & Stepson, 120/124 King Street, London W6. Tel: 081-748 0821

Day & Shindler Ltd., 98 Druid Street, London SE1. Tel: 071-231 8863

DK Engineering, Unit D, 200 Rickmansworth Road, Watford, Herts. Tel: (0923) 55246

Ivan Dutton, Peacehaven Farm, Worminghall Road, Ickford, Aylesbury, Bucks. Tel: (08447) 457

Earlsway Classics Ltd., Earls Way, Halesowen, West Midlands. Tel: 021-585 6003

Ely Service, Lynn Road, Ely, Cambridgeshire. Tel: (0353) 662981

Epsom Mini Centre, 26 Waterloo Road, Epsom, Surrey. Tel: (03727) 40702

Keith Evans, Malthouse Garage, Halfway House, Shrewsbury, Shropshire. Tel: (0743) 884468

Nick Faure, Whitley, Surrey. Tel: (042879) 4708

Five Star Ford, Unit 12 Industrial Estate, Milkwood Road, London SE24.

Forward Engineering, Walsh Lane, Meriden, Nr Coventry. Tel: (0676) 23526

G. T. Foulds, Firth Street, Huddersfield, West Yorks. Tel: (0484) 534743

4.2 Motors, Unit 6, Claggy Road, Kimpton, Herts. Tel: (0438) 833434

Gatwick Alfa, Charlwood Garage, The Street, Charlwood, Surrey.

B. Gillies, Barn Elms Farm, Dark Lane, Bradfield, Berks. Tel: (0734) 744134

Goldsmith & Young, Unit 1D, Quarryfield Industrial Estate, Mere, Wilts. Tel: (0747) 866715

Graypaul, The Corneries, Loughborough. Tel: (0509) 232233

Greystoke, Witch Hazel Plantation, Tylney Hall, Rotherwick, Basingstoke, Hants. Tel: (0256) 766137

GTC Engineering, Unit 5, Sanders Lodge Industrial Estate, Rushden, Northants. Tel: (0933) 315530

A. J. Hickman, 85 Worthington Road, Fradley, Lichfield, Staffs. Tel: (0543) 252196

Hightone Restorations, Unit 5, Enstone Airfield, Enstone. Tel: (0608) 677328

Geoff Hine, Moorland Classic Cars, Forest Side, Parknook, Ipstones, Stoke-on-Trent. Tel: (0538) 266459

Hofmann & Mountford Ltd., Fairfield Works, Reading Road, Henley-on-Thames, Oxon. Tel: (0491) 573953

Huntsworth, 24-28 Boston Place, London NW1. Tel: 071-724 0269

Hypertronics Ltd., 50 Sapcoge Trading Estate, 374 High Road, London NW10. Tel: 081-459 3725

Jensen Car Company, Kelvin Way, West Bromwich, West Midlands. Tel: 021-553 6741

JME, 18 Green Parmend, Kineton, Warwickshire. Tel: (0926) 640031

Johnson Coachwork Restorations, Berkhamsted, Herts. Tel: (0442) 874114

Rod Jolley Coachbuilding, 37 Gordleton Industrial Park, Sway Road, Lymington, Hants. Tel: (0590) 683702

L & C Auto Services, BMW House, 39 St Johns Road, Tunbridge Wells, Kent. Tel: (0892) 39355

Rod Leach, Nostalgia, Briar Forge, Vicarage Causeway, Hertford Heath, Herts. Tel: (0992) 500007

Michael Leake Classic Cars, Painswick, Gloucester. Tel: (0452) 813152

Lifes Motors Ltd., West Street, Southport, Lancs. Tel: (0704) 32975

Lombarda, 2-10 Railway Mews, Ladbroke Grove, London W10. Tel: 071-243 0636

Lotus Service Centre, 214A Wanstead Park Road, Ilford, Essex. Tel: 081-554 6194

Bill McGrath, Units 8-9, Claggy Lane Industrial Estate, Kimpson, Herts. Tel: (0438) 832161

Maranello, Egham Bypass, Egham, Surrey. Tel: (0784) 436431

Ian Mason, 139A Freston Road, London W10. Tel: 071-727 7678

Paul Matty Sports Cars, 12 Old Birmingham Road, Bromsgrove, Worcs. Tel: (0527) 35656

Medway Renovations. Tel: (0634) 718482

MG Centre Cardiff, Unit 10, Alexandra Industrial Estate, Wentloog Road, Rumney, Cardiff. Tel: (0222) 777834

Modena, Station Garage, East Horsley, Surrey. Tel: (04865) 4663

Motobuild Ltd., 328 Bath Road, Hounslow, Middlesex. Tel: 081-572 5437

The Morris Minor Centre, Avon House, Lower Bristol Road, Bath. Tel: (0225) 315449

Avon M M Centre, Grove House, Beeches Industrial Estate, Stoner Road, Yate, Bristol. Tel: (0454) 310589

The M M Centre, Birmingham Parade Service, Station Parade, Birmingham. Tel: 021-236 1341

The Minor Clinic, The Old Brickworks, The Meadway, Reading, Berks. Tel: (0734) 572283

Original Morris Traveller Centre, 282-300 Leabridge Road, London E10. Tel: 081-558 9235

Moto-Technique, Pycroft Road, Chertsey, Surrey. Tel: (0932) 564706

P. Nardelli, 68 Windermere Avenue, Finchley, London N3. Tel: 081-346 8628

Christopher Neil Ltd., Middlewich Road, Northwich, Cheshire. Tel: (0606) 47914

Newman & Jones, 128 Stonehouse Street, Clapham, London SW4. Tel: 071-622 1918

NSU HME, 10-16 Abury Avenue, Foleshill, Coventry. Tel: (0203) 661357

The Oak's Classic Cars. Tel: (0279) 777216

Omicron Engineering Ltd., The Malthouse, Mulbarton, Norwich. Tel: (0508) 70351

Orchard Restorations, High Street, Horam, Sussex. Tel: (04353) 2374

Panelcraft. Tel: (04027) 25295

Tim Pettifer, Tove Trimming, Towcester. Tel: (0327) 53667/50264

Pleiades, Green End House, Scotney Way, Shawtry, Cambridgeshire. Tel: (0487) 831239

I S Polson, Mill Farm, Ashfield Green, Wickham Brook, Newmarket, Suffolk. Tel: (0440) 82037

Portman, Unit 3, Ealing Road Industrial Estate, Ealing Road, Brentford, Middlesex. Tel: 081-568 1949

Luxury & Power, 31 Gillian Street, Ladywell Village, London SE13. Tel: 081-690 8088

Prestbury Restorations. Tel: (0625) 827884

Radbourne Racing, 213-217 The Broadway, London SW19

W. Rawles, Unit 10, Bumpers Farm Estate, Long Sutton, Hants. Tel: (0256) 862001

Red Triangle, Cherry Street, Warwick. Tel: (0926) 410176

Rees Bros, 69 Gordon Road, Aldershot, Hants. Tel: (0252) 23038

Riverside Works, Cropredy, Banbury, Oxon. Tel: (029 575) 8444

Roverline, 7 High Street, Clowne, Nr Chesterfield, Derbyshire. Tel: (0246) 819585

Rover Part, 18 Cheriton Court, Selhurst Road, London SE2. Tel: 081-653 4790

Melvyn Rutter Ltd., The Morgan Garage, Little Hallingbury, Nr Bishops Stortford, Herts. Tel: (0279) 725725

Schmit Auto Services Ltd., 109 Goldhurst Terrace, London NW6. Tel: 071-624 0884

School Street Renovations, School Street, Dudley, West Midlands. Tel: (0384) 392798

Herb Schofield, Lagonda Garage, Rear 44 London Road, Oldham, Lancs. Tel: 061-633 7356

D. Scott-Moncreiff, Britannia Works, West Street, Leek, Staffs. Tel: (0384) 392798

Sherwood Restorations, 10 Dalesworth Road, Sutton in Ashfield, Nottinghamshire. Tel: (0623) 440313

Stags 'N' Jags. Tel: (0792) 581166

Straight 8, 152-160 Goldhawk Road, London W12. Tel: 081-743 1599

Straight 6, Gemini House, High Street, Edgware, Middx. Tel: 081-951 0188

Martin Stretton, Unit 30, Bewdley Commercial Centre, Longbank, Bewdley, Worcs. Tel: (0299) 266793

SC Austin Healey, 13 Cobham Way, Gatwick Road, Crawley, West Sussex

Streber, Station Road, Hemylock, Devon. Tel: (0823) 680748

Stretton Summers, High Street, Cleobury Mortimer, Nr Kidderminster, Worcs. Tel: (0299) 27021

Swallow Engineering, Basildon, Essex. Tel: (0268) 558418

Tidy Engineering, Brook Farm, Horsham Road, Cowfold, West Sussex. Tel: (0403) 864507

Thompson & Potter, High Street, Borrelton, Blairgowrie, Perthshire. Tel: (08287) 247

2002 Centre, Jaymic, Norwich Road, Cromer. Tel: (0263) 511710

Vicarage Classic Car Co. Ltd., Building 13, Stanmore Industrial Estate, Nr Bridgnorth, Shropshire. Tel: (0746) 766031

Voiture Technique, 10-11 Catell Road, Warwick. Tel: (0926) 402101

Tim Walker Restorations. Tel: (0296) 77596

Ray Weekley, Unit 1, 3 St Agatha's Road, Stoke, Coventry. Tel: (0203) 635274

David Wells Restoration, 564-566 Wickham Road, Shirley, Croydon, Surrey. Tel: 081-777 2775

Wykehams Ltd., 6 Kendricks Place, Reece Mews, London SW7. Tel: 071-589 6894

XK Engineering, Unit 15, Netherwood Industrial Estate, Ratcliffe Road, Atherstone, Warwicks. Tel: (0827) 717885

Insurance

Broadoak Insurance, 114A High Street, Brentwood, Essex. Tel: (0277) 211606

Hyperformance Insurance. Tel: 081-941 7552

R.F.O. plc, Fleet House, 310 High Street, Sutton, Surrey. Tel: 081-770 0065

Esprit (Finance & Leasing) Ltd. Tel: (0371) 856661

Bryant Kesek & Partners, Exeter House, Tylers Court, Cranleigh, Surrey. Tel: (0483) 274792

Heritage Classic Car Insurance, 115 Hagley Road, Birmingham. Tel: 021-455 6644

Vintage Car Insurance Associates, 124 High Street, Godstone, Surrey. Tel: (0883) 744040

Headley Mitchell Insurance, Fakenham. Tel: (0328) 863358

Gott & Wynne Insurance Brokers, 11 Madoc Street, Llandudno, Gwynedd. Tel: (0492) 870991

Moffatt & Co. Ltd., Percy House, 796 High Road, London N17. Tel: 081-808 3020

Instruments

Complete Automobilist Ltd., The Old Rectory, Greatford, Stamford, Lincolnshire. Tel: (077 836) 312

Renown Instruments, Stonehenge Road, Durrington, Wilts. Tel: (0980) 53800

Speedy Cables (London) Ltd., The Mews, St. Paul Street, Islington, London N1. Tel: 071-226 9228

Vintage Restorations, The Old Bakery, Windmill Street, Tunbridge Wells, Kent. Tel: (0892) 25899

Jaguar Specialists

M. R. Buckeridge Ltd., Hirstlane Garage, Hirst Lane, Shipley, West Yorks. Tel: (0274) 589389

Marcus Barclay, Unit 10, Middle Green Trading Estate, Langley, Berks. Tel: (0753) 693778

Kirk Rylands, Carlisle. Tel: (0228) 74626

Reincarnation, Lower Rainham Road, Rainham, Kent. Tel: (0634) 362161/405475

Ken Shergold, Waltham Cross. Tel: (0992) 24721

Lamborghini Specialists

Portman Lamborghini. Tel: 081-568 1949

Lamps

D.C.M. & Co., 94 Matilda Street, Sheffield, Yorks. Tel: (0742) 700229/739799/750479

Leather Upholstery

Leathercare Renovations, 2 Aston Court, Kingsland Grange, Woolston, Warrington. Tel: (0925) 851621

Fortes Luxury Leather Redressers, S.E. London. Tel: (0860) 381379

D.S. Automobile Upholstery, Guildford. Tel: (0483) 225203

Sovereign Leather Renovation Services. Tel: (0831) 270909

Gary Jackson, Newlife Service Systems, Co. Durham. Tel: (0388) 420678

Fine Leather Refinishing. Tel: 081-683 2408

Lotus Specialists

Performance Unlimited, 290 Westborough Road, Westcliff-on-Sea, Essex. Tel: (0702) 340954

Magneto and Dynamo Specialists

F.T.W. Magnetos, 178 Peniston Road North, Hillborough, Sheffield. Tel: (0742) 336269

Independent Ignition Supplies, AM Boat Yard, Myrtle Street, Appledore, Bideford, Devon. Tel: (0237) 475986

Maserati Specialists

Maserati, Units 8 and 9, Claggy Lane Industrial Estate, Kimpton, Herts. Tel: (0438) 832161

Mercedes Specialists

Portfield Mercedes, Quarry Lane, Chichester, West Sussex. Tel: (0243) 776111

MG Specialists

Charmons Coachworks, 7 St George's Avenue, Parkstone, Poole, Dorset. Tel: (0202) 722755/872127

A & C The Complete MG Centre. Tel: 081-303 0955

Lancecliff MG Services, Botley. Tel: (0836) 556874

Morris Minor Specialists

Alan James, Dept. AC6, Unit 7, Willow Green Farm, Threemilestone, Truro, Cornwall. Tel: (0872) 70210

Number Plates

Premier Plates, 23 Laurel Avenue, Ripley, Derbys. Tel: (0773) 747295

Overdrive Repair

Overdrive Repair Service, Unit C4, Ellisons Road, Norwood Trading Estate, Killamarsh, Sheffield. Tel: (0742) 482632

Paintwork

Courtenay Garage, Woking. Tel: (0483) 721658

Frank Taylor Ltd., Station Road, Hinckley, Leics. Tel: (0455) 632478

Pro Paint. Tel: (0629) 55233

Bob Jenkins, Bristol. Tel: (0272) 615944

Bill's Paint Shop, Chertsey. Tel: (0932) 569622

Plating

Derby Plating Services Ltd., 148 Abbey Street, Derby. Tel: (0332) 382408

Electro Plating Services Ltd., Unit 7, Napier Road, Hillington Estate, Glasgow. Tel: 041-882 3335

Weldmet, Unit 8, 55 Weir Road, Wimbledon SW19. Tel: 081-947 1288

Plugs

The Green Spark Plug Co., 340 Washway Road, Sale, Cheshire. Tel: (061 973) 6755

Powder Coating

Airoblast, Unit K, Loddon Industrial Estate, Norwich, Norfolk. Tel: (0508) 28037

Racing Car Specialists

Scott Ellis Racing Ltd., Unit 17, Crane Way, Woolsbridge Industrial Park, Three Legged Cross, Wimborne, Dorset. Tel: (0202) 813245

Huddart Racing Engines, 5-7 Collins Street, Crewe, Cheshire. Tel: (0270) 665405

Radiators

Northampton Autorads, 51/53 Robert Street, Northampton. Tel: (0604) 35937

British & Continal Radiators. Tel: 081-459 6230

Rebore

Sutton Rebore Service Ltd., 34-38 Lind Road, Sutton, Surrey. Tel: 081-642 5685/3419

Rolls-Royce and Bentley Specialists

T. Stevens, Unit 6, Hanbury Road, Stoke Prior, Bromsgrove, Worcs. Tel: (0527) 36477

Rover Specialists

B.D. & G. Rover Parts Centre, 318 Lea Bridge Road, Leyton, London E10. Tel: 081-558 2975/556 5442

Ray Weekley, Unit One, 3 St Agatha's road, Coventry. Tel: (0203) 635274

Rust Proofing

Vintage & Classic Specialists. Tel: 081-301 2244

Scimitar Specialists

Robin Rew Ltd., Unit 12, Silverstone Circuit, Silverstone, Northants. Tel: (0327) 857903

Shock Absorbers

J. W. E. Banks Ltd., Crowland, Peterborough. Tel: (0733) 210316

Seatbelts

Quickfit, 39 Kenton Park Parade, Kenton Road, Harrow. Tel: 081-907 1162

Springs

Springs Only. Tel: (0922) 410096

Steering Wheels

Auto Image, 260 Gospel Lane, Acocks Green, Birmingham. Tel: 021-707 7677

Sunroofs

R & S Coachbuilts, 123a Old Dover Road, Blackheath. Tel: 081-858 4312

Tools

Auto Restoration Techniques Ltd., Crawford Street, Rochdale. Tel: (0706) 58619

Tracy Tools (Garage) Ltd., 2 Mayors Avenue, Dartmouth, South Devon. Tel: (0803) 833134

A. E. Charlesworth, 28 Middleton Road, Mansfield Woodhouse, Notts. Tel: (0623) 23634

A.B.C. Spares, Holt Forest Farm, Holt, Nr Wimborne, Dorset. Tel: (0258) 840309

FORTHCOMING EVENTS 1991

February
11th-16th	Monte Carlo Challenge
15th-24th	Retromobile, Paris
17th	Bug Freeze, Stafford

March
2nd-3rd	London International Classic Car Show, Alexandra Palace
7th-10th	RAC International Historic Rally of Great Britain
8th-10th	Techno-Classica, Essen, Germany
16th-17th	Bristol Classic Car Show

April
13th	Collectors Car Spectacular, Bingley Hall
20th	VSCC Historic Racing, Silverstone

May
2nd-5th	Mille Miglia, Italy
4th-5th	HSCC Historic Racing, Donington
4th-6th	Classic and Sportscars International, NEC
5th	Benson and Hedges Classic
26th	Norwich Union RAC Classic Run

June
1st-2nd	HSCC Historic Racing, Brands Hatch
9th	Benson and Hedges Classic, Syon Park
15th	VSCC Historic Racing, Silverstone

23rd	London-Brighton Classic Car Run Benson and Hedges Classic, Glasgow
30th	Bromley Pageant, Kent

July
14th	Uxbridge Auto Show, Middlesex Benson and Hedges Classic, Swansea
20th-21st	HSCC Historic Racing, Donington Americana '90
26th-28th	International Historic Festival, Silverstone

August
2nd-4th	Oldtimer Grand Prix, Nurburgring, Germany
3rd-4th	American Lifestyle Show
11th	Benson and Hedges Classic, Ulster
25th	Benson and Hedges Classic, Beaulieu
26th	Luton Hoo Classic Car Run

September
7th-8th	Beaulieu Autojumble
21st-22nd	VSCC Historic Racing, Donington

November
3rd	London-Brighton Veteran Car Run
9th-10th	National Classic Car Show, NEC
29th-8th Dec	Motor Show Essen, Germany

448

DIRECTORY OF AUCTIONEERS

United Kingdom

ADT, Prospect House, The Broadway, Farnham Common, Slough, Bucks. Tel: (0753) 645622

Anglian Automobile Auctions, North Weald Airfield, Epping, Essex. Tel: (0284) 754902

Arlington Auctions Ltd, Kingston Wharf, Brighton Road, Shoreham-by-Sea, West Sussex. Tel: (0273) 595952

Bonhams, 65-69 Lots Road, Chelsea, London SW10. Tel: 071-351 7111

Brooks, 81 Westside, London SW4. Tel: 071-228 8000

Central Motor Auctions plc, Barfield House, Britannia Road, Morley, Leeds. Tel: (0532) 527722

Christie's, 8 King Street, St James, London SW1. Tel: 071-839 9060

Classic Motor Auctions, PO Box 20, Fishponds, Bristol. Tel: (0272) 701370

Coys of Kensington, 2-4 Queens Gate Mews, London SW7. Tel: 071-584 7444

Hampson Ltd, Road 4, Winsford Industrial Estate, Winsford, Cheshire. Tel: (0606) 559054

Hamptons Collectors Cars, 71 Church Street, Malvern, Worcs. Tel: (0684) 893110

Holloways, 49 Parsons Street, Banbury, Oxon. Tel: (0295) 253197

Husseys, Alphin Brook Road, Exeter. Tel: (0392) 50441

James Auctioneers, 33 Timberhill, Norwich. Tel: (0603) 625369

Lambert & Foster, 97 Commercial Road, Paddock Wood, Tonbridge, Kent. Tel: (0892) 832325

Phillips, West Two, 10 Salem Road, London W2. Tel: 071-229 9090

Premier Auctions, 45 Murrain Drive, Downswood, Maidstone, Kent. Tel: (0622) 862854

Renaissance, 36-38 London Road, Hazel Grove, Nr Stockport, Cheshire. Tel: 061-483 9427

RTS Auctions Ltd, 11 Telford Close, Sweet Briar Industrial Estate, Norwich. Tel: (0603) 409677

Russell, Baldwin & Bright, Ryelands Road, Leominster, Herefordshire. Tel: (0568) 611166

Sentries Auctions, Huntworth Manor, Huntworth, Somerset. Tel: (0278) 663263

Shoreham Car Auctions, 5-6 Brighton Road, Kingston Wharf, Shoreham-by-Sea, West Sussex. Tel: (0273) 595250

Sotheby's, 34-35 New Bond Street, London W1. Tel: 071-493 8080

Walton & Hipkiss, 111 Worcester Road, Hagley, West Midlands. Tel: (0562) 885555

International

C. Boisgirard, 2 Rue de Provence, 75009 Paris, France. Tel: (010 33) 147708136

Carlisle Productions, The Flea Marketeers, 1000 Bryn Mawr Road, Carlisle, PA 17013-1588, USA

Christie's Australia Pty Ltd, 1 Darling Street, South Yarra, Melbourne, Victoria 3141. Tel: (03) 820 4311

Christie's (Monaco), S.A.M., Park Palace, 98000 Monte Carlo. Tel: 010 339 325 1933

Christie, Manson & Woods International Inc, 502 Park Avenue, New York, NY10022. Tel: (212) 546 1000

Classic Automobile Auctions B.V., Goethestrasse 10, 6000 Frankfurt 1. Tel: (010 49) 69 28666/8

Kruse International Inc, PO Box 190-Co.Rd. 11-A, Auburn, Indiana, USA 46706

Orion Auction House, Victoria Bldg-13, Bd Princess Charlotte, Monte Carlo, MC 98000 Monaco. Tel: (010 3393) 301669

Silver Collector Car Auctions, E204, Spokane, Washington 99207, USA. Tel: (0101) 509 326 4485

Sotheby's, Summers Place, Billingshurst, West Sussex. Tel: (0403) 783933

Sotheby's, 1334 York Avenue, New York, NY 10021. Tel: (212) 606 7000

Sotheby's, B.P. 45, Le Sporting d'Hiver, Place du Casino, MC 98001 Monaco/Cedex. Tel: 33 (93) 30 88 80

DIRECTORY OF MUSEUMS

Avon
Bristol Industrial Museum, Princes Wharf, City Docks, Bristol 1. Tel: (0272) 251470

Bedfordshire
Shuttleworth Collection, Old Warden Aerodrome, Nr Biggleswade. Tel: (096 727) 288

Buckinghamshire
West Wycombe Motor Museum, Cockshoot Farm, Chorley Road, West Wycombe

Cambridgeshire
Vintage M/C Museum, South Witham, Nr Peterborough

Cheshire
Mouldsworth Motor Museum, Smithy Lane, Mouldsworth. Tel: (0928) 31781

Cornwall
Automobilia Motor Museum, The Old Mill, St Stephen, St Austell

Co Durham
North of England Open Air Museum, Beamish

Cumbria
Lakeland Motor Museum, Holker Hall, Cark-in-Cartmel, Nr Grange over Sands. Tel: (0448) 53314

Cars of the Stars Motor Museum, Standish Street, Keswick. Tel: (07687) 73757

Derbyshire
The Donington Collection, Donington Park, Castle Donington. Tel: (0332) 810048

Riber Castle Fauna Reserve and Wildlife Park, Riber Castle, Matlock

Devon
Totnes Motor Museum, Steamer Quay, Totnes. Tel: (0803) 862777

Essex
Ford Historic Car Collection, Ford Motor Co, Eagle Way, Brentwood

The Motor Museum, Mill Lane, Malden

Gloucestershire
Bugatti Molsheim, Prescott, Gotherington, Cheltenham. Tel: (0242) 677201

Cotswolds Motor Museum, Old Mill, Bourton-on-the-Water, Nr Cheltenham. Tel: (0451) 21255

Hampshire
Cothey Bottom Heritage Centre, Brading Road, Ryde, Isle of Wight

Gangbridge Collection, Gangbridge House, St Mary Bourne, Andover

The National Motor Museum, Beaulieu, Brockenhurst. Tel: (0590) 612345

Hertfordshire
Hatfield House Motor Museum, Hatfield House, Hatfield

Humberside
Automobilia Transport Museum, Billy Lane, Old Town, Hebden Bridge. Tel: (0422) 844775

Peter Black Collection, Lawkholme Lane, Keighley

Bradford Industrial Museum, Moorside Mills, Moorside Road, Bradford. Tel: (0274) 631756

Hull Transport Museum, 36 High Street, Kingston upon Hull. Tel: (0482) 22311

Museum of Army Transport, Flemingate, Beverley. Tel: (0482) 860445

Sandtoft Transport Centre, Sandtoft, Nr Doncaster

Kent
Historic Vehicles Collection of C. M. Booth, Falstaff Antiques, High Street, Rolvenden

The Motor Museum, Dargate, Nr Faversham

Ramsgate Motor Museum, West Cliff Hall, Ramsgate. Tel: (0843) 581948

Lancashire
The British Commercial Vehicles Museum, King Street, Leyland, Preston. Tel: (0772) 451011

Bury Transport Museum, Castlecroft Road, off Bolton Street, Bury

Manchester Museum of Transport, Boyle Street, Manchester

St Annes-on-Sea Motor Museum, St Annes-on-Sea

Tameside Transport Collection, Warlow Brook, Frietland, Greenfield, Oldham

Leicestershire
Stanford Hall Museum, Stanford Hall, Lutterworth. Tel: (0788) 860250

London
British Motor Industry Heritage Trust, Syon Park, Brentford. Tel: 081-560 1378

Science Museum, South Kensington SW7. Tel: 071-938 8000

Merseyside
Lark Lane Motor Museum, 1 Hesketh Street, Liverpool. Tel: 051-727 7557

Norfolk
Caister Castle Motor Museum, Caister on Sea, Nr Great Yarmouth. Tel: (0572) 84251/84202

Sandringham Museum, Sandringham. Tel: (0553) 772675

Nottinghamshire
Nottingham Industrial Museum, Courtyard Buildings, Wallaton Park

Shropshire
Midland Motor Museum, Stourbridge Road, Bridgnorth. Tel: (0746) 761761

Somerset
Haynes Sparkford Motor Museum, Sparkford, Nr Yeovil. Tel: (0963) 40804

Suffolk
Easton Farm Park and Motorcycle Collection, Easton, Wickham Market

Surrey
Brooklands Museum, Brooklands Road, Weybridge. Tel: (0932) 859000

The Land Rover Museum, Alford Road, Dunsfold, Nr Godalming

Sussex
Bentley Motor Museum, Bentley Wildfowl Trust, Halland. Tel: (082 584) 711

Effingham Motor Museum, Effingham Park, Copthorne

Tyne and Wear
Newburn Hall Motor Museum, 35 Townfield Garden, Newburn

Warwickshire
Stratford-upon-Avon Motor Museum, 1 Shakespeare Street, Stratford-upon-Avon. Tel: (0789) 69413

West Midlands
Birmingham Museum of Science, Newhall Street, Birmingham. Tel: 021-236 1022

Black Country Museum, Tipton Road, Dudley

Museum of British Road Transport, St Agnes Lane, Hales Street, Coventry. Tel: (0203) 832425

The Patrick Collection, 180 Lifford Lane, Kings Norton, Birmingham. Tel: 021-459 9111

Wiltshire
Science Museum, Red Barn Gate, Wroughton, Nr Swindon. Tel: (0793) 814466

Eire
The National Museum of Irish Transport, Scotts Garden, Killarney, Co Derry

Isle of Man
Manx Motor Museum, Crosby. Tel: (0624) 851236

Port Erin Motor Museum, High Street, Port Erin. Tel: (0624) 832964

Jersey
Jersey Motor Museum, St Peter's Village. Tel: (0534) 21080

Northern Ireland
Ulster Folk and Transport Museum, Cultra Manor, Holywood, Co Down. Tel: (0232) 428428

Scotland
Doune Motor Museum, Carse of Cambus, Doune, Perthshire. Tel: (078 684) 203

Grampian Transport Museum, Alford, Aberdeenshire. Tel: (0336) 2292

Highland Motor Heritage, Bankford, Perthshire

Melrose Motor Museum, Annay Road, Melrose. Tel: (089 6822) 2624

Moray Motor Museum, Bridge Street, Elgin. Tel: (0343) 544933

Museum of Transport, Kelvingrove, Glasgow. Tel: 041-357 3929

Myreton Motor Museum, Aberlady, East Lothian. Tel: (087) 57288

Royal Scottish Museum, Department of Transport, Chambers Street, Edinburgh. Tel: 031-225 7534

Wales
Conwy Valley Railway Museum Ltd, The Old Goods Yard, Betws-y-Coed, Gwynedd. Tel: (069 02) 568

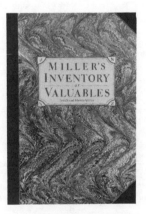

INDEX